The Compact Compendium of Experimental Philosophy

The Compact Compendium of Experimental Philosophy

—

Edited by
Alexander Max Bauer and Stephan Kornmesser

DE GRUYTER

ISBN 978-3-11-221375-9
e-ISBN (PDF) 978-3-11-071693-1
e-ISBN (EPUB) 978-3-11-071702-0

Library of Congress Control Number: 2023942139

Bibliographic information published by the Deutsche Nationalbibliothek
The Deutsche Nationalbibliothek lists this publication in the Deutsche Nationalbibliografie; detailed bibliographic data are available on the internet at http://dnb.dnb.de.

© 2025 Walter de Gruyter GmbH, Berlin/Boston.
This volume is text- and page-identical with the hardback published in 2024.
Cover image: M.C. Escher's "Doric Columns" © 2023 The M.C. Escher Company – The Netherlands. All rights reserved. www.mcescher.com
Printing and binding: CPI books GmbH, Leck

www.degruyter.com

Contents

List of Abbreviations —— VII

Stephan Kornmesser and Alexander Max Bauer
Introduction —— 1

Part 1: The Philosophy of Experimental Philosophy

Justin Sytsma, Joseph Ulatowski, and Chad Gonnerman
History and Philosophy of Experimental Philosophy: All in the Family —— 9

Eugen Fischer and Justin Sytsma
Projects and Methods of Experimental Philosophy —— 39

Joachim Horvath
Intuitions in Experimental Philosophy —— 71

Theodore Bach
Limitations and Criticism of Experimental Philosophy —— 101

Part 2: Topics from Theoretical Philosophy

Paul Henne
Experimental Metaphysics: Causation —— 133

James R. Beebe
Experimental Epistemology: Knowledge and Gettier Cases —— 163

Edouard Machery
Experimental Philosophy of Language: Proper Names and Predicates —— 183

Igor Douven, Shira Elqayam, and Karolina Krzyżanowska
The Experimental Philosophy of Logic and Formal Epistemology: Conditionals —— 211

Jonathan Waskan
Experimental Philosophy of Science: Scientific Explanation —— 237

Mark Phelan
Experimental Philosophy of Mind: Conscious State Attribution —— 263

Part 3: Topics from Practical Philosophy

Justin Bruner
Experimental Political Philosophy: Social Contract —— 291

Raff Donelson
Experimental Legal Philosophy: General Jurisprudence —— 309

Thomas Nadelhoffer
Experimental Philosophy of Action: Free Will and Moral Responsibility —— 327

Rodrigo Díaz
Experimental Philosophy of Emotion: Emotion Theory —— 353

Ian M. Church
Experimental Philosophy of Religion: Problem of Evil —— 371

Florian Cova
Experimental Philosophy of Aesthetics: Aesthetic Judgment —— 393

List of Contributors —— 417

Index —— 421

List of Abbreviations

CNS	Central Nervous System
COCA	Corpus of Contemporary American
CPU	Central Processing Unit
DIY	Do it Yourself
DSM	Distributional Semantic Model
FEO	Fair Equality of Opportunity
FIDE	Fédération Internationale des Échecs (World Chess Federation)
GAP	German Society for Analytic Philosophy
HIV	Human Immunodeficiency Virus
ISIS	Islamic State
JTB	Justified True Belief
MISC	Mischaracterization Claim
MP	Modus Ponens
MR/FW	Moral Responsibility and Free Will
OSC	Open Science Collaboration
SEE	Side-Effect Effect
WEIRD	Western, Educated, Industrialized, Rich, and Democratic

Stephan Kornmesser and Alexander Max Bauer
Introduction

As Wesley Buckwalter and Justin Sytsma (2016, p. 1) once put it, experimental philosophy (or "x-phi", for short) "is a way of doing philosophy". A way that, in its broadest definition, uses the methods of empirical science – e.g., from psychology, the social sciences, or experimental economics, to name but a few – to explore philosophical questions from a somewhat new point of view. Following this way is highly contested and one might argue that experimental philosophy, after all, fails to contribute in a significant way to philosophical issues for fundamental reasons. However, for others, us included, x-phi is one of the most exciting developments in contemporary philosophy. And one that is rapidly evolving. Over the last two decades, research in this area has steadily increased, skyrocketed even, one might say. Nowadays, a wide variety of experimental methods – from vignette studies to corpus analyses or eye-tracking measurements – is used to approach an even wider variety of philosophical topics and issues. The rapid growth of x-phi within the last few years may be understood as a growing interest and recognition of the field. However, as the number of contributions to experimental philosophy increases, it becomes increasingly difficult to get an overview of its various topics and branches, especially for the interested novice.

This is where our *Compact Compendium of Experimental Philosophy* comes in. With the volume at hand, we want to provide – especially for newcomers or researchers unfamiliar with a particular branch of x-phi – a quick introduction and a sound orientation. To this end, the volume is divided into three parts. While the first part takes a look at x-phi as such from a metaphilosophical point of view, the second and third parts focus on specific topics of x-phi. For the sake of organization, we follow the distinction between theoretical and practical philosophy; in Part 2, you will find the philosophical areas that primarily belong to theoretical philosophy, while in Part 3, you will find those that mainly belong to practical philosophy. However, how can this volume provide a *brief but substantial* introduction to the philosophical areas of, say, experimental metaphysic or experimental political philosophy? For each of these philosophical areas, there are several topics and issues that are debated and experimentally explored. To briefly touch on each topic would result in a rather superficial introduction; to go into each topic in depth would cause the book's scope to sprawl and would undermine the idea of a *compact* compendium. This is why we have decided to structure the chapters of Parts 2 and 3 in the following way: Each chapter presents a specific *core topic* that is prototypical of a specific area of experimental

---

Note: We are grateful to De Gruyter for the opportunity to compile this compendium, which we hope will offer many a curious reader a good introduction to the subject. At De Gruyter, we are especially thankful to Christoph Schirmer, who found interest in our idea, and Mara Weber, who helped with production. Moreover, we owe thanks to Konrad Vorderobermeier for careful copy editing. We also thank an anonymous reviewer. Of course, our gratitude goes to all the authors who have put so much effort into their contributions.

philosophy (e.g., causation as a core topic from experimental metaphysics or the social contract as a core topic from experimental political philosophy). The core topics are the main subjects of the respective chapters. However, each chapter also includes an additional section showing what further topics exist in the area besides the core topic in order to provide a brief overview of the experimental research of this area as a whole.

1 Philosophy of Experimental Philosophy (Part 1)

Now, what awaits you in the following? Part 1 of this volume is concerned with experimental philosophy as such, or with "the philosophy of experimental philosophy". It situates x-phi within the history of Western philosophy (Chapter 1) and shows exemplarily how it lends methods from the social sciences and digital humanities (Chapter 2). Chapters 3 and 4 are dedicated to criticisms of experimental philosophy. This criticism is particularly important because experimental philosophy is once again igniting a dispute about what philosophy is. This is about nothing less than the important question of who we – as philosophers – actually are. And about the question, "what are we doing here anyway?" (as Bauer 2020, par. 15, put it). That's why we consider it important to include these debates here as well. We will leave it at this point; this exciting debate will surely be continued in other places with many passionate voices and interesting perspectives.

Let's take a closer look at the chapters of Part 1. First, Justin Sytsma, Joseph Ulatowski, and Chad Gonnerman (Chapter 1) focus on the *History and Philosophy of Experimental Philosophy*. They demonstrate that empirical claims and references to empirical observations are not uncommon in the history of Western philosophy. After a general discussion of the relevance of history for experimental philosophy, they highlight important stages from antiquity to the early and late moderns as well as to the present.

Next, Eugen Fischer and Justin Sytsma (Chapter 2) examine *Projects and Methods of Experimental Philosophy*. They identify a metaphilosophical naturalism as a central new methodological perspective; philosophical questions about certain phenomena are investigated by empirically studying how people think about the phenomena in question. The authors explore the question of how the results of these investigations can contribute to answering philosophical questions and highlight the potential of methods from psycholinguistics and corpus methods from the digital humanities.

Joachim Horvath (Chapter 3) illuminates the role of *Intuitions in Experimental Philosophy*. X-phi challenges the role of intuitive judgments in philosophical thought experiments by experimentally examining intuitive folk judgments. Horvath discusses two strategies to defend the traditional method of cases against the challenge posed by x-phi, the so-called expertise defense and the mischaracterization objection. The expertise defense assumes that, contrary to expert intuitions, laypeople's intuitions are susceptible to irrelevant factors. Hence, they do not contribute to case judgments in a meaningful way. According to the mischaracterization objection, on the other hand, laypeople's intuitions are irrelevant to the method of cases because philosophers do not judge intuitively but *argue* for case judgments. Horvath concludes that the expertise defense should be rejected, but he finds arguments supporting the mischaracterization objection and, in doing so, challenges x-phi's challenge to the method of cases.

Theodore Bach (Chapter 4) takes a further look at the *Limitations and Criticism of Experimental Philosophy*. He distinguishes between the limitations of x-phi, on the one hand, indicating what x-phi cannot do due to conceptual, confirmational, as well as empirical factors, and criticisms of x-phi, on the other hand, containing negative evaluative claims about x-phi's basic idea of using experimental methods to investigate philosophical issues. In doing so, Bach points out synergistic relationships between certain limitations and/or criticisms.

2 Topics from Theoretical Philosophy (Part 2)

Part 2 of our volume deals with experimental philosophical approaches to relevant topics in theoretical philosophy. First, in *Experimental Metaphysics*, Paul Henne (Chapter 5) explores the core topic of *Causation*. Henne reviews work on causal judgments based on omissions and normality effects. He further explains how the temporality of actions affects causal judgments in preemption and overdetermination scenarios and discusses problems of the counterfactual account of causation due to cases of double prevention.

James Beebe (Chapter 6) is concerned with *Experimental Epistemology*, focusing on *Knowledge and Gettier Cases*. He discusses experimental evidence on the ordinary concept of knowledge and points out differences between laypeople's and philosophers' judgments on Gettier cases due to the distinction between what he calls merely apparent and authentic evidence in the evidential basis of beliefs.

In *Experimental Philosophy of Language*, Edouard Machery (Chapter 7) provides an overview of the discussion on the semantics of *Proper Names and Predicates*. To this end, he reviews cross-cultural work on the reference of proper names and examines experimental results on the question of whether laypeople are committed to an internalist or externalist account of the semantics of predicates.

Igor Douven, Shira Elqayam, and Karolina Krzyżanowska (Chapter 8) showcase contributions to the *Experimental Philosophy of Logic and Formal Epistemology*, focusing on *Conditionals*. Given that everyday reasoning shows not to be based on the material conditional of classical logic – as, for example, prominently shown by the Wason selection task (see Wason 1968) – they discuss the theory of inferentialism to model everyday conditional reasoning.

Jonathan Waskan (Chapter 9) is concerned with the *Experimental Philosophy of Science*, introducing empirical work on *Scientific Explanation*. Traditionally, philosophers of science reject influences from psychology or cognitive science as being psychologistic. However, Waskan shows, with reference to studies in experimental philosophy, that the claims for the autonomy of the philosophy of science rest on judgments incompatible with those of practicing scientists.

Mark Phelan (Chapter 10) is concerned with the *Experimental Philosophy of Mind*, taking a closer look at *Conscious State Attribution*. He reviews answers to the questions of whether ordinary people possess a concept of phenomenal consciousness and what features of an entity lead people to attribute phenomenally conscious mental states to that entity.

3 Topics from Practical Philosophy (Part 3)

Part 3 of our volume brings together contributions from the vast field of practical philosophy. First, in *Experimental Political Philosophy*, Justin Bruner (Chapter 11) introduces research on the *Social Contract*. He highlights experimental political philosophy's characteristic of using methods from experimental economics before introducing research on stability, efficiency, and fairness in collaborations.

Raff Donelson (Chapter 12) sheds light on *Experimental Legal Philosophy*, focusing on *General Jurisprudence*. He discusses the question of its relevance and introduces work on the concept and nature of law before touching further work on consent and causation in law. Donelson concludes with general thoughts about the future of experimental jurisprudence.

Exemplarily for the *Experimental Philosophy of Action*, Thomas Nadelhoffer (Chapter 13) gives a rundown of recent research on *Free Will and Moral Responsibility*, highlighting studies that investigate the compatibility of determinism and moral agency as well as the influence of advances in neuroscience research on free will beliefs. He then goes on to discuss two error theories, namely bypassing and intrusion.

In *Experimental Philosophy of Emotion*, Rodrigo Díaz (Chapter 14) takes a closer look at the *Nature of Emotion* and investigates whether bodily perceptions and evaluative beliefs are perceived as necessary or sufficient for emotion, before briefly giving an outlook on research about happiness, pain, being moved, and basic emotions.

In *Experimental Philosophy of Religion*, Ian Church (Chapter 15) turns to the *Problem of Evil*, at the center of which is – a little abbreviated – the fundamental issue that there are instances of intense suffering that an omnipotent, omniscient being could prevent. Since an omniscient, wholly good being would do so but – apparently – does not actually do, there is no such being, or so the argument goes.

Last but not least, in *Experimental Aesthetics*, Florian Cova (Chapter 16) presents research on *Aesthetic Judgment*. He focuses on the question of whether people consider aesthetic properties to be objective rather than subjective and introduces work on the nature of guilty pleasures and aesthetic taste, the possibility of aesthetic disagreement, and the value of aesthetic testimony.

Bibliography

Bauer, Alexander Max (2020): "'Was mache ich hier überhaupt?' Experimentelle Philosophie zwischen Lehnstuhl und Labor". *philosophie.ch*. https://www.philosophie.ch/2020-06-08-bauer/, last accessed May 19, 2023.

Buckwalter, Wesley, and Justin Sytsma (2016): "Introduction", in: Justin Sytsma and Wesley Buckwalter (Eds.): *A companion to experimental philosophy.* Chichester: Wiley-Blackwell, pp. 1–2.

Wason, Peter Cathcart (1968): "Reasoning about a rule", *Quarterly Journal of Experimental Psychology* 20 (3), pp. 273–281.

Part 1: The Philosophy of Experimental Philosophy

Justin Sytsma, Joseph Ulatowski, and Chad Gonnerman

History and Philosophy of Experimental Philosophy: All in the Family

Abstract: Experimental philosophy (or "x-phi") is a way of doing philosophy. It is "traditional" philosophy, but with a little something extra: In addition to the expected philosophical arguments and engagement, x-phi involves the use of empirical methods to test the empirical claims that arise. This extra bit strikes some as a new, perhaps radical, addition to philosophical practice. We don't think so. As this chapter will show, empirical claims have been common across the history of Western philosophy, as have appeals to empirical observation in attempting to support or subvert these claims. While conceptions of philosophy have changed over time, across these changes we find philosophers employing empirical methods in pursuing their philosophical questions. Our primary aim in this chapter is to illustrate this fact. We begin by discussing the relevance of history to experimental philosophy (Section 2), then offer a necessarily condensed and highly selective history of empirical work in Western philosophy, ranging from the ancients (Section 3), to the early moderns (Section 4), to the late moderns (Section 5), and on to the present (Section 6).

Keywords: Experimental Philosophy; History and Philosophy of Science; History of Philosophy; Metaphilosophy; Philosophical Methods; Philosophy of Psychology

1 Introduction

Experimental philosophy is philosophy *with a little something extra*. Work in experimental philosophy (or "x-phi") addresses philosophical issues or questions, just like other work in philosophy. It puts forward philosophical arguments and offers reasons to believe key premises in those arguments, just like other work in philosophy. And it often appeals to empirical evidence in laying out these reasons, just like *much* other work in contemporary philosophy. The twist – the *something extra* – is that experimental philosophers do not merely call on the empirical work of others, mining the scientific literature for their evidence, but report the results of their own studies. That is, experimental philosophers *do* empirical science as part of *doing* philosophy.[1]

Note: The authors would like to thank the volume editors for helpful comments on a previous draft. This chapter was a collaborative effort and, after we each expressed that we should be third author, the order was determined by a random number generator.

[1] Thus, we disagree with overly simplistic readings of Knobe's (2016) "Experimental Philosophy is Cognitive Science". It is tempting to interpret the title as claiming that all of experimental philosophy belongs to the area of research or inquiry categorized as "cognitive science". But that interpretation fails to capture experimental philosophical work that doesn't have much to do with cognitive scientific matters

As we understand it, experimental philosophy involves the use of scientific methods for the purpose of casting light on philosophical issues or helping to answer philosophical questions. This is a *broad* definition. It does not specify what these scientific methods are, nor does it prescribe what the philosophical target of these investigations must be. As such, it does not restrict x-phi to the use of questionnaires (or surveys), nor does it restrict it to the study of people's intuitions, let alone people's intuitions about philosophical thought experiments.

Many have interpreted experimental philosophy more *narrowly*, however, including both critics and proponents. This was especially notable in the early days of twenty-first-century x-phi, where metaphilosophical debates generally focused on the use of questionnaire methods to study people's judgments about philosophical cases, often specifically targeting non-philosophers ("the folk") and interpreting the judgments elicited in terms of "intuitions". In our opinion this was never the sole extent of experimental philosophy, though, as is evidenced by early works within x-phi like Nichols' (2002) and Schwitzgebel's (2009), which we discuss briefly in the next section. And over the past ten years, a broad conception of x-phi has become increasingly prevalent, even if some critics continue to assume a narrow focus.[2]

It is particularly tough to maintain a narrow conception of experimental philosophy today if you pay attention to the recent literature. The diversity of methods employed by experimental philosophers (as illustrated by Fischer and Sytsma in Chapter 2), and the range of targets that they explore (as illustrated by the chapters in Parts 2 and 3),[3] are simply too large, far outstripping the use of questionnaires to probe intuitions about philosophical cases. Nonetheless, it remains true that a good deal of work employs questionnaire methods and targets case intuitions, as detailed by Horvath in Chapter 3. But we contend that it includes much, much more besides.[4]

(cf. Barnard et al. 2021). And when combined with the common picture of cognitive science as an interdisciplinary area of research that somehow goes over and beyond its contributing disciplines (e.g., Bechtel 1986), the overly simplistic interpretation leads to the conclusion that x-phi isn't philosophy at all. But it is. As Gonnerman (2018, p. 465) writes, "The 'experimental' in 'experimental philosophy' is not like the 'fake' in 'fake diamonds'. It's more like the 'good' in 'good ideas'. It modifies a noun to identify a subset".

2 For an explanation of the diversity of projects in x-phi, see Barnard et al. (2021), and to understand this diversity as an exemplification of intellectual humility, see Ulatowski (forthcoming). For some examples of experimental philosophers explicitly adopting a broad definition, see Sytsma and Machery (2013), Rose and Danks (2013), O'Neill and Machery (2014), Sytsma and Livengood (2015), Schupbach (2016), Buckwalter and Sytsma (2016), Stich and Tobia (2016), Weinberg (2016), and Cova et al. (2021).

3 For surveys of an even wider array of topics, see Sytsma and Buckwalter (2016).

4 For instance, recent papers have focused on qualitative interview methods (Thompson 2022) and computer simulations (Sytsma et al. 2021). Another clear illustration is the increasing body of work calling on methods from corpus linguistics – the branch of linguistics that aims to collect and analyze pre-existing "real world" data on the use of words (McEnery and Wilson 2002, McCarthy and O'Keefe 2010). Philosophers have increasingly called on such methods, ranging from simple web searches, to more balanced corpora, to sophisticated computational approaches. See the discussion by Fischer and Sytsma in Chapter 2 for an illustration, and Bluhm (2016), Sytsma et al. (2019), Caton (2020), and Ulatowski et al.

Recognizing this, we might ask, "What unites the various research being done in experimental philosophy today?" This is the potential downside to diversity. A bigger tent often means a less clear agenda. On a particularly narrow conception, x-phi is quite focused: it is the scientific study of intuitions about philosophical cases. On a broad conception, however, x-phi is not so readily encapsulated. In fact, we believe that it is not best thought of as an area of study at all. Rather, experimental philosophy is an approach to philosophy – *a way of doing philosophy* – whatever the topic or area. Thought of in this way, we believe that, at a minimum, what unites experimental philosophers is simply a basic methodological commitment – that empirical claims call for empirical support (Sytsma 2017, Ulatowski 2017) – along with a certain DIY attitude, a kind of self-initiative where the experimentalist is willing to deploy empirical methods where needed to fill in the gaps of the existing empirical record, especially when the extant evidence fails to adequately speak to empirical claims that matter for philosophical purposes.

As we will see, this methodological commitment and DIY attitude is neither new nor radical. Empirical claims have been common across the history of Western philosophy, as have appeals to empirical observation in attempting to support or subvert these claims. And while conceptions of philosophy have changed over time, in most, if not all, stages we find philosophers employing empirical methods in their philosophical explorations. Our primary aim in this chapter is to illustrate this fact. We begin by discussing the relevance of history to experimental philosophy (Section 2), then offer a necessarily condensed and highly selective history of empirical work in Western philosophy,[5] ranging from the ancients (Section 3), to the early moderns (Section 4), to the late moderns (Section 5), and on to the present (Section 6).

2 Appeals to History

There are many ways in which the history of philosophy can be relevant to present-day experimental philosophy. One is that history can serve as a kind of breeding ground for hypotheses that the experimentalist might explore. Eric Schwitzgebel and Joshua Rust's work on the moral behavior of ethicists illustrates this kind of relationship (for an

---

(2020) for further examples and discussion. See Sytsma (2022) for an extended bibliography for English-language work employing corpus methods. Below we'll argue that contemporary experimental philosophy is a continuation of a much longer tradition of employing empirical methods for philosophical purposes, and this includes the use of corpus methods such as in Patrick (1888), McKinnon (1970), and Meiuner et al. (1976). Perhaps a paper or chapter not too much unlike this one would argue that present-day corpus analysis is an extension of such work.

5 Further, restricting ourselves to just Western philosophy leaves out many examples of fruitful empirical work in other traditions, such as work in Igbo metaphysics on the theory of being that rarely, if ever, gets noticed (Edeh 1985). We hope that future work will be able to rectify this limitation by giving a global history of the role of empirical work in philosophical explorations.

overview see Schwitzgebel and Rust 2016). For example, to motivate his examination of rates at which philosophy books go missing from academic libraries, Schwitzgebel (2009) notes that prominent historical figures such as Aristotle, Kant, and Mill were committed to the idea that philosophical reflection on the moral domain will tend to improve moral behavior. Whether this idea is correct or not, however, is an empirical issue. And, as far as library holdings go, the claim generates the prediction that books more likely to appeal to professional ethicists will be stolen or left unreturned due to negligence at lower rates than books more likely to attract the attention of philosophers who are not ethicists. This prediction is not borne out by Schwitzgebel's data, however. Indeed, he found that relatively obscure books in ethics were more likely to be missing from library holdings than obscure books from other areas of philosophy.

Another way in which the history of philosophy may be relevant to experimental philosophy is nearly the opposite of the preceding relationship. Rather than serving as a source of hypotheses worthy of empirical assessment, philosophy's history can also function as a kind of data stream for evaluating philosophical claims. Consider Shaun Nichols' (2002) work on the genealogy of norms. He considers the question of how norms come to be accepted and maintained in a culture, putting forward the hypothesis that emotional response is an important factor in the process. To test this, he focuses on norms related to core disgust (i.e., disgust elicited by body by-products, spoiled food, and the like), deriving a list of prohibitive manner norms from the first known book on manners in the Western tradition, categorizing these based on their relation to core disgust, and then having a set of independent coders judge whether they are part of contemporary Western manners. Nichols found that while 92% of the norms related to core disgust remained part of contemporary manners, only 27% of those not related to core disgust were still in force, supporting his hypothesis.

The history of philosophy can also help inform our metaphilosophical considerations, as it does in this chapter. And we are hardly alone in turning to the history of philosophy to help situate experimental philosophy within the larger discipline. Here are but three examples. First, Joshua Knobe (2007a, 2007b; see also Knobe and Nichols 2008) points to earlier philosophers in his argument that modern-day experimental philosophy is a return to a vision of philosophy centered on human nature, especially how the human mind operates, as we find for Hume in Section 4. Second, Guy Longworth (2018) reflects on the ordinary language philosophy of John Cook Wilson and J.L. Austin, in part, in order to highlight a form of experimental philosophy closer to experimental mathematics than the form he believes to be common in experimental philosophy these days. We'll return to ordinary language philosophy briefly in Section 5 (see also Chapter 2). And, third, Tom Sorrell (2018) portrays some experimental philosophers, such as Sytsma and Livengood (2015), as calling on philosophy's history with the goal of defending the claim that experimental philosophy is in fact philosophy and not merely psychology or some other social science. Sytsma and Livengood (2019) deny that their aim was to defend x-phi from this charge (which they don't take seriously in the first place); rather, they called on the history of philosophy to show how x-phi fits into the wider practice of philosophy as understood by practitioners at the time. We expand on this here, suggesting that experimental philosophy has a long, nearly uninterrupted, connection to the way that philosophy has got done over at least the last four centuries, if not the last two millennia.

To a large extent, what sets our historical appeals in this chapter apart from the three examples above, then, is our argumentative goal. It is our claim that appeals to empirical evidence have long figured in philosophy's past. And often it has been (self-proclaimed) philosophers collecting this evidence. As such, we suggest that far from representing a radical departure from philosophy's past, as some suggest, experimental philosophy is in fact continuous with many of its traditions (Sytsma and Livengood 2015, 2019; Barnard and Ulatowski 2016; Ulatowski 2016).

In the remainder of this chapter we aim to illustrate this point by reporting a few of the many examples from the history of Western philosophy in which philosophers have employed empirical methods in their philosophical inquiries. However, this aim raises an issue immediately: How are we to identify which inquirers were *philosophers* and which of their inquiries were *philosophical*? This is not an easy question to answer. How to draw disciplinary boundaries today is a contentious issue, and it only gets thornier as we shift our view further back in time. We find that many thinkers who considered themselves to be philosophers are now most often classified in another way. And even among those considered canonical philosophers, we find that many of the inquiries that they considered philosophical concerned questions that would not be deemed so today. Accepting this, we see two basic choices: at one extreme we could defer to the thinkers themselves, accepting their identification as philosophers and their judgments about their inquiries; at the other, we could hold fast to our contemporary judgments, imposing one or another modern conception of philosophy on historical figures.

It is well beyond the scope of the present chapter to attempt to settle this issue, although we have trouble imagining what could reasonably justify the claim that some current conception of philosophy best delineates its true and immutable boundaries, let alone what would justify the claim that philosophy has such true and immutable boundaries in the first place.[6] As such, in what follows we will largely focus on

---

[6] This perhaps comes into focus when thinking about the future of philosophy. Given that conceptions of philosophy have changed over time, it is quite plausible they will continue to do so. But, then, why think that we're currently occupying the crucial moment in which we're getting it right? Furthermore, we strongly suspect that any such delineation of philosophy's boundaries would not only eject many historical "philosophers" from the tradition but would exclude many present-day "philosophers" as well – many folks with all the trappings of academic philosophers (PhD's in the subject, appointments in philosophy departments, publishing in philosophy journals). See Sytsma and Livengood (2015, ch. 2) for discussion. We personally find such practices rather distasteful. One cause for concern is that the development and deployment of such restrictive conceptions is often insufficiently attentive to the ways in which they contribute to what Kristie Dotson (2012) calls a "culture of justification" in philosophy, wherein a premium is placed on "legitimation narratives". Importantly, these narratives are not aimed at, say, the central and supporting claims of a piece of research; rather, they endeavor to establish the research's status as philosophy in the first place. One common exemplification of philosophy's cul-

thinkers' self-conceptions with regard to philosophers and philosophical enquiry, although we'll highlight some places where this plausibly diverges from contemporary impressions of the canon or the extent of philosophical inquiry. Regardless, we believe that you are likely to find *many* examples of philosophers employing empirical methods in philosophical inquiries in the brief survey we turn to now, even if you discard other examples as not being *true* philosophers or *true* philosophical inquiries. And, insofar as the central argument of this paper is concerned, that should be enough.

3 Ancient Philosophy

Reflection on ancient philosophy helps to reveal that, where we find philosophers, we rarely have to search long to find empirical evidence being deployed towards philosophical ends. Consider Thales of Miletus. In addition to the remarkably parsimonious picture of the universe he is most known for, Thales is reported to have asserted that lodestones have souls (Aristotle 1984, 1.2, 405a19 – 405a21), distinguishing them from inanimate things (Lorenz 2009). It is hard to see what would have undergirded Thales' assertion about magnets if not experience with them. They do, after all, display something like "contingent interactive behavior", as when they attract certain other objects (on the importance of such behavior in triggering mental state attributions, see, e.g., Arico et al. 2011). Sure, Thales' assertion is likely to strike many as rather silly today. But the merits or demerits of the assertion are largely beside the point. What matters for current purposes is that we have a recognizably philosophical claim, by either contemporary or historical standards, being put forward on the basis of empirical observation. And as we will see, this is hardly an anomaly.

Then again, one might worry that this example from Thales does not quite serve the argumentative ends of the present chapter, even if you accept it as an example of a philosopher conducting a philosophical enquiry. While Thales' evidence must have been at least partially empirical, it might be urged that in distinguishing between empirical and non-empirical (or "armchair") philosophy, we need to allow that *some* empirical observation can be called on while remaining firmly in the armchair. Exactly which tools in the philosopher's toolkit qualify as armchair implements is not perfectly clear, however. Mortensen and Nagel (2016, p. 56) provide some suggestions, registering the likes of Plato's dialectical method, Descartes' introspective examinations in the *Meditations*, Locke's method of relying on his observations about how knowledge is acquired and how words are used, as well as more formal methods such as the use of

---

ture of justification is a question often heard by Dotson, which experimental philosophers will be quite familiar with: "How is this paper philosophy?" As Dotson argues, one problem with philosophy's culture of justification is that the burden of legitimation falls on philosophy's diverse and would-be diverse practitioners, which, in turn, helps to contribute to philosophy's underrepresentation problems, including along racial, ethnic, gender, sexual, and ability lines but also in connection to diverse approaches to and topics in philosophy.

logic, decision theory, and semantics. In Section 3, we show how it could be a mistake to maintain that these armchair methods were the only ones deployed by early modern philosophers. Descartes, for example, was far more experimental than many care to admit.

This list is likely to strike some as possibly missing an important item. To get at this, consider direct realism, which we might characterize as the view that perceptual experience is individuated in terms of relations that the perceiver bears to external-world objects, relations that are unmediated by, or perhaps unanalyzable by appeal to, inner states of the perceiver (Lyons 2016, sec. 2.3.3). One kind of argument often given against direct realism is a perceptual relativity argument. Berkeley's *Three Dialogues Between Hylas and Philonous* provides an example. There, through his mouthpiece Philonous, Berkeley argues against the view by noting that a bowl of water may feel hot to one hand while cold to another and that what tastes sweet to one person may strike another as bitter (Berkeley [1713] 1901, 476). What we have is an argument that appeals to an empirical discovery, namely, the fact that perception can (and indeed often does) vary across presentations and perceivers. But the argument will strike many, if not all, as a bit of armchair philosophy, perhaps because of the now commonplace nature of the empirical evidence called on. Indeed, to capture arguments like Berkeley's, Fumerton suggests that armchair philosophers can appeal to "'familiar' facts" (Fumerton 1999, p. 22), or "the kind of empirical data that one can't help getting by simply living one's life" (Fumerton 1999, p. 23). Assuming that the behavior of magnets could be treated as familiar facts for the ancients, then Thales and his ensouled lodestone might be better characterized as an instance of armchair philosophy. And there is certainly something compelling about this suggestion. At the very least, we have no reason to think that the empirical basis for Thales's assertion was arrived at through anything like the systematic empirical investigations characteristic of the sciences today.

Even adopting a suitably broad conception of armchair philosophy and suitably strict expectations about the sophistication of ancient science, however, will only push our origin story forward at most a few hundred years. Aristotle provides some rather clear examples of an ancient philosopher making empirical claims in their philosophical investigations on the basis of less readily accessible empirical evidence, perhaps even evidence of the sort that we might associate with the sciences properly speaking.

In an 1882 letter to his friend William Ogle, Charles Darwin wrote, "Linnaeus and Cuvier have been my two gods […] but they were mere schoolboys to old Aristotle" (Darwin Correspondence Project n.d.).[7] This quote helps to remind us of Aristotle's immense accomplishments in biology (among a wide range of scientific topics). Indeed, about 20 % of his extant writings were biological, and in these he put forward an im-

---

7 It is sometimes suggested that Darwin's praise of Aristotle was insincere. Gotthelf (1999) argues that a close examination of Darwin's writings shows that the praise was genuine.

pressive body of information about the physiology, behavior, and classification of over 500 species (Mason 1962, pp. 412–434). It is clear that systematic empirical research and inquiry helped to inform Aristotle's biological writings. True, he obviously didn't leave us with any detailed descriptions of his studies, as in the form of lab notes, but it appears that Aristotle did rely on dissections that he performed or directed as well as on the testimony of people working closely with animals including beekeepers, fisherman, and sponge divers (Lennox 2021, sec. 3). And, of course, it seems fairly undeniable that Aristotle was a philosopher. Indeed, he is generally considered one of the greatest ever.

In Aristotle, then, we have a rather clear example of a philosopher who engaged in systematic empirical research and inquiry. At first blush, what is perhaps a bit less clear is how to characterize the relationship between his biological research and philosophical inquiries. It is perhaps tempting to say that Aristotle was simply a polymath – sometimes he wore the hat of a biologist and at others he donned the hat of a philosopher (among many others). The problem with this story is that it fails to capture the ways in which Aristotle's biological research interacted with his philosophical thinking, even drawing such a whiggish distinction. The idea that these two were deeply intertwined is well captured in the historical scholarship on Aristotle. For example, Grene and Depew (2004, p. 1) write that "[o]ne cannot read him for any length of time without seeing that his central philosophical concerns were closely related to his biological interests". Further, Tipton (2014, p. 9) refers to both "Aristotle's philosophical biology" and his "biological philosophy", two phrases that hint at deep interconnections between Aristotle's biology and his philosophy. And Lennox notes that

> there are important connections between the theoretical approach to the relationship between body and soul defended in [*De Anima*] and the distinctive way that Aristotle approaches the investigations of animals. (Lennox 2021, sec. 1)

What the historical scholarship suggests, then, is that Aristotle engaged in and relied on systematic biological research in order to draw philosophical conclusions, even when we operate with today's standards of what qualifies as philosophy.

4 Early Modern Philosophy

We've just seen that the use of empirical observation in philosophy has a long history. And while we've focused on just a pair of examples, more could be given (e.g., Theophrastus' biological observations and his claims about animal minds and prohibitions against animal sacrifices; see Ierodiakonou 2020), and similar examples could be highlighted among the Romans and Medievals (e.g., Buridan's theory of impetus and its role in explaining the behavior of virtuous people and in distinguishing occurrent from dispositional thought; see Zupko 2018). But it is in the early modern period, especially in the late 1650s and early 1660s, that the use of empirical methods really began to flourish in Western philosophy. What may be called "early modern experimental philosophy", like contemporary x-phi, was a broad movement that eschewed speculative philosophical inquiry, especially within the realm of natural philosophy (Anstey and Vanzo 2016). Dmitri Levitin gives a terse description of the distinction between speculative and experimental philosophy in early modern philosophy:

> At its simplest level, the distinction was a polemical one, emphasising that any natural philosophy not founded on observation and experiment was invalid, and especially that "hypotheses" formed without recourse to experience were to be avoided, and lay at the historical origins of natural philosophical error. (Levitin 2019, p. 230)

Such investigations held a powerful grip on philosophy and eventually spread to medicine, moral philosophy, and aesthetics (cf. Anstey 2005, 2012).

Early modern experimental philosophers were finished with speculations and theories about the world that were based on empirical claims in the absence of sufficient empirical evidence. And similar points hold for contemporary experimental philosophers, with one driving force behind the rise of x-phi in the twentieth century being dissatisfaction with speculative appeals to philosophers' own intuitions, which were often assumed to be widely shared and supposed to be highly reliable. Despite the similarities, however, there are also important differences between early modern and contemporary experimental philosophy. These include that early modern experimental philosophy was notably broader in ambition than x-phi today, likely in part reflecting the relatively early stages of systematic scientific inquiry and specialization found during the early modern period.

While early modern experimental philosophy can be seen as a general approach to the study of nature, contemporary x-phi is more modest in its aspirations, reflecting a narrowing of our sense of what reflects distinctly philosophical issues or questions. The flip side of this is that both our understanding of science and the sophistication of scientific methods has dramatically increased since the early modern period, resulting in a steep increase in specialization. Alongside this progression, early modern experimental philosophy went through various incarnations as key methodological notions (hypothesis, experiment, confirmation, and so forth) were elucidated. For example, for its first four decades it was generally held that experimental philosophy should be done using the method of Baconian natural history. The success of Newton's *Principia* changed all that, however. By contrast, contemporary x-phi has a sophisticated, robust, and tested set of methodological practices and principles it can draw on, borrowing from the expertise of various established sciences.

Not surprisingly, there are ample examples of self-proclaimed philosophers employing empirical methods during the early modern period. For instance, Gottfried Wilhelm Leibniz made careful observations of fossils collected from mountaintops and Blaise Pascal famously followed up on experiments by Galileo and Torricelli, carrying a barometer up a mountain to show that the air had weight. As these two examples help to hint at, many of the people calling themselves experimental philosophers, however, were primarily working on problems in what we might now call science, especially physics or chemistry. For instance, much of Robert Boyle's experimental work was directed at questions about the nature of matter, including the so-called spring of the air (see Shapin 1994, Shapin and Schaffer 1995). In one ingenious experiment, he hung a watch by a thread within a bell jar, which was then connected to an air pump. Boyle then listened carefully to the sound of the watch as the pump was used to remove the air, noting that it steadily decreased in volume as the air was removed. Thus, Boyle convincingly demonstrated that sound is transmitted through air and could not be transmitted in a vacuum.

Early modern experimental philosophy was not a short-lived trend. For instance, a search of the *Eighteenth Century Collections Online* database turns up more than 100 entries with "experimental philosophy" in the title alone (and 2,750 with the phrase in the document).[8] Even removing repetitions and irrelevant entries, we're still left with more than 30 distinct works on experimental philosophy. And authors continued to publish on experimental philosophy well into the nineteenth century. For example, corrected editions of Parker's 1852 *School Compendium of Natural and Experimental Philosophy*, written for use by Boston school children, were published as late as 1870. While much of this work would be described as part of the physical sciences today, and not philosophy proper, it is important to note that through much of this period, researchers considered their empirical explorations of the natural world to be philosophical investigations. To give but one example, in Michael Faraday's public lectures on *The Chemical History of a Candle*, he remarks that "we come here to be philosophers" (Faraday 2008, p. 9).

In line with the issue raised above, it might be objected that while experimental philosophers of the period described themselves as philosophers, what we mean by "philosophy" has shifted over time and that their empirical research is philosophy in name only by today's standards. Indeed, many prominent experimental philosophers are no longer typically thought of as philosophers. For instance, Newton is most often described as a physicist today, despite the first known use of this term coming over 100 years after his death. We find this to be unfortunate and misleading, as a historical survey of the work of figures like Boyle, Newton, and Faraday reveal much that strikes us as straightforwardly philosophical.

Even if you are inclined to exclude figures like these from the philosophical canon, however, the point remains that many *self-described* philosophers have traditionally employed empirical methods in trying to answer questions that *they* considered philosophical. And contemporary experimental philosophers do the same. Further, even if we set aside figures like Boyle, Newton, and Faraday, many philosophers of the early modern period that are considered canonical today employed empirical methods. One example that stands out is René Descartes. Descartes is often portrayed as an armchair philosopher, perhaps the quintessential armchair philosopher, but he was also an ex-

---

8 See https://www.gale.com/primary-sources/eighteenth-century-collections-online/, last accessed May 25, 2023.

perimentalist. Focusing just on the *Meditations* and the method of doubt, one might well think of Descartes as being anti-empirical, with the primary aim of his method being to rid us of our mistaken empirical beliefs. Skeptical scenarios involving evil demons are said to have cleansed us of our sinful dependence upon experience, heading us off from the mistaken belief that anything to do with experience could be the foundation of knowledge (Newman 1994, 2006). This, however, hardly tells the whole story. Indeed, in our opinion, Descartes' experimental and scientific work is as much a part of his philosophical legacy as are his more speculative arguments.[9]

To offer but one of many examples, in the *Optics*, Descartes gives an account of visual perception, calling on a number of empirical observations in doing so. For instance, Descartes argues that while images in the mind need not resemble the things perceived, they nonetheless "do imprint very perfect images on the back of our eyes" (Descartes 2001, p. 91). To demonstrate this he then describes the process of dissecting "the eye of a newly deceased man, or, for want of that, of an ox or some other large animal" as follows:

> carefully cut through to the back the three membranes which enclose it, in such a manner that a large part of the humor M [...] which is there remains exposed without any of it spilling out because of this. Then, having covered it over with some white body thin enough to let the daylight pass through it, as for example with a piece of paper or with an eggshell, RST, place this eye in the hole of a specially made window such as Z, in such a manner so that it has its front, BCD, turned toward some location where there are various objects, such as V, X, Y, illuminated by the sun; and the back of it, where the white body RST is located, toward the inside of the chamber P (where you will be), into which no other light is allowed to enter except that which will be able to penetrate through this eye, all of whose parts, from C to S, you know to be transparent. For when this has been done, if you look at that white body RST, you will see there, not perhaps without admiration and pleasure, a picture which will represent in natural perspective all the objects which will be outside of it toward VXY. (Descartes 2001, p. 93)

This was not simply an empirical aside for Descartes. Rather, the experiment played a key role in elucidating his account of vision, which was part of his philosophical treatment of perception. Thus, Descartes states that by explaining at length how the picture is formed in this experiment, he "can enable you to understand several things which pertain to vision" (Descartes 2001, p. 93; for an account of how Descartes' optics figure in his theory of visual spatial perception, see Wolf-Devine 2000).

Further, other philosophers focused on the use of empirical methods in the study of human nature. For instance, in *A Treatise of Human Nature*, David Hume wrote that "we can hope for success in our philosophical researches" by studying "all those scien-

---

[9] Also, it is notable that Gassendi, one of Descartes' interlocutors who had an overwhelming influence upon the formation of *Meditations on First Philosophy*, offered in his work a defense of experiment very different from Bacon's, which had largely won favor amongst their contemporaries. Instead of following Bacon's eliminative induction with the goal of establishing an experimental science based on solid principles, Gassendi formulated a probabilistic logic that worked within a semiotics, which moved the experimentalists beyond what was evident to the senses (see Cassan 2012 on Gassendi 1658).

ces, which more intimately concern human life" (Hume 1975, I.4). Hume's thought was that we could begin to understand philosophical phenomena like morality, perception, or causation by first studying our own minds. Indeed, when it comes to studying the human mind, Hume (1975, I.6–8) claimed that it was "impossible to form any notion of its powers and qualities otherwise than from careful and exact experiments". This is an attitude that resonates clearly with experimental philosophers today, as noted above.

5 Late Modern Philosophy

By the end of the nineteenth century, the label "experimental philosophy" which was so prominently used in the early modern period, had largely fallen into disuse. And one may suspect that the use of empirical methods in philosophy largely died with the label as philosophy increasingly came to be distinguished from the sciences. Indeed, this is the standard story. Looking across the history of philosophy since the early modern period, we find a process of specialization as the sciences steadily break away from the mother discipline of philosophy. As this process of specialization continued, theoretical speculation increasingly came to overshadow empirical investigation. Despite this, it is important to recognize that empirical work never disappeared from Western philosophy, as we detail in some length in this section. As we will see, regardless of the standard story about early analytic philosophy, a clear lineage can be found between nineteenth- and twentieth-century philosophy and contemporary x-phi.

The standard story is that the rise of analytic philosophy pushed any remaining vestiges of empirical work from mainstream philosophy around the time of Gottlob Frege and Bertrand Russell. Despite the impact that some philosophers had in the emerging scientific psychology, and despite inroads being made using empirical methods by philosophers, their overwhelming influence turned many philosophers' gaze toward language, ontology, and the foundations of mathematics. Accordingly, the view that predominated analytic philosophy from the 1880s through the early part of the twentieth century was that formal and speculative approaches, in contrast to empirical or experimental approaches, form the basis of resolving philosophical problems (cf. Dummett 1993; Soames 2003a, 2003b, 2014, 2018, 2019; Stroll 2001).

This is not the whole story of early analytic philosophy's relationship with empirical work, however. One part of the larger story is the role that philosophers played working at the intersection with psychology. This includes philosophers who both conducted experiments and made careful observations in order to advance their philosophical (and psychological) theses, such as Charles Sanders Peirce and William James. While they often published in philosophy journals, some of their most prominent work was published in early issues of *Psychological Review* and *The American Journal of Psychology*. Similarly, Henri Bergson's first scholarly publication (1886) was based on his observations of hypnosis sessions, and he was elected president of the Society for Psychical Research in 1913. Moreover, John Dewey and Josiah Royce, in addition to William James – people that we typically categorize as American philosophers – each served as President of the American Psychological Association around the turn of the century. The end of the nineteenth and beginning of the twentieth century was rife with philosophical activity in psychology labs, as we illustrate over the next several paragraphs.

Even a cursory glance at philosophy journals such as *The Philosophical Review* or *Mind* and psychology journals such as *Psychological Review* or *The American Journal of Psychology* published in the 1880s and 1890s illustrates just how much overlap there was between the two disciplines, and makes clear that empirical investigations were still being pursued by philosophers despite the standard story.[10] Philosophical topics were under experimental investigation by philosophers, psychologists, and medical practitioners, and included aesthetics (Calkins et al. 1900, Martin 1905), belief and knowledge (Sumner 1898), corpus analysis of Heraclitus (Patrick 1888), foreknowledge and free will (Jastrow 1891), epistemological implications of optical illusions (Jastrow 1891, 1892), happiness (Brinton 1893), logic (Howison 1896, Lloyd 1896, Stratton 1896), memory (Burnham 1889, Kennedy 1898), and the longitudinal effect of teaching moral arguments to students (Street 1897). In fact, we believe that so many empirical studies exist from this period, which have largely gone unnoticed in recent times, that it is critical that we return to them if we hope to truly understand what is "traditional" in Western philosophy.

Many philosophers – especially those working at the boundary with psychology – pursued projects that look quite different from the supposed tradition. Some were reporting the results of experiments that they had run on their own, sometimes with the help of colleagues at other institutions. One study in particular stands out. Alexander Fraser reports finding individual differences in some data on the nature of perception. He writes:

> Thought has often been designated, by prominent philosophical critics, a kind of natural language; but that, like language, it varies with different classes of individuals, and to what extent this fact may be regarded as the source from which arises the great variety of philosophical theory which exists in the world, has as yet been barely noticed. Just as men of different nationalities speak in different verbal languages, so do different types of individuals think in different thought-languages and, just as in the case of verbal languages, each thought-language is made up from various different sources, but has one dominant, characteristic foundation. (Fraser 1891, p. 230)

Fraser's experiments were meant to undermine a popular view that thought was a "kind of natural language" that has as its source the data of the five senses. This was called "sensationalism". Fraser argued that the predominant source of thought, especially for those philosophers working in the early modern period such as Hobbes,

---

[10] We should mention that studies undertaken to explore the history of philosophical topics in peer-reviewed journals will tend to return skewed, and perhaps idiosyncratic, results if they fail to take up corpora from psychology and sociology journals. For one prominent example of such a study, see Weatherson (2020).

Locke, Berkeley, and Hume, was vision. He performed experiments testing whether people relied more upon their vision for thought, and he completed a corpus analysis of the works of Hobbes, Locke, Berkeley, and Hume. In addition, he cited famous studies by Galton and Huxley in which it was shown, e.g., that from childhood to adulthood people "accustomed to hard abstract thinking" relied more and more upon "verbal images" as they grew older. Through these different methods, Fraser argued that the natural language of thought arises from visualization alone, thus undermining the vastly more popular view of sensationalism.

Fraser's study of "visualization" was not the last time that he defended the use of psychological methods and data to discover something interesting about philosophy. In 1892, relying on, e.g., Goldscheider's empirical work on the sensation of touch and a close examination of the writings of Thomas Reid, Fraser defended the claim that natural realism has its source in the sense of touch.

Following on from that study, a later study of his traces the origin of Hegel's systemic philosophy to the discovery of galvanism. According to Fraser, the value of "Hegelism" may be derived from the very general conclusion that a whole metaphysical system may be founded upon "possible world conception" (the absolute) and, second:

> [I]n his endeavor to make the so-called ultimate principles of reason as exhibited in the science of logic conform to his newly conceived principle, Hegel necessarily freed thought from the fixed and apparently ultimate forms in which it had lain bound for centuries. (Fraser 1893, p. 494)

The famous discoveries of Galvani and Volta concerning the first principle of electricity showed how it was "the most satisfactory explanation possible of the fundamental facts of nearly all departments of knowledge" (Fraser 1893, p. 474). Through a careful analysis of experiments completed in morphology, mineralogy, physiology, and chemistry, Fraser explained how Hegel used results in galvanism to lay out the foundation of his philosophical system. Through his close engagement with early empirical research, Fraser intended to build a "psychology of philosophy", a phrase that he had coined in his metaphilosophical reflections that appeared in print between the two empirical studies (cf. Fraser 1892).

Around the same time that Fraser was exploring the sources of thought, natural realism, and Hegelism in the wild, there was a crisis brewing over the "function of philosophy" in the University (see Dodson 1908) and the role that the study of philosophy played in tertiary education generally (see Brown 1921).[11] Another figure who saw value in philosophy's practical application was Jay William Hudson (1910, 1912), who strikes a chord by noting the clear need for an empirical approach:

---

[11] Even William James and Josiah Royce were concerned with philosophy's fate at the hands of the mechanical arts and vocational studies that were becoming popularized by the industrial wing of academic life (cf. Veysey 1965).

> It is a commendable fashion to tell those entering upon the study of metaphysics that, after all, metaphysics is not a thing apart from the ordinary business of life, that even common-sense attitudes involve an unconscious theory of reality. But, supplementing this statement, little or no explicit reference is made concerning what particular attitudes of common-sense imply what particular metaphysics. [...] [N]obody has attempted an empirical history of the popular judgments of any people concerning the true, the real, and the right, as expressed or implied in what one broadly calls social institutions. Yet nobody can deny the explicit and general use by any civilized society of the epistemological, ontological and moral predicates; nor can any one deny that these predicates are decisively implied in certain classes of social deeds. (Hudson 1910, p. 570)

Such a concern with the empirical history is a precursor to the ordinary language philosophy of the mid-twentieth century, with its concern with how we actually use words. And while ordinary language philosophy was often carried out from the armchair, there are also clear examples of empirical work from the period.

While many philosophers came to embrace methods that have been thought to be independent of empirical investigation, such as conceptual analysis, there was a preoccupation among many empirically minded philosophers that mere speculation would not be sufficient to settle philosophical questions. This is a refrain we see especially in ordinary language philosophy. For example, John Herman Randall (1956) complained that philosophers often do too much talking and not enough looking, a view he had likely inherited from Ludwig Wittgenstein.[12] Likewise, Anthony Douglas Woozley (1953), despite being a critic of ordinary language philosophy, cautioned philosophers against departing too significantly from what has been said in ordinary language. Space does not permit us a more detailed treatment of ordinary language philosophy, but see Hanfling (2000), Hansen (2014), and Laugier (2013), as well as Chapter 2 of this volume for more on its connection to experimental philosophy. Let us close, however, with two clear examples of experimental philosophy in the mid-twentieth century, starting with perhaps the most famous – Arne Næss.

In much of his early philosophical work, Næss promoted an empirical approach to resolving philosophical problems. Although at the time of its publication, Næss's work was often derided (cf. Hempel 1950, Moore 1939, Nagel 1939), it later garnered respect (cf. Carnap 1955, p. 46; a letter from Carnap to Quine published in Creath 1991), including from contemporary experimental philosophers. Næss focused especially on how non-philosophers use ordinary terms of philosophical interest, such as "truth", holding that philosophers can come to a more thorough understanding of a term's usage by engaging ordinary people. In this he recognized that philosophers had been ignoring a valuable research tool.

Næss advocated for taking a more empirical stance in developing an account of truth (cf. Næss 1953a, 1953b). Toward this he describes how a philosopher might start

---

[12] As you might expect, a similar sentiment is found among many experimental philosophers today, including that some have taken Wittgenstein's (2009, sec. 66) slogan – "don't think, but look!" – as a motivation for their empirical pursuits (e.g., Sytsma and Livengood 2015, p. 43; Zahorec et al. forthcoming).

by reviewing dictionary definitions, or operational definitions of truth from specific sciences, or by constructing "a formal definition suited to logical purposes" (Næss 1938, p. 13). But, when this process leads to "various types of theories which deal with the non-philosopher's opinion on the notion of truth" – with the "opinion of the man in the street" (Næss 1938, p. 14) – Næss questions how one can come to such conclusions without rising from the armchair. In line with the motivation we suggested above for contemporary x-phi, his view is that these are clearly empirical questions and since philosophers have not done the empirical research – have not asked non-philosophers for their views – the value of the work is dubious.

In this context, Næss points out an array of common phrases that philosophers of the period employed, each of which suggested a body of empirical knowledge that they were not in a position to opine on. These include many of the types of appeals to ordinary or common-sense judgments that contemporary experimental philosophers have frequently targeted, such as "the opinion of the man in the street on the truth-notion is", "to naive people truth means", "[i]f common-sense had been asked to formulate what is meant by the truth of a belief, this is probably what it would have written", and so on (Næss 1938, pp. 14–15). In regard to such appeals, Næss rightly asks, "how do philosophers *know* these things?" Indeed, he notes that "even superficial questioning of non-philosophers makes it hard for anyone to believe that the philosopher has got his 'knowledge' about peasant's and other's use of the word 'true' – or about the views of non-philosophers of truth – by asking any other person than himself" (Næss 1938, p. 40).

In light of this, Næss took an experimental turn, using questionnaires to investigate the accuracy of such claims about the ordinary use of terms like "truth". In these questionnaires Næss asked people a range of open-ended questions, including:

> What is to be understood by the expression "something is true"? Define the expression. (Næss 1938, p. 24)
>
> What is the c.c. [common characteristics] of that which is wrong? (Næss 1938, p. 23)
>
> Give me an example of something that is true. (Næss 1938, p. 23)
>
> Do you employ the expression "the truth"? (If answered positively:) On which occasions? (Næss 1938, p. 26)

Subjects' responses to these questions were recorded by an assistant, and the data were then analyzed. Even as Næss conducted this work, however, he laments the fact that it was necessary in the first place, noting that much of the work Næss and his lab assistants performed could have been prevented if philosophers had told us of how they came to know what the non-philosopher thinks. Næss writes:

> [T]he fact remains: [Philosophers'] writings contain almost nothing of [how they arrived at the conception of truth among non-philosophers]. Perhaps some of them have asked their wives or assistants for their opinions on the truth-notion, but there is very little to prove that they actually employed such a method. […] Even very superficial questioning of non-philosophers would make it

> almost impossible for anyone to believe that the philosophers writing about the opinions of ordinary people actually ask others than themselves. (Næss 1938, p. 15)

Since philosophers failed to support their views of the non-philosopher with anything more than mere speculation, Næss believed that a more systematic accounting was needed.

It seems that Næss was conflicted with regard to the ordinary notion. The questionnaire method, though fruitful, did not lead Næss to a uniform view. For instance, he writes that "we have gathered more than 1000 examples from non-philosophers and a great many from philosophic literature, but it is by no means plain how we from this collection should be able to infer any *general* statement resembling definitions" (Næss 1938, p. 71). Given the wide variety of ordinary notions of truth he had collected using the questionnaire method, none of them stand alone as *the* ordinary notion or commonsense view – a conclusion that prefigures the pluralistic conclusions many contemporary experimental philosophers have arrived at in studying ordinary beliefs (see, e. g., Gonnerman et al. 2018, 2021 on knowledge-how; Tierney et al. 2014 on personal identity; Goldberg et al. forthcoming on pain; Ulatowski 2017 on truth).

We close by noting one further episode from the largely forgotten empirical history of philosophy. A bit later in the mid-twentieth century, over a two-year span Haskell Fain and Eugene Francis Kaelin (1960) conducted a longitudinal study of the philosophical beliefs of students in beginning philosophy classes. Their aim was two-fold: "to find out what some of the philosophical beliefs of students beginning philosophy actually are and to examine opinion shifts that occur during the semester" (Fain and Kaelin 1960, p. 138).[13] Interestingly, Fain and Kaelin found that some views remained the same across the term, despite being taught material that might alter their opinions, while others showed notable changes. We'll detail two examples.

First, Fain and Kaelin asked students the following question about explanation:

> Suppose one were asked why the ducks flew south this year. Which of the following statements would you consider the best explanation?
> (a) Ducks always fly south in the winter.
> (b) Ducks desire a warmer climate.
> (c) Ducks have an instinct to fly south.
> (d) No explanation is possible.
> (e) Cold produced a change in the pineal gland which is located near the duck's brain. (Fain and Kaelin 1960, p. 140)

Fain and Kaelin report that at the start of the semester, the majority of respondents favored either (b) – the teleological explanation – or (c) – an explanation by instinct. And when the same test was administered at the end of the semester, they found that there was no notable change in respondents' answers, despite having been introduced

---

[13] A notable comparison of their second aim is recent work completed by Schwitzgebel et al. (2021) and Buckland et al. (2022).

to Hume's analysis of causation in the meantime, which could have given rise to a shift towards answer (a).

A second example showed a notable change, however. Fain and Kaelin asked students the following question about the relativity of truth:

> All truths are relative. What is true for one person could be false for another. What do you think?
> (a) I think all truths are relative.
> (b) I think most truths are relative.
> (c) I think most truths are not relative.
> (d) I think no truths are relative. (Fain and Kaelin 1960, p. 141)

The distribution of responses at the beginning and at the end of the semester is shown in Figure 1. Fain and Kaelin (1960, p. 142) conclude that since 56% of the students "still held that all or most truths are relative" at the end of the term, they must be relativists about truth. Unfortunately, they did not perform statistical tests on the data, relying instead on the descriptive data, and their conclusion is in fact not well supported by their data, given the significant shift over the course of the term and the fact that the 56% figure was not significantly different from chance.[14]

One often hears that analytic philosophy pushed empirically oriented work out of the discipline, starting around the time of Frege and Russell. But, as we've seen, the use of empirical methods and data remained in some circles of analytic philosophy, perhaps percolating beneath the surface due to concerns with the "educational crisis" and the value of philosophy outside narrow academic confines. Nonetheless, many philosophers who had become hypnotized by the linguistic turn ignored the experimental work of the late nineteenth and twentieth century, much to the detriment of philosophy, in our opinion. Only recently has experimental philosophy emerged from the shadow cast upon it by mainstream analytic philosophy.

6 Contemporary Philosophy

While the label "experimental philosophy" had fallen out of use by the end of the nineteenth century, and was all but forgotten by the end of the twentieth century, a new group of researchers picked up the phrase in the early years of the twenty-first century – seemingly with little knowledge of its previous use and the tradition it tied them to. The *new* experimental philosophy, as Sytsma and Livengood (2015) call it, was kicked

---

14 Fain and Kaelin performed a follow-on study asking members of the same class how much they agree with statements such as: "If someone believes that there are men on Mars, then the statement 'There are men on Mars' is true for him". From the data collected on these statements, they recommend that when someone says that x is true *for them*, what the person actually means is that "the same proposition can be believed and disbelieved by different people at the same time" (Fain and Kaelin, p. 142). Some of this work may be contrasted with recent work on the objectivity of truth (see Barnard and Ulatowski 2021).

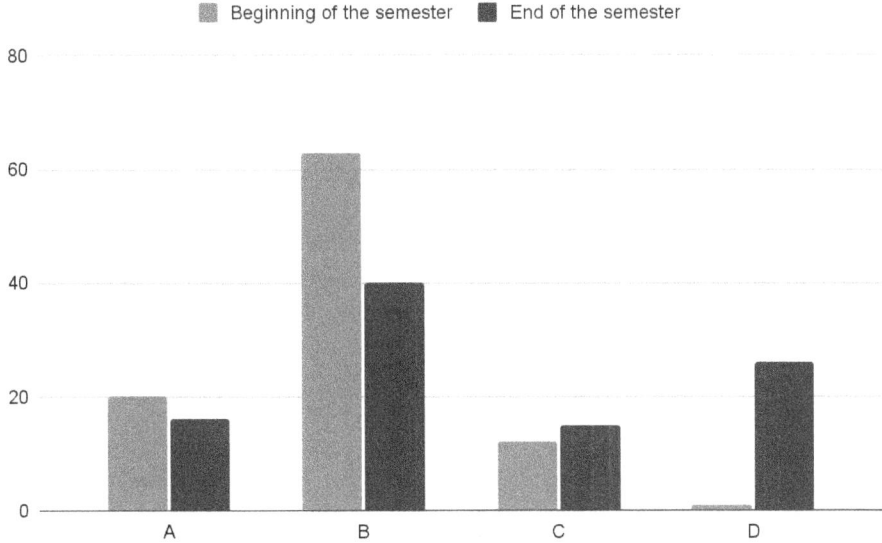

Figure 1: Longitudinal study of students' views on the objectivity of truth (Fain and Kaelin 1960)

off by the "Rutgers Posse": Stephen Stich, Ron Mallon, Shaun Nichols, and Jonathan Weinberg, as well as Joshua Knobe, Edouard Machery, Eddy Nahmias, and Thomas Nadelhoffer, among others, and philosophically-inclined psychologists like Joshua Greene, Tania Lombrozo, and Jennifer Cole Wright. Other contributors to this volume cover the span of work in the new experimental philosophy. As such, we will close by briefly discussing three trends in the new experimental philosophy over its first two decades and what these portend for its future.

We believe that there are five seminal papers from the first half of the aughts that really kicked off the new experimental philosophy, formed philosophers' initial impressions of the sub-discipline, and contributed to its rapid growth: Weinberg, Nichols, and Stich (2001) on cross-cultural differences in epistemic intuitions (see Chapter 6 of this volume for a general discussion); a pair of papers by Knobe (2003a, 2003b) on intuitions about intentionality that introduced the side-effect effect (also known as the Knobe effect); Machery, Mallon, Nichols, and Stich (2004) on intuitions about reference (see Chapter 7); and Nahmias, Morris, Nadelhoffer, and Turner (2005) on intuitions about free will (see Chapter 13). Topically, these four projects might seem to inhabit rather disparate worlds of philosophical thought,[15] but they also share much in com-

---

[15] And, to add to their differences, it may be worth noting that the five publications have not weathered subsequent empirical research equally well. For instance, replication efforts have tended to fail when it comes to the finding from Weinberg et al. (2001) that university students of Western cultural backgrounds were more likely than students of East Asian and South Asian backgrounds to report that the Gettier protagonist in their thought experiments lacks knowledge despite having a justified true belief. Not only have fairly close replication attempts failed to unveil this result (e.g., Kim and Yuan 2015,

mon. Each of these papers employs a vignette design, giving lay participants (i.e., non-philosophers) a description of a philosophical case and soliciting their judgments (or "intuitions") about it. As such, these papers suggest a narrow definition of experimental philosophy, as described in Section 1, with x-phi being concerned with the empirical study of intuitions about philosophical cases. While this was never the whole of the empirical work being done by philosophers, it did set the standard impression of what x-phi is all about.

With this standard impression as background, the first trend in the new experimental philosophy we want to highlight is a broadening of approaches. While experimentalists have continued to explore judgments about philosophical cases using vignette methods, they've increasingly done a great deal more besides. They've conducted empirical studies to explore questions that have little directly to do with case intuitions, as illustrated by Nichols (2002) and Schwitzgebel (2009) in Section 2. And they've called on a much wider range of empirical methods, including methods from psycholinguistics and the digital humanities, as discussed in the next chapter. What we think this means is that it is now simply inappropriate to adopt a narrow view of experimental philosophy, and doing so promises to miss much of the most fascinating work being done in x-phi today. Looking toward the future, we only expect things to accelerate, with new cohorts of experimentalists bringing an even wider array of tools to bear on an ever expanding set of philosophical concerns.

The second trend we want to highlight also concerns acceleration; now not specifically with regard to methods and topics, but the amount of empirical work being done in philosophy. That there has been some such an acceleration is probably pretty clear, although its precise extent is less so. We can go some ways towards developing a more detailed picture, however, by turning to empirical methods – doing a bit of experimental metaphilosophy.

Knobe (2015) is a great example of this approach, and his work helps to establish the acceleration of x-phi as part of a more general trend within philosophy – that there has been an increase in the use of systematic empirical data, whether produced by the philosophers themselves (experimental philosophy) or not (empirical philosophy more generally). What Knobe did was to compare highly cited philosophical publications on the mind from two time periods: 1960 to 1999 and 2009 to 2013. He reports that there

---

Nagel et al. 2013, Seyedsayamdost 2015), but also efforts at expanding on the original have not delivered clear successes (e.g., Machery 2017, Machery et al. 2017; but see Gonnerman et al. 2022 for an argument that claims to the effect that the Gettier intuition is universal are premature; see Cova et al. 2021 for a general look at the replicability of x-phi). On the other hand, subsequent research has largely tended to reinforce and deepen the original results for others. For example, Machery et al. (2004) show that East Asian participants are more likely than Western participants to report referential intuitions that track descriptions that speakers associate with the name, and thus to have intuitions that align more closely with the descriptive theory of reference. This finding has been further developed and replicated (e.g., Machery et al. 2009, Sytsma and Livengood 2011, Machery 2012, Machery et al. 2015, Sytsma et al. 2015, Beebe and Undercoffer 2016), although the case is not settled (for a recent meta-analysis, see van Dongen et al. 2021).

was a radical shift in the extent to which these works relied on systematic empirical research. Whereas only a minority (though still fairly substantial) proportion (37.6%) of the papers from 1960 to 1999 turned on empirical research, a majority (61.8%) of the contemporary papers depended on such research, with an additional proportion (26.8%) reporting original experimental results. All told, Knobe's work suggests that, in a span of around 50 years, there has been a substantial drop – from 62.4% to a mere 11.5% – in philosophical publications on the mind that rely on purely armchair methods.

Further evidence that there has been an acceleration in philosophy's reliance on systematic empirical research comes from Ashton and Mizrahi (2018). Applying the tools of data science and text mining to JSTOR (a digital library whose holdings include a wide range of philosophy journals), Ashton and Mizrahi report evidence of a slow but steady increase in the use of inductive arguments in philosophy. More specifically, they found that, while the percentages of philosophical publications from 1840 to 2012 that contain deductive argument indicators (e.g., "therefore necessarily") do reliably exceed the percentages of publications that contain inductive argument indicators (e.g., "therefore probably"), nonetheless these percentages have been narrowing over time. This pattern of results is taken to indicate that the difference in ratios of philosophical publications advancing deductive arguments and those putting forward inductive arguments have been gradually declining over time. What matters for current purposes is that a decrease of just this sort is to be expected if there has been an acceleration in philosophical deployments of systematic empirical inquiry.

These two pieces of research suggest that in recent years philosophy has been swinging back toward serious engagement with empirical research, and provide a bit of evidence for an acceleration in experimental philosophy specifically. We can add to this evidence by turning to PhilPapers, which provides an expansive record of philosophical work broken down by topic or category at multiple taxonomic levels, including experimental philosophy. We exported a record of all publications in this category as of mid-January 2022 and then tallied them by year. Figure 2 shows the results across the first two decades of the twenty-first century. As the figure makes clear, the number of publications has rapidly increased across this span. And, indeed, a simple regression supports this conclusion: A negative binomial model found that publication year is a significant predictor of the number of publications ($B = 0.15$, $SEB = 0.04$, $p < 0.001$, CI: [0.07, 0.24]).

A third trend is drawn out by another piece of experimental metaphilosophy from Joshua Knobe. It is common to divide experimental philosophy into a negative program and a positive program. These programs have been characterized in different ways, but are often distinguished with regard to their attitude toward the evidential value of judgments about philosophical cases ("intuitions"). Knobe (2016) phrases this a bit more broadly, focusing on conceptual analysis (which has prominently featured case judgments). He then takes negative x-phi to involve work that "aims to engage negatively by providing evidence against the methodological assumptions of conceptual analysis itself" while positive x-phi, by contrast, "aims to make a positive contribution to con-

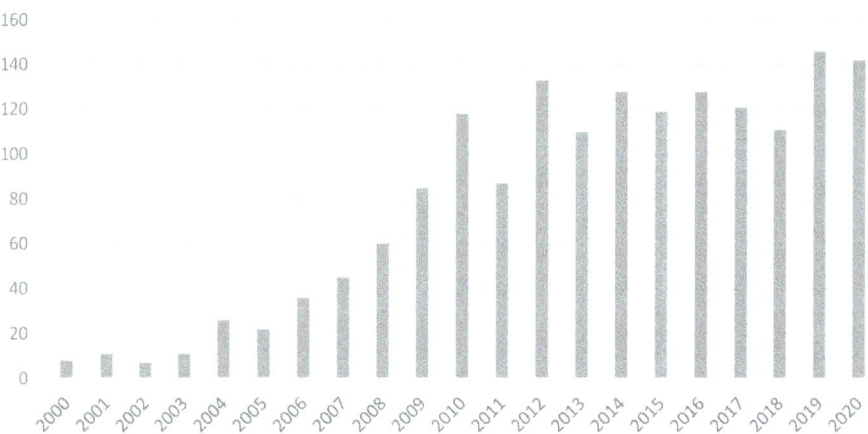

Figure 2: Publication counts for the "Experimental Philosophy" category on PhilPapers for 2000–2022

ceptual analysis" (Knobe 2016, p. 38). In line with the first trend noted above, it is worth noting that some have drawn further divisions, including highlighting work that does not target intuitions in the first place, as well as noting experimental work that targets intuitions but isn't focused on their evidential value – what has been termed the neutral program (Sytsma and Machery 2013, Sytsma and Livengood 2015; see Chapter 2 of this volume for further discussion).

Knobe hypothesizes that despite what we might expect focusing on classic projects from the early years of the new experimental philosophy, most work in x-phi is not positive or negative. To test this, Knobe and Ike Silver used the PhilPapers database to generate a dataset of empirical studies from 2009 to 2013. Knobe then classified the studies based on whether they fell within the positive or negative programs. By his characterization, only 10.4% were positive and a mere 1.3% were negative. While one might question this classification, even if the numbers were several times what Knobe found, it would still indicate that a majority of work in x-phi over this period wasn't engaged with either the negative or positive programs. So, what are experimental philosophers doing? According to Knobe (2016, p. 39), "they are revealing surprising new effects and then offering explanations [of] those effects in terms of certain underlying cognitive processes".

There is a great deal to be said about Knobe's findings. The lesson we want to suggest, though, is that they indicate that the new experimental philosophy is maturing as a sub-discipline. While experimental philosophers are, of course, still engaged in classic philosophical debates like those concerning accounts of the reference of proper names and the relationship between free will and determinism, they are also increasingly forging their own paths, generating new topics of debates, often centered around understanding and explaining new insights that their empirical results have brought to light.[16] And this is a key trend we expect to see continue during the new experimental philosophy's third decade and beyond.

7 Conclusion

As we noted in the introduction, x-phi is philosophy with a little something extra. It does all the basic things we associate with philosophy in the analytic tradition – drawing distinctions, presenting arguments, engaging with the surrounding literature, and so on – but it also adds a further ingredient, presenting empirical results in support of the claims being made. We take this to reflect a base motivation behind contemporary experimental philosophy, with experimentalists being united by the methodological conviction that empirical claims call for empirical support and the attitude that they can do the work to provide this support when needed. This commitment to empirical support is neither new nor radical, however. As we have illustrated throughout this chapter, empirical claims have been common across the history of Western philosophy and appeals to empirical observation to support or subvert these claims have been equally common. While conceptions of philosophy have changed over time, in most, if not all, stages we find philosophers employing empirical methods in their philosophical explorations. From the earliest Greek philosophers to often overlooked projects from the twentieth century, we find the embryonic origins of a range of approaches and methods that we associate with x-phi. Thus, we shouldn't think of experimental philosophy in its current incarnation as an outlier, doing something odd, unique, or completely different; instead, we should think of x-phi as a living descendant that has inherited methods and approaches from the same origin as other philosophical methods and approaches.

Bibliography

Anstey, Peter (2005): "Experimental versus speculative natural philosophy", in: Peter Anstey and John Schuster (Eds.): *The science of nature in the seventeenth century. Patterns of change in early modern natural philosophy.* Dordrecht: Springer, pp. 214–242.

Anstey, Peter (2012): "Francis Bacon and the classification of natural history", *Early Science and Medicine* 17 (1), pp. 11–31.

---

[16] The literature growing out of Knobe's discovery of the side-effect effect is a prime example. Similar effects have been found for other types of judgments besides intentionality, spinning off literatures of their own. For instance, a wide range of studies have found that normative judgments matter for people's causal judgments (e.g., Knobe and Fraser 2008, Hitchcock and Knobe 2009, Sytsma et al. 2012, Kominsky et al. 2015, Icard et al. 2017, Henne et al. 2017, Livengood et al. 2017, Kominsky and Phillips 2019, Livengood and Sytsma 2020), leading to an extended back-and-forth as experimentalists attempt to explain these findings (see the discussions in Chapters 2 and 5 of this volume).

Anstey, Peter, and Alberto Vanzo (2016): "Early modern experimental philosophy", in: Justin Sytsma and Wesley Buckwalter (Eds.): *A companion to experimental philosophy.* Oxford: Wiley-Blackwell, pp. 87–102.

Arico, Adam, Brian Fiala, Robert Goldberg, and Shaun Nichols (2011): "The folk psychology of consciousness", *Mind & Language* 26 (3), pp. 327–352.

Aristotle (1984): "On the soul", in: Aristotle: *The complete works of Aristotle.* Vol. 1. Ed. by Jonathan Barnes. Princeton: Princeton University Press, pp. 641–692.

Ashton, Zoe, and Moti Mizrahi (2018): "Intuition talk is not methodologically cheap. Empirically testing the 'received wisdom' about armchair philosophy", *Erkenntnis* 83 (3), pp. 595–612.

Barnard, Robert, and Joseph Ulatowski (2016): "Tarski's 1944 polemical remarks and Næss' 'experimental philosophy'", *Erkenntnis* 81 (3), pp. 457–477.

Barnard, Robert, and Joseph Ulatowski (2021): "The objectivity of truth. A core truism?", *Synthese* 198 (2), pp. 717–733.

Barnard, Robert, Joseph Ulatowski, and Jonathan Weinberg (2021): "The fourfold route to empirical enlightenment. Experimental philosophy's adolescence and the changing body of work", *Filozofia Nauki* 29 (2), pp. 77–113.

Bechtel, William (1986): "The nature of scientific integration", in: William Bechtel (Ed.): *Integrating scientific disciplines.* Dordrecht: Martinus Nijhoff, pp. 3–54.

Beebe, James, and Ryan Undercoffer (2016): "Individual and cross-cultural differences in semantic intuitions. New experimental findings", *Journal of Cognition and Culture* 16 (3–4), pp. 322–357.

Bergson, Henri (1886): "De la simulation inconsciente dans l'hypnotisme", *Revue philosophique de la France et de l'etranger* 22, pp. 525–531.

Berkeley, George (1901): "Three dialogues between Hylas and Philonous the design of which is plainly to demonstrate the reality and perfection of human knowledge, the incorporeal nature of the soul, and the immediate providence of a deity, in opposition to sceptics and atheists, also to open a method for rendering the sciences more easy, useful, and compendious", in: George Berkeley: *The complete works of George Berkeley.* Vol. 1. *Philosophical works, 1705–1721.* Ed. by Alexander Campbell Fraser. Oxford: Clarendon Press, pp. 452–595.

Bluhm, Roland (2016): "Corpus analysis in philosophy", in: Martin Hinton (Ed.): *Evidence, experiment, and argument in linguistics and the philosophy of language.* Berlin: Peter Lang, pp. 91–109.

Brinton, Daniel (1893): *The pursuit of happiness. A book of studies and strowings.* Philadelphia: David McKay.

Brown, William Adams (1921): "The future of philosophy as a university study", *The Journal of Philosophy* 18 (25), pp. 673–682.

Buckland, Luke, Matthew Lindauer, David Rodríguez-Arias, and Carissa Véliz (2022): "Testing the motivational strength of positive and negative duty arguments regarding global poverty", *Review of Philosophy and Psychology* 13, pp. 699–717.

Buckwalter, Wesley, and Justin Sytsma (2016): "Introduction", in: Justin Sytsma and Wesley Buckwalter (Eds.): *A companion to experimental philosophy.* Oxford: Wiley-Blackwell, pp. 1–3.

Burnham, William (1889): "Memory, historically and experimentally considered", *The American Journal of Psychology* 2 (4), pp. 568–622.

Calkins, Mary Whiton, Helen Buttrick, and Mabel Young (1900): "Wellesley college psychological studies. An attempted experiment in psychological æsthetics", *Psychological Review* 7 (6), pp. 580–591.

Carnap, Rudolf (1955): "Meaning and synonymy in natural languages", *Philosophical Studies* 6 (3), pp. 33–47.

Cassan, Elodie (2012): "The status of Bacon in Gassendi's syntagma philosophicum history of logic", *Societate si Politica* 6 (1), pp. 80–89.

Caton, Jacob (2020): "Using linguistic corpora as a philosophical tool", *Metaphilosophy* 51 (1), pp. 51–70.

Cova, Florian, Brent Strickland, Angela Abatista, Aurélien Allard, James Andow, Mario Attie, James Beebe, Renatas Berniūnas, Jordane Boudesseul, Matteo Colombo, Fiery Cushman, Rodrigo Díaz, Noah N'Djaye Nikolai van Dongen, Vilius Dranseika, Brian Earp, Antonio Gaitán Torres, Ivar Hannikainen,

José Hernández-Conde, Wenjia Hu, François Jaquet, Kareem Khalifa, Hanna Kim, Markus Kneer, Joshua Knobe, Miklos Kurthy, Anthony Lantian, Shen-Yi Liao, Edouard Machery, Tania Moerenhout, Christian Mott, Mark Phelan, Jonathan Phillips, Navin Rambharose, Kevin Reuter, Felipe Romero, Paulo Sousa, Jan Sprenger, Emile Thalabard, Kevin Tobia, Hugo Viciana, Daniel Wilkenfeld, and Xiang Zhou (2021): "Estimating the reproducibility of experimental philosophy", *Review of Philosophy and Psychology* 12 (1), pp. 9–44.

Creath, Richard (Ed.) (1991): *Dear Carnap, dear Van. The Quine-Carnap correspondence and related work.* Berkeley: University of California Press.

Darwin Correspondence Project (Ed.) (n.d.): "Letter no. 13622". https://www.darwinproject.ac.uk/letter/?docId=letters/DCP-LETT-13622.xml, last accessed May 19, 2023.

Descartes, René (2001): *Discourse on method, optics, geometry, and meteorology.* Transl., with an introduction, by Paul Olscamp. Indianapolis: Hackett.

Dodson, George (1908): "The function of philosophy as an academic discipline", *The Journal of Philosophy, Psychology, and Scientific Method* 5 (17), pp. 454–458.

Dotson, Kristie (2012): "How is this paper philosophy?", *Comparative Philosophy* 3 (1), pp. 3–29.

Dummett, Michael (1993): *Origins of analytical philosophy.* Cambridge: Harvard University Press.

Edeh, Emmanuel (1985): *Towards an Igbo metaphysics.* Chicago: Loyola University Press.

Fain, Haskell, and Eugene Francis Kaelin (1960): "Student philosophical opinions. A survey", *Inquiry* 3 (1–4), pp. 137–152.

Faraday, Michael (2008): *The chemical history of a candle.* Cirencester: Echo Library.

Fraser, Alexander Campbell (1891): "Visualization as a chief source of the psychology of Hobbes, Locke, Berkeley, and Hume", *The American Journal of Psychology* 4 (2), pp. 230–247.

Fraser, Alexander Campbell (1892): "The psychological foundation of natural realism", *The American Journal of Psychology* 4 (3), pp. 429–450.

Fraser, Alexander Campbell (1893): "The psychological basis of Hegelism", *The American Journal of Psychology* 5 (4), pp. 472–495.

Fumerton, Richard (1999): "A priori philosophy after an a posteriori turn", *Midwest Studies in Philosophy* 23 (1), pp. 21–33.

Gassendi, Peter (1658): *Opera omnia.* 6 vols. Lyon: Anisson & Ioan. Bapt. Devenet.

Goldberg, Benjamin, Kevin Reuter, and Justin Sytsma (forthcoming): "A brief history of pain concepts", in: Kristien Hens and Andreas De Block (Eds.): *Advances in experimental philosophy of medicine.* London: Bloomsbury.

Gonnerman, Chad (2018): "Consciousness and experimental philosophy", in: Rocco Gennaro (Ed.): *The Routledge handbook of consciousness.* London: Routledge, pp. 463–477.

Gonnerman, Chad, Kaija Mortensen, and Jacob Robbins (2018): "The ordinary concept of knowledge how", in: Tania Lombrozo, Shaun Nichols, and Joshua Knobe (Eds.): *Oxford studies in experimental philosophy.* Vol. 2. Oxford: Oxford University Press, pp. 104–115.

Gonnerman, Chad, Kaija Mortensen, and Jacob Robbins (2021): "Knowing how as a philosophical hybrid", *Synthese* 199 (3–4), pp. 11323–11353.

Gonnerman, Chad, Banjit Singh, and Grant Toomey (2022): "Authentic and apparent evidence Gettier cases across American and Indian nationalities", *Review of Philosophy and Psychology.*

Gotthelf, Allan (1999): "Darwin on Aristotle", *Journal of the History of Biology* 32 (1), pp. 3–30.

Grene, Marjorie, and David Depew (2004): *The philosophy of biology. An episodic history.* Cambridge: Cambridge University Press.

Hanfling, Oswald (2000): *Philosophy and ordinary language. The bent and genius of our tongue.* London: Routledge.

Hansen, Nat (2014): "Contemporary ordinary language philosophy", *Philosophy Compass* 9 (8), pp. 556–569.

Hempel, Carl (1950): "Review of Arne Næss. Toward a theory of interpretation and preciseness. Theoria, vol. 15 (1949), pp. 220–241", *The Journal of Symbolic Logic* 15 (2), p. 154.

Henne, Paul, Ángel Pinillos, and Felipe De Brigard (2017): "Cause by omission and norm. Not watering plants", *Australasian Journal of Philosophy* 95 (2), pp. 270–283.

Hitchcock, Christopher, and Joshua Knobe (2009): "Cause and norm", *Journal of Philosophy* 106 (11), pp. 587–612.

Howison, George Holmes (1896): "Psychology and logic. Further views", *Psychological Review* 3 (6), pp. 652–657.

Hudson, Jay William (1910): "An introduction to philosophy through the philosophy in history", *The Journal of Philosophy, Psychology, and Scientific Methods* 7 (21), pp. 569–574.

Hudson, Jay William (1912): "The aim and content of the first college course in ethics", *The Journal of Philosophy, Psychology, and Scientific Methods* 9 (17), pp. 455–459.

Hume, David (1975): *A treatise of human nature.* 2nd edition. Ed. by Lewis Amherst Selby-Bigge and Peter Harold Nidditch. Oxford: Clarendon.

Icard, Thomas, Jonathan Kominsky, and Joshua Knobe (2017): "Normality and actual causal strength", *Cognition* 161, pp. 80–93.

Ierodiakonou, Katerina (2020): "Theophrastus on Plato's theory of vision", *Rhizomata* 7 (2), pp. 249–268.

Jastrow, Joseph (1891): "Studies from the laboratory of experimental psychology of the University of Wisconsin", *The American Journal of Psychology* 4 (2), pp. 198–223.

Jastrow, Joseph (1892): "Studies from the laboratory of experimental psychology of the University of Wisconsin. II", *The American Journal of Psychology* 4 (3), pp. 381–428.

Kennedy, Francis (1898): "On the experimental investigation of memory", *Psychological Review* 5 (5), pp. 477–499.

Kim, Minsun, and Yuan Yuan (2015): "No cross-cultural differences in the Gettier car case intuition. A replication study of Weinberg et al. 2001", *Episteme* 12 (3), pp. 355–361.

Knobe, Joshua (2003a): "Intentional action and side effects in ordinary language", *Analysis* 63 (3), pp. 190–193.

Knobe, Joshua (2003b): "Intentional action in folk psychology. An experimental investigation", *Philosophical Psychology* 16 (2), pp. 309 324.

Knobe, Joshua (2007a): "Reason explanation in folk psychology", *Midwest Studies in Philosophy* 31 (1), pp. 90–107.

Knobe, Joshua (2007b): "Folk psychology. Science and morals", in: Daniel Hutto and Matthew Ratcliffe (Eds.): *Folk psychology reassessed.* Dordrecht: Springer, pp. 157–174.

Knobe, Joshua (2015): "Philosophers are doing something different now: quantitative data", *Cognition* 135, pp. 36–38.

Knobe, Joshua (2016): "Experimental philosophy is cognitive science", in: Justin Sytsma and Wesley Buckwalter (Eds.): *A companion to experimental philosophy.* Oxford: Wiley-Blackwell, pp. 37–52.

Knobe, Joshua, and Ben Fraser (2008): "Causal judgement and moral judgement. Two experiments", in: Walter Sinnott-Armstrong (Ed.): *Moral psychology. Vol. 2. The cognitive science of morality. Intuition and diversity.* Cambridge: The MIT Press, pp. 441–448.

Knobe, Joshua, and Shaun Nichols (Eds.) (2008): *Experimental philosophy.* Vol. 1. Oxford: Oxford University Press.

Kominsky, Jonathan, and Jonathan Phillips (2019): "Immoral professors and malfunctioning tools. Counterfactual relevance accounts explain the effect of norm violations on causal selection", *Cognitive Science* 43 (11), e12792.

Kominsky, Jonathan, Jonathan Phillips, Tobias Gerstenberg, David Lagnado, and Joshua Knobe (2015): "Causal superseding", *Cognition* 137, pp. 196–209.

Laugier, Sandra (2013): *Why we need ordinary language philosophy.* Chicago: The University of Chicago Press.

Lennox, James (2021): *Aristotle on inquiry. Erotetic frameworks and domain-specific norms.* Cambridge: Cambridge University Press.

Levitin, Dmitri (2019): "Early modern experimental philosophy. A non-anglocentric overview", in: Alberto Vanzo and Peter Anstey (Eds.): *Experiment, speculation and religion in early modern philosophy*. London: Routledge, pp. 229–291.

Livengood, Jonathan, and Justin Sytsma (2020): "Actual causation and compositionality", *Philosophy of Science* 87 (1), pp. 43–69.

Livengood, Jonathan, Justin Sytsma, and David Rose (2017): "Following the FAD. Folk attributions and theories of actual causation", *Review of Philosophy and Psychology* 8 (3), pp. 273–294.

Lloyd, Alfred (1896): "A psychological interpretation of certain doctrines in formal logic", *Psychological Review* 3 (4), pp. 422–426.

Longworth, Guy (2018): "The ordinary and the experimental. Cook Wilson and Austin on method in philosophy", *British Journal for the History of Philosophy* 26 (5), pp. 939–960.

Lorenz, Hendrik (2009): "Ancient theories of soul", in: Edward Zalta (Ed.): *The Stanford encyclopedia of philosophy*. Summer 2009 edition. https://plato.stanford.edu/archives/sum2009/entries/ancient-soul/, last accessed May 19, 2023.

Lyons, Jack (2016): "Epistemological problems of perception", in: Edward Zalta (Ed.): *The Stanford encyclopedia of philosophy*. Spring 2017 edition. https://plato.stanford.edu/archives/spr2017/entries/perception-episprob/, last accessed May 19, 2023.

Machery, Edouard (2012): "Delineating the moral domain". *The Baltic International Yearbook of Cognition, Logic, and Communication* 7, 6.

Machery, Edouard (2017): *Philosophy within its proper bounds*. Oxford: Oxford University Press.

Machery, Edouard, Ron Mallon, Shaun Nichols, and Stephen Stich (2004): "Semantics, cross-cultural style", *Cognition* 92 (3), pp. B1–B12.

Machery, Edouard, Christopher Olivola, and Molly de Blanc (2009): "Linguistic and metalinguistic intuitions in the philosophy of language", *Analysis* 69 (4), pp. 689–694.

Machery, Edouard, Stephen Stich, David Rose, Anjan Chatterjee, Kaori Karasawa, Noel Struchiner, Smita Sirker, Naoki Usui, and Takaaki Hashimoto (2015): "Gettier across cultures", *Noûs* 51 (3), pp. 645–664.

Machery, Edouard, Stephen Stich, David Rose, Mario Alai, Adriano Angelucci, Renatas Berniūnas, Emma Buchtel, Amita Chatterjee, Hyundeuk Cheon, In Rae Cho, Daniel Cohnitz, Florian Cova, Vilius Dranseika, Ángeles Eraña Lagos, Laleh Ghadakpour, Maurice Grinberg, Ivar Hannikainen, Takaaki Hashimoto, Amir Horowitz, Evgeniya HristovaYasmina Jraissati, Veselina Kadreva, Kaori Karasawa, Hackjin Kim, Yeonjeong Kim, Minwoo Lee, Carlos Mauro, Masaharu Mizumoto, Sebastiano Moruzzi, Christopher Olivola, Jorge Ornelas, Barbara Osimani, Carlos Romero, Alejandro Rosas López, Massimo Sangoi, Andrea Sereni, Sarah Songhorian, Paulo Sousa, Noel Struchiner, Vera Tripodi, Naoki Usui, Alejandro Vázquez del Mercado, Giorgio Volpe, Hrag Abraham Vosgerichian, Xueyi Zhang, and Jing Zhu (2017): "The Gettier intuition from South America to Asia", *Journal of the Indian Council of Philosophical Research* 34 (4), pp. 517–541.

Martin, Lillien (1905): "Psychology of æsthetics. I. Experimental prospecting in the field of the comic", *The American Journal of Psychology* 16 (1), pp. 35–118.

Mason, Stephen Finney (1962): *A history of the sciences*. London: Collier.

McCarthy, Michael, and Anne O'Keeffe (2010): *The Routledge handbook of corpus linguistics*. London: Routledge.

McEnery, Tony, and Andrew Wilson (2001): *Corpus linguistics. An introduction*. Edinburgh: Edinburgh University Press.

McKinnon, Alastair (1970): *The Kierkegaard indices*. 4 vols. Leiden: Brill.

Meiuner, Jean-Guy, Stanislaus Rolland, and François Daoust (1976): "A system for text and content analysis", *Computers and the Humanities* 10 (5), pp. 281–286.

Moore, Jared Sparks (1939): "'Truth' as conceived by those who are not professional philosophers by Arne Ness", *The American Journal of Psychology* 52 (3), pp. 489–490.

Mortensen, Kaija, and Jennifer Nagel (2016): "Armchair-friendly experimental philosophy", in: Justin Sytsma and Wesley Buckwalter (Eds.): *A companion to experimental philosophy*. Oxford: Wiley-Blackwell, pp. 53–70.

Næss, Arne (1938): *"Truth" as conceived by those who are not professional philosophers*. Oslo: Kommisjon Hos Jacob Dybwad.

Næss, Arne (1953a): *Interpretation and preciseness. A contribution to the theory of communication*. Oslo: Kommisjon Hos Jacob Dybwad.

Næss, Arne (1953b): *An empirical study of the expressions "true", "perfectly certain", and "extremely probable"*. Oslo: Kommisjon Hos Jacob Dybwad.

Nagel, Ernst (1939): "'Truth' as conceived by those who are not professional philosophers", *The Journal of Philosophy* 36 (3), pp. 78–80.

Nagel, Jennifer, Valerie San Juan, and Raymond Mar (2013): "Lay denials of knowledge for justified true beliefs", *Cognition* 129 (3), pp. 652–661.

Nahmias, Eddy, Stephen Morris, Thomas Nadelhoffer, and Jason Turner (2005): "Surveying freedom. Folk intuitions about free will and moral responsibility", *Philosophical Psychology* 18 (5), pp. 561–584.

Newman, Lex (1994): "Descartes on unknown faculties and our experience of the external world", *Philosophical Review* 103 (3), pp. 489–531.

Newman, Lex (2006): "Descartes' rationalist epistemology", in: Alan Nelson (Ed.): *A companion to rationalism*. Oxford: Wiley-Blackwell, pp. 179–204.

Nichols, Shaun (2002): "Norms with feeling. Towards a psychological account of moral judgment", *Cognition* 84 (2), pp. 221–236.

O'Neill, Elizabeth, and Edouard Machery (2014): "Experimental philosophy. What is it good for?", in: Edouard Machery and Elizabeth O'Neill (Eds.): *Current controversies in experimental philosophy*. London: Routledge, pp. 3–16.

Parker, Richard Green (1852): *A school compendium of natural and experimental philosophy*. New York: A.S. Barnes & Co.

Patrick, George Thomas White (1888). "A further study of Heraclitus", *The American Journal of Psychology* 1 (4), pp. 557–690.

Randall, John Herman (1956): "Talking and looking", *Proceedings of the Aristotelian Society* 30, pp. 5–24.

Rose, David, and David Danks (2013): "In defense of a broad conception of experimental philosophy", *Metaphilosophy* 44 (4), pp. 512–532.

Schwitzgebel, Eric (2009): "Do ethicists steal more books?", *Philosophical Psychology* 22 (4), pp. 711–725.

Schwitzgebel, Eric, Brad Cokelet, and Peter Singer (2021): "Do ethics classes influence student behavior? Case study. Teaching the ethics of eating meat", *Cognition* 203, 104397.

Schwitzgebel, Eric, and Joshua Rust (2016): "The behavior of ethicists", in: Justin Sytsma and Wesley Buckwalter (Eds.): *A companion to experimental philosophy*. Oxford: Wiley-Blackwell, pp. 225–233.

Seyedsayamdost, Hamid (2015): "On normativity and epistemic intuitions. Failure of replication", *Episteme* 12 (1), pp. 96–116.

Shapin, Steven (1994): *A social history of truth. Civility and science in seventeenth-century England*. Chicago: The University of Chicago Press.

Shapin, Steven, and Simon Schaffer (1985): *Leviathan and the air pump. Hobbes, Boyle, and the experimental life*. Princeton: Princeton University Press.

Soames, Scott (2003a): *Philosophical analysis in the twentieth century*. Vol. 1. Princeton: Princeton University Press.

Soames, Scott (2003b): *Philosophical analysis in the twentieth century*. Vol. 2. Princeton: Princeton University Press.

Soames, Scott (2014): *The analytic tradition in philosophy*. Vol. 1. Princeton: Princeton University Press.

Soames, Scott (2018): *The analytic tradition in philosophy*. Vol. 2. Princeton: Princeton University Press.

Soames, Scott (2019): *The world philosophy made. From Plato to the digital age*. Princeton: Princeton University Press.

Sorrell, Thomas (2018): "Experimental philosophy and the history of philosophy", *British Journal for the History of Philosophy* 26 (5), pp. 829–849.

Stich, Stephen, and Kevin Tobia (2016): "Experimental philosophy and the philosophical tradition", in: Justin Sytsma and Wesley Buckwalter (Eds.): *A companion to experimental philosophy*. Oxford: Wiley-Blackwell, pp. 3–21.

Stratton, George (1896): "The relation between psychology and logic", *Psychological Review* 3 (3), pp. 313–320.

Street, Jacob Richard (1897): "A study in moral education", *The Pedagogical Seminary* 5 (1), pp. 5–40.

Stroll, Avrum (2001): *Twentieth-century analytic philosophy*. New York: Columbia University Press.

Sumner, Francis Bertody (1898): "A statistical study of belief", *The Psychological Review* 5 (6), pp. 616–631.

Sytsma, Justin (2017): "Two origin stories for experimental philosophy", *teorema* 36 (3), pp. 23–43.

Sytsma, Justin (2022): "Crossed wires. Blaming artifacts for bad outcomes", *The Journal of Philosophy* 119 (9), pp. 489–516.

Sytsma, Justin, Roland Bluhm, Pascale Willemsen, and Kevin Reuter (2019): "Causal attributions and corpus analysis", in: Eugen Fischer and Mark Curtis (Eds.): *Methodological advances in experimental philosophy*. London: Bloomsbury, pp. 209–238.

Sytsma, Justin, and Wesley Buckwalter (Eds.) (2016): *A companion to experimental philosophy*. Oxford: Wiley-Blackwell.

Sytsma, Justin, and Jonathan Livengood (2011): "A new perspective concerning experiments on semantic intuitions", *Australasian Journal of Philosophy* 89 (2), pp. 315–332.

Sytsma, Justin, and Jonathan Livengood (2015): *The theory and practice of experimental philosophy*. New York: Broadview.

Sytsma, Justin, and Jonathan Livengood (2019): "On experimental philosophy and the history of philosophy. A reply to sorrell", *British Journal for the History of Philosophy* 27 (3), pp. 635–647.

Sytsma, Justin, Jonathan Livengood, and David Rose (2012): "Two types of typicality. Rethinking the role of statistical typicality in ordinary causal attributions", *Studies in the History and Philosophy of Biological and Biomedical Sciences* 43 (4), pp. 814–820.

Sytsma, Justin, Jonathan Livengood, Ryoji Sato, and Mineki Oguchi (2015): "Reference in the land of the rising sun. A cross-cultural study on the reference of proper names", *Review of Philosophy and Psychology* 6 (2), pp. 213–230.

Sytsma, Justin, and Edouard Machery (2012): "On the relevance of folk intuitions. A reply to Talbot", *Consciousness and Cognition* 21 (4), pp. 654–660.

Sytsma, Justin, Ryan Muldoon, and Shaun Nichols (2021): "The meta-wisdom of crowds", *Synthese* 199, pp. 11051–11074.

Thompson, Kyle (2022): "Qualitative methods show that surveys misrepresent 'ought implies can' judgments". *Philosophical Psychology* 36 (1), pp. 29–57.

Tierney, Hannah, Chris Howard, Victor Kumar, Trevor Kvaran, and Shaun Nichols (2014): "How many of us are there?", in: Justin Sytsma (Ed.): *Advances in experimental philosophy of mind*. London: Bloomsbury, pp. 181–202.

Tipton, Jason (2014): *Philosophical biology in Aristotle's parts of animals*. Dordrecht: Springer.

Ulatowski, Joseph (2016): "Ordinary truth in Tarski and Næss", in: Adrian Kuźniar and Joanna Odrowąż-Sypniewska (Eds.): *Uncovering facts and values. Studies in contemporary epistemology and political philosophy*. Leiden: Brill, pp. 67–90.

Ulatowski, Joseph (2017): *Commonsense pluralism about truth. An empirical defence*. Basingstoke: Palgrave Macmillan.

Ulatowski, Joseph (forthcoming): "Experimental philosophy", in: Marcus Rossberg (Ed.): *The Cambridge handbook of analytical philosophy*. Cambridge: Cambridge University Press.

Ulatowski, Joseph, Dan Weijers, and Justin Sytsma (2020): "Cognitive science of philosophy symposium. Corpus analysis". *The Brains Blog*. https://philosophyofbrains.com/2020/12/15/cognitive-science-of-philosophy-symposium-corpus-analysis.aspx, last accessed May 19, 2023.

van Dongen, Noah, Matteo Colombo, Felipe Romero, and Jan Sprenger (2021): "Intuitions about the reference of proper names. A meta-analysis", *Review of Philosophy and Psychology* 12 (4), pp. 745–774.

Veysey, Laurence (1965): *The emergence of the American university*. Chicago: The University of Chicago Press.

Weatherson, Brian (2020): "A history of philosophy journals. Vol. 1. Evidence from topic modelling 1876–2013". *University of Michigan*. http://www-personal.umich.edu/~weath/lda/, last accessed May 19, 2023.

Weinberg, Jonathan (2016): "Experimental philosophy, noisy intuitions, and messy inferences", in: Jennifer Nado (Ed.): *Advances in experimental philosophy and philosophical methodology*. London: Bloomsbury, pp. 11–34.

Weinberg, Jonathan, Shaun Nichols, and Stephen Stich (2001): "Normativity and epistemic intuitions", *Philosophical Topics* 29 (1–2), pp. 429–460.

Wittgenstein, Ludwig (2009): *Philosophical investigations*. Transl. by Gertrude Elizabeth Margaret Anscombe, Peter Michael Stephan Hacker, and Joachim Schulte. 4th edition. Oxford: Wiley-Blackwell.

Wolf-Devine, Celia (2000): "Descartes theory of visual spatial perception", in: Stephen Gaukroger, John Schuster, and John Sutton (Eds.): *Descartes' natural philosophy*. London: Routledge, pp. 506–523.

Woozley, Anthony Douglas (1953): "Ordinary language and common sense", *Mind* 64 (247), pp. 301–312.

Zahorec, Michael, Robert Bishop, Nat Hansen, John Schwenkler, and Justin Sytsma (forthcoming): "Linguistic corpora and ordinary language. On the dispute between Ryle and Austin about the use of 'voluntary', 'involuntary', 'voluntarily', and 'involuntarily'", in: David Bordonaba (Ed.): *Experimental philosophy of language. Perspectives, methods and prospects*. Dordrecht: Springer.

Zupko, John (2018): "Acts and dispositions in John Buridan's faculty psychology", in: Nicolas Faucher and Magali Roques (Eds.): *The ontology, psychology, and axiology of habits in medieval philosophy*. Dordrecht: Springer, pp. 333–346.

Eugen Fischer and Justin Sytsma
Projects and Methods of Experimental Philosophy

Abstract: How does experimental philosophy address philosophical questions and problems? That is: What projects does experimental philosophy pursue? What is their philosophical relevance? And what empirical methods do they employ? Answers to these questions will reveal how experimental philosophy can contribute to the long-standing ambition of placing philosophy on the "secure path of a science", as Kant put it. We argue that experimental philosophy has introduced a new methodological perspective – a "meta-philosophical naturalism" that addresses philosophical questions about a phenomenon by empirically investigating how people think about this phenomenon. This chapter asks how this novel perspective can be successfully implemented: How can the empirical investigation of how people think about something address genuinely philosophical problems? And what methods – and, specifically, what methods beyond the questionnaire – can this investigation employ? We first review core projects of experimental philosophy and raise the question of their philosophical relevance. For ambitious answers, we turn to experimental philosophy's most direct historical precursor, mid-twentieth-century ordinary language philosophy, and discuss empirical implementations of two of its research programs that use experimental methods from psycholinguistics and corpus methods from the digital humanities.

Keywords: Corpus Methods; Experimental Philosophy; Foundations of Experimental Philosophy; Metaphilosophy; Naturalism; Philosophical Methodology; Philosophy as Science; Psycholinguistic Experiments

1 Introduction

Philosophers have long wondered how their discipline can be placed on the "secure path of a science", with methods that go beyond "groping among mere concepts" (cf. Kant 2003, p. 21). Much of the excitement attached to experimental philosophy arises from the fact that it holds out the promise of fresh answers to this question. Experimental philosophy recruits empirical methods to address philosophical questions and problems. The empirical methods are taken mainly from the social and the cognitive sciences, although increasingly also from linguistics and the digital humanities. Many of these methods are impeccably scientific and reasonably well understood, and certainly go beyond "mere groping". To answer the Kantian question, though, we need to get clear on how these methods can be deployed for *specifically* philosophical projects, and this question is itself philosophically difficult and divisive.

Note: The authors would like to thank the volume editors for helpful comments on a previous draft.

Experimental philosophy has already addressed questions from almost all areas of philosophy, with a focus on ethics (26% of current experimental philosophy papers, as categorized by the PhilPapers database), the philosophy of action (12%), epistemology (10%), philosophy of language (8%), philosophy of mind (7%), and metaphysics (6%).[1] Within each area, experimental literatures have developed around specific topics, such as free will and intentional action in the philosophy of action, causation and personal identity in metaphysics, or contextualism in epistemology. Some of these foci have emerged from philosophically unexpected findings in seminal studies – such as, for example, the finding that judgments traditionally regarded as merely descriptive or explanatory, such as attributions of intentionality or causal efficacy, are influenced by the moral valence of the relevant outcomes (Knobe 2003, Nadelhoffer 2006, Knobe and Fraser 2008). Other foci have emerged from well-established theoretical debates that explicitly rely on straightforwardly empirical assertions. For instance, epistemological debates about contextualism rely on claims about how contextual factors influence ordinary speakers' attributions of knowledge (DeRose 1992, Buckwalter 2010, Schaffer and Knobe 2012). Epistemologists advanced competing claims to account for the same intuitions about the same hypothetical cases. This clearly called for empirical investigation of competing explanations. However, the dynamic growth of experimental philosophy – from under 100 papers in 2007, to over 700 papers listed under this heading in PhilPapers in April 2014, to more than 2,750 papers listed in March 2022 – has seen topical coverage extend well beyond these foci of interest (see subsequent chapters in this volume; also Sytsma and Buckwalter 2016). Given this diversity in topics, projects in experimental philosophy in general can be usefully discussed only at the meta-philosophical level.

At the grandest meta-philosophical level, experimental philosophers are united by a commitment to methodological naturalism. Naturalism as a methodological stance is independent from naturalism as a metaphysical position (De Caro 2008; Haug 2014, pt. 1). Methodological naturalism recommends we address philosophical problems by drawing on empirical findings from the sciences (whose findings need not be consistent with metaphysical naturalism; Collins 2015). Traditional methodological naturalism seeks to address philosophical problems about a topic (say, vision, or intentional action) by drawing on empirical findings about that topic (say, findings from the psychology or neuroscience of vision, or of action control). Experimental philosophers go further by conducting their own empirical investigations when called for, distinguishing their practice from empirically informed "empirical philosophy" (Prinz 2008).

Crucially, however, experimental philosophers are conducting empirical investigations with two very different directions of thrust, one of which is genuinely novel. To address, for example, philosophical questions or problems about vision, experimental

---

[1] These figures are based on PhilPapers listings, as of November 9, 2021. They indicate lower bounds, since listings under the generic "Experimental Philosophy" heading include more non-experimental papers (e.g., on foundations of experimental philosophy) than sub-categories. (e.g., "Experimental Philosophy of Action").

philosophers have not only built on the psychology and neuroscience of vision and added their own investigations of the mechanisms of vision (e.g., Schwenkler and Weksler 2019, Weksler, Jacobson, and Bronfman 2021). Rather, experimental philosophers of perception have also built on the psychologies *of judgment and language*, and have empirically investigated how people *think and speak about* vision (e.g., Fischer et al. 2021; Fischer, Engelhardt, and Sytsma 2021; Roberts, Allen, and Schmidtke 2018, 2021). Similarly, to address philosophical questions about color, experimental philosophers have primarily investigated not color perception but color *cognition* (e.g., Cohen and Nichols 2010, Sytsma 2010, Hansen and Chemla 2017, Roberts and Schmidtke 2019), and similarly with regard to other topics, such as pain (e.g., Sytsma and Reuter 2017, Liu 2020, Reuter and Sytsma 2020, Salomons et al. 2021). Where traditional ("object-level") methodological naturalism addresses philosophical questions and problems about a topic (e.g., vision or color) by drawing on scientific findings about that topic, experimental philosophy has added a novel ("meta-level" or) *meta-philosophical naturalism* that addresses those questions and problems through empirical study of *how people think about* the topic of interest (Fischer and Collins 2015).

This distinctive new stance motivates our guiding question: How can empirical findings about how people think about a topic be used to address philosophical questions and problems about that topic? Our chapter will develop this question and make a start on answering it. We will develop and address the question through a review of experimental philosophy's two major strands – evidential and explanatory experimental philosophy (Section 2.2). We then propose fresh answers through two case studies (Sections 2.3–2.4).

The case studies explore how recent work in experimental philosophy has developed and transformed research programmes initially formulated by experimental philosophy's most direct historical precursor: Ordinary language philosophy, as pioneered by John Langshaw Austin (1957, 1962) and – on a liberal understanding of the movement – Arne Næss (1956, 1961), was analytic philosophy's first attempt to overcome limitations of armchair reflection through the use of (informal) experiments (Hansen and Chemla 2015), (peer-based) focus groups (Urmson 1969), and empirical surveys (Murphy 2014). This precursor of experimental philosophy[2] suggests answers to our guiding question: Ordinary language philosophy adopted a similar "meta-level" perspective and deployed insights into *how people talk about* a topic in order to address philosophical questions and problems about that topic. The two main strands of ordinary language philosophy explored different approaches in this vein. To answer our guiding question, our case studies will therefore consider how experimental philosophy has developed, respectively, the programs of *critical* ordinary language philosophy (Section 2.3) and *constructive* ordinary language philosophy (Section 2.4). So far, experimental philosophy has relied mainly on questionnaire-base methods (explained in Sytsma and Livengood 2015), while further methods are increasingly being taken up from two sources:

---

[2] See Chapter 1 for discussion of further precursors of experimental philosophy.

behavioral experiments from the social sciences and empirical and computational methods from the digital humanities (see Fischer and Curtis 2019). Our case studies will illustrate new uses, in experimental philosophy, of such further methods, namely, experimental methods from psycholinguistics (Section 2.3) and corpus methods from the digital humanities (Section 2.4).

2 Experimental Philosophy – Evidential and Explanatory

While experimental philosophy ranges considerably more widely, its two most prominent strands examine philosophically relevant intuitions (Fischer and Collins 2015, Sytsma and Livengood 2015). In several areas of philosophy, theory construction involves the "method of cases": In thought experiments, philosophers consider (typically) hypothetical cases (like Gettier cases, trolley cases, Frankfurt cases, and so forth), elicit intuitive judgments about them, and deploy these judgments as defeasible evidence for or against philosophical theories. These theories are typically required to be consistent with the case judgments and are often meant to explain or justify them. This approach has been used to assess analyses of concepts (e.g., "knowledge"), modal claims (e.g., that, provided current chemistry is correct, water must be H_2O), and moral claims (e.g., the moral equivalence of killing people or letting them die), among others (for reviews, see Daly 2010; Machery 2017, pp. 11–44). Philosophical theory construction guided by the method of cases often proceeds by working back and forth between intuitions elicited by different thought experiments and various background beliefs, until "reflective equilibrium" and a coherent set of judgments and beliefs has been achieved. While used most explicitly in moral and political philosophy (e.g., Foot 1967, Rawls 1971), this approach is sufficiently common to have been characterized as analytic philosophy's "standard justificatory procedure" (Bealer 1996, p. 4). Indeed, some philosophers have regarded it as "characteristic, perhaps definitive, of philosophical argumentation throughout its history" (Levin 2005, p. 193). Methodological rationalists have invoked the approach, as practiced from the armchair, to argue for the disciplinary autonomy of philosophy as a subject, holding that it can gain insight through a priori methods that rely on intuition and pure reason alone (e.g., Bealer 1996, 2000).

The main strands of experimental philosophy are responses to such intuition-driven philosophizing: *Evidential experimental philosophy* seeks to assess the evidential value of philosophically relevant intuitive judgments ("philosophical intuitions"), while *explanatory experimental philosophy* seeks to explain such intuitions.[3] The for-

---

3 See Sytsma and Livengood (2015). We employ the more expressive label "explanatory experimental philosophy" for what they termed the "cognitive program". On this first rough characterization, the programs overlap: Many (e.g., debunking) explanations are developed to contribute to epistemological evaluation.

mer may appear to make at most indirect contributions to philosophical theorizing; the latter might seem to be of primarily psychological interest. In the following, we examine the philosophical ambitions and rationales of these two enterprises.

2.1 Evidential Experimental Philosophy

Evidential experimental philosophy is pursued with two different ambitions (for reviews, see Stich and Tobia 2016, Mallon 2016) – what are often labeled the *positive* and *negative* programmes. We begin with the *positive programme*, which shares the key ambitions and methodological commitments of the pre-experimental philosophical work it engages with and introduces empirical methods to better sort the evidential wheat from the chaff.

Many philosophical debates take for granted the existence of "common-sense" conceptions of the phenomena of interest, and accord these conceptions an epistemic default status that places the burden of proof on critics (e.g., Daly 2010, Jackson 1998, Strawson 1959). This assumption is common, for example, in debates about free will (e.g., O'Connor and Franklin 2021, Jackson 1998, p.31), consciousness (e.g., Chalmers 1996, Lewis 1972), color (e.g., Allen 2016, Johnston 1992), and time (e.g., Callender 2017, Price 2011), among others. Seminal contributions to the positive programme sought to verify this assumption, as made in debates about free will. In these debates, common-sense status has been claimed for both compatibilist and incompatibilist conceptions of free will (see Chapter 13). Nahmias and colleagues (2004, 2005, 2006) examined whether laypeople's intuitive attributions of moral responsibility to hypothetical agents in deterministic and non-deterministic universes, respectively, are consistent with these conceptions. Other studies have examined lay conceptions of consciousness (e.g., Sytsma and Machery 2010; see Chapter 10), color (e.g., Roberts and Schmidtke 2019), or time (e.g., Latham, Miller, and Norton 2021), among others. A prominent motivation of these studies has been to settle which of competing conceptions is the clear majority view among adult laypeople and can lay claim to being "common sense" and enjoying epistemic default status. Viewed thus, these studies adjudicate on burdens of proof.

Other contributions to the positive programme have sought to enhance the use of the method of cases in conceptual analysis – e.g., on the concepts of *knowledge* (Buckwalter 2010, Schaffer and Knobe 2012; see Chapter 6) or *intention* (for a review see Cova 2016). Much work of this kind accepts the method's fundamental assumption that "possessing a concept makes one disposed to have pro-intuitions toward correct applications and con-intuitions toward incorrect applications – correct, that is, relative to the contents of the concept as it exists in the subject's head" (Goldman 2007, p. 15; cf. Chalmers and Jackson 2001, Ludwig 2007) – and seek to arrive at characterizations of conceptual contents through abductive inferences from (patterns of) intuitive application judgments. But this body of work questions the related assumption that individual philosophers, simply in virtue of being competent speakers of a shared language like English, can effectively examine folk concepts by eliciting just their own intuitions.[4]

Some critics of standard uses of the method of cases have suggested that philosophers' judgments may be unduly influenced by philosophical *theories* of the concepts of interest (*knowledge, moral permissibility, intention*, and so forth), rather than accurately reflecting folk concepts (e.g., Goldman 2007, Weinberg, Nichols, and Stich 2001). This suggestion motivates turning to case judgments from laypeople. This turn is warranted by findings that the intuitive judgments of philosophers sometimes diverge systematically from the judgments of laypeople or even other academics (e.g., Starmans and Friedman 2020 on intuitive knowledge attributions; cf. Horvath and Wiegmann 2016), and by patterns of responses from laypeople that philosophers failed to anticipate (e.g., Knobe's (2003) discovery that intention attributions are influenced by the moral valence of actions' outcomes).[5] Thus, the traditional assumption that philosophers' case intuitions are representative of competent speakers' intuitions more generally and can be safely taken to reflect widely shared folk concepts clearly stands in need of empirical investigation for any given case of interest. Empirical studies examining this assumption help determine whether philosophers' case judgments provide relevant evidence for the analysis of folk concepts and provide relevant evidence where philosophers' own judgments won't do.

By contrast, the *negative programme* in evidential experimental philosophy puts the method of cases more directly to the test by examining how epistemically irrelevant factors influence intuitions. To spell out the challenge raised by the negative programme, it is worth distinguishing between two different uses of the method of cases: in the "formal mode" the method is used to analyze concepts; in the "material mode" it is used to establish truths about the world. In different ways, both uses are put into doubt by the sensitivity of case judgments to irrelevant factors.

The "formal" use assumes that case judgments reflect the content of the underlying concepts. This assumption will not hold if case judgments are notably influenced by factors that have nothing to do with the content of the concept at issue. Factors examined include presentational factors such as purely verbal differences between equivalent case descriptions, the order in which cases are presented, or physical circumstances under which cases are presented (e.g., Horvath and Wiegmann 2021; for reviews, see Machery 2017, Stich and Tobia 2016). They further include individual differences in personality traits or cognitive traits like reflectiveness that may influence how a speaker applies a concept to a case, irrespective of the concept's represented content. Differences between demographic groups can raise similar worries. Sensitivity to cultural or socio-economic background can raise doubts about whether the use of a con-

---

[4] A related body of research on folk concepts is more profoundly skeptical of the method of cases and has employed psycholinguistic methods, instead (perhaps first: Powell, Horne, and Pinillos 2014, for a recent example, see Beisbart and Reuter 2021).

[5] Stich and Machery (2022, Table 2) list 20 studies contributing to conceptual analysis that elicit lay judgments that arguably differ from the case intuitions capturing or close to a "textbook consensus".

cept of interest is universal and have us ask whether different communities employ different concepts and, if so, which of these concepts is better, for which purposes (Stich and Tobia 2016, p. 14). Such findings move philosophical research on the concepts of interest from the traditional concerns of conceptual analysis to the ameliorative concerns of conceptual engineering (for a review see Cappelen and Plunkett 2020). Experimental philosophy can then contribute to this new enterprise in various ways – for example, by examining to what extent people are prone to reason badly with extant concepts (which are therefore in need of improvement) or are able to reason correctly, or as intended, with supposedly improved concepts (e.g., Fischer 2020, Machery 2021).

The "material" use of the method of cases assumes that intuition is a reliable source of the case judgments of interest. The basic assumption is that these judgments are true (at least) more often than not. This is meant to warrant the further assumption that they are generated by an underlying cognitive process that is reliable. If so, the fact that we have these intuitions, as and when we do, speaks for their truth. The basic assumption is called into doubt by sensitivity to presentational factors and individual differences as well as by sensitivity to demographic factors: If any of these factors lead to different judgments, the judgments made under some conditions, or by some people, must be wrong. In the absence of error theories that allow us to understand when and why people make the wrong judgments, or under what conditions and in what kind of people the underlying process is unreliable, however, we cannot tell which intuitions provide evidence for claims about the world.

The negative programme thus examines basic assumptions that motivate different uses of the method of cases, for individual classes of intuitive case judgments. Findings help philosophers identify classes of intuitions that cannot serve as evidence for or against philosophical hypotheses – or at any rate, cannot serve as such evidence in the absence of error theories and, more generally, a better understanding of the underlying processes. This allows philosophers to restrict their use of the method of cases to kinds of judgments that are not otiose due to inexplicable sensitivity.

To sum up, evidential experimental philosophy stands to make a variety of contributions to philosophy: its findings help to adjudicate on burdens of proof, to prevent premature generalization from philosophers' intuitions, and to avoid reliance on dubious evidence and methods incapable of supporting or assessing claims of interest. While the positive programme also generates fresh evidence about common-sense conceptions and folk concepts, both the positive and the negative programme in evidential experimental philosophy contribute mostly at the meta-level, where they address philosophical questions about the phenomenon of interest indirectly, by answering methodological questions about how those philosophical questions should be addressed, and what evidence should be admitted.

2.2 Explanatory Experimental Philosophy

Many contributions to evidential experimental philosophy involved explanations of the intuitions at issue – e.g., on free will (Nichols and Knobe 2007, Nadelhoffer et al. 2020; see Chapter 13), consciousness attributions (Arico et al. 2011, Fischer and Sytsma 2021; see Chapter 10), or knowledge attributions (Alexander, Gonnerman, and Waterman 2014, Gerken et al. 2020; see Chapter 6). In this work, explanation (debunking and other) is at the service of epistemological evaluation.

Other work in experimental philosophy pursues explanatory aims for their own sake. This work can be regarded as giving rise to a distinct strand of experimental philosophy that is continuous with cognitive science. It follows the same pattern as cognitive science, where researchers seek to identify new effects and explain them in terms of cognitive processes, typically with an aim of explaining a maximum number of effects in terms of a minimum number of processes. This pattern is well-illustrated by work sparked by the side-effect effect. For example, Chandra Sripada (2010, 2012) proposed the "deep self" hypothesis that explains this effect by positing a process whereby people attribute to agents a set of deeply held values and determine whether the agent's action concords with this "deep self". The hypothesis was invoked from the start to explain not only the targeted effect on intention attributions, but also effects on assessments of moral responsibility (Sripada 2010) and freedom (Sripada 2012). The proposal then swiftly motivated further research on the process that examined its impact on yet further phenomena (starting with Newman, Bloom, and Knobe 2014).

Discerning the characteristic course of cognitive science research in much experimental philosophy, Joshua Knobe (2016, p. 50) concludes that "the vast majority of [experimental philosophy] research is *cognitive science*". We propose a more nuanced approach that takes into account how such explanations are intended to fit into the philosophical dialectic. Where explanatory efforts are motivated by the aim to contribute to the epistemological assessment of philosophical intuitions, claims, or arguments, we see such work as an extension of evidential experimental philosophy. By contrast, where the explanans (e.g., people's "deep self" conception) is treated as a phenomenon of philosophical interest in its own right, regardless of how explanations invoking it might bear on further (meta-)philosophical questions, we hold that it forms a distinct strand of experimental philosophy: *explanatory experimental philosophy*.

As it unfolds, a line of research may well, by these lights, change from evidential experimental philosophy to explanatory, and back again. Explanatory work initially motivated by an evidential question may come to be pursued for its own sake, and the insights gained in this pursuit might later be applied to a new set of evidential questions. For instance, as Knobe (2016) points out, work sparked by the side-effect effect that follows the trajectory of cognitive science works against the ambitions of conceptual analysis: As standardly conceived, conceptual analysis seeks to explain patterns of case judgments, first and foremost, by reference to the content of the concept of interest. Work following the cognitive science trajectory aims to explain those patterns by reference to cognitive processes that affect the use of several concepts. But the more substantive the theories of these underlying cognitive processes become, the less explanatory work remains to be done by accounts of individual contents. Work on theories of such cognitive processes is hence set to leave the ambit of conceptual analysis. At the same time, some such theories can in principle be repurposed for the negative programme: Where they expose biases – like the "blame bias account" of the side-effect effect (Nadelhoffer 2006, Alicke 2008) – they can potentially provide a basis for error theories that allow us to understand when and why people make wrong judgments. Without such theories, the negative programme can infer from intuitional sensitivity only that certain kinds of intuitions are unreliable. With suitable error theories, it can go beyond purely negative findings and hope to identify conditions under which people may trust their intuitive case judgments (Weinberg 2015).[6]

Explanatory experimental philosophy thus seems to face a tougher question about its philosophical relevance than evidential experimental philosophy. The latter seemed to contribute to philosophical questions and problems mainly indirectly, by answering methodological questions about how those questions should be addressed, and what evidence should be admitted. Where explanatory efforts are put to these uses, they share this indirect relevance. By contrast, explanatory experimental philosophy, which undertakes explanatory work for its own sake, might be accused of doing something else entirely. Insofar as cognitive science is taken to be distinct from philosophy, accepting with Knobe that evidential experimental philosophy is cognitive science raises a critical question – "Why is this work *philosophy?*" (Stich and Tobia 2016, fn. 10). At this point, intuitional experimental philosophy appears to face a dilemma: the critic can charge that it either contributes to philosophy only indirectly (through the evidential strand) or not at all (if the explanatory strand reduces to "mere psychology").

3 Critical Ordinary Language Philosophy – Psycholinguistic Experiments

Much experimental philosophy seeks to address philosophical problems about a topic by examining how people think and speak about that topic. The apparent dilemma we now face motivates the question, how an approach along these lines can make a direct and substantive contribution to resolving distinctively or characteristically philosophical problems. For a first answer, we turn to experimental philosophy's most direct historical precursor, ordinary language philosophy. Much work in this mid-twentieth-century movement focused on "philosophical puzzles" which, ordinary language philosophers maintained, arise from the way we think and speak about the phenom-

---

[6] For example, Fischer and Sytsma (2021) expose a framing effect in judgments about philosophical zombies and explain it by reference to a comprehension bias. This explanation allows to go beyond the conclusion that intuitions about philosophical zombies are unreliable, and identify a more and a less helpful frame.

ena that puzzle us (e.g., Austin 1946, 1962; Ryle 1954; Waismann 1997; cf. Fischer 2019, 2023; Schroeder 2006, pp. 151–168; Wittgenstein 1953). Understanding these ways – and their errors – was regarded as an essential step in resolving the resulting problems. We now consider such "puzzles" (Section 3.1), spell out how experimental philosophy can provide much-needed empirical foundations for an approach to them that is in line with critical ordinary language philosophy (Section 3.2), and explain how experimental methods from psycholinguistics can be employed for the purpose (Section 3.3).

3.1 Philosophical Puzzles

Plato regarded a sense of wonder in the face of the familiar as the starting point of philosophizing (2004, 155b–d). He had in mind puzzlement about *the very possibility* of familiar facts, rather than curiosity about their causes – not "what makes the apple drop?" but "how is it even possible for the apple to reach the ground?" (or for the tortoise to overtake Achilles). This sort of puzzlement is the hallmark of *one* kind of characteristically philosophical problems, exemplified by skeptical problems and the problems of mental causation, free will, perception, and induction.[7] These philosophical puzzles (let's call them "Platonic puzzles") are motivated by intuitive lines of thought that suggest certain common-sense convictions *cannot* be true. These lines of thought, often conceptualized as paradoxes, appear to bring out antinomies and motivate philosophical questions like: How is it possible to know anything at all about the physical environment? How can our beliefs and desires make a difference to our bodily movements? How is it possible that people are morally responsible for their actions? How is sense-perception, as we ordinarily understand it, even possible?

Relevant lines of thought typically rely on apparently common-sense convictions and intuitive judgments, and suggest a conclusion at odds with further common-sense convictions. These lines of thought thus appear to bring out conflicts between extant beliefs, namely, between the beliefs invoked by the arguments and the belief(s) challenged by them. To the extent to which these beliefs are deeply held, these conflicts are both puzzling and troubling, causing cognitive dissonance (see Gawronski and Strack 2012, Kruglanski et al. 2018). Philosophical responses typically seek to show that these conflicts are merely apparent. Responses may include revisionary elements (some common-sense convictions get revised) and diagnostic elements (some steps of the arguments are shown fallacious). But, typically, they focus on reconciliation: on showing that, and explaining why, the common-sense conviction or conception challenged (or as much of it as survives revision) is consistent with as much of the argu-

---

[7] The entries in the *Stanford Encyclopedia of Philosophy* on mental causation (Robb and Heil 2021), free will (O'Connor and Franklin 2021), the problem of perception (Crane and French 2021) and the problem of induction (Henderson 2020) all conceptualize at least key versions or components of these problems in a manner consistent with the following characterization.

ments challenging them as theorists feel obliged to accept (see Fischer 2011 for a review).

Platonic puzzles are developed by, and perhaps even arise from, intuitive reasoning about the world. These puzzles therefore seem a particularly plausible target for the meta-philosophical naturalism promoted by experimental philosophy (Section 2.1): They should help us identify some ways in which empirical findings about how people think about a topic can be used to address philosophical problems about that topic. For a start, experimental philosophy can support and complement the responses reviewed:

- Experimental philosophy can help establish whether supposed common-sense convictions – invoked or apparently challenged – are indeed common sense. Similarly, it can assess whether people indeed make any such intuitive judgments as the arguments rely on.
- Going a step further, it can help *assess* these convictions and intuitions, e.g., by developing debunking explanations of the relevant beliefs and judgments. Together, these first two steps assess the need for revision of common sense and identify the parties in need of reconciliation.
- Finally, experimental philosophy can help assess the arguments that rely on those beliefs or judgments, for example, by exposing biases that lead to typically overlooked fallacies. The identification of fallacies supports diagnostic responses.

We now consider a case-study that develops the last and most novel of these applications and demonstrates how experimental philosophy can directly address Platonic puzzles (see also Fischer 2023).

3.2 A New Experimental Project – Critical Ordinary Language Philosophy

This case-study is on an experimental implementation of critical ordinary language philosophy, as pioneered by John Langshaw Austin (1946, 1962). This purely diagnostic approach seeks to "dissolve" philosophical ("Platonic") puzzles by exposing fallacies already in the opening moves of the arguments that raise them; the aim is to reveal that these arguments fail to get off the ground, so that the apparent conflict between extant beliefs does not even begin to arise and is *merely* apparent. Following Austin (1962), the approach has been developed most fully for the "problem of perception" (Crane and French 2021, Smith 2002). As standardly conceived today, this problem is developed by arguments "from illusion" and "from hallucination". These arguments invoke the uncontroversial beliefs that illusions occur and hallucinations are possible, and derive the conclusion that perceivers are directly aware of subjective sense-data, rather than physical objects. The arguments thus appear to challenge the common-sense conception of sense-perception (folk direct realism), and bring out a conflict between this conception and those uncontroversial premises. They motivate the question, how sense-perception, as we ordinarily understand it, is even possible – given the evident possibility of illusions and hallucinations.

Critical ordinary language philosophy seeks to expose "seductive (mainly verbal) fallacies" as "concealed motives" for formulating philosophical paradoxes (Austin 1962, p. 5). That the fallacious inferences are "concealed" means that thinkers are not conscious of making them and presupposing their conclusions, in the relevant arguments. In today's terms, the approach focuses on exposing automatic default inferences that are contextually inappropriate (Fischer et al. 2021). This approach is in need of experimental implementation and empirical validation: Thinkers have no privileged access to automatic inferences, which can be documented only experimentally (Bargh et al. 2012). Moreover, principles of charity demand that fallacies be attributed to competent thinkers only in the light of an empirically supported explanation of when and why competent thinkers commit such fallacies (Thagard and Nisbett 1983). An extension of evidential experimental philosophy that turns from the assessment of intuitions to that of inferences in verbal reasoning can provide – and has provided – just what is needed.

The need for a validating explanation is pressing for attributions of inappropriate default inferences: Nouns and verbs automatically activate associated stereotypes (prototypes and situation schemas, respectively) that represent knowledge about typical and diagnostic features of objects and events (Engelhardt and Ferreira 2016). These stereotypes support defeasible inferences (the "secretary" is female) that are triggered by words almost irrespective of context (Levinson 2000). These inferences are swiftly complemented, as combinations of nouns and verbs ("the mechanic checked…") activate knowledge about the typical features of more specific situations (car inspections) that are not activated by either word alone (Bicknell et al. 2010, Matsuki et al. 2011). In sentence comprehension, these different inferences need to be integrated with each other and with information from wider discourse context (Metusalem et al. 2012), in building the *situation model:* the mental representation of the situation described by the text or speech, which provides the basis for further judgments and reasoning about that situation (Kintsch 1988, Zwaan 2016). Initial inferences decay when lacking contextual support (Oden and Spira 1983) and may get effortfully suppressed where they conflict with contextual information ("the secretary, Mr. Smith") or with background beliefs (Faust and Gernsbacher 1996). Competent language users are good at this task (for a review see Butterfuss and Kendeou 2018), and can, e.g., suppress default inferences that conflict with background beliefs within one second (Fischer and Engelhardt 2017). In consequence, inappropriate default inferences hardly influence further judgment and reasoning.

One explanation of when and why contextually inappropriate default inferences influence further cognition, even so, is provided by the linguistic salience bias hypothesis (Fischer and Engelhardt 2020, Fischer and Sytsma 2021): Subordinate uses of markedly unbalanced polysemes (like "see") can give rise to fallacies of equivocation. That is: Subordinate uses ("Jack saw her point") are often interpreted by retaining the initially activated stereotype (situation schema) associated with the dominant sense (e.g., the visual sense of *S sees X*) and suppressing its irrelevant component features (e.g., *S looks at X*, *X is in front of S*, and so forth, retaining only *S knows X is there*, *S knows what X is*) (Giora 2003; cf. Brocher et al. 2018). Where some, but not all, of the stereotypical features associated with the dominant sense are contextually relevant, and the dominant sense is far more frequent than all others, general principles of activation ensure that suppression remains partial.[8] In consequence, stereotypical inferences supported only by the dominant sense are made also from the subordinate use. This explains experimentally documented spatial inferences (*X is in front of Y*) from purely epistemic uses of "see" ("He saw her point") (Fischer and Engelhardt 2017, 2019, 2020), doxastic inferences (*S believes that X is F*) from purely phenomenal uses of appearance verbs (*X appears F to S*) (Fischer et al. 2021, Fischer, Engelhardt, and Sytsma 2021), and inferences of stereotypical zombie properties from philosophical uses of "zombie" (Fischer and Sytsma 2021). Professional academic philosophers proved as susceptible to this bias as laypeople (Fischer, Engelhardt, and Herbelot 2022).

These empirical findings warrant new reconstructions of arguments from illusion and hallucination that develop the problem of perception. These arguments employ appearance- and perception-verbs in a "phenomenal" or "phenomenological" sense (Ayer 1956, p. 90; Robinson 1994, pp. 51–53) which lacks many of the implications – factive, epistemic, or doxastic – of ordinary uses of these verbs, as it serves only to describe the character of perceivers' subjective experience (e.g., "Macbeth sees$_{PHEN}$ a dagger" means "Macbeth had an experience like that of seeing a dagger"). The linguistic salience bias hypothesis predicts that even competent thinkers will make contextually inappropriate stereotypical inferences from these uses that lead to fallacies of equivocation.

For example, an influential statement of the argument from hallucination assumes that

(1) Macbeth saw a dagger,

and immediately infers "but still not a real dagger" (Ayer 1956, p. 90). Since the hallucinator is meant to have an experience just like that of seeing a physical dagger, this inference is fallacious: In the relevant phenomenal sense, Macbeth is seeing a physical dagger – he merely fails to see such a thing in the dominant visual sense. The linguistic salience bias hypothesis suggests the step is driven by existential or spatial inferences that are supported by the dominant visual sense but are made from the special phenomenal use in (1), anyway.[9] They lead to implicit conclusions that are defeated by contextual information but are tacitly assumed, even so, in further reasoning:

---

8 The two most relevant principles of activation are that senses get activated more strongly when encountered more frequently than other senses (Giora 2003), and that frequently co-activated stereotype components exchange lateral cross-activation (McRae et al. 2005).

9 On some interpretations of (1), Macbeth hallucinates a purely imaginary dagger; on others, he hallucinates the actual murder weapon he will use (which just is not around at this point), and the following

(2) There was something there that Macbeth saw. But, by assumption:

(3) There was no physical object there for Macbeth to see. By (2) and (3):

(4) There was a non-physical object that Macbeth saw.

Here, the inference from (1) leads to an implicit conclusion (2) that is immediately defeated (by 3) but tacitly assumed in the inference from (1) and (3) to (4) (see Fischer and Engelhardt 2020, pp. 432–433). The second half of the argument then generalizes from this case of hallucination to all – qualitatively indistinguishable – cases of visual perception (Ayer 1956, p. 90; McPherson 2013, pp. 15–16; Smith 2002, pp. 196–197).

Such diagnostic reconstructions of arguments from hallucination (Fischer 2019, Fischer and Engelhardt 2020) and from illusion (Fischer et al. 2021, Fischer, Engelhardt, and Sytsma 2021) promise to "dissolve" the problem of perception by showing that the apparent conflict between belief in the occurrence or possibility of illusions and hallucinations, on the one hand, and folk direct realism, on the other, is only due to fallacious reasoning. The puzzle is an artefact of a verbal reasoning bias.

Such diagnostic accounts have two key elements: reconstructions of specific arguments that expose fallacies in these arguments, and explanations of why even competent thinkers commit those fallacies, e.g., by reference to a cognitive bias. Both elements are in need of empirical support. To support the proposed reconstruction of the argument from hallucination, for instance, we need to document factive inferences from phenomenal uses of perception-verbs. To support the proposed explanation, we need to provide evidence of linguistic salience bias, more generally. Methods from psycholinguistics allow us to address both tasks.

3.3 Psycholinguistic Methods

We now illustrate how psycholinguistic methods that were initially developed to study language comprehension can be adapted for the new purpose of studying verbal reasoning. To do so, we consider experiments that assessed the linguistic salience bias hypothesis.

Hypotheses about automatic inferences from words can be tested with the psycholinguistic cancellation paradigm (for a review, see Fischer and Engelhardt 2019): Participants read or hear sentences where the word of interest is followed by sequels that are respectively consistent and inconsistent with the conclusion of the hypothesized inference. If these inferences are made, the resulting clashes with inconsistent sequels engender comprehension difficulties which require effort to overcome. Increased cog-

---

steps (2) and (3) (below) quantify over locally restricted domains, with the second "there" understood as "before Macbeth". In the former case, the argument involves parallel existential and spatial inferences from (1); in the latter case, the argument relies exclusively on spatial inferences (Fischer and Engelhardt 2020).

nitive effort shows up through pupil dilations (Laeng et al. 2012), longer reading times (Rayner et al. 2004), and signature electrophysiological responses in the brain (Kutas and Federmeier 2011). Experimental philosophers have taken up all these methods: pupillometry (e.g., Fischer and Engelhardt 2017, 2020), reading-time measurements with eye-tracking (e.g., Fischer, Engelhardt, and Sytsma 2021), as well as electroencephalography (e.g., Cosentino et al. 2017). We discuss the method that strikes us as the most helpful for the investigation of inferences in philosophical arguments: reading-time measurements with eye-tracking, combined with plausibility ratings.

Readers fixate most words as their eyes move forward (skipping the words easiest to predict from the context) *and* backwards ("regressions" at points of difficulty). Readers immediately construct local interpretations over small numbers of adjacent words. If the task at hand demands it, and only then, they subsequently integrate these local interpretations into more comprehensive interpretations of longer sentences and passages, which take long-distance dependencies into account (Swets et al. 2008; cf. Ferreira and Lowder 2016). In reading, we thus need to recognize words and integrate them into local and more comprehensive interpretations. Difficulties at these different stages manifest themselves in different eye-tracking measures (first-pass reading times, re-reading times, and so forth). Where default inferences from words get cancelled by subsequent context, readers have difficulties integrating information from the initial "source region" with information from the subsequent cancellation or "conflict region". Such difficulties lead to longer re-reading times, for either of these two regions (Rayner et al. 2004, Clifton et al. 2016). Automatic inferences can therefore be studied by examining re-reading times.

Fischer and Engelhardt (2019) used this approach to document inappropriate spatial inferences from epistemic uses of "see", predicted by their linguistic salience bias hypothesis. Materials manipulate verb, object, and post-verbal context, in a 2×2×2 design (Table 1).

Table 1: Example stimuli and regions of interest for eye movement analysis (from Fischer and Engelhardt 2019)

	Verb	Object		Context	
		Visual			
(1)	Sheryl sees	the picture	on the wall	behind her.	(s-inconsistent)
(2)	Sheryl sees	the picture	on the wall	facing her.	(s-consistent)
(3)	Sheryl is aware of	the picture	on the wall	behind her.	(s-inconsistent)
(4)	Sheryl is aware of	the picture	on the wall	facing her.	(s-consistent
		Epistemic			
(1)	Joe sees	the problems	that lie	ahead of him.	(s-consistent)
(2)	Joe sees	the problems	that lie	behind him.	(s-inconsistent)
(3)	Joe is aware of	the problems	that lie	ahead of him.	(s-consistent)
(4)	Joe is aware of	the problems	that lie	behind him.	(s-inconsistent)

Concrete versus abstract objects (e. g., "picture" versus "problems") invite visual versus epistemic interpretations of the verb. Post-verbal contexts are amenable to literal spatial and metaphorical temporal interpretation (whereby ahead = in the future; behind = in the past). These facilitate purely metaphorical interpretations of epistemic items (*Joe knows what problems he will have in the future* and *Joe knows what problems he had in the past*). If any spatial inferences from "see" are suppressed from the local interpretation, e. g., of "Joe sees the problems", readers have no trouble winning through to this interpretation. The space–time metaphors in our items give rise to embodied cognition effects (Boroditsky and Ramscar 2002, Bottini et al. 2015) and support spatial reasoning about temporal relations (Casasanto and Boroditsky 2008, Gentner, Imai and Boroditsky 2002). If spatial inferences from "see" cannot be suppressed from the local interpretation of the previous words, they will engage spatial reasoning, and engender integration difficulties in sentences like "Joe sees the problems that lie behind him". Such inferences will hence show up through longer re-reading times for spatially inconsistent than spatially consistent contexts.

Even when they persist long enough to cause integration difficulties, inappropriate default inferences may be suppressed within one second. To examine their influence of further cognition, Fischer and Engelhardt (2019) therefore combined the reading task with a subsequent plausibility rating task: If spatial inferences persist long enough to influence further judgment and reasoning, they will engender the impression of a conflict in spatially inconsistent items, which will reduce the items' plausibility. Accordingly, lower plausibility ratings for spatially inconsistent than consistent "see"-sentences provide evidence that spatial inferences from "see" influence further cognition, as do lower ratings for spatially inconsistent sentences with "see" than with the contrast verb "be aware of" that does not give rise to persistent spatial inferences. This experimental paradigm has been used to garner evidence for contextually inappropriate stereotypical inferences. It permits to examine, more generally, automatic inferences in verbal reasoning. Findings can provide much-needed empirical foundations for the promising approach of critical ordinary language philosophy, and assess diagnostic analyses proposed for specific philosophical arguments.

4 Constructive Ordinary Language Philosophy – Corpus Analyses

In contrast to the critical project that seeks to dissolve ("Platonic") philosophical puzzles, constructive ordinary language philosophy aims to draw positive conclusions about phenomena of philosophical interest. As Hansen (2020, p. 2434) puts it, "the constructive project consists of observations about how philosophically significant expressions are ordinarily used and uses those observations to support conclusions about non-linguistic aspects of the world". Of course, the inferences one draws from how we talk about the world to how the world actually is can be stronger or weaker –

and one can be more or less skeptical about such inferences. Minimally, we can see constructive ordinary language philosophy as seeking to use "a sharpened awareness of words to sharpen our perception of, though not as the final arbiter of, the phenomena" (Austin 1957, p. 8). The hope is that such sharpened perception will result in improved understanding of the non-linguistic phenomena and, in particular, their roles in our lives. This enterprise has an empirical side: empirical methods are required to investigate how we use words, the situations in which we apply them, and the ends to which they are put.

The empirical side of constructive ordinary language philosophy corresponds with what Sytsma and Livengood (2015) term the *descriptive programme* of experimental philosophy. As they put it, practitioners "aim to describe how people actually talk about philosophically interesting topics" (Sytsma and Livengood 2015, p. 43), hoping to detail "the contours of our concepts" (Sytsma and Livengood 2015, p. 76). While Sytsma and Livengood focus on how this can be done by using the classic, case-based questionnaire methods, we now consider how constructive ordinary language philosophy can be aided by an expanded set of tools, especially tools from corpus linguistics. As an example, we look at Sytsma and Livengood's responsibility account of ordinary causal attributions. We now introduce work on causal attributions (Section 4.1) and corpus methods (Section 4.2), and suggest how findings can serve the aims of constructive ordinary language philosophy (Section 4.3).

4.1 Causal Attributions and Injunctive Norms

What is causation? The recent philosophical literature has tended to treat causation as a non-linguistic aspect of the world, and yet has focused on "our folk-theoretical notion of 'cause'" (Paul and Hall 2003, p. 2) in examining it, often calling on case judgments about the applicability of this lemma[10] for purposes of giving an analysis of the concept, which is in turn treated as evidence with regard to the nature of causation. Frequently, the cases employed have had a clear normative dimension. For example, Carolina Sartorio calls on several cases involving life and death decisions to set "a constraint on the concept of cause" and thereby help "carve up the concept" (Sartorio 2005, p. 71). The first is the Assassination Case, which is taken to provide an obvious counterexample to a simple counterfactual account of causation:

> Assassin shoots Victim and, as a result, Victim dies. However, Backup is waiting in reserve. Had Assassin not shot, Backup would have, and Victim would still have died (in a very similar way, at around the same time, etc.). (Sartorio 2005, p. 72)

---

[10] A lemma is the dictionary form of a set of words or the word they are indexed by. To illustrate, the concern here is presumably not simply with the word "cause" but would also include "caused", "causes", and "causing".

Despite calling on norm-laden cases like this, philosophers have generally assumed that the concept of causation is a purely descriptive concept, such that the normative dimension might be seen as simply adding a bit of color to the discussion. As Helen Beebee (2004, p. 293) puts it, "no philosopher working within the tradition I'm concerned with here thinks that the *truth* conditions for causal claims contain a moral element".

Seminal work in experimental philosophy has cast grave doubt on the assumption that the moral aspects of cases can simply be ignored, however, at least insofar as we hope to analyze the folk concept of causation (see Chapter 5). Perhaps the most discussed example, the Pen Case, comes from Knobe and Fraser:

> The receptionist in the philosophy department keeps her desk stocked with pens. The administrative assistants are allowed to take the pens, but faculty members are supposed to buy their own.
> The administrative assistants typically do take the pens. Unfortunately, so do the faculty members. The receptionist has repeatedly e-mailed them reminders that only administrative assistants are allowed to take the pens.
> On Monday morning, one of the administrative assistants encounters Professor Smith walking past the receptionist's desk. Both take pens. Later that day, the receptionist needs to take an important message… but she has a problem. There are no pens left on her desk. (Knobe and Fraser 2008, p. 443)

In this case, two agents perform the same action, jointly bringing about a bad outcome. The only difference is that one violates an injunctive norm in doing so – in this case doing something that is proscribed by established rules – while the other does not. Despite this, when participants are asked who caused the problem, ratings are very notably higher for the norm-violating agent (Professor Smith) than for the norm-conforming agent (the administrative assistant). And similar findings have been found using a range of different vignettes, using both within- and between-participant designs, and employing a variety of types of questions, including using Likert-scales, binary and multiple-choice answers, rank-ordering, and fill-in-the-blank (e.g., Alicke 1992, 2000; Hitchcock and Knobe 2009; Kominsky et al. 2015; Icard et al. 2017; Kominsky and Phillips 2019; Sytsma and Livengood 2021; Sytsma 2022a).

One key question that the experimental literature has focused on is how we should explain the effect of norms on causal attributions. A number of different types of accounts have been offered, although we'll focus on just two here.[11] Perhaps the most prominent are *counterfactual accounts*, such as that offered by Hitchcock and Knobe (2009), building off the work of Knobe and Fraser (2008) discussed above.[12] Hitchcock and Knobe's work can be categorized most cleanly as an example of explanatory experimental philosophy: they note the effect of norms on causal attributions and lay out a cognitive mechanism to explain it. Specifically, they hold that norm violations matter

---

11 See also the bias account put forward by Alicke and colleagues (e.g., Alicke 1992, 2000; Alicke, Rose, and Bloom 2011) as well as the pragmatic account put forward by Samland and Waldmann (2016).
12 This type of account has been developed in a large number of papers, including Halpern and Hitchcock (2015), Kominsky et al. (2015), and Icard et al. (2017), among others.

for causal attributions because people arrive at such judgments by considering counterfactuals, but don't do so indiscriminately; rather, they are more likely to consider counterfactuals on which a norm violation is replaced with something more normal. If the outcome doesn't occur on this counterfactual, they then treat the abnormal event as the cause. For instance, in the Pen Case, Professor Smith violates a norm in taking a pen (while the administrative assistant does not). According to Hitchcock and Knobe, this renders Professor Smith's action more salient, with people then being more likely to consider the counterfactual on which Professor Smith does not take a pen. Since the problem doesn't occur on this counterfactual, people then tend to judge that Professor Smith caused the problem. This type of view is in accord with the philosophical consensus, treating the ordinary concept of causation as purely descriptive, while explaining the impact of norms indirectly, holding that norms affect the process by which we apply the descriptive concept.

Sytsma, Livengood, and Rose (2012) offered a rather different type of explanation. Pushing against the philosophical consensus, they suggested that the ordinary concept of causation is not purely descriptive, but in part normative, such that ordinary causal attributions are akin to responsibility or accountability attributions.

Projects in experimental philosophy seldom map cleanly onto theoretical divisions between programmes, and the work of Sytsma and colleagues is no exception. Thus, the responsibility account has been pushed in ways that align with evidential experimental philosophy, stressing the divergence between ordinary causal attributions and philosophical assumptions (e.g., Livengood, Sytsma, and Rose 2017, Livengood and Sytsma 2020, Sytsma 2022b). And, in line with explanatory experimental philosophy, the responsibility account is given as an explanation of effects like that shown by Knobe and Fraser (2008) for the Pen Case. Nonetheless, Sytsma and colleagues' primary claim concerns how English speakers typically use the lemma "cause", and the main goal of their work is to help detail the contours of this usage. In other words, the evidential and explanatory ends follow from a project starting in descriptive experimental philosophy. This is perhaps most clear in the work of Sytsma and colleagues (2019), which goes beyond the case-based questionnaire methods that have most commonly been employed in experimental philosophy of causation by calling on the methods of corpus linguistics.

4.2 Corpus Methods

While questionnaire methods have been the dominant approach in experimental philosophy, they are not the only methods that have been used. One set of methods that has been becoming increasingly popular in recent years are corpus methods, which have often been employed with the goal of supplementing data collected in experimental settings with information about the use of words "in the wild" so as to provide a consilience of evidence (Bluhm 2016, Ulatowski et al. 2020).[13]

Corpus linguistics aims to collect and analyze pre-existing, "real world" linguistic data (McEnery and Hardie 2015, O'Keefe and McCarthy 2022). Corpus analysis starts with corpora. These are collections of written or oral texts, typically supplemented with additional information (e.g., where the texts were drawn from, parts of speech, and so on). Corpora are often built with the aim of giving a balanced picture of the target domain, which might be rather general (e.g., contemporary American English) or quite specific (e.g., the utterances of children). Many corpora are available online, often with extensive search features that, among other things, allow users to easily compare how often different words occur and the contexts in which they are used. Perhaps the most common corpus in recent work in experimental philosophy is the Corpus of Contemporary American English (COCA).[14] This is a contemporary, balanced corpus, comprised of some one billion words drawn from a range of sources (including magazines and newspapers, blogs and webpages, books and academic texts, transcripts and subtitles). And COCA is the corpus used by Sytsma and colleagues (2019).

Their main goals were to determine whether the use of causal attributions tends to be sensitive to normative information outside of experimental contexts and whether they are similar to responsibility attributions, as predicted by the responsibility account. To do this, they used the COCA in two different ways: They began by using the online search features to compare contexts for key phrases of interest, then confirmed their findings by applying computational methods to the full text of the corpus.

As a proxy for the presence of normative information in the texts, Sytsma and colleagues looked at what events people tend to attribute causation for, noting that people are generally more focused on blame than praise (Prinz 2007). As such, they expected that if causal attributions are used in a normative way, we would expect them to be disproportionately directed toward bad outcomes. By contrast, if the ordinary concept of causation is purely descriptive, we would have no a priori reason to expect it to be used in contexts with any particular valence. To test this, Sytsma and colleagues compiled the nouns that occur most frequently after the phrases standardly used to elicit causal attributions ("caused the") and responsibility attributions ("responsible for the") in the experimental literature, as well as a range of possible synonyms, using the non-academic portions of the COCA. This resulted in a list of 260 distinct items. They then had independent coders judge the valence of each item.

As expected, Sytsma and colleagues found that "caused the" was disproportionately used to describe items that the coders judged to be negative. To illustrate, the five most common nouns were "death", "accident", "crash", "problem", and "explosion". And a similar result held for responsibility attributions, but not for most of the poten-

---

13 While the use of corpus methods in philosophy dates back to at least the 1970s (e.g., Meunier et al. 1976, McKinnon 1970), its use has grown notably in the past five years. For an extensive, if incomplete, set of references, see Sytsma (2023, fn. 3).
14 See https://www.english-corpora.org/coca/, last accessed May 19, 2023.

tial synonyms tested, such as "created the" or "produced the", which were mainly used in a neutral fashion. Based on these results, as well as further analyses aimed at testing potential confounds, Sytsma and colleagues (2019, p. 223) conclude that "the data suggests that the notion of causation is in itself inherently normative".

To further test this finding, Sytsma and colleagues turned to more computational methods, constructing distributional semantic models (DSMs) from the full text of the non-academic portions of the COCA. While the details can be daunting, the basic idea behind this approach is that "you shall know a word by the company it keeps" (Firth 1957, p. 11).[15] To do this, DSMs look at the contexts in which terms occur across the corpus, typically representing each term as a geometric vector in a high-dimensional space. Closeness in the space is interpreted in terms of relatedness of meaning, and standardly measured by taking the cosine of the vectors. In their final DSM, Sytsma and colleagues used the *word2vec* algorithm to build a high-performing semantic space[16] with the key phrases from above ("caused the", "responsible for the") treated as individual terms. As predicted, they found that these were quite close together in the semantic space, indicating that they are used in very similar ways. In fact, each of them was one of the five nearest terms to the other in the space. Further, other close terms suggested, again, that each is used in predominately negative contexts. These findings lend further strength to the more qualitative analysis, as well as prior experimental results, supporting the key contention of the responsibility account – that causal attributions are typically used in a normative fashion.

4.3 From Descriptive to Constructive

The responsibility account suggests that the folk concept of causation is normative. In "descriptive experimental philosophy" (Sytsma and Livengood 2015), such a descriptive conclusion is treated as an end in itself. But it can also form the basis for inferences about non-linguistic phenomena. In the case at hand, the sharpened perception of the ordinary use of "cause" plausibly suggests a shift in how philosophers should think about the phenomenon of causation, resituating it from the non-social to the social realm: Rather than see the normative aspect of our causal attributions as reflecting a mistake or a bias that threatens to distract us from the a more fundamental descriptive relation, we can recalibrate our thinking to recognize the centrality of normative concerns to our daily lives. Thus, Sytsma (2021) suggests that the responsibility account fits neatly with a general view of how humans tend to think about the world – that "we

---

[15] For more detailed discussion of DSMs, see Baroni et al. (2014a), Erk (2012), as well as Turney and Pantel (2010). For further examples illustrating different philosophical applications, see Fischer, Engelhardt, and Herbelot (2015, 2022), Fischer and Sytsma (2021), Sytsma and Snater (2023), Zahorec et al. (2023).

[16] As measured by the MEN benchmark (Bruni et al. 2013), for which it produced a Spearman's ρ of 0.80, which is on par with the best performing models in Baroni et al. (2014b).

are moralizing creatures through and through" (Knobe 2010, p. 328), tending to focus not just on how things came about, but also on how to apportion praise and blame for what has occurred. This is exactly the kind of conclusion constructive ordinary language philosophy aims for: a conclusion that is drawn from an examination of the ordinary uses of words and that helps to situate our thinking about non-linguistic phenomena.

5 Conclusion – Experimental Philosophy and the Kantian Ambition

This chapter considered how experimental philosophy can help realize the Kantian ambition of placing philosophy – or notable parts of it – on the secure path of a science. Among other things, experimental philosophy uses scientific methods to investigate how people think and speak about phenomena of philosophical interest. To discern how such an investigation can help realize the Kantian ambition, we need to understand how an improved understanding of how people think and speak about phenomena can help address philosophical questions and problems about these phenomena.

We have suggested that two main strands of experimental philosophy potentially face a dilemma: the critic can contend that evidential experimental philosophy at best makes indirect contributions to philosophy, while explanatory experimental philosophy reduces to mere psychology. To identify ways in which experimental philosophy can play a more substantive role and contribute more directly to addressing characteristically philosophical problems, we turned to its most direct historical precursor, ordinary language philosophy.

Constructive ordinary language philosophy seeks to advance from claims about folk concepts to a better understanding of the non-linguistic phenomena these concepts are used to conceptualize, as well as the role these phenomena play in our lives. We have noted that descriptive experimental philosophy offers a base for this practice, aiming to detail the contours of our concepts. And we have suggested that methods from corpus linguistics can play an important role in the practice, supplementing more common questionnaire methods. By calling on a diversity of methods, we can gain insight into our language, and with it our underlying concepts, setting the stage for constructive inferences about the non-linguistic world.

Critical ordinary language philosophy assumes that many philosophical puzzles – "Platonic puzzles", as we called them – result from fallacious reasoning about the phenomena of interest. The approach then seeks to resolve such puzzles by exposing fallacies in the relevant reasoning. We considered an experimental implementation of the approach that addresses the "problem of perception" that is engendered by arguments from illusion and hallucination. The implementation develops and assesses explanations of pertinent fallacies, and documents the particular fallacious inferences that are hypothesized to drive the targeted puzzle-generating arguments. Diagnostic analyses that expose fallacies in the early stages of all arguments that contribute to the relevant puzzle would then "dissolve" this puzzle (e.g., the problem of perception).

A potentially complementary approach builds on findings from experimental philosophy that suggest persistent inter- or even intrapersonal conflicts between beliefs. The negative program's investigation of intuitional sensitivity prompted still ongoing debates about the extent and relevance of such sensitivity (Knobe 2021, Stich and Machery 2022). Regardless of how these debates pan out, however, this work has revealed a considerable amount of interpersonal conflict (for a review, see Knobe 2021): Both where intuitions of interest proved sensitive to the epistemically irrelevant parameters investigated and where they proved stable, considerable minorities disagreed with the majority judgments, and were typically too large to be easily explained away as performance errors. Indeed, in some cases, people across cultures appear to be almost evenly split between competing judgments (e.g., compatibilism versus incompatibilism about free will; see Hannikainen et al. 2019). In addition, sensitivity to presentational factors may sometimes be indicative of intrapersonal conflicts: People may feel torn between opposing judgments, and even minor presentational factors, such as small differences in wording, may sway them in different directions.

Such intrapersonal conflicts may be the ultimate source of many philosophical puzzles and problems. "Fragmentation accounts" of belief storage suggest that people's beliefs are often "fragmented" and conflicted (Bendaña and Mandelbaum 2021, Leiser 2001): Different cognitive processes, operating under different conditions, generate conflicting beliefs, which are never systematically screened for coherence; they are stored at different locations in long-term memory, in different "belief fragments", which are internally coherent, but may conflict with one another. As a result, different, and conflicting conceptions of the same phenomenon may be held not only by members of different communities (as findings from Berniūnas et al. 2021 suggest for free will) and different members of the same community (as findings from Latham, Miller, and Norton 2021 suggest for time), but even by the same individual (as findings from Fischer, Allen, and Engelhardt 2023 suggest for vision).

Philosophical puzzles may thus arise from direct conflicts between different belief fragments. For instance, the problem of perception may be exacerbated by arguments from illusion and hallucination, but ultimately arise from a conflict between equally pre-scientific beliefs about vision that are consistent with direct realism and indirect realism, respectively, and are frequently held by the same individuals (Fischer, Allen, and Engelhardt 2023). In this case, debunking explanations of one of the two parties to the conflict could help "dissolve" the puzzle. For instance, a grossly simplified implicit model of attention that is used to track others' and one's own focus of visual attention (Webb and Graziano 2015) could account for indirect realist beliefs about vision. The resulting explanation would debunk these beliefs and thus contribute to "dissolving" the problem of perception.

Alternatively, empirical insight into how fragmented and conflicted folk belief is may have us regard conflicts between folk beliefs as unavoidable parts of the human condition. Due to their incoherence, we would then simply set aside folk beliefs in efforts to explain phenomena and would accept as unavoidable any cognitive dissonance that arises from conflicts between different belief fragments (cf. Fischer 2023). This attitude would lead us to stop bothering about philosophical puzzles that arise from such conflicts. Either way, be it through diagnostic analyses, debunking explanations, or meta-cognitive insight into the workings and extent of belief fragmentation, empirical insights of a kind to which experimental philosophy aspires can make key contributions to overcoming longstanding puzzles and problems of a distinctively philosophical nature.

Bibliography

Alexander, Joshua, Chad Gonnerman, and John Waterman (2014): "Salience and epistemic egocentrism. An empirical study", in: James Beebe (Ed.): *Advances in experimental epistemology*. London: Bloomsbury, pp. 97–118.

Alicke, Mark (1992): "Culpable causation", *Journal of Personality and Social Psychology* 63 (3), pp. 368–378.

Alicke, Mark (2000): "Culpable control and the psychology of blame", *Psychological Bulletin* 126 (4), pp. 556–574.

Alicke, Mark (2008): "Blaming badly", *Journal of Cognition and Culture* 8 (1–2), pp. 179–186.

Alicke, Mark, David Rose, and Dori Bloom (2011): "Causation, norm violation and culpable control", *Journal of Philosophy* 108 (12), pp. 670–696.

Allen, Keith (2016): *A naïve realist theory of colour*. Oxford: Oxford University Press.

Arico, Adam, Brian Fiala, Robert Goldberg, and Shaun Nichols (2011): "The folk psychology of consciousness", *Mind & Language* 26 (3), pp. 327–352.

Austin, John Langshaw (1946): "Other minds", *Proceedings of the Aristotelian Society* 20, pp. 148–197.

Austin, John Langshaw (1957): "A plea for excuses", *Proceedings of the Aristotelian Society* 57 (1), pp. 1–30.

Austin, John Langshaw (1962): *Sense and sensibilia*. Oxford: Oxford University Press.

Ayer, Alfred Jules (1956): *The problem of knowledge*. London: Penguin.

Bargh, John, Kay Schwader, Sarah Hailey, Rebecca Dyer, and Erica Boothby (2012): "Automaticity in social-cognitive processes". *Trends in Cognitive Sciences* 16 (12), pp. 593–605.

Baroni, Marco, Raffaella Bernardi, and Roberto Zamparelli (2014a): "Frege in space. A program for compositional distributional semantics", *Linguistic Issues in Language Technology* 9, pp. 241–346.

Baroni, Marco, Georgiana Dinu, and German Kruszewski (2014b): "Don't count, predict! A systematic comparison of context-counting vs. context-predicting semantic vectors", in: Kristina Toutanova and Hua Wu (Eds.): *Proceedings of the 52nd annual meeting of the association for computational linguistics*. Baltimore: Association for Computational Linguistics, pp. 238–247.

Bealer, George (1996): "On the possibility of philosophical knowledge", *Philosophical Perspectives* 10, pp. 1–34.

Bealer, George (2000): "A theory of the a priori", *Pacific Philosophical Quarterly* 81 (1), pp. 1–30.

Beebee, Helen (2004): "Causing and nothingness", in: John Collins, Ned Hall, and Laurie Paul (Eds.): *Causation and counterfactuals*. Cambridge and London: The MIT Press, pp. 291–308.

Beisbart, Claus, and Kevin Reuter (2021): "What is the folk concept of life?", *Australasian Journal of Philosophy* 101 (2), pp. 486–507.

Bendaña, Joseph, and Eric Mandelbaum (2021): "The fragmentation of belief", in: Cristina Borgoni, Dirk Kindermann, and Andrea Onofri (Eds.): *The fragmented mind*. Oxford: Oxford University Press, pp. 78–107.

Berniūnas, Renatas, Audrius Beinorius, Vilius Dranseika, Vytis Silius, and Paulius Rimkevičius (2021): "The weirdness of belief in free will", *Consciousness and Cognition* 87, 103054.

Bicknell, Klinton, Jeffrey Elman, Mary Hare, Ken McRae, and Marta Kutas (2010): "Effects of event knowledge in processing verbal arguments", *Journal of Memory and Language* 63 (4), pp. 489–505.

Bluhm, Roland (2016): "Corpus analysis in philosophy", in: Martin Hinton (Ed.): *Evidence, experiment, and argument in linguistics and the philosophy of language.* Berlin: Peter Lang, pp. 91–109.

Boroditsky, Lera, and Ramscar, Michael (2002): "The roles of body and mind in abstract thought", *Psychological Science* 13 (2), pp. 185–188.

Bottini, Roberto, Davide Crepaldi, Daniel Casasanto, Virgine Crollen, and Olivier Collignon (2015): "Space and time in the sighted and blind", *Cognition* 141, pp. 67–72.

Brocher, Andreas, Jean-Pierre Koenig, Gail Mauner, and Stephani Foraker (2018): "About sharing and commitment. The retrieval of biased and balanced irregular polysemes", *Language, Cognition and Neuroscience* 33 (4), pp. 443–466.

Bruni, Elia, Nam Khahn Tran, and Marco Baroni (2013): "Multimodal distributional semantics", *Journal of Artificial Intelligence Research* 49, pp. 1–47.

Buckwalter, Wesley (2010): "Knowledge isn't closed on Saturdays", *Review of Philosophy and Psychology* 1 (3), pp. 395–406.

Butterfuss, Reese, and Panayiota Kendeou (2018): "The role of executive functions in reading comprehension", *Educational Psychology Review* 30 (3), pp. 801–826.

Callender, Craig (2017): *What makes time special?* Oxford: Oxford University Press.

Casasanto, Daniel, and Lera Boroditsky (2008): "Time in the mind. Using space to think about time", *Cognition* 106 (2), pp. 579–593.

Chalmers, David (1996): *The conscious mind.* New York: Oxford University Press.

Chalmers, David, and Frank Jackson (2001): "Conceptual analysis and reductive explanation", *Philosophical Review* 110 (3), pp. 315–360.

Clifton, Charles, Fernanda Ferreira, John Henderson, Albrecht Inhoff, Simon Liversedge, Erik Reichle, and Elizabeth Schotter (2016): "Eye movements in reading and information processing. Keith Rayner's 40 year legacy", *Journal of Memory and Language* 86, pp. 1–19.

Cohen, Jonathan, and Shuan Nichols (2010): "Colours, colour relationalism and the deliverances of introspection", *Analysis* 70 (2), pp. 218–228.

Collins, John (2015): "Naturalism without metaphysics", in: Eugen Fischer and John Collins (Eds.): *Experimental philosophy, rationalism, and naturalism.* London: Routledge, pp. 85–109.

Cosentino, Erica, Giosue Baggio, Jarmo Kontinen, and Markus Werning (2017): "The time-course of sentence meaning composition. N400 effects of the interaction between context-induced and lexically stored affordances", *Frontiers in Psychology* 8, 813.

Cova, Florian (2016): "The folk concept of intentional action. Empirical approaches", in: Justin Sytsma and Wesley Buckwalter (Eds.): *A companion to experimental philosophy.* Chichester: Wiley-Blackwell, pp. 121–141.

Crane, Tim, and Craig French (2021): "The problem of perception", in: Edward Zalta (Ed.): *The Stanford Encyclopedia of Philosophy.* Fall 2021 edition. https://plato.stanford.edu/archives/fall2021/entries/perception-problem/, last accessed May 19, 2023.

Daly, Christopher (2010): *An introduction to philosophical methods.* Buffalo: Broadview.

De Caro, Mario, and David Macarthur (Ed.) (2008): *Naturalism in question.* Cambridge: Harvard University Press.

DeRose, Keith (1992): "Contextualism and knowledge attributions", *Philosophy and Phenomenological Research* 52 (4), pp. 913–929.

Engelhardt, Paul, and Fernanda Ferreira (2016): "Reaching sentence and reference meaning", in: Pia Knoeferle, Pirita Pyykkonen-Klauck, and Matthew Crocker (Eds.): *Visually situated language comprehension.* Amsterdam and Philadelphia: John Benjamins, pp. 127–150.

Erk, Katrin (2012): "Vector space models of word meaning and phrase meaning. A survey", *Language and Linguistics Compass* 6 (10), pp. 635–653.

Faust, Mark, and Morton Gernsbacher (1996): "Cerebral mechanisms for suppression of inappropriate information during sentence comprehension", *Brain and Language* 53 (2), pp. 234–259.

Ferreira, Fernanda, and Matthew Lowder (2016): "Prediction, information structure, and good-enough language processing", *Psychology of Learning and Motivation* 65, pp. 217–247.

Firth, John Rupert (1957): "A synopsis of linguistic theory 1930–55", in: John Rupert Firth: *Studies in linguistic analysis*. Oxford: Blackwell, pp. 1–32.

Fischer, Eugen (2011): *Philosophical delusion and its therapy. Outline of a philosophical revolution.* New York: Routledge.

Fischer, Eugen (2019): "Linguistic legislation and psycholinguistic experiments. Redeveloping Waismann's approach", in: Dejan Makovec and Stewart Shapiro (Eds.): *Friedrich Waismann. The open texture of analytic philosophy*. Cham: Palgrave Macmillan, pp. 211–241.

Fischer, Eugen (2020): "Conceptual control. On the feasibility of conceptual engineering", *Inquiry*.

Fischer, Eugen (2023): "Critical ordinary language philosophy. A new project in experimental philosophy", *Synthese* 201, 102.

Fischer, Eugen, Keith Allen, and Paul Engelhardt (2023): "Fragmented and conflicted. Folk beliefs about vision", *Synthese* 201, 84.

Fischer, Eugen, and John Collins (2015): "Rationalism and naturalism in the age of experimental philosophy", in: Eugen Fischer and John Collins (Eds.): *Experimental philosophy, rationalism, and naturalism*. London: Routledge, pp. 1–33.

Fischer, Eugen, and Mark Curtis (Eds.) (2019): *Methodological advances in experimental philosophy*. London: Bloomsbury.

Fischer, Eugen, and Paul Engelhardt (2017): "Stereotypical inferences. Philosophical relevance and psycholinguistic toolkit", *Ratio* 30 (4), pp. 411–442.

Fischer, Eugen, and Paul Engelhardt (2019): "Eyes as windows to minds. Psycholinguistics for experimental philosophy", in: Eugen Fischer and Mark Curtis (Eds.): *Methodological advances in experimental philosophy*. London: Bloomsbury, pp. 43–100.

Fischer, Eugen, and Paul Engelhardt (2020): "Lingering stereotypes. Salience bias in philosophical argument", *Mind & Language* 35 (4), pp. 415–439.

Fischer, Eugen, Paul Engelhardt, and Aurelie Herbelot (2015): "Intuitions and illusions. From experiment and explanation to assessment", in: Eugen Fischer and John Collins (Eds.): *Experimental philosophy, rationalism and naturalism*. London: Routledge, pp. 259–292.

Fischer, Eugen, Paul Engelhardt, and Aurelie Herbelot (2022): "Philosophers' linguistic expertise. A psycholinguistic approach to the expertise objection against experimental philosophy", *Synthese* 200, 33.

Fischer, Eugen, Paul Engelhardt, Joachim Horvath, and Hiroshi Ohtani (2021): "Experimental ordinary language philosophy. A cross-linguistic study of defeasible default inferences, *Synthese* 198, pp. 1029–1070.

Fischer, Eugen, Paul Engelhardt, and Justin Sytsma (2021): "Inappropriate stereotypical inferences? An adversarial collaboration in experimental ordinary language philosophy", *Synthese* 198, pp. 10127–10168.

Fischer, Eugen, and Justin Sytsma (2021): "Zombie intuitions", *Cognition* 215, e104807.

Foot, Philippa (1967): "The problem of abortion and the doctrine of double effect", *Oxford Review* 5, pp. 5–15.

Gawronski, Bertram, and Fritz Strack (Eds.) (2012): *Cognitive consistency. A fundamental principle in social cognition*. New York: Guilford Press.

Gentner, Dedre, Mutsumi Imai, and Lera Boroditsky (2002): "As time goes by. Evidence for two systems in processing space time metaphors", *Language and Cognitive Processes* 17 (5), pp. 537–565.

Gerken, Mikkel, Chad Gonnerman, Joshua Alexander, and John Waterman (2020): "Salient alternatives in perspective", *Australasian Journal of Philosophy* 98 (4), pp. 792–810.

Giora, Rachel (2003): *On our mind. Salience, context, and figurative language.* Oxford: Oxford University Press.

Goldman, Alvin (2007): "Philosophical intuitions. Their target, their source, and their epistemic status", *Grazer Philosophische Studien* 74, pp. 1–26.

Halpern, Joseph, and Christopher Hitchcock (2015): "Graded causation and defaults", *British Journal for the Philosophy of Science* 66 (2), pp. 413–457.

Hannikainen, Ivar, Edouard Machery, David Rose, Stephen Stich, Christopher Olivola, Paulo Sousa, Florian Cova, Emma Buchtel, Mario Alai, Adriano Angelucci, Renatas Berniūnas, Amita Chatterjee, Hyundeuk Cheon, In-Rae Cho, Daniel Cohnitz, Vilius Dranseika, Ángeles Eraña Lagos, Laleh Ghadakpour, Maurice Grinberg, Takaaki Hashimoto, Amir Horowitz, Evgeniya Hristova, Yasmina Jraissati, Veselina Kadreva, Kaori Karasawa, Hackjin Kim, Yeonjeong Kim, Minwoo Lee, Carlos Mauro, Masaharu Mizumoto, Sebastiano Moruzzi, Jorge Ornelas, Barbara Osimani, Carlos Romero, Alejandro Rosas López, Massimo Sangoi, Andrea Sereni, Sarah Songhorian, Noel Struchiner, Vera Tripodi, Naoki Usui, Alejandro Vázquez del Mercado, Hrag Vosgerichian, Xueyi Zhang, and Jing Zhu (2019): "For whom does determinism undermine moral responsibility? Surveying the conditions for free will across cultures", *Frontiers in Psychology* 10, 2428.

Hansen, Nat (2020): "'Nobody would really talk that way!'. The critical project in contemporary ordinary language philosophy", *Synthese* 197, pp. 2433–2464.

Hansen, Nat, and Emmanuel Chemla (2015): "Linguistic experiments and ordinary language philosophy", *Ratio* 28 (4), pp. 422–445.

Hansen, Nat, and Emmanuel Chemla (2017): "Color adjectives, standards, and thresholds. An experimental investigation", *Linguistics and Philosophy* 40, pp. 239–278.

Haug, Matthew (Ed.) (2014): *Philosophical methodology. The armchair or the laboratory?* London: Routledge.

Henderson, Leah (2020): "The problem of induction", in: Edward Zalta (Ed.): *The Stanford Encyclopedia of Philosophy.* Spring 2020 edition. https://plato.stanford.edu/archives/spr2020/entries/induction-problem/, last accessed May 19, 2023.

Hitchcock, Christopher, and Joshua Knobe (2009): "Cause and norm", *The Journal of Philosophy* 106 (11), pp. 587–612.

Horvath, Joachim, and Alex Wiegmann (2016): "Intuitive expertise and intuitions about knowledge", *Philosophical Studies* 173 (10), pp. 2701–2726.

Horvath, Joachim, and Alex Wiegmann (2021): "Intuitive expertise in moral judgements", *Australasian Journal of Philosophy* 100 (2).

Icard, Thomas, Jonathan Kominsky, and Joshua Knobe (2017): "Normality and actual causal strength", *Cognition* 161, pp. 80–93.

Jackson, Frank (1998): *From metaphysics to ethics. A defense of conceptual analysis.* New York: Oxford University Press.

Johnston, Mark (1992): "How to speak of the colors", *Philosophical Studies* 68, pp. 221–263.

Kant, Immanuel (2003): *Critique of pure reason.* 2nd edition. Transl. by Norman Kemp Smith. Basingstoke: Palgrave Macmillan.

Kintsch, Walter (1988): "The role of knowledge in discourse comprehension. A construction-integration model", *Psychological Review* 95 (2), pp. 163–182.

Knobe, Joshua (2003): "Intentional action in folk psychology. An experimental investigation", *Philosophical Psychology* 16 (2), pp. 309–324.

Knobe, Joshua (2010): "Person as scientist, person as moralist", *Behavioral and Brain Sciences* 33 (4), pp. 315–365.

Knobe, Joshua (2016): "Experimental philosophy is cognitive science", in: Justin Sytsma and Wesley Buckwalter (Eds.): *A companion to experimental philosophy.* Chichester: Wiley-Blackwell, pp. 37–52.

Knobe, Joshua (2021): "Philosophical intuitions are surprisingly robust across demographic differences", *Filozofia Nauki* 29 (2), pp. 11–76.

Knobe, Joshua, and Ben Fraser (2008): "Causal judgments and moral judgment. Two experiments", in: Walter Sinnott-Armstrong (Ed.): *Moral Psychology. Vol. 2. The cognitive science of morality*. Cambridge: The MIT Press, pp. 441–447.

Kominsky, Jonathan, and Jonathan Phillips (2019): "Immoral professors and malfunctioning tools. Counterfactual relevance accounts explain the effect of norm violations on causal selection", *Cognitive Science* 43 (11), e12792.

Kominsky, Jonathan, Jonathan Phillips, Tobias Gerstenberg, David Lagnado, and Joshua Knobe (2015): "Causal superseding", *Cognition* 137, pp. 196–209.

Kruglanski, Arie, Katarzyna Jasko, Maxim Milyavsky, Marina Chernikova, David Webber, Antonio Pierro, and Daniela di Santo (2018): "Cognitive consistency theory in social psychology. A paradigm reconsidered", *Psychological Inquiry* 29 (2), pp. 45–59.

Kutas, Marta, and Kara Federmeier (2011): "Thirty years and counting. Finding meaning in the N400 component of the event-related brain potential (ERP)", *Annual Review of Psychology* 62, pp. 621–647.

Laeng, Bruno, Sylvain Sirois, and Gustaf Gredebäck (2012): "Pupillometry. A window to the preconscious?", *Perspectives on Psychological Science* 7 (1), pp. 18–27.

Latham, Andrew, Kristie Miller, and James Norton (2021): "Is our naïve theory of time dynamical?", *Synthese* 198 (5), pp. 4251–4271.

Leiser, David (2001): "Scattered naïve theories. Why the human mind is isomorphic to internet web", *New Ideas in Psychology* 19 (3), pp. 175–202.

Levin, Janet (2005): "The evidential status of philosophical intuition", *Philosophical Studies* 121 (3), pp. 193–224.

Levinson, Stephen (2000): *Presumptive meanings. The theory of generalized conversational implicature*. Cambridge and London: The MIT Press.

Lewis, David (1972): "Psychophysical and theoretical identifications", *Australasian Journal of Philosophy* 50 (3), pp. 249–258.

Liu, Michelle (2020): "The intuitive invalidity of the pain-in-mouth argument", *Analysis* 80 (3), pp. 463–474.

Livengood, Jonathan, and Justin Sytsma (2020): "Actual causation and compositionality", *Philosophy of Science* 87 (1), pp. 43–69.

Livengood, Jonathan, Justin Sytsma, and David Rose (2017): "Following the FAD. Folk attributions and theories of actual causation", *Review of Philosophy and Psychology* 8 (2), pp. 274–294.

Ludwig, Kurt (2007): "The epistemology of thought experiments. First person versus third person approaches", *Midwest Studies in Philosophy* 31 (1), pp. 128–159.

Machery, Edouard (2017): *Philosophy within its proper bounds*. Oxford: Oxford University Press.

Machery, Edouard (2021): "A new challenge to conceptual engineering", *Inquiry*.

Macpherson, Fiona (2013): "The philosophy and psychology of hallucination", in: Fiona Macpherson and Dimitris Platchias (Eds.): *Hallucination. Philosophy and psychology*. Cambridge and London: The MIT Press, pp. 1–38.

Mallon, Ron (2016): "Experimental philosophy", in: Herman Cappelen, Tamar Szabo Gendler, and John Hawthorne (Eds.): *Oxford handbook of philosophical methodology*. Oxford: Oxford University Press, pp. 410–433.

Matsuki, Kazunaga, Tracy Chow, Mary Hare, Jeffrey Elman, Christoph Scheepers, and Ken McRae (2011): "Event-based plausibility immediately influences on-line language comprehension", *Journal of Experimental Psychology – Learning, Memory and Cognition* 37 (4), pp. 913–934.

McEnery, Tony, and Andrew Hardie (2015): *Corpus linguistics. Method, theory and practice*. Cambridge: Cambridge University Press.

McKinnon, Alastair (1970): *The Kierkegaard indices*. Leiden: Brill.

McRae, Ken, Mary Hare, Jeffrey Elman, and Todd Ferretti (2005): "A basis for generating expectancies for verbs from nouns", *Memory & Cognition* 33, pp. 1174–1184.

Metusalem, Ross, Marta Kutas, Thomas Urbach, Mary Hare, Ken McRae, and Jeffrey Elman (2012): "Generalized event knowledge activation during online sentence comprehension", *Journal of Memory and Language* 66 (4), pp. 545–567.

Meunier, Jean-Guy, Stanislas Rolland, and Francois Daoust (1976): "A system for text and content analysis", *Computers and the Humanities* 10 (5), pp. 281–286.

Murphy, Taylor (2014): "Experimental philosophy 1935–1965", in: Joshua Knobe, Tania Lombrozo, and Shaun Nichols (Eds.): *Oxford studies in experimental philosophy.* Vol. 1. Oxford: Oxford University Press, pp. 325–368.

Nadelhoffer, Thomas (2006): "Bad acts, blameworthy agents, and intentional actions. Some problems for juror impartiality", *Philosophical Explorations* 9 (2), pp. 203–219.

Nadelhoffer, Thomas, David Rose, Wesley Buckwalter, and Shaun Nichols (2020): "Natural compatibilism, indeterminism, and intrusive metaphysics", *Cognitive Science* 44 (8), e12873.

Næss, Arne (1956): "Logical equivalence, intentional isomorphism and synonymity as studied by questionnaires", *Synthese* 10, pp. 471–479.

Næss, Arne (1961): "A study of 'or'", *Synthese* 13, pp. 49–60.

Nahmias, Eddy, Stephen Morris, Thomas Nadelhoffer, and Jason Turner (2004): "The phenomenology of free will", *Journal of Consciousness Studies* 11 (7–8), pp. 162–179.

Nahmias, Eddy, Stephen Morris, Thomas Nadelhoffer, and Jason Turner (2005): "Surveying freedom. Folk intuitions about free will and moral responsibility", *Philosophical Psychology* 18 (5), pp. 561–584.

Nahmias, Eddy, Stephen Morris, Thomas Nadelhoffer, and Jason Turner (2006): "Is incompatibilism intuitive?", *Philosophy and Phenomenological Research* 73 (1), pp. 28–53.

Newman, George, Paul Bloom, and Joshua Knobe (2014): "Value judgments and the true self", *Personality and Social Psychology Bulletin* 40 (2), pp. 203–216.

Nichols, Shaun, and Joshua Knobe (2007): "Moral responsibility and determinism. The cognitive science of folk intuitions", *Noûs* 41 (4), pp. 663–685.

O'Connor, Timothy, and Christopher Franklin (2021): "Free will", in: Edward Zalta (Ed.): *Stanford Encyclopedia of Philosophy.* Spring 2021 edition. https://plato.stanford.edu/archives/spr2021/entries/freewill/, last accessed May 19, 2023.

O'Keefe, Anne, and Michael McCarthy (2022): *The Routledge handbook of corpus linguistics.* 2nd edition. London and New York: Routledge.

Oden, Gregg, and James Spira (1983): "Influence of context on the activation and selection of ambiguous word senses", *Quarterly Journal of Experimental Psychology* 35 A (1), pp. 51–64.

Paul, Laurie, and Ned Hall (2003): *Causation. A user's guide.* Oxford: Oxford University Press.

Plato (2004): *Theaetetus.* Transl. by Joe Sachs. Newburyport: Focus.

Plunkett, David, and Herman Cappelen (2020): "A guided tour of conceptual engineering and conceptual ethics", in: Harman Cappelen, David Plunkett, and Alexis Burgess (Eds.): *Conceptual engineering and conceptual ethics.* Oxford: Oxford University Press, pp. 1–34.

Powell, Derek, Zachary Horne, and Ángel Pinillos (2014): "Semantic integration as a method for investigating concepts", in: James Beebe (Ed.): *Advances in experimental epistemology.* London: Bloomsbury, pp. 119–144.

Price, Huw (2011): "The flow of time", in: Craig Callender (Ed.): *The Oxford handbook of philosophy of time.* Oxford: Oxford University Press, pp. 276–311.

Prinz, Jesse (2007): *The emotional construction of morals.* Oxford: Oxford University Press.

Prinz, Jesse (2008): "Empirical philosophy and experimental philosophy", in: Joshua Knobe and Shaun Nichols (Eds.): *Experimental philosophy.* Oxford: Oxford University Press, pp. 189–208.

Rawls, John (1971): *A theory of justice.* Cambridge: Harvard University Press.

Rayner, Keith, Tessa Warren, Barbara Juhasz, and Simon Liversedge (2004): "The effect of plausibility on eye movements in reading", *Journal of Experimental Psychology – Learning, Memory, and Cognition* 30 (6), pp. 1290–1301.

Reuter, Kevin, and Justin Sytsma (2020): "Unfelt pain", *Synthese* 197 (4), pp. 1777–1801.

Robb, David, and John Heil (2021): "Mental causation", in: Edward Zalta (Ed.): *The Stanford Encyclopedia of Philosophy*. Spring 2021 edition. https://plato.stanford.edu/archives/spr2021/entries/mental-causation, last accessed May 19, 2023.

Roberts, Pendaran, Keith Allen, and Kelly Ann Schmidtke (2018): "Folk intuitions about the causal theory of perception", *Ergo* 3 (28), pp. 729–749.

Roberts, Pendaran, Keith Allen, and Kelly Ann Schmidtke (2021): "Reflective intuitions about the causal theory of perception across sensory modalities", *Review of Philosophy and Psychology* 12, pp. 257–277.

Roberts, Pendaran, and Kelly Ann Schmidtke (2019): "Folk core beliefs about color", *Review of Philosophy and Psychology* 10, pp. 849–869.

Robinson, Howard (1994): *Perception*. London: Routledge.

Ryle, Gilbert (1954): *Dilemmas*. Cambridge: Cambridge University Press.

Salomons, Tim, Richard Harrison, Nat Hansen, James Stazicker, Astrid Sorensen, Paula Thomas, and Emma Borg (2021): "Is pain 'all in your mind'? Examining the general public's views of pain", *Review of Philosophy and Psychology* 13, pp. 683–698.

Samland, Jana, and Michael Waldmann (2016): "How prescriptive norms influence causal inferences", *Cognition* 156, pp. 164–176.

Sartorio, Carolina (2005): "Causes as difference-makers", *Philosophical Studies* 123 (1–2), pp. 71–96.

Schaffer, Jonathan, and Joshua Knobe (2012): "Contrastive knowledge surveyed", *Noûs* 46 (4), pp. 675–708.

Schroeder, Severin (2006): *Wittgenstein. The way out of the fly bottle*. Cambridge: Polity.

Schwenkler, John, and Assaf Weksler (2019): "Are perspectival shapes seen or imagined? An experimental approach", *Phenomenology and the Cognitive Sciences* 18 (6), pp. 855–877.

Smith, David (2002): *The problem of perception*. Cambridge: Harvard University Press.

Sripada, Chandra (2010): "The Deep Self Model and asymmetries in folk judgments about intentional action", *Philosophical Studies* 151 (2), pp. 159–176.

Sripada, Chandra (2012): "What makes a manipulated agent unfree?", *Philosophy and Phenomenological Research* 85 (3), pp. 563–593.

Starmans, Christina, and Ori Friedman (2020): "Expert or esoteric? Philosophers attribute knowledge differently than all other academics", *Cognitive Science* 44 (7), e12850.

Stich, Stephen, and Edouard Machery (2022): "Demographic differences in philosophical intuition. A reply to Joshua Knobe", *Review of Philosophy and Psychology*.

Stich, Stephen, and Kevin Tobia (2016): "Experimental philosophy and the philosophical tradition", in: Justin Sytsma and Wesley Buckwalter (Eds.): *A companion to experimental philosophy*. Chichester: Wiley-Blackwell, pp. 5–21.

Strawson, Peter Frederick (1959): *Individuals*. London: Methuen.

Swets, Benjamin, Timothy Desmet, Charles Clifton, and Fernanda Ferreira (2008): "Underspecification of syntactic ambiguities. Evidence from self-paced reading", *Memory & Cognition* 36, pp. 201–216.

Sytsma, Justin (2010): "Dennett's Theory of the folk theory of consciousness", *Journal of Consciousness Studies* 17 (3–4), pp. 107–130.

Sytsma, Justin (2021): "Causation, responsibility, and typicality", *Review of Philosophy and Psychology* 12 (4), pp. 699–719.

Sytsma, Justin (2022a): "The responsibility account", in: Pascale Willemsen and Alex Wiegmann (Eds.): *Advances in experimental philosophy of causation*. London: Bloomsbury, pp. 145–164.

Sytsma, Justin (2022b): "Crossed wires. Blaming artifacts for bad outcomes", *The Journal of Philosophy*, 119(9), pp. 489–516.

Sytsma, Justin (2023): "Ordinary meaning and consilience of evidence", in: Stefan Magen and Karolina Prochownik (Eds.): *Advances in experimental philosophy of law*. London: Bloomsbury, pp. 171–191.

Sytsma, Justin, Roland Bluhm, Pascale Willemsen, and Kevin Reuter (2019): "Causal attributions and corpus analysis", in: Eugen Fischer and Mark Curtis (Eds.): *Methodological advances in experimental philosophy*. London: Bloomsbury, pp. 209–238.

Sytsma, Justin, and Wesley Buckwalter (Eds.) (2016): *A companion to experimental Philosophy*. Chichester: Wiley-Blackwell.

Sytsma, Justin, and Jonathan Livengood (2015): *The theory and practice of experimental philosophy*. Peterborough: Broadview.

Sytsma, Justin, and Jonathan Livengood (2021): "Causal attributions and the trolley problem", *Philosophical Psychology* 34 (8), pp. 1167–1191.

Sytsma, Justin, Jonathan Livengood, and David Rose (2012): "Two types of typicality. Rethinking the role of statistical typicality in ordinary causal attributions", *Studies in History and Philosophy of Biological and Biomedical Sciences* 43 (4), pp. 814–820.

Sytsma, Justin, and Edouard Machery (2010): "Two conceptions of subjective experience", *Philosophical Studies* 151 (2), pp. 299–327.

Sytsma, Justin, and Kevin Reuter (2017): "Experimental philosophy of pain", *Journal of Indian Council of Philosophical Research* 34 (3), pp. 611–628.

Sytsma, Justin, and Melissa Snater (2023): "Consciousness, phenomenal consciousness, and free will", in: Paul Henne and Samuel Murray (Eds.): *Advances in experimental philosophy of action*. London: Bloomsbury, pp. 13–32.

Thagard, Paul, and Richard Nisbett (1983): "Rationality and charity", *Philosophy of Science* 50 (2), pp. 250–267.

Turney, Peter, and Patrick Pantel (2010): "From frequency to meaning. Vector space models of semantics", *Journal of Artificial Intelligence Research* 37 (1), pp. 141–188.

Ulatowski, Joseph, Dan Weijers, and Justin Sytsma (2020): "Cognitive science of philosophy symposium. Corpus analysis". *The Brains Blog*. https://philosophyofbrains.com/2020/12/15/cognitive-science-of-philosophy-symposium-corpus-analysis.aspx, last accessed May 19, 2023.

Urmson, James Opie (1969): "A symposium on Austin's method. Part I", in: Kuang Tih Fann (Ed.): *Symposium on J.L. Austin*. London: Routledge, pp. 76–86.

Waismann, Friedrich (1997): *Principles of linguistic philosophy*. 2nd edition. Ed. by Rom Harré. London: Macmillan.

Webb, Taylor, and Michael Graziano (2015): "The attention schema theory. A mechanistic account of subjective awareness", *Frontiers in Psychology* 6, 500.

Weinberg, Jonathan (2015): "Humans as instruments, on the inevitability of experimental philosophy", in: Eugen Fischer and John Collins (Eds.): *Experimental philosophy, rationalism, and naturalism*. London: Routledge, pp. 171–187.

Weinberg, Jonathan, Shaun Nichols, and Stephen Stich (2001): "Normativity and epistemic intuitions", *Philosophical Topics* 29 (1–2), pp. 429–460.

Weksler, Assaf, Hilla Jacobson, and Zohar Bronfman (2021): "The transparency of experience and the neuroscience of attention", *Synthese* 198 (5), pp. 4709–4730.

Wittgenstein, Ludwig (1953): *Philosophical investigations*. Oxford: Blackwell.

Zahorec, Mike, Robert Bishop, Nat Hansen, John Schwenkler, and Justin Sytsma (2023): "Linguistic corpora and ordinary language. On the dispute between Ryle and Austin about the use of 'voluntary', 'involuntary', 'voluntarily', and 'involuntarily'", in: David Bordonaba Plou (Ed.): *Experimental philosophy of language. Perspectives, methods and prospects*. Dordrecht: Springer, pp. 121–149

Zwaan, Rolf (2016): "Situation models, mental simulations, and abstract concepts in discourse comprehension", *Psychonomic Bulletin and Review* 23 (4), pp. 1028–1034.

Joachim Horvath
Intuitions in Experimental Philosophy

Abstract: This chapter proceeds from the standard picture of the relation between intuitions and experimental philosophy: the alleged evidential role of intuitions about hypothetical cases, and experimental philosophy's challenge to these judgments. I will survey some of the main defenses of this standard picture against the x-phi challenge, most of which fail. Concerning the most popular defense, the expertise defense, I will draw the pessimistic conclusion that intuitive expertise of the envisaged kind is largely a myth. Next, I will consider the mischaracterization objection, which states that philosophers do not appeal to intuitions as evidence for their case judgments, but instead argue for them. I will then consider a few instructive replies to the mischaracterization objection, which are all unconvincing on further inspection. Finally, I will discuss some potential normative consequences of the mischaracterization objection, and I will argue that it recommends a shift away from the excessive focus on intuitions about cases in metaphilosophy and experimental philosophy, towards more work on the role of argumentation in the method of cases.

Keywords: Argumentation; Expertise Defense; Experimental Philosophy; Intuitions; Intuitive Expertise; Metaphilosophy; Method of Cases; Mischaracterization Objection; Thought Experiments

1 Introduction

The standard picture of how philosophical intuitions and experimental philosophy are related looks as follows. In accordance with one of philosophy's key methods, the *method of*

Note: First, I would like to thank the editors of this volume, Alexander Max Bauer und Stephan Kornmesser, for inviting me to contribute this chapter, and for their patience with my delays in delivering the manuscript as well as their helpful editorial comments. Second, I would like to thank several audiences of talks that provided the basis for this chapter's two main sections on "The myth of intuitive expertise" and "The mischaracterization objection and its consequences" at the *Ringvorlesung Theoretische Philosophie*, Institute for Philosophy, Carl von Ossietzky Universität Oldenburg, June 2021, at the *Institutskolloquium*, Institute for Philosophy, *Technische Universität Dresden*, June 2021, at the *Research Seminar – Chair of Theoretical Philosophy*, Heinrich-Heine-University Düsseldorf, December 2020, at the Workshop *Conceptual Analysis, Conceptual Engineering and Experimental Philosophy*, University of Zürich, November 2019, at my *Inaugural Lecture*, Faculty of Philosophy and Educational Research, Ruhr University Bochum, May 2019, at the *EXTRA Workshop.1 "Experimental Philosophy and the Method of Cases"*, Ruhr University Bochum, May 2019, at the *Book Symposium "Philosophy Within Its Proper Bounds" by Edouard Machery*, Ruhr University Bochum, December 2017, at the *II. Workshop of the Experimental Philosophy Group Germany*, Universität Osnabrück, November 2017, at the *XXIV. Deutscher Kongress für Philosophie*, Humboldt-University Berlin, September 2017, and at the Workshop *Intuitions and the Expertise Defense*, University of Aarhus, September 2017. My work on this paper was generously funded by the Deutsche Forschungsgemeinschaft (DFG; German Research Foundation; project number 391304769).

cases, philosophers routinely appeal to *intuitive judgments* about hypothetical thought experiment cases, which are then used to support or refute philosophical theories that make a prediction about how these judgments should turn out. A classic example would be Gettier's (1963) refutation of an account of knowledge in terms of justified true belief (JTB) by his case judgments that the protagonist of his two hypothetical cases lacks knowledge, despite having a belief that is both justified and true. Hence, the story goes, Gettier has provided two *intuitive counterexamples* to the traditional JTB-account of knowledge, which is typically considered as one of the greatest successes of the method of cases – illustrated by the thousands of citations of Gettier's two-and-a-half-page paper and the hundreds of papers and books that try to resolve the ensuing "Gettier problem".[1] But then, in the early 2000s, experimental philosophy (or "x-phi", for short) enters the scene with various experiments on people's intuitive judgments about well-known philosophical thought experiment cases, such as versions of Gettier's cases (in Weinberg, Nichols, and Stich 2001). The surprising finding is, again and again, that these intuitive judgments vary with factors that are arguably irrelevant to their truth. Well-known examples are the variation of judgments about Gettier cases with people's *cultural background* (Weinberg et al. 2001), or the variation of Truetemp and Trolley cases with *order of presentation* (Swain, Alexander, and Weinberg 2008, Wiegmann, Okan, and Nagel 2012). This challenges the epistemic trustworthiness or reliability of people's judgments about philosophical cases, and might thus require a serious restriction on the use of the method of cases in philosophy – or even its abandonment (Alexander and Weinberg 2007, Machery 2017). In any case, that's how the standard picture about intuitions and experimental philosophy is frequently painted.

One way in which this standard picture is clearly too narrow by now is in its neglect of *other methods* and *other targets* of experimental philosophy. For example, apart from using *case-based questionnaires* to elicit people's intuitive judgments about hypothetical cases, experimental philosophers also collect *behavioral evidence* (e.g., Schwitzgebel 2009, Schwitzgebel et al. 2012) or use *corpus studies* (e.g., Hansen, Porter, and Francis 2021, Sytsma and Reuter 2017) and the *tools of psycholinguistics* (e.g., Fischer et al. 2021, Fischer, Engelhardt, and Herbelot 2022) – to offer just a few well-known examples. Moreover, and relatedly, today's experimental philosophers do not only target *intuitive judgments* about cases, but also, for example, the *ethical behavior* of ethicists and other people (e.g., Schwitzgebel et al. 2012, Schwitzgebel, Cokelet, and Singer 2020), the *cognitive mechanisms* that underlie people's case judgments (e.g., Nichols and Knobe 2007), or the *effectiveness of arguments* for case judgments (e.g., Horvath and Wiegmann n.d., Wysocki 2017).

While it is important to acknowledge this increasing diversity of both research methods and topics in current experimental philosophy (see also Fischer and Curtis

---

[1] The precise numbers are hard to assess, though, given that many authors do not (fully) cite Gettier's original paper from 1963. In any case, a *Google Scholar* search of "Gettier justified true belief knowledge" generates about 13,600 results, and a search of "Gettier problem" even about 15,000 results (on June 8, 2022).

2019, Machery and O'Neill 2014), the issue of intuitive case judgments and the x-phi challenge to the method of cases still take center stage in the metaphilosophical debate about x-phi. Moreover, a lot of unfinished philosophical business remains even in this relatively narrow area of metaphilosophical concern. For example, it is still an open question how serious the experimental challenge to the method of cases really is, and whether or how the method of cases can be defended against it (for an overview, see, e. g., Horvath and Koch 2021, Machery 2017, Nado 2016a). For these reasons, the current chapter will mostly be concerned with the predominant issue of intuitions about hypothetical cases and the x-phi challenge.

With respect to this challenge, one can distinguish two main camps on the side of champions of the method of cases. One camp basically accepts the standard picture but tries to defend the method of cases against the x-phi challenge nevertheless – let us call it the camp of *intuition apologists*. This defense can take many forms – from objecting that experimental philosophers have studied the *wrong subjects*, e. g., laypeople instead of philosophical experts (e. g., Hales 2006, Horvath 2010, Ludwig 2007, Williamson 2011), to complaining that they have investigated the *wrong cognitive states*, e. g., spontaneous judgments instead of genuine intuitions or reflective judgments (e. g., Bengson 2013, Kauppinen 2007), to arguing that the experimental results are in fact *compatible with the method of cases*, e. g., because they only indicate a merely verbal or conceptual difference (e. g., Sosa 2009, 2010).

The second camp tackles the more fundamental assumption that the standard picture of the method of cases and the presumed role of intuitive case judgments in this method is basically correct – let us call this the camp of *intuition detractors*. There are more moderate forms of intuition detraction, e. g., as a mere denial that case judgments are *intuitive* judgments, yet without questioning their standardly assumed methodological role (e. g., Ichikawa 2014, Machery 2017, Williamson 2004), or more radical forms, e. g., as rejecting the standard picture as a severe *mischaracterization* of the actual practice of the method of cases in philosophy (e. g., Cappelen 2012, Deutsch 2015).

One might even distinguish a third camp here, whose members attack the robustness of the empirical findings of experimental philosophy, e. g., by challenging the experimental design or replicability of particular studies (e. g., Cullen 2010, Nagel 2012, Seyedsayamdost 2015, Ziółkowski 2019). Important as this third camp and its contributions may be, I will nevertheless put it aside here, for it has become clear by now that this approach does not allow for a principled answer to the experimental philosophy challenge – simply because most x-phi studies replicate fairly well and do not suffer from any serious methodological flaws (see, e. g., Cova et al. 2018, Machery 2017, Sytsma and Livengood 2016).

In the following, I will first consider various well-known replies to the experimental philosophy challenge by *intuition apologists*, and briefly explain why they are largely unconvincing. My main focus will be on the most popular reply, the *expertise defense*. According to this defense, the susceptibility of laypeople's intuitive case judgments to philosophically irrelevant factors is irrelevant to the practice of *philosophical experts*, who can be expected to be resistant to the influence of such factors. However, I will argue that, by now, the available evidence suggests that this kind of intuitive expertise is largely a myth. To this end, I will distinguish between the *master model* and the *immunity model* of intuitive expertise, and then explain why neither of them delivers what proponents of the expertise defense would need in order to successfully rebut the x-phi challenge.

So, if there is any hope for practitioners of the method of cases to simply shrug off the experimental philosophy challenge, then it would have to come from the second camp of *intuition detractors*. Indeed, the *mischaracterization objection*, mainly developed by Max Deutsch (e.g., 2015) and Herman Cappelen (e.g., 2012), promises no less than to expose the irrelevance of the x-phi challenge to the method of cases. How so? By arguing, on the basis of detailed textual analyses, that philosophers do not appeal to intuitions about hypothetical cases, but instead *argue* for their case judgments. If this *argument view* were correct, then it would indeed follow that experimental findings about intuitive case judgments have little relevance to philosophers' actual practice of the method of cases. I will therefore briefly analyze the mischaracterization objection and defend it against a few instructive objections. Lastly, I will consider what follows for the *methodological role* of intuitions in philosophy if the mischaracterization objection is indeed correct, and I will consider some interesting consequences, both descriptive and normative, for the future practice of the method of cases and related work in experimental philosophy.

2 A Brief Survey of Intuition Apologetics

The main aim of *intuition apologists* is to defend the standard intuition-based picture of the method of cases against the challenge from experimental philosophy. That is, intuition apologists argue, in one way or another, that the surprising variation of intuitive case judgments with philosophically irrelevant factors is no obstacle to practicing the method of cases in more or less the same way – captured by the standard picture – as before the advent of experimental philosophy. However, it has proven difficult to achieve this goal, which I will illustrate with a brief survey of the main defensive moves of intuition apologists.

To begin with, some philosophers have complained that the x-phi studies merely track "answers" to questionnaires, but *not "genuine" philosophical intuitions*, which may differ crucially in epistemic value (see, e.g., Bengson 2013, Ludwig 2007). For example, maybe only those judgments are based on genuine intuitions that "express solely the subject's competence in the deployment of the concepts involved" (Ludwig 2007, p. 144), or that solely reflect one's rational intuitions or intellectual seemings (cf. Bengson 2013). The main problem for this response is that the alleged difference between genuine intuitions and mere questionnaire-answers is rarely transparent to the thought experimenting subject, which threatens to make the defense methodologically idle. For, it would then be equally unclear whether philosophers themselves rely on genuine intuitions in their thought experiments, and so the response would fail as a defense of actual philosophical practice (cf. Horvath 2010, p. 2; Weinberg, Crowley, et al. 2012; Weinberg and Alexander 2014).

Other philosophers have objected that people's responses to questionnaires are primarily spontaneous and unreflective judgments, while the verdicts that really matter for philosophical theorizing are of a more *reflective* kind (see, e.g., Kauppinen 2007). One might put this objection in terms of the psychological distinction between System 1 and System 2 cognition (see, e.g., Evans 2003): questionnaires typically elicit fast, automatic, and unconscious System 1 responses, but philosophy requires slow, deliberate, and conscious System 2 responses. However, System 2 cognition is subject to its own biases and limitations, and so its superiority to System 1 cognition cannot simply be taken for granted (see, e.g., Kahneman 2011). Moreover, experimental philosophers have already gathered evidence that the influence of irrelevant factors on intuitive case judgments is not mitigated in more reflective subjects (cf. Kneer et al. 2021, Weinberg, Alexander, et al. 2012).

According to the *different-concepts objection*, the findings of x-phi merely suggest that the tested subjects have different concepts of, e.g., knowledge or free will, and not that their intuitive judgments are influenced by philosophically irrelevant factors (see, e.g., Sosa 2009, 2010). But first, it seems questionable to ascribe different concepts to people who only disagree about a few hypothetical cases. More plausibly, some of these people are simply mistaken in their application of a widely shared concept. Second, this objection is at best applicable to *some* of the tested factors, such as cultural background, yet it seems implausible as a response to, for example, order effects or the influence of affective content (see, e.g., Alexander and Weinberg 2007, Horvath 2010, Nichols, Stich, and Weinberg 2003).

A more promising response raises *skeptical worries* about the epistemic implications of the x-phi challenge. For example, the claim that intuitive judgments about cases are unreliable or untrustworthy threatens to challenge ordinary, everyday judgments about cases as well, and might thus lead to a debilitating form of "judgment skepticism" (see, e.g., Williamson 2007, ch. 7). Relatedly, the challenge might even be *self-defeating*, because it relies on epistemic principles that themselves seem to be justified on the basis of intuitive case judgments (see, e.g., Horvath 2010). In response, experimental philosophers have limited the scope of their challenge to, for example, intuitive judgments about "esoteric, unusual, far-fetched, or generally outlandish" cases (Weinberg 2007, p. 321; see also Machery 2017). If successful, this strategy might avoid the skeptical "spill-over" to judgments about ordinary cases. The main problem is to distinguish verdicts about ordinary and "esoteric" cases in a non-arbitrary way (cf. Horvath 2010). It is not clear, however, why experimental philosophers could not simply pick out the problematic case judgments via their methodological role in philosophy. For example, philosophers typically use judgments about hypothetical cases to establish a modal conclusion of some sort (see, e.g., Horvath 2023), and this kind of usage seems far removed from everyday judgments about ordinary cases. So, maybe experimental philosophers can simply dodge skeptical worries about their challenge by focusing on case judgments *as they are typically used in philosophical contexts*. In any case, the debate about skeptical worries concerning the x-phi challenge has not been very active in recent years, but it seems that the available options have not been exhausted yet. The current status of this attempted defense is thus inconclusive.

So far, I have not mentioned the most popular strategy of intuition apologists, the *expertise defense*. The intensity of the metaphilosophical debate about this defense and the richness of the available empirical evidence merit a more in-depth analysis, which I will turn to in the following section.

3 The Myth of Intuitive Expertise

The core idea of the expertise defense against the x-phi challenge is that only the intuitive judgments of the relevant *philosophical experts* matter – as in other academic disciplines too (e.g., Devitt 2011, Hales 2006, Horvath 2010, Ludwig 2007, Williamson 2011). Accordingly, lay intuitions about philosophical thought experiment cases would be largely irrelevant to the practice of professional philosophy, just as lay intuitions about physical matters are largely irrelevant to professional physicists. Now, at the time when the expertise defense became popular (around the year 2010), almost all of the available x-phi studies had been conducted with philosophical laypeople (in fact, mostly with U.S. undergraduate students). So, from the perspective of the expertise defense, these studies have almost no bearing on the philosophical method of cases. It is easy to see the metaphilosophical attraction of this defense, which would allow for an uncompromising defense of the standard picture of the method of cases in professional philosophy – in addition to the "self-congratulatory" appeal of seeing ourselves as "expert intuiters" who can safely ignore the intuitions of the *hoi polloi*.

There are several ways of motivating the expertise defense. I have already mentioned the *argument from analogy* with professional practitioners of other academic disciplines, such as math, physics, or law (e.g., Hales 2006, Ludwig 2007, Williamson 2011). One can also appeal to a *general presumption of expertise* for the professional practitioners of any respectable discipline (in a broad sense), even in non-academic fields like chess or cooking (e.g., Horvath 2010, Williamson 2011). Finally, one can also appeal to *specific cognitive skills* that professional philosophers are more likely to have than laypeople, such as their higher sensitivity to conceptual distinctions and a better understanding of the point and purpose of doing thought experiments (e.g., Horvath 2010, Ludwig 2007).

None of these motivations for the expertise defense are uncontroversial even among its proponents, however, and all of them are subject to various concerns or problems (see, e.g., Horvath 2010, Nado 2015, Weinberg et al. 2010). For example, how analogous is philosophy really to other academic disciplines, given the amount of disagreement that is so characteristic of philosophy since its very beginning (see, e.g., Chalmers 2015)? One key point about the expertise defense should nevertheless be acknowledged by proponents and opponents alike: that it is not enough to establish that professional philosophers are *experts in one way or another* – which they surely are, if only by knowing a lot more about philosophy than laypeople. Rather, what is needed for the specific purpose of countering the x-phi challenge to the method of cases is the assumption that professional philosophers have *intuitive expertise* in judging hypothetical cases in their respective field (cf. Weinberg et al. 2010). This highly specific intuitive expertise does not automatically follow from the general philosophical expertise that professional philosophers undeniably have. To claim such intuitive expertise for professional philosophers is, on the one hand, more difficult to motivate than some general assumption of philosophers' expertise, and, on the other hand, it is also a straightforwardly testable empirical claim. But before I start to evaluate this claim, let me propose some clarifications and helpful distinctions regarding the key notion of *intuitive expertise*.

How should we understand both the *intuitive* and the *expertise* in intuitive expertise? With respect to the *intuitive* judgments that would result from an exercise of intuitive expertise, it is, unfortunately, not easy to say something reasonably uncontroversial about them – given the welter of views about the nature of intuitions in philosophy (see, e.g., Pust 2017). So, the best we can do for present purposes is to roughly demarcate intuitions and intuitive judgments from other mental states and judgments – yet without aiming for anything like a strict definition in terms of necessary and sufficient conditions (for simplicity, I will focus on intuitive judgments in the following). One key feature of intuitive judgments is that their psychological origin is not (fully) transparent from an introspective or reflective perspective. Typically, all we can say when we make an intuitive judgment is that it is not (wholly) based on conscious inference, reasoning, perception, memory, or other consciously accessible sources. This leads to the characteristic impression that intuitive judgments are, in some sense, automatic or spontaneous, and not subject to conscious control or influence (psychologically, this is often cached out in terms of System 1 and 2 cognition; see above). In any case, one important upshot for the following discussion is that judgments that are (wholly) based on some conscious argument, inference, or reasoning process would clearly *not* be intuitive judgments – or else the distinction between reflective judgments and intuitive judgments would simply collapse.

With an eye on the expertise defense, what should we say about the *expertise* in intuitive expertise? Mainly what I have already highlighted above, namely, that it should be understood as the very *specific expertise* for judging hypothetical cases about the philosophical topic in question. Given the well-established *domain-specificity* of expertise in general (see, e.g., Ericsson and Lehmann 1996), we should think of the intuitive expertise in question as at least relative to established philosophical subfields, such as epistemology, ethics, or metaphysics. Thus, we should not simply assume that professional philosophers are equally competent in judging thought experiment cases from all areas of philosophy. But *if* there is such a thing as intuitive expertise in philosophy, we should at least find it in those professional philosophers who have the relevant subfield as one of their areas of specialization or competence.

Finally, let me introduce a distinction between two very different models of how one can conceive of expertise in general and intuitive expertise in particular, which will be helpful for organizing the following discussion. These two models are the *master model* and the *immunity model* of intuitive expertise (see also Machery 2017, Sytsma and Livengood 2016). According to the *master model*, the intuitive judgments of experts would be highly superior to laypeople across the board in their respective domain of expertise. In contrast, the *immunity model* only claims that experts are less sensitive to biases and other distorting influences on their domain-related intuitive judgments. I will further elaborate on these two models below, but I want to emphasize right away that this is a primarily analytic and thus somewhat idealized distinction. In practice, there will be all kinds of hybrid combinations between these analytically distinguishable models of expertise. However, if neither expertise in the master sense nor expertise in the immunity sense can be plausibly ascribed to professional philosophers, then the expertise defense is definitely bound to fail.

3.1 The Myth of Intuitive Mastery

A good way to illustrate the *master model* is with an example from one of the "model domains" of mastery that features in a lot of empirical research on expertise as well (see, e.g., Gobet and Simon 1996): the game of *chess*. Here, the differences in both playing ability and the quality of (intuitive) judgments about chess positions are simply astounding. The relative strength of chess players is measured by the *Elo rating system* (named after its developer, the Hungarian-American physicist Arpad Elo), which is also the basis for the chess world rankings by the world chess federation FIDE.[2] For example, the probability that a chess player at the level of an average international master with an Elo rating of 2400 loses against an average club player with an Elo rating of 1800 is a strikingly low 0.57% (so, it basically never happens in practice; see Table 1).[3] This is to bear in mind that the gulf between a chess master and a chess amateur is even more pronounced if we consider a player at the grandmaster (about Elo 2500) or even super-grandmaster level (above Elo 2700) – with the latter reducing the amateur's chances of winning to a staggering 0.013% or less.[4] Therefore, chess mastery is an excellent paradigm for what *genuine mastery* in some field or discipline would have to look like when it comes to expert-lay comparisons (other professional sports or the mastery of musical instruments would be instructive here as well).

---

[2] For details, see, e.g., https://en.wikipedia.org/wiki/Elo_rating_system, last accessed May 25, 2023.
[3] One big advantage of the Elo rating system over many other rating systems in sports is that it allows for a relatively accurate and ecologically valid estimate of the probability of a given result between two Elo-rated players. This makes chess an especially apt and fruitful field for the empirical study of expertise.
[4] The source for all Elo calculations can be found here: https://wismuth.com/elo/calculator.html, last accessed May 25, 2023.

Table 1: Probability of the outcome of a game of chess between a master-level player (Elo 2400) and an average club player (Elo 1800)

Result	Probability
Player 1 (Elo 2400) wins	0.969960018
Player 2 (Elo 1800) wins	0.005688859
Draw	0.024351123

Now, if professional philosophers were indeed *master intuiters* with respect to thought experiments in their areas of specialization, then the variation with irrelevant factors observed in x-phi studies would not matter very much for whether we can trust philosophers' intuitive judgments a lot more than those of laypeople. Even chess masters are influenced by certain *order effects* (Bilalić, McLeod, and Gobet 2008), for example. But all that follows is that even masters are not infallible in their intuitive judgments (we already knew that!) – but not that the judgments of masters do not count for a lot more than laypeople's judgments on practically all occasions. In other words, if philosophers were indeed master intuiters, then the challenge from experimental philosophy would at best be a minor issue that hardly recommends any significant change to philosophical practice.

Thus, let us turn to the crucial question: is there any reason to think that professional philosophers have intuitive expertise in the master sense? To structure the discussion, I will first consider *direct experimental evidence* that bears on this issue, and then move on to more *indirect evidence*, such as observations about our actual philosophical practice and results from the science of expertise. In comparison to chess, however, where we have the Elo rating system and powerful computer software in order to double-check even the judgments of world-class players, the situation for studying intuitive expertise in philosophy is less straightforward. For example, given that even world-class philosophical experts disagree on many issues in their domains of expertise, and that we lack independent procedures for checking the quality of philosophers' judgments, we can only work with a *minimal condition* on intuitive mastery in philosophy.[5] My proposal for this minimal condition is that there must be at least a *very large difference* between the intuitive judgments of master intuiters and laypeople.

---

5 One could also supplement the minimal condition with a selection of thought experiment cases on which expert philosophers largely agree, and use these as a further "benchmark" for assessing the differences between philosophical experts and laypeople (see, e.g., Horvath and Wiegmann 2016, Schindler and Saint-Germier 2022). While this procedure would complicate things a bit, it would not change all that much in the general picture that emerges from the discussion. For example, there is a high level of philosophical agreement on Gettier's cases (1963), but cases of this kind are also judged in the philosophers' way by a clear majority of lay subjects – even across cultures and languages (Machery et al. 2017).

So, we can now ask the more focused question: is there a very large difference between the intuitive case judgments of philosophical experts and laypeople?

Let us first consider the extant *experimental evidence.* Unfortunately, there are only a few studies that bear on intuitive philosophical expertise in the master sense (the situation is a bit better in case of intuitive expertise in the immunity sense, as we will see below). Still, the available evidence points to a relatively clear conclusion about intuitive mastery in philosophy, as I will argue in the following.

First, there is a study by Machery (2012) in which he compared intuitions about *reference* in laypeople and various groups of language experts from philosophy and linguistics. More specifically, he investigated a version of Kripke's (1980) famous Gödel-Schmidt case (taken from Machery et al. 2004) in order to test whether participants' intuitions about the reference of proper names are influenced by descriptions associated with the name. In Kripke's hypothetical Gödel-Schmidt case, the description that most people associate with the mathematician Kurt Gödel – being the man who discovered the incompleteness of arithmetic – is actually true of an unknown mathematician called "Schmidt", from whom Gödel stole the incompleteness theorem. So, this case poses the question whether the name "Gödel" in fact refers to Schmidt, who actually discovered the incompleteness of arithmetic (Kripke 1980, pp. 83–92). To the extent that people are not influenced by associated descriptions, and thus respond that the name "Gödel" does not refer to Schmidt, their intuitions would be more in line with Kripke's semantic externalism about proper names, which holds that reference is not determined by associated descriptions, but rather by certain causal-historical relations between a name and its referent. What Machery (2012, pp. 47f.) found is that the proportion of Kripkean intuitions about the tested case was roughly at the same level for philosophers of language (83.9%) and laypeople (76.9%), with no significant difference between these two groups. An interesting additional finding was that the various groups of language experts also disagreed significantly among each other.

Second, Horvath and Wiegmann (2016) report two experiments in which they compared the knowledge-intuitions of laypeople and expert epistemologists about three thought experiment cases, inspired by the epistemological literature, and a clear case of knowledge and non-knowledge, respectively. Overall, they found no dramatic differences between experts and laypeople, although expert and lay verdicts differed significantly in some cases. But even here, the mean expert and lay ratings were still on the same side of the employed Likert scale (i.e., above or below the midpoint), ranging from 1 ("strongly disagree") to 6 ("strongly agree"), and so there was no "hard" disagreement about whether the cases should more be seen as cases of knowledge or non-knowledge. Moreover, Horvath and Wiegmann found that expert intuitions about cases of the fake-barn-type (cf. Goldman 1976) were on average judged as cases of knowledge by both laypeople and experts – contrary to the relevant "textbook consensus" (see, e.g., Shope 2004, Steup 2014). In cases of this kind, the subject correctly perceives an object, such as a barn or a painting, which is, however, surrounded by fake objects of the same kind, i.e., by fake barns or fake paintings. Expert judgments about these cases were also fairly polarized (see Horvath and Wiegmann 2016, p. 2).

Third, in a more recent study, Horvath and Wiegmann (2022) compared the intuitive case judgments of expert ethicists and laypeople in five moral cases. The main purpose of the study was to test expert-lay differences with respect to five well-known framing effects. The results are thus primarily relevant to the immunity model of intuitive expertise (see below), but they also bear on our present discussion of the master model. For, Horvath and Wiegmann found significant expert-lay differences in only two of the five tested cases, and a few of their expert-lay comparisons even were – descriptively speaking – strikingly similar (Horvath and Wiegmann 2022, p. 1). So, once again, the overall pattern of expert-lay differences runs counter to what the master model of intuitive expertise would predict.

Fourth, Schindler and Germier (2022) compared the intuitive judgments of professional philosophers and laypeople for six thought experiments from theoretical philosophy. They found a significant difference between laypeople's and philosophers' case verdicts in only three of the six tested cases, and the overall difference between philosophers' and laypeople's case judgments did not amount to any "hard" disagreement either (in the sense explained above).[6] In addition, Schindler and Germier (2022) compared philosophers and laypeople in terms of three interpretative skills that are closely related to thought experiment judgments, such as evaluating the possibility of the cases or the relevance of particular case features. While there was a significant philosopher-lay difference concerning these interpretative skills, the overall pattern of responses was still fairly similar, and thus not indicative of any pronounced expert-lay differences.

The available empirical evidence therefore does not support an understanding of intuitive expertise in philosophy along the lines of the master model, because it disconfirms a key prediction of the master model: that we should find pronounced expert-lay differences in intuitive judgments about philosophical cases. This stands in striking contrast to areas of proven master expertise, such as chess, where we find very large differences in (intuitive) judgments between masters and laypeople.

There are also *indirect considerations* based on observations about our actual philosophical practice and findings from the science of expertise that militate against the master model in philosophy. For example, even world-leading philosophical experts are not treated as master intuiters in philosophical practice. Think about high-level expert epistemologists, such as Alvin Goldman or Ernest Sosa: neither students of philosophy nor "second-rate" epistemologists treat their judgments about, e.g., fake-barn cases as the pronouncements of a superior epistemic authority to whom they would defer in cases of disagreement. Rather, the intuitive case judgments of all reasonable

---

[6] The same is true of philosopher-lay differences in five of the six tested cases individually. The only outlier is Schindler and Germier's fake-barn-type case (see https://osf.io/mhs9t/, last accessed May 25, 2023), which is inspired by Horvath and Wiegmann's (2016) Sculpture case. Here, the mean ratings of laypeople's and philosophers' case verdicts fall on different sides of the midpoint of Schindler and Germier's 5-point Likert scale, which is a finding that does not fit into the general pattern of experimental results concerning fake-barn-type cases (see, e.g., Turri 2017).

interlocutors, that is, people who exhibit a basic understanding of the relevant thought experiment and its purpose, are roughly treated alike, i.e., as having roughly the same epistemic status. So, for example, even a philosopher like Ernest Sosa, with decades of experience as a professional epistemologist, would treat it as prima facie problematic if his students did not share his verdict about a particular hypothetical case. This, again, stands in clear contrast to the pronouncements of a world-leading chess grandmaster vis-à-vis the intuitive judgments of a chess amateur, for the latter will typically defer to the grandmaster in cases of disagreement. If a high-level grandmaster like Judit Polgár, for example, says that a certain move feels or seems wrong to her, then amateur players will typically take her judgment very seriously, and revise their own judgments about the position accordingly.

Moreover, one key result that has emerged from the *science of expertise* is that the development of genuine expertise typically requires a training regimen called *deliberative practice* (see, e.g., Ericsson et al. 2006). The specific features of deliberative practice have been studied in many undeniable areas of genuine expertise, such as chess, math, or musical virtuosity. What it requires, among other things, is *timely, clear, and reliable feedback in a large number of cases* and *clear guiding standards of excellence.* In the domain of chess, for example, this amounts to being exposed to thousands of chess positions over a training period of up to several decades, followed by timely, clear, and reliable feedback on how to best judge and play the relevant positions from chess masters or computer engines that vastly outperform even the best human players. Whatever exactly the typical training in philosophy may look like, we can say without exaggeration that it is miles away from the intensity, level of precision, and systematicity that we find in the education of budding chess masters (cf. Clarke 2013, Weinberg et al. 2010). So, even if we do find *some* of the elements of deliberate practice in the way we train philosophical novices in their judgments about thought experiments (as, e.g., Williamson 2011, argues), it still does not even come close to what the inculcation of genuine expertise in the master sense would require.

Therefore, I conclude that both the available experimental evidence and the more indirect evidence from philosophical practice and the science of expertise clearly suggest that the master model is not a plausible model of intuitive expertise in philosophy.

3.2 The Myth of Intuitive Immunity

Now, you might object that the master model was never a plausible candidate for intuitive philosophical expertise in the first place, because many key philosophical concepts, such as *knowledge* or *truth*, are actually shared by philosophers and laypeople, and the excessively high standard of mastery is thus not really needed to support the expertise defense. Rather, it suffices if philosophical experts are simply less influenced by philosophically irrelevant factors, such as order of presentation or framing effects, regardless of whether their intuitive judgments are overall much better than those of laypeople. In other words, an assumption of intuitive expertise in the *immunity sense* is more than enough to defend the intuitive judgments of philosophical experts from the x-phi challenge. One key idea here is that philosophical experts draw on roughly the same cognitive resources as laypeople, for example, their competence with the relevant concepts, but that they are also much better at "screening off" the influence of irrelevant and distorting psychological factors on their intuitive judgments about hypothetical cases.

Prima facie, this seems plausible enough to get the expertise defense going. However, even the more modest claim that philosophical experts enjoy this kind of intuitive immunity in their areas of expertise involves two crucial empirical assumptions that will turn out to be problematic on closer inspection. The *first empirical assumption* is that immunity expertise is psychologically separable from master expertise. For, tellingly, there do not seem to be any clear paradigm cases of "free-standing" immunity expertise. The *second empirical assumption* is, once again, that philosophical experts really have the immunity expertise in question. I will now first revisit the available *experimental evidence* that bears directly on this second assumption, and then consider some more *indirect evidence* from philosophical practice, psychology, and the science of expertise. In this connection, I will also return to the first empirical assumption and offer some evidence for its questionability.

Let us begin by considering the available *experimental evidence* that bears on intuitive expertise in the immunity sense. Even though the number of relevant studies is still not exactly large here, the situation is nevertheless better than in the case of intuitive mastery, because the last decade has seen a series of experimental work on intuitive immunity in philosophical experts. Before we turn to these studies, however, we should first consider what they would have to show in order to substantiate the expertise defense. Fortunately, the crucial issue itself – whether experts are less susceptible to philosophically irrelevant factors than laypeople – is directly empirically testable by comparing relevant groups of philosophical experts with laypeople. As a minimal requirement on intuitive immunity – and thus for a successful rebuttal of the x-phi challenge – I would propose that philosophical experts must be substantially more resistant to the influence of philosophically irrelevant factors than laypeople in a wide range of cases in their respective areas of expertise (such as ethics, epistemology, metaphysics, or philosophy of language). The assumption that the factors in question are indeed philosophically irrelevant is, of course, crucial for this kind of research, but it is also fairly uncontroversial in many cases, such as the influence of order of presentation (for discussion, see, e.g., Wiegmann, Horvath, and Meyer 2020).

Let us begin with an early study by Hitchcock and Knobe (2009), which compares intuitions about actual causation (or "token" causation) in professional philosophers and laypeople. Judgments about actual causation are not judgments about the overall causal structure that is operative in a certain situation, but rather judgments that a particular event A caused another event B, such as the impact of the ball causing the breaking of the window. What they found is that the relevant causal intuitions of professional philosophers (inclusion criteria: professor of philosophy or PhD in philosophy) are equally affected by *norm violations* as those of lay people (even in cases where questions of blame and responsibility were not an issue). However, it is somewhat controversial whether norm violations are in fact irrelevant to judgments about actual causation, with Hitchcock and Knobe arguing, for example, that sensitivity to norm violations is a constitutive feature of our pre-theoretical concept of causation.

Another early study by Schulz, Cokely, and Feltz (2011) reports that expert judgments on free will and moral responsibility were not immune to the influence of the heritable personality trait *extraversion* (more specifically, a sub-trait of extraversion called *warmth*), which predicts compatibilist intuitions in both experts and laypeople (as determined by the "Free Will Skill Test" developed by the authors). Roughly speaking, compatibilism allows for actions out of free will and genuine moral responsibility even in a universe where every action is completely causally determined by previous conditions. At least for laypeople, the influence of extraversion on compatibilist intuitions was also shown to be robust in a recent meta-study (Feltz and Cokely 2019).

In Schwitzgebel and Cushman's (2012) seminal study on the expertise defense, they report that *order effects* about a number of ethical cases, including classic trolley cases, were equally large in expert ethicists (inclusion criteria: area of specialization or competence in ethics and/or PhD in philosophy) and laypeople. Order effects are influences on cognition that merely depend on the order in which certain items, such as various hypothetical cases, are presented to the subject in question, which is almost always an irrelevant or distorting factor – both in- and outside of philosophy (for discussion, see Wiegmann et al. 2020). In a follow-up study, Schwitzgebel and Cushman (2015) successfully replicated their earlier finding about *order effects* in expert ethicists, and they also found that the influence of order of presentation is not mitigated by forced reflection, self-reported familiarity with the tested cases, self-reported stability of previous opinion on the tested cases, and self-reported expertise.

Another study by Tobia, Buckwalter, and Stich (2013) reports that professional philosophers exhibit an equally large *actor-observer bias* as laypeople concerning various ethical cases. One speaks of an actor-observer bias if certain judgments or intuitions are influenced merely by whether otherwise identical situations are described from a third-person or first-person point of view. Tobia, Chapman, and Stich (2013) confirmed this earlier finding. In addition, they also reported that professional philosophers' moral judgments are equally influenced by *priming* with the smell of the disinfectant Lysol (i.e., exposure to this smell before the actual experimental task), which is psychologically strongly associated with cleanliness. However, both of these findings seem highly questionable in light of the recent replication crisis in psychology and other experimental disciplines (see, e.g., Open Science Collaboration 2015): the initial finding about actor-observer bias has been disconfirmed by a high-powered experiment of Horvath and Wiegmann (2022), and priming studies of the Lysol-kind have generally been shown to lack empirical robustness (see, e.g., Johnson, Cheung, and Donnellan 2014).

In a more recent study, Löhr (2019) tests various hypotheses about Nozick's (1974) experience-machine thought experiment with laypeople and professional philosophers. In this thought experiment, Nozick wants us to imagine a machine that artificially induces a stream of experience or consciousness in us that is qualitatively indistinguishable from our actual experience. This raises the question whether we would prefer to enter this machine for the rest of our lives if our conscious experience were as happy and pleasurable as we can possibly imagine it – or whether we would rather prefer to live in "the real world" with all its hardships and frustrations. While philosophers were somewhat more consistent in their answers to different versions of the experience-machine scenario than laypeople, a remarkable 29% of them still gave inconsistent answers (in a within-subject design).

Even more recently, Wiegmann, Horvath, and Meyer (2020) presented evidence that expert ethicists (inclusion criteria: PhD or MA in philosophy *and* moral philosophy as area of specialization or competence) are no less susceptible to *order effects* and the influence of *irrelevant options* on their moral judgments about trolley scenarios of the push-type (i.e., cases with the option of *pushing* a person on the track to stop a train from killing several people versus the option of *doing nothing*, and a six-option version of the case with four additional intermediate options). Most strikingly, the difference between first seeing the original dilemma version of the push-type trolley case versus first seeing the six-option version was highly significant in expert ethicists, but non-significant in laypeople. Since the two basic options of the dilemma version, i.e., *pushing* and *doing nothing* (see above), are equally available in the six-option version of the case, it is puzzling – and arguably the influence of a morally irrelevant factor – that philosophers' intuitive judgments about these two basic options would change merely as a result of having further intermediate options.

Finally, Horvath and Wiegmann (2022) tested five previously investigated framing effects from the literature on judgment and decision-making (most of which had been shown to be empirically robust) in five ethical cases with laypeople and expert moral philosophers (inclusion criteria: PhD or MA in philosophy *and* moral philosophy as area of specialization or competence). They found that expert moral philosophers are also susceptible to these well-known biases over all five cases, as well as in some individual cases, such as one that implements Tversky and Kahneman's (1981) "Asian disease" framing. In this kind of framing effect, people respond very differently to an identical prospect concerning how many people will survive a certain intervention to control the outbreak of a rare disease, depending on whether the prospect is framed in terms of losses (people killed) or gains (people saved). However, expert ethicists also turned out to be unsusceptible to the influence of a simple framing of the response option in terms of "people killed" versus "people saved" in a trolley-style scenario. As the authors emphasize, it is hard to predict the cases in which expert philosophers may in fact enjoy some "immunity advantage" in advance of experimental testing. Therefore, Horvath and Wiegmann's findings still do not support typical versions of the expertise defense "from one's philosophical armchair" – but they may open the door to a more qualified *empirical expertise defense* for some cases.

The picture that emerges from this brief survey of empirical evidence concerning intuitive expertise in the immunity sense is that philosophical experts, by and large, enjoy no clear advantage over laypeople in their susceptibility to philosophically irrelevant factors. Just as laypeople, philosophers fall prey to many of the same distorting influences on their intuitive case judgments, such as heritable personality traits, order of presentation, or various framing effects. From an experimental perspective, the proposed condition for the intuitive immunity of philosophical experts is not satisfied: in comparison to laypeople, philosophical experts are *not* substantially more resistant to the influence of irrelevant factors on their intuitive judgments in a wide range of cases in their areas of expertise.

Let us now consider the *indirect evidence* concerning intuitive expertise in the immunity sense. First, although the evidence on this issue is relatively scarce, it seems likely that immunity expertise mainly occurs as a *byproduct* of high degrees of mastery. This is supported, for example, by a study in the domain of chess, which reports that, while *chess masters* are susceptible to *order effects* when solving chess problems, *chess grandmasters* were not affected by them (Bilalić et al. 2008). A plausible hypothesis would be that immunity expertise is not a psychologically self-standing form of expertise at all, but only the result of very high degrees of master expertise. In any case, this would explain why convincing paradigms of immunity expertise without master expertise are hard to come by. Relatedly, it would also cast doubt on the *first empirical assumption* identified above, namely, that immunity expertise is psychologically separable from master expertise. Instead, if the reported finding about chess masters and chess grandmasters should generalize, it might be practically impossible or at least highly unlikely to acquire substantial immunity expertise independently of acquiring high-level master expertise – and given that the evidence against intuitive master expertise in philosophy is strong, this would indirectly also tell against philosophers' immunity expertise.

Second, it is unclear *why* philosophical experts should be immune to the influence of irrelevant factors in the first place, such as well-known biases of judgment and decision-making, or *how* they may have acquired such expertise. For example, philosophers typically get no feedback on whether their intuitive judgments about hypothetical cases are influenced by irrelevant factors – in fact, before the advent of experimental philosophy, such issues were hardly ever discussed in philosophy. At any rate, it seems clear that inculcating immunity expertise is *not* an explicit goal of any standard philosophical training. If one adds to this that the influence of, say, order of presentation or inheritable personality traits, is introspectively opaque and not easily accessible on reflection, then it is indeed quite mysterious how professional philosophers should have acquired any intuitive immunity expertise at all (apart from acquiring it as a byproduct of intuitive mastery, which they very likely don't have; see above).

Third, there are tricky general obstacles to the acquisition of immunity expertise as well, such as the phenomenon of *bias blindspot*, which makes us unwilling to accept our own biases even in light of explicit information about them – while we have little problem to accept that other people are variously biased (see, e.g., Pronin 2007). For many philosophically irrelevant factors, it is also unclear whether we can (fully) resist them at all, or what the best way of achieving such resistance might be (see, e.g., Ahlstrom-Vij 2013). In any case, the best guess is that a truly effective form of "immunity training" would have to be very different from (what is part of) our current philosophical training.

Let me thus conclude that both the available experimental evidence and various indirect considerations tell against the assumption that philosophical experts possess anything like the intuitive immunity expertise that would be needed in order to rebut the x-phi challenge. In combination with the equally negative conclusion about intuitive expertise in the master sense, it seems no exaggeration to conclude that the intuitive expertise that proponents of the expertise defense are hoping for is largely a myth. So, to the extent that one regards the x-phi challenge as a serious problem for the philosophical method of cases, a more promising defense would be badly needed. Given this sobering conclusion, let us now turn to the *mischaracterization objection*, which may already be one of the last straws that champions of the traditional method of cases can hold onto.

4 The Mischaracterization Objection and Its Consequences

Let us set the failed defenses of intuition apologists aside for now and turn to the camp of *intuition detractors* and their main reply to the x-phi challenge: the *mischaracterization objection* (cf. Sytsma and Livengood 2016). This objection is mainly based on the work of Max Deutsch (e. g., 2009, 2010, 2015) and Herman Cappelen (e. g., 2012, 2014), with some influence from Timothy Williamson's (e. g., 2004) work as well (for a recent overview, see Horvath 2022). The mischaracterization objection, as I will understand it here, can be decomposed into a *descriptive* and a *methodological* (i. e., *normative*) part. The descriptive part can again be distinguished into a *negative, intuition-detraction* claim, and a *positive, argument-affirming* claim.[7] While the intuition-detraction aspect of the mischaracterization objection has generated the most controversy (see, e. g., Boghossian 2014, Chalmers 2014, Nado 2016b, Weinberg 2014), the argument-affirming claim is in fact equally important for the overall view. For, without some positive story about *what other than intuition* philosophers' case judgments might be based on, the mischaracterization view would be a lot less persuasive, because it would seem rather mysterious *on what* judgments about hypothetical cases could be based *at all*. Finally, the *methodological part* of the mischaracterization objection draws certain normative lessons about philosophical methodology from its descriptive part, most

---

[7] These distinctions, as well as the following discussion, are heavily based on my much more comprehensive analysis and defense of the mischaracterization objection in "Mischaracterization Reconsidered" (Horvath 2022). What I add to this previous paper here are new experimental results on the psychologically efficacy of arguments for thought experiment judgments, and further reflections on the metaphilosophical consequences of mischaracterization.

notably that the x-phi challenge is simply misdirected at intuitions about cases instead of arguments for case judgments.

But let us first step back and consider in some more detail what the descriptive part of the mischaracterization objection really involves, and what the evidence for it is supposed to be. First, the *intuition-detraction claim* roughly holds that philosophers do not appeal to intuitions or intuitive judgments as crucial evidence for their judgments about hypothetical cases – contrary to widespread metaphilosophical opinion (see, e.g., DePaul and Ramsey 1998, Pust 2017). The positive, *argument-affirming claim*, in turn, holds that philosophers instead argue and give reasons for their judgments about hypothetical cases. Taken together, these two claims amount to the following *mischaracterization claim:*

(MISC) Philosophers do not appeal to intuitions or intuitive judgments about thought experiment cases as crucial evidence for their case judgments; instead, they give reasons and arguments for their case judgments.[8]

In light of philosophers' well-known enthusiasm for arguing with each other, this should be a highly plausible and acceptable metaphilosophical claim, but it has nevertheless been met with striking and fierce resistance (see, e.g., Bengson 2014, Boghossian 2014, Brogaard 2014, Chalmers 2014, Chudnoff 2017, Colaço and Machery 2017, Egler 2020, Nado 2016b, Sytsma and Livengood 2016, Weinberg 2014). So, what is Deutsch and Cappelen's evidence for this "infamous" view about the method of cases? It is simply a series of case studies in which they carefully analyze how various seminal thought experiments are presented and introduced into the philosophical literature (mainly developed in Cappelen 2012, Deutsch 2015), such as Gettier cases (Gettier 1963), Burge's arthritis case (Burge 1979), or Jackson's Mary case (Jackson 1982). In these case studies, Deutsch and Cappelen spend significant effort on elaborating that there are few, if any, indications that the authors of the relevant texts appeal to intuitions as crucial evidence for their case judgments, while there are plenty of indications that the authors argue for their case judgments (and often quite extensively).

For example, consider the following key passage from Gettier (1963), where he presents his verdict about the second of his two hypothetical cases that are meant to refute the traditional analysis of knowledge as justified true belief:

> But imagine now that two further conditions hold. First, Jones does *not* own a Ford, but is at present driving a rented car. And secondly, by the sheerest coincidence, and entirely unknown to Smith, the place mentioned in proposition (h) ["Either Jones owns a Ford, or Brown is in Barcelona"] happens really to be the place where Brown is. If these two conditions hold then Smith does *not* know that (h) is true [...]. (Gettier 1963, p. 123)

---

8 This is a simplified version of my more detailed presentation in Horvath (2022, sec. 2).

The final sentence here summarizes Gettier's (brief) informal argument for his case verdict that Smith does not know that the proposition "Either Jones owns a Ford, or Brown is in Barcelona" is true. Moreover, Gettier also indicates that the main reason why Smith does not know this proposition is that it is true "by the sheerest coincidence" in light of Smith's evidence (which only concerns Jones' ownership of a Ford, but not the current location of Brown). In other words, Gettier appeals to a certain kind of epistemic luck here, which is still one of the main reasons for accepting Gettier's case verdict in contemporary epistemology (see, e.g., Engel 2015, Pritchard 2005). Finally, there is no compelling indication in Gettier's paper that intuitions about the case play any role for why one should accept his suggested case judgment (for further discussion, see Horvath 2022).

However, despite the considerable efforts of Deutsch and Cappelen, they have nevertheless failed to convince the philosophical community of their case for the mischaracterization claim, and also of the need to take it seriously as one of the main metaphilosophical views about the method of cases. Therefore, one might think that there must be some exceptionally powerful objections to such an attractive and natural view that might explain its near-universal rejection. Not so, however. For, as I have argued elsewhere (Horvath 2022), all extant objections to the mischaracterization claim are unconvincing, and so we remain with a puzzling situation that I have expressed as follows:

> The most charitable explanation that I can come up with is that analytic (meta)philosophers are still so much in the grip of the intuition-based view of the method of cases that they tend to automatically reinterpret Gettier (1963) and other seminal texts in this light. (Horvath 2022, p. 9)

Although I cannot offer a full defense of the above claims here, I still want to briefly explain why some of the most prominent and salient replies to the mischaracterization objection are unconvincing (see Horvath 2022, sec. 3, for the full monty).

The most direct way of challenging Deutsch and Cappelen's case for the descriptive mischaracterization claim is to challenge the case studies on which it is crucially based. For example, one might suspect that their *choice* of case studies is somehow *biased* against the intuition-based view. However, it is hard to see how it could be, given that they simply consider some of the most prominent examples of the method of cases in philosophy, such as Gettier (1963) or Kripke (1980), which are frequently cited as paradigmatic instances by proponents of the intuition-based view as well (e.g., Bealer 1996).

Nevertheless, one might object that a *more systematic analysis* of the philosophical literature will reveal that "while arguments may sometimes support philosophers' assessment of thought experiments, [it is dubious that] this is true in general" (Colaço and Machery 2017, p. 179). Unfortunately, philosophers who express such concerns have not presented anything like the carefully analyzed case studies of Deutsch and Cappelen, let alone a systematic review of the philosophical literature. So, at present, the objection in question is more a vague hypothesis, pending empirical investigation, than a properly substantiated challenge to the mischaracterization claim.

Still, it is true that there are a few clear cases of philosophers who explicitly subscribe to an intuition-based method of cases as metaphilosophers, and who also apply this method in their first-order philosophical practice. One example in epistemology would be Laurence BonJour, who is well-known for his book-length defense of a rationalist, intuition-involving conception of philosophy (1998), and who also explicitly appeals to intuition in his first-order epistemological work (e. g., BonJour 1980). Another case in point is Frances Kamm, who both endorses an intuition-based methodology at the metaphilosophical level and also applies it in her first-order work in moral philosophy (e. g., Kamm 2007).

However, it would be a mistake to think that the existence of a few clear counterexamples to the mischaracterization claim simply rehabilitates the standard intuition-based picture of the method of cases. For, suppose that the overall share of clear instances of an intuition-based method of cases is only 20 %, while the other 80 % fit much better with the argument view. Even though both theoretical and experimental work on intuitions and their role in philosophy would still be warranted in this scenario, the excessive metaphilosophical focus on intuitions of the last few decades would clearly not be justified. Rather, our "division of cognitive labor" (cf. Kitcher 1990) in metaphilosophy should then better shift towards a majority of work on the role of arguments in the method of cases, while only a much smaller share of work should be devoted to intuitions. This would also hold for experimental philosophy, which should then prioritize research on arguments for case judgments over research on intuitions about cases (see below for some actual examples).

Admittedly, we currently just do not know the real figures about the proportion of intuition-based versus argument-based instances of the method of cases in philosophy. But even in light of the preliminary and anecdotical evidence from Deutsch and Cappelen's case studies, it would be surprising if argument-based instances were so few and far between that they hardly justify any metaphilosophical attention. Moreover, once it is established that there is a non-negligible number of argument-based instances of the method of cases, this also creates considerable *normative pressure* on the intuition-based view. For, given the many problems with the intuition-based view – due to both theoretical unclarities about intuitions (see, e. g., Nado 2014, Williamson 2004) and the difficulties with rebutting the x-phi challenge (see above) – it would then be a serious methodological question whether philosophers *should* continue to appeal to intuitions about cases, given that arguing for case judgments has been established as a viable alternative (see also below).

But let us also consider a more concessive response to the mischaracterization objection, which grants most of its descriptive content (at least for the sake of the argument), yet nevertheless tries to maintain a key role for appeals to intuition. For example, it might be conceded that philosophers often argue for their case judgments, but only to add that the story doesn't end there. For, arguments require *premises*, and these premises must be based on something as well. It is here that intuition apologists claim to have spotted a lacuna in the case for the mischaracterization view, because they argue that there is often *no obvious alternative epistemic source* for the premises in question *but intuition* (see, e.g., Brogaard 2014, Chalmers 2014, Chudnoff 2017, Nado 2016b). The main problem with this reply is that it basically just concedes the main point of the mischaracterization objection: that philosophers' case judgments are *not* directly based on intuition or their intuitiveness, but rather on further premises and reasons. It is true that this is compatible with the claim that some of those premises and reasons may eventually turn out to be intuition-based – but then they may also not. To really carve out some key role for intuitions in the method of cases with this strategy, considerable additional work is still needed, for example, by analyzing the argumentative chains in question deeply enough to be able to tell that they do – or even must – end with intuitions somewhere. Once again, this kind of work has not been done with anything like the care or level of detail that one finds in Deutsch and Cappelen's case studies. Moreover, the present reply, even if successful, would still have drastic consequences for the x-phi challenge to the method of cases, given that almost all relevant x-phi work has been done on *intuitive judgments about particular cases.* However, the premises and reasons offered in support of philosophical case judgments will often *not* be judgments about particular cases, but rather more *general claims or principles*, such as "knowledge is incompatible with accidentally true belief" or "it is morally wrong to treat another person as a mere means to an end" (see, e.g., Brown 2017, Landes 2020). So far, almost no extant work in experimental philosophy tackles intuitions of this more general kind (maybe with the exception of Andow 2018). The present reply to the mischaracterization objection would thus have the startling "side-effect" that the x-phi challenge to the method of cases is successfully rebutted for now.

Finally, let us have a look at some attempts to unsettle the mischaracterization objection on the basis of *empirical results* from experimental metaphilosophy. Since the descriptive part of the mischaracterization objection is an empirical claim about actual philosophical practice, there is no mystery why experimental findings can be relevant to its assessment. One such attempt is based on a survey by Kuntz and Kuntz (2011) on *philosophers' self-reported attitude* concerning the role of intuitions in philosophy (see, e.g., Sytsma and Livengood 2016, p. 91). The results of this study are quite mixed, however, because less than 30% of the surveyed philosophers agree with the strong pro-intuition claim "Intuitions are *essential* to *justification* in philosophical methods". Moreover, Kuntz and Kuntz' questions are not specifically targeted at *intuitions about particular cases*, which are the main focus of the mischaracterization claim. Lastly, given that the mischaracterization claim concerns the *practice* of the method of cases (as in the seminal texts analyzed by Deutsch and Cappelen), one might legitimately question the probative value of self-reported attitudes with respect to how the method of cases is actually carried out in practice.

A more interesting experimental challenge to the mischaracterization claim is based on findings about the psychological efficacy of arguments for thought experiment judgments. In a pioneering study, Wysocki (2017) reports that neither an argument for nor an argument against ascribing knowledge in a Gettier case of the stopped-clock type had any significant effect on participants' case judgments. But why would it be a problem for the mischaracterization objection if it were generally true that arguments had no effect on people's judgments about philosophical cases? First, one could challenge the *descriptive mischaracterization claim* by arguing that, given the psychologically inefficacy of arguments, these arguments are probably just *post-hoc rationalizations* of our case judgments, which therefore must be really based on something else – with intuition as the most plausible candidate. Second, one could also challenge the mischaracterization objection *on normative grounds*, namely, by claiming that philosophers *should not* argue for their judgments about hypothetical cases if such arguments have no psychological effect on people's case judgments. The issue of the psychological efficacy of arguments for case judgments is thus both metaphilosophically pressing and also interesting in its own right. The "natural expectation" would be that good arguments for (or against) a given case judgment should at least make *some* noticeable difference here. In any case, the contrary expectation would amount to an extremely bleak view about the power of (philosophical) arguments.

In fact, there are several reasons to be critical of Wysocki's (2017) investigation of argument efficacy (cf. Horvath 2022), most notably that his argument for ascribing knowledge in the tested Gettier case is even prima facie a bad one, because it only appeals to the practical usefulness of the protagonist's belief. To address these shortcomings, Horvath and Wiegmann (2023) first replicated Wysocki's original design, and then conducted an improved follow-up experiment that includes two further Gettier cases in addition to Wysocki's stopped-clock case. While the replication of Wysocki's original experiment was indeed successful, Horvath and Wiegmann also found that merely adding a condition with a better argument for ascribing knowledge to Wysocki's otherwise unchanged design already led to a highly significant effect (in comparison to the con-argument condition). In Horvath and Wiegmann's second experiment, they presented both the case descriptions and the arguments for and against ascribing knowledge in the more natural setting of a little dialogue between friends, and they also used arguments that are at least prima facie convincing. In this improved design, and with a statistically high-powered sample, they found a clear pattern of influence of the presented arguments on people's case judgments, both over all three cases combined, and also for most of the individual comparisons between pro-, con- and baseline-conditions. Even though a lot more research about the efficacy of arguments for case judgments is surely needed, the improved and broadened study by Horvath and Wiegmann clearly indicates a significant influence of prima facie good arguments on case judgments – also in line with pre-theoretical expectations. Thus, it seems unlikely that the issue of argument efficacy will pose a serious challenge to the mischaracterization objection.

For reasons of space, I could only cover a relatively small selection of extant replies to the mischaracterization objection here (but see Horvath 2022, for a much more comprehensive discussion). But I hope that even my limited treatment already illustrates that these replies fall short of exposing the mischaracterization objection as being just an annoying distraction from the "proper business" of intuition-based philosophy. Quite to the contrary, some of these replies only help to bring out the full force of the mischaracterization objection, especially with respect to the x-phi challenge to the method of cases. For, if the descriptive mischaracterization claim turns out to be correct, most relevant work in experimental metaphilosophy has been directed at the wrong target, and the x-phi challenge to the method of cases as we know it simply collapses.

Let me finally turn to the *normative consequences* of the mischaracterization claim for philosophical methodology, which I have already touched upon at various places in my discussion of the descriptive mischaracterization claim. To start with the simplest case, let us assume that the mischaracterization claim MISC is true of all instances of the method of cases in philosophy. What would follow for the x-phi challenge, and also for metaphilosophy more generally? For the *x-phi challenge*, this would be the worst-case scenario, for almost all extant experimental work focuses exclusively on *intuitions* or *intuitive judgments* about hypothetical cases (or, more neutrally, on non-inferential judgments that are not crucially supported by arguments and reasons). Since MISC holds that intuitions play no crucial evidential role for philosophers' case judgments, which are instead supported by reasons and arguments, the respective work from experimental philosophy would basically be irrelevant to the metaphilosophy of the method of cases. This would not, of course, make experimental philosophy irrelevant to the method of cases as a matter of principle, but other target phenomena and research questions would definitely be needed in order to reassert its metaphilosophical relevance. I have already given one example of this "mischaracterization-friendly" experimental metaphilosophy above: the recent work on the psychological efficacy of arguments for case judgments (Horvath and Wiegmann 2023, Wysocki 2017). This is just the beginning, of course, because many other issues about arguments and argumentation in philosophy are amenable to experimental investigation as well (see, e.g., Fischer et al. 2021). Moreover, experimental philosophers could also direct their attention to intuitions about general principles and claims, which might still play a key evidential role in philosophy even if MISC were completely true – for example, with respect to some of the premises of philosophers' arguments for case judgments (see above). What is true, however, is that experimental philosophy would have to change its research focus quite drastically in order to maintain its metaphilosophical relevance if MISC were correct.

What would follow for metaphilosophy more generally if MISC were completely true? This would certainly expose the enormous attention that intuitions, and intuitions about hypothetical cases in particular, have received over the last few decades (see, e.g., Booth and Rowbottom 2014, DePaul and Ramsey 1998, Pust 2017) as overly excessive and at least partly misguided. Complementary to that, it would also suggest that the role of arguments and argumentation in the method of cases – and probably elsewhere in philosophy as well – has been unduly neglected by recent metaphilosophy. One suggestive piece of evidence for this claim is that the first article on argument and argumentation in the *Stanford Encyclopedia of Philosophy* has only been published very recently (Dutilh Novaes 2021).

However, what if the actual situation with the method of cases is a lot more complicated than what is suggested by intuition detractors and intuition apologists alike? What if the truth about how philosophers justify their judgments about hypothetical cases lies in a much grayer area – with some instances of the argument view, some instances of the intuition-based view, some hybrid cases, and various unclear or much harder to classify instances of the method of cases? I believe that the truth about the method of cases lies indeed somewhere in this gray area, but that we currently have no clear sense about the relative proportion of its different types of instances – another issue that would require considerably more empirical investigation. Still, almost any location of the method of cases in this gray area raises a host of interesting and novel metaphilosophical questions. For a start, one might ask whether there are also ways in which philosophers support their judgments about hypothetical cases that are different from all previously considered options. Moreover, once there are alternatives on the table, one might ask which of those alternatives should be preferred: should we now always justify our case judgments by arguing for them, or should we always justify them primarily on intuitive grounds – or should we rather decide this on a case-by-case basis, or maybe even always offer both kinds of justification (if possible)? Needless to say, it would complicate things even further if there should be other viable options beyond intuitions and arguments.

Even though I can only scratch the surface here, I want to close this section by offering some considerations *why we should almost always argue for our case judgments in philosophy* (maybe with the exception of case judgments that are clearly part of the common ground of the relevant philosophical debate; cf. Cappelen 2012). First, offering explicit reasons and arguments for case judgments makes the evidential situation a lot more transparent and therefore greatly facilitates the subsequent philosophical debate, because other philosophers can then directly respond to those publicly available reasons and arguments. In contrast, purely intuition-driven debates often lead to fruitless stalemate-situations, where philosopher A simply finds P intuitive, while philosopher B just does not share A's intuition or even finds P counterintuitive. As an aside, I think that philosophers who take their case judgments to be solely justified on an intuitive basis should also explicitly say so in their talks and published research, because this would clarify things considerably for their hearers and readers. Second, if case judgments are non-trivial claims or have non-trivial consequences – as almost always in philosophy – it seems even normatively required to offer explicit reasons or evidence for those claims, simply as a basic norm of how academic and scientific work should be presented to other researchers. In other words, "Always argue for your non-trivial claims!" seems to be one of the most basic methodological imperatives of academia (in contrast to other spheres of human activity, such as religion or one's personal life). Finally, analyzing arguments and arguing about difficult and abstract matters is one of the most plausible kinds of expertise that philosophers can legitimately claim for themselves – unlike intuitive expertise in judging hypothetical cases, for example, which is very likely a myth (as I have argued above). To put it differently, arguing is simply "core business" for professional philosophers, while the case intuitions of philosophers, by and large, seem to be just as amateurish as those of laypeople.

5 Conclusion

I opened this chapter with the standard picture of the relation between intuitions and experimental philosophy: the alleged key evidential role of intuitive judgments about hypothetical cases in the philosophical method of cases, and experimental philosophy's challenge to the epistemic trustworthiness of these judgments, based on their variation with philosophically irrelevant factors. Then I surveyed some of the main ways in which intuition apologists try to defend this standard picture against the x-phi challenge, and found most of them wanting. For the most popular of these defensive strategies, the expertise defense, I have provided a more in-depth analysis. Based on the distinction between the master model and the immunity model of intuitive expertise, I surveyed the available experimental and indirect evidence that bears on philosophers' intuitive expertise for judging hypothetical cases in their areas of expertise. From this discussion, I have drawn the rather bleak conclusion that intuitive expertise of the envisaged kind is probably a myth on either of these two models. For, the available experimental evidence tells against both the claim that the intuitive case judgments of philosophical experts are massively superior to those of laypeople (i.e., the master model) and the claim that philosophical experts are immune to the influence of irrelevant factors on their case judgments (i.e., the immunity model). In addition, the indirect evidence from philosophical practice and the science of expertise also speak against the assumption of philosophers' intuitive expertise because, for example, first-rate philosophers are not treated as master intuiters by other philosophers, the acquisition of immunity expertise without mastery is psychologically unlikely, and it is not plausibly inculcated by our actual philosophical training. Next, I considered the main "defensive weapon" in the intuition detractors' arsenal, the mischaracterization objection, which has been mainly developed by Max Deutsch and Herman Cappelen (and more recently also by Horvath 2022). According to this objection, which is based on the textual analysis of seminal presentations of philosophical thought experiments, philosophers do not actually appeal to intuitions as crucial evidence for their case judgments, but instead argue for them. If correct, this would render the x-phi challenge to the method of cases irrelevant, because experimental philosophers have focused almost exclusively on intuitive judgments about hypothetical cases. The mischaracterization objection can be decomposed into a descriptive mischaracterization claim, with a negative, intuition-detraction part and a positive, argument-affirming part, and its normative, methodological consequences for philosophical practice. In light of these distinctions, I have considered a few instructive replies to the mischaracterization objection, which are, however, unconvincing on further inspection, and which sometimes even cause significant "collateral damage", for example, by actually supporting the metaphilosophical irrelevance of the x-phi challenge. Finally, I have considered some normative consequences of the mischaracterization objection, based on the assumption that it is either wholly or partly correct. In any case, the mischaracterization objection clearly recommends a shift away from the excessive focus on intuitions about cases in metaphilosophy and experimental philosophy, and towards more work on the role of arguments and argumentation in the method of cases. In a somewhat more speculative fashion, I have also argued for the normative claim that philosophers should always argue for their case judgments, even if they have strong intuitions about them, because an argument-based methodology would be both more transparent and philosophically fruitful – apart from directly tapping into one of professional philosophers' "core skills". Last but not least, my overall assessment of the role of intuitions in experimental philosophy is that the mischaracterization objection – currently the most promising defense against the x-phi challenge – recommends that we should scale back our obsession with intuitions about cases in both experimental philosophy and metaphilosophy. So, even if intuitions about thought experiment cases may still play a large role in many philosophical corners, they arguably shouldn't.

Bibliography

Ahlstrom-Vij, Kristoffer (2013): "Why we cannot rely on ourselves for epistemic improvement", *Philosophical Issues* 23 (1), pp. 276–296.

Alexander, Joshua, and Jonathan Weinberg (2007): "Analytic epistemology and experimental philosophy", *Philosophy Compass* 2 (1), pp. 56–80.

Andow, James (2018): "Are intuitions about moral relevance susceptible to framing effects?", *Review of Philosophy and Psychology* 9 (1), pp. 115–141.

Bealer, George (1996): "'A priori' knowledge and the scope of philosophy", *Philosophical Studies* 81 (2–3), pp. 121–142.

Bengson, John (2013): "Experimental attacks on intuitions and answers", *Philosophy and Phenomenological Research* 86 (3), pp. 495–532.

Bengson, John (2014): "How philosophers use intuition and 'intuition'", *Philosophical Studies* 171 (3), pp. 555–576.

Bilalić, Merim, Peter McLeod, and Fernand Gobet (2008): "Inflexibility of experts – reality or myth? Quantifying the Einstellung effect in chess masters", *Cognitive Psychology* 56 (2), pp. 73–102.

Boghossian, Paul (2014): "Philosophy without intuitions? A reply to Cappelen", *Analytic Philosophy* 55 (4), pp. 368–381.

BonJour, Laurence (1980): "Externalist theories of empirical knowledge", *Midwest Studies in Philosophy* 5 (1), pp. 53–74.

BonJour, Laurence (1998): *In defense of pure reason. A rationalist account of a priori justification.* Cambridge: Cambridge University Press.

Booth, Anthony Robert, and Darrell Rowbottom (Eds.) (2014): *Intuitions.* Oxford: Oxford University Press.

Brogaard, Berit (2014): "Intuitions as intellectual seemings", *Analytic Philosophy* 55 (4), pp. 382–393.

Brown, Jessica (2017): "The Gettier case and intuition", in: Rodrigo Borges, Claudio de Almeida, and Peter Klein (Eds.): *Explaining knowledge. New essays on the Gettier problem.* Oxford: Oxford University Press, pp. 191–211.

Burge, Tyler (1979): "Individualism and the mental", *Midwest Studies in Philosophy* 4 (1), pp. 73–121.

Cappelen, Herman (2012): *Philosophy without intuitions.* Oxford: Oxford University Press.

Cappelen, Herman (2014): "X-phi without intuitions?", in: Anthony Robert Booth and Darrell Rowbottom (Eds.): *Intuitions*. Oxford: Oxford University Press, pp. 269–286.
Chalmers, David (2014): "Intuitions in philosophy. A minimal defense", *Philosophical Studies* 171 (3), pp. 535–544.
Chalmers, David (2015): "Why isn't there more progress in philosophy?", *Philosophy* 90 (1), pp. 3–31.
Chudnoff, Elijah (2017): "The reality of the intuitive", *Inquiry* 60 (4), pp. 371–385.
Clarke, Steve (2013): "Intuitions as evidence, philosophical expertise and the developmental challenge", *Philosophical Papers* 42 (2), pp. 175–207.
Colaço, David, and Edouard Machery (2017): "The intuitive is a red herring", *Inquiry* 60 (4), pp. 403–419.
Cova, Florian, Brent Strickland, Angela Abatista, Aurélien Allard, James Andow, Mario Attie, James Beebe, Renatas Berniūnas, Jordane Boudesseul, Matteo Colombo, Fiery Cushman, Rodrigo Díaz, Noah N'Djaye Nikolai van Dongen, Vilius Dranseika, Brian Earp, Antonio Gaitán Torres, Ivar Hannikainen, José Hernández-Conde, Wenjia Hu, François Jaquet, Kareem Khalifa, Hanna Kim, Markus Kneer, Joshua Knobe, Miklos Kurthy, Anthony Lantian, Shen-Yi Liao, Edouard Machery, Tania Moerenhout, Christian Mott, Mark Phelan, Jonathan Phillips, Navin Rambharose, Kevin Reuter, Felipe Romero, Paulo Sousa, Jan Sprenger, Emile Thalabard, Kevin Tobia, Hugo Viciana, Daniel Wilkenfeld, and Xiang Zhou (2018): "Estimating the reproducibility of experimental philosophy", *Review of Philosophy and Psychology* 2, pp. 9–44.
Cullen, Simon (2010): "Survey-driven romanticism", *Review of Philosophy and Psychology* 1 (2), pp. 275–296.
DePaul, Michael, and William Ramsey (Eds.) (1998): *Rethinking intuition. The psychology of intuition and its role in philosophical inquiry*. Lanham: Rowman & Littlefield.
Deutsch, Max (2009): "Experimental philosophy and the theory of reference", *Mind & Language* 24 (4), pp. 445–466.
Deutsch, Max (2010): "Intuitions, counter-examples, and experimental philosophy", *Review of Philosophy and Psychology* 1 (3), pp. 447–460.
Deutsch, Max (2015): *The myth of the intuitive. Experimental philosophy and philosophical method*. Cambridge: The MIT Press.
Devitt, Michael (2011): "Experimental semantics", *Philosophy and Phenomenological Research* 82 (2), pp. 418–435.
Dutilh Novaes, Catarina (2021): "Argument and argumentation", in: Edward Zalta: *The Stanford Encyclopedia of Philosophy*. Fall 2021 edition.
https://plato.stanford.edu/archives/fall2021/entries/argument/, last accessed May 19, 2023.
Egler, Miguel (2020): "No hope for the irrelevance claim", *Philosophical Studies* 177 (11), pp. 3351–3371.
Engel, Mylan Jr. (2015): "Epistemic Luck", in: James Fieser and Bradley Dowden (Eds.): *Internet Encyclopedia of Philosophy*. http://www.iep.utm.edu/epi-luck/, last accessed May 19, 2023.
Ericsson, Anders, Neil Charness, Paul Feltovich, and Robert Hoffman (Eds.) (2006): *The Cambridge handbook of expertise and expert performance*. New York: Cambridge University Press.
Ericsson, Anders, and Andreas Lehmann (1996): "Expert and exceptional performance. Evidence of maximal adaptation to task constraints", *Annual Review of Psychology* 47 (1), pp. 273–305.
Evans, Jonathan (2003): "In two minds. Dual-process accounts of reasoning", *Trends in Cognitive Sciences* 7 (10), pp. 454–459.
Feltz, Adam, and Edward Cokely (2019): "Extraversion and compatibilist intuitions. A ten-year retrospective and meta-analyses", *Philosophical Psychology* 32 (3), pp. 388–403.
Fischer, Eugen, and Mark Curtis (Eds.) (2019): *Methodological advances in experimental philosophy*. London: Bloomsbury.
Fischer, Eugen, Paul Engelhardt, and Aurélie Herbelot (2022): "Philosophers' linguistic expertise. A psycholinguistic approach to the expertise objection against experimental philosophy", *Synthese* 200 (1), pp. 1–33.

Fischer, Eugen, Paul Engelhardt, Joachim Horvath, and Hiroshi Ohtani (2021): "Experimental ordinary language philosophy. A cross-linguistic study of defeasible default inferences", *Synthese* 198 (2), pp. 1029–1070.

Gettier, Edmund (1963): "Is justified true belief knowledge?", *Analysis* 23 (6), pp. 121–123.

Gobet, Fernand, and Herbert Simon (1996): "Recall of rapidly presented random chess positions is a function of skill", *Psychonomic Bulletin & Review* 3 (2), pp. 159–163.

Goldman, Alvin (1976): "Discrimination and perceptual knowledge", *The Journal of Philosophy* 73 (20), pp. 771–791.

Hales, Steven (2006): *Relativism and the foundations of philosophy*. Cambridge: The MIT Press.

Hansen, Nat, Jack Porter, and Kathryn Francis (2021): "A corpus study of 'know'. On the verification of philosophers' frequency claims about language", *Episteme* 18 (2), pp. 242–268.

Hitchcock, Christopher, and Joshua Knobe (2009): "Cause and norm", *Journal of Philosophy* 106 (11), pp. 587–612.

Horvath, Joachim (2010) "How (not) to react to experimental philosophy", *Philosophical Psychology* 23 (4), pp. 447–480.

Horvath, Joachim (2022): "Mischaracterization reconsidered", *Inquiry*.

Horvath, Joachim (2023): "Gettier's thought experiments", in: Duško Prelević and Anand Vaidya (Eds.): *Epistemology of modality and philosophical methodology*. London: Routledge, pp. 302–326.

Horvath, Joachim, and Steffen Koch (2021): "Experimental philosophy and the method of cases", *Philosophy Compass* 16 (1), e12716.

Horvath, Joachim, and Alex Wiegmann (2016): "Intuitive expertise and intuitions about knowledge", *Philosophical Studies* 173 (10), pp. 2701–2726.

Horvath, Joachim, and Alex Wiegmann (2022): "Intuitive expertise in moral judgments", *Australasian Journal of Philosophy* 100 (2), pp. 342–359.

Horvath, Joachim, and Alex Wiegmann (2023): "Arguing about thought experiments", *Synthese* 201 (6), 217.

Ichikawa, Jonathan Jenkins (2014): "Who needs intuitions? Two experimentalist critiques", in: Anthony Robert Booth and Darrell Rowbottom (Eds.): *Intuitions*. Oxford: Oxford University Press, pp. 232–255.

Jackson, Frank (1982): "Epiphenomenal qualia", *Philosophical Quarterly* 32 (127), pp. 127–136.

Johnson, David, Felix Cheung, and Brent Donnellan (2014): "Does cleanliness influence moral judgments? A direct replication of Schnall, Benton, and Harvey (2008)", *Social Psychology* 45 (3), pp. 209–215.

Kahneman, Daniel (2011): *Thinking, fast and slow*. New York: Farrar, Straus and Giroux.

Kamm, Frances (2007): *Intricate ethics. Rights, responsibilities, and permissible harm*. New York: Oxford University Press.

Kauppinen, Antti (2007): "The rise and fall of experimental philosophy", *Philosophical Explorations* 10 (2), pp. 95–118.

Kitcher, Philip (1990): "The division of cognitive labor", *The Journal of Philosophy* 87 (1), pp. 5–22.

Kneer, Markus, David Colaço, Joshua Alexander, and Edouard Machery (2021): "On second thought. Reflections on the reflection defense", in: Tania Lombrozo, Joshua Knobe, and Shaun Nichols (Eds.): *Oxford studies in experimental philosophy*. Vol. 4. Oxford: Oxford University Press, pp. 257–296.

Kripke, Saul (1980): *Naming and necessity*. Cambridge: Harvard University Press.

Kuntz, Joana, and Joseph Kuntz (2011): "Surveying philosophers about philosophical intuition", *Review of Philosophy and Psychology* 2 (4), pp. 643–665.

Landes, Ethan (2020): "The threat of the intuition-shaped hole", *Inquiry* 66 (4), pp. 539–564.

Löhr, Guido (2019): "The experience machine and the expertise defense", *Philosophical Psychology* 32 (2), pp. 257–273.

Ludwig, Kirk (2007): "The epistemology of thought experiments. First person versus third person approaches", *Midwest Studies in Philosophy* 31 (1), pp. 128–159.

Machery, Edouard (2012): "Expertise and intuitions about reference", *Theoria* 27 (1), pp. 37–54.

Machery, Edouard (2017): *Philosophy within its proper bounds*. Oxford: Oxford University Press.

Machery, Edouard, Ron Mallon, Shaun Nichols, and Stephen Stich (2004): "Semantics, cross-cultural style", *Cognition* 92 (3), B1–B12.

Machery, Edouard, and Elizabeth O'Neill (Eds.) (2014): *Current controversies in experimental philosophy.* London: Routledge.

Machery, Edouard, Stephen Stich, David Rose, Amita Chatterjee, Kaori Karasawa, Noel Struchiner, Smita Sirker, Naoki Usui, and Takaaki Hashimoto (2017): "Gettier across cultures", *Noûs* 51 (3), pp. 645–664.

Nado, Jennifer (2014): "Why intuition?", *Philosophy and Phenomenological Research* 89 (1), pp. 15–41.

Nado, Jennifer (2015): "Philosophical expertise and scientific expertise", *Philosophical Psychology* 28 (7), pp. 1026–1044.

Nado, Jennifer (Ed.) (2016a): *Advances in experimental philosophy and philosophical methodology.* London: Bloomsbury.

Nado, Jennifer (2016b): "The intuition deniers", *Philosophical Studies* 173 (3), pp. 781–800.

Nagel, Jennifer (2012): "Intuitions and experiments. A defense of the case method in epistemology", *Philosophy and Phenomenological Research* 85 (3), pp. 495–527.

Nichols, Shaun, and Joshua Knobe (2007): "Moral responsibility and determinism. The cognitive science of folk intuitions", *Noûs* 41 (4), pp. 663–685.

Nichols, Shaun, Stephen Stich, and Jonathan Weinberg (2003): "Metaskepticism. Meditations in ethno-epistemology", in: Steven Luper (Ed.): *The skeptics. Contemporary essays.* Aldershot: Ashgate, pp. 227–247.

Nozick, Robert (1974): *Anarchy, state, and utopia.* New York: Basic Books.

Open Science Collaboration (2015): "Estimating the reproducibility of psychological science", *Science* 349 (6251).

Pritchard, Duncan (2005): *Epistemic luck.* Oxford: Oxford University Press.

Pronin, Emily (2007): "Perception and misperception of bias in human judgment", *Trends in Cognitive Sciences* 11 (1), pp. 37–43.

Pust, Joel (2017): "Intuition", in: Edward Zalta (Ed.): *The Stanford encyclopedia of philosophy.* Summer 2017 edition. https://plato.stanford.edu/archives/sum2017/entries/intuition/, last accessed May 19, 2023.

Schindler, Samuel, and Pierre Saint-Germier (2022): "Philosophical expertise put to the test", *Australasian Journal of Philosophy.*

Schulz, Eric, Edward Cokely, and Adam Feltz (2011): "Persistent bias in expert judgments about free will and moral responsibility. A test of the expertise defense", *Consciousness and Cognition* 20 (4), pp. 1722–1731.

Schwitzgebel, Eric (2009): "Do ethicists steal more books?", *Philosophical Psychology* 22 (6), pp. 711–725.

Schwitzgebel, Eric, Bradford Cokelet, and Peter Singer (2020): "Do ethics classes influence student behavior? Case study: Teaching the ethics of eating meat", *Cognition* 203, 104397.

Schwitzgebel, Eric, and Fiery Cushman (2012): "Expertise in moral reasoning? Order effects on moral judgment in professional philosophers and non-philosophers", *Mind & Language* 27 (2), pp. 135–153.

Schwitzgebel, Eric, and Fiery Cushman (2015): "Philosophers' biased judgments persist despite training, expertise and reflection", *Cognition* 141, pp. 127–137.

Schwitzgebel, Eric, Joshua Rust, Linus Ta-Lun Huang, Alan Moore, and Justin Coates (2012): "Ethicists' courtesy at philosophy conferences", *Philosophical Psychology* 25 (3), pp. 331–340.

Seyedsayamdost, Hamid (2015): "On normativity and epistemic intuitions. Failure of replication", *Episteme* 12 (1), pp. 95–116.

Shope, Robert (2004): "The analysis of knowing", in: Ilkka Niiniluoto, Matti Sintonen, and Jan Wolenski (Eds.): *Handbook of epistemology.* Dordrecht: Kluwer, pp. 283–329.

Sosa, Ernest (2009): "A defense of the use of intuitions in philosophy", in: Dominic Murphy and Michael Bishop (Eds.): *Stich and his critics.* Oxford: Blackwell, pp. 101–112.

Sosa, Ernest (2010): "Intuitions and meaning divergence", *Philosophical Psychology* 23 (4), pp. 419–426.

Steup, Matthias (2014): "Epistemology", in: Edward Zalta (Ed.): *The Stanford encyclopedia of philosophy.* Spring 2014 edition. https://plato.stanford.edu/archives/spr2014/entries/epistemology/, last accessed May 19, 2023.

Swain, Stacey, Joshua Alexander, and Jonathan Weinberg (2008): "The instability of philosophical intuitions. Running hot and cold on truetemp", *Philosophy and Phenomenological Research* 76 (1), pp. 138–155.

Sytsma, Justin, and Jonathan Livengood (2016): *The theory and practice of experimental philosophy.* Peterborough: Broadview.

Sytsma, Justin, and Kevin Reuter (2017): "Experimental philosophy of pain", *Journal of Indian Council of Philosophical Research* 34 (3), pp. 611–628.

Tobia, Kevin, Wesley Buckwalter, and Stephen Stich (2013): "Moral intuitions. Are philosophers experts?", *Philosophical Psychology* 26 (5), pp. 629–638.

Turri, John (2017): "Knowledge attributions in iterated fake barn cases", *Analysis* 77 (1), pp. 104–115.

Tversky, Amos, and Daniel Kahneman (1981): "The framing of decisions and the psychology of choice", *Science* 211 (4481), pp. 453–458.

Weinberg, Jonathan (2007): "How to challenge intuitions empirically without risking skepticism", *Midwest Studies in Philosophy* 31 (1), pp. 318–343.

Weinberg, Jonathan (2014): "Cappelen between rock and a hard place", *Philosophical Studies* 171 (3), pp. 545–553.

Weinberg, Jonathan, and Joshua Alexander (2014): "The challenge of sticking with intuitions through thick and thin", in: Anthony Robert Booth and Darrell Rowbottom (Eds.): *Intuitions.* Oxford: Oxford University Press, pp. 187–212.

Weinberg, Jonathan, Joshua Alexander, Chad Gonnerman, and Shane Reuter (2012): "Restrictionism and reflection. Challenge deflected, or simply redirected?", *The Monist* 95 (2), pp. 200–222.

Weinberg, Jonathan, Stephen Crowley, Chad Gonnerman, Ian Vandewalker, and Stacey Swain (2012): "Intuition & calibration", *Essays in Philosophy* 13 (1), pp. 257–284.

Weinberg, Jonathan, Chad Gonnerman, Cameron Buckner, and Joshua Alexander (2010): "Are philosophers expert intuiters?", *Philosophical Psychology* 23 (3), pp. 331–355.

Weinberg, Jonathan, Shaun Nichols, and Stephen Stich (2001): "Normativity and epistemic intuitions", *Philosophical Topics* 29 (1–2), pp. 429–460.

Wiegmann, Alex, Joachim Horvath, and Karina Meyer (2020): "Intuitive expertise and irrelevant options", in: Tania Lombrozo, Joshua Knobe, and Shaun Nichols (Eds.): *Oxford studies in experimental philosophy.* Vol. 3. Oxford: Oxford University Press, pp. 275–310.

Wiegmann, Alex, Yasmina Okan, and Jonas Nagel (2012): "Order effects in moral judgment", *Philosophical Psychology* 25 (6), pp. 813–836.

Williamson, Timothy (2004): "Philosophical 'intuitions' and scepticism about judgement", *Dialectica* 58 (1), pp. 109–153.

Williamson, Timothy (2007): *The philosophy of philosophy.* Malden: Blackwell.

Williamson, Timothy (2011): "Philosophical expertise and the burden of proof", *Metaphilosophy* 42 (3), pp. 215–229.

Wysocki, Tomasz (2017): "Arguments over intuitions?", *Review of Philosophy and Psychology* 8 (2), pp. 477–499.

Ziółkowski, Adrian (2019): "The stability of philosophical intuitions. Failed replications of Swain et al. (2008)", *Episteme* 18 (12), pp. 328–346.

Theodore Bach
Limitations and Criticism of Experimental Philosophy

Abstract: Experimental philosophy involves subjecting philosophical methods and judgments to empirical scrutiny. I begin by exploring conceptual, confirmational, and empirical factors that limit the significance of experiment-based and survey-based approaches to the evaluation of philosophical epistemic activities. I then consider specific criticisms of experimental philosophy: its experimental conditions lack ecological validity; it wrongly assumes that philosophers rely on psychologized data; it overlooks the reflective and social elements of philosophical case analysis; it misconstrues the importance of both procedural and evaluative forms of philosophical expertise; it incorrectly views psychological bias as incompatible with reliability; and it generalizes to a global, self-defeating skepticism about case judgment. I explain why these criticisms should be understood as converging and interdependent. I also set out a three-level model of philosophical case judgment that frames the criticisms.

Keywords: Criticisms of Experimental Philosophy; Ecological Validity; Empirical Confirmation; Experimental Philosophy; Expertise; Intuition; Metaphilosophy; Method of Cases; Philosophical Judgment

1 Introduction – Limitations versus Criticisms

Here are three factors that limit the performance of my decade-old station wagon: the earth's gravity limits its vertical mobility, an outdated audio system limits listening choices to compact discs and radio, and a weak engine limits its ability to accelerate quickly onto highways. Some of these limitations are grounds for justified critique (the third, which is a design flaw), and some are not (surely the first). The example suggests a rough but serviceable account of the difference between an item's or method's limitations, on the one hand, and grounds for its (justified) critique, on the other. A limitation indicates something that an item or method cannot do. Some limitations are more or less permanent (the first above), and some are not (the second). Some deserve scrutiny (the third), and some are uninteresting (the first). A criticism, on the other hand, is an evaluative claim about an item or method that is made relative to what that item is designed to do, what someone purports it can do, or more generally some type of error with respect to that item's or method's output. Not all criticisms are justified.

After discussing the boundaries and aims of experimental philosophy, I sketch general limitations (Section 3) and general criticisms (Section 4) so understood of the epistemic activity of experimental philosophy, targeting mostly the interesting and justified varieties.

2 Experimental Philosophy – What It Is and Aims to Do

We first need a handle on what experimental philosophy (commonly dubbed "x-phi") is and aims to do. The matter is not simple.[1]

X-phi overviews typically distinguish a broad and narrow conception. Rose and Danks advance the former, claiming that x-phi is "philosophical work that uses various empirical results, particularly from the cognitive sciences, in philosophical theorizing", with the further condition that the experiments "happen to have been done by the same individual[s]" (Rose and Danks 2013, p. 515) who are doing the philosophical theorizing.[2] This counts the epistemic projects of Piaget, Helmholtz, and Kohlberg as instances of x-phi. Knobe and Nichols (2017) also invoke a broad conception, claiming that x-phi "brings together" the questions and frameworks of traditional philosophy, on the one hand, and "the kinds of experimental methods traditionally associated with psychology and [the] cognitive [and social] science[s]" (Knobe and Nichols 2017, p. 1), on the other. This counts Fodor, Crick and Koch, Ruth Millikan, and nearly all philosophical naturalists as experimental philosophers.

The narrow conception understands x-phi as the application of experimental results (generally survey-centered studies) to the evidential use of philosophical intuition or, more generally, the dialectical use of "the method of cases" (see below, Section 4.2). Most but not all instances of x-phi fall into this category.[3]

With respect to the aims of x-phi, it is standard to distinguish "positive" and "negative" programs.[4] The positive program aims to make progress on the questions that philosophers traditionally seek to answer, e.g., *what is knowledge?* Advocates of this program claim that if eliciting intuitive verdicts about cases is useful for adjudicating competing philosophical models, then it is better to canvas intuitions empirically than to rely on armchair assumptions about (say) their uniformity (see, e.g., Knobe 2003, Nahmias et al. 2006). In contrast, the negative program emphasizes that intuitions, or more generally case judgments, are often steered by epistemically irrelevant factors. In light of this influence, advocates of the negative program claim that philosophers

---

1 See Chapter 2 of this volume.
2 Stich and Tobia advance a similarly broad conception, but they drop Rose and Dank's "colocation" condition: "experimental philosophy is empirical work undertaken with the goal of contributing to a philosophical debate [...] sometimes people doing experimental philosophy conduct the experiments, but sometimes they don't" (Stich and Tobia 2016, p. 5).
3 Paradigmatic examples include survey-centered studies that suggest philosophical case judgments (about knowledge possession, to pick one of many topics) vary with the order of case presentation (Swain et al. 2008), the font of case presentation (Weinberg et al. 2012), and the cultural background of the person making the judgment (Machery et al. 2004). Readers should consult Machery (2017, ch. 2) and the chapters in this volume for an overview of the experimental findings.
4 Some commentators mention a third program, which is (very roughly) to advance our understanding of psychological explananda, for example mechanisms of belief-formation.

should not rely uncritically on intuitions as sources of evidence. The kernel of the negative program is "the Restrictionist Challenge" (Alexander and Weinberg 2007, Weinberg et al. 2010): until intuition-users can show that they have corrected their evidential use of intuition to sufficiently insulate them from non-truth tracking influences – or until they can show that the intuitions were never so influenced in the first place – they ought to stop using the intuitions evidentially in the error-prone contexts.

There is a clear difference in emphasis between the negative and positive program, but the distinction may also be misleading. Those aligned with the negative program are just as interested in, and believe x-phi is instrumental to, answering philosophical questions accurately as those aligned with the positive program. Moreover, the negative program is not committed to the claim that the method of cases or the evidential use of philosophical intuitions is necessarily or universally epistemically unreliable (Weinberg 2017).[5]

At this point it is fair to ask whether unclarity about x-phi's boundaries and aims could itself mark an important limitation on x-phi's capacity to reform first-order philosophy or generate metaphilosophical insight. If there is a limitation or grounds for criticism here, then given similar doctrinal debates in nearly all philosophical sub-disciplines (especially so given the recent surge in metaphilosophical discussion), it would generalize broadly. It would be a limitation of philosophical discourse generally, not a limitation of x-phi specifically.[6]

But perhaps a stronger case can be made for there being a natural kind of epistemic project to which many (but not all) self-claimed instances of x-phi belong. I submit that a methodological or metaphilosophical conception of x-phi deserves consideration here. On this conception, x-phi's essential feature is its application of experimental results to philosophical methodology – to whatever psychological, social, and even biological mechanisms underwrite philosophical output, whether that output is a private judgment about a philosophical case or a trend in professional philosophers' credences. This conception encompasses paradigmatic, survey-based studies of philosophers' method of cases. Less obviously, it counts Kathy Davis's (2008) "Intersectionality as Buzzword" as x-phi, as that article applies Murray Davis's (1971, 1986) empirical investigations of the properties that causally explain an academic paper's professional uptake to philosophy. Contrary to the broad conception, it does not count Helmholtz, Crick and Koch, Piaget or Millikan as conducting x-phi, as these researchers are not

---

5 But see the "radical restrictionism" advocated for in Machery (2017), though Machery's restrictionism applies only to cases that elicit modal philosophical claims.
6 One is reminded of complaints in the 1980s and 1990s that philosophical feminism lacked doctrinal unity or that its subject matter (the category *woman*) was ill-defined (see, e.g., Young 1994). These types of concerns are generally worth exploring, but they are also reflections of ongoing disagreements about deeply theoretical issues concerning classification, reference, conceptual change, natural kinds, and so forth. I do not think that experimental philosophers (or philosophical feminists) should feel any more hamstrung about these doctrinal debates than evolutionary biologists should feel hamstrung about the ever-increasing number of species concepts (currently around 27). See also Boyd (2021, p. 2874).

bringing to bear experimental results specifically on philosophical methodology (even if these researchers are addressing philosophical questions in the spirit or empirically informed philosophy).

I will assume this methodological conception of x-phi in what follows, with a focus on paradigmatic x-phi (i.e., the narrow conception).

3 Three Limitations of Experimental Philosophy

Here I discuss three factors that limit the type and strength of evaluative claim about philosophical method that is warranted given the empirical findings of x-phi. These discussions are not advanced here as criticisms. However, and as will become clear below, it is possible to leverage these limitations in support of specific lines of x-phi critique.

3.1 The Central Limitation of Experimental Philosophy

We generally do not have access to – or empirical knowledge of – which specific material conditions can in principle, let alone in practice, distinguish the correctness of two rival but empirically adequate philosophical models. For example, when philosophers disagree about whether all human motivation reduces to self-directed desires, or whether free will requires an indeterministic world, or whether the possession of meaningful mental states requires a certain type of history, there is no empirical state of affairs the observation of which will tell us who is correct and who is incorrect.[7] And while it is tempting here to appeal to episodes of agreement among professional philosophers as a capable substitute for the empirical confirmation of philosophical accuracy (at least for that small subset of philosophical models for which there is something like a consensus), there is (perhaps ironically) disagreement about the merits of such a method (see, e.g., Kelly 2016). Moreover, the history of philosophical consensus has a worrisome track-record.[8]

---

7 For discussion, see Williamson (2007), Sosa (2011), Papineau (2011), Paul (2012), Ryberg (2013), Nolan (2015), Ludwig (2018) and Bach (2019, 2021). Note that this confirmational limit on the assessment of philosophical models applies regardless of whether the disagreeing parties espouse material (synthetic) or semantic (analytic) aims when employing philosophical case analysis (see Section 4.1 below for further discussion of the distinction between these aims). Note that it also applies to many disagreements about which facts obtain in philosophical thought experiments.

8 As Lycan (2017, p. 109 f.) remarks: "There are periods of very wide agreement, but they are pathetically short and geographically local. Just in my lifetime, we Anglo-Americans have seen sense-datum theory reign and then be scorned, mind-body materialism reign and then come under heavy attack, and so forth. The late Jerry Katz once predicted to me that Moorean moral intuitionism would make a big comeback; and I would never doubt that idealism will too, possibly still within my lifetime. Philosophical consensus is far more the result of Zeitgeist, fad, fashion, and careerism than of accumulation of probative argument".

This confirmational predicament limits how effective the empirical methods of experimental philosophy can be for indicating whether particular influences on the construction and judgment of philosophical models are truth-tracking or non-truth-tracking. For example, with respect to the x-phi negative program, while experimental philosophers might demonstrate that a particular factor (order of case presentation, cultural background, and so forth) exerts a causal influence on philosophical judgment, they are far more limited in their ability to demonstrate that this influence is epistemically "distorting". To make this stronger claim about epistemic distortion, one needs to add a metaphilosophical assumption (e.g., that the influence of cultural background on philosophical case judgment is non-truth-tracking) the truth of which is difficult to confirm empirically. And if one is able to secure such a stronger claim, one still needs to show that the effect of the distorting factor is significant – that its size and relationship to philosophers' case analysis renders that judgment-type, or its underlying mechanism, unreliable (see below, Section 4.4).[9]

To put this point into focus, it is helpful to consider how the *absence* of similar confirmational limitations in *non*-philosophical domains permits evaluators of those domains more effective use of empirical methods for performance assessment. In fact, there is an extensive empirical literature on the accuracy of professional judgment (including forms of judgment that many philosophers will classify as intuition-based) for a wide variety of non-philosophical domains (chess, clinical psychology, finance, livestock judging, and so on). A central and surprising finding is that in many domains, credentialed experts often fail to outperform both novices and statistical models.[10] Putting aside the question of *why* this is (but see below), we should ask: *how* are empirical researchers able to make these determinations? The answer, in brief, is that the researchers have a clear and quantifiable success metric relative to which they can assess the accuracy of (non-philosophical) expert judgment and methodology. Financial advisors predict the market will turn bullish, clinicians judge that intervening with medication y will bring about improvement z, parole experts predict that inmates with property x are the most likely to reoffend, and so forth. In all these cases, there is a (future) fact of the matter that indicates whether the expert's judgment – as a prediction, intervention, or rule-following consideration – was correct or incorrect. The auditors' epistemic access to this metric – their knowledge of the truth-determining material events – is what allows them to assess accurately the epistemic quality of the experts' judgments.

But as discussed above, in the philosophical case, we do not have access to such a metric. For example, we do not know which specific material conditions can in principle distinguish the correctness of competing but empirically equivalent philosophical

---

[9] Nor can one resolve this issue simply by generalizing criteria for effect significance from non-philosophical experimental contexts (but see Weinberg 2016 and Machery 2017 for attempts to address this concern).

[10] See, e.g., Shanteau (1992). These domains include finance, criminal justice, clinical psychology, graduate admissions, and political forecasting.

models of causation. As a result, we are limited in our ability to know which causal influences on philosophical model-building and judgment are epistemically distorting versus epistemically relevant.

We should not take this point too far. Some assumptions about epistemically distorting influences are warranted regardless of whether we can empirically confirm the accuracy or inaccuracy of theoretical models the construction of which were subject to those influences. For example, surely the influence of font-type (Weinberg et al. 2012) or racially coded name changes (Uhlmann et al. 2009) on case judgment does not reliably steer towards greater accuracy, and this is something that we can affirm prior to knowing which philosophical models are most accurate. The concern, however, is that the range of causal influences to which that type of warrant applies may be quite limited. For example, many researchers had assumed that the influence of presentation order on philosophical case judgment must be epistemically distorting (non-truth-tracking), but as Horne and Livengood (2017) point out, there are grounds for claiming that ordering effects can reveal an epistemically virtuous form of "updating" (that is, learning). Similarly, Ludwig (2010, 2018) has pointed out that the influence of cultural background on philosophical case judgment about the reference of proper names is not epistemically irrelevant if different cultural backgrounds underwrite different exposures to factors that inform accurate versus inaccurate views about the nature of reference.[11] Even with respect to font-type, a case can be made that its influence on judgment is epistemically relevant (particularly if the font-type is hard to read and thus more likely to induce deeper thinking).[12]

It is not uncommon for experimental philosophers to respond to such proposals by requesting empirical support for the purported epistemic relevance of the influencing factor (see, e.g., Weinberg et al. 2010, Alexander 2012, Sytsma and Livengood 2015, Machery 2017). If the relevant types of empirical tests are available, then this is a sensible request. The problem – and this stems from the central limitation discussed here – is that often such tests are not available. For example, if researchers do not know in advance what philosophical model of reference is correct, then it is unclear how to isolate via empirical tools subtle developmental differences that might causally explain why one group's judgments are slightly more aligned with the correct model (whatever that model is). We should certainly be on guard against post-hoc or "just-

---

[11] In Ludwig's (2018, p. 391) terms: "all that can be shown by these results is that not everyone is getting it right, and that there can be factors that correlate with different cultural, ethnic, or socio-economic backgrounds that can contribute to errors". Some restrictionists charge this type of suggestion with "chauvinism" or "ethnocentrism" (e.g., Machery 2017, p. 106). It is not clear that the charge is warranted. The claim about epistemic relevance does not require that "we" are getting it more correct than "them" – it only requires that some group is getting it more correct. If there *are* reasons to privilege the view of a particular group – perhaps one of the groups has received expert training – then one might side with Jackson's (2011, p. 469) suggestion that "talk of chauvinism is a misdirection" in this context. I discuss some of these issues below in the context of the expertise defense (see Section 4.3.3).
[12] See Weinberg et al. (2012, p. 218, fn. 22).

so" stories about the epistemic virtue of a causal influence on philosophical judgment. But we should also be careful not to weaponize dialectically, sometimes through verificationist claims about burdens of proof, the confirmational predicament of much philosophical discourse.

Some experimental philosophers invoke empirical data on non-philosophical expert performance to bridge (or rather, circumvent) the impasse generated by the confirmational limitation discussed above. The basic idea is to identify the features that causally explain poor versus superior expert performance in non-philosophical domains (domains for which the confirmational limitation does not apply), and then investigate whether those features manifest in philosophy (see especially Weinberg et al. 2010, Clarke 2013, Ryberg 2013). We know that, in the case of many non-philosophical domains, exposure during training and job experience to direct and environmental learning feedback about the quality of one's judgments leads to superior performance (and its absence leads to inferior performance). Is that type of direct and environmental learning feedback available to philosophers? Experimental philosophers provide reasons – reasons connected to the confirmation issue discussed throughout this section – for why it is not.[13] They then reason inductively: given this shared developmental condition between philosophy and the poor-performing non-philosophical expert domains, we should doubt (even if we cannot empirically confirm it) whether expert philosophical training and experience promotes more accurate theorizing and case judgment.

This is a good example of experimental philosophy – the use of empirical methods and data to evaluate philosophical methodology. Notably, it does not rely on surveys. Nonetheless, we should raise some objections. First, the types of non-philosophical judgment that according to the empirical literature require direct and environmental learning feedback for superior performance are generally rule-following, predictive, or intervention-based judgments. However, these aims and types of judgment content are unrepresentative of philosophical theories and judgment. Philosophical theories and judgments typically have unificatory and explanatory aims rather than predictive or rule-following aims. If that is correct, we should reject generalizations to philosophy that are drawn from data about professional domains that have non-representative goals and success conditions. Second and related, if our goal is to locate an empirically studied non-philosophical base from which to generalize to philosophy, and if we take seriously the abstract unificatory aims of much philosophical theorizing (e.g., Paul 2012), then we are led to areas of the empirical literature on expertise that are much more encouraging for expert philosophers. Empirical studies indicate that experts in feedback-deficient environments demonstrate superior performance with respect to relational (as opposed to superficial) retrieval, simulation, ability to discover

---

[13] Clarke (2013, p. 193) is especially clear on this point: "In the case of philosophical intuitions, however, direct feedback from the environment is typically unavailable. We cannot directly discover what knowledge really is or what morality really demands".

important causal-explanatory relationships and categories, and ability to grasp the meaning and importance of unusual events (see Bach 2021).

3.2 Empirical Limitations of Experimental Philosophy

The previous section examined how the distinctive targets and aims of philosophical analysis impose limits on what we can learn about the epistemic success of philosophical analysis based on empirical investigation of its underlying methods. This section sketches limitations sourced in the specific empirical methods commonly employed by experimental philosophers.

An immediate concern is that x-phi's adoption of the experimental methods of the social sciences will inherit whatever limitations apply to those methods generally. One limiting factor – replication failure – is especially salient here (see, e.g., Woolfolk 2013, Seyedsayamdost 2015). Some influential x-phi findings, for example gender effects on semantic judgments (Buckwalter and Stich 2014) and cultural background effects on epistemic judgments (Weinberg, Nichols, and Stich 2001), have failed to replicate. Many other influential findings have been reproduced. Researchers participating in the "XPhi Replicability Project" (Cova et al. 2021) provide evidence that suggests there is greater replication of x-phi results than there is of results in social psychology generally (see also Stuart et al. 2019, Colombo et al. 2018, Machery 2017).

If we grant that many of the empirical findings of x-phi are genuine and replicable, we should still inquire if there are features of survey-centered reports that limit their philosophical and metaphilosophical significance. One feature of concern is that they are sourced in self-report data. The goal of much x-phi is to uncover epistemically irrelevant influences on "intuitions" or a type of cognitive judgment that is evidentially (or at least dialectically) instrumental to "the method of cases". But given possible differences between what people say about philosophical cases and what they believe about philosophical cases, data restricted to the former provide a limited and potentially misleading understanding of the latter (Kauppinen 2007, Cullen 2010, Woolfolk 2013).

There are various ways that experimental philosophers have addressed this limitation, for example developing more carefully designed studies (e.g., incorporating pilot testing of subject comprehension). As Rose and Danks (2013, p. 525) suggest, experimental philosophers can also support survey self-report data with "behavioral measures, neuroimaging data, and other measures or cognitive functioning", although these additional tools come with their own, mostly logistical, limitations.

Regardless of the increasing sophistication of x-phi studies, this limitation continues to inform several lines of criticism of both positive and negative x-phi programs. Some critics allege that ambiguous vignettes and probe questions stoke verbal disagreement rather than reveal distorting influences (particularly with respect to vignettes about reference, which several critics have claimed are ambiguous between speaker's reference and semantic reference – see Ludwig 2007, Deutsch 2009, and

Heck 2018).[14] Sosa (2009, 2015) suggests that verbal disagreement, in addition to being caused by vignette ambiguity and contextual variation, results when survey participants draw from different conceptual backgrounds to fill in differently the missing details of a vignette (much like how people draw from their unique conceptual backgrounds to flesh out differently scenes from a novel). Other critics claim that x-phi survey studies lack ecological validity. An experiment lacks ecological validity if it includes artificial conditions (e.g., asking human subjects to memorize a series of nonsense syllabus) that are importantly different from the part of the actual world that we are trying to understand (e.g., school learning) (Neisser 1976, p. 33).[15] According to these critics, x-phi surveys misrepresent philosophers' actual dialectical employment of the method of cases (see Section 4.2 below). Related to this, many critics claim that x-phi surveys are inadequate for the purpose of informing us about the types of philosophical case judgment that dialectically matter – "reflective" judgments and "expert" judgments (see Section 4.3.2 and Section 4.3.3 below).

3.3 Conceptual Limitations of Experimental Philosophy

A third and conditional limitation of specifically restrictionist x-phi projects is the following: to the extent that restrictionist claims about philosophical methodology are warranted, one is thereby limited in which conceptual, philosophical resources are available for the construction of philosophical theories and arguments. If per the restrictionist challenge we ought to treat judgments elicited by various thought experiments as epistemically suspect, then we ought to treat whichever philosophical concepts or theoretical frameworks centrally depend on those judgments as also epistemically suspect. This limits the pool of claims and theories from which we can construct philosophical arguments, including those that might inform the evaluative and interpretive claims of x-phi.

The extent of this limitation will depend on at least two factors. First, it depends on the strength of the restrictionist claim. Machery's radical restrictionism (see Machery 2017), which employs inductive arguments and metaphilosophical assumptions to restrict the use of all (modally ambitious) instances of the method of cases, cordons off more conceptual resources than moderate forms of restrictionism that target only judgment-types shown empirically to exhibit susceptibility to irrelevant influencers. Second, the extent of this limitation depends on whether there are alternative ways

---

14 For example, in the case of x-phi surveys that ask participants to say who John is talking about when John uses the name "Gödel", participants might interpret this as asking about the language conventions for the referent of "Gödel" (semantic reference) or about who John intends to use that name to talk about (speaker's reference).
15 As Neisser also points out, criticisms based on this notion lack force if they do not identify the specific real-world features that the experiment leaves out. In Sections 4.2 and 4.3, I specify the omitted real-world features that inform ecological validity-based criticisms of x-phi.

of supporting the conceptual resource. Here it is helpful to have a positive account of what makes evidential practices reliable and that does not recruit the problematic evidential appeals (see, e.g., Weinberg 2007; for discussion, see Section 4.5 below).

At any rate, it is not difficult to see how this limitation might be directed critically at x-phi itself, making it a victim of its own success. Indeed, some critics claim that x-phi is in this sense self-defeating, while others allege that it leads to a generalized and unacceptable form of judgment skepticism. I discuss these objections in Section 4.5.

4 Specific Criticisms of Experimental Philosophy

It has become standard to chunk up criticisms of x-phi into distinct categories or "defenses" (e.g., Sytsma and Livengood 2015, Machery 2017): mischaracterization, expertise defense, reflection defense, and so on. I will be doing some of that here, but I think that the practice is misleading. It gives the impression that the criticisms are isolated – that the defender of x-phi can deal with one type of criticism, then move on to deal with the next type, and so on. It obscures synergistic relationships between the criticisms. We would do well, I suggest, to think of x-phi criticisms in terms of Duncker's radiation problem (see Gick and Holyoak 1980): they are individual rays of radiation launched from different angles towards a central target, and while no single ray may be powerful enough on its own to eradicate the target, when considered as a converging network their overall destructive effect is considerably more compelling. I will flag examples of this converging effect as I move through the individual criticisms.

4.1 X-phi Findings Are Not Relevant to Philosophical Methodology Because Philosophers Do Not Rely on Intuitions

Much early x-phi resourced experimental findings to challenge philosophers' evidential use of intuitions about cases. Several critics, particularly Williamson (2007), Deutsch (2009), and Cappelen (2012), rejected that philosophers employ cases for the purpose of eliciting "intuitions" – intellectually compelling seemings of some sort – that are supposed to serve an important evidential or argumentative role.[16] If these critics are correct, then empirical reports about distorting influences on philosophical intuitions would not seem relevant to actual philosophical argumentation and theorizing.

Both Deutsch (2009, 2015) and Cappelen (2012) develop this criticism through detailed analysis of actual philosophical texts. Such textual scrutiny, they claim, reveals that philosophers' psychological states (i.e., intuitions) do not play the evidential

---

[16] A related criticism was that experimentalists did not provide sufficient clarity about what their target is (i.e., intuitions). See especially Williamson (2011, 2013) on this point. See Cappelen (2012, ch. 7), Nado (2016), Pust (2019), and Horvath (this volume) for x-phi-themed overviews of what intuitions are or are supposed to be.

role that the restrictionists and positive experimental philosophers suppose. In Section 3.2, I mentioned that x-phi surveys may be limited in their capacity to recreate the conditions of real-life philosophy. We can view Deutsch's and Cappelen's text-based criticism in this light – as illustrating how a chasm between x-phi lab conditions and real-life philosophy conditions permits a misleading picture of philosophical case analysis and the purported evidential role of intuitions.

According to Deutsch and Cappelen, philosophers mostly construct arguments rather than rely on intuitions, and they use all manner of (non-psychological) data and methods to do so (see, e.g., Cappelen 2012, p. 196). One standard method of argumentation, employed in both philosophical and non-philosophical contexts, is offering or ostending to a counterexample to challenge a generalization. Deutsch reports that Kripke's discussion of the Gödel case does just this: it is "no different in principle from the method someone might use in arguing against the generalization that, for example, *all mushrooms are edible*, namely by pointing to a poisonous variety of mushroom" (Deutsch 2009, p. 447). The point generalizes. Similarly, Williamson claims that in Gettier cases, it is simply a fact that there is not knowledge. For both Williamson and Deutsch, then, it is an objective state of affairs (a poisonous mushroom, an opportunistic Gödel) and not some psychological feature of the apprehension of that state of affairs that grounds the counterexample.[17]

One might counter that it is the hypothetical nature of philosophical cases that makes their contemplation and classification as counterexamples intuition-based rather than fact-based. After all, these are thought experiments that we conduct in our imaginations, so it would seem that any dialectically relevant "facts" will be psychological rather than material. In response, Williamson and others have pointed out that there are real-world analogues of many such cases (e.g., Gettier cases in which stopped clocks show the correct time). And if judgments about these actual cases are similarly construed as intuition-based, then negative x-phi's restrictionism appears to generalize into a global skepticism about the everyday (and scientific) judgment of actual cases (see Section 4.5).

But what about philosophers who explicitly describe themselves as appealing to special psychological states – intuitions – as a form of philosophical evidence, and who also provide explicit arguments for the epistemic importance of doing so (e.g., Bealer 1998, Goldman and Pust 1998, BonJour 1998)? These would be philosophers who, pace Cappelen (2012), insist that their intuition-talk is neither stylistic nor disposable scaffolding for non-intuition depending philosophical argument. And what about philosophers who claim that a central goal of philosophical theorizing and argumentation is probing the analytic commitments of one's own concepts (e.g., Jackson 1998)?

---

17 Thus Williamson (2007, ch. 7) cautions against the urge to psychologize philosophical evidence (an urge made stronger by the confirmational limitation discussed in Section 3.1). See Alexander (2010) for a contrary view.

Aren't at least *these* philosophers and their self-described methods worthy targets of both negative and positive x-phi programs?

The first thing to observe here is that, given the on-going trend of philosophical naturalism and empirically informed philosophy, this group of philosophers appears small and growing smaller.

Second, one can challenge whether these philosophers are correctly describing their own methods. This challenge can be made empirically by: (a) citing evidence that people are prone to confabulation and, more generally, are not very good at identifying their own cognitive processes, and (b) flagging that there is no current or foreseeable empirical evidence that warrants positing a special cognitive faculty dedicated to intuition. The challenge can also be made on conceptual grounds. Papineau (2009, 2011) offers compelling arguments that philosophers who claim to employ the case method for the purpose of making analytic judgments (e.g., about the application conditions of their own concepts) are, ultimately, invoking cases to make synthetic judgments.

Third, even if we were to grant that there is a faction of philosophers for whom it is descriptively accurate to characterize as relying evidentially on a richly-construed notion of philosophical intuition (or philosophers who truly employ the case method only for the purposes of conceptual analysis), then we might urge these philosophers to stop doing so (and for reasons not deriving from, but not incompatible with, negative program x-phi findings).[18] See Millikan (2000), Papineau (2009), Kornblith (2014), and Boyd (2021) for compelling arguments in this direction.[19]

4.2 X-phi Findings (and Evaluative Claims) Are Not Relevant to Philosophical Methodology Because They Are Based on Surveys (and a Conception of Philosophical Method) That Overlook or Mischaracterize Important Dialectical Features of the "Method of Cases"

More recent x-phi evaluative claims about philosophical practice do not assume that philosophers rely on psychologically unique events or states called "intuitions" as evidence. As Machery explains:

> It is thus unfortunate that experimental philosophers, including myself, have followed the philosophical tradition in describing the method of cases as eliciting intuitions, and have given the im-

---

[18] In contrast, this position is incompatible with the aims of the positive x-phi program.
[19] The three considerations set out above, along with the arguments made by Deutsch and Cappelen, also apply to, and limit the significance of, x-phi surveys (see Kuntz and Kuntz 2011; see Sytsma and Livengood 2015 for discussion) in which 23.5 % of surveyed professional philosophers said that intuitions were essential for philosophical justification and half said that they were useful for philosophical justification.

pression that their argument was directed at the alleged use of intuitions in philosophy. It is not; the target is the method of cases. (Machery 2017, p. 178)

On this construal, when philosophers evaluate cases, they deploy the same judgment-forming cognitive mechanisms that they and others use generally (Machery 2017, p. 21). The epistemic concern derives from a set of "disturbing" characteristics of the types of cases that philosophers tend to consider, for example the unusual and hypothetical nature of these cases. These disturbing characteristics purportedly corrupt philosopher's judgments about what facts obtain in the target cases, and the evidence for that corruption is x-phi's findings of presentation and demographic effects on philosopher's judgments about these cases (see Section 4.5).

Critics of x-phi restrictionism allow that this construal's omission of intuition-talk makes progress – its characterization of philosophical methodology is more closely aligned with what philosophers actually do, which is provide arguments and employ judgments about facts rather than defer to psychologized forms of evidence called "intuitions". Nonetheless, they insist that this "minimalist" conception of philosophical case judgment, and especially its attempted simulation in the lab by experimental philosophers (i.e., survey studies), omits essential dialectical features of philosophers' actual use of cases. Given this disparity, we are sharply limited in what evaluative inferences about actual philosophical practice we are warranted drawing from the experimental studies.

What are the omitted dialectical features? Critics point out that philosophers' actual dialectical use of cases is socially embedded (Williamson 2007, 2013; Ludwig 2007, 2018; Kauppinen 2007, 2018). As Ludwig writes:

> Philosophers aim to arrive at a reflective judgment about a case and then to review it in the light of other judgments (their own and others) and more general theoretical considerations. They do not simply record their spontaneous judgments and take the third person stance toward them as neutral observations to be explained. […] we do not do this like hermits in the woods: we try out ideas and thought experiments on others, give and publish papers, take criticism, make revisions, try out new ideas generated in this process, and so on. (Ludwig 2018, p. 388)

Critics point out that the cases considered by philosophers are eclectic, possessing non-generalizing domain-specific epistemic features (Cappelen and Deutsch 2018, Cappelen 2022). As Cappelen puts it:

> The term "method of cases" doesn't denote a theoretically useful class. It encourages the thought that there's uniformity where there isn't. The thing we call "cases" come in too many varieties. The source of their degree of difficulty is multifaceted and cannot be separated from their specific subject matter. (Cappelen 2022, p. 314)

They point out that the case method it is extended through time, both interpersonally and intrapersonally (e.g., Jackson 2011, Williamson 2009). Williamson says that the application of x-phi data ignores the difference between one-off individual judgments and consensus reached through the interaction of many participants in a public philosophical debate, conducted over several years in conferences and journals. (Williamson 2009, p. 474)

They point out that philosophers appeal to cases to reveal truths rather than cognitive judgments. Deutsch claims that the method of cases

does not involve everyday judgments as opposed to intuitive judgments. Rather, it does not involve judgments, period – not as a component of the method itself. (Deutsch 2020, p. 769 f.)

The overarching objection here is that, by overlooking these central features of the case method in both description and experimental simulation, experimental philosophers, including those that have dropped reference to intuition, continue to target "a mythical conception of 'the method of cases'" (Kauppinen 2018, p. 69), a "caricature of philosophical method" (Ludwig 2018, p. 388), and "a fictional class" (Cappelen 2022, p. 314).

4.3 Philosophical Reflection and Expertise

The above criticism is a bridge to other, more fine-grained objections, particularly the criticisms that x-phi fails to take sufficiently into account philosophers' "reflective" and "expert" judgments. To unpack those specific criticisms, we need a richer, three-level model of the psychology and sociology of the method of cases to which we can appeal. Such a model needs to be empirically adequate, and it needs to make explicit the resources used by x-phi critics who assert the importance of philosophical expertise and reflection.[20]

4.3.1 A Three-Level Model of Philosophical Judgment

At the bottom level (Level 1) are snap judgments about category membership. These might be unbidden, immediate, not fully conscious judgments concerning the classification of features of the target case. Still, these judgments do not emerge from an epistemic vacuum. They are sprung from some schema, theory, or other cognitively stored knowledge representations (see, e.g., Kahneman and Klein 2009, Hornsby 2007), and in that respect they are theory-laden. At the next level, Level 2, are considered, reflective judgments. Here, one thinks carefully about reasons for making the classificatory judgment. One might uncover to some extent the reasons that drove the snap judgment. One might sift through alternative reasons that lead to contrary judgments. One considers arguments, implications, and explanatory values of competing classifica-

---

[20] For a somewhat similar model of philosophical case judgment, see Strevens (2019, sec. 4.3).

tory judgments. And so on. At the last level (Level 3), the reflective procedures of Level 2 are extended through time as well as the social, expert community. One talks with other philosophers, receives feedback from commentators and peer reviewers, reads articles and arguments, and so on. Given that Level 1 judgments are theory-laden, the fruits of Level 2 and Level 3 judgments feed back causally into Level 1 judgments, affirming or changing them in various ways. This is like how if one receives decades of formal chess training, then one's snap judgments about position classification will change as a result.

These judgment levels might function in a philosophical context as follows. When first confronting the Swampman thought experiment, one tokens the snap (Level 1) judgment that Swampman has contentful (meaningful) thoughts. But then (Level 2) one reflects more carefully on the case. One considers whether one's association between skilled behavior and underlying contentful cognition was the source of the snap judgment and, if so, whether that provides sufficient warrant for the classification. One considers analogous cases, for example that of a collection of twigs on a beach randomly wind-blown to form H-E-L-P but that does not carry the semantic information *help*. One is now inclined to override and revise the Level 1 snap judgment. At Level 3, one talks with other philosophers about Swampman. One writes about Swampman, receiving feedback from commentators and peer reviewers. One reads the arguments from all the articles in the 1996 *Mind and Language* journal forum on Swampman. One considers again and affirms one's decision to revise the snap judgment.

4.3.2 Reflection

The various references to "reflecting" and "considering" above, as well as some of the quotes from Section 4.2, make clear how an objection based on reflection will run (as well as why that objection is a species of the mischaracterization objection). On this view, any attempt to evaluate or simulate the method of cases will fail to the extent that it misleadingly construes philosophers as epistemically beholden to Level 1 snap classificatory judgments. The very purpose of developing and socially disseminating philosophical cases, the objection continues, is to spur an extended process of careful and socially mediated reflection on competing classificatory judgments – a process that includes socially mediated reflection on different sets of arguments for the competing judgments, comparison of the explanatory and unificatory profiles of the competing classifications, and so on. Versions of this objection can be found in Ludwig (2007), Kauppinen (2007, 2018), Kornblith (2007), Williamson (2009), Cullen (2010), Bengson (2013), and Hannon (2018).

To address this appeal to reflective judgments, experimental philosophers have developed survey studies that they claim incorporate the reflective features. However, it is unclear whether x-phi surveys can in principle, let alone in practice, probe the types of extended and socially mediated reflective judgment processes that according to critics are central to philosopher's actual use of cases (Kauppinen 2007). For example, it is unclear how experimental surveys can capture the three levels of judgment – and diachronic interactions between them – as sketched above. Kneer and colleagues, conceding that the reflection-based critique of x-phi "has not yet received enough attention" (Kneer et al. 2022, p. 1), attempt to simulate in surveys only what they term a "thin characterization of reflective judgment" (Kneer et al. 2022, p. 7), "leaving thicker versions of the defense to the side for now" (Kneer et al. 2022, p. 9). They do this in part because the thinly characterized judgments are "most easily tractable by means of experimental tools – the tools we intend to deploy" (Kneer et al. 2022, p. 9). This is grist for the mill of critics who view philosophical case analysis as an extended, reflective, socially mediated activity and who object that x-phi's experimental studies lack ecological validity.

4.3.3 Expertise

The above points lead directly to the related issue of philosophical expertise. The initial expertise-based objection to both positive and negative x-phi ambitions was that, because the subjects of x-phi surveys were undergraduates with little to no training in philosophy, the surveys were not informative about the epistemology and psychology of professional philosophical methodology. Critics motivated this objection with suggestive analogies. Ludwig (2007) observed that the discipline of mathematics is unthreatened by survey studies revealing distorting influences on math amateurs. And Williamson (2011, p. 217) pointed out that "we do not expect physicists to suspend their current projects in order to carry out psychological investigations of their capacity as laboratory experimentalists, on the basis of evidence that undergraduates untrained in physics are bad at conducting laboratory experiments".[21]

Pushing past these analogies, what is it that experts (specifically philosophy experts) have that novices lack such that empirically scrutinizing the novice's use of cases will not inform about the pro's use of cases? How one responds to this question will (or should) be informed by how one understands the purpose of philosophical case analysis in the first place – whether that method is used to delineate the borders of one's own (or the folk's) concepts (ala the Canberra Plan) or to illuminate the nature of objective structures and kinds (ala the "synthetic" aims described in Papineau (2009), Devitt (2012), and Kornblith (2002); the "material", as opposed to "conceptual", aims described in Machery (2017); see also Section 4.1 above). Moreover, we should not assume uniformity across philosophical sub-disciplines on this matter; some sub-disciplines (e.g., philosophy of biology, philosophy of psychology, naturalized ontology and

---

[21] See Hales (2006) and Sorenson (2014) for more analogies along these lines. See Nado (2015a) for discussion.

epistemology) likely espouse mostly synthetic aims, while other sub-disciplines (e.g., logic and perhaps metaethics) are more likely to espouse conceptual aims.

At any rate, proponents of the expertise objection characterize the philosophy expert-novice skill difference in various ways. We can use the three-level model of philosophical case analysis to express the core idea: the philosophy expert has learned to progress more skillfully and knowledgeably through the three levels of case judgment, using those levels (and the cases that prompt their cycling) to generate classificatory judgments and theoretical commitments that, assuming synthetic aims, more accurately capture explanatorily important kinds and structures relative to what novices generate (with or without similar case prompts). Indeed, a developmental progression like this is (nearly) the whole point of philosophical training.

It deserves emphasis that the progression includes both a procedural and evaluative (or content) component. Regarding the procedural component, Williamson claims that philosophers learn how "to apply general concepts to specific examples with careful attention to the relevant subtleties" (Williamson 2007, p. 191) and to "decompose the task of thought-experimentation into consciously discernible sub-tasks" (Williamson 2011, p. 224). Horvath claims that training makes philosophers "much more sensitive to potential ambiguities, unclarities or incoherencies" (Horvath 2010, p. 467). And Ludwig states that trained philosophers are skilled at "sorting out the various confusing factors that may be at work" (Ludwig 2007, p. 149) in a complex philosophical case. Applied to our judgment model, these types of procedural skills are often employed in the context of Level 2 judgments (e.g., as a means of interrogating Level 1 judgments), and they inform much Level 3 discourse as well.[22]

The evaluative (or content) improvement, which is not disconnected from procedural expertise, concerns the ability to correctly judge the probative value of different arguments given for different classificatory judgments and thereafter adjusting one's credences accordingly. As we saw in Section 4.1, Deutsch and Cappelen emphasize that case analysis involves a competition between arguments rather than between intuitions. Philosophical training teaches you the historical and vetted arguments. It also teaches you how to evaluate arguments and how to construct new ones, where this involves, among other things, evaluating the explanatory profiles of competing classificatory schemes (and what counts as a good explanation in the first place). Indeed, the purpose of many thought experiments just is to lay bare a theory's explanatory commitments: the Swampman case illustrates that teleosemanticist's unificatory theory of content excludes the possibility of behaviorally sophisticated creatures that have accidental origins; Gettier cases illustrate that the JTB theory of knowledge includes lucked-into true beliefs; and so forth. It is then a matter of argument and the judicious

---

[22] For example, the emerging understanding, facilitated by procedurally skilled public philosophical debate, that Jackson's knowledge argument, whatever its merits, was not guilty of committing the intensional fallacy. See Stoljar (2017, p. 10).

weighing of explanatory merit as to whether these exclusions and inclusions indicate epistemic deficiency. As Jackson explains in the context of Gettier cases:

> true justified belief isn't suited to the special role we give knowledge in epistemology. We want knowledge to be a kind of gold standard in epistemology. The state we are in if and only if things have gone right, epistemically speaking. True justified belief had seemed to be such a state. Gettier cases taught us that it need not be. (Jackson 2011, p. 475)

We should not expect lay persons to understand what would count as the "gold standard in epistemology" (especially if we are assuming synthetic, material aims), as lay persons are not in a good position to know what theoretical itch "knowledge" is scratching.[23] To know *that* generally requires training in both the methods and history of philosophy.[24] Sosa makes a related point:

> Compare how we have been led to classify the tomato as a fruit, not a vegetable, and the whale as a mammal, not a fish, even if that departs from how many conceive of fruits, vegetables, mammals, and fish. It may of course turn out that philosophers, some of us, are led to a distinctive concept or conception of knowledge through our interest in knowledge itself, and through our search for an account of its nature. [...] The disagreement between philosophers and folk respondents on street corners might conceivably be analogous to the early disagreement among scientists and ordinary folk on what counts as a fruit, or as a fish. (Sosa 2015, p. 16 f.)

Again, the idea here is that the philosophy expert has the requisite training and historical knowledge to judge more accurately when explanatory gain trumps departure from semantic defaults and snap judgments.[25] This is neither chauvinism nor dogmatism if the explanatory gains are real and the descriptions of kinds or structures more accurate (just as it is not chauvinistic or dogmatic for expert biologists to privilege the whale-excluding fish concept despite folk push-back).[26]

---

[23] When Deutsch and Williamson say that Gettier cases are *counterexamples* – that these cases reveal the *fact* that there is not knowledge – we might view them as claiming that there is no question about the deficient explanatory value of theories of knowledge that classify otherwise.
[24] See especially Millikan (2012) on the importance of extended philosophical training in the history of philosophy in this sense.
[25] There is an emerging trend of labeling this sort of proposal "conceptual engineering". In the context of synthetic aims, which I suspect are the dominant (and correct) aims, I submit that the label "conceptual engineering" threatens to be either misleading or trivial, as just about every philosopher who has ever advanced a new theory about a part of the world when old theories were descriptively inadequate becomes a "conceptual engineer". Whether the label is appropriate or interesting for explicitly norm-driven category revisions (e. g., in the sense of Haslanger 2012) or for those who are invested in the Canberra Plan is perhaps another matter.
[26] This evaluative (or content) component of expert skill is played out – and developed through repeated iterations of – all three levels of our judgment model. It manifests at Level 1 judgment in so far as expert's snap judgments grow increasingly conditioned by acquired knowledge schemas. See, e. g., Kornblith (2007) and Devitt (2011).

4.3.3.1 Three Objections to the Expertise Criticism, and Responses to the Objections

As the expertise criticism has figured prominently in debates about the metaphilosophical relevance of x-phi studies, it is worth sketching some objections as well as responses to the objections.

The first is that expert philosophers' acquired theories and schemas are "just as likely to contaminate as they are to clarify" (Alexander 2012, p. 95; Weinberg et al. 2010). In response, Williamson (2013, p. 473 f.), Kornblith (2014, p. 165 f.), and Devitt (2011, sec. 5.5) have each pointed out that given the theory-ladenness of observation generally, one can raise this skeptical worry for any intellectual endeavor or discipline.[27]

The second objection we already discussed in Section 3.1. As reported there, several experimental philosophers have argued that the developmental conditions in philosophy are the same as the developmental conditions in domains in which experts are deluded about the quality of their expertise. As explained in Section 3.1, this argument overlooks important differences between philosophical epistemic activities and non-philosophical epistemic activities, thus undercutting the generalization about virtuous developmental conditions. The argument also overlooks empirical evidence indicating that non-philosophical experts who engage in tasks that are relevantly similar to philosophical case analysis (simulation, relational retrieval, grasping the importance of rare events, the discovery of new categories) are led to superior performance in direct feedback-deficient domains (Bach 2021). Still, one hopes for a positive, empirically informed account of the development of philosophical content expertise. Such an account is needed to address more forcefully the concern that expert philosophers' distinctive content judgments are tracking indoctrination rather than gold-standard explanatory categories – a concern raised by Starmans and Friedman (2020, p. 22). For attempts at an empirically informed developmental account of philosophical content expertise, see Nolan (2015) and Bach (2019, sec. 4.3).

The third objection is advanced on empirical grounds and consists of several recent x-phi survey studies that suggest distorting influences on specifically professional philosophers' case judgments.[28] These findings should concern philosophers, but here are five observations that mitigate their significance for philosophical methodology.

The first we have already covered, which is that this new wave of empirical studies, like the prior wave, lack ecological validity. As Kauppinen explains, "the experiments attempt to study an aspect of philosophical expertise *in isolation from the theoretical and practical context in which such expertise is originally exercised*"

---

[27] To better support the theory contamination objection to the expertise defense, the restrictionist might address head-on the sorts of explanatory considerations put forward for the theories themselves (e.g., contesting whether justified true beliefs fall short of the "gold standard" in epistemology; see Section 4.3.3 above).

[28] These include Hitchcock and Knobe (2009), Schulz, Cokely, and Feltz (2011), Schwitzgebel and Cushman (2012, 2015), Tobia, Buckwalter, and Stich (2013), as well as Wiegmann, Horvath, and Meyer (2020).

(Kauppinen 2018, p. 50, emphasis in original), and thus the findings of those experiments do not undermine the assumption that philosophers' skills enable reliable case analysis.

Second, one can argue that the studies assume an overly simplistic view of philosophical expertise. Recall the above distinction between procedural and evaluative (or content) philosophical expertise. Probably all philosophy PhDs possess considerable procedural expertise – they understand distinctions, focus on relevant features, recognize fallacies, and so on. However – and here we must remind ourselves of how difficult and unforgiving philosophy is – probably not all (maybe a minority) of professional philosophers are truly skilled at adjudicating between competing explanatory considerations.[29] While the new wave of x-phi studies screens out those without procedural expertise, they likely fail to screen out those who lack content expertise. Analogously, consider that there are lots of sushi chefs these days (several at my local grocery, in fact), all with professional training. Consider also that high-end sushi work requires unusually sharp knives. In the hands of lesser sushi chefs, those knives are more likely to bring about nicked fingers and botched cuts than exemplary cuisine. The point is that the same item – a knife, a thought experiment – can function as an essential trade tool for one professional and a "disturbing" tool for another. But to register this point, one must first accept the quasi-elitist (if platitudinous) conception of philosophical expertise sketched above. Note that the resulting view is not incompatible with selective applications of restrictionism. For example, if we have reason to believe that a particular tool – a specific knife, a specific thought experiment – is so poorly designed that it is likely to damage a high percentage of users, then perhaps that item should be taken off the market entirely (see also Dennett 1996). X-phi studies will aid the discovery of such defective items.[30]

Third, x-phi studies of professional philosophers have been mostly restricted to cases that have normative content (e.g., trolly and footbridge cases). There are independent reasons to be suspicious about philosopher's ability to think clearly about this domain (i.e., Mackie 1977), so it is a live possibility that these experimental findings will not generalize to professional philosophers' judgments about mind, epistemology, metaphysics, and other theoretical areas of philosophy (the objective targets of which may be more conducive to accurate philosophical theorizing). It also remains to be seen to whether the findings of this new wave of x-phi studies can be replicated.

---

[29] That might sound elitist – and to be clear I don't count myself as one of the skilled adjudicators – but it is also a sociological platitude. That is, most philosophers think that most other philosophers are wrong much of the time, and they think this not because they regard other philosophers as procedurally sloppy. See Bach (2019, sec. 3.2) for discussion of the contrast between the distribution of content expertise and the distribution of procedural expertise.

[30] But given our inability to confirm the accuracy of first-order philosophical theoretical models (Section 3.1), we are strongly limited outside of the normal modes of (empirically informed) philosophical argumentation in terms of what conclusive decisions we can make in this context (but see Levy 2013).

Fourth, there are x-phi studies that appear to vindicate the objection based on expertise. For example, Starmans and Friedman (2020) show that both laypersons and non-philosophy academics are considerably more likely than academic philosophers to attribute knowledge in Gettier cases.[31] This is exactly what the expertise objection (particularly the synthetic version) predicts – that philosophy experts' developmental history has guided them to distinct (and more accurate) judgments about epistemological categories – what Jackson termed the "gold standard".[32] This is analogous to the folk's favoring of the whale-inclusive fish category versus the expert biologist's grasp of which taxonomic schemes have greater explanatory payoff (a sure sign that those schemes are tracking the world's real kinds and structures).[33]

Fifth, despite restrictionists' claims to the contrary, we should not expect expert philosophers who (by hypothesis) use the method of cases reliably to be "insulated" from distorting influences. This point deserves separate discussion, below.

4.4 The Reliable and Expert-Superior Analysis of Philosophical Cases Is Compatible with That Analysis Being Influenced by Epistemically Irrelevant Factors

Several restrictionists claim that expertise-based defenses of philosophical case analysis require that experts' judgments are sufficiently "inoculated", "immune" to, or "insulated" from the influence of epistemically irrelevant factors. Various commentators on the expertise discussion have rejected this requirement.[34] Non-philosophical examples help demonstrate the general compatibility between reliability and instability. For example, Sorensen (2014, p. 137) points out that "order effects have been demonstrated for master chess players and many other types of experts […] Since the chess masters perform well despite these shortcomings, the impact on performance must be minor".

At issue here is whether x-phi's documented presentational and demographic effects are mere "foibles" (Ludwig 2018) – the sorts of general biases that you would expect to find accompanying any intellectual (or perceptual, see Sosa 2007) endeavor, in-

---

[31] Starmans and Friedman (2020, p. 22) interpret the results of their study along these lines only for a "more focused" version of the expertise defense. They interpret their results as worrisome for what they consider to be the standard version of that defense (because, they say, the results show that non-philosophy academic experts judge differently than philosophers). As made clear both above and below, I think the best way (and the more common way) to formulate the expertise objection is the "focused" version. This version resources not only intellectual reflection (which appears to distinguish Starmans and Friedman's generic version) but also familiarity with philosophical explananda, established arguments, historical texts, and other components of a philosophical training regimen.
[32] See Sosa (2015, p. 16 f.); see also Papineau (2009), Jackson (2011), Strevens (2019), and Bach (2019).
[33] See Griffiths (1999) and Millikan (2000) on this point.
[34] See Sosa (2007), Devitt (2011), Williamson (2011), Papineau (2011), Nagel (2012), Kornblith (2014), Sorensen (2014), Rini (2015), and Kauppinen (2018).

cluding epistemically fruitful and expert-superior endeavors – or whether they are symptomatic of an underlying epistemically deficient methodology.[35] At this dialectical juncture, restrictionists might ask for demonstration of the reliability (or "hopefulness", see below) of the relevant philosophical methodology. However, if meeting that request presupposes confirmation of correct answers to first-order philosophical questions, then one might respond that the request illegitimately exploits the confirmational reality of philosophical analysis described earlier (Section 3.1).

4.5 X-phi Restrictionist Claims Lead to Over-Generalization and Self-Defeat

Several philosophers have claimed that x-phi's negative program leads to an unacceptable and general form of skepticism about everyday and scientific judgment (Ludwig 2007; Sosa 2007; Williamson 2007, 2011; Horvath 2010). This critique is advanced in at least two ways. The first way claims that the inference from demographic and presentational effects to unreliability leads to an unacceptable skepticism. For example, if we view ordering effects as indicating epistemic unreliability, then it would seem that we need to view chess experts' judgments about mating positions, which are also subject to ordering effects (Section 4.4), as unreliable. And if we treat demographic effects as indicating epistemic unreliability, then we seem forced to accept overly skeptical views about (at least) the status of scientific judgment. As Papineau (2011, p. 83 f.) observes in this spirit, "we wouldn't expect physicists to throw up their hands in excitement just because somebody shows that different cultures have different views about the origin of the universe". The second way locates the generalizing factor at the level of the judgment-forming mechanisms. If the judgment mechanisms that drive philosophical case analysis are the same as the judgment mechanisms that drive the everyday application of general concepts, then deeming those mechanisms unreliable in the philosophical case invites an overly skeptical stance towards the everyday application of concepts.

In an extension, or application, of this overgeneralization critique, some philosophers charge that the restrictionist interpretation of x-phi's experimental findings is self-defeating because that interpretation derives from philosophical concepts the justifications of which depend on the restricted evidential practices (see Williamson 2009, Horvath 2010, Ludwig 2018).[36] Because this charge is a species of the more general, over generalizing criticism, we can focus on the latter.

---

[35] Note the synergies between this and other criticisms of x-phi; we should expect general psychological biases to manifest in contexts that diverge (e.g., are non-socially mediated, non-reflective, non-extended) from those in which evaluative philosophical expertise is standardly developed and employed.
[36] As Ludwig (2018, p. 399) summarizes: "It [is] a point of mild irony that the use of survey results to argue against the use of thought experiments in philosophy relies on an epistemology which could only be supported by the sources which it aims to undermine".

The over-generalizing critique is directed at both intuition-based (Section 4.1) and non-intuition-based (Section 4.2) forms of restrictionism. Weinberg (2007) is a notable and ambitious attempt to defend the former type of restrictionism from this objection. He claims that philosophers' evidential use of intuitions lacks the external corroboration and means of error detection needed to confer reliability to an evidential practice. On this view, the restrictionist challenge stays local to philosophers' uses of intuitions because scientific and perceptual evidential practices, unlike philosophers' evidential sourcing of intuitions, possess these epistemically "hopeful" features. It is fair to ask whether the epistemic standards that Weinberg imposes here capitalize on the confirmational predicament that applies to philosophical theory-building generally (Section 3.1, see also Sosa 2011). At any rate, readers should consult Horvath (2010), Grundmann (2010), Brown (2011), Sosa (2011), Ichikawa (2012), and Nado (2015b) for discussion of whether Weinberg's attempt succeeds.[37]

In Section 4.1, I critically examined the descriptive claim that philosophers appeal to intuitions as evidence. In Section 4.2, following the arguments of Deutsch, Cappelen, and Williamson, I suggested that a model of philosophical case judgment that did not psychologize evidence was more descriptively accurate. Machery advances such a model, claiming that "philosophical cases do not elicit attitudes distinct in kind from the application of concepts in everyday life" (Machery 2017, p. 21). To escape the overgeneralization worry, this type of view needs to indicate why specifically philosophical cases interact with otherwise reliable judgment mechanisms to make them function unreliably. This is the point of Machery's discussion of the "disturbing characteristics" of philosophical cases (briefly mentioned in Section 4.2). Several commentators have claimed that this appeal to disturbing characteristics does not block the slide to skepticism. It is beyond the scope of this chapter to examine this interesting debate in detail, but readers can consult Machery (2011, 2017, sec. 3.5), Williamson (2016), Deutsch (2020), and Nado (2022) for discussion.

Finally, it is important to observe that the overgeneralization objection has a distinct application to the developmental argument (see Sections 3.1 and 4.4 above) made by experimental philosophers against the reliability of expert philosophers' theories and theory-based judgments. Weinberg et al. (2010) claim that the epistemic virtue of expert philosophers' (theory-laden) intuitions cannot be defended in reference to the epistemic virtue of expert philosophers' theories because philosophers do not receive the good, direct kind of learning feedback that is needed for the development of epistemically virtuous theories.[38] Weinberg and colleagues are aware that this view suggests an overly skeptical stance towards philosophical theories generally. In response, they state that there are a few "successful" and "key" distinctions (they men-

---

37 Note that the philosophical naturalist who construes a theory's explanatory and unificatory payoff (and lack thereof) as an indicator of success (and error), and who views intuitions as both theory-laden and instrumental to the construction of further theories, has resources to claim that philosophers' evidential uses of intuitions are in this sense "hopeful".
38 See Weinberg et al. (2010, p. 340 f.).

tion the use-mention and the epistemological-metaphysical distinctions) that "philosophers have wrung from their theorizing" (Weinberg et al. 2010, p. 342), that have "proved useful" (Weinberg et al. 2010, p. 351), and that are "exceptions that prove the rule" (Weinberg et al. 2010, p. 342).[39] It is not clear how this response is satisfactory; one can make similar claims about success and usefulness for just about any philosophical proposal (which is what philosophers do when they argue for their theories). What appears to distinguish Weinberg and colleagues' exempted theoretical distinctions is the extent of agreement among professional philosophers about the epistemic virtue of these distinctions. If that is what explains their privileged epistemic status, then it reframes Weinberg and colleagues' developmental argument against expert philosophical theorizing in a way that seems to confuse the conditions required for professional belief convergence, on the one hand, and the conditions needed for the development of accurate philosophical theoretical models, on the other. The defender of epistemically virtuous philosophical theories (and theory-laden judgments) does not need to make a case that the developmental conditions of philosophical discourse are conducive to professional agreement (they are not). They only need to defend the claim that the developmental conditions are conducive to the construction of philosophical theoretical models (and associated classificatory judgments) that describe their targets with reasonable accuracy.

5 Conclusion

Philosophy is difficult, which we already knew. But it is especially difficult if one is not taking the time to reflect carefully, if one is not engaging with epistemic peers in dialogue, if one is led into verbal disagreements, if one is less than highly skilled at evaluating the explanatory profiles of competing but empirically equivalent philosophical models, if one's judgments are expected to be insulated from general types of psychological bias, if one is expected to use psychological rather than objective data, or if one is not allowed use of conceptual practices considered trustworthy in everyday and scientific contexts. That, at least, is one way to understand an interdependent network of criticisms directed at x-phi's (primarily) restrictionist evaluations of philosophical methods. According to these criticisms, x-phi's evaluative claims, as well as the experimental simulations and descriptive models on which they are premised, impose additional epistemic burdens on philosophical case analysis, thereby construing an already

---

[39] Weinberg and colleagues (2010, p. 342) also state that we are very good at training philosophy students to use these distinctions correctly. That may be correct, but it is beside the point. One can also train students to be very effective and sensitive in their application of the rules of snake-oil medicine. What needs explaining is what accounts for the success – e. g., correspondence to natural kinds or properties – of the rules themselves, as well as what enabled expert philosophers to develop that theoretical success. See Bach (2019, p. 15 f.) for further discussion.

challenging epistemic activity as considerably more challenging – and hence less trustworthy – than it in fact is.

Whatever we make of these criticisms, there is no question that the experimental studies and metaphilosophical explorations generated by and through experimental philosophy have improved our understanding of the psychology and epistemology of philosophical analysis, and moreover they inform how best to approach traditional philosophical questions. The extent of this type of improvement, however, is ultimately limited by the empirical unverifiability of the accuracy of first-order philosophical theoretical models.

Bibliography

Alexander, Joshua (2010): "Is experimental philosophy philosophically significant?", *Philosophical Psychology* 23 (3), pp. 377–389.
Alexander, Joshua (2012): *Experimental philosophy*. Cambridge: Polity.
Alexander, Joshua, and Jonathan Weinberg (2007): "Analytic epistemology and experimental philosophy", *Philosophy Compass* 2 (1), pp. 56–80.
Bach, Theodore (2019): "In defence of armchair expertise", *Theoria* 85 (5), pp. 350–382.
Bach, Theodore (2021): "Why the empirical study of non-philosophical expertise does not undermine the status of philosophical expertise", *Erkenntnis* 86 (4), pp. 999–1023.
Bealer, George (1998): "Intuition and the autonomy of philosophy", in: Michael DePaul and William Ramsey (Eds.): *Rethinking intuition. The psychology of intuition and its role in philosophical inquiry*. Lanham: Rowman & Littlefield, pp. 201–240.
Bengson, John (2013): "Experimental attacks on intuitions and answers", *Philosophy and Phenomenological Research* 86 (3), pp. 495–532.
BonJour, Laurence (1998): *In defense of pure reason*. Cambridge: Cambridge University Press.
Boyd, Richard (2021): "Rethinking natural kinds, reference and truth. Towards more correspondence with reality, not less", *Synthese* 198 (12), pp. 2863–2903.
Brown, Jessica (2013): "Intuitions, evidence and hopefulness", *Synthese* 190 (12), pp. 2021–2046.
Buckwalter, Wesley, and Stephen Stich (2013): "Gender and philosophical intuition", in: Joshua Knobe and Shaun Nichols (Eds.): *Experimental philosophy*. Vol. 2. Oxford: Oxford University Press, pp. 307–346.
Cappelen, Herman (2012): *Philosophy without intuitions*. Oxford: Oxford University Press.
Cappelen, Herman (2022): "Experimental philosophy without intuitions. An illustration of why it fails", *Philosophical Studies* 179, pp. 309–317.
Cappelen, Herman, and Max Deutsch (2018): "The crisis of method in contemporary analytic philosophy", *Notre Dame Philosophical Reviews* 1 (5).
Clarke, Steve (2013): "Intuitions as evidence, philosophical expertise and the developmental challenge", *Philosophical Papers* 42 (2), pp. 175–207.
Colombo, Matteo, Georgi Duev, Michèle Nuijten, and Jan Sprenger (2018): "Statistical reporting inconsistencies in experimental philosophy", *PLOS ONE* 13 (4), e0194360.
Cova, Florian, Brent Strickland, Angela Abatista, Aurélien Allard, James Andow, Mario Attie, James Beebe, Renatas Berniūnas, Jordane Boudesseul, Matteo Colombo, Fiery Cushman, Rodrigo Díaz, Noah N'Djaye Nikolai van Dongen, Vilius Dranseika, Brian Earp, Antonio Gaitán Torres, Ivar Hannikainen, José Hernández-Conde, Wenjia Hu, François Jaquet, Kareem Khalifa, Hanna Kim, Markus Kneer, Joshua Knobe, Miklos Kurthy, Anthony Lantian, Shen-Yi Liao, Edouard Machery, Tania Moerenhout, Christian Mott, Mark Phelan, Jonathan Phillips, Navin Rambharose, Kevin Reuter, Felipe Romero, Paulo Sousa, Jan Sprenger, Emile Thalabard, Kevin Tobia, Hugo Viciana, Daniel Wilkenfeld, and Xiang

Zhou (2018): "Estimating the reproducibility of experimental philosophy", *Review of Philosophy and Psychology* 2, pp. 9–44.
Cullen, Simon (2010): "Survey-driven romanticism", *Review of Philosophy and Psychology* 1 (2), pp. 275–296.
Davis, Kathy (2008): "Intersectionality as buzzword. A sociology of science perspective on what makes a feminist theory successful", *Feminist Theory* 9 (1), pp. 67–85.
Davis, Murray (1971): "That's interesting! Towards a phenomenology of sociology and a sociology of phenomenology", *Philosophy of the Social Sciences* 1 (2), pp. 309–344.
Davis, Murray (1986): "'That's classic!' The phenomenology and rhetoric of successful social theories", *Philosophy of the Social Sciences* 16 (3), pp. 285–301.
Dennett, Daniel (1996): "Cow-sharks, magnets, and swampman", *Mind & Language* 11 (1), pp. 76–77.
Deutsch, Max (2009): "Experimental philosophy and the theory of reference", *Mind & Language* 24 (4), pp. 445–466.
Deutsch, Max (2015): *The myth of the intuitive*. Cambridge: The MIT Press.
Deutsch, Max (2020): "The method of cases unbound", *Analysis* 80 (4), pp. 758–771.
Devitt, Michael (2012): "Whither experimental semantics?", *Theoria* 27 (1), pp. 5–36.
Gick, Mary, and Keith Holyoak (1980): "Analogical problem solving", *Cognitive Psychology* 12 (3), pp. 306–355.
Goldman, Alvin, and Joel Pust (1998): "Philosophical theory and intuitional evidence", in: Michael DePaul and William Ramsey (Eds.): *Rethinking intuition. The psychology of intuition and its role in philosophical inquiry.* Lanham: Rowman & Littlefield, pp. 179–200.
Griffiths, Paul (1999): "Squaring the circle. Natural kinds with historical essences", in: Robert Wilson (Ed.): *Species. New interdisciplinary essays.* Cambridge and London: The MIT Press, pp. 209–228.
Grundmann, Thomas (2010): "Some hope for intuitions. A reply to Weinberg", *Philosophical Psychology* 23 (4), pp. 481–509.
Hales, Steven (2006): *Relativism and the foundations of philosophy.* Cambridge and London: The MIT Press.
Hannon, Michael (2018): "Intuitions, reflective judgments, and experimental philosophy", *Synthese* 195 (9), pp. 4147–4168.
Haslanger, Sally (2012): *Resisting reality. Social construction and social critique.* Oxford and New York: Oxford University Press.
Heck, Richard (2018): "Speaker's reference, semantic reference, and intuition", *Review of Philosophy and Psychology* 9 (2), pp. 251–269.
Hitchcock, Christopher, and Joshua Knobe (2009): "Cause and norm", *Journal of Philosophy* 106 (11), pp. 587–612.
Horne, Zachary, and Jonathan Livengood (2017): "Ordering effects, updating effects, and the specter of global skepticism", *Synthese* 194 (4), pp. 1189–1218.
Horvath, Joachim (2010): "How (not) to react to experimental philosophy", *Philosophical Psychology* 23 (4), pp. 447–480.
Horvath, Joachim, Karina Meyer, and Alex Wiegmann (2020): "Intuitive expertise and irrelevant options", in: Tania Lombrozo, Shaun Nichols, and Joshua Knobe (Eds.): *Oxford studies in experimental philosophy.* Vol. 3. Oxford: Oxford University Press, pp. 275–310.
Ichikawa, Jonathan (2012): "Experimentalist pressure against traditional methodology", *Philosophical Psychology* 25 (5), pp. 710–753.
Jackson, Frank (1998): *From metaphysics to ethics. A defence of conceptual analysis.* Oxford: Clarendon.
Jackson, Frank (2011): "On Gettier holdouts", *Mind & Language* 26 (4), pp. 468–481.
Kahneman, Daniel, and Gary Klein (2009): "Conditions for intuitive expertise. A failure to disagree", *American Psychologist* 64 (6), pp. 515–526.
Kauppinen, Antti (2007): "The rise and fall of experimental philosophy", *Philosophical Explorations* 10 (2), pp. 95–118.
Kauppinen, Antti (2018): "Who's afraid of trolleys?", in: Jussi Suikkanen and Antti Kauppinen (Eds.): *Methodology and moral philosophy.* New York and London: Routledge, pp. 49–72.

Kelly, Thomas (2016): "Disagreement in philosophy", in: Herman Cappelen, Tamar Szabó Gendler, and John Hawthorne (Eds.): *The Oxford handbook of philosophical methodology*. Oxford: Oxford University Press, pp. 374–394.

Kneer, Markus, David Colaço, Joshua Alexander, and Edouard Machery (2022): "On second thought. Reflections on the reflection defense", in: Tania Lombrozo, Joshua Knobe, and Shaun Nichols (Eds.): *Oxford studies in experimental philosophy*. Vol. 4. Oxford: Oxford University Press, pp. 257–296.

Knobe, Joshua (2003): "Intentional action and side effects in ordinary language", *Analysis* 63 (3), pp. 190–194.

Knobe, Joshua, and Shaun Nichols (2017): "Experimental philosophy", in: Edward Zalta (Ed.): *The Stanford encyclopedia of philosophy*. Winter 2017 edition. https://plato.stanford.edu/archives/win2017/entries/experimental-philosophy/, last accessed May 19, 2023.

Kornblith, Hilary (2002): *Knowledge and its place in nature*. Oxford: Oxford University Press.

Kornblith, Hilary (2007): "Naturalism and intuitions", *Grazer Philosophische Studien* 74 (1), pp. 27–49.

Kornblith, Hilary (2014): *A naturalistic epistemology. Selected papers*. Oxford: Oxford University Press.

Kuntz, Joana, and Joseph Kuntz (2011): "Surveying philosophers about philosophical intuition", *Review of Philosophy and Psychology* 2 (4), pp. 643–665.

Levy, Neil (2013): "Intuitions and experimental philosophy. Comfortable bedfellows", in: Matthew Haug (Ed.): *Philosophical methodology. The armchair or the laboratory?* London and New York: Routledge, pp. 381–397.

Ludwig, Kirk (2007): "The epistemology of thought experiments. First person versus third person approaches", *Midwest Studies in Philosophy* 31 (1), pp. 128–159.

Ludwig, Kirk (2010): "Intuitions and relativity", *Philosophical Psychology* 23 (4), pp. 427–445.

Ludwig, Kirk (2018): "Thought experiments in experimental philosophy", in: Mike Stuart, James Robert Brown, and Yiftach Fehige (Eds.): *The Routledge companion to thought experiments*. New York: Routledge, pp. 385–405.

Lycan, William (2017): "On evidence in philosophy", *Proceedings and Addresses of the American Philosophical Association* 91, pp. 102–117.

Machery, Edouard (2011): "Thought experiments and philosophical knowledge", *Metaphilosophy* 42 (3), pp. 191–214.

Machery, Edouard (2017): *Philosophy within its proper bounds*. Oxford: Oxford University Press.

Machery, Edouard, Ron Mallon, Shaun Nichols, and Stephen Stich (2004): "Semantics, cross-cultural style", *Cognition* 92 (3), pp. B1–B12.

Mackie, Jonh (1977): *Ethics. Inventing right and wrong*. Harmondsworth: Penguin.

Millikan, Ruth (2000): *On clear and confused ideas. An essay about substance concepts*. Cambridge: Cambridge University Press.

Millikan, Ruth (2012): "Accidents", *Proceedings and Addresses of the American Philosophical Association* 86 (2), pp. 92–103.

Nado, Jennifer (2015a): "Philosophical expertise and scientific expertise", *Philosophical Psychology* 28 (7), pp. 1026–1044.

Nado, Jennifer (2015b): "Intuition, philosophical theorizing, and the threat of skepticism", in: Eugen Fischer and John Collins (Eds.): *Experimental philosophy, rationalism, and naturalism. Rethinking philosophical method*. London and New York: Routledge, pp. 212–229.

Nado, Jennifer (2016): "The intuition deniers", *Philosophical Studies* 173 (3), pp. 781–800.

Nado, Jennifer (2022): "Philosophizing out of bounds", *Philosophical Studies* 179 (1), pp. 319–327.

Nagel, Jennifer (2012): "Intuitions and experiments. A defense of the case method in epistemology", *Philosophy and Phenomenological Research* 85 (3), pp. 495–527.

Nahmias, Eddy, Stephen Morris, Thomas Nadelhoffer, and Jason Turner (2006): "Is incompatibilism intuitive?", *Philosophy and Phenomenological Research* 73 (1), pp. 28–53.

Neisser, Ulric (1976): *Cognition and reality. Principles and implications of cognitive psychology.* San Francisco: W.H. Freeman.

Nolan, Daniel (2015): "The a posteriori armchair", *Australasian Journal of Philosophy* 93 (2), pp. 211–231.

Papineau, David (2009): "The poverty of analysis", *Aristotelian Society Supplementary Volume* 83 (1), pp. 1–30.

Papineau, David (2011): "What is x-phi good for?", *The Philosophers' Magazine* 52, pp. 83–88.

Paul, Laurie (2012): "Metaphysics as modeling. The handmaiden's tale", *Philosophical Studies* 160 (1), pp. 1–29.

Pust, Joel (2019): "Intuition", in: Edward Zalta (Ed.): *The Stanford encyclopedia of philosophy.* Summer 2019 edition. https://plato.stanford.edu/archives/sum2019/entries/intuition/, last accessed May 19, 2023.

Rini, Regina (2015): "How not to test for philosophical expertise", *Synthese* 192 (2), pp. 431–452.

Rose, David, and David Danks (2013): "In defense of a broad conception of experimental philosophy", *Metaphilosophy* 44 (4), pp. 512–532.

Ryberg, Jesper (2013): "Moral intuitions and the expertise defence", *Analysis* 73 (1), pp. 3–9.

Schulz, Eric, Edward Cokely, and Adam Feltz (2011): "Persistent bias in expert judgments about free will and moral responsibility. A test of the expertise defense", *Consciousness and Cognition* 20 (4), pp. 1722–1731.

Schwitzgebel, Eric, and Fiery Cushman (2012): "Expertise in moral reasoning? Order effects on moral judgment in professional philosophers and non-philosophers", *Mind & Language* 27 (2), pp. 135–153.

Schwitzgebel, Eric, and Fiery Cushman (2015): "Philosophers' biased judgments persist despite training, expertise and reflection", *Cognition* 141, pp. 127–137.

Seyedsayamdost, Hamid (2015): "On gender and philosophical intuition. Failure of replication and other negative results", *Philosophical Psychology* 28 (5), pp. 642–673.

Shanteau, James (1992): "Competence in experts. The role of task characteristics", *Organizational Behavior and Human Decision Processes* 53 (2), pp. 252–266.

Sorensen, Roy (2014): "Novice thought experiments", in: Anthony Robert Booth and Darrell Rowbottom (Eds.): *Intuitions.* Oxford: Oxford University Press, pp. 135–147.

Sosa, Ernest (2007): "Experimental philosophy and philosophical intuition", *Philosophical Studies* 132 (1), pp. 99–107.

Sosa, Ernest (2009): "A defense of the use of intuitions in philosophy", in: Michael Bishop and Dominic Murphy (Eds.): *Stich and his critics.* Chichester: Wiley-Blackwell, pp. 101–112.

Sosa, Ernest (2011): "Can there be a discipline of philosophy? And can it be founded on intuitions?", *Mind & Language* 26 (4), pp. 453–467.

Sosa, Ernest (2015): "Philosophical intuitions and metaphysical analysis", *Discipline filosofiche* 25 (1), pp. 9–22.

Starmans, Christina, and Ori Friedman (2020): "Expert or esoteric? Philosophers attribute knowledge differently than all other academics", *Cognitive Science* 44 (7), e12850.

Stich, Stephen, and Kevin Tobia (2016): "Experimental philosophy and the philosophical tradition", in: Justin Sytsma and Wesley Buckwalter (Eds.): *A companion to experimental philosophy.* Chichester: Wiley-Blackwell, pp. 5–21.

Stoljar, Daniel (2017): *Philosophical progress. In defence of a reasonable optimism.* Oxford: Oxford University Press

Strevens, Michael (2019): *Thinking off your feet. How empirical psychology vindicates armchair philosophy.* Cambridge and London: Belknap.

Stuart, Michael, David Colaço, and Edouard Machery (2019): "P-curving x-phi. Does experimental philosophy have evidential value?", *Analysis* 79 (4), pp. 669–684.

Swain, Stacey, Joshua Alexander, and Jonathan Weinberg (2008): "The instability of philosophical intuitions. Running hot and cold on truetemp", *Philosophy and Phenomenological Research* 76 (1), pp. 138–155.

Sytsma, Justin, and Jonathan Livengood (2015): *The theory and practice of experimental philosophy.* Peterborough: Broadview.

Tobia, Kevin, Wesley Buckwalter, and Stephen Stich (2013): "Moral intuitions. Are philosophers experts?", *Philosophical Psychology* 26 (5), pp. 629–638.

Uhlmann, Eric, David Pizarro, David Tannenbaum, and Peter Ditto (2009): "The motivated use of moral principles", *Judgment and Decision Making* 4 (6), pp. 479–491.

Weinberg, Jonathan (2007): "How to challenge intuitions empirically without risking skepticism", *Midwest Studies in Philosophy* 31 (1), pp. 318–343.

Weinberg, Jonathan (2016): "Going positive by going negative. On keeping x-phi relevant and dangerous", in: Justin Sytsma and Wesley Buckwalter (Eds.): *A companion to experimental philosophy.* Chichester: Wiley-Blackwell, pp. 71–86.

Weinberg, Jonathan (2017): "What is negative experimental philosophy good for?", in: Giuseppina D'Oro and Søren Overgaard (Eds.): *The Cambridge companion to philosophical methodology.* Cambridge: Cambridge University Press, pp. 161–183.

Weinberg, Jonathan, Joshua Alexander, Chad Gonnerman, and Shane Reuter (2012): "Restrictionism and reflection. Challenge deflected, or simply redirected?", *The Monist* 95 (2), pp. 200–222.

Weinberg, Jonathan, Chad Gonnerman, Cameron Buckner, and Joshua Alexander (2010): "Are philosophers expert intuiters?", *Philosophical Psychology* 23 (3), pp. 331–355.

Weinberg, Jonathan, Shaun Nichols, and Stephen Stich (2001): "Normativity and epistemic intuitions", *Philosophical Topics* 29 (1–2), pp. 429–460.

Williamson, Timothy (2007): *The philosophy of philosophy.* Oxford: Blackwell.

Williamson, Timothy (2009): "Replies to Ichikawa, Martin and Weinberg", *Philosophical Studies* 145 (3), pp. 465–476.

Williamson, Timothy (2011): "Philosophical expertise and the burden of proof", *Metaphilosophy* 42 (3), pp. 215–229.

Williamson, Timothy (2013): "Review of Joshua Alexander, experimental philosophy", *Philosophy* 88 (3), pp. 467–474.

Williamson, Timothy (2016): "Philosophical criticisms of experimental philosophy", in: Justin Sytsma and Wesley Buckwalter (Eds.): *A companion to experimental philosophy.* Chichester: Wiley-Blackwell, pp. 22–36.

Woolfolk, Robert (2013): "Experimental philosophy. A methodological critique", *Metaphilosophy* 44 (1–2), pp. 79–87.

Young, Iris Marion (1994): "Gender as seriality. Thinking about women as a social collective", *Signs* 19 (3), pp. 713–738.

Part 2: Topics from Theoretical Philosophy

Paul Henne
Experimental Metaphysics: Causation

Abstract: In this chapter, I review some issues in the metaphysics of causation that have been widely discussed by experimental philosophers. After I review the work investigating the effects of normality on causal judgment, I discuss the work on action-omission differences, temporal differences (late-preemption), and double-prevention scenarios. I review some explanations for the patterns of causal judgments that experimental philosophers observe in all of these cases. I then identify some new issues for the experimental philosophy of causation and experimental metaphysics more generally.

Keywords: Causal Judgment; Causal Pluralism; Causation; Counterfactual Thinking; Experimental Philosophy

1 Introduction

Experimental philosophers have investigated the judgments that are relevant to metaphysical theories in many domains (Rose 2017). And some metaphysicians have called for and suggested a role for experimental philosophy in many of these (Paul 2010b, Thomasson 2012). In this chapter, I review the work on one topic in experimental metaphysics – causation – and identify some general projects for future research.

2 Experimental Philosophy of Causation

In this section, I review some of the major issues in the experimental philosophy of causation – specifically, the effects of normality, action-omission, and temporal differences on causal judgments and double-prevention cases – I outline some of the major lingering debates, and I identify general projects for future work.

2.1 Normality

In the *It's Always Sunny in Philadelphia* episode "Reynolds vs. Reynolds – The Cereal Defense", Frank is driving in his car at 10:19 AM on a Friday (Keen 2012). He is listening to a cassette tape of his roommate, Charlie, giving him directions. "Okay – making a right", Frank responds. As the tape expectedly gets out of synch with Frank's driving,

---

Note: I would like to thank Kevin O'Neill for numerous discussions over the years about this work and for reading various parts of this chapter.

Frank exclaims, "You don't know where I am, tape!" Becoming increasingly frustrated with the cassette, he begins to hit his dashboard and yell at Charlie who is not in his car. Unbeknownst to Frank, his stepson, Dennis, is a block ahead of Frank's increasingly erratic driving. While driving, Dennis calmly listens to a public-radio story on composting. He comes to a gentle stop at a red light, and he then – surprisingly – takes a bite of cereal. Frank, who continues his erratic driving, suddenly runs into the rear of Dennis' car, causing Dennis to spill his cereal inside of his Range Rover. When they return to their bar, Frank exclaims, "I didn't cause any damages, Dennis!" Dennis replies, "not to the exterior of my car, but to the interior of my car – my interior is ruined!" Frank explains to the gang that the only damages to the car were to the interior because of the bowl of cereal that Dennis was eating while driving. In this quixotic scenario, Frank claims that he did not cause Dennis' damages and that Dennis did. Dennis engaged in highly unusual, or abnormal, behavior – i.e., having a bowl of cereal while driving – so Frank claims that Dennis caused the damages.

While you might not see this absurd example in an actual courtroom, Frank's causal judgment accords with some findings in experimental studies. In fact, many experimental philosophers have found that normality affects causal judgments such that people are more inclined to judge norm-violating actions or events – like eating a bowl of cereal while driving – as causes than norm-conforming ones (Alicke 1992, Icard et al. 2017, Knobe and Fraser 2008). For ease, I will refer to this effect as *abnormal inflation* (Icard et al. 2017, Morris et al. 2019).

In one study on abnormal inflation, Knobe and Fraser gave participants the following vignette:

> The receptionist in the philosophy department keeps her desk stocked with pens. The administrative assistants are allowed to take the pens, but faculty members are supposed to buy their own. The administrative assistants typically do take the pens. Unfortunately, so do the faculty members. The receptionist has repeatedly emailed them reminders that only administrative assistants are allowed to take the pens.
>
> On Monday morning, one of the administrative assistants encounters Professor Smith walking past the receptionist's desk. Both take pens. Later that day, the receptionist needs to take an important message… but she has a problem. There are no pens left on her desk. (Knobe and Fraser 2008, p. 443)

The authors then asked participants the extent to which they agreed with the following statements:

> Professor Smith caused the problem.
> The administrative assistant caused the problem.

Knobe and Fraser (2008) found that people overwhelmingly agreed more with the causal statement about the professor (the norm-violating agent) than the statement about the administrative assistant (the norm-conforming agent). Just as Frank thought that Dennis' norm-violating action – eating the bowl of cereal while driving – caused the damage, participants thought that the person who violated the norm by taking a pen caused the receptionist's problem.

The effect of norms on causal judgments is pervasive (cf. Danks et al. 2014). Knobe and Fraser's study has been replicated many times (Kirfel and Phillips 2022, Knobe and Szabó 2013, Phillips et al. 2015). And abnormal inflation replicates using a variety of scenarios (Clarke et al. 2015, Cova et al. 2018, Gill et al. 2022, Icard et al. 2017, Kominsky et al. 2015, Morris et al. 2019, O'Neill, Henne, Bello, et al. 2022, O'Neill, Henne, Pearson, et al. 2022), children participants (Samland et al. 2016), and non-agential stimuli (Gerstenberg and Icard 2020, Hitchcock and Knobe 2009, Sytsma 2022a).[1] Importantly, abnormal inflation does not only occur for prescriptive norm violations as in the pen case; researchers also find this effect for statistical norms[2] (Icard et al. 2017, Roxborough and Cumby 2009)[3] and for norms of proper functioning (Kominsky and Phillips 2019).

At this point, it may seem like abnormal inflation is an interesting psychological phenomenon, but also it might be unclear why philosophers would be interested in it at all. While some philosophers argue that causal selection involves normative considerations (McGrath 2005), this is an interesting question for those who think that causation is not at all normative (Bernstein 2017, Lewis 1974).

Philosophers have good reason to think that norms should not affect causal judgments at all. If we are in a good epistemic position, we ought to be more egalitarian and scientific about causal judgments; we should not privilege particular events over others simply because norms make them more salient (Beebee 2004). Abnormal inflation might represent a bias or a pragmatic feature of language that is distinct from the true causal structure – as some have argued (Blanchard and Schaffer 2017). If norms distort or bias causal judgments in this way, then we probably ought to reject them when developing metaphysical theories of causation. Some argue – noting other limi-

---

[1] It may be helpful to distinguish abnormal inflation from abnormal selection. Abnormal inflation uses a continuous scale to measure the extent to which people think that an event is a cause of some outcome. Abnormal selection, however, uses a categorical selection to measures people's tendency to select an event as a cause. Samland and colleagues is an example where researchers investigated abnormal selection (Samland et al. 2016), and there are many more examples of this kind of investigation (Henne et al. 2017, Henne, O'Neill, et al. 2021).
[2] Experimental philosophers of causation distinguish between prescriptive and statistical norms (Icard et al. 2017, Kominsky et al. 2015). To see this difference, consider diving a car above the speed limit. There is a prescription by law that one ought to drive below the speed limit, so it is prescriptively normal to drive below the speed limit and prescriptively abnormal to drive at speeds above the limit. In some areas of the world, however, it might be very common (statistically normal) to drive at speeds above the prescribed speed limit – that is, it is statistically normal to drive at speeds above the speed limit and statistically abnormal to drive at speeds below the speed limit. For further discussion, see Bear and Knobe (2017).
[3] Interestingly, there is some evidence that abnormal inflation for statistical norms varies whether this norm violation is a population-level norm violation or an agent-level norm violation (Sytsma 2020, Sytsma et al. 2012). Moreover, some have found that Roxborough and Cumby (2009) fail to replicate Liao and Cova (2017), but more work ought to be done to investigate these variations in findings (Cova et al. 2018).

tations as well – that this is grounds to reject the experimental evidence in the domain of metaphysics (Bernstein 2017).

Others argue, however, that if norms are a core part of our conceptual competence in making causal judgments, then we have no reason to reject just any causal judgment that is affected by normality (Hitchcock and Knobe 2009, Knobe 2010, Knobe and Doris 2010). Instead, we might integrate these findings into more general theories. Because of this disagreement, the cognitive mechanism that produces causal judgments and abnormal inflation is critical to philosophers who work to understand causation. Whether there is some kind of bias at work or whether norms are an essential feature of people's causal conceptual competence seems to affect the extent to which philosophers ought to rely on certain judgments when developing their metaphysical theories.

2.1.1 What Explains the Effect of Normality on Causal Judgments?

As I just explained, it is important for philosophers to understand the cognitive mechanism producing abnormal inflation. So, why does it happen? There are a variety of explanations (Knobe 2010, Willemsen and Kirfel 2019). In this section, I review some of the most widely discussed explanations.

One explanation for abnormal inflation relies on differences in what agents know about the norm violation (Kirfel and Lagnado 2021, Kirfel and Phillips 2022, Samland and Waldmann 2016). On one version of this *epistemic-advantage view*, abnormally-acting agents in these scenarios have an epistemic advantage – that is, the abnormally-acting agent is more inclined to know that the normally-acting agent would perform their action than the normally-acting agent is to know that the abnormally-acting agent would perform their action. And because of the epistemic advantage, people attribute more foresight to the abnormally-acting agent, increasing their causal judgments about that agent (Kirfel and Lagnado 2021).

To see this, consider the pen case from Knobe and Fraser (2008). Professor Smith has an epistemic advantage: he should know that the administrative assistant would take the pen because administrative assistants are allowed to take them. The administrative assistant, on the other hand, does not have such an epistemic advantage – they do not know that the professor would act abnormally and take a pen. Observing this epistemic advantage, people attribute more foresight to the professor, which accounts for the stronger causal judgments about the norm-violating action.

The epistemic advantage view has some strong evidence to support it. In a series of experiments, Kirfel and Lagnado (2021) tested this view. In one experiment, they had participants watch videos of two employees who shared workspace that had two electric appliances in it. They told participants that the company had a policy that using both appliances simultaneously on Friday would produce a power outage. In the videos, one employee used one appliance every day, and the other employee used the appliance either everyday (normal condition) or only on Friday (abnormal condition). In both conditions, both employees used the appliances on Friday, and there was a power outage. Kirfel and Lagnado asked participants to rate the degree to which each agent caused the outage and the degree to which each employee expected the other to act as they did. Participants judged the abnormally-acting agent as more causal then the normally-acting agent. Participants also judged that the abnormally-acting agent had a greater expectation that the normally-acting agent would act relative to the normally-acting agent's expectation that the abnormally-acting agent would act – i.e., the abnormally-acting agent had greater foresight that the power outage would happen if they acted (Experiment 1). In another experiment, Kirfel and Lagnado (2021) also manipulated whether the agents knew about each other's behavior. When neither agent knew about what the other was doing – because they worked in completely different floors of the company building – participants showed no differences in causal judgments between the abnormally-acting and normally-acting agents (Experiment 2). In other words, when there is no epistemic advantage that participants attribute to the abnormally-acting agent, abnormal inflation disappears. This result yields strong evidence in support of the epistemic-advantage view.

Another set of explanations for the effect of norms on causal judgment is what I will refer to as *blame explanations*. These models hold that people's tendency to blame agents for their actions affects their causal judgments about those agents (Alicke 1992, 2000, 2008; Alicke et al. 2011, 2015; Güver and Kneer forthcoming; Rogers et al. 2019). Alicke's culpable-control model in particular puts this cognitive process into a temporal sequence (Alicke 2000). First, people spontaneously evaluate the agent in a scenario negatively or positively. This initial, spontaneous evaluation then stimulates a blame-validation mode of cognitive processing. People who are in this mode of cognitive processing then make judgments about agents' causal role such that their judgments validate the blame or praise that they attributed to the agent who elicited the initial negative or positive evaluation (Alicke 2000; Alicke et al. 2011, 2015).

Blame explanations naturally explain abnormal inflation (Alicke et al. 2011, Rogers et al. 2019). In a famous study, participants read a vignette about John who got into a car accident on his way home (Alicke 1992). Participants either read about John returning home to hide an anniversary gift or to hide cocaine. Consistent with abnormal inflation, people were more inclined to judge John as the cause of the accident when the vignette described him as returning home to hide cocaine than when the vignette described him as returning home to hide an anniversary gift. On this model, people go through a series of processes. First, people react negatively toward John when he plans to hide cocaine and react positively toward John when he plans to hide the anniversary gift. This initial, spontaneous, and negative evaluation of John when wants to hide cocaine stimulates a blame-validation mode of cognitive processing. Participants then identify John's actions as the cause of the accident when he plans to hide cocaine because this causal judgment validates the blame that they attributed to him.

Another prominent explanation for abnormal inflation is the *responsibility account* (Sytsma 2022b). On this view, normative evaluations – like responsibility judgments – are part of what someone considers when they make a causal judgment; so, causal statements – like "X caused Y" – are similar to judgments of responsibility – like "X is responsible for Y" (Sytsma 2022a, 2022b; Sytsma and Livengood 2021). As such, when people, for instance, judge that Professor Smith *caused* the receptionist's problem, they express in part that the agent is responsible for that outcome (Sytsma 2022a).

This account naturally explains abnormal inflation. Because people tend to be responsible for norm violations, causal judgments will show abnormal inflation. Consider again the pen case from above. Professor Smith is more responsible than the administrative assistant because he violated a norm, while the administrative assistant did not. Since causal judgments are in part judgments about responsibility, people judge Professor Smith as more causal, too.

There is some evidence in support of the responsibility account. In a series of studies, Sytsma adapted a case from Hitchcock and Knobe (2009):

> A machine is set up in such a way that it will short circuit if both the black wire and the red wire touch the battery at the same time. The machine will not short circuit if just one of these wires touches the battery. The black wire is designated as the one that is supposed to touch the battery, while the red wire is supposed to remain in some other part of the machine.
>
> One day, the black wire and the red wire both end up touching the battery at the same time. There is a short circuit. (Sytsma 2022a, p. 604)

Not only did he ask for participants' causal judgments about each wire, but he also asked about the responsibility people attributed to both. Participants' judgments of responsibility displayed the abnormal-inflation effect – just like causal judgments – and these two kinds of judgments were correlated (Sytsma 2022a). Importantly, although this vignette was not about agents at all, people still attributed responsibility to the wires. This finding suggests that any finding of abnormal inflation with non-agential stimuli does not mean that responsibility attributions fail to explain the effect. Because people consider responsibility generally when making causal judgments, responsibility attributions can explain abnormal inflation.

One last explanation is the counterfactual explanation. There are a variety of these recent, general accounts that differ in their technical details (Gerstenberg et al. 2021, Halpern and Hitchcock 2015, Icard et al. 2017, Johnson-Laird and Khemlani 2017, Khemlani et al. 2014, Quillien 2020).[4] But the approach of many of these accounts is similar. When people think about whether an event caused some outcome, they imagine that the event had not happened and then ask if the outcome would still have happened in that imagined counterfactual alternative. If it would not have happened, then the event made a difference – it caused the outcome. So, if someone wanted to know if Frank bumping into Dennis' car caused the damages to the interior, they imagine that he had not done so. In that alternative scenario, the damages would not have occurred,

---

4 See the following for helpful comparisons of recent models and data that compares the them: Morris et al. (2019), O'Neill, Henne, Bello, et al. (2022), O'Neill, Henne, Pearson, et al. (2022), Quillien and Barlev (2022).

so Frank's action caused the damages. This simple overview does not explain the intricacies of the case that I discuss above or abnormal inflation, but many of the accounts are adjusted and amended to accommodate these nuances.

One such account, the *necessity-sufficiency model*, was specifically designed to explain abnormal inflation (Icard et al. 2017), and it has recently been extended to account for omissive causation (Henne et al. 2019), late-preemption (Henne, Kulesza, et al. 2021), and double-prevention cases (Henne and O'Neill 2022). This account relies on a widely studied phenomenon: people are more inclined to imagine counterfactual alternatives to abnormal events (Byrne 2016, Kahneman et al. 1982). For instance, when people encounter something abnormal like a person driving while eating cereal, they are more inclined to imagine a normal situation like where someone is just driving – not eating a bowl of cereal. Moreover, the more inclined people are to imagine counterfactual alternatives to an event – where the outcome does not happen in those alternatives – the more causal people judge the event to be. As such, people judge abnormal events to be more causal (Icard et al. 2017).

To see this explanation, consider again the pen case. On the assumptions of necessity-sufficiency model, people are more inclined to imagine Professor Smith not taking a pen – just as he should – than they are to imagine the administrative assistant not taking one. When people consider the counterfactual alterative the Professor Smith's action, people are reminded that Professor Smith taking the pen was necessary for the receptionist's problem, so people judge Professor Smith's action as more causal. People are not inclined to imagine the counterfactual to the administrative assistant's action – the administrative assistant was just acting normally – so people are not more inclined to judge the administrative assistant's action as causal.

The most compelling evidence for the necessity-sufficiency model comes from its novel predictions that are derived from some details of the model (Icard et al. 2017). Without explaining all of the technical details, the necessity-sufficiency model weights two features of a potential cause:

Necessity Strength: the degree to which a potential cause is necessary for the outcome
Sufficiency Strength: the degree to which a potential cause is sufficient for the outcome

The model weights necessity strength by the probability of imagining a counterfactual alternative to it, and it weights sufficiency strength by the probability of imagining what actually happened. As such, if people tend to imagine a counterfactual alternative to a potential cause, there is greater weight on necessity strength, and if people tend to think of the potential cause happening as it did, then there is greater weight on sufficiency strength. As such, the degree to which people consider a potential cause to be the cause of an outcome – or *causal strength* – is the weighted sum of the necessity strength and the sufficiency strength.

The necessity-sufficiency model predicts patterns of causal judgments that vary depending on the causal structure of the situation. At this point, it would be helpful to define two common kinds of causal structures:

Joint-Causation Structures: the potential causes are jointly sufficient and individually necessary for the outcome

Overdetermination: the potential causes are individually sufficient but not individually necessary for the outcome

For joint-causation structures, each potential cause is individually required for the outcome and only jointly sufficient for the outcome. The pen case has a joint-causation structure; Professor Smith's and the administrative assistant's actions were each required for the receptionist's problem, but neither action alone would have brought it about. For overdetermination structures, each potential cause is individually sufficient for the outcome but not individually necessary for the outcome. To see a case of overdetermination, suppose Billy and Suzie throw rocks at a jar at the exact same time with the exact same force, and each rock hitting it would be sufficient for the jar to shatter, but neither alone is necessary because the other rock hitting the jar would shatter it.

With this general framework in mind, the unique predictions of the necessity-sufficiency model follow. First, the model explains abnormal inflation. Recall that the necessity-sufficiency model assumes that people just naturally tend to consider the counterfactuals to abnormal events more than they consider the counterfactuals to normal events (Byrne 2016, Icard et al. 2017). If people are more inclined to consider the counterfactual to an abnormal event, then there is more weight on necessity strength. Hence, in cases of joint causation, there is *abnormal inflation* because the potential cause is necessary and only jointly sufficient for the outcome.

Second, the model explains a new effect that is not predicted by other explanations of abnormal inflation – *abnormal deflation*: in cases of overdetermination, people should judge abnormal events to be *less* causal than normal events. If people just imagine the potential cause happening as it did – when the event is normal – there is greater weight on sufficiency strength. Moreover, if people tend to imagine the counterfactual alternative to the potential cause, there is a lower weight on sufficiency strength. And, in cases of overdetermination, the potential cause is only individually sufficient but not necessary. As such, in cases of overdetermination people should judge abnormal events as *less* causal than normal events – i.e., *abnormal deflation* – because potential causes are not necessary and normal events have greater weight on the sufficiency strength than abnormal events. To see this, consider the Billy and Suzy example above. Suppose though that Billy is terrible at throwing, and he never hits anything. And suppose that Suzy is great at throwing, and she hits anything she aims for. In this case, it seems that Suzy's normal action (i.e., hitting the jar) was relatively more causal than Billy's abnormal action. This is an example of abnormal deflation, and it has been found in many studies (Icard et al. 2017, Morris et al. 2019, O'Neill, Henne,

Bello, et al. 2022, O'Neill, Henne, Pearson, et al. 2022), yielding strong evidence in support of the necessity-sufficiency model, a counterfactual explanation for abnormal inflation.

Experimental philosophers continue to discuss these competing explanations for abnormal inflation, and finding an adequate explanation ought to be the aim of future work in the coming years (Willemsen and Kirfel 2019). Understanding the cognitive processes underlying causal judgments in these cases yields important results relevant to metaphysicians and other philosophers interested in causation and causal modeling (Woodward 2021).

2.2 Omissions

Omissions – absences, failures, non-doings, and nothingness – create many problems for metaphysicians, but they are of special interest to those who work on causation (Bernstein 2015). Some philosophers deny that omissions are causal (Beebee 2004, Dowe 2004, Salmon 1994, Varzi 2007), others accept that omissions are causal (Hitchcock 2007, Lewis 2004, McGrath 2005, Schaffer 2000), and still others think that they are part of the motivation for causal pluralism – where there is both a generative (i.e., productive, transference, or oomphy) and a counterfactual concept of causation (Hall 2004). There is generally disagreement of whether omissions – unlike ordinary positive events and actions – are causal.[5]

While there is a variety of reasons for this disagreement, part of it might result from what I will refer to as the action effect for causal judgment: people tend to judge omissions as less causal than positive events or actions (Henne et al. 2019). To see this tendency, consider a recent article on the action effect (Henne et al. 2019). We gave some participants a vignette that described an action (Henne et al. 2019):

> Tom works for a demolition company, and today he is demolishing a building by implosion.
> The building will implode automatically at 5:00 PM if both the safety switch is off and knob A is switched on.
> At 4:00 PM, the safety switch is off, and knob A is off. At that time, Tom checks to see if knob A is on, and he sees that it's off. So, he changes the position of knob A to the on position.
> Because the building would implode if both the safety switch is off and knob A is switched on, the building implodes at 5:00 PM.

We then asked participants the extent to which they agreed with the following causal statement:

> The building imploded because Tom changed the position of knob A.

---

[5] For discussions of whether and when omissions are causes at all, I point the reader to the following: Beebee (2004), Bernstein (2017), Clarke et al. (2015), Henne et al. (2017), Livengood and Machery (2007).

We gave another group of participants an inaction (omission) version of the same scenario:

> Tom works for a demolition company, and today he is demolishing a building by implosion.
> The building will implode automatically at 5:00 PM if both the safety switch is off and knob A is switched on.
> At 4:00 PM, the safety switch is off, and knob A is on. At that time, Tom checks to see if knob A is on, and he sees that it's on. So, he does not change the position of knob A at all.
> Because the building would implode if both the safety switch is off and knob A is switched on, the building implodes automatically at 5:00 PM.

We then asked these participants to what extent they agreed with the following statement:

> The building imploded because Tom did not change the position of knob A.

Across a range of vignettes just like this one, participants agreed more with the causal statement about the action than with the causal statement about the inaction (Henne et al. 2019).

The action effect for causal judgment has replicated using a range of moral and non-moral vignettes (Cushman and Young 2011, Henne et al. 2019, Jamison et al. 2020, Siegel et al. 2017, Spranca et al. 1991, Walsh and Sloman 2011, Willemsen and Reuter 2016), and the discussion of the effects for causal judgments are critical in the discussion of the omission bias in the moral domain (Handfield et al. 2021). Some recent work, however, suggests that while the action effect occurs when an agent performs the action or omission, the action effect may not occur when patients, or victims, perform an action or omission that is necessary to bring about an outcome (Niemi and Henne 2022).

The action effect might illuminate some of the philosophical disagreement about omissive causation. Just like in the case of abnormal inflation though, experimental philosophers need to understand what explains this pattern of judgments. Understanding the underlying cognitive mechanisms will help determine the warrant for accepting or rejecting these patterns of judgments.

2.2.1 What Explains the Action Effect for Causal Judgments?

There are a few very natural explanations for the action effect in causal judgment. One view is an extension of the responsibility account discussed in Section 2.1.1 (Sytsma 2022b). When investigating abnormal inflation, Sytsma and Livengood (2021) found what seems to be a case of the action effect. In one experiment, they gave some participants a version of a trolley problem where the agent performs an action (Sytsma and Livengood 2021, p. 9):

> A runaway trolley is headed toward five innocent people who are on the track and who will be killed unless something is done. Marcy is too far away to warn the people to get off the track, but she is standing next to a switch that she can flip to redirect the trolley onto a second track. If Marcy flips the switch, the five people on the original track will be saved. However, an innocent bystander is standing on the second track. If Marcy flips the switch, the trolley will hit and kill the bystander.
>
> Marcy flips the switch, redirecting the trolley onto the second track. The trolley hits and kills the bystander, but not the five people.

They gave another set of participants a version of the vignette where the agent refrains from acting and only the last paragraph differs:

> Marcy does not flip the switch and the trolley continues down the original track. The trolley hits and kills the five people, but not the bystander.

In the action version, the authors asked participants the extent to which the agreed with the following statement:

> Marcy caused the death of the bystander.

In the inaction version, the authors asked participants the extent to which they agreed with the following statement:

> Marcy caused the death of the five people.

Consistent with previous work, people agreed more with the causal statement in the action case than with the causal statement in the inaction case (Sytsma and Livengood 2021).

The authors argue that while it might seem that this is an action effect, which is driven by an action-omission difference, a normative difference in the two conditions actually explains the effect in this case (Sytsma and Livengood 2021). Their reasoning is intuitive. People tend to think that the agent ought to switch in bystander trolley-style cases and that it is more appropriate to switch, so they themselves claim that they would switch (Awad et al. 2020). However – Sytsma and Livengood (2021) reason – people would judge agents as more responsible when they got involved in the scenarios and switched the tracks relative to when they did nothing and refrained from acting. Sytsma and Livengood (2021) found exactly this in many of their experiments. As such, people's tendency to attribute more responsibility to the agents who switch is what people express in their agreement with the causal statements (see Section 2.1.1), thus it accounts for the purported action effect.

Sytsma and Livengood (2021) support their view with many experiments. First, the authors run additional studies similar to the experiment described above where they emphasize a positive event (i.e., making a decision). The idea is that if they vary the same conditions in a trolley case but focus on and ask about the agents' decisions rather than an action or inaction, then an action effect fails to explain their findings; rather, the responsibility account explains the findings: people attribute more responsibility when the agent switches and becomes involved in the scenario, and this accounts for the greater causal judgments. Consistently, Sytsma and Livengood (2021) find exactly this result.

Second, Sytsma and Livengood (2021) run an additional study where they vary action and omission without people on the alternative tracks. In the action condition, participants read:

> Tom is walking to the trolley station when he finds himself in a dangerous situation: A runaway trolley is hurtling down the tracks. The only thing that Tom can do is to flip the switch next to him to divert the trolley onto a secondary track, which has a single person on it.
> Tom is faced with a decision:
>
> If he decides to flip the switch, the trolley will be diverted and the person on the secondary track will die.
> If he decides to do nothing, the trolley will not be diverted and will continue along the original track, eventually slowing to a stop with nobody getting hurt.
>
> Tom decides to flip the switch. The trolley is diverted onto the secondary track. The person on the track is hit and dies.

And the authors asked participants for their level of agreement with the following causal statement:

> Tom's decision caused the death of the person on the secondary track.

In the inaction condition, participants read:

> Tom is walking to the trolley station when he finds himself in a dangerous situation: A runaway trolley is hurtling down the tracks toward five people. All five people will be killed if the trolley proceeds on its present course. The only thing that Tom can do is to flip the switch next to him to divert the trolley onto a secondary track, which has nobody on it.
> Tom is faced with a decision:
>
> If he decides to flip the switch, the trolley will be diverted and will continue along the secondary track, eventually slowing to a stop with nobody getting hurt.
> If he decides to do nothing, the trolley will not be diverted and the five people on the original track will die.
>
> Tom decides to do nothing. The trolley proceeds down the original track. The five people on the track are hit and die.

And the authors asked participants for their level of agreement with the following causal statement:

> Tom's decision caused the death of the five people on the original track.

In this experiment, Sytsma and Livengood (2021) actually found no evidence that people judged the agent's decision in the action case as more causal than the agent's decision in the inaction case. The lack of an action effect here, the authors argue, is in line with the responsibility account (Sytsma and Livengood 2021); action and omission difference alone did not produce an action effect in this case. While the authors do not present this as a general account of the action effect – they were discussing causal judgments, norms, and trolley cases – the account can be extended more generally, and more work ought to be done to explore this view.

There is another explanation for the action effect that I will call the *generative explanation* (for discussion, see Henne et al. 2019, Walsh and Sloman 2011). A lot of work on force dynamics in cognitive science (Wolff 2007, Wolff and Thorstad 2017) and on causation as a transference of energy in the philosophy of science (Dowe 2004, Salmon 1994) supports this kind of view. If causal judgments depend on the perception of force interaction, actions are more causal than inactions because actions transfer energy but inactions or omissions do not. Consider the implosion case from the previous section. Tom changing the position of knob A transfers energy that produces the implosion, but Tom not changing the position of knob A does not. As such, Tom's action is more causal than his relevant inaction in the other condition. This kind of explanation is intuitively plausible – and some work has explored force dynamic views with omissive causation (Wolff et al. 2010) – but more work ought to be done to investigate the generative explanation in light of recent findings that challenge it (Henne et al. 2019).

Another explanation relies on counterfactual thinking. There have been a few counterfactual models of omissive causation proposed in recent years (Bello and Khemlani 2015; Gerstenberg and Stephan 2021; Khemlani et al. 2018, 2021). Here, I focus on one that is an extension of the necessity-sufficiency model that I discussed in Section 2.1 (Henne et al. 2019, Icard et al. 2017). Similar to how the model handles norms, the extended necessity-sufficiency model assumes that people tend to imagine the counterfactual alternative to actions more than omissions (Byrne 2016, Byrne and McEleney 2000). This extended model then explains the action effect in a similar way to how the necessity-sufficiency model explains abnormal inflation. In joint-causation cases, there is an action effect because people tend to imagine the counterfactual alternative to actions, and when they do this reminds them that the action is necessary for the outcome, thus increasing the causal strength of the action.

To see this explanation at work, consider again the implosion case. People are more inclined to imagine Tom not changing the position of knob A in the action condition than they are to imagine Tom changing the position of knob A in the inaction condition. Because of this difference in people's tendency to imagine counterfactual alternatives, people who read the action condition are reminded more than those who read the inaction condition that Tom's action was necessary for the outcome. Hence, there is greater causal strength for actions relative to inactions – an action effect.

This counterfactual model's unique predictions for action-inaction differences are the best evidence for it. In cases of overdetermination this extended necessity-sufficiency model predicts that people should actually judge that inactions are *more* causal than actions – i.e., there should be a reverse-action effect (Henne et al. 2019) that parallels the abnormal-deflation effect. The reverse-action effect happens because people tend to imagine the counterfactual alternative to actions, and when they do in cases of overdetermination, this reminds them that the action is not necessary for the outcome at all, thus decreasing the causal strength of the action relative to the inaction (Henne et al. 2019).

To test this unique prediction, my colleagues and I modified the implosion case so that they were about cases of overdetermination rather than joint causation (Henne et al. 2019). One group of participants read the action version of this vignette (Henne et al. 2019):

> Tom works for a demolition company, and today he is demolishing a building by implosion.
> The building will implode automatically at 5:00 PM if either the safety switch is off or knob A is switched on.
> At 4:00 PM, the safety switch is off, and knob A is off. At that time, Tom checks to see if knob A is on, and he sees that it's off. So, he changes the position of knob A to the on position.
> Because the building would implode if either the safety switch is off or knob A is switched on, the building implodes at 5:00 PM.

Another group of participants read an inaction version:

> Tom works for a demolition company, and today he is demolishing a building by implosion.
> The building will implode automatically at 5:00 PM if either the safety switch is off or knob A is switched on.
> At 4:00 PM, the safety switch is off, and knob A is on. At that time, Tom checks to see if knob A is on, and he sees that it's on. So, he does not change the position of knob A at all.
> Because the building would implode if either the safety switch is off or knob A is switched on, the building implodes automatically at 5:00 PM.

The dependent measures were the same as in the joint-causation cases above. Notably, for this vignette and others like it, participants judged inactions to be *more* causal than actions in cases of overdetermination (Henne et al. 2019). This reverse-action effect is uniquely predicted by the counterfactual account, yielding strong evidence in its favor. More work, however, ought to be done to explore whether other models can accommodate this new finding.

2.3 Preemption and Temporality

So far, I have described findings showing that normality and action-omission differences affect causal judgments. Time also affects causal judgments; that is, the temporal ordering of events – i.e., potential causes – seems to affect the extent to which people think that the events are a cause of the outcome. Consider a case:

> Billy and Suzie would win a bet only if both hit a homerun during the baseball game. Billy hit one out of the park in the first inning, and Suzie did so at the bottom of the ninth. So, they won the bet.

In this example, it seems that Suzie hitting a homerun in the ninth inning caused them to win the bet – at least her homerun in the last inning seems more causal than Billy's in the first. As my students and I put it, "[t]his [kind of apparent] difference in judgments is an example of the recency effect for causal judgment: in cases of joint-causation, people tend to judge that recent events are more causal than earlier ones" (Henne, Kulesza, et al. 2021, p. 1; Lagnado and Channon 2008; Reuter et al. 2014; Spellman 1997; Ziano and Pandelaere 2022).

The temporal order of events also affects people's causal judgments when the causal structure is different. Consider a case of overdetermination – specifically a case of so-called late-preemption. In these cases, "two events occur; each event is individually sufficient but not individually necessary for the outcome; if the first event failed to bring about the outcome, then the second would have brought it about; and the first event brings about the outcome" (Henne, Kulesza, et al. 2021, p. 2; see also Paul and Hall 2013). Consider a case in this causal structure:

> Billy and Suzie would win a bet if either hit a homerun during the baseball game. Billy hit one out of the park in the first inning, and Suzie did so at the bottom of the ninth. So, they won the bet.

In this example, it seems that Billy hitting a homerun in the first inning caused them to win the bet – at least his homerun in the first inning seems more causal than Suzie's in the last. As my students and I put it, "[t]his [kind of apparent] apparent difference in judgments is an example of […] the primacy effect for causal judgment: in cases of overdetermination – specifically cases of late-preemption – people tend to judge that earlier events are more causal than recent ones" (Chang 2009; Henne, Kulesza, et al. 2021, p. 1; Lombrozo 2010; Walsh and Sloman 2011).

While the recency effect has not be directly investigated much by experimental philosophers (cf. Henne, Kulesza, et al. 2021, Reuter et al. 2014), the primacy effect – i.e., the pattern of judgments in cases of late preemption – has been investigated by experimental philosophers because these cases have important consequences for counterfactual theories of causation and causal pluralism (Lombrozo 2010). In a foundational study on late-preemption judgments, Lombrozo gave participants vignettes like the following:

> Alice, Bob, and Carol have spent the afternoon juggling and listening to music. At the moment, Alice and Carol are juggling and the music is not playing. Alice wants to listen to music, so she deliberately throws a juggling ball, which heads straight for the stereo's "on" button. Meanwhile, Bob switches on his laptop to check his e-mail. And at the same time, Carol decides she wants to listen to music, so she also deliberately throws a juggling ball, which heads straight for the stereo's "on" button. Alice happens to throw first and her juggling ball reaches the stereo's "on" button before Carol's ball does. As a result of these events, the music starts to play. (Lombrozo 2010, p. 311)

Across a range of conditions, participants judged that Alice throwing her ball – the first action – caused the music to start (Lombrozo 2010). This finding of the primacy effect is consistent with metaphysicians' judgments in late-preemption cases (Paul and Hall 2013).

An explanation for the primacy effect is crucial for philosophers of causation because late-preemption cases famously cause trouble for counterfactual accounts of causation and causal cognition (Gerstenberg et al. 2021; Lewis 1987, 2004; Paul and Hall 2013). Specifically, cases of late preemption suggest that counterfactual thinking is not necessary for causation. Because of this trouble, there is doubt whether counterfactual accounts can explain causal judgments at all.

To see this trouble, consider how counterfactual accounts handle the primacy effect. Recall that counterfactual accounts say that when people make causal judgments, they imagine the counterfactual alternative to the potential cause, ask if the outcome come would have happened in that alternative scenario, and then determine if that potential cause made a difference to the outcome. In cases of late preemption, if people imagine that the event that happened earlier had not happened, then the outcome still would have happened; the later event alone would be sufficient to produce it. So, it seems that the earlier event did not make a difference. But, as I mentioned, philosophers and non-philosophers make judgments in line with the primacy effect – that the event that happened earlier caused the outcome (Henne, Kulesza, et al. 2021, Lombrozo 2010, Paul and Hall 2013).

For a concrete example, consider the overdetermination variation of the baseball case from above. It seems that Billy hitting a homerun in the first inning caused them to win the bet. When people make this judgment on a counterfactual account, people imagine that Billy had not hit a homerun at all. In this alternative scenario, however, Billy and Suzie still would have won the bet because Suzie hit a homerun in the ninth inning. Even though his homerun did not seem to make a difference to the outcome, it seems that Billy hitting a homerun in the first inning caused them to win the bet. In other words, the counterfactual account seems unable to explain causal judgments here – and maybe more generally.[6]

2.3.1 What Explains the Effect of Temporality on Causal Judgments?

Given the importance to metaphysicians and philosophers of science, we ought to know what explains the recency and primacy effects. We might also wonder whether there are distinct explanations for each effect or if there is a unified explanation for both.

A common approach to explaining cases of late preemption – the primacy effect – is causal pluralism (Hall 2004, Lombrozo 2010). If the primacy effect is pervasive in cases of late preemption, then we might assume that counterfactual thinking is not nec-

---

6 This discussion is based on the background discussion from Henne, Kulesza, and colleagues (2021).

essary for causal judgments. But rather than thinking that the primacy effect undermines the relationship between causal judgments and counterfactual thinking altogether, some take late-preemption cases – among cases of causation by omission and double prevention – to motivate causal pluralism, where there are two concepts of causation (Hall 2004). Some posit that there is both a productive – or generative (see Section 2.2.1) – concept of causation and a counterfactual concept (Hall 2004, Lombrozo 2010). On this view, people sometimes employ the generative concept – like in cases of late preemption – and other times a counterfactual one – like in cases involving omissions. Such pluralist views can accommodate a wide range of cases like preemption.

But the cases of late preemption might not be detrimental to counterfactual views altogether. Some philosophers and cognitive scientists have tried to explore ways for counterfactual view to accommodate these important cases (Gerstenberg et al. 2021, Henne, Kulesza, et al. 2021).

Recently, my students and I did just this (Henne, Kulesza, et al. 2021). We extended the necessity-sufficiency model (see Section 2.1.1) to explain both the recency and primacy effects (Henne, Kulesza, et al. 2021). To recall, the original necessity-sufficiency model that was designed to explain abnormal inflation assumed that people are more inclined to imagine counterfactual alternatives to abnormal events (Icard et al. 2017). As I described in Section 2.2.1, my colleagues and I extended this model to omissions (Henne et al. 2019) to explain the action effect by adding the assumption that people are more inclined to consider the counterfactual alternative to actions than to inactions or omissions. In our recent work (Henne, Kulesza, et al. 2021), we extended this model to incorporate another established finding in cognitive science: people are more inclined to imagine counterfactual alternatives to more recent events than to earlier events (Byrne et al. 2000, Henne, Kulesza, et al. 2021, Meehan and Byrne 2005, Miller and Gunasegaram 1990, Segura et al. 2002, Walsh and Byrne 2004).

With this critical assumption, this extended version of the necessity-sufficiency model explains both the recency and primacy effect. The extended model critically assumes that – regardless of causal structure – people tend to imagine the counterfactual alternative to the more recent event (Henne, Kulesza, et al. 2021). In joint-causation structures, the extended model explains the recency effect similarly to how it explains abnormal inflation and the action effect. People's simulations of the imagined alternative to the recent event remind people that the recent event made a difference. As such, there is a recency effect. In the language of the model, an increase in the weight of the necessity strength of the recent event accounts for the recency effect. In cases of overdetermination, the extended model explains the primacy effect similarly to how it explains abnormal deflation and the reverse-action effect. People's simulations of the imagined alternative to the recent event show that the recent event did not make a difference. As such, there is a primacy effect. In the language of the model, a decrease in the weight of the sufficiency strength of the recent event accounts for the primacy effect. In our experiments, my students and I manipulated people's counterfactual thinking and found that it affected the recency and primacy effect in just the ways predicted by the extended necessity-sufficiency model (Henne, Kulesza, et al. 2021), yielding further evidence for this counterfactual model and – critically – for a counterfactual explanation for judgments in late-preemption cases. As such, we might not have to abandon counterfactual accounts of causal judgment simply because of the patterns of judgments in late-preemption cases. More work ought to explore whether any other models can explain these new findings for experimental philosophers.[7]

2.4 Double Prevention

Another critical case for philosophers of causation are cases of double prevention (Paul and Hall 2013). In these cases, an event happens, and a would-be preventer is prevented from preventing the initial event from bringing about the outcome, which allows the outcome to happen. To see this concretely, consider the following vignette, a standard case of double prevention:

> Mike, Jack, and Peter were at a party, and there was an open bottle of beer on the table.
> Mike turned around and accidentally knocked against the bottle.
> Jack saw that the bottle was about to fall. It was easily within his reach. Jack was just about to catch the bottle when Peter accidentally knocked against him, making Jack unable to catch the bottle.
> Jack didn't manage to grab the bottle, and it fell to the ground and spilled. (Henne and O'Neill 2022, p. 5)

In this double-prevention case, the outcome – the bottle spilling – counterfactually depends on multiple actions. If Mike had not knocked into the bottle, it would not have spilled. If Peter had not knocked into Jack, it would not have spilled. But Mike knocking into the bottle seems to cause it to spill, while Peter knocking into Jack does not. Philosophers and non-philosophers alike show this double-prevention effect (Chang 2009, Henne and O'Neill 2022, Lombrozo 2010, Paul and Hall 2013): that is, people agree that the productive factor (like Mike knocking into the bottle) is more causal than the double preventer (like Peter knocking into Jack) – even though if either event did not happen the outcome would not have happened, too.

Double-prevention cases are a critical, famous counterexample to counterfactual accounts (Hall 2004, Paul 2010a, Paul and Hall 2013, Woodward 2012). People show the double-prevention effect, but counterfactual accounts have no immediate way to explain this difference in people's causal judgments; the outcome counterfactually depends on both the productive factor and the double preventer, but people judge that the productive factor, but not the double preventer, caused the outcome. In other words, counterfactual models seem insufficient to explain causal judgments.

---

[7] Interested readers should also explore Spellman's Crediting Causality Model (Spellman 1997) and the recent discussion of this model in light of recent findings (Henne, Kulesza, et al. 2021).

2.4.1 What Explains the Double-Prevention Effect for Causal Judgments?

Researchers note that double-prevention cases are critical because it seems that counterfactual theories – one of the most reliable, general accounts of causal judgments – fail to explain the double-prevention effect (Hall 2004, Lombrozo 2010). The patterns of judgments in response to these cases show that counterfactuals are insufficient for causation; the outcome is counterfactually dependent on both the productive factor and the double preventer, but it seems that the productive factor causes the outcome while the double preventer does not.

A very natural explanation for the double-prevention effect is a form of the generative explanation that I mentioned in Section 2.2.1. On this explanation, the reason people judge the productive factor as more causal than the double preventer is because the productive factor transfers force to the outcome, while the double preventer does not at all transfer force. Mike knocking into the bottle transfers force to the bottle that results in the bottle spilling, so it causes the bottle to spill. Peter knocking Jack, however, does not transfer force to the bottle at all, so this event is not a cause of the bottle spilling.

In seeing this intuition about the transference of energy or force, some have also taken this case as motivation for causal pluralism (Hall 2004, Lombrozo 2010). That is, when people judge that the productive factor caused the outcome, they are employing a generative concept of causation, and other times people are employing a counterfactual concept of causation. To support this kind of pluralism, Lombrozo (2010) ran experiments using double-prevention cases where the agents acted intentionally or unintentionally. In one experiment, where the agents acted unintentionally (as in the example above), there was a double-prevention effect. But when the agents acted intentionally, there was no evidence for a double-prevention effect: people judged both the productive factor and the double preventer to be the cause of the outcome. On this view, people who encounter unintentional double-prevention cases tend to think about mechanisms and force dynamics involved in what I have described as the generative explanation. Intentionality attributions, however, prompt people to think teleologically, thus invoking a counterfactual concept (Lombrozo 2010). On this account, causal judgment – in double-prevention cases and more generally – involves both a generative and a counterfactual concept of causation – only if the relation between events is described mechanistically, there is greater weight on the generative concept, and if it is described teleologically, there is greater weight on the counterfactual concept.

Some have argued, however, that there may be a way to explain double-prevention cases in terms of counterfactual thinking alone – avoiding pluralism altogether (Gerstenberg et al. 2021, Henne and O'Neill 2022, Lombrozo 2010, Woodward 2006). This important case for causal judgments in metaphysics and philosophy of science deserves more attention in the coming years.

2.5 New Issues

In the above sections, I highlighted some of the core issues in the philosophy of causation that experimental philosophers have been working on for the last two decades. In the coming years, it will be critical to determine which explanation that I mentioned (or some other explanation) can account for all of these findings. The recent attempts to unify explanations of causal judgment on counterfactual models (Gerstenberg et al. 2021), responsibility accounts (Sytsma 2022b), epistemic advantage views (Kirfel and Lagnado 2021), or something else is one of the critical tasks for experimental philosophers of causation in the coming years.

But there are many new areas in the experimental philosophy of causation that have an impact on these unifying explanations and other philosophical puzzles. The study of causation involves many cases and complex structures, and it affects many areas of philosophy. So, experimental philosophers of causation are now exploring many of these issue like compositionality (Bauer and Kornmesser 2023, Bauer and Romann 2022, Livengood and Sytsma 2020), some applied issues for causal judgment like the exclusion problem in philosophy of mind (Blanchard et al. 2021), and some concepts that are thought to affect causal cognition like sensitivity (Blanchard et al. 2018, Vasilyeva et al. 2018), and they are expanding this work to better understand the relationship between causal judgment and moral judgment (Engelmann and Waldmann 2022). Experimental philosophers are also using new methods like corpus analysis (Sytsma et al. 2019), implicit causality measurements (Niemi et al. 2020), and memory techniques (Henne et al. 2017) to investigate these issues. Some of these areas and new methods deserve more attention in the coming years.

More recently experimental philosophers of causation have started to explore whether differences in linguistic constructions of causal statements affect causal judgments (Rose et al. 2021, Schwenkler and Sievers 2022, Siegal et al. 2021). It turns out that they do – and in some really critical cases.

In one recent series of studies on this issue, the authors rely on some distinctions from linguistics and some linguistic observations from previous studies in experimental philosophy (Rose et al. 2021). The authors hold that it is common for people not to use the word "cause" when making causal judgments; instead, they frequently use the simple causal verbs like "spill" – as in "Shaun spilled the wine." But the authors note that experimental philosophers often ask about the periphrastic construction using the verb "cause" – as in "Shaun caused the wine to spill." The authors suggest that the simple causal verbs like "spill" might involve a generative concept of causation, while the periphrastic constructions that experimental philosophers often rely on might involve a counterfactual concept (Rose et al. 2021). As such, it is critical to investigate these distinct linguistic constructions.

The authors provide a number of pieces of evidence in support of their account (Rose et al. 2021). In one experiment on omissions, Rose and Colleagues asked participants to read a series of vignettes like the following:

> Jane is spending the afternoon at the beach. Typically, she wears sunscreen when she is on the beach but today she forgets to bring any. As a result, her skin becomes burned. (Rose et al. 2021, p. 3)

They then asked participants the extent to which they agreed or disagreed with a number of causal statements about the scenarios like the following:

(1) The lack of sunscreen caused Jane's skin to burn.
(2) The lack of sunscreen burned Jane's skin.
(3) The sun caused Jane's skin to burn.
(4) The sun burned Jane's skin.

Importantly, statements (1) and (2) are about omissions, while (3) and (4) are not, and statements (1) and (3) are periphrastic constructions (i.e., using the verb "caused"), while (2) and (4) are simple causatives (i.e., using the verb "burned"). Critically, the authors found a difference in judgments as a result of the varying linguistic constructions. People showed an action effect for the simple constructions – i.e., people agreed more with statements like (4) than those like (2). They also found no evidence of an action effect for the periphrastic constructions – i.e., there was no evidence that people agreed more with statements like (3) than those like (1) (Rose et al. 2021).[8]

These findings and others might suggest that the periphrastic constructions that experimental philosophers have used involve a counterfactual concept of causation, while the simple causal constructions that people typically use involve a generative concept (Rose et al. 2021); Rose and colleagues find an action effect with these simple causal constructions (see Section 2.2.1 for a discussion of the generative explanation of the action effect). Regardless of what these findings show or what inferences we can draw from them, this is a major developing challenge for experimental philosophers of causation, and future work must respond to it.

3 Further Topics

In this chapter, I focused on a narrow part of the burgeoning field of experimental metaphysics. While there is still a lot of work to do on the topic of causation (Rose and Danks 2012, Willemsen and Wiegmann 2022), there is much more work that has been done and much more to be done in experimental metaphysics.

Any reader who is interested in further exploring experimental metaphysics will first want to explore the work in Rose's (2017) *Experimental Metaphysics*. Rose's volume explores not only some core issues in this field but also some of the metaphilosophical

---

[8] Notably, this finding differs from some previous work that found the action effect (see Section 2.2). Some may wonder if this finding has to do with differences about asking about events as opposed to objects or whether there are normative factors in the vignettes that the authors used. More work should be done to explore why there is no action effect here.

issues about the use of experimental evidence in metaphysical theorizing. Anyone interested in experimental metaphysics should engage with these metaphilosophical issues (Cappelen 2012; Deutsch 2010, 2015; Goldman 1987, 2010; Goldman and McLaughlin 2019; Kneer et al. 2021; Machery 2017; Novick 2017; Paul 2010b, 2016; Rose 2019; Rose and Danks 2013; Schaffer 2019; Thomasson 2012; Thomasson et al. 2017; Williamson 2016; Woodward 2014).

There are also many issues in experimental metaphysics that deserve more exploration. Growing topics of interest to experimental metaphysicians include mereology (Rose and Schaffer 2017), persistence (Rose et al. 2020), essentialism (Joo and Yousif 2022; Neufeld 2021; Ritchie and Knobe 2020; Rose and Nichols 2019, 2020), teleology and explanation (Joo et al. 2021, 2022; Liquin and Lombrozo 2018), simplicity and explanation (Bonawitz and Lombrozo 2012, Lombrozo 2007, Lombrozo and Vasilyeva 2017, Pacer and Lombrozo 2017, Vrantsidis and Lombrozo 2022), personal identity (Finlay and Starmans 2022, Starmans and Bloom 2018, Strohminger et al. 2017, Strohminger and Nichols 2014, Tobia 2022), counterfactual plausibility (De Brigard et al. 2021, Stanley et al. 2017), the perception of possibility (Guan and Firestone 2020) and shape (Morales et al. 2020), time (Latham et al. 2020b, 2020a, 2021; Latham and Miller 2020, 2022; Norton 2021), and much more. And there is plenty of work to do as more experimental metaphysicians move to use new methods (Chartrand 2022) and do cross-cultural studies (Hannikainen et al. 2019, Rose 2020).

Bibliography

Alicke, Mark (1992): "Culpable causation", *Journal of Personality and Social Psychology* 63 (3), pp. 368–378.
Alicke, Mark (2000): "Culpable control and the psychology of blame", *Psychological Bulletin* 126 (4), pp. 556–574.
Alicke, Mark (2008): "Blaming badly", *Journal of Cognition and Culture* 8 (1–2), pp. 179–186.
Alicke, Mark, David Mandel, Denis Hilton, Tobias Gerstenberg, and David Lagnado (2015): "Causal conceptions in social explanation and moral evaluation. A historical tour", *Perspectives on Psychological Science* 10 (6), pp. 790–812.
Alicke, Mark, David Rose, and Dori Bloom (2011): "Causation, norm violation, and culpable control", *The Journal of Philosophy* 108 (12), pp. 670–696.
Awad, Edmond, Sohan Dsouza, Azim Shariff, Iyad Rahwan, and Jean-François Bonnefon (2020): "Universals and variations in moral decisions made in 42 countries by 70,000 participants", *Proceedings of the National Academy of Sciences* 117 (5), pp. 2332–2337.
Bauer, Alexander Max, and Stephan Kornmesser (2023): "Poisoned babies, shot fathers, and ruined impairments. Experimental evidence in favor of the compositionality constraint of actual causation", *Philosophy of Science* 90, pp. 489–517.
Bauer, Alexander Max, and Jan Romann (2022): "Answers at gunpoint. On Livengood and Sytsma's revolver case", *Philosophy of Science* 89 (1), pp. 180–192.
Bear, Adam, and Joshua Knobe (2017): "Normality. Part descriptive, part prescriptive", *Cognition* 167, pp. 25–37.
Beebee, Helen (2004): "Causing and nothingness", in: John Collins, Ned Hall, and Laurie Paul (Eds.): *Causation and counterfactuals*. Cambridge and London: The MIT Press, pp. 291–308.

Bello, Paul, and Sangeet Khemlani (2015): "A model-based theory of omissive causation", in: David Noelle, Rick Dale, Anne Warlaumont, Jeff Yoshimi, Teenie Matlock, Carolyn Jennings, and Paul Maglio (Eds.): *Proceedings of the 37th annual conference of the cognitive science society*. Red Hook: Curran, pp. 214–219.

Bernstein, Sara (2015): "The metaphysics of omissions", *Philosophy Compass* 10 (3), pp. 208–218.

Bernstein, Sara (2017): "Intuitions and the metaphysics of causation", in: David Rose (Ed.): *Experimental metaphysics*. London: Bloomsbury, pp. 75–95.

Blanchard, Thomas, Dylan Murray, and Tania Lombrozo (2021): "Experiments on causal exclusion", *Mind & Language* 37 (5), pp. 1067–1089.

Blanchard, Thomas, and Jonathan Schaffer (2017): "Cause without default", in: Helen Beebee, Christopher Hitchcock, and Huw Price (Eds.): *Making a difference*. Oxford: Oxford University Press, pp. 175–214.

Blanchard, Thomas, Nadya Vasilyeva, and Tania Lombrozo (2018): "Stability, breadth and guidance", *Philosophical Studies* 175 (9), pp. 2263–2283.

Bonawitz, Elizabeth Baraff, and Tania Lombrozo (2012): "Occam's rattle. Children's use of simplicity and probability to constrain inference", *Developmental Psychology* 48 (4), pp. 1156–1164.

Byrne, Ruth (2016): "Counterfactual thought", *Annual Review of Psychology* 67 (1), pp. 135–157.

Byrne, Ruth, and Alice McEleney (2000): "Counterfactual thinking about actions and failures to act", *Journal of Experimental Psychology – Learning, Memory, and Cognition* 26 (5), pp. 1318–1331.

Byrne, Ruth, Susana Segura, Ronan Culhane, Alessandra Tasso, and Pablo Berrocal (2000): "The temporality effect in counterfactual thinking about what might have been", *Memory & Cognition* 28 (2), pp. 264–281.

Cappelen, Herman (2012): *Philosophy without intuitions*. Oxford: Oxford University Press.

Chang, Winston (2009): "Connecting counterfactual and physical causation", *Proceedings of the Annual Meeting of the Cognitive Science Society* 31, pp. 1983–1987.

Chartrand, Louis (2022): "Modeling and corpus methods in experimental philosophy", *Philosophy Compass* 17 (6), e12837.

Clarke, Randolph, Joshua Shepherd, John Stigall, Robyn Repko Waller, and Chris Zarpentine (2015): "Causation, norms, and omissions. A study of causal judgments", *Philosophical Psychology* 28 (2), pp. 279–293.

Cova, Florian, Brent Strickland, Angela Abatista, Aurélien Allard, James Andow, Mario Attie, James Beebe, Renatas Berniūnas, Jordane Boudesseul, Matteo Colombo, Fiery Cushman, Rodrigo Díaz, Noah N'Djaye Nikolai van Dongen, Vilius Dranseika, Brian Earp, Antonio Gaitán Torres, Ivar Hannikainen, José Hernández-Conde, Wenjia Hu, François Jaquet, Kareem Khalifa, Hanna Kim, Markus Kneer, Joshua Knobe, Miklos Kurthy, Anthony Lantian, Shen-Yi Liao, Edouard Machery, Tania Moerenhout, Christian Mott, Mark Phelan, Jonathan Phillips, Navin Rambharose, Kevin Reuter, Felipe Romero, Paulo Sousa, Jan Sprenger, Emile Thalabard, Kevin Tobia, Hugo Viciana, Daniel Wilkenfeld, and Xiang Zhou (2018): "Estimating the reproducibility of experimental philosophy", *Review of Philosophy and Psychology* 12, pp. 9–44.

Cushman, Fiery, and Liane Young (2011): "Patterns of moral judgment derive from nonmoral psychological representations", *Cognitive Science* 35 (6), pp. 1052–1075.

Danks, David, David Rose, and Edouard Machery (2014): "Demoralizing causation", *Philosophical Studies* 171 (2), pp. 251–277.

De Brigard, Felipe, Paul Henne, and Matthew Stanley (2021): "Perceived similarity of imagined possible worlds affects judgments of counterfactual plausibility", *Cognition* 209, 104574.

Deutsch, Max (2010): "Intuitions, counter-examples, and experimental philosophy", *Review of Philosophy and Psychology* 1 (3), pp. 447–460.

Deutsch, Max (2015): *The myth of the intuitive. Experimental philosophy and philosophical method*. Cambridge and London: The MIT Press.

Dowe, Phil (2004): "Causation and misconnections", *Philosophy of Science* 71 (5), pp. 926–931.

Engelmann, Neele, and Michael Waldmann (2022): "How causal structure, causal strength, and foreseeability affect moral judgments", *Cognition* 226, 105167.

Finlay, Melissa, and Christina Starmans (2022): "Not the same same. Distinguishing between similarity and identity in judgments of change", *Cognition* 218, 104953.

Gerstenberg, Tobias, Noah Goodman, David Lagnado, and Joshua Tenenbaum (2021): "A counterfactual simulation model of causal judgments for physical events", *Psychological Review* 128 (5), pp. 936–975.

Gerstenberg, Tobias, and Thomas Icard (2020): "Expectations affect physical causation judgments", *Journal of Experimental Psychology – General* 149 (3), pp. 599–607.

Gerstenberg, Tobias, and Simon Stephan (2021): "A counterfactual simulation model of causation by omission", *Cognition* 216, 104842.

Gill, Maureen, Jonathan Kominsky, Thomas Icard, and Joshua Knobe (2022): "An interaction effect of norm violations on causal judgment", *Cognition* 228, 105183.

Goldman, Alvin (1987): "Cognitive science and metaphysics", *The Journal of Philosophy* 84 (10), pp. 537–544.

Goldman, Alvin (2010): "Philosophical naturalism and intuitional methodology", *Proceedings and Addresses of the American Philosophical Association* 84 (2), pp. 115–150.

Goldman, Alvin, and Brian McLaughlin (2019): *Metaphysics and cognitive science.* Oxford: Oxford University Press.

Guan, Chenxiao, and Chaz Firestone (2020): "Seeing what's possible. Disconnected visual parts are confused for their potential wholes", *Journal of Experimental Psychology – General* 149 (3), pp. 590–598.

Güver, Levin, and Markus Kneer (forthcoming): "Causation and the silly norm effect", in: Stefan Magen and Karolina Prochownik (Eds.): *Advances in experimental philosophy of law.* London: Bloomsbury.

Hall, Ned (2004): "Two concepts of causation", in: John Collins, Ned Hall, and Laurie Ann Paul (Eds.): *Causation and counterfactuals.* Cambridge and London: The MIT Press, pp. 225–276.

Halpern, Joseph, and Christopher Hitchcock (2015): "Graded causation and defaults", *The British Journal for the Philosophy of Science* 66 (2), pp. 413–457.

Handfield, Toby, John Thrasher, Andrew Corcoran, and Shaun Nichols (2021): "Asymmetry and symmetry of acts and omissions in punishment, norms, and judged causality", *Judgment and Decision Making* 16 (4), pp. 796–822.

Hannikainen, Ivar, Edouard Machery, David Rose, Stephen Stich, Christopher Olivola, Paulo Sousa, Florian Cova, Emma Buchtel, Mario Alai, Adriano Angelucci, Renatas Berniūnas, Amita Chatterjee, Hyundeuk Cheon, In-Rae Cho, Daniel Cohnitz, Vilius Dranseika, Ángeles Eraña Lagos, Laleh Ghadakpour, Maurice Grinberg, Takaaki Hashimoto, Amir Horowitz, Evgeniya Hristova, Yasmina Jraissati, Veselina Kadreva, Kaori Karasawa, Hackjin Kim, Yeonjeong Kim, Minwoo Lee, Carlos Mauro, Masaharu Mizumoto, Sebastiano Moruzzi, Jorge Ornelas, Barbara Osimani, Carlos Romero, Alejandro Rosas López, Massimo Sangoi, Andrea Sereni, Sarah Songhorian, Noel Struchiner, Vera Tripodi, Naoki Usui, Alejandro Vázquez del Mercado, Hrag Vosgerichian, Xueyi Zhang, and Jing Zhu (2019): "For whom does determinism undermine moral responsibility? Surveying the conditions for free will across cultures", *Frontiers in Psychology* 10, 2428.

Henne, Paul, Aleksandra Kulesza, Karla Perez, and Augustana Hewali (2021): "Counterfactual thinking and recency effects in causal judgment", *Cognition* 212, 104708.

Henne, Paul, Laura Niemi, Ángel Pinillos, Felipe De Brigard, and Joshua Knobe (2019): "A counterfactual explanation for the action effect in causal judgment", *Cognition* 190, pp. 157–164.

Henne, Paul, and Kevin O'Neill (2022): "Double prevention, causal judgments, and counterfactuals", *Cognitive Science* 46 (5), e13127.

Henne, Paul, Kevin O'Neill, Paul Bello, Sangeet Khemlani, and Felipe De Brigard (2021): "Norms affect prospective causal judgments", *Cognitive Science* 45 (1), e12931.

Henne, Paul, Ángel Pinillos, and Felipe De Brigard (2017): "Cause by omission and norm. Not watering plants", *Australasian Journal of Philosophy* 95 (2), pp. 270–283.

Hitchcock, Christopher (2007): "Prevention, preemption, and the principle of sufficient reason", *The Philosophical Review* 116 (4), pp. 495–532.

Hitchcock, Christopher, and Joshua Knobe (2009): "Cause and norm", *The Journal of Philosophy* 106 (11), pp. 587–612.

Icard, Thomas, Jonathan Kominsky, and Joshua Knobe (2017): "Normality and actual causal strength", *Cognition* 161, pp. 80–93.

Jamison, John, Tijen Yay, and Gilad Feldman (2020): "Action–inaction asymmetries in moral scenarios. Replication of the omission bias examining morality and blame with extensions linking to causality, intent, and regret", *Journal of Experimental Social Psychology* 89, 103977.

Johnson-Laird, Philip, and Sangeet Khemlani (2017): "Mental models and causation", in: Michael Waldmann (Ed.): *The Oxford handbook of causal reasoning*. Oxford: Oxford University Press, pp. 169–187.

Joo, Sehrang, and Sami Yousif (2022): "Are we teleologically essentialist?", *Cognitive Science* 46 (11), e13202.

Joo, Sehrang, Sami Yousif, and Frank Keil (2022): "Understanding 'why'. How implicit questions shape explanation preferences", *Cognitive Science* 46 (2), e13091.

Joo, Sehrang, Sami Yousif, and Joshua Knobe (2021): "Teleology beyond explanation", *Mind & Language*.

Kahneman, Daniel, Paul Slovic, and Amos Tversky (1982): *Judgment under uncertainty. Heuristics and biases.* Cambridge: Cambridge University Press.

Keen, Richie (2012): *Reynolds vs. Reynolds. The cereal defense.* Written by Charlie Day, Glenn Howerton, and Rob McElhenney. Season 8, Episode 10 of *It's Always Sunny in Philadelphia.*

Khemlani, Sangeet, Aron Barbey, and Philip Johnson-Laird (2014): "Causal reasoning with mental models", *Frontiers in Human Neuroscience* 8, 849.

Khemlani, Sangeet, Paul Bello, Gordon Briggs, Hillary Harner, and Christina Wasylyshyn (2021): "Much ado about nothing. The mental representation of omissive relations", *Frontiers in Psychology* 11, 609658.

Khemlani, Sangeet, Christina Wasylyshyn, Gordon Briggs, and Paul Bello (2018): "Mental models and omissive causation", *Memory & Cognition* 46 (8), pp. 1344–1359.

Kirfel, Lara, and David Lagnado (2021): "Causal judgments about atypical actions are influenced by agents' epistemic states", *Cognition* 212, 104721.

Kirfel, Lara, and Jonathan Scott Phillips (2022): *The pervasive impact of ignorance.* Manuscript.

Kneer, Markus, David Colaço, Joshua Alexander, and Edouard Machery (2021): "On second thought. Reflections on the reflection defense", in: Tania Lombrozo, Joshua Knobe, and Shaun Nichols (Eds.): *Oxford studies in experimental philosophy*. Vol. 4. Oxford: Oxford University Press, pp. 257–296.

Knobe, Joshua (2010): "Person as scientist, person as moralist", *Behavioral and Brain Sciences* 33 (4), pp. 315–329.

Knobe, Joshua, and John Doris (2010): "Responsibilitys", in: John Doris (Ed.): *The moral psychology handbook*. Oxford: Oxford University Press, pp. 321–354.

Knobe, Joshua, and Ben Fraser (2008): "Causal judgment and moral judgment. Two experiments", in: Walter Sinnott-Armstrong (Ed.): *Moral psychology. Vol. 2. The cognitive science of morality. Intuition and diversity.* Cambridge: The MIT Press, pp. 441–447.

Knobe, Joshua, and Zoltán Gendler Szabó (2013): "Modals with a taste of the deontic", *Semantics & Pragmatics* 6, pp. 1–42.

Kominsky, Jonathan, and Jonathan Phillips (2019): "Immoral professors and malfunctioning tools. Counterfactual relevance accounts explain the effect of norm violations on causal selection", *Cognitive Science* 43 (11), e12792.

Kominsky, Jonathan, Jonathan Phillips, Tobias Gerstenberg, David Lagnado, and Joshua Knobe (2015): "Causal superseding", *Cognition* 137, pp. 196–209.

Lagnado, David, and Shelley Channon (2008): "Judgments of cause and blame. The effects of intentionality and foreseeability", *Cognition* 108 (3), pp. 754–770.

Latham, Andrew, and Kristie Miller (2020): "Time in a one-instant world", *Ratio* 33 (3), pp. 145–154.

Latham, Andrew, and Kristie Miller (2022): "Are the folk functionalists about time?", *The Southern Journal of Philosophy* 60 (2), pp. 221–248.

Latham, Andrew, Kristie Miller, and James Norton (2020a): "An empirical investigation of purported passage phenomenology", *The Journal of Philosophy* 117 (7), pp. 353–386.

Latham, Andrew, Kristie Miller, and James Norton (2020b): "Do the folk represent time as essentially dynamical?", *Inquiry*.

Latham, Andrew, Kristie Miller, and James Norton (2021): "An empirical investigation of the role of direction in our concept of time", *Acta Analytica* 36 (1), pp. 25–47.

Lewis, David (1974): "Causation", *The Journal of Philosophy* 70 (17), pp. 556–567.

Lewis, David (1987): *Philosophical papers*. Vol. 2. New York and Oxford: Oxford University Press.

Lewis, David (2004): "Causation as influence", *The Journal of Philosophy* 97 (4), pp. 182–197.

Liao, Shen-Yi, and Florian Cova (2017): "Replication of Roxborough and Cumby (2009), 'Folk psychological concepts. Causation', Philosophical Psychology". *Open Science Framework*. https://osf.io/5eanz/, last accessed May 19, 2023.

Liquin, Emily, and Tania Lombrozo (2018): "Structure-function fit underlies the evaluation of teleological explanations", *Cognitive Psychology* 107, pp. 22–43.

Livengood, Jonathan, and Edouard Machery (2007): "The folk probably don't think what you think they think. Experiments on causation by absence", *Midwest Studies in Philosophy* 31 (1), pp. 107–127.

Livengood, Jonathan, and Justin Sytsma (2020): "Actual causation and compositionality", *Philosophy of Science* 87 (1), pp. 43–69.

Lombrozo, Tania (2007): "Simplicity and probability in causal explanation", *Cognitive Psychology* 55 (3), pp. 232–257.

Lombrozo, Tania (2010): "Causal-explanatory pluralism. How intentions, functions, and mechanisms influence causal ascriptions", *Cognitive Psychology* 61 (4), pp. 303–332.

Lombrozo, Tania, and Nadya Vasilyeva (2017): "Causal explanation", in: Michael Waldmann (Ed.): *The Oxford handbook of causal reasoning*. Oxford: Oxford University Press, pp. 415–432.

Machery, Edouard. (2017): *Philosophy within its proper bounds*. Oxford: Oxford University Press, pp. 415–432.

McGrath, Sarah (2005): "Causation by omission. A dilemma", *Philosophical Studies* 123 (1–2), pp. 125–148.

Meehan, Julie, and Ruth Byrne (2005): "The temporal order effect in children's counterfactual thinking", in: Bruno Bara, Lawrence Barsalou, and Monica Bucciarelli (Eds.): *Proceedings of the 27th Annual Conference of the Cognitive Science Society*. Mahwah: Lawrence Erlbaum, pp. 1467–1473.

Miller, Dale, and Saku Gunasegaram (1990): "Temporal order and the perceived mutability of events. Implications for blame assignment", *Journal of Personality and Social Psychology* 59 (6), pp. 1111–1118.

Morales, Jorge, Axel Bax, and Chaz Firestone (2020): "Sustained representation of perspectival shape", *Proceedings of the National Academy of Sciences* 117 (26), pp. 14873–14882.

Morris, Adam, Jonathan Phillips, Tobias Gerstenberg, and Fiery Cushman (2019): "Quantitative causal selection patterns in token causation", *PLOS ONE* 14 (8), e0219704.

Neufeld, Eleonore (2021): "Against teleological essentialism", *Cognitive Science* 45 (4), e12961.

Niemi, Laura, Joshua Hartshorne, Tobias Gerstenberg, Matthew Stanley, and Liane Young (2020): "Moral values reveal the causality implicit in verb meaning", *Cognitive Science* 44 (6), e12838.

Niemi, Laura, and Paul Henne (2022): "Victim omissions. How doing nothing affects judgments of cause and blame", in: Thomas Nadelhoffer and Andrew Monroe (Eds.): *Advances in experimental philosophy of free will and responsibility*. London: Bloomsbury.

Norton, James (2021): "Experimental philosophy on time", *Philosophy Compass* 16 (11), e12779.

Novick, Aaron (2017): "Metaphysics and the vera causa ideal. The nun's priest's tale", *Erkenntnis* 82 (5), pp. 1161–1176.

O'Neill, Kevin, Paul Henne, Paul Bello, John Pearson, and Felipe De Brigard (2022): "Confidence and gradation in causal judgment", *Cognition* 223, 105036.

O'Neill, Kevin, Paul Henne, John Pearson, and Felipe De Brigard (2022): "Measuring and modeling confidence in human causal judgment", *Proceedings of the Annual Meeting of the Cognitive Science Society* 44, pp. 446–452.

Pacer, Michael, and Tania Lombrozo (2017): "Ockham's razor cuts to the root. Simplicity in causal explanation", *Journal of Experimental Psychology – General* 146 (12), pp. 1761–1780.

Paul, Laurie (2010a): "Counterfactual theories", in: Helen Beebee, Christopher Hitchcock, and Peter Menzies (Eds.): *The Oxford handbook of causation.* Vol. 1. Oxford and New York: Oxford University Press, pp. 158–184.

Paul, Laurie (2010b): "A new role for experimental work in metaphysics", *Review of Philosophy and Psychology* 1 (3), pp. 461–476.

Paul, Laurie (2016): "Experience, metaphysics, and cognitive science", in: Justin Sytsma and Wesley Buckwalter (Eds.): *A companion to experimental philosophy.* Chichester: Wiley-Blackwell, pp. 419–433.

Paul, Laurie, and Ned Hall (2013): *Causation. A user's guide.* Oxford: Oxford University Press.

Phillips, Jonathan, Jamie Luguri, and Joshua Knobe (2015): "Unifying morality's influence on non-moral judgments. The relevance of alternative possibilities", *Cognition* 145, pp. 30–42.

Quillien, Tadeg (2020): "When do we think that X caused Y?", *Cognition* 205, 104410.

Quillien, Tadeg, and Michael Barlev (2022): "Causal judgment in the wild. Evidence from the 2020 US presidential election", *Cognitive Science* 46 (2), e13101.

Reuter, Kevin, Lara Kirfel, Raphael van Riel, and Luca Barlassina (2014): "The good, the bad, and the timely. How temporal order and moral judgment influence causal selection", *Frontiers in Psychology* 5, 1336.

Ritchie, Katherine, and Joshua Knobe (2020): "Kindhood and essentialism. Evidence from language", *Advances in Child Development and Behavior* 59, pp. 133–164.

Rogers, Ross, Mark Alicke, Sarah Taylor, David Rose, Teresa Davis, and Dori Bloom (2019): "Causal deviance and the ascription of intent and blame", *Philosophical Psychology* 32 (3), pp. 404–427.

Rose, David (2017): *Experimental metaphysics.* London: Bloomsbury.

Rose, David (2019): "Cognitive science for the revisionary metaphysician", in: Alvin Goldman and Brian McLaughlin (Eds.): *Metaphysics and cognitive science.* New York: Oxford University Press, pp. 364–383.

Rose, David (2020): "The ship of Theseus puzzle", in: Tania Lombrozo, Joshua Knobe, and Shaun Nichols (Eds.): *Oxford studies in experimental philosophy.* Vol. 3. Oxford: Oxford University Press, pp. 158–174.

Rose, David, and David Danks (2012): "Causation. Empirical trends and future directions", *Philosophy Compass* 7 (9), pp. 643–653.

Rose, David, and David Danks (2013): "In defense of a broad conception of experimental philosophy", *Metaphilosophy* 44 (4), pp. 512–532.

Rose, David, and Shaun Nichols (2019): "Teleological essentialism", *Cognitive Science* 43 (4), e12725.

Rose, David, and Shaun Nichols (2020): "Teleological essentialism. Generalized", *Cognitive Science* 44 (3), e12818.

Rose, David, and Jonathan Schaffer (2017): "Folk mereology is teleological", *Noûs* 51 (2), pp. 238–270.

Rose, David, Jonathan Schaffer, and Kevin Tobia (2020): "Folk teleology drives persistence judgments", *Synthese* 197 (12), pp. 5491–5509.

Rose, David, Eric Sievers, and Shaun Nichols (2021): "Cause and burn", *Cognition* 207, 104517.

Roxborough, Craig, and Jill Cumby (2009): "Folk psychological concepts. Causation", *Philosophical Psychology* 22 (2), pp. 205–213.

Salmon, Wesley (1994): "Causality without counterfactuals", *Philosophy of Science* 61 (2), pp. 297–312.

Samland, Jana, Marina Josephs, Michael Waldmann, and Hannes Rakoczy (2016): "The role of prescriptive norms and knowledge in children's and adults' causal selection", *Journal of Experimental Psychology – General* 145 (2), pp. 125–130.

Samland, Jana, and Michael Waldmann (2016): "How prescriptive norms influence causal inferences", *Cognition* 156, pp. 164–176.

Schaffer, Jonathan (2000): "Causation by disconnection", *Philosophy of Science* 67 (2), pp. 285–300.

Schaffer, Jonathan (2019): "Cognitive science and metaphysics. Partners in debunking", in: Alvin Goldman and Brian McLaughlin (Eds.): *Metaphysics and cognitive science*. New York: Oxford University Press, pp. 38–70.

Schwenkler, John, and Eric Sievers (2022): "Cause, 'cause', and norm", in: Pascale Willemsen and Alex Wiegmann (Eds.): *Advances in experimental philosophy of causation*. London: Bloomsbury, pp. 123–143.

Segura, Susana, Pablo Fernandez-Berrocal, and Ruth Byrne (2002): "Temporal and causal order effects in thinking about what might have been", *The Quarterly Journal of Experimental Psychology – Section A* 55 (4), pp. 1295–1305.

Siegal, Elitzur Avraham Bar-Asher, Noa Bassel, and York Hagmayer (2021): "Causal selection. The linguistic take", *Experiments in Linguistic Meaning* 1, pp. 27–38.

Siegel, Jenifer, Molly Crockett, and Raymond Dolan (2017): "Inferences about moral character moderate the impact of consequences on blame and praise", *Cognition* 167, pp. 201–211.

Spellman, Barbara (1997): "Crediting causality", *Journal of Experimental Psychology – General* 126 (4), pp. 323–348.

Spranca, Mark, Elisa Minsk, and Jonathan Baron (1991): "Omission and commission in judgment and choice", *Journal of Experimental Social Psychology* 27 (1), pp. 76–105.

Stanley, Matthew, Gregory Stewart, and Felipe De Brigard (2017): "Counterfactual plausibility and comparative similarity", *Cognitive Science* 41 (S5), pp. 1216–1228.

Starmans, Christina, and Paul Bloom (2018): "Nothing personal. What psychologists get wrong about identity", *Trends in Cognitive Sciences* 22 (7), pp. 566–568.

Strohminger, Nina, Joshua Knobe, and George Newman (2017): "The true self. A psychological concept distinct from the self", *Perspectives on Psychological Science* 12 (4), pp. 551–560.

Strohminger, Nina, and Shaun Nichols (2014): "The essential moral self", *Cognition* 131 (1), pp. 159–171.

Sytsma, Justin (2020): "Causation, responsibility, and typicality", *Review of Philosophy and Psychology* 12 (4), pp. 699–719.

Sytsma, Justin (2022a): "Crossed wires. Blaming artifacts for bad outcomes", *Journal of Philosophy* 119 (9), pp. 489–516.

Sytsma, Justin (2022b): "The responsibility account", in: Pascale Willemsen and Alex Wiegmann (Eds.): *Advances in experimental philosophy of causation*. London: Bloomsbury, pp. 145–164.

Sytsma, Justin, Roland Bluhm, Pascale Willemsen, and Kevin Reuter (2019): "Causal attributions and corpus analysis", in: Eugen Fischer and Mark Curtis (Eds.): *Methodological advances in experimental philosophy*. London: Bloomsbury, pp. 209–238.

Sytsma, Justin, and Jonathan Livengood (2021): "Causal attributions and the trolley problem", *Philosophical Psychology* 34 (8), pp. 1167–1191.

Sytsma, Justin, Jonathan Livengood, and David Rose (2012): "Two types of typicality. Rethinking the role of statistical typicality in ordinary causal attributions", *Studies in History and Philosophy of Science – Part C* 43 (4), pp. 814–820.

Thomasson, Amie (2012): "Experimental philosophy and the methods of ontology", *The Monist* 95 (2), pp. 175–199.

Thomasson, Amie, Giuseppina D'Oro, and Søren Overgaard (2017): "What can we do, when we do metaphysics?", in: Giuseppina D'Oro and Søren Overgaard (Eds.): *The Cambridge companion to philosophical methodology*. Cambridge: Cambridge University Press, pp. 101–121.

Tobia, Kevin (2022): *Experimental philosophy of identity and the self*. London: Bloomsbury.

Varzi, Achille (2007): "Omissions and causal explanations", in: Francesca Castellani and Josef Quitterer (Eds.): *Agency and causation in the human sciences*. Paderborn: mentis, pp. 153–167.

Vasilyeva, Nadya, Thomas Blanchard, and Tania Lombrozo (2018): "Stable causal relationships are better causal relationships", *Cognitive Science* 42 (4), pp. 1265–1296.

Vrantsidis, Thalia, and Tania Lombrozo (2022): "Simplicity as a cue to probability. Multiple roles for simplicity in evaluating explanations", *Cognitive Science* 46 (7), e13169.

Walsh, Clare, and Ruth Byrne (2004): "Counterfactual thinking. The temporal order effect", *Memory & Cognition* 32 (3), pp. 369–378.

Walsh, Clare, and Steven Sloman (2011): "The meaning of cause and prevent. The role of causal mechanism", *Mind & Language* 26 (1), pp. 21–52.

Willemsen, Pascale, and Lara Kirfel (2019): "Recent empirical work on the relationship between causal judgements and norms", *Philosophy Compass* 14 (1), e12562.

Willemsen, Pascale, and Kevin Reuter (2016): "Is there really an omission effect?", *Philosophical Psychology* 29 (8), pp. 1142–1159.

Willemsen, Pascale, and Alex Wiegmann (Eds.) (2022): *Advances in experimental philosophy of causation*. London: Bloomsbury.

Williamson, Timothy (2016): "Philosophical criticisms of experimental philosophy", in: Justin Sytsma and Wesley Buckwalter (Eds.): *A companion to experimental philosophy*. Chichester: Wiley-Blackwell, pp. 22–36.

Wolff, Phillip (2007): "Representing causation", *Journal of Experimental Psychology – General* 136 (1), pp. 82–111.

Wolff, Phillip, Aron Barbey, and Matthew Hausknecht (2010): "For want of a nail. How absences cause events", *Journal of Experimental Psychology – General* 139 (2), pp. 191–221.

Wolff, Phillip, and Robert Thorstad (2017): "Force dynamics and causation", in: Michael Waldmann (Ed.): *The Oxford handbook of causal reasoning*. Oxford: Oxford University Press, pp. 147–168.

Woodward, James (2006): "Sensitive and insensitive causation", *The Philosophical Review* 115 (1), pp. 1–50.

Woodward, James (2012): "Causation. Interactions between philosophical theories and psychological research", *Philosophy of Science* 79 (5), pp. 961–972.

Woodward, James (2014): "Causal reasoning. Philosophy and experiment", in: Joshua Knobe, Tania Lombrozo, and Shaun Nichols (Eds.): *Oxford studies in experimental philosophy*. Vol. 1. Oxford: Oxford University Press, pp. 294–324.

Woodward, James (2021): *Causation with a human face. Normative theory and descriptive psychology*. New York: Oxford University Press.

Ziano, Ignazio, and Mario Pandelaere (2022): "Late-action effect. Heightened counterfactual potency and perceived outcome reversibility make actions closer to a definitive outcome seem more causally impactful", *Journal of Experimental Social Psychology* 100, 104290.

James R. Beebe
Experimental Epistemology: Knowledge and Gettier Cases

Abstract: The central focus of post-Gettier epistemology was the attempt to find necessary and sufficient conditions that captured "the ordinary concept of knowledge" – on the assumption that there was a single, widely shared concept to be found. A guiding assumption behind this project was that the competent epistemic judgments of ordinary individuals were relevant to whether an analysis is correct. Against this backdrop, experimental epistemology emerged as the systematic empirical study of epistemic judgments. Expecting to find cross-cultural differences, experimental philosophers have instead uncovered broad agreement. Notably, researchers have found that most people agree that false beliefs and unjustified beliefs do not count as knowledge and that justified true beliefs in Gettier cases do not count as knowledge when they are based upon *merely apparent* rather than *authentic evidence*. However, contrary to received philosophical wisdom, non-philosophers judge that justified true beliefs formed on the basis of authentic evidence do count as knowledge even when the putative knower is in a classic Gettier situation. What the distinction between authentic and apparent evidence amounts to and what other differences in epistemic intuitions across demographic groups there might be are important issues that mainstream and experimental philosophers need to work together to understand.

Keywords: Analysis of Knowledge; Authentic Evidence; Experimental Epistemology; Folk Epistemology; Gettier Cases; Knowledge Attributions

1 Introduction

Under the banner of epistemology, one might investigate (*inter alia*) what knowledge is, what people think knowledge is, what our ordinary concept of knowledge is, what people think our ordinary concept of knowledge is, what the meaning of the word "knows" is, or what people think the meaning of "knows" is. In the second half of the twentieth century, epistemologists did not typically distinguish between knowledge (understood as something like a relation between a knower and a known proposition or fact), the concept of knowledge (understood as a type of psychological representation, a Fregean sense, or some other kind of intension), and the meaning of "knows". Epistemologists at this time also largely assumed that the essential features of this undifferentiated target of epistemological theorizing could be apprehended by reflection upon general epistemic principles and our intuitive judgments about particular cases. According to this set of guiding assumptions, if ordinary people competently judge that someone can know that *p* even though that person clearly does not satisfy some condition *X*, then *X* is not a necessary condition for knowledge (alternatively, *X* does not figure in the intension of knowledge, the meaning of "knows", and so forth). Performance errors are of course possible, and thus folk judgments can benefit from the guidance of philosophical experts. Nevertheless, the late-twentieth century, post-Gettier approach to epistemology charted a fairly direct path from the competent epistemic judgments of ordinary individuals about concrete cases to fundamental facts about the central target of epistemological theorizing.

In this context, experimental epistemology arose as the attempt to marshal the methods and tools of the cognitive and social sciences to investigate folk epistemic practices in a systematic, empirical fashion. The most immediate goal of this project was to see whether patterns of folk epistemic judgments matched philosophers' armchair predictions about them and thus matched philosophers' intuitions about what those epistemic judgments ought to be. Does the folk conception of knowledge recognize – as philosophers have maintained – a distinction between knowledge, on the one hand, and confidently-held belief, mere true belief, and mere justified belief, on the other? Does ordinary knowledge require something less than certainty? A number of experimental philosophers predicted that folk judgments would diverge significantly from armchair predictions. Nearly all experimental philosophers agreed that at least some surprising patterns of competent epistemic judgments would be found and that various kinds of performance errors, cognitive biases, or epistemically irrelevant factors that influence epistemic judgments would also be brought to light.

Prior research in cross-cultural psychology (e.g., Nisbett et al. 2001) led early experimental philosophers to expect significant differences in the epistemic intuitions of individuals from diverse backgrounds. It was known that individuals from highly individualistic cultures that encourage analytic styles of thinking which involve the detachment of objects from their contexts have been observed to differ in the ways they describe, predict, and explain events and categorize objects from individuals in highly interdependent cultures that encourage holistic styles of thinking. Although it was not clear how a tendency to prefer analytic over holistic thinking or other culturally variable factors might affect folk knowledge attributions, the wealth of cross-cultural variation documented in the social sciences made it seem quite likely that some kind of variation in the epistemic domain would be observed as well.

Given the centrality of thought experiments in the mainstream epistemological debates of the late-twentieth century, experimental philosophers began their research on folk epistemic intuitions by presenting participants from different cultural backgrounds with some of the most widely discussed vignettes in epistemology. These included Gettier cases (Gettier 1963) that probed participants' intuitions about the relationship between knowledge and justified true belief, Truetemp cases (BonJour 1980) that examined intuitions about epistemic internalism and externalism, and bank cases (DeRose 1992) that focused on whether raising the stakes of being wrong about a belief might require one to be in a stronger epistemic position in order to have knowledge.

The present contribution focuses on empirical work that has examined attributions and denials of knowledge in Gettier cases. Section 2.1 reviews work by Jonathan

Weinberg, Shaun Nichols, and Stephen Stich (2001) that helped give birth to the new field of experimental philosophy and that reported cross-cultural differences in epistemic intuitions about Gettier cases. Sections 2.2 and 2.3 describe subsequent research on Gettier cases that failed to find any cross-cultural differences but uncovered a surprising degree of universality instead. Section 2.4 reviews the unexpected finding by Christina Starmans and Ori Friedman (2012) that laypeople are inclined to attribute knowledge in Gettier cases when they take the evidence upon which Gettiered beliefs are founded to be authentic or reliable in some way. Section 3 briefly surveys other topics in experimental epistemology that would benefit from further investigation.

2 The Folk Epistemology of Gettier Cases

2.1 Initial Reports of Cross-Cultural Differences

In one of the founding documents of experimental philosophy, Weinberg, Nichols, and Stich (2001) presented American undergraduates from different cultural backgrounds with the following version of a classic Gettier case:

> **American Car:** Bob has a friend, Jill, who has driven a Buick for many years. Bob therefore thinks that Jill drives an American car. He is not aware, however, that her Buick has recently been stolen, and he is also not aware that Jill has replaced it with a Pontiac, which is a different kind of American car. Does Bob really know that Jill drives an American car, or does he only believe it?

Although Edmund Gettier (1963) was not the first philosopher to formulate such cases,[1] he is credited with popularizing the idea that someone can have a justified true belief (JTB) without having knowledge. According to the prevailing consensus in Anglophone epistemology, the following statements are true of the case above:

(J)   Intuitively, Bob is justified in thinking that Jill drives an American car.
(T)   It is true that Jill drives an American car.
(B)   Bob believes that Jill drives an American car.
(No-K) Intuitively, Bob does not really know that Jill drives an American car.

---

[1] Jennifer Nagel (2014, p. 58) reports that the eighth-century Indian philosopher Dharmottara formulated the following "Gettier" cases: "A fire has just been lit to roast some meat. The fire hasn't started sending up any smoke, but the smell of the meat has attracted a cloud of insects. From a distance, an observer sees the dark swarm above the horizon and mistakes it for smoke. 'There's a fire burning at that spot,' the distant observer says. A desert traveler is searching for water. He sees, in the valley ahead, a shimmering blue expanse. Unfortunately, it's a mirage. But fortunately, when he reaches the spot where there appeared to be water, there actually is water, hidden under a rock".
    Not long before Gettier, Bertrand Russell (1948, pp. 170 f.) offered the following "Gettier" case: "There is the man who looks at a clock which is not going, though he thinks it is, and who happens to look at it at the moment when it is right; this man acquires a true belief as to the time of day, but cannot be said to have knowledge".

When experimental philosophers hear certain claims being described as intuitive, they tend to ask, "Intuitive to whom?" and "What evidence do you have for thinking your intuition is widely shared?" Weinberg, Nichols and Stich (2001) reported that three-fourths of their participants from Western backgrounds agreed that (No-K) was true but that half of their East Asian participants and two-thirds of their South Asian participants thought that (No-K) was false – i.e., they judged that Bob really did know that Jill drives an American car. On the basis of findings like this, Weinberg, Nichols, and Stich draw the following conclusion:

> Our data indicate that when epistemologists advert to "our" intuitions when attempting to characterize epistemic concepts or draw normative conclusions, they are engaged in a culturally local endeavor – what we might think of as *ethno-epistemology*. […] [I]t is difficult to see why a process that relies heavily on epistemic intuitions that are local to one's own cultural and socioeconomic group would lead to genuinely normative conclusions. Pending a detailed response to this problem, we think that the best reaction to the high-SES Western philosophy professor who tries to draw normative conclusions from the facts about "our" intuitions is to ask: What do you mean "we"? (Weinberg, Nichols, and Stich 2001, p. 454 f.)

When philosophers consult their intuitions about epistemic thought experiments and use these intuitive judgments to guide their epistemological theorizing, they take themselves to be uncovering fundamental truths about knowledge and related epistemic concepts rather than engaging in a merely autobiographical or auto-ethnographic exercise. However, when faced with the possibility that many other people do not share their intuitions, important questions arise about the nature of this activity. Are people who do not share your intuitions simply mistaken about whether Bob knows that Jill drives an American car? If so, how could you know or show this? If your only evidence for the correctness of your intuition is the intuition itself, it is difficult to see how this can serve as adequate grounds for concluding that another person's intuitive judgment is mistaken – since the other person could argue that your intuition is mistaken because it conflicts with theirs. Joshua Alexander and Jonathan Weinberg (2007) have argued that this line of questioning raises significant doubts about the ability of intuitive judgments to function as evidence for or against any substantive philosophical claim.

Another response to apparent diversity in epistemic intuitions is to think that perhaps the reason why members of different demographic groups respond to the same thought experiment in significantly different ways is that they are employing nonequivalent epistemic concepts – in which case they are talking past each other more than actually disagreeing (Sosa 2007). Thorny questions arise here about the difficulty of knowing when two groups are employing distinct concepts and when they simply have conflicting beliefs about the same concepts. Even if it were established that individuals who report conflicting intuitions are talking about the same knowledge relation, there would still remain the difficulty of knowing how to privilege some individuals' intuitions over those of others. If it were established that individuals who seem to be reporting conflicting intuitions are in fact employing distinct epistemic concepts, we would need to do more than simply note that these individuals may not be fully disagreeing with one another. We would also need to grapple with the difficult question of determining which epistemic concepts are most appropriately or valuably employed in the situation(s) under discussion – a question to which philosophers have given insufficient attention. Regardless of how reports of diversity in epistemic intuitions are interpreted, they point to important but previously neglected metaphilosophical questions about the nature of philosophical inquiry. This is perhaps the central reason why the rise of metaphilosophy has been coextensive with the rise of experimental philosophy.

2.2 Failed Replications and New Findings of Universality

The groundbreaking work of Weinberg, Nichols, and Stich (2001) generated a tremendous amount of discussion, with most early responses (e. g., Sosa 2007; Williamson 2004, 2011) focusing on the strong philosophical conclusions the authors wished to draw from their data. For a number of years, scholars took for granted that the cross-cultural and other demographic differences in epistemic judgments reported by Weinberg, Nichols, and Stich were robust. In more recent years, however, attempts to replicate their findings have failed – in large part it seems because of the rather small sample sizes employed in the original studies.

Various teams of researchers – including Jennifer Nagel, Valerie San Juan, and Raymond Mar (2013), Hamid Seyedsayamdost (2015), as well as Minsun Kim and Yuan Yuan (2015) – presented Weinberg, Nichols, and Stich's (2001) American car Gettier case (and a number of other epistemological thought experiments) to larger samples of North American and British participants of Western, East Asian, and South Asian descent but found no significant cross-cultural differences in participants' epistemic judgments. Moreover, a solid majority of participants from each group gave the philosophically orthodox response to common Gettier cases – i.e., that Gettiered justified true belief does not count as knowledge.

Edouard Machery and colleagues (2017a) presented participants from four different cultural groups (Brazil, India, Japan, and the United States) the following two Gettier cases (borrowed from Nagel et al. 2013) in their native languages:

Hospital: Paul Jones was worried because it was 10 pm and his wife Mary was not home from work yet. Usually she is home by 6 pm. He tried her cell phone but just kept getting her voicemail. Starting to worry that something might have happened to her, he decided to call some local hospitals to ask whether any patient by the name of "Mary Jones" had been admitted that evening. At the University Hospital, the person who answered his call confirmed that someone by that name had been admitted with major but not life-threatening injuries following a car crash. Paul grabbed his coat and rushed out to drive to University hospital. As it turned out, the patient at University Hospital was not Paul's wife, but another woman with the same name. In fact, Paul's wife had a heart attack as she was leaving work, and was at that moment receiving treatment in Metropolitan Hospital, a few miles away.

Trip: Luke works in an office in New York with two other people, Victor and Monica. All winter Victor has been describing his plans to go to Las Vegas on his vacation, even showing Luke the website of the hotel where he has reservations. When Victor is away on vacation, Luke receives a very nice email from Victor together with photos of Victor posing in front of Las Vegas landmarks. When he gets back to work, Victor talks a lot to Luke about how much fun he had vacationing in Las Vegas. However, Victor didn't really go on the trip; he has just been pretending. His tickets and reservations were cancelled because his credit card was maxed out, and he secretly stayed home in New York, very skillfully faking the photos he sent Luke. Meanwhile, Monica just spent a weekend vacationing in Las Vegas, but kept this a secret from all her co-workers. (Machery et al. 2017a, p. 4)

Machery and colleagues (2017a) presented these Gettier cases along with a clear case of knowledge and a case describing a false belief. The clear case of knowledge described an agent with good eyesight who observed a bright red table in a furniture store under good lighting conditions and then formed the true belief that the table was red. In the false belief case, a customer in a jewelry store formed the belief that the object she was looking at was a genuine diamond when in fact it was a fake. Instead of asking whether the protagonist in each case "really knows" or "only believes" the proposition in question (as Weinberg and colleagues 2001 did), Machery and his collaborators asked participants two knowledge attribution questions about each case (Machery et al. 2017a, p. 5; derived from Nagel et al. 2013). For the Hospital case, the knowledge probes were the following:

Knowledge 1: When Paul rushed out to drive to University Hospital, did he know that his wife was hospitalized?
– Yes, he knew.
– No, he did not know.

Knowledge 2: In your view, which of the following sentences better describes Paul's situation?
– When Paul rushed out to drive to University Hospital, he knew that his wife was hospitalized.
– When Paul rushed out to drive to University Hospital, he thought he knew that his wife was hospitalized, but he did not actually know this.

For the Trip case, participants were asked a Yes/No question about whether Luke knows that someone in his office went on a vacation to Las Vegas (Knowledge 1) and a second question about whether Luke knows or merely thinks he knows the same proposition (Knowledge 2). Participants were also asked how justified they thought each protagonist was in thinking the relevant proposition was true, indicating their responses on a seven-point scale ranging from "Completely unjustified" to "Completely justified". Machery and colleagues (2017a) excluded from analysis participants who selected an answer below the neutral midpoint in response to the justification question for all four thought experiments employed in their study. The rationale for this exclusion was that the researchers wanted to examine whether participants thought that Gettiered justified true beliefs failed to count as knowledge, but individuals who thought that no beliefs were ever justified might deny knowledge in such cases for reasons that had nothing to do with Gettier-related considerations.

Machery and colleagues (2017a) found that individuals from all four participant groups were much more likely to select knowledge-attributing answers to both the Knowledge 1 and the Knowledge 2 questions in response to a clear case of knowledge than in response to a Gettier case. Importantly they found that participants from all four cultures responded to Knowledge 2 in basically the same way – viz., by strongly agreeing that the protagonist failed to have knowledge.

In another study, Machery and colleagues (2017b) presented the Hospital Gettier case to 2,838 participants in 24 locations in 23 countries (including individuals from large cities to small-scale societies) in 17 different languages. Participants were again asked the Knowledge 1, Knowledge 2, and justification questions and were excluded from analysis if they selected an answer to the justification question that was below the midpoint. In response to the Knowledge 1 question about whether Paul knew that his wife was hospitalized, a majority of individuals in 10 out of 24 cultures selected the knowledge-denying answer ("No, he did not know"). However, in response to the Knowledge 2 question, a majority of individuals in 23 out of 24 cultures selected the knowledge-denying answer ("When Paul rushed out to drive to University Hospital, he thought he knew that his wife was hospitalized, but he did not actually know this"). The only exception to this came from a very small sample ($n = 19$) of Bedouins. Approximately 70% to 90% of participants in the other 23 cultures reported the standard Gettier intuition. Although Machery and colleagues (2017b, p. 532) note some limitations to their study, they take these results to provide convergent evidence for the claim that "[t]he Gettier intuition is robust across cultures and languages, suggesting that it is part of a core epistemology".

The lower percentages of participants who selected the knowledge-denying answer to the Knowledge 1 question in both studies reported by Machery and his collaborators reveal the importance of asking questions like Knowledge 2, which Buckwalter (2014), Nagel and colleagues (2013), as well as Machery and colleagues (2017a) argue controls for the phenomenon of protagonist projection. Richard Holton first identified and described protagonist projection as follows:

> I suggest that these sentences work by projecting us into the point of view of the protagonist; let us call the phenomenon protagonist projection. In each case the point of view into which we are projected involves a false belief. We describe the false belief using words that the protagonists might use themselves, words that embody their mistake. So we deliberately use words in ways that do not fit the case. (Holton 1997, p. 626)

Protagonist projection in knowledge attribution is perhaps most clearly seen in cases where a (living) storyteller says, "That's when I knew I was going to die" (Buckwalter 2014). Intuitively, the person could not have actually known this – otherwise they would not be alive to tell the story. The idea is that even if some participants are initially more inclined to endorse knowledge-attributing sentences in response to questions such as Knowledge 1 in ways that involve protagonist projection, when questions like Knowledge 2 prompt them to reflect more carefully upon whether protagonists literally know certain propositions, participants will be much more likely to provide answers that are free from protagonist projection.

In light of both the failures to replicate the original cross-cultural findings of Weinberg, Nichols, and Stich (2001) and the cross-cultural universality observed by Machery and his collaborators, it seems that at present there is no evidence for any substantive cross-cultural differences in epistemic intuitions about Gettier cases.

2.3 Other Reports of Universality

Until recently, the contentious nature of the cross-cultural findings reported by Weinberg, Nichols, and Stich (2001) and the strong metaphilosophical conclusions they sought to draw from these results overshadowed patterns of cross-cultural universality that have been consistently reported in cross-cultural studies in experimental epistemology. For a number of years after the publication of Weinberg, Nichols, and Stich's (2001) original article, few philosophers paused to reflect upon the significance of the strong agreement observed among all of their participants that unjustified true beliefs such as the following do not count as knowledge:

> **Coinflip:** Dave likes to play a game with flipping a coin. He sometimes gets a "special feeling" that the next flip will come out heads. When he gets this "special feeling", he is right about half the time, and wrong about half the time. Just before the next flip, Dave gets that "special feeling", and the feeling leads him to believe that the coin will land heads. He flips the coin, and it does land heads. Did Dave really know that the coin was going to land heads, or did he only believe it?

Adrian Ziółkowski (2021) reports the same result with Polish participants. After asking participants to indicate the extent to which they agreed or disagreed that Dave knew the coin was going to land heads on a scale ranging from 1 ("Strongly disagree") to 5 ("Strongly agree"), the mean rating of Ziółkowski's participants was 1.03 – which is about as close to complete unanimity in knowledge denial as one can expect to find.

Other cross-cultural patterns of uniformity in epistemic assessments have been reported by a number of research teams. For example, Nagel and colleagues (2013), Machery and colleagues (2017a), John Turri and YeounJun Park (2018), as well as Ziółkowski (2021) found that individuals from the United States, Canada, Brazil, India, Japan, Korea, and Poland agree that unGettiered justified true beliefs do count as knowledge. Machery and colleagues (2017a) as well as Turri and Park (2018) report agreement among individuals from the United States, Brazil, India, Japan, and Korea that justified false beliefs do not count as knowledge. David Rose and colleagues (2019) probed the intuitions of 4,504 individuals from 19 sites in 16 different countries about the extent to which raising the stakes of being wrong about a belief raises the bar for obtaining knowledge. They report that their participants' intuitions were uniformly in accord with the view that knowledge is not sensitive to practical stakes.

Turri and Park (2018) found cross-cultural agreement among Korean and American participants regarding the knowledge norm of assertion. The epistemic side-effect

effect – wherein blameworthy agents are more likely to be viewed as possessing knowledge – has been observed among American (Beebe and Buckwalter 2010, Beebe and Jensen 2012), German (Dalbauer and Hergovich 2013), Mandarin Chinese, Korean (Yuan and Kim 2021), and Polish (Ryszkowska et al. n.d., Zaręba n.d.) participants. Yuan and Kim (2021) observed the perceptual versus probabilistic evidence effect (where individuals are less willing to attribute knowledge to beliefs based upon probabilistic rather than perceptual evidence; cf. Friedman and Turri 2015) among North American, South Korean, Mainland Chinese, and Taiwanese participants.

Although cross-cultural studies in experimental epistemology need to be expanded in terms of both the research materials they employ and the participant populations they study, the cross-cultural uniformity in epistemic judgments that has thus far been uncovered has been greater than many (if not most) experimental philosophers expected and perhaps than the broader philosophical community realizes.

2.4 Authentic versus Merely Apparent Evidence

In a surprising[2] turn of events, two psychologists have identified an important distinction between two fundamentally different kinds of Gettier case that escaped the notice of epistemologists for at least half a century. Starmans and Friedman (2012) found that laypeople are inclined to attribute knowledge in Gettier cases when a person's belief is based upon authentic evidence but not when that person's belief is based upon merely apparent evidence. According to Starmans and Friedman (2012, p. 278), apparent evidence is "evidence that only *appears* to be informative about the world, but coincidentally leads to a true belief", whereas authentic evidence is actually informative about reality. In a subsequent paper, Starmans and Friedman (2020, p. 21) characterize apparent evidence as evidence that is faulty at the time of belief formation and authentic evidence as evidence that is not faulty in this way. Starmans and Friedman contend that most of the Gettier cases discussed since 1963 have involved merely apparent evidence. In the Hospital case, for example, the employee who tells Paul Jones that someone named "Mary Jones" had been admitted to the University Hospital was not talking about Paul Jones's wife. Learning the location of someone distinct from Paul Jones's wife is (*ceteris paribus*) not informative about the location of Jones's wife. In the Trip case, Luke forms the belief that one of his co-workers recently vacationed in Las Vegas on the basis of deceptive testimony from Victor; and deception is of course faulty or unreliable by design.

In contrast, Starmans and Friedman contend that cases like the following do not involve flawed evidence at the time of belief formation, even though they would be normally classified as Gettier cases by philosophers:

---

2 Surprising to philosophers at least, but perhaps to no one else.

> **Watch:** Peter is in his locked apartment reading, and is about to have a shower. He puts his book down on the coffee table, and takes off his black plastic watch and leaves it on the coffee table. Then he goes into the bathroom. As Peter's shower begins, a burglar silently breaks into the apartment. The burglar takes Peter's black plastic watch, replaces it with an identical black plastic watch, and then leaves. Peter is still in the shower, and did not hear anything. (Starmans and Friedman 2012, p. 274)

When Peter forms the belief that there is a watch on the table before taking a shower, his evidential basis is faultless, according to Starmans and Friedman, because he has direct perceptual evidence about the watch's actual location. Strikingly, 72 % of their American participants judged that while Peter is still in the shower, he really knows (rather than only thinks) that there is a watch on the table. This judgment runs strongly counter to the consensus in contemporary epistemology, according to which every Gettiered justified true belief fails to count as knowledge. Importantly, these findings also fail to comport with epistemologists' armchair predictions about what non-philosophers would say about such cases.

It is often remarked that the distinctive feature of Gettier cases is an important kind of "double luck" (Zagzebski 1994). An instance of bad luck makes a justified belief false, but then an instance of good luck intervenes to make the belief true after all. The result is usually that the protagonist's belief is true for one reason but justified for some other reason, resulting in a crucial mismatch between two necessary conditions for knowledge. Starmans and Friedman (2012) note that in Watch, the agent who steals Peter's watch intentionally replaces it with an identical one, so that the two components of the double luck in this case are causally connected. Wondering whether making these two elements causally disconnected and unrelated might reduce individuals' willingness to attribute knowledge in Gettier cases with authentic evidence, in a subsequent experiment Starmans and Friedman had a thief absentmindedly leave behind an exact copy of the stolen item. However, that this made no difference to participants' epistemic assessments – 69 % still attributed knowledge to the protagonist.

To further explore folk judgments regarding authentic and apparent evidence, Starmans and Friedman created an additional pair of closely matched cases that differ only in the quality of the evidence agents possess at the time of belief formation, the authentic evidence version of which reads as follows:

> **Yogurt:** Julie buys a container of yogurt at the local deli. Although, Julie is not aware of it, the yogurt in the container is exceptionally sweet – a mixup at the factory caused the yogurt to get a triple dose of sweetener. Julie comes home, puts it her fridge, and then goes into her bedroom. Julie's neighbor Sam has been spying on her. While she is in her bedroom, he picks the lock to her apartment, and enters. He takes the yogurt container from the fridge, and replaces it with a sealed container of yogurt from his own fridge. Then he goes back into his own apartment with Julie's yogurt container. Julie has only been in the bedroom for a few minutes, and did not hear anything. (Starmans and Friedman 2012, p. 282)

In the apparent evidence version, the second sentence is replaced with "Although, Julie is not aware of it, there is no yogurt in the container – a mixup at the factory caused the container to be filled with sour cream instead". In both versions, the end result is that there is a yogurt container in Julie's fridge. According to Starmans and Friedman, in the first version of the Yogurt case Julie possesses authentic evidence for her belief that there is a yogurt container in her fridge because at the time of belief formation the label on the container accurately reflects its contents. However, in the second version of the case, the label does not accurately reflect its contents. In the merely apparent evidence version, the label is an accurate indicator of what is inside the container only at the end of the story but not at the time of belief formation. Combing data from Yogurt and a structurally similar case, Starmans and Friedman found that participants attributed knowledge to the protagonists 67% of the time when they possessed authentic evidence but only 30% of the time when they possessed merely apparent evidence. Gonnerman and colleagues (2022) partially replicated this result with individuals from the United States and India.

Starmans and Friedman's findings seem to upend decades of philosophical wisdom about Gettier cases. Professional philosophers have overwhelmingly agreed not only that cases like Watch and Yogurt feature agents who lack knowledge but also that ordinary individuals would agree with this judgment.

Recognizing that their findings "point to a major difference between the epistemic intuitions of laypeople and those of philosophers" (Starmans and Friedman 2020, p. 272), they conducted an interesting pair of follow-up studies, in which they presented an authentic evidence Gettier case – together with an unGettiered JTB case and another epistemological thought experiment – to professional philosophers, laypeople, and scholars from seven other disciplines (including physics, chemistry, biology, history, English, mathematics, and psychology). The idea was to see whether "training and experience in the pursuit of knowledge" could explain the difference between the intuitions of the folk and those of philosophers. If spending time reflecting upon knowledge and how to acquire it makes people more likely to share the standard Gettier intuition, scholars from other disciplines should agree with philosophers' judgments about authentic evidence Gettier cases.

In each of their studies, Starmans and Friedman (2020) found that a majority of laypeople attributed knowledge in both the unGettiered justified true belief case and the authentic evidence Gettier case but that a majority of non-philosophy academics denied knowledge in both cases. Philosophers responded as expected (see Table 1).

Table 1: Majority responses in each study from Starmans and Friedman (2020) from the three participant groups in regard to whether the central protagonist possessed knowledge

	JTB	Gettier case
Philosophers	Y	N
Non-philosophy academics	N	N
Laypeople	Y	Y

Although slightly fewer laypeople attributed knowledge in the Gettier case than in the unGettiered JTB case, the difference was not statistically significant. The same thing was true for non-philosophy academics. It was only the philosophers who gave sharply different responses to the two kinds of cases.

Starmans and Friedman (2020) contend that the difference between the responses of philosophers and laypeople to Gettier cases cannot be explained in terms of an "expertise defense", according to which laypeople provide lower quality responses to epistemological thought experiments due to their lack of sufficient education, training, or reflection. Starmans and Friedman's (2020) findings show that highly educated, highly reflective professional academics from disciplines other than philosophy who have dedicated their lives to the pursuit of knowledge also fail to draw a sharp distinction between Gettiered and unGettiered justified true beliefs. Starmans and Friedman note that these results raise the following questions:

> If training in philosophy leads philosophers to have different intuitions about what knowledge is than any other group of people, then it is not clear whether we should think of this divergence as a type of expertise, or if it is better thought of as a type of indoctrination. Further, it raises important questions about whether an analysis of knowledge that captures only the judgments of a small, highly trained group is the analysis that philosophers are (or should be) interested in pursuing. (Starmans and Friedman 2020, p. 22)

Starmans and Friedman (2020, p. 26) argue that philosophers need to confront the possibility that "the study of philosophy leads to a narrowing of acceptable theories about knowledge that results in a sort of echo chamber of intuitions disconnected from how concepts are used by others". The distinction between authentic and apparent evidence that Starmans and Friedman (2012, 2020) have uncovered is thus theoretically significant in a number of ways. It appears to be an important but previously unappreciated part of folk epistemology, and it points to an unnoticed divide between the epistemic intuitions of ordinary individuals and professional philosophers.

Additional empirical and theoretical work needs to be done to shed light on the distinction between authentic and apparent evidence, as it is currently not well understood. Starmans and Friedman (2012, p. 280) acknowledge that the distinction is "largely intuitive" and that they have not provided clear criteria for determining when evidence is authentic or merely apparent. At one point, they make the following suggestion:

> A more precise way of drawing the distinction is to note that in cases of apparent evidence, the agent is unaware of facts about the evidence that if known would prevent the agent from forming the belief. (Starmans and Friedman 2012, p. 280)

Depending upon how this suggestion is understood, it could potentially (and unwittingly) entail infallibilism about evidence by ruling out the possibility of ever having evidence in favor of false beliefs. Suppose that a piece of evidence intuitively supports a false proposition. If the fact that the evidence supports a false proposition is a fact about the evidence in the relevant sense, then since knowing that a proposition is false would prevent a rational agent from believing the proposition is true, there can be no authentic evidence in favor of false propositions. Such an idea seems not only counterintuitive but also to be absent from folk epistemology.

Furthermore, in many Gettier cases where the folk deny that protagonists have knowledge, the evidence possessed by the protagonists appears to be authentic (at least in some sense of the term). For example, in the apparent evidence version of the Yogurt case above, Starmans and Friedman contend that Julie's evidence is merely apparent because the information on the container label is not a reliable indicator of what is inside. The label says that it contains yogurt, but there is in fact sour cream inside. However, yogurt container labels are, in general, highly reliable indicators of what is inside their containers, even if this particular one led Julie to form a false belief about the contents. To deny that a generally reliable indicator provides authentic evidence on any occasion when it happens to lead to a false belief again appears to entail an implausibly strong form of infallibilism about evidence.

Also consider Bob's evidence in the American car case above. His evidence for his belief that Jill drives an American car – at least as far as the story tells us – appears to be faultless at the time of belief formation. Jill's car has recently been stolen, but this act of theft has taken place long after Bob's belief formation. Denying that Bob's evidence is authentic merely because his belief is now false – although it was true at the time of belief formation – would again seem implausible. Thus, an accurate and illuminating account of what the distinction between authentic and apparent evidence amounts to is needed.

The research of Starmans and Friedman (2012, 2020) is a good example of how systematic empirical investigation can surprise and upend armchair philosophical speculation about matters in the real world. It appears that not even Starmans and Friedman anticipated they would uncover the distinction between authentic and apparent evidence. However, it should be noted that investigations in experimental philosophy do not need to overturn philosophical tradition in order to count as substantive scholarly contributions. Many epistemologists have written – in complete ignorance of many years of social scientific research that have revealed a variety of cross-cultural differences in human behavior and cognition – as if they expected that every person in every culture who possessed the concept of knowledge will think about it in the same way they do and thus that there would be no significant cross-cultural differences in epistemic intuitions. When, as in the studies described in Sections 2.2 and 2.3, empirical investigation delivers findings that accord with armchair predictions, those pontificating from the armchair deserve little credit for being right when these empirical claims are made without any recognition of the need for empirical support.

2.5 Topics for Future Research

2.5.1 Cross-Cultural Differences

Although we have seen that cross-cultural investigations in experimental epistemology have revealed more cross-cultural universality than many experimental (and otherwise empirically minded) philosophers expected, there are a number of reasons for thinking that significant cross-cultural differences in epistemic judgments and practices await our examination and discovery. One is simply that some reports of cross-cultural differences in experimental philosophy have proven to be quite robust. Machery, Mallon, Nichols, and Stich (2004), for example, famously observed East-West differences in participants' intuitions about the semantic properties of proper names. Despite strong initial skepticism from many philosophers of language (e.g., Ludwig 2007, Deutsch 2009, Martí 2009, Devitt 2011), these results have been consistently replicated – even if their explanation remains elusive (cf. Machery 2014, Haukioja 2015, Beebe and Undercoffer 2016).

Furthermore, consider the following instances of broad diversity in human psychology and behavior that Henrich, Heine, and Norenzayan (2010) canvass in their widely discussed paper comparing WEIRD (Western, Educated, Industrialized, Rich, and Democratic) people to the rest of the world:

- Individuals' intuitions about what counts as a fair offer in economic games and inclinations to reject unfair offers or punish free riders vary considerably.
- Individuals' tendencies to be risk-averse or rise-prone with monetary gambles, the degree to which they discount the future in situations of inter-temporal choice, and the degree to which they make prosocial contributions to public goods games vary widely.
- There are significant differences in the ways in which people understand themselves in terms of their internal psychological characteristics versus their roles and relationships within social networks and these self-conceptions significantly affect (1) the degree to which people engage in self-serving biases, (2) their attitudes about conformity, self-worth, and the value of personal choice, (3) their preference for explaining behavior in terms individuals' internal dispositions versus situational factors, (4) their preferences for rule-based versus family resemblance-based approaches to categorization.

In light of these and many other cross-cultural differences that have been reported in the social scientific literature, it seems practically impossible for there to be no cross-cultural differences in epistemic intuitions and practices.

There may well be, as some of the authors described above suggest, a universal folk epistemology that includes the intuition that false beliefs, unjustified true beliefs, and Gettiered justified true beliefs based upon merely apparent evidence do not count as knowledge. Further investigation is needed to confirm this speculation. But future research is also likely to reveal cross-cultural variation outside of whatever core folk epistemology may exist. The core could potentially be quite small or rather large. For example, people around the world might well agree about false beliefs, unjustified beliefs, and one class of Gettier cases while disagreeing widely about the merits of foundationalism and coherentism, reductionism and non-reductionism in regard to testimony, fallibilism and infallibilism, skepticism and anti-skepticism, and epistemic internalism and externalism. There are also likely to be other factors such as the one driving the difference in intuitions about authentic evidence versus apparent evidence Gettier cases that we at present have no theoretical reason to expect but which will be revealed only by empirical happenstance. While the studies discussed above may suggest that a great deal of work in cross-cultural experimental epistemology has been done, the empirical investigation of epistemic folkways is still very much in its early stages.

2.5.2 Weaker Than Expected Patterns

One issue in experimental epistemology that needs to be examined in more careful detail going forward is the fact that even when there are fairly clear patterns in the knowledge attributions and denials of laypeople, it is at times puzzling that the patterns are not even clearer. Nagel and colleagues, for example, write:

> Although the broad pattern of responses was consistent with the standard philosophical handling of the cases we examined, participants did not exhibit perfect consensus on these cases. Although Standard True Belief cases attracted the highest rates of knowledge attribution, these cases were not always rated as exemplifying knowledge. [...] Similarly, the Justified False Belief stories were not always judged to involve a failure of knowledge. Although a large majority of participants did deny knowledge for these stories, it is potentially troubling that the rate of knowledge ascription was not lower still. (Nagel et al. 2013, p. 658)

Participants from Nagel and colleagues (2013) firmly attributed knowledge in standard justified true belief cases only 75% of the time, at least 14% of the time in false belief cases, and 32% to 35% of the time in response to Gettier cases. Starmans and Friedman made similar observations:

> While baseline levels of knowledge attribution were not the focus of our studies, it is worth noting that both laypeople and non-philosophy academics attributed knowledge to protagonists with false beliefs at fairly high rates (52% and 29%, respectively). (Starmans and Friedman 2020, p. 23)

These higher or lower than expected rates of knowledge attribution appear to be too high or too low to be readily explained in terms of low-effort responding by participants. A closer examination of the factors that may be responsible for these findings is needed.

Strikingly, Machery and colleagues (2017a) excluded from analysis the responses of 59% of participants for thinking that none of the protagonists in four thought experiments had justified beliefs. Machery and colleagues (2017b) excluded 21% of their participants for the same reason. These numbers highlight the fact – which should have already been obvious – that experimental epistemologists need to carefully examine folk practices of justification attribution and not focus solely on practices of knowledge attribution.

More generally, the observed patterns described in this section suggest that there are likely to be more ways in which the epistemic intuitions of laypeople depart from those of professional philosophers than experimental philosophy have thus far discovered and that more sustained and detailed investigation is needed to understand their nature and significance.

3 Further Topics

Empirical research on knowledge attributions and denials in response to Gettier cases, false belief cases, and unjustified true belief cases has been the central focus of experimental epistemology during its two-decade history. However, a number of other issues have received a degree of attention but would benefit from further investigation. As briefly noted above, the question of whether it is more difficult to know a proposition when the stakes of being wrong about the proposition are higher has been examined by both mainstream and experimental epistemologists (DeRose 1992, 2011; Pinillos 2012; Pinillos and Simpson 2014; Rose et al. 2019). Some experimental philosophers (Rose et al. 2019) contend that existing data settle the debate in favor of the view that folk epistemological norms about knowledge acquisition are insensitive to practical stakes. Others (Buckwalter 2017, 2021; Turri 2017b) argue that a more nuanced examination of the issue reveals that folk norms about knowledge are sensitive to stakes – but not in a way that is friendly to the views of epistemic contextualists (DeRose 1992, 2011) who are largely responsible for the philosophical attention paid to the issue. Despite some strong pronouncements on the issue from different contributors to the debate, the debate seems to remain open – if only because we still lack a good theoretical understanding of how folk norms of epistemic rationality are related to norms of practical rationality. Keith DeRose's (1992) widely discussed case of the person who needs to know that the bank will be open on Saturday because things will go very poorly for him financially if his belief is wrong and he is unable to make an important deposit to his account represents only the tip of the iceberg that is the intersection between epistemology and decision theory. It points in the direction of a number of important but poorly understood issues about folk epistemic norms – e.g., whether epistemic norms are more fundamental than, reducible to, or independent of practical or prudential norms and issues concerning the nature of the normativity involved in each kind of norm (cf. Turri and Buckwalter 2017). Collaboration between experimental epistemologists, mainstream epistemologists, formal epistemologists, decision theorists, and decision scientists will likely be needed in order to construct illuminating answers to these questions.

A number of other topics in experimental epistemology have the following, somewhat curious feature: they have been investigated by John Turri (sometimes with one or more collaborators, e.g., Wesley Buckwalter) and almost no one else. Turri has blazed more new trails in experimental epistemology than anyone else, examining (*inter alia*) the knowledge norm of assertion (Turri 2016a, 2017a), knowledge attributions and denials in lottery cases (Turri and Friedman 2014, Turri 2022), knowledge and epistemic luck (Turri, Buckwalter, and Blouw 2015), the unexpected prevalence of factive norms in folk epistemology (Turri 2016b), whether knowledge can be acquired via false premises (Turri 2019), doxastic voluntarism (Buckwalter and Turri 2020b), and whether knowledge requires merely approximate truth (Buckwalter and Turri 2020a). Turri's groundbreaking work includes a number of surprising and theoretically significant findings and constitutes an invaluable contribution to the expansion of experimental epistemology into new domains. However, not enough experimental philosophers have followed Turri down the trails he has initially or provisionally cleared. Thus, our knowledge of these areas of folk epistemology is severely limited. Some good advice for graduate students wishing to make original contributions to experimental epistemology is simply to survey the novel work of Turri and think about what subsequent steps can be taken from the jumping off points he has created.

Bibliography

Alexander, Joshua, and Jonathan Weinberg (2007): "Analytic epistemology and experimental Philosophy", *Philosophy Compass* 2 (1), pp. 56–80.

Beebe, James, and Wesley Buckwalter (2010): "The epistemic side-effect effect", *Mind & Language* 25 (4), pp. 474–498.

Beebe, James, and Mark Jensen (2012): "Surprising connections between knowledge and action. The robustness of the epistemic side-effect effect", *Philosophical Psychology* 25 (5), pp. 689–715.

Beebe, James, and Ryan Undercoffer (2016): "Individual and cross-cultural differences in semantic intuitions. New experimental findings", *Journal of Cognition and Culture* 16 (3–4), pp. 322–357.

BonJour, Laurence (1980): "Externalist theories of empirical knowledge", *Midwest Studies in Philosophy* 5 (1), pp. 53–73.

Buckwalter, Wesley (2014): "Factive verbs and protagonist projection", *Episteme* 11 (4), pp. 391–409.

Buckwalter, Wesley (2017): "Epistemic contextualism and linguistic behavior", in: Jonathan Jenkins Ichikawa (Ed.): *Handbook of epistemic contextualism*. London: Routledge, pp. 44–56.

Buckwalter, Wesley (2021): "Error possibility, contextualism, and bias", *Synthese* 198, pp. 2413–2426.

Buckwalter, Wesley, and John Turri (2020a): "Knowledge, adequacy, and approximate truth", *Consciousness and Cognition* 83 (4), 102950.

Buckwalter, Wesley, and John Turri (2020b): "Inability and obligation in intellectual evaluation", *Episteme* 17 (4), pp. 475–497.

Dalbauer, Nikolaus, and Andreas Hergovich (2013): "Is what is worse more likely? The probabilistic explanation of the epistemic side-effect effect", *Review of Philosophy and Psychology* 4 (4), pp. 639–657.

DeRose, Keith (1992): "Contextualism and knowledge attributions", *Philosophy and Phenomenological Research* 52 (4), pp. 913–929.

DeRose, Keith (2011): "Contextualism, contrastivism, and x-phi surveys", *Philosophical Studies* 156 (1), pp. 81–110.
Deutsch, Max (2009): "Experimental philosophy and the theory of reference", *Mind & Language* 24 (4), pp. 445–466.
Devitt, Michael (2011): "Experimental semantics", *Philosophy and Phenomenological Research* 82 (2), pp. 418–435.
Friedman, Ori, and John Turri (2015): "Is probabilistic evidence a source of knowledge?", *Cognitive Science* 39 (5), pp. 1062–1080.
Gettier, Edmund (1963): "Is justified true belief knowledge?", *Analysis* 23 (6), pp. 121–123.
Goldman, Alvin (2007): "Philosophical intuitions. Their target, their source, and their epistemic status", *Grazer Philosophische Studien* 74 (1), pp. 1–26.
Gonnerman, Chad, Banjit Singh, and Grant Toomey (2022): "Authentic and apparent evidence Gettier cases across American and Indian nationalities", *Review of Philosophy and Psychology*.
Haukioja, Jussi (Ed.) (2015): *Advances in experimental philosophy of language*. London: Bloomsbury.
Henrich, Joseph, Steven Heine, and Ara Norenzayan (2010): "The weirdest people in the world?", *Behavioral and Brain Sciences* 33 (2–3), pp. 61–83.
Holton, Richard (1997): "Some telling examples. A reply to Tsohatzidis", *Journal of Pragmatics* 28 (5), pp. 625–628.
Ichikawa, Jonathan Jenkins, and Mattias Steup (2018): "The analysis of knowledge", in: Edward Zalta (Ed.): *The Stanford encyclopedia of philosophy*. Summer 2018 edition. https://plato.stanford.edu/archives/sum2018/entries/knowledge-analysis/, last accessed May 19, 2023.
Kim, Minsun, and Yuan Yuan (2015): "No cross-cultural differences in the Gettier car case intuition. A replication study of Weinberg et al. 2001", *Episteme* 12 (3), pp. 355–361.
Ludwig, Kirk (2007): "The epistemology of thought experiments. First person versus third person approaches", *Midwest Studies in Philosophy* 31 (1), pp. 128–159.
Machery, Edouard (2014): "What is the significance of the demographic variation in semantic intuitions?", in: Edouard Machery and Elizabeth O'Neill (Eds.): *Current controversies in experimental philosophy*. New York and London: Routledge, pp. 3–16.
Machery, Edouard, Ron Mallon, Shaun Nichols, and Stephen Stich (2004): "Semantics, cross-cultural style", *Cognition* 92 (3), pp. B1–B12.
Machery, Edouard, Stephen Stich, David Rose, Amita Chatterjee, Kaori Karasawa, Noel Struchiner, Smita Sirker, Naoki Usui, and Takaaki Hashimoto (2017a): "Gettier across cultures", *Noûs* 51 (3), pp. 645–664.
Machery, Edouard, Stephen Stich, David Rose, Mario Alai, Adriano Angelucci, Renatas Berniūnas, Emma Buchtel, Amita Chatterjee, Hyundeuk Cheon, In-Rae Cho, Daniel Cohnitz, Florian Cova, Vilius Dranseika, Ángeles Eraña Lagos, Laleh Ghadakpour, Maurice Grinberg, Ivar Hannikainen, Takaaki Hashimoto, Amir Horowitz, Evgeniya Hristova, Yasmina Jraissati, Veselina Kadreva, Kaori Karasawa, Hackjin Kim, Yeonjeong Kim, Minwoo Lee, Carlos Mauro, Masaharu Mizumoto, Sebastiano Moruzzi, Christopher Olivola, Jorge Ornelas, Barbara Osimani, Carlos Romero, Alejandro Rosas López, Massimo Sangoi, Andrea Sereni, Sarah Songhorian, Paulo Sousa, Noel Struchiner, Vera Tripodi, Naoki Usui, Alejandro Vázquez del Mercado, Giorgio Volpe, Hrag Abraham Vosgerichian, Xueyi Zhang, and Jing Zhu (2017b): "The Gettier intuition from South America to Asia", *Journal of Indian Council of Philosophical Research* 34 (3), pp. 517–541.
Martí, Genoveva (2009): "Against semantic multi-culturalism", *Analysis* 69 (1), pp. 42–48.
Nagel, Jennifer (2014): *Knowledge. A very short introduction*. New York: Oxford University Press.
Nagel, Jennifer, Valerie San Juan, and Raymond Mar (2013): "Lay denial of knowledge for justified true beliefs", *Cognition* 129 (3), pp. 652–661.
Nisbett, Richard, Kaiping Peng, Incheol Choi, and Ara Norenzayan (2001): "Culture and systems of thought. Holistic versus analytic cognition", *Psychological Review* 108 (2), pp. 291–310.

Pinillos, Ángel (2012): "Knowledge, experiments and practical interests", in: Jessica Brown and Mikkel Gerken (Eds.): *Knowledge ascriptions.* New York: Oxford University Press, pp. 192–221.

Pinillos, Ángel, and Shawn Simpson (2014): "Experimental evidence supporting anti-intellectualism about knowledge", in: James Beebe (Ed.): *Advances in experimental epistemology.* London: Bloomsbury, pp. 9–43.

Rose, David, Edouard Machery, Stephen Stich, Mario Alai, Adriano Angelucci, Renatas Berniūnas, Emma Buchtel, Amita Chatterjee, Hyundeuk Cheon, In-Rae Cho, Daniel Cohnitz, Florian Cova, Vilius Dranseika, Ángeles Eraña Lagos, Laleh Ghadakpour, Maurice Grinberg, Ivar Hannikainen, Takaaki Hashimoto, Amir Horowitz, Evgeniya Hristova, Yasmina Jraissati, Veselina Kadreva, Kaori Karasawa, Hackjin Kim, Yeonjeong Kim, Minwoo Lee, Carlos Mauro, Masaharu Mizumoto, Sebastiano Moruzzi, Christopher Olivola, Jorge Ornelas, Barbara Osimani, Carlos Romero, Alejandro Rosas López, Massimo Sangoi, Andrea Sereni, Sarah Songhorian, Paulo Sousa, Noel Struchiner, Vera Tripodi, Naoki Usui, Alejandro Vázquez del Mercado, Giorgio Volpe, Hrag Abraham Vosgerichian, Xueyi Zhang, Jing Zhu (2019): "Nothing at stake in knowledge", *Noûs* 53 (1), pp. 224–247.

Russell, Bertrand (1948): *Human knowledge. Its scope and limits.* London: George Allen & Unwin.

Ryszkowska, M., K. Skrzecz, and U. Wiśniewska (n.d.): "The group Knobe effect. Data from Polish speakers". Manuscript.

Seyedsayamdost, Hamid (2015): "On normativity and epistemic intuitions. Failure of replication", *Episteme* 12 (1), pp. 95–116.

Sosa, Ernest (2007): "Experimental philosophy and philosophical intuition", *Philosophical Studies* 132 (1), pp. 99–107.

Starmans, Christina, and Ori Friedman (2012): "The folk conception of knowledge", *Cognition* 124 (3), pp. 272–283.

Starmans, Christina, and Ori Friedman (2020): "Expert or esoteric? Philosophers attribute knowledge differently than all other academics", *Cognitive Science* 44 (7), e12850.

Turri, John (2016a): *Knowledge and the norm of assertion. An essay in philosophical science.* Cambridge: Open Book.

Turri, John (2016b): "The radicalism of truth-insensitive epistemology. Truth's profound effect on the evaluation of belief", *Philosophy and Phenomenological Research* 93 (2), pp. 348–367.

Turri, John (2017a): "Experimental work on the norms of assertion", *Philosophy Compass* 12 (7): e12425.

Turri, John (2017b): "Epistemic contextualism. An idle hypothesis", *Australasian Journal of Philosophy* 95 (1), pp. 141–156.

Turri, John (2019): "Knowledge from falsehood. An experimental study", *Thought* 8 (3), pp. 167–178.

Turri, John (2022): "Knowledge attributions and lottery cases. A review and new evidence", in: Igor Douven (Ed.): *Lotteries, knowledge, and rational belief.* Cambridge: Cambridge University Press, pp. 28–47.

Turri, John, and Wesley Buckwalter (2017): "Descartes's schism, Locke's reunion. Completing the pragmatic turn in epistemology", *American Philosophical Quarterly* 54 (1), pp. 25–46.

Turri, John, Wesley Buckwalter, and Peter Blouw (2015): "Knowledge and luck", *Psychonomic Bulletin and Review* 22 (2), pp. 378–390.

Turri, John, and Ori Friedman (2014): "Winners and losers in the folk epistemology of lotteries", in: James Beebe (Ed.): *Advances in experimental epistemology.* London: Bloomsbury, pp. 45–69.

Turri, John, and YeounJun Park (2018): "Knowledge and assertion in Korean", *Cognitive Science* 42 (6), pp. 2060–2080.

Weinberg, Jonathan, Shaun Nichols, and Stephen Stich (2001): "Normativity and epistemic intuitions", *Philosophical Topics* 29 (1–2), pp. 429–460.

Williamson, Timothy (2004): "Philosophical 'intuitions' and scepticism about judgement", *Dialectica* 58 (1), pp. 109–153.

Williamson, Timothy (2011): "Philosophical expertise and the burden of proof", *Metaphilosophy* 42 (3), pp. 215–229.

Yuan, Yuan, and Minsun Kim (2021): "Cross-cultural convergence of knowledge attribution in East Asia and the US", *Review of Philosophy and Psychology* 14 (1), pp. 267–294.
Zagzebski, Linda (1994): "The inescapability of Gettier problems", *The Philosophical Quarterly* 44 (174), pp. 65–73.
Zaręba, Marta (n.d.): "Epistemic side-effect effect in Polish language". Manuscript. University of Warsaw.
Ziółkowski, Adrian (2021): "The stability of philosophical intuitions. Failed replications of Swain et al. (2008)", *Episteme* 18 (2), pp. 328–346.

Edouard Machery
Experimental Philosophy of Language: Proper Names and Predicates

Abstract: One of the most successful research areas in experimental philosophy examines people's judgments about semantic properties. This chapter reviews results of experimental philosophy of language that focus on the reference of proper names (the causal-historical view versus the descriptivist view), investigating in particular the cross-cultural variation in judgments about reference, as well as the semantics of predicates (semantic externalism versus semantic internalism).

Keywords: Cultural Variation; Experimental Philosophy; Reference; Saul Kripke; Semantic Intuitions

1 Introduction

One of the most successful research areas in experimental philosophy examines people's judgments about semantic properties. Much of the literature has focused on the reference of proper names in a cross-cultural context, although recent work has turned to the extension of predicates such as natural kind terms. In this chapter, I review this literature, with an eye to identifying open questions that call for more theoretical and empirical work. Section 2.1 examines the cross-cultural work about the reference of proper names and the debates it has given rise to. Section 2.2 examines the burgeoning work on the extension of predicates. Section 3 gives a short overview regarding other areas of research in experimental semantics. Section 4 summarizes.

2 Experimental Semantics of Proper Names and Predicates

This section examines experimental work on judgments about the reference of proper names across cultures (Section 2.1) and about the semantics of predicates, with a special focus on natural kind terms (Section 2.2).

2.1 Proper Names

2.1.1 Gödel in Asia

In *Naming and Necessity*, Kripke discusses at some length a theory of reference that he attributes to Frege (1892), Russell, and Searle (1958) and describes as follows:

> According to this view, and a locus classicus of it is Searle's article on proper names, the referent of a name is determined not by a single description but by some cluster or family. Whatever in some sense satisfies enough or most of the family is the referent of the name. (Kripke 1980, p. 18)

This theory, which we will call "the descriptive theory of reference" or "descriptivism" (Kripke calls it "the description theory of names") is contrasted, not to a theory proper, but, as Kripke himself insists, to a "picture":

> for most speakers, unless they are the ones who initially give an object its name, the referent of the name is determined by a "causal" chain of communication rather than a description. (Kripke 1980, p. 59)

Despite Kripke's disclaimer, I will call this picture "the causal-historical theory of reference". As understood here, descriptivism and the causal-historical theory are not about the meaning of proper names (i.e., what a proper name contributes to the truth conditions of the sentences containing it); rather, they are about how their reference is determined (i.e., about the facts in virtue of which a proper name refers to what it refers to).

Kripke brought a battery of considerations to bear against descriptivism, which includes some famous thought experiments. The most famous one is the so-called Gödel case:

> Suppose that Gödel was not in fact the author of [Gödel's] theorem. A man called "Schmidt" [...] actually did the work in question. His friend Gödel somehow got hold of the manuscript and it was thereafter attributed to Gödel. On the [descriptivist] view in question, then, when our ordinary man uses the name "Gödel", he really means to refer to Schmidt, because Schmidt is the unique person satisfying the description "the man who discovered the incompleteness of arithmetic." [...] But it seems we are not. We simply are not. (Kripke 1980, p. 83f.)

Descriptivism entails that in this scenario "Gödel" refers to the man called "Schmidt" by Kripke. By contrast, the causal-historical theory entails that this proper name refers to the man called "Gödel".

Naming and Necessity gave rise to a lively literature about how the reference of proper names is fixed, with some attempting to amend the simple version of descriptivism that Kripke had attacked (e.g., Jackson 1998), others fleshing out the picture proposed by Kripke (Devitt 1981), and yet others finding a compromise between the two approaches contrasted by Kripke (e.g., Evans 1973). What was *not* examined in this literature was the thought experiments Kripke had used: Did people react to the cases put forward as Kripke did? Did judgments[1] vary? And what would follow if they did?

---

[1] Philosophers often call the judgments elicited by thought experiments "intuitions", but this terminology is at best misleading (Machery 2017, ch. 1). No property distinguishes these judgments from the judgments we make in everyday life (e.g., while reading fictions or newspapers).

Machery and colleagues (2004) were the first to raise and address these questions. They contrasted two different views about the reference of proper names. Following Kripke (1980, p. 71), descriptivism was characterized by two theses:

D1. Competent speakers associate a description with every proper name. This description specifies a set of properties.

D2. An object is the referent of a proper name if and only if it uniquely or best satisfies the description associated with it. (Machery et al. 2004, p. B2)

An object uniquely satisfies a description when the description is true of it and only it. If no object entirely satisfies the description, many philosophers claim that the proper name refers to the unique individual that satisfies most of the description (Lewis 1970, Searle 1958). If the description is not satisfied at all or if many individuals satisfy it, the name does not refer.

Two theses also characterized the causal-historical theory:

C1. A name is introduced into a linguistic community for the purpose of referring to an individual. It continues to refer to that individual as long as its uses are linked to the individual via a causal chain of successive users: every user of the name acquired it from another user, who acquired it in turn from someone else, and so on, up to the first user who introduced the name to refer to a specific individual.

C2. Speakers may associate descriptions with names. After a name is introduced, the associated description does not play any role in the fixation of the referent. The referent may entirely fail to satisfy the description. (Machery et al. 2004, pp. B2f.)

Machery and colleagues acknowledged the existence of more sophisticated views about the reference of proper names, but focused on these two precisifications of Kripke's descriptivism and causal-historical theory.

They then developed two types of cases, based on two of Kripke's own thought experiments: the Gödel case and the Jonah case. In a Gödel case, a proper name is associated by a speaker or a community of speakers with a description that is not satisfied by the original bearer of this name, but by someone else. In a Jonah case (Kripke 1980, p. 67), a proper name is associated by a speaker or a community of speakers with a description that is not satisfied by anyone, including by the original bearer of this name. Machery and colleagues wrote a version of the Gödel case framed in a Chinese context, and one framed in a Western context (which closely followed Kripke's own wording); they did the same for the Jonah case. The Western Gödel case read as follows:

Suppose that John has learned in college that Gödel is the man who proved an important mathematical theorem, called the incompleteness of arithmetic. John is quite good at mathematics and he can give an accurate statement of the incompleteness theorem, which he attributes to Gödel as the discoverer. But this is the only thing that he has heard about Gödel. Now suppose that Gödel was not the author of this theorem. A man called "Schmidt", whose body was found in Vienna under mysterious circumstances many years ago, actually did the work in question. His friend Gödel somehow got hold of the manuscript and claimed credit for the work, which was thereafter attributed to Gödel. Thus, he has been known as the man who proved the incompleteness of arithmetic. Most people who have heard the name "Gödel" are like John; the claim that Gödel discovered the incompleteness theorem is the only thing they have ever heard about Gödel. When John uses the name "Gödel", is he talking about:

(A) the person who really discovered the incompleteness of arithmetic? Or
(B) the person who got hold of the manuscript and claimed credit for the work? (Machery et al. 2004, p. B6)

An (A) answer is a descriptivist judgment (i.e., a judgment in line with what descriptivism entails about the case), a (B) answer is a causal-historical answer (i.e., a judgment in line with what the causal-historical theory entails about the case).

Machery and colleagues hypothesized that people in East Asia and in the West would tend to make different judgments on the basis of the then emerging view in cultural psychology that there are systematic cognitive differences between East Asia and the West (Nisbett 2004). In particular, East Asians appeared less likely to emphasize causal relations in describing situations and in classifications (Norenzayan et al. 2002; but see Klein et al. 2018 for concerns about this result's replicability). This led Machery and colleagues to the following prediction:

> When presented with Kripke-style thought experiments, [Westerners] would be more likely to respond in accordance with causal-historical accounts of reference, while [East Asians] would be more likely to respond in accordance with descriptivist accounts of reference. (Machery et al. 2004, p. B5)

Data were collected in Hong Kong and in the United States, using vignettes in English. Figure 1 reports the results for the Gödel case. As predicted, Chinese were more likely than Americans to make descriptivist judgments in response to the Gödel case; in fact, a majority of Chinese made descriptivist judgments, while a majority of Americans made causal-historical judgments. However, Americans turned out to be divided about what to say in response to this case.

One of the two Jonah cases read as follows:

> In high-school, German students learn that Attila founded Germany in the second century A.D. They are taught that Attila was the king of a nomadic tribe that migrated from the east to settle in what would become Germany. Germans also believe that Attila was a merciless warrior and leader who expelled the Romans from Germany, and that after his victory against the Romans Attila organized a large and prosperous kingdom.
>
> Now suppose that none of this is true. No merciless warrior expelled the Romans from Germany, and Germany was not founded by a single individual. Actually, the facts are the following. In the fourth century A.D., a nobleman of low rank, called "Raditra", ruled a small and peaceful area in what today is Poland, several hundred miles from Germany. Raditra was a wise and gentle man who managed to preserve the peace in the small land he was ruling. For this reason, he quickly became the main character of many stories and legends. These stories were passed on from one generation of peasants to the next. But often when the story was passed on the peasants would

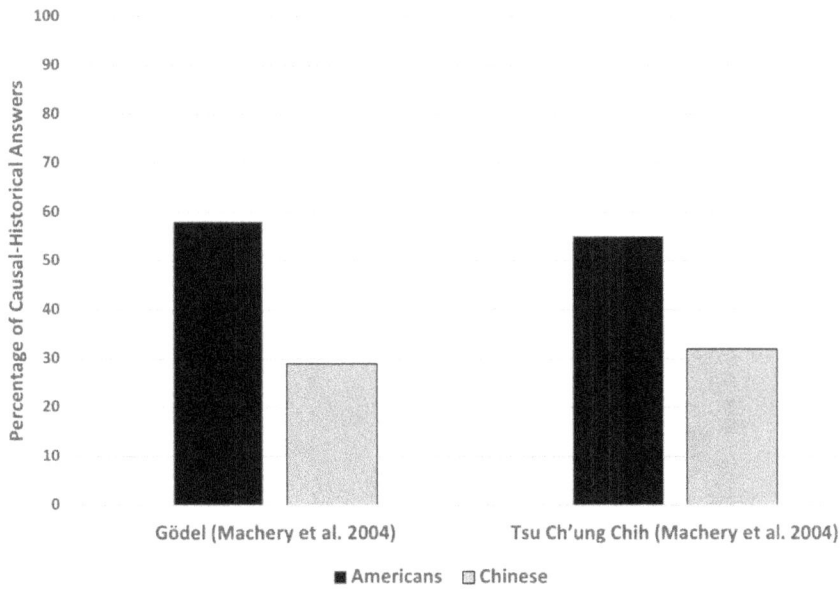

Figure 1: Proportion of causal-historical answers in two Gödel cases in Machery et al. (2004)

embellish it, adding imaginary details and dropping some true facts to make the story more exciting. From a peaceful nobleman of low rank, Raditra was gradually transformed into a warrior fighting for his land. When the legend reached Germany, it told of a merciless warrior who was victorious against the Romans. By the eighth century A.D., the story told of an Eastern king who expelled the Romans and founded Germany. By that time, not a single true fact remained in the story.

Meanwhile, as the story was told and retold, the name "Raditra" was slowly altered: it was successively replaced by "Aditra", then by "Arritrak" in the sixth century, by "Arrita" and "Arrila" in the seventh and finally by "Attila". The story about the glorious life of Attila was written down in the eighth century by a scrupulous Catholic monk, from whom all our beliefs are derived. Of course, Germans know nothing about these real events. They believe a story about a merciless Eastern king who expelled the Romans and founded Germany.

When a contemporary German high-school student says "Attila was the king who drove the Romans from Germany", is he actually talking about the wise and gentle nobleman, Raditra, who is the original source of the Attila legend, or is he talking about a fictional person, someone who does not really exist?

(A) He is talking about Raditra.
(B) He is talking about a fictional person who does not really exist. (Machery et al. 2004, p. B10)

Figure 2 reports the results for the Jonah cases. No difference was found between Chinese and Americans. Both groups leaned toward making causal-historical judgments. Machery and colleagues concluded provocatively as follows:

our data indicate that philosophers must radically revise their methodology. Since the intuitions philosophers pronounce from their armchairs are likely to be a product of their own culture

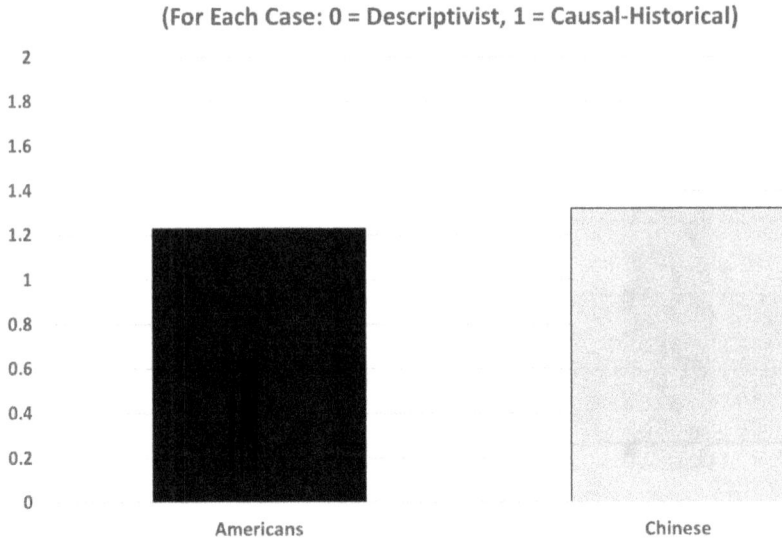

Figure 2: Aggregated causal-historical answers in two Jonah cases in Machery et al. (2004)

and their academic training, in order to determine the implicit theories that underlie the use of names across cultures, philosophers need to get out of their armchairs. And this is far from what philosophers have been doing for the last several decades. (Machery et al. 2004, p. B9)

These findings gave rise to a large literature (e. g., Ludwig 2007; Devitt 2011, 2012a, 2012b; Mallon et al. 2009; Martí 2009, 2012, 2014; Ichikawa et al. 2012; Machery 2011, 2012a, 2012b, 2014, 2015; Ostertag 2013; Machery et al. 2013; Beebe and Undercoffer 2015, 2016; Kallestrup 2016; Nado and Johnson 2016; Izumi et al. 2018; Vignolo and Domaneschi 2018; Devitt and Porot 2019; Domaneschi and Vignolo 2020; Li 2021; for further discussion of some of the issues raised by these papers, see Machery 2020). In the remainder of Section 2, I highlight some important threads of this literature.

2.1.2 Are the Gödel Case Data Robust?

The replication crisis in the behavioral sciences (OSC 2015, Machery and Doris 2017) has taught us to treat empirical results, particularly from single studies, with great care. So, do Machery and colleagues' results replicate? As can be seen in Figure 3, the basic finding has been replicated many times, using slightly different formulations.

Sytsma and Livengood had noted an ambiguity in the probes used by Machery and colleagues (i. e., the questions at the end of the vignettes), which they describe as follows:

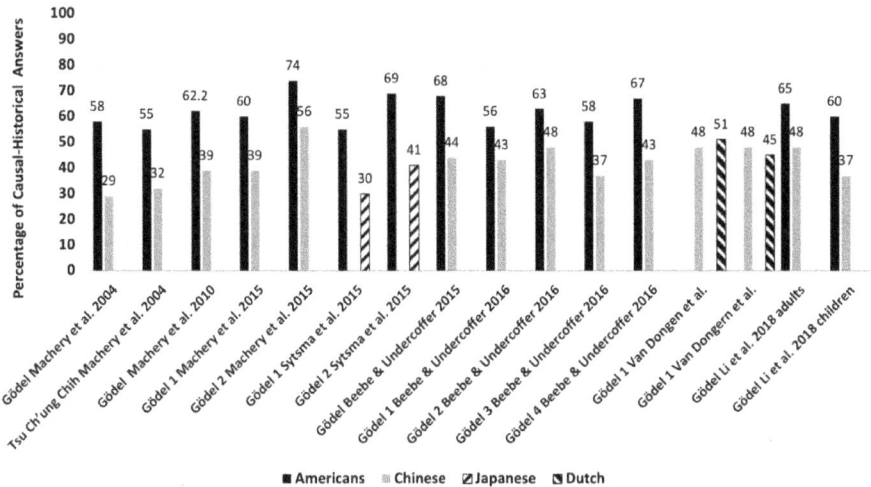

Figure 3: Proportion of causal-historical answers in Gödel cases across studies

> One problem with this question is that it does not adequately specify whose epistemic perspective should be adopted in deciding who these descriptions denote, raising the possibility that different participants might associate the same description with different people from the story. While Machery et al. expect the descriptions to be read from the narrator's perspective, the question might plausibly lead participants to instead adopt John's [the character in the thought experiment] perspective. (Sytsma and Livengood 2011, p. 319)

That is, the probe could ask what the reference of the proper name "Gödel" is from the perspective of the narrator or from the perspective of the case's character. They had also suggested a way to disambiguate between these two interpretations, and they showed that among Westerners the proportion of causal-historical judgments increases when the probe is so disambiguated. Further work has however shown that this disambiguation had little impact on the observed cross-cultural difference (Sytsma et al. 2015, Machery et al. 2015).

Second, the cross-cultural difference is not limited to the original comparison between China and the United States, but it has been extended to Japan (Sytsma et al. 2015). This finding provides evidence for the cultural hypothesis originally put forward by Machery et al. (2004).

Third, Machery and colleagues' work with adults raises the question of when the difference between East Asians and Westerners emerges. Li and colleagues (2018) wrote children-appropriate versions of the Gödel case, such as the following one:

> Long ago, there was a race called the Super Dog Race. Max, Pickles and Blaze participated in the race. Max crossed the finish line first, winning the race, but he got too excited and ran all the way to the North Pole. Pickles crossed the finish line second. He stopped and watched Max run away. The race announcer mistakenly thought that Pickles won the race. He told every newspaper in the world that Pickles won. He also told them that another dog, Blaze, ran very fast despite his short

legs. Since then, everyone learned that Pickles won the race. They don't know anything else about Pickles. Tom and Emily learned at school that Pickles won the Super Dog Race. This is the only thing they know about the dog race and Pickles. They don't know anything about Max. That night, their dad asked: Do you know who won the Super Dog Race?

Tom replied: Blaze was the dog that won the Super Dog Race.
Emily said: Pickles was the dog that won the Super Dog Race. (Li et al. 2018, p. 109)

Participants were asked whether they agreed with Tom (a control question) and with Emily. Agreement with Emily indicated a descriptivist answer, disagreement a causal-historical answer. Not only did they replicate the cultural difference, but they also found it with 6- to 8-year-old children.

Finally, not all replication attempts were successful. Cova and colleagues (2021) report an unsuccessful attempt conducted by Romero and colleagues (2017). Follow-up work by the same team however replicated the cross-cultural difference originally reported by Machery and colleagues (2004).

In addition to the impressive list of studies replicating the cross-cultural difference in reference judgments in response to the Gödel case, van Dongen and colleagues (2021) have recently conducted a meta-analysis of the literature on judgments about reference. Their conclusion is worth quoting:

> our meta-analysis supports the hypothesis that cross-cultural factors affect semantic intuitions about proper names. [...] Neither do specific analysis tools aimed at detecting publication bias or QRPs (e.g., funnel plots, p-curves) provide evidence of systematic suppression of negative results. (van Dongen et al. 2021, p. 763)

They also found that the effect varies across studies, and they highlight the "high inter-study variability of the data" (van Dongen et al. 2021, p. 763).

While this meta-analysis is an important contribution to the literature, it is unfortunately undiscerning with respect to the studies it meta-analyzes: Very different studies are aggregated, some of which have demonstrable flaws that have been discussed in the literature, and it is no wonder that van Dongen and colleagues find heterogeneous results. Some of their meta-analytic analyses aggregate results obtained with the Gödel and Jonah cases. Lam's (2010) vignettes and the replications by Machery and colleagues (2010) are also included among the studies meta-analyzed for some meta-analyses. Lam's study aimed at showing that Machery and colleagues' (2004) findings were due to the imperfect linguistic competence of their Chinese participants. Lam describes his findings as follows:

> This new data concerning the intuitions of Cantonese-speakers raises questions about whether cross-cultural variation in answers to questions on certain vignettes reveal genuine differences in intuitions, or whether such differences stem from non-intuitional differences, such as differences in linguistic competence. (Lam 2010, p. 320)

To support this conclusion, Lam presented Asian participants in the USA with Gödel cases in Cantonese, and reports that the cross-cultural difference observed by Machery and colleagues (2004) disappears. However, this is not the only modification that Lam made: The vignette and the probe were also modified; they read as follows:

> Suppose there is a group of people who do not know anything of the English author Shakespeare except the name and that he is the author of "Romeo and Juliet". Unbeknownst to this group of people, Shakespeare did not in fact write the play "Romeo and Juliet"; in fact, a German man named "Spencer" wrote the play, but Spencer was an obscure writer who died before the play was published. Shakespeare in fact found the play and published it as his own. Nobody knows this. This group of people otherwise use the name "Shakespeare" and can use it in conversation, for instance, they may ask each other, "I wonder whether Shakespeare was English or German?" When these people use the name "Shakespeare" in a conversation, is their use of the name to talk about
> (A) Shakespeare
> (B) Spencer (Lam 2010, p. 322)

In contrast to the probes used elsewhere, Lam's probe uses and cites "Shakespeare". Follow-up work has shown that these modifications, and not the language of the vignette, was the crucial factor (Machery et al. 2010): Presenting the Gödel case in English and Mandarin to Mandarin speakers elicit similar results; the same is true of presenting Lam's modified vignette in English and Mandarin to Mandarin speakers. What's more, Machery and colleagues argued that the modifications introduced by Lam are inappropriate for testing reference judgments because they bias people to give apparently causal-historical answers by both quoting and using the name: It primes people to answer "Shakespeare" when they are asked a question about whom "Shakespeare" may refer to.[2]

2.1.3 The Debate about Speaker's Reference

Machery and colleagues (2004) as well as the following experimental studies aim at assessing whether judgments about reference vary across and within cultures. Some have however objected that the judgments elicited by the Gödel case and other cases are not about reference in the relevant sense (Ludwig 2007, Deutsch 2009, Vignolo and Domaneschi 2018, Heck 2018). This objection builds on Kripke's (1977) distinction between semantic reference and speaker's reference. Semantic reference is the reference a proper name has because it belongs to a given language; speaker reference is the reference a proper name has on a given occasion of use because of the speaker's referential intention. Speaker's reference and semantic reference often coincide, but at times they can diverge. So, the objection is that the Gödel case elicits (or, more weakly, might elicit)

---

[2] Unsurprisingly, whether a study uses Lam's vignettes predicts East Asians' answers (van Dongen et al. 2021, fn. 13): East Asians give more causal-historical answers when given Lam's vignettes.

judgments about speaker's reference, not semantic reference, and as a result that the empirical findings are irrelevant for the type of semantic project Kripke and others have been engaged in.

In addition to theoretical responses (Machery 2011, 2014; Machery and Stich 2012), Machery and colleagues (2015) have attempted to address this objection head-on by designing experiments that increase the probability that participants genuinely report a judgment about semantic reference. Their first experimental strategy consists in reformulating the probe so as to make clear that the question was not about the intention of the speaker (in English in Study 2 and Chinese in Study 3):

> When John uses the name "Gödel", *regardless of whom he might intend to be talking about*, he is *actually* talking about:
> (A) the person who really discovered the incompleteness of arithmetic;
> (B) the person who got hold of the manuscript and claimed credit for the work. (Machery et al. 2015, p. 69)

Their second experimental strategy consisted in making it clear that the speaker has the intention to refer to the man who stole the theorem (Study 4 of Machery et al. 2015). A participant that still answered (A) must then be reporting a judgment about semantic reference. The results were all in line with Machery and colleagues' (2004) original finding.

Machery and colleagues (2015) conceded that their experiments didn't conclusively demonstrate that the judgments elicited by the Gödel case and other vignettes were genuinely about semantic reference, but they insisted that "taken together, our findings provide strong evidence that genuine intuitions about semantic reference vary both across and within cultures" (Machery et al. 2015, p. 74). Not everyone has been convinced (Heck 2018).

2.1.4 The Jonah Case

Machery and colleagues (2004) failed to find any difference between Chinese and American responses to the Jonah case, but this negative result could be explained in various ways. The vignettes used by them, for example, were long and intricate, and thus might have confused readers. Chinese participants might also have been reluctant to assert that the speaker was talking about nothing. Their apparently causal-historical answers may have been driven by a charitable interpretation of what the speaker could be saying.

Further work tentatively suggests that the Jonah case elicits the same cross-cultural pattern as the Gödel case. In two studies that used shortened, simplified versions of Machery and colleagues' Jonah case and changed the probe, Beebe and Undercoffer (2016) report that Americans are more likely than Chinese to give a causal-historical answer in their version of the Jonah case (Figure 4). Additional work is needed to determine whether judgments about reference vary cross-culturally when they are elicited by a Jonah case, and how answers to the Jonah and Gödel case are related.

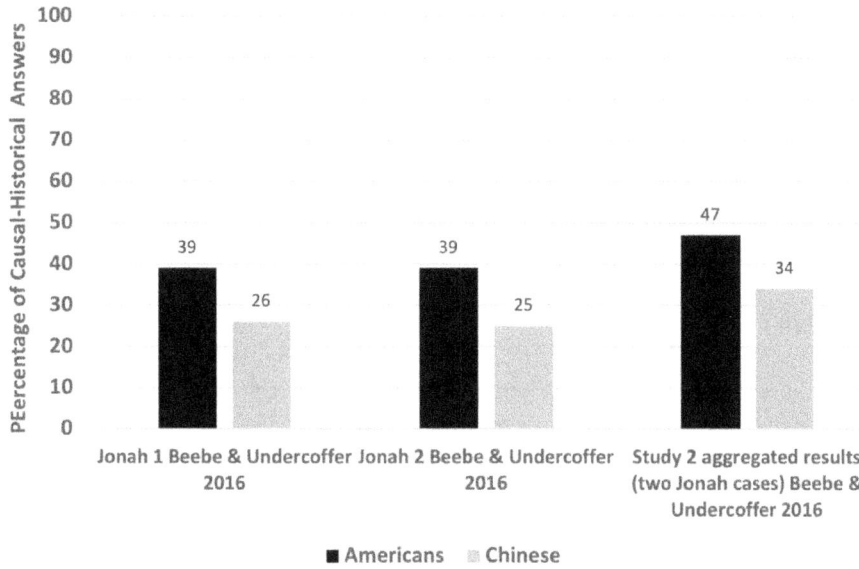

Figure 4: Proportion of causal-historical answers in two Jonah cases in Beebe and Undercoffer (2016)

2.1.5 The Methodology of Experimental Semantics

An important area of discussion concerns the methodology of experimental semantics, a debate initiated by Martí (2009, 2012, 2014). According to Martí, experimental semanticists should examine how proper names are used instead of asking metalinguistic questions about the reference of proper names or the referential intentions of proper name users (for discussion, see Machery et al. 2009, Machery and Stich 2012, Machery 2014). Methodological debates have focused on the significance of, and relations between, three types of data:

(1) Metalinguistic judgments about reference (or about referential intentions);
(2) Truth-value judgments;
(3) The use of words.

Machery and colleagues (2004) asked whom the speaker "is talking about", an instance of the first type of data. Machery and colleagues (2009) asked instead the following question: "when Ivy says, 'Tsu Ch'ung Chih was a great astronomer,' do you think that her claim is: (A) true or (B) false?", an instance of the second type of data. More recently, Devitt and Porot (2019) as well as Domaneschi, Vignolo, and Di Paola

(2017) have elicited uses of proper names, an instance of the third type of data (for critical discussion of these attempts, see Machery 2020).

Machery and colleagues (2009) provided evidence that truth-value judgments were in line with metalinguistic judgments (see also Li et al. 2018, Devitt and Porot 2019), and they argued that truth-value judgments provide defeasible evidence about how one would use words: If someone judges that it is true that in the Gödel case Gödel has proven that arithmetic is incomplete, then she would be inclined to assert that Gödel has proven that arithmetic is incomplete. Devitt and Porot (2018) concur with the latter point, but Vignolo and Domaneschi (2018) have cast some doubts about its cogency (for further discussion, see Machery 2020).

2.1.6 Future Research

While the existing research has established that judgments about the reference of proper names vary across cultures, it is limited in some important respects. Experimental philosophers have examined whether and how variation in the vignettes or probes influences reference judgments. Beebe and Undercoffer (2015, 2016) have shown that the cross-cultural variation in judgments about reference does not depend on the vignette describing a bad action (i.e., stealing) or on the use of the verb "to learn" in the vignette. Sytsma and Livengood (2011) have examined the impact of various formulations of the probe (see also Machery et al. 2010). However, most vignettes are versions of the same original cases presented by Machery and colleagues (2004) (but see Li et al. 2018), and a broader range of vignettes would be needed to establish the results firmly.

Second, the findings from Sytsma and colleagues (2015) as well as Li and colleagues (2018) support the hypothesis that the cultural differences between the West and East Asia, often described as a contrast between individualism and collectivism (e.g., Oyserman et al. 2002) or between independence and interdependence (e.g., Markus and Kitayama 1991), are related to the variation in judgments about reference, but much more cultural work should be conducted to map cultural variation. Very little is known about most cultures in the world. In addition, experimental philosophers should examine whether other demographic variables or other types of judgment also correlate with variation in judgments about reference (for some fascinating results, see Grau and Pury 2014, Machery et al. 2020).

Third, we do not know how to explain the cross-cultural difference between East Asians and Westerners. The few explanatory accounts were all speculative (Ludwig 2007, Lam 2010, Izuwi et al. 2018) and have turned out to be dubious (see Machery 2020 on Izuwi et al. 2018). Future research should investigate theoretically *and* empirically the factors that lead people to make different types of judgments about reference.

2.1.7 Further Readings

Dacey and Mallon (2016) provide a complementary overview of the early work on proper names. Li and Xu (2022) examine 20 years of experimental philosophy of language by bibliometric means. Readers interested in learning about experimental philosophy should consult Sytsma and Livengood (2015).

2.2 Predicates

2.2.1 Externalism and Internalism

As Kripke himself noted, the question of how the reference of proper names is fixed is bound to raise questions about other types of words: In particular, how is the extension of predicates fixed? What determines whether this, but not that, object belongs to the extension of, say, "cat"? And should semantic distinctions be drawn between types of predicates? Does "cat" (a predicate referring to a biological kind) refer in the same way as "pen" (a predicate referring to kind of artifacts)?

Kripke (1980) and Putnam (1975a, 1975b) both rejected a descriptivist account of the extension of words like "cat", "trees", and "gold", which they called "natural kind terms". According to Kripke:

> Terms for natural kinds are much closer to proper names than is ordinarily supposed. The old term "common name" is thus quite appropriate for predicates marking out species or natural kinds, such as "cow" or "tiger". My considerations apply also, however, to certain mass terms for natural kinds, such as "gold", "water", and the like. (Kripke 1980, p. 127)

Similarly, Putnam rejected the idea that meaning is determined by a description (1975a).

Their positive views are often grouped together under the label "externalism". In contrast to the causal-historical theory, which is a theory of reference determination, externalism is a theory of meaning: It asserts that the meaning of a natural kind term is not determined by speakers' beliefs (i.e., what they believe about its extension), but rather by possibly unknown facts about the kind or substance some particular samples or objects this term has been applied to are samples of or belong to. The meaning of "water" is not determined by speakers' beliefs about its extension (perhaps that water is a watery substance, i.e., a substance that is wet, transparent, and quelches thirst), but by possibly unknown facts about the substance called "water" (perhaps by their molecular structure). By contrast, internalism holds that meaning is determined by some beliefs held by speakers. Externalism must be complemented by two things: A theory of the nature of kinds and substances and a theory of extension determination (to identify which samples or objects matter to determine the relevant kind). Concerning the former, Kripke and Putnam embraced a naïve form of essentialism: For instance, chemical structures are supposed to constitute the nature of chemical kinds. (This essentialism is naïve because no effort was made to examine how scientists think of kinds.) Kripke characterizes the latter as follows:

> the species-name may be passed from link to link, exactly as in the case of proper names, so that many who have seen little or no gold can still use the term. Their reference is determined by a causal (historical) chain, not by use of any items. (Kripke 1980, p. 139)

Putnam writes as follows:

> what does determine the reference of the terms "aluminum," and "molybdenum" in my idiolect? In the previous papers, I suggested that the reference is fixed by a test known to experts; it now seems to me that this is just a special case of my use being causally connected to an introducing event. (Putnam 1975b, p. 205)

Externalism was also associated with a sociolinguistic hypothesis (sometimes called "the division of linguistic labor"): Speakers defer to scientific experts, when those appear to have identified the essence of kinds (Putnam 1975a).

Both Kripke and Putnam relied on thought experiments to support externalism. The most famous among them is Putnam's twin-earth thought experiment:

> Somewhere in the galaxy there is a planet we shall call Twin Earth. Twin Earth is very much like Earth; in fact, people on Twin Earth even speak English. In fact, apart from the differences we shall specify in our science-fiction examples, the reader may suppose that Twin Earth is exactly like Earth. [...] One of the peculiarities of Twin Earth is that the liquid called "water" is not H_2O but a different liquid whose chemical formula is very long and complicated. I shall abbreviate this chemical formula simply as XYZ. I shall suppose that XYZ is indistinguishable from water at normal temperatures and pressures. In particular, it tastes like water and it quenches thirst like water. Also, I shall suppose that the oceans and lakes and seas of Twin Earth contain XYZ and not water, that it rains XYZ on Twin Earth and not water, etc. If a spaceship from Earth ever visits Twin Earth, then the supposition at first will be that "water" has the same meaning on Earth and on Twin Earth. This supposition will be corrected when it is discovered that "water" on Twin Earth is XYZ, and the Earthian spaceship will report somewhat as follows: "On Twin Earth the word 'water' means XYZ." (Putnam 1975a, pp. 139 f.)

I will call cases that have this structure "kind-negative cases": In this type of cases, samples or objects that fulfill the description associated with a predicate do not have the expected kind-determining properties. In another type of thought experiments, the samples or objects that have some kind-determining properties do not fulfill the description associated with the term associated with this kind. For instance:

> the case of pencils turning out to be organisms is complementary to the case [...] of cats turning out to be robots (remotely controlled from Mars). [...] in the case I described, "Cats have turned out to be robots remotely controlled from Mars" is surely nondeviant, and "There are no cats in the world" is highly deviant. (Putnam 1975a, p. 262)

I will call this second type of cases "kind-positive case". Kind-negative and -positive cases can involve either transformations (the superficial or kind-determining properties are transformed) or discoveries (as in the twin-earth thought experiment).

While externalism turned out to be very influential, giving rise to a large literature (e.g., Devitt 1981), a few voices have dissented, objecting to the idea that the use of words in science guides everyday uses and criticizing the erroneous historical accounts of the use of natural kind terms as well as the naïve take on science (e.g., Dupré 1981, Hacking 2007, Bursten 2014).

What about words referring to artifacts? Putnam (1975a) thought their semantics and metasemantics worked similarly to those of natural kind terms, but others have disagreed, rejecting the application of an externalist semantics to this class of words (Schwartz 1978).

2.2.2 Testing Externalist Judgment

In contrast to the research on judgment about the reference of proper names, largely driven by the finding of Machery and colleagues (2004), research on judgments about the extension of predicates is not centered around a single finding and a particular experimental paradigm (the Gödel case). Research mostly focused on determining whether the extension of so-called natural kind terms is fixed by the nature of the kind (e.g., cats) or substance (e.g., water or light), which is discovered by science (for water, philosophers' typical example is H_2O), or rather by superficial, diagnostic properties that plausibly correspond to the descriptions speakers associate with these words (e.g., *furry, meow, four-legged, mammal*). All in all, this literature suggests that (1) both the essence of a kind and the superficial, diagnostic properties associated with it matter, in contrast to what one would expect on the basis of Kripke's and Putnam's externalism and (2) that there is tremendous variation across speakers and across uses for a given speaker. Overall, people do not appear to have the kind of strict linguistic commitments that either externalism or internalism would lead us to expect.

Jylkkä and colleagues' (2009) Study 1 described a scenario where a fictitious substance (zircaum) is thought to have some chemical structure (ACB). A new sample with the superficial properties of zircaum is reported to have that very chemical structure, and participants are asked whether this sample is made of zircaum (I will call their answer "their original judgment"). Participants are then told that it has been discovered that zircaum has in fact another chemical structure (KML). They are then asked the following question:

> When in the earlier situation you judged that "the substance found in Northern Norway is/is not zircaum", was your answer

(A) Justified
(B) strictly speaking correct?[3] (Jylkkä et al. 2009, p. 49)

If participants are committed to externalism about natural kind terms, they should say that their original judgment was erroneous; if they are internalists, they should say that they made no mistake because the extension of "zircaum" is not determined by unknown properties, but by the description associated with "zircaum". First- and third-person versions of this basic scenario were used: In the former case, participants are asked to evaluate whether their original judgment was erroneous, in the latter case whether the judgments of scientists (e. g., scientists thought the substance found in Norway was zircaum) was erroneous. Furthermore, in half of the scenarios, the sample is originally thought to have the same molecular structure as the fictitious substance, but turns out to have a different chemical structure, while in the other half, the sample is originally thought to have a different molecular structure from that of the fictitious substance, but turns out to have the same structure. These two manipulations had no effect. Vignettes described three substances and three animal species, although this manipulation appeared to make no difference. Most answers were in line with externalism, but only a third of participants were consistently externalist: Most participants answered sometimes along externalist, sometimes along internalist lines. Similar results were found in Study 2, which was structurally similar.

Genone and Lombrozo (2012) used a different design, inspired in part by Burge's (1979) famous arthritis thought experiment. In the vignettes, two speakers use a given word, such as "tyleritis", that is either causally associated with a single phenomenon (e. g., a single disease) or with two distinct phenomena (e. g., two diseases), one for each speaker. The vignette also specified that the speakers had more or less overlapping beliefs associated with this word by listing the beliefs they shared. Participants are asked the following question:

> When Alex and his doctor each have a thought in the examination room, are they having a thought about the same disease?
>
> (A) Yes, they are both thinking about the same disease.
> (B) No, they are not thinking about the same disease. (Genone and Lombrozo 2012, p. 725)

Externalists should answer (A) when the word is associated with a single condition, and (B) when it is associated with two phenomena, independently of how much the beliefs of the two speakers overlap; internalists should answer (A) when the beliefs of the two speakers overlap, (B) when they don't. Genone and Lombrozo used fictitious predicates for diseases ("tyleritis"), minerals, and artifacts as well as a legal term.

Roughly, half of the participants answered (A) and half (B) when the target word was associated with a single phenomenon (i. e., when its uses have a single causal ori-

---

[3] Participants had to answer to both (A) and (B).

gin), and the speakers had different beliefs, or when the target word was associated with two distinct phenomena (i.e., different causal origins), but the speakers had the same beliefs. The more similar the beliefs of the two speakers, the more likely it was that people answered that the two speakers were having the same thought. Participants were not consistent in their answers, and no difference was found between the types of predicates used. Study 2 replicated these results, and showed that asking participants to justify their answers had no detectable effect.

Nichols and colleagues (2016) used yet another design. They used an actual predicate ("catoblepas"), instead of fictitious ones, although speakers were not familiar with it. Participants were told that this predicate had been associated with false beliefs, which were however "based on reports of encounters with" real animals (Nichols et al. 2016, p. 153). Participants were then asked the following question:

> Obviously there are some species that really exist and some that really don't. Rabbits really exist; goblins don't really exist. Please indicate to what extent you think catoblepas are more like rabbits or goblins in this regard. Are catoblepas more like rabbits (really exist) or goblins (don't really exist)? (Nichols et al. 2016, p. 153)

Externalists should say that catoblepas exist because of the historical connection between the use of the word "catoblepas" and real animals; internalists should say that catoblepas don't exist because nothing satisfies speakers' beliefs. In Study 1, participants were primed to answer the question by being either given a text describing how a referring predicate (e.g., "Triceratops") was originally associated with false beliefs or they were given a neutral text. Participants were more likely to give internalist answers (more like goblins – don't really exist) in the neutral-text condition than in the Triceratops condition, although the mean answer was barely below the neutral point in the neutral-text condition and barely above it in the Triceratops condition.

In Study 2, participants were presented with the following vignette followed by two assertations, (1) and (2) below, without any framing:

> In the Middle Ages, animal researchers described a distinctive kind of mammal. They called it catoblepas. The catoblepas was said to be like a bull but with a head so heavy that the animal has to keep its head down at all times. It was also thought that the catoblepas had scales on its back. Of course there is nothing that meets this description, but researchers think that it was based on reports of encounters with wildebeests. [...]
>
> (1) "Catoblepas" refers to wildebeests
> (2) Catoblepas exist. (Nichols et al. 2016, p. 155)

Participants had to express their agreement with both assertions on a 6-point scale. Externalists should agree with assertions (1) and (2), internalists disagree. Both assertions elicited externalist answers on average, but some participants didn't give consistent answers to these two questions. An even more pronounced inconsistency was found in Study 3 when participants were asked to express their agreement with the following two assertions: "Catoblepas are wildebeests" (on average externalist answers) and "Catoblepas exist" (on average internalist answers).

Devitt and Porter (2021) have extended Nichols and colleagues' (2016) research by eliciting use of predicates instead of asking questions about them or asking questions using them. Participants were presented with the following story:

> Researchers in the Middle Ages, who are now considered early biologists, described a distinctive kind of animal which they called "catoblepas". They claimed that these animals were like bulls, but with heads so heavy they had to keep their heads down at all times. These early biologists also thought that these animals had scales on their backs, and that their breath was poisonous to humans. We now know, of course, that there have never been any animals that meet this description. Historians have recently discovered, however, that the descriptions arose from some of those biologists observing some actual animals, and coming to mistaken views about them. The animals they observed were in fact wildebeests, which are migratory antelopes that still roam Africa today. Wildebeests are not bulls, but they do have large heads with horns. They do not keep their heads down at all times, but they often hold their heads low to the ground in order to eat grass. They do not have scales, but it is now thought that the biologists wrongly took their rough manes for scales. Furthermore, the diet of wildebeests does include many poisonous plants, and the early biologists seem to have mistakenly thought that this would make their breath poisonous. (Devitt and Porter 2021, p. 7)

They were then asked to "say what if anything [they] think textbooks on the history of science should say about Catoblepas" and to "give reasons" (Devitt and Porter 2021, p. 8). In line with the results reviewed here, about half of the answers were aligned with externalism, that is, they identified catoblepas with wildebeests. Study 2 used the same vignette and asked participants to assess the truth of one of two assertions:

> Catoblepas were real animals that were falsely described in the Middle Ages.
> Catoblepas did not really exist. (Devitt and Porter 2021, p. 10)

Surprisingly, answers were not consistent: The first question elicited causal-historical answers, the second descriptivist answers. Study 3 was similar, but asked participants to assess both assertions: Inconsistency was found, not merely across participants (as in Study 2), but within participants.

Some studies have directly examined the judgments elicited by twin-earth thought experiments. Their results converge with the findings reported in this section. Tobia and colleagues (2019) wrote twin-earth scenarios for two substances (water and gold) and a species (tiger). The water vignette[4] read as follows:

> Suppose that in a few years, humans are able to travel to other galaxies. While exploring, they land on a planet that looks nothing like Earth in virtually any respect. It is populated by plants and animals that look totally different from the familiar plants and animals on Earth. Its landscapes and ecosystems look and function totally differently from those on Earth. They dub this planet "Twin Earth". The astronauts remove their helmets and find that they can breathe freely. They drink a

---

[4] Available in the paper's supplementary materials at https://osf.io/f44hq/, last accessed May 29, 2023.

liquid not found in any of the planet's lakes and rivers and find the liquid does not look and taste at all like water. They do not at all quench their thirst on the liquid they collect while they explore the planet. When they perform a chemical analysis of this liquid, they find out that it does not contain any compound molecules. The liquid in Twin Earth's lakes and rivers is entirely composed of elemental atoms. In contrast, scientists long ago discovered that all the samples of water on Earth are composed of a particular compound. [That compound was named "H_2O".] Scientists theorize (correctly) that some compound molecules and atoms will never behave in exactly the same way. This means that they will never be completely indistinguishable and interchangeable outside the lab. Scientists issue a report stating that the liquid in Twin Earth's lakes and rivers is not at all identical to the liquid in Earth's lakes and rivers in any observable properties and also does not belong to the same scientific category.

Study 1 participants were then asked to choose one of three options:

1. The liquid from Twin Earth is water.
2. The liquid from Twin Earth is not water.
3. There is a sense in which the liquid from Twin Earth is water, but ultimately, if you think about what it really means to be water, you would have to say there is a sense in which the liquid from Twin Earth is not truly water at all. (Tobia et al. 2019, p. 193)

Slightly more than half of participants chose the third option on average, although the exact proportion varied across types of entities (largest for gold, smallest for tiger). A follow-up study used different prompts, and asked participants whether they agreed with the following two statements on a 7-point scale:

1. There is a sense in which the liquid from Twin Earth is water.
2. Ultimately, if you think about what it really means to be water, you would have to say there is a sense in which the liquid from Twin Earth is not truly water at all. (Tobia et al. 2019, p. 184)

While the mean was above the neutral point (and no difference was detected among stimuli), the difference from the neutral point was small.

Tobia and colleagues also showed that the proportion of externalist answers is influenced by the context of the judgment participants are asked to make: Participants make more externalist judgments in a scientific context than in a legal context (Studies 2 and 3). Again, no effect of kind was observed.

Haukioja and colleagues (2021) also examined twin-earth thought experiments, with various types of natural kind terms (for chemicals, species, and so forth). After reading a kind-negative[5] (which they call "TE-case") or a kind-positive (which they call "reverse-TW-case") scenario, participants in Experiments 1 and 2 were asked three questions. The first one elicited production, as Devitt and Porter (2021) had done:

---

[5] In a kind-negative case, samples or objects that fulfill the description associated with a predicate do not have the expected kind-determining properties. In a kind-positive case, samples and objects that have the kind-determining properties do not fulfill the description.

> Right after having been informed of these discoveries, you are told to report on your findings about the [liquid (TE-case for water)/substance (reverse-TE-case for water), etc.] back to your base on Earth. Draft a report in your own words. (Haukioja et al. 2021, p. 384)

They were then asked whether they agree with one of two statements (for the kind-negative scenarios – this question was adapted for the kind-positive scenarios):

> There is disagreement among your group on how to report your findings back to Earth, and you decide to take a vote. In the vote, you are given two options, (a) and (b):
>
> a. We have found a new water-like substance on this planet, but it is not water. It consists of XYZ, not H_2O.
> b. We have found a new kind of water on this planet. It consists of XYZ rather than H_2O. (Haukioja et al. 2021, p. 384)

Finally, Haukioja and colleagues tested deference to experts:

> Suppose that you find out that all the chemists in your expedition have voted unlike you, and chosen the other alternative. How confident are you, after learning of this, that the option you chose was the more accurate one? (Haukioja et al. 2021, p. 386)

On average participants made externalist answers to both the elicitation and the agreement prompts for the kind-negative scenario, but not for the kind-positive one; what's more, they report some variation among natural kind terms, although at a qualitative level natural kind terms behaved similarly. Experiment 3 shows that superficial similarities between the substance discovered on twin-earth (e.g., twater) and the earthly substance (water) matter for classification judgments. Given the findings of Tobia and colleagues (2019), it is noteworthy that Haukioja and colleagues' scenarios all were set in a scientific context.

Machery and colleagues (2023) have also shown that reactions to kind-negative (based on twin-earth thought experiments) and kind-positive cases vary across cultures and that they vary depending on how the question is formulated. For instance, participants in India were substantially less likely to make externalist judgment in a twin-earth thought experiment (with the prompt, "Would you say that in those conditions, mantup is water?") than Americans, French, and South Koreans. What's more, after a kind-positive case, answers varied depending on how the probe was framed. "Would you say that in those conditions there are still lemons?" elicited a minority of externalist judgments while "Would you say that in those conditions lemons are now oranges?", "Would you say that in those conditions lemons have become oranges?", and "What are they now, lemons or oranges?" elicited about 50% of externalist judgments.

Finally, using a twin-earth thought experiment Koch and Wiegmann (2021) examined whether people judge that the extension of natural kind terms can change. They report that describing speakers as interacting for decades with a watery substance that has a chemical structure different from H_2O leads them to judge that the extension of "water" has changed.

2.2.3 Discussion

Experimental philosophers have used a variety of experimental materials and have probed participants' commitment to externalism in various ways:
1. Metalinguistic questions about predicates (e.g., Nichols et al. 2016, Koch and Wiegmann 2021);
2. Metalinguistic questions about the truth of past statements (Jylkkä et al. 2009);
3. Questions about the identity of the object of thoughts (Genone and Lombrozo 2012);
4. Truth-value judgments about existence (e.g., Nichols et al. 2016, Machery et al. 2023);
5. Truth-value judgments about identity across changes (e.g., Machery et al. n.d. b), despite superficial or essential differences (e.g., Tobia et al. 2019, Machery et al. 2023), and despite what speakers believe (e.g., Nichols et al. 2016);
6. Use (Devitt and Porter 2021, Haukioja et al. 2021).

The exact formulation of these questions itself varies across studies in a way that seems to influence participants' willingness to make externalist judgments, as discussed by Nichols and colleagues (2016), Devitt and Porter (2021), and Machery and colleagues (2023).

Devitt and Porter (2021) usefully distinguish three different interpretations of the overall pattern of results. According to what they call "the Ambiguity Theory" (e.g., Nichols et al. 2016, Tobia et al. 2019), which should be rather called "the polysemy interpretation", natural kind terms, and perhaps other predicates, are polysemous: They can have an externalist and an internalist reading, and conversational cues prime one interpretation rather than the other. Devitt and Porter reject the polysemy interpretation on the grounds that speakers are not aware of the plurality of senses that is hypothesized. Their objection assumes that polysemy must be conventionalized and that speakers must know about it, and in this respect at least it assimilates polysemy to ambiguity, but awareness of a plurality of senses is not required for all forms of polysemy: Some forms of polysemy are conventionalized, others are not, and speakers need not be aware that they are using a word in slightly different senses. According to "hybrid theories" (e.g., Genone and Lombrozo 2012), people use both externalist and internalist elements to determine the truth conditions of sentences including natural kind terms. Hybrid theories do not have the resources to explain the contextual variation in judgments about the extensions of natural kind terms.

Devitt and Porter themselves believe that the stimuli used to investigate people's commitment to externalism are the culprit ("the faulty test hypothesis"). On their view, speakers do not have any preformed linguistic habits about how to use fictional or unfamiliar predicates, which many studies rely on. Devitt and Porter write the following, referring to "catoblepas" in Nichols and colleagues' studies:

"catoblepas" has no meaning in [the participant's] language. So, our experiments could not test the way that the linguistic meaning of the biological kind term "catoblepas" determines reference. (Devitt and Porter 2021, p. 23)

Not all studies have used fictional or unfamiliar predicates, however, and the results of those using predicates such as "water" and "oranges" are in line with the findings with fictional and unfamiliar predicates. What's more, if people really have an externalist commitment about the meaning of natural kind terms, they should be inclined to treat new words in an externalist manner. To address this point, Devitt and Porter add that outlandish thought experiments such as the twin-earth thought experiment are too esoteric. While this point is plausible (Machery 2017, p. 239), participants report high confidence in the judgments made in response to twin-earth thought experiments (Machery et al. 2023).

Devitt and Porter do not consider a fourth interpretation of the overall pattern of data: People do not have any semantic commitment concerning predicates ("water", "triceratops", and so forth) as types; rather, they assign a meaning to each occurrence of predicates in line of various contextual factors, and they attempt to make sense of what the speaker might intend to refer to. This process is straightforward in many situations – people understand what others intend to say and know what they would themselves say in those situations if they intended to say what others intend to say – but this process is puzzling and challenging in other situations, including when people interpret the vignettes used in experimental semantics. This proposal is similar to the Strawsonian idea that expressions, including proper names, do not refer, but that people refer using expressions like proper names (Strawson 1950, Machery and Stich 2012, Machery 2015, Chomsky 2000). As Strawson put it:

> [An] expression [...] cannot be said to mention, or refer to, anything, any more than the sentence can be said to be true or false. [...] "Mentioning," or "referring," is not something an expression does; it is something that someone can use an expression to do. (Strawson 1950, p. 250)

This Strawsonian proposal differs from both the hybrid and the polysemy interpretations discussed earlier, both of which are making a claim about the semantics of predicates qua types. It explains why people might be inconsistent, and why context matters for the assignment of meaning to predicates.

2.2.4 Further Readings

Hansen (2014) reviews the literature on proper names and natural kind terms. He also examines empirical work on the reliability of metalinguistic judgments (so-called "linguistic intuitions") in linguistics and the role of expertise in relation to linguistic judgments.

3 Further Topics

Experimental philosophers are increasingly examining issues at the intersection of philosophy of language, formal semantics, and experimental philosophy. This section briefly reviews some of these developments. The work reviewed tends to combine formal and empirical approaches to the relevant issues about language.

Experimental philosophers have contributed to the study of the semantics of conditionals (e.g., Douven 2015; Douven et al. 2018, 2020; see Chapter 8) and of epistemic modals (e.g., Knobe and Yalcin 2012, Khoo and Phillips 2018, Del Pinal and Waldon 2019), as well as to the debate between relativism and contextualism (Kneer et al. 2017, Kneer 2022). Experimental philosophers have also examined the meaning of particular kinds of words, such as taste predicates (e.g., Kneer 2021a, 2021b), moral predicates (Khoo and Knobe 2018), and slurs (e.g., Mandelbaum and Young forthcoming).

Another area of research focuses on the norm of assertion: To be entitled to assert that *p*, must one know that *p*? Turri has provided a wealth of theoretical arguments and empirical evidence (Turri 2013, 2014, 2015, 2016), but the debate is ongoing (Kneer 2018, 2021c; Reuter and Brössel 2019).

The factivity of "knowing that" and of other so-called factive verbs has also been discussed in experimental philosophy. Buckwalter (2014) has argued that apparent non-factive uses of "knowing that" could be explained by appealing to protagonist projection (for discussion, see Domaneschi and Di Paola 2019). Recent work by the Geography of Philosophy Project suggests that the factive behavior of "know that" and its typical translations varies substantially across languages (Machery et al. n.d.).

4 Conclusion

This chapter has reviewed the increasingly large literature in experimental semantics about proper names and natural kind terms. It is now clear that judgments about the reference of proper names vary across cultures, although the contours and explanation of this variation remain mysterious. The literature on natural kind terms has failed to find any evidence of a deep commitment to an externalist semantics for natural kind terms, perhaps because speakers do not have any such commitment.

Bibliography

Beebe, James, and Ryan Undercoffer (2015): "Moral valence and semantic intuitions", *Erkenntnis* 80 (2), pp. 445–466.

Beebe, James, and Ryan Undercoffer (2016): "Individual and cross-cultural differences in semantic intuitions. New experimental findings", *Journal of Cognition and Culture* 16 (3–4), pp. 322–357.

Buckwalter, Wesley (2014): "Factive verbs and protagonist projection", *Episteme* 11 (4), pp. 391–409.

Burge, Tyler (1979): "Individualism and the mental", *Midwest Studies in Philosophy* 4 (1), pp. 73–121.

Bursten, Julia (2014): "Microstructure without essentialism. A new perspective on chemical classification", *Philosophy of Science* 81 (4), pp. 633–653.

Chomsky, Noam (2000): *New horizons in the study of language and mind.* Cambridge: Cambridge University Press.

Cohnitz, Daniel, and Jussi Haukioja (2015): "Intuitions in philosophical semantics", *Erkenntnis* 80 (3), pp. 617–641.

Cova, Florian, Brent Strickland, Angela Abatista, Aurélien Allard, James Andow, Mario Attie, James Beebe, Renatas Berniūnas, Jordane Boudesseul, Matteo Colombo, Fiery Cushman, Rodrigo Díaz, Noah N'Djaye Nikolai van Dongen, Vilius Dranseika, Brian Earp, Antonio Gaitán Torres, Ivar Hannikainen, José Hernández-Conde, Wenjia Hu, François Jaquet, Kareem Khalifa, Hanna Kim, Markus Kneer, Joshua Knobe, Miklos Kurthy, Anthony Lantian, Shen-Yi Liao, Edouard Machery, Tania Moerenhout, Christian Mott, Mark Phelan, Jonathan Phillips, Navin Rambharose, Kevin Reuter, Felipe Romero, Paulo Sousa, Jan Sprenger, Emile Thalabard, Kevin Tobia, Hugo Viciana, Daniel Wilkenfeld, and Xiang Zhou (2021): "Estimating the reproducibility of experimental philosophy", *Review of Philosophy and Psychology* 12 (1), pp. 9–44.

Dacey, Michael, and Ron Mallon (2016): "Reference", in: Justin Sytsma and Wesley Buckwalter (Eds.): *A companion to experimental philosophy.* Chichester: Wiley-Blackwell, pp. 371–390.

Del Pinal, Guillermo, and Brandon Waldon (2019): "Modals under epistemic tension", *Natural Language Semantics* 27 (2), pp. 135–188.

Deutsch, Max (2009): "Experimental philosophy and the theory of reference", *Mind & Language* 24 (4), pp. 445–466.

Devitt, Michael (1981): *Designation.* New York: Columbia University Press.

Devitt, Michael (2011): "Experimental semantics", *Philosophy and Phenomenological Research* 82 (2), pp. 418–435.

Devitt, Michael (2012a): "Whither experimental semantics?", *Theoria* 27 (1), pp. 5–36.

Devitt, Michael (2012b): "Semantic epistemology. Response to Machery", *Theoria* 27 (2), pp. 229–233.

Devitt, Michael, and Nicolas Porot (2018): "The reference of proper names. Testing usage and intuitions", *Cognitive Science* 42 (5), pp. 1552–1585.

Devitt, Michael, and Brian Porter (2021): "Testing the reference of biological kind terms", *Cognitive Science* 45 (5), e12979.

Domaneschi, Filippo, and Simona Di Paola (2019): "Relevance and non-factive knowledge attributions", *Acta Analytica* 34 (1), pp. 83–115.

Domaneschi, Filippo, and Massimiliano Vignolo (2020): "Reference and the ambiguity of truth-value judgments", *Mind & Language* 35 (4), pp. 440–455.

Domaneschi, Filippo, Massimiliano Vignolo, and Simona Di Paola (2017): "Testing the causal theory of reference", *Cognition* 161, pp. 1–9.

Douven, Igor (2015): *The epistemology of indicative conditionals. Formal and empirical approaches.* Cambridge: Cambridge University Press.

Douven, Igor, Shira Elqayam, Henrik Singmann, and Janneke van Wijnbergen-Huitink (2018): "Conditionals and inferential connections. A hypothetical inferential theory", *Cognitive Psychology* 101, pp. 50–81.

Douven, Igor, Shira Elqayam, Henrik Singmann, and Janneke van Wijnbergen-Huitink (2020): "Conditionals and inferential connections. Toward a new semantics", *Thinking & Reasoning* 26 (3), pp. 311–351.

Dupré, John (1981): "Natural kinds and biological taxa", *The Philosophical Review* 90 (1), pp. 66–90.

Evans, Gareth (1973): "The causal theory of names", *Supplementary Proceedings of the Aristotelian Society* 47 (1), pp. 187–208.

Frege, Gottfried (1892): "Über Sinn und Bedeutung", *Zeitschrift für Philosophie und Philosophische Kritik* 100 (1), pp. 25–50.

Genone, James, and Tania Lombrozo (2012): "Concept possession, experimental semantics, and hybrid theories of reference", *Philosophical Psychology* 25 (5), pp. 717–742.

Grau, Christopher, and Cynthia Pury (2014): "Attitudes towards reference and replaceability", *Review of Philosophy and Psychology* 5 (2), pp. 155–168.

Hacking, Ian (2007): "The contingencies of ambiguity", *Analysis* 67 (4), pp. 269–277.

Hansen, Nat (2014): "Experimental philosophy of language", in: Oxford Handbooks Editorial Board (Ed.): *The Oxford handbook of topics in philosophy*.
https://academic.oup.com/edited-volume/42642/chapter/358144189, last accessed June 1, 2023.

Haukioja, Jussi, Mons Nyquist, and Jussi Jylkkä (2021): "Reports from twin earth. Both deep structure and appearance determine the reference of natural kind terms", *Mind & Language* 36 (3), pp. 377–403.

Heck, Richard (2018): "Speaker's reference, semantic reference, and intuition", *Review of Philosophy and Psychology* 9 (1), pp. 251–269.

Ichikawa, Jonathan, Ishani Maitra, and Brian Weatherson (2012): "In defense of a Kripkean dogma", *Philosophy and Phenomenological Research* 85 (1), pp. 56–68.

Izumi, Yu, Masashi Kasaki, Yan Zhou, and Sobei Oda (2018): "Definite descriptions and the alleged east-west variation in judgments about reference", *Philosophical Studies* 175 (3–4), pp. 1183–1205.

Jackman, Henry (2009): "Semantic intuitions, conceptual analysis, and cross-cultural variation", *Philosophical Studies* 146 (2), pp. 159–177.

Jackson, Frank (1998): "Reference and description revisited", *Philosophical Perspectives* 12, pp. 201–218.

Jylkkä, Jussi, Henry Railo, and Jussi Haukioja (2009): "Psychological essentialism and semantic externalism. Evidence for externalism in lay speakers' language use", *Philosophical Psychology* 22 (1), pp. 37–60.

Kallestrup, Jespere (2016): "Counteractuals, counterfactuals and semantic intuitions", *Review of Philosophy and Psychology* 7 (1), pp. 35–54.

Khoo, Justin, and Joshua Knobe (2018): "Moral disagreement and moral semantics", *Noûs* 52 (1), pp. 109–143.

Khoo, Justin, and Joshua Phillips (2018): "New horizons for a theory of epistemic modals", *Australasian Journal of Philosophy* 97 (2), pp. 309–324.

Klein, Richard, Michelangelo Vianello, Fred Hasselman, Byron Adams, Reginald Adams, Jr., Sinan Alper, Mark Aveyard, Jordan Axt, Mayowa Babalola, Štěpán Bahník, Rishtee Batra, Mihály Berkics, Michael Bernstein, Daniel Berry, Olga Bialobrzeska, Evans Dami Binan, Konrad Bocian, Mark Brandt, Robert Busching, Anna Cabak Rédei, Huajian Cai, Fanny Cambier, Katarzyna Cantarero, Cheryl Carmichael, Francisco Ceric, Jesse Chandler, Jen-Ho Chang, Armand Chatard, Eva Chen, Winnee Cheong, David Cicero, Sharon Coen, Jennifer Coleman, Brian Collisson, Morgan Conway, Katherine Corker, Paul Curran, Fiery Cushman, Zubairu Dagona, Ilker Dalgar, Anna Dalla Rosa, William Davis, Maaike de Bruijn, Leander De Schutter, Thierry Devos, Marieke de Vries, Canay Doğulu, Nerisa Dozo, Kristin Nicole Dukes, Yarrow Dunham, Kevin Durrheim, Charles Ebersole, John Edlund, Anja Eller, Alexander Scott English, Carolyn Finck, Natalia Frankowska, Miguel-Ángel Freyre, Mike Friedman, Elisa Maria Galliani, Joshua Gandi, Tanuka Ghoshal, Steffen Giessner, Tripat Gill, Timo Gnambs, Ángel Gómez, Roberto González, Jesse Graham, Jon Grahe, Ivan Grahek, Eva Green, Kakul Hai, Matthew Haigh, Elizabeth Haines, Michael Hall, Marie Heffernan, Joshua Hicks, Petr Houdek, Jeffrey Huntsinger, Ho Phi Huynh, Hans IJzerman, Yoel Inbar, Åse Innes-Ker, William Jiménez-Leal, Melissa-Sue John, Jennifer Joy-Gaba, Roza Kamiloğlu, Heather Barry Kappes, Serdar Karabati, Haruna Karick, Victor Keller, Anna Kende, Nicolas Kervyn, Goran Knežević, Carrie Kovacs, Lacy Krueger, German Kurapov, Jamie Kurtz, Daniël Lakens, Ljiljana Lazarević, Carmel Levitan, Neil Lewis, Jr., Samuel Lins, Nikolette Lipsey, Joy Losee, Esther Maassen, Angela Maitner, Winfrida Malingumu, Robyn Mallett, Satia Marotta, Janko Međedović, Fernando Mena-Pacheco, Taciano Milfont, Wendy Morris, Sean Murphy, Andriy Myachykov, Nick Neave, Koen Neijenhuijs, Anthony Nelson, Félix Neto, Austin Lee Nichols, Aaron Ocampo, Susan O'Donnell, Haruka Oikawa, Masanori Oikawa, Elsie Ong, Gábor Orosz, Malgorzata Osowiecka, Grant Packard, Rolando Pérez-Sánchez, Boban Petrović, Ronaldo Pilati, Brad Pinter, Lysandra Podesta, Gabrielle Pogge, Monique Pollmann, Abraham Rutchick, Patricio Saavedra, Alexander Saeri, Erika Salomon, Kathleen Schmidt, Felix Schönbrodt, Maciej Sekerdej, David Sirlopú, Jeanine Skorinko, Michael Smith, Vanessa Smith-Castro, Karin Smolders, Agata Sobkow, Walter

Sowden, Philipp Spachtholz, Manini Srivastava, Troy Steiner, Jeroen Stouten, Chris Street, Oskar Sundfelt, Stephanie Szeto, Ewa Szumowska, Andrew Tang, Norbert Tanzer, Morgan Tear, Jordan Theriault, Manuela Thomae, David Torres, Jakub Traczyk, Joshua Tybur, Adrienn Ujhelyi, Robbie van Aert, Marcel van Assen, Marije van der Hulst, Paul van Lange, Anna Elisabeth van 't Veer, Alejandro Vásquez-Echeverría, Leigh Ann Vaughn, Alexandra Vázquez, Luis Diego Vega, Catherine Verniers, Mark Verschoor, Ingrid Voermans, Marek Vranka, Cheryl Welch, Aaron Wichman, Lisa Williams, Michael Wood, Julie Woodzicka, Marta Wronska, Liane Young, John Zelenski, Zeng Zhijia, and Brian Nosek (2018): "Many Labs 2. Investigating variation in replicability across samples and settings", *Advances in Methods and Practices in Psychological Science* 1 (4), pp. 443–490.

Kneer, Markus (2018): "The norm of assertion. Empirical data", *Cognition* 177, pp. 165–171.

Kneer, Markus (2021a): "Predicates of personal taste, semantic incompleteness, and necessitarianism", *Linguistics and Philosophy* 44 (5), pp. 981–1011.

Kneer, Markus (2021b): "Predicates of personal taste. Empirical data", *Synthese* 199 (3), pp. 6455–6471.

Kneer, Markus (2021c): "Norms of assertion in the United States, Germany, and Japan", *Proceedings of the National Academy of Sciences* 118 (37), e2105365118.

Kneer, Markus (2022): "Contextualism versus relativism. More empirical data", in: Jeremy Wyatt, Julia Zakkou, and Dan Zeman (Eds.): *Perspectives on taste. Aesthetics, language, metaphysics, and experimental philosophy.* New York: Routledge, pp. 109–140.

Kneer, Markus, Agustin Vicente, and Dan Zeman (2017): "Relativism about predicates of personal taste and perspectival plurality", *Linguistics and Philosophy* 40 (1), pp. 37–60.

Knobe, Joshua, and Seth Yalcin (2014): "Epistemic modals and context. Experimental data", *Semantics and Pragmatics* 7 (10), pp. 1–21.

Koch, Steffen, and Alex Wiegmann (2021): "Folk intuitions about reference change and the causal theory of reference", *Ergo* 8 (25), pp. 31–57.

Kripke, Saul (1977): "Speaker's reference and semantic reference", *Midwest Studies in Philosophy* 2 (1), pp. 255–276.

Kripke, Saul (1980): *Naming and necessity.* Cambridge: Harvard University Press.

Lam, Barry (2010): "Are Cantonese speakers really descriptivists? Revisiting cross-cultural Semantics", *Cognition* 115 (2), pp. 320–329.

Lewis, David (1970): "How to define theoretical terms", *Journal of Philosophy* 67 (13), pp. 427–446.

Li, Jesse, and Xiaozhen Zhu (2022): "A bibliometric study of the research field of experimental philosophy of language", *Forum for Linguistic Studies* 4 (1), pp. 18–35.

Li, Jincai (2021): "The origin of cross-cultural differences in referential intuitions. Perspective taking in the Gödel case", *Journal of Semantics* 38 (3), pp. 415–440.

Li, Jincai, Longgen Liu, Elizabeth Chalmers, and Jesse Snedeker (2018): "What is in a name. The development of cross-cultural differences in referential intuitions", *Cognition* 171, pp. 108–111.

Ludwig, Kirk (2007): "The epistemology of thought experiments. First-person approach versus third-person approach", *Midwest Studies in Philosophy* 31 (1), pp. 128–159.

Machery, Edouard (2011): "Variation in intuitions about reference and ontological disagreements", in: Steven Hales (Ed.): *A companion to relativism.* Chichester: Wiley-Blackwell, pp. 118–136.

Machery, Edouard (2012a): "Expertise and intuitions about reference", *Theoria* 27 (1), pp. 37–54.

Machery, Edouard (2012b): "Semantic epistemology. A brief response to Devitt", *Theoria* 27, pp. 223–227.

Machery, Edouard (2014): "What is the significance of the demographic variation in semantic intuitions?", in: Edouard Machery and Elizabeth O'Neill (Eds.): *Current controversies in experimental philosophy.* London: Routledge, pp. 3–16.

Machery, Edouard (2015): "A broad Rylean argument against reference", in: Jussi Haukioja (Ed.): *Advances in experimental philosophy of language.* London: Bloomsbury, pp. 65–83.

Machery, Edouard (2017): *Philosophy within its proper bounds.* Oxford: Oxford University Press.

Machery, Edouard (2020): "Cross-cultural semantics at 15", in: Stephen Biggs and Heimir Geirsson (Eds.): *The Routledge handbook of linguistic reference.* New York: Routledge, pp. 535–550.

Machery, Edouard, Surabhi Awasthi, Kelli Barr, Abdellatif Bencheriffa, Dasa Bombjakova, Yasuo Deguchi, Alejandro Erut, Emanuele Fabiano, Kim Hackjin, Joshua Homan, Martin Kanovsky, Kaori Karasawa, Jordan Kiper, Minha Lee, Xiaofei Liu, Veli Mitova, Rukmini Nair, Ljiljana Pantovic, Brian Porter, Pablo Quintanilla, Josien Reijer, Pedro Romero, Pritika Sejwal, Purnima Singh, Salma Tber, Daniel Wilkenfeld, Stephen Stich, and Clark Barrett (n.d.): "Factivity across languages". Manuscript.

Machery, Edouard, Max Deutsch, Ron Mallon, Shaun Nichols, Justin Sytsma, and Stephen Stich (2010): "Semantic intuitions. Reply to Lam", *Cognition* 117 (3), pp. 361–366.

Machery, Edouard, and John Doris (2017): "An open letter to our students. Doing interdisciplinary moral psychology", in: Benjamin Voyer and Tor Tarantola (Eds.): *Moral psychology. A multidisciplinary guide*. Berlin: Springer, pp. 119–143.

Machery, Edouard, Christopher Grau, and Cynthia Pury (2020): "Love and power. Grau and Pury (2014) as a case study in the challenges of x-phi replication", *Review of Philosophy and Psychology* 11 (4), pp. 995–1011.

Machery, Edouard, Ron Mallon, Shaun Nichols, and Stephen Stich (2004): "Semantics, cross-cultural style", *Cognition* 92 (3), pp. B1–B12.

Machery, Edouard, Ron Mallon, Shaun Nichols, and Stephen Stich (2013): "If folk intuitions vary, then what?", *Philosophy and Phenomenological Research* 86 (3), pp. 618–635.

Machery, Edouard, Christopher Olivola, and Molly de Blanc (2009): "Linguistic and metalinguistic intuitions in the philosophy of language", *Analysis* 69 (4), pp. 689–694.

Machery, Edouard, Christopher Olivola, Hyundeuk Cheon, Irma Kurniawan, Carlos Mauro, Noel Struchiner, and Harry Susianto (2023): "Is identity essentialism a fundamental feature of human cognition?", *Cognitive Science* 47 (5), e13292.

Machery, Edouard, and Stephen Stich (2012): "Experimental philosophy of language", in: Gillian Russell and Delia Graff Fara (Eds.): *Routledge companion to the philosophy of language*. New York: Routledge, pp. 495–512.

Machery, Edouard, Justin Sytsma, and Max Deutsch (2015): "Speaker's reference and cross-cultural semantics", in: Andrea Bianchi (Ed.): *On reference*. Oxford: Oxford University Press, pp. 62–76.

Mallon, Ron, Edouard Machery, Shaun Nichols, and Stephen Stich (2009): "Against arguments from reference", *Philosophy and Phenomenological Research* 79 (2), pp. 332–356.

Mandelbaum, Eric, and Steven Young (forthcoming): "The sound of slurs. Bad sounds for bad words", in: Joshua Knobe and Shaun Nichols (Eds.): *Oxford Studies in Experimental Philosophy*. Vol. 5. Oxford: Oxford University Press.

Markus, Hazel, and Shinobu Kitayama (1991): "Culture and the self. Implications for cognition, emotion, and motivation", *Psychological Review* 98 (2), pp. 224–253.

Martí, Genoveva (2009): "Against semantic multi-culturalism", *Analysis* 69 (1), pp. 42–48.

Martí, Genoveva (2012): "Empirical data and the theory of reference", in: William Kabasenche, Michael O'Rourke, and Matthew Slater (Eds.): *Reference and referring. Topics in contemporary philosophy*. Cambridge: The MIT Press, pp. 63–82.

Martí, Genoveva (2014): "Reference and experimental semantics", in: Edouard Machery and Elizabeth O'Neill (Eds.): *Current controversies in experimental philosophy*. London: Routledge, pp. 17–26.

Murray, Dylan (2020): "Maggots are delicious, sunsets hideous", in: Tania Lombrozo, Joshua Knobe, and Shaun Nichols (Eds.): *Oxford studies in experimental philosophy*. Vol. 3. Oxford: Oxford University Press, pp. 64–96.

Nado, Jennifer, and Michael Johnson (2016): "Intuitions and the theory of reference", in: Jennifer Nado (Ed.): *Advances in experimental philosophy and philosophical methodology*. London: Bloomsbury, pp. 125–154.

Nichols, Shaun, Ángel Pinillos, and Ron Mallon (2016): "Ambiguous reference", *Mind* 125 (497), pp. 145–175.

Nisbett, Richard (2004): *The geography of thought*. New York: The Free Press.

Norenzayan, Ara, Edward Smith, Beom Jun Kim, and Richard Nisbett (2002): "Cultural preferences for formal versus intuitive reasoning", *Cognitive Science* 26 (5), pp. 653–684.
Open Science Collaboration (OSC) (2015) "Estimating the reproducibility of psychological science", *Science* 349 (6251), aac4716.
Ostertag, Gary (2013): "The 'Gödel' effect", *Philosophical Studies* 166 (1), pp. 65–82.
Oyserman, Daphna, Heather Coon, and Markus Kemmelmeier (2002): "Rethinking individualism and collectivism. Evaluation of theoretical assumptions and meta-analyses", *Psychological Bulletin* 128 (1), pp. 3–72.
Putnam, Hilary (1975a): "The meaning of 'meaning'", in: Hilary Putnam: *Philosophical papers. Vol. 2. Mind, language and reality.* Cambridge: Cambridge University Press, pp. 215–271.
Putnam, Hilary (1975b): "Explanation and reference", in: Hilary Putnam: *Philosophical papers. Vol. 2. Mind, language and reality.* Cambridge: Cambridge University Press, pp. 196–214.
Reuter, Kevin, and Peter Brössel (2019): "No knowledge required", *Episteme* 16 (3), pp. 303–321.
Romero, Felipe, Matteo Colombo, Noah van Dongen, and Jan Sprenger (2017): "Replication of Machery, Mallon, Nichols and Stich (2004)". *Open Science Framework.* https://osf.io/qdekc/, last accessed May 19, 2023.
Schwartz, Stephen (1978): "Putnam on artifacts", *The Philosophical Review* 87 (4), pp. 566–574.
Searle, John (1958): "Proper names", *Mind* 67 (266), pp. 166–173.
Strawson, Peter (1950): "On referring", *Mind* 59 (235), pp. 320–344.
Sytsma, Justin, and Jonthan Livengood (2011): "A new perspective concerning experiments on semantic intuitions", *Australasian Journal of Philosophy* 89 (2), pp. 315–332.
Sytsma, Justin, Jonathan Livengood, Ryoji Stato, and Mineki Oguchi (2015): "Reference in the land of the rising sun. A cross-cultural study on the reference of proper names", *Review of Philosophy and Psychology* 6 (2), pp. 213–230.
Tobia, Kevin, George Newman, and Joshua Knobe (2019): "Water is and is not H_2O", *Mind & Language* 35 (2), pp. 183–208.
Turri, John (2013): "The test of truth. An experimental investigation of the norm of assertion", *Cognition* 129 (2), pp. 279–291.
Turri, John (2014): "Knowledge and suberogatory assertion", *Philosophical Studies* 167 (3), pp. 557–567.
Turri, John (2015): "Knowledge and the norm of assertion. A simple test", *Synthese* 192 (2), pp. 385–392.
Turri, John (2016): *Knowledge and the norm of assertion. An essay in philosophical science.* Cambridge: Open Book.
van Dongen, Noah, Matteo Colombo, Felipe Romero, and Jan Sprenger (2021): "Intuitions about the reference of proper names. A meta-analysis", *Review of Philosophy and Psychology* 12 (4), pp. 745–774.
Vignolo, Massimiliano, and Filippo Domaneschi (2018): "Referential intuitions are still problematic", *Analysis* 78 (3), pp. 472–483.

Igor Douven, Shira Elqayam, and Karolina Krzyżanowska
The Experimental Philosophy of Logic and Formal Epistemology: Conditionals

Abstract: Classical logic was long believed to provide the norms of reasoning. But more recently researchers interested in the norms of reasoning have shifted their attention toward probability theory and various concepts and rules that can be defined in probabilistic terms. In philosophy, this shift gave rise to formal epistemology, while in psychology, it led to the New Paradigm psychology of reasoning. Whereas there has traditionally been a clear division of labor between philosophers and psychologists working on reasoning, the past decade has seen an increasing collaboration between philosophers and psychologists, from which an experimental philosophy of logic and formal epistemology emerged. An area in which the fruits of this collaboration have been particularly in evidence is the research concerned with conditionals and conditional reasoning. This chapter showcases contributions to this area to underline the value of the said branch of experimental philosophy more generally.

Keywords: Conditionals; Experimental Philosophy; Formal Epistemology; Logic; New Paradigm Psychology of Reasoning; Pragmatics; Probability; Semantics

1 Introduction

When we argue, we typically present some premises as warranting a given conclusion: so-and-so is true, thus/hence/therefore/such-and-such is true as well. Although people start to use words like "thus", "therefore", and their ilk early in life, and they use them frequently, the use of these words can easily spark controversies, disputes of the following form being nothing out of the ordinary:

Speaker 1: A, B, and C, hence D.
Speaker 2: No! I grant you A, B, and C. But D doesn't follow!

How are we to arbitrate such disputes? Can anything systematic be said about when "thus", "hence", and so on, are used correctly and when incorrectly?

Classical logic was long believed to provide the norms of reasoning, so that "thus", "hence", and kindred terms were thought to be used correctly as long as their use conformed to the laws of logic. For instance, in the preceding dispute, the first speaker used "hence" correctly if, and only if, D can be derived, using the rules of logic, from premises A, B, and C, or equivalently (by the completeness theorem for logic), if, and only if, the joint truth of A, B, and C guarantees the truth of D.

Note: We are indebted to the editors for valuable comments on a previous version.

But in everyday English, it can be perfectly fine to present an argument using "thus" to indicate that a conclusion follows from certain premises even if the truth of the premises does *not* guarantee the truth of the conclusion. For example, it can be perfectly fine to argue

(1) So far, Alice passed all her math exams with flying colors, thus she'll pass her upcoming math exam as well.

We may have reason to suspect that the upcoming exam is particularly challenging, or that this time Alice has not been able to prepare properly. But barring such reasons, the use of "thus" in (1) is pre-theoretically entirely appropriate.

Here, we are reminded that modern classical logic was primarily devised (by Frege, Russell, Whitehead, and others) to facilitate mathematical reasoning, and that our everyday reasoning is in many respects different from that. (Throughout the paper, by "logic", we mean "classical logic", given that virtually all experimental work on logical reasoning has been concerned with classical logic; in fact, it has been predominantly concerned with classical propositional logic.)[1] In particular, our everyday reasoning does not normally consist of deriving, one step at a time, theorems from a system of axioms, where each step can be seen to be fully secure. Rather, we are typically trying to reason our way to a conclusion taking into account all sorts of uncertainties. For instance, in reasoning why we expect Alice to pass the upcoming exam, we may not be able to rule out entirely that Alice was unable to prepare for the exam in her usual thorough manner. So, we may not be one hundred percent certain that Alice will pass the exam even though she passed all previous ones with flying colors. And yet, the argument can be valid in a pre-theoretic sense.

Backed by such observations, philosophers have proposed to regard probability theory, and possibly principles definable in probabilistic terms (such as, e.g., rules for responding to new information), as embodying the norms of reasoning. For instance, it could be argued that the first speaker in the dispute stated above used "hence" correctly if, and only if, the probability of D conditional on the conjunction of A, B, and C is close to 1. From the 1980s onward, philosophy saw a broader shift in attention from logic to probability theory, leading to the field now commonly called "formal epistemology", which among other things studies the norms of correct non-deductive reasoning. Note that this is not to dismiss logic as being irrelevant to reasoning: probability theory *builds* on logic. It is just to say that logic can be taken to give the norms of reasoning only under very special circumstances, in which we are not dealing with uncertainties.

There has been a parallel development in the psychology of reasoning. Peter Wason, who many regard as the founding father of that field in its modern form,

---

[1] This is not to say that there are no exceptions; see, e.g., Stenning and van Lambalgen (2012) on non-monotonic logic.

took for granted that classical logic embodies the standards of correct reasoning and was interested in whether, and the extent to which, people are able to live up to those standards. He is most famous for reporting experimental work on reasoning, apparently showing that people do quite badly in this respect (Wason 1968). In what is known as "Wason's selection task", replicated many times since, he showed participants four cards and told them those cards had a letter on one side and a number on the reverse. In the abstract, indicative version of the task, participants were given an indicative conditional rule of the form "If [antecedent condition] on one side, than [consequent condition] on the other side", such as "If there is an A on one side of the card, then there is a 2 on the other side of the card", then shown four cards, for example, cards showing an "A", a "K", a "2" and a "7". Their task was to turn over all the cards, and only the cards, that would allow them to find out if the rule is true or false. Given that the cards that show the "A" and the "7" are the only ones that could provide falsifying evidence, logic suggests that those ought to be turned. That is, the normatively sanctioned selection is the [antecedent condition] card and the not-[consequent condition] card. But most participants select either the cards showing the "A" and the "2" or the "A" card alone. The standard explanation is that participants *match:* they select the cards named in the rule.

However, in psychology, too, researchers came to question the assumption that the laws of logic constitute the standards of correct reasoning. The first cracks in the wall came from examining deontic conditionals, such as "If a person drinks beer, then this person must be over 18 years of age" (Griggs and Cox 1982). This version substantially facilitated performance, with 75% of participants selecting the normatively sanctioned [antecedent condition] ∧ ¬[consequent condition] cards, instead of the more usual 10% in the indicative abstract task. It turned out that, contrary to the previous hypothesis, it is not familiarity alone that facilitates performance; it is the use of a deontic operator alongside clearly identified utility (see also Bonnefon 2009).

More substantively still, Nick Chater, Mike Oaksford, David Over, and several other researchers started to draw attention to the fact that reasoning usually takes place in a sea of uncertainty and that hence we should rather be looking for norms governing uncertain reasoning, which logic does not cover. Their proposal to look at probability theory instead led to the emergence of the so-called New Paradigm psychology of reasoning (Over 2009, Elqayam and Over 2013). An early success of this approach was Oaksford and Chater's (1994, 1996) work on the selection task, which argued that the predominant response in Wason's experiment was the one we should expect to find if people followed something close to an optimal probabilistic strategy for seeking information. The core idea is that people will tend to interpret the task before them as one of discovering a statistical dependence between "A" cards and "2" cards, and that by turning the "A" card and the "2" card in front of them, they are gaining the most informative evidence regarding such a dependence; at least, that is so given assumptions about people's priors and about how best to measure information gain, which Oaksford and Chater argue to be plausible in the context of Wason's task. One advantage of the New Paradigm is that the focus on probability and utility enables better cross-disciplinary communication with the vast and important literature on judgment and decision making. In other words, reasoning and decision-making are two facets of human thinking.

The clash between what logic would seem to prescribe and apparently sound everyday thinking and reasoning was particularly evident in studies on how people reason with indicative conditionals – sentences of the form "If A, [then] B" or "B if A", with the antecedent being in the indicative mood – and how they evaluate the truth values and probabilities of conditionals.[2] Logic gives us the so-called material conditional,[3] which is true if its antecedent is false or its consequent is true; otherwise it is false. However, not many people are willing to infer

(2) If Jeff Bezos went broke, he is a billionaire,

from

(3) Jeff Bezos is a billionaire.

Yet, if conditionals are to be interpreted materially, the inference is valid. Furthermore, on the same supposition, and given Bezos' net worth, (2) is *true*, which few people may be inclined to agree with. Relatedly, whereas most people will be fully convinced that Bezos is a billionaire, few would want to assign (2) a probability of 1, even though anyone who is fully convinced of the consequent *should* do that, again assuming that natural-language conditionals are material conditionals.

Of course, once we have abandoned the idea that the laws of classical logic are the norms of reasoning, it becomes natural to explore other interpretations of the ordinary English conditional beyond the material one. That is what both philosophers and psychologists have done. In spite of all the work that went into this, however, there is little to no consensus on even the most basic questions concerning conditionals. What is the majority view on what the truth conditions of conditionals are? What is the majority view on whether conditionals have truth conditions to begin with, on the conditions under which we can assert or accept a conditional, on how we ought to evaluate the probabilities of conditionals, on how we ought to respond to the receipt of conditional information, and on and on? The answer is always the same, to wit, that there *is* no majority view. Importantly, it is not that philosophers tend to hold views very different from those held by psychologists. Rather, there is widespread disagreement on these matters in both camps.

---

[2] We will only be concerned with indicative conditionals and therefore refer to them simply as "conditionals" throughout this chapter. Note that we include in this deontic conditionals, as long as they are not in the subjunctive mood.

[3] Strictly speaking, classical logic defines the relation of the material implication, which was not intended to capture the meaning of the natural language conditional. For more on this, see Kyburg, Teng, and Wheeler (2007). There are, however, logics of conditionals that are devised specifically to account for empirical findings on how people use conditional sentences. See, e.g., Crupi and Iacona (2022), or Berto and Özgün (2021), for recent developments.

Given that this has been the situation for years, one starts wondering whether there is any hope of making progress on our theoretical understanding of conditionals. Is there any one method that recommends itself here? We want to explain why we are betting on an experimental approach.

Philosophers and psychologists working on conditionals have largely focused on the same questions: questions regarding the truth conditions of conditionals, questions regarding their acceptability or assertability conditions, and questions regarding their probabilities. However, for many years, the two research communities used different methods to address these questions. Where philosophers tended to rely on conceptual analysis and formal modeling, psychologists mostly used empirical methods. But along with a growing general concern among philosophers about the reliability of conceptual analysis (which gave rise to experimental philosophy), the method came to appear especially unsuited for addressing the key questions about conditionals as experimental work showed some of the main philosophical accounts of conditionals, seemingly backed by sound intuitions, to be inconsistent with real-world data about how people use conditionals.

There is always the option for philosophers to dismiss such findings by saying that all these do is showing that ordinary people get confused by conditionals and have a tendency to be mistaken about their truth value, or to assign a wrong probability to them, or to deem them acceptable or assertable when in fact they are not and vice versa. But this response is not only uncharitable to ordinary people, it also makes one wonder what the point could be of having norms putatively governing conditionals if ordinary people are not able to generally stick to them, not even approximately. More importantly, it is unclear where the norms are to derive from. For example, advocates of the so-called material conditional account, according to which the semantics of the conditional is that of the material conditional, may say that one ought to respect *Modus ponens* and *Modus tollens*, and that one's probability for "If A, B" ought to equal one's probability for "not-A or B", that one should be willing to accept "If A, B" as soon as one is willing to accept at least one of "¬A" and "B", and so on. But it is not as though philosophers had produced an argument to the effect that, unless we bring our use of conditionals in line with the material conditional account, then we are liable to something like a Dutch book argument, say, or we are likely to engage in other behavior supposedly betokening irrationality on our part. The same holds true of any other semantics of conditionals that philosophers have developed.

In other words, there is no practical rationality justification to support the normative rationality of the material conditional – or of classical logic, for that matter. But one might ask, then, whether the use of empirical methods does not wipe out the boundary between philosophy and psychology. Why do we need two disciplines, in that case? Are we advocating for philosophers to forgo conceptual analysis, or for psychologists to become empirical philosophers? The answer, as far as we can tell, is that psychologists and philosophers differ in the research questions they tend to ask. Marr (1982) famously distinguished between three levels of analysis in conceptualizing cognitive systems: first, the computational level of analysis, the level of what the system does and why; second, the algorithmic level of analysis, the level of how this is done; and third, the implementational level of analysis, the level of hardware or wetware supporting the system. Leaving aside the latter for now, we can identify both the overlaps and the differences between psychological and philosophical research questions in this domain. Both psychologists and philosophers are interested in the computational level of analysis, especially in characterizing what the system does. In this case, for example, the semantics of conditionals as a description of how humans use conditionals in language. The difference between psychologists and philosophers is twofold: first, psychologists tend to ask more research questions about processing and representations, focusing on the algorithmic level of analysis. Second, within the computational level of analysis, philosophers ask more normative research questions (what ought we to do or to think?), whereas psychologists ask more function-related questions (what is this for?). That said, we note that psychology of reasoning is unusual within psychological science in that it attends to normative issues as well, although this has been criticized (Elqayam and Evans 2011).

If a priori theorizing about conditionals has not brought the returns that philosophers were hoping for, then perhaps philosophers should also start investing more heavily in empirical approaches. To be sure, we already said that the empirical work done by psychologists did not bring us any closer to a consensus view. But much is still to be explored. So far, psychologists have mostly focused, on one hand, on the material conditional account, and on the other hand, on probabilistic approaches to conditionals. In this chapter, we want to make a case for an experimental philosophy of conditionals and conditional reasoning by drawing attention to a recent development, which takes important cues from philosophical work on conditionals that, we believe, has been unduly ignored. In this development – which has gone under the banner of "inferentialism" – philosophers and psychologists have joined forces from the start, and philosophical theorizing has, from the start, gone hand in hand with experimentation. Although there are still some important open questions to be answered, the empirical results obtained so far show inferentialism to be a promising new theory of conditionals.

2 The Experimental Philosophy of Conditionals – The Case of Inferentialism

Humans are hardwired, from an early age on, to be attuned to all sorts of connections in the world. We often use conditionals to store and transmit the fruits of those endeavors. A parent teaching his or her child that if A, B is, in a way, handing the child a license to infer B from A. At least in principle, should the child ever receive the information that A, it can immediately draw the conclusion that B is the case if it does not believe B already at that time. We say "in principle" because there can be countervailing considerations. Perhaps the child already knows B *not* to be the case when it comes to know that A *is* the case. Then it may want to abandon the conditional that if A, B. All of this is compatible with the idea that conditionals embody some sort of inferential connection between their antecedent and consequent.

Pre-theoretically plausible though it may be, the idea that conditionals embody inferential connections has never become mainstream, neither in philosophy nor in psychology. Indeed, it is glaringly absent from any of the better-known semantics of conditionals. For instance, according to the material conditional account, (2) is true, as we said, even though no parent would want to hand this conditional as an inference ticket to his or her child. Similarly for Stalnaker's (1968) possible worlds account, according to which a conditional is true if, and only if, its consequent is true in the world in which its antecedent is true that is closest to the actual world. On this account, any conditional with a true antecedent and a true consequent, however unrelated they are (e.g., "If Paris is the capital of France, Bezos is a billionaire"), comes out true. To mention a third popular proposal, according to Adams (1975), conditionals are neither true nor false, but they can be acceptable, provided their probability is sufficiently close to 1. For Adams and his followers, the probability of a conditional is the conditional probability of its consequent given its antecedent. If you are subjectively certain that a proposition A is false, then – Adams stipulates – the conditional probability of any self-consistent proposition given A is 1. So, assume that you are subjectively certain that Bezos did not go broke – if he did, it would have been all over the news and you would have heard about it. Then (2) is acceptable on Adams' account, which conflicts with our pre-theoretical judgment. And, of course, the account also faces the problem that Stalnaker's faces, to wit, that any conditional about whose consequent one is subjectively certain has a conditional probability of 1 and thus is acceptable, irrespective of whether there is any pre-theoretically sensible connection between its antecedent and consequent.

This is not to say that no one ever ventured a semantics for conditionals starting from the thought that, for a conditional to be true, its consequent must be inferrable from its antecedent. The Stoic philosopher Chrysippus did (Kneale and Kneale 1962), as did, much later, Mill, who writes the following:

> When we say, If the Koran comes from God, Mahomet is the prophet of God, we do not intend to affirm either that the Koran does come from God, or that Mahomet is really his prophet. Neither of these simple propositions may be true, and yet the truth of the [conditional] may be indisputable. What is asserted is not the truth of either of the propositions, but the inferribility of the one from the other. (Mill 1843/1872, p. 91)

Still later, we find Ramsey explicitly endorsing Mill's idea:

> In general we can say with Mill that "If p, then q" means that q is inferrible from p, that is, of course, from p together with certain facts and laws not stated but in some way indicated by the context. (Ramsey 1990, p. 156)

We find related ideas in Ryle (1950) and Mackie (1973), and in psychology in Braine and O'Brien (1991).

Mill possibly being an exception (Skorupski 1989, p. 73 f.), what the aforementioned authors meant by a consequent being inferrible from an antecedent is that the consequent follows *deductively* from the antecedent. But as Krzyżanowska, Wenmackers, and Douven (2014) point out, thus interpreted, the idea that a conditional means that its consequent is inferrible from its antecedent is difficult to maintain. Douven and colleagues (2018) give the example

(4) If Betty misses her bus, she will be late for the movies,

which, as these authors argue, could well be true in a situation in which there is still a remote possibility that, after she missed the bus, Betty is transported from where she is now to the cinema to still make it in time for the movies.

It is easy to come up with further examples of plausibly true conditionals whose consequent does not follow deductively from its antecedent. That may be why the idea that conditionals embody inferential connections never gained much traction. However, as argued in Krzyżanowska, Wenmackers, and Douven (2014), there is no reason why someone attracted to the idea should want to commit to a reading of "inference" as meaning *deductive* inference.[4] In its place, these authors propose a broader understanding on which a consequent is inferrable from an antecedent if a compelling argument can be made for the consequent starting from the antecedent and whatever background assumptions are available in the context of evaluation. As they emphasize, an argument can be compelling without being conclusive. And for an argument to be compelling, it is not necessary that it consists only of deductive steps. It may include, or consists only of, inductive steps (roughly, steps based on statistical considerations), abductive steps (roughly, steps based on explanatory considerations), and perhaps other inferential steps as well (e.g., steps based on analogical considerations; see Carnap 1980, or Paris and Vencovská 2018).

To be more exact, the new proposal to cash out the idea that conditionals are intimately connected to inference – which was dubbed "inferentialism" – is both contextualist and three-valued and goes as follows: A conditional "If A, B" is true if there is a compelling argument from A plus contextually determined background premises to B, with A being pivotal to that argument (i.e., with A removed, the argument would cease to be compelling), false if there is a compelling argument from A plus contextually determined background premises to the *negation* of B, and indeterminate otherwise. As Douven, Elqayam, and Krzyżanowska (2022) remark, the intuitive understanding is that any person who is justified in believing A becomes justified to believe B as soon as she becomes justified to believe "If A, B" (e.g., on the basis of testimony), supposing her being informed that if A, B, does not undermine whatever justifies her belief in A.

---

4 See also Krzyżanowska (2015), Douven (2016, 2017), Douven et al. (2018, 2020), Douven, Elqayam, and Krzyżanowska (2023).

The broad idea here is that compelling arguments allow one to carry over any justification one has for their premises to their conclusion.[5]

There is already considerable empirical support for inferentialism, some experiments also contrasting inferentialism with the earlier-mentioned mainstream semantics of conditionals. The following subsections discuss this support, which concerns the truth values assigned to conditionals (Section 2.1); probabilities assigned to conditionals (Section 2.2); and reasoning with conditionals (Section 2.3).

2.1 Truth Assignments

Douven and colleagues (2018) report the outcomes of an experiment that was designed around the color patches seen in Figure 1. These patches form a so-called soritical series in that the colors of adjacent patches are very similar, while the patches get slightly greener as we move to the right, ending in a clearly green patch, and having started from a clearly blue one. The materials of the experiment consisted of conditionals pertaining to this series of patches. Each conditional had the form

If patch number i is X, then patch number j is X,

and the participants were asked to evaluate several instances of this schema. Each instance referred to one of the patches 2, 7, 8, 9, 10, or 13, and X was either "blue" or "green", depending on whether the participant had been assigned to the blue condition or to the green condition, a split between participants that was made for control purposes. An orthogonal split was that between the small and the large condition, which determined the values j could take. For participants in the small condition, the patch referred to in the consequent was either one or *two* steps away from the patch referred to in the antecedent, whereas for participants in the large condition, the distance between the patches was either one or *three* steps.

Douven and colleagues point out that, with each of the resulting conditionals, one can readily associate an argument. Consider, for instance,

(5) If patch number 6 is green, then so is patch number 7.

---

[5] Related proposals are to be found in Oaksford and Chater (2010, 2013, 2014, 2017, 2020) as well as in van Rooij and Schulz (2019). These authors analyze the connection between a conditional's component parts in terms of causality. It may be difficult to experimentally distinguish between these authors' proposals and inferentialism for everyday conditionals, given that both inductive and abductive considerations tend to rest on causal relations (e.g., most explanations are causal explanations, and regularities that warrant inductive inferences are often grounded in some causal mechanism). However, Douven and colleagues (2018) found evidence for abstract conditionals, where causal relations cannot underlie the inference.

Figure 1: The soritical color series from the materials of Douven et al. (2018)

This conditional can be backed by the following argument: Patches become greener as we move to the right in the color series, so from the premise that patch number 6 is green, infer that patch number 7 is green (given that patch number 7 is to the right of patch number 6). Or consider

(6) If patch number 6 is green, then so is patch number 5,

with which we can associate this argument: Adjacent patches are very similar in color, so from the premise that patch number 6 is green, infer that patch number 5 is green as well (given that patch number 5 and patch number 6 are adjacent).

As Douven and co-authors further point out, the arguments that can be associated with the conditionals in their materials can vary in strength. This is already clear from (5) and (6). Although both these conditionals refer to adjacent pairs of patches, in (5) the consequent patch is to the "greener" side of the antecedent patch, whereas in (6) the consequent patch is to the "bluer" side of the antecedent patch. While the argument we can associate with (6) is not weak, it is not quite as strong as the argument we can associate with (5). After all, for the former argument, there is a consideration that at least somewhat weakens the conclusion, which is not the case for the latter argument.

In the analysis of Douven and colleagues, there were two key determinants for argument strength in the context of their materials, to wit, *direction* (is the consequent patch to the left or to the right of the antecedent patch?) and *distance* (how close is the consequent patch to the antecedent patch?). As to why direction matters to argument strength, compare again (5) and (6) above: the argument associated with the former is stronger than that associated with the latter, given that in the former we move in the "greener" direction whereas in the latter we move in the "bluer" direction. To see why distance matters to argument strength, it is enough to compare (6) with

(7) If patch number 6 is green, then so is patch number 4.

We would associate essentially the same argument with (6) and (7), except that the argument associated with the latter is slightly weaker than that associated with the former because immediately adjacent patches are more similar to each other than patches that are separated by an intermediate patch.

The statistical analysis reported by Douven and colleagues shows that direction and distance were highly accurate predictors of the rates at which participants judged the conditionals in the materials to be true. That that would be so was predicted by inferentialism. Thus, the results of the experiment provide clear support for that semantics.[6]

Douven and colleagues (2020) further strengthen their case for inferentialism. In this paper, they compare inferentialism with the semantics of conditionals mentioned above – the material conditional account, Stalnaker's possible worlds semantics, and Adams' proposal – as well as some further semantics (notably, De Finetti's three-valued semantics and some variants of that; see, e.g., De Finetti 1995 and McDermott 1996). The comparison shows inferentialism to be clearly superior to any of the other semantics in predicting the data from Douven and colleagues (2018).[7]

We also briefly mention very recent work looking at truth evaluations of conditionals embodying *analogical* arguments. An analogical argument is one were the premise or premises support the conclusion in virtue of some similarity relation holding between items referred to in the premises and conclusion. Paris and Vencovská (2017) give the following example:

My son likes the movie *Toy Story.*
_____
My son likes the movie *The Sound of Music.*

Plausibly, and supposing you have a son, how compelling you deem this argument will depend on how similar you deem *The Sound of Music* to be to *Toy Story.* Inferentialism predicts that, the more compelling you find the argument, the more likely you are to judge (8) to be true:

(8) If my son likes *Toy Story*, then he'll like *The Sound of Music.*

This idea inspired Douven and colleagues (2022a) to run a two-part experiment, one part of which presented participants with various analogical arguments, and the other part of which presented them with conditionals each of which corresponded to one of the arguments presented in the first part. The analysis of the participants' responses strongly supported inferentialism, showing that how compelling an argument was to the eyes of a participant reliably predicted how likely that same participant was to judge the corresponding conditional to be true.[8]

---

[6] To be more exact, the experiment had 532 participants, and the analysis, using mixed-effects models, revealed a main effect of direction, $\chi^2(1) = 201.66$, $p < .0001$, as well as a main effect of distance, $\chi^2(2) = 80.00$, $p < .0001$.

[7] This conclusion was based on a re-analysis of the experiment from Douven et al. (2018). This analysis looked at combinations of and patterns in truth evaluations of the conditionals that were part of the materials of the said experiment as well as of their antecedents and consequents. The analysis, which was akin to (though more complicated than) a χ^2 test, compared frequencies of combinations and patterns that counted as hits or as misses, according to the various semantics. See Douven et al. (2022, sec. 4) for details.

[8] In this experiment, there were 93 participants. Douven and colleagues conducted a Bayesian mixed-effects logistic regression analysis, the main finding of which was that for every one-point increase on

2.2 Probabilities of Conditionals

We sometimes express conditional probabilities using "if" instead of "given that" or "conditional on". For example, it seems perfectly fine to say that the probability of throwing a 6 with a die if you throw an even number is ⅓. From this observation, it is a small step to the idea that the probability of a conditional is the probability of its consequent given its antecedent, an idea now mostly referred to as either "Stalnaker's Thesis" or the "Equation". However, Lewis (1976) showed that, given seemingly incontrovertible assumptions, the Equation has all sorts of absurd consequences.[9] This result stunned the community at the time, given that the Equation does sound reasonable. What made the result look even more stunning is that when psychologists turned their attention to the Equation, they did find strong empirical support for it: people's conditional probabilities appeared to predict quite accurately their probability assignments to the corresponding conditionals.[10]

Both in light of its intuitive appeal and in light of the apparently massive empirical support, many believe the right response to Lewis' result is to abandon the thought that conditionals express propositions. More exactly, according to this proposal conditionals are neither true nor false, and the "probabilities" we assign to conditionals are not standard probabilities of truth but rather degrees of acceptability. This blocks Lewis' argument against the Equation, given that that requires the usual logical operators – which are *propositional* operators – to apply to conditionals. But it also comes at a steep cost, precisely because now it becomes puzzling how conditionals can truth-functionally combine with other parts of the language, as it would seem they can. For example, we have no difficulty understanding conjunctions or disjunctions of conditionals.

Recent experimental results suggest that there may be no need to address Lewis' result head on, simply because there may be independent reason to abandon the Equation. Spohn (2015) may have been the first to question the empirical results supposedly supporting the Equation. As he rightly notes, all materials used in the relevant experiments consisted of conditionals whose antecedent was positively probabilistically relevant to their consequent, meaning that the probability of the consequent given the antecedent was higher than the unconditional probability of the consequent. This is not

---

the 7-point Likert scale that these authors had used to elicit judgments of argument strength, one could expect a close to 75 % increase in the odds that the conditional with the given argument's premise as an antecedent and its conclusion as a consequent would be judged true. See Douven et al. (2021, sec. 4.2) for details.

9 Douven and Verbrugge (2013) show that the assumptions underlying Lewis' argument may not all be innocuous, but we let that pass.

10 See, e.g., Oaksford and Chater (2003, 2007), Over and Evans (2003), Evans and Over (2004), Oberauer, Weidenfeld, and Fischer (2007), Over et al. (2007), Douven and Verbrugge (2010, 2013), Fugard et al. (2011), Over, Douven, and Verbrugge (2013), as well as van Wijnbergen-Huitink, Elqayam, and Over (2015).

because the conditionals were explicitly selected to have that feature. It is rather that most or even all conditionals we encounter in quotidian speech *have* that feature, and psychologists working on conditionals were interested in people's responses to *normal* conditionals. Would conditional probabilities still be found to predict the probabilities of the corresponding conditionals if experimenters presented participants with conditionals whose antecedent is negatively probabilistically relevant to their consequent, or is probabilistically irrelevant to the consequent?

Skovgaard-Olsen, Singman, and Klauer (2016) set out to answer this question. They found that conditional probabilities reliably predict people's probability assignments to conditionals as long as the positive relevance condition holds, but that they fail to do so quite badly in those cases in which the said condition does not hold. While Skovgaard-Olsen and colleagues explain their findings by postulating that the relevance belongs to the "core meaning" of conditional, that is its semantic content, others, for instance, Over and colleagues (2007, p. 92), suggested that "the use of a conditional *pragmatically suggests*, in certain ordinary contexts, that p raises the probability of q or that p causes q".

Elsewhere, we have explained why we prefer semantic over pragmatic explanations of the relevance effect in the data from Skovgaard-Olsen, Singmann, and Klauer (2016).[11] And as shown by Douven and colleagues (2022b), inferentialism provides a perfectly good semantic explanation. These authors start by working out the implications of inferentialism for the probabilities of conditionals. Unpacking the truth conditions that inferentialism assigns to conditionals, Douven and co-authors note that, as standardly understood, probabilities are probabilities of *truth*. Thus, the probability of "If A, B" is the probability that "If A, B" is *true*, which is the probability that the truth conditions of "If A, B" are realized, which finally, assuming inferentialism, is the probability that there is a compelling argument from the conditional's antecedent (plus background knowledge) to the conditional's consequent.

Douven and colleagues (2022b) further note that it is often not immediately obvious to us whether there is a compelling argument for a given proposition starting from a second proposition in conjunction with whatever our background knowledge happens to be. Right now, for instance, we are inclined to believe that a compelling case can be made for the claim that the United States will get the COVID-19 outbreak under control on the supposition that its government can convince at least 80% of the population to get a vaccine. At the moment, however, this is really only an inclination: we are by no means sure and would have to think the matter through more carefully and see in particular whether we are not overlooking factors that might contribute to a continuation of the pandemic even in a fully or near-to-fully vaccinated population (such as, most notably, the emergence of new variants of the SARS-CoV-2

---

11 See Douven, Elqayam, and Krzyżanowska (2023); see also Krzyżanowska, Collins, and Hahn (2021) as well as Rostworowski, Pietrulewicz, and Będkowski (2021).

virus that the current vaccines offer insufficient protection to). But if we now had to answer the question what probability we assign to

(9) If the United States government can convince at least 80% of its population to get vaccinated, they will get the COVID-19 outbreak under control,

we would estimate the likelihood that we can make a compelling case for the consequent, starting from the antecedent plus background knowledge, and would give that as our answer. Douven and colleagues (2022b) argue that we do this by relying on a heuristic of gauging the inferential strength between antecedent and consequent.

Douven and colleagues (2022b) report two experiments designed to test this "inference heuristic". Each experiment presented participants with three tasks, which used the same set of 50 conditionals. One task asked participants for their probability for each of those conditionals; a second task, which participants received a week after the first, asked them to indicate, for each conditional, how strongly in their opinion the consequent followed from the antecedent; and the third task, which the participants received a week after the second, determined their conditional probabilities corresponding to the conditionals, these conditional probabilities being measured via a probabilistic truth-table task in one experiment and by asking participants to engage in suppositional thinking in the other experiment. For instance, one of the conditionals they were presented in the first part was

(10) If a cure for AIDS will be discovered, condom sales will drop.

They were asked to indicate how probable this conditional was, in their opinion. Then in the second part, participants were asked, among other things, "Suppose that a cure for AIDS is discovered. How strongly do you agree that it then follows that condom sales will drop?" They were supposed to answer on a 7-point Likert scale that ranged from "Strongly disagree" to "Strongly agree", with "Neither agree nor disagree" as the midpoint. And then the corresponding question in the final task was, in the first experiment, to rate each of the following situations on a probability scale ranging from 0 to 100%:

> It is TRUE that a cure for AIDS will be discovered and it is also TRUE that condom sales will drop ...
> It is TRUE that a cure for AIDS will be discovered but it is FALSE that condom sales will drop ...
> It is FALSE that a cure for AIDS will be discovered but it is TRUE that condom sales will drop ...
> It is FALSE that a cure for AIDS will be discovered and it is also FALSE that condom sales will drop ...
>
> 100

Here, participants were instructed to make sure that the probabilities summed to 100. In the second experiment, they were not shown such probabilistic truth tables but asked to suppose that a cure for AIDS will be discovered and then to assess, under that supposition, the probability that condom sales will drop.

Across both experiments, inference strength judgments were found to accurately predict probability ratings, in line with what one would expect on the basis of inferentialism. Moreover, inference strength judgments were also found to predict probability ratings much more accurately than conditional probability ratings, an outcome that strongly favors inferentialism over Adams' (1975) account.[12]

2.3 Reasoning with Conditionals

A third major research area concerning conditionals, next to their truth conditions and probabilities, is the inferences they license. While this is again an area of vast disagreement, virtually all researchers agree that the conditional operator should validate *Modus ponens* (MP): from A and "If A, B" we should be allowed to infer B. After all, this is a rule we rely on quite routinely in our reasoning. However, as Krzyżanowska, Wenmackers, and Douven (2014) acknowledged right away, their position does *not* validate MP, simply because we may deem an argument from a true premise A to a conclusion B compelling (making "If A, B" true, given our background knowledge), but, unbeknownst to us, B may be false.[13]

As Krzyżanowska and co-authors also pointed out, however, the fact that inferentialism invalidates MP does not mean that, from an inferentialist perspective, there is anything wrong with our practice of relying on that rule of inference. To the contrary, from that perspective, the designated practice is perfectly fine. For consider that, typically, when we have a compelling argument from A to B, and A is true, then B will be true as well. As Schurz and Hertwig (2019) argue, we rely on compelling-but-inconclusive arguments much more frequently in our daily lives than we rely on deductively valid arguments. Thus, it would be a serious problem if the arguments we judge to be compelling were not highly truth-conducive. But if that is so, then, from an inferentialist perspective, MP is a highly reliable inference rule, which typically yields a true conclusion when applied to true premises. Also, as McGee (1985) argued, it suffices to account for the intuition that it is perfectly alright to rely on MP that MP be highly reliable, given that we cannot expect our intuitions about the validity of an inference rule

---

[12] In the first experiment there were 118 participants, in the second there were 204. The data from both experiments were analyzed using Bayesian mixed-effects linear models. In both analyses, the best models were those with both inference strength responses and conditional probabilities as predictors of the probabilities of conditionals. However, also in both analyses, the former had a much bigger impact than the latter. For details, see Sections 2.2 and 3.2.

[13] We say "unbeknownst to us" because we are unlikely to regard any argument as compelling if we know its conclusion to be false.

to be sensitive to the difference between that rule being guaranteed to preserve truth and it preserving truth with near-certainty.

In fact, psychologists have been long looking at MP. In multiple experiments, they found that whereas MP was typically *highly* endorsed, it seldom was *universally* endorsed.[14] That is due to processing factors and perhaps some noise – but not entirely. As New Paradigmers argued, experimenters can request their participants to suppose the premises of an argument, but they should still reckon with the possibility that a participant's own beliefs about those premises will have some impact on his or her judgments about whether a certain conclusion follows. Most notably, Stevenson and Over (2001) found that uncertainty about the major premise in an MP argument tends to diminish a participant's willingness to endorse the conclusion.

Mirabile and Douven (2021) examined the endorsement rates of the conclusions of MP arguments with an eye toward testing inferentialism. More specifically, they were interested in whether a participant's judgment of the strength of the argument embodied by the major premise of an MP argument would predict the likelihood that that participant would endorse the conclusion of the argument. They were further interested in contrasting the predictive power of such inferential strength judgments with that of the judged probability of the consequent of the major premise given its antecedent.

They conducted a three-part experiment whose main materials consisted of a number of MP arguments. One part of the experiment was meant to measure the conditional probabilities corresponding to the conditionals that served as major premises in those argument, another part was meant to measure the strength of the inferential connection between those conditionals' antecedents and consequents, and the third was meant to measure endorsement rates of the conclusions of the arguments. In their analysis, Mirabile and Douven found, in support of inferentialism, that whereas conditional probability was a good predictor of conclusion endorsement, argument strength was a significantly better predictor.[15]

It may be helpful to explain in a little more detail how Mirabile and Douven see their results as supporting inferentialism. As they point out, from an inferentialist perspective, conditionals look a bit like *pipes* or *conduits* in that, if accepted, a conditional allows one to transfer whatever grounds one has for believing its antecedent to its consequent. That, after all, is what a compelling argument does: transferring whatever grounds one has for believing the premises to grounds for believing the conclusion. As mentioned, however, that an argument is compelling does not imply that it is conclusive. Because of that – Mirabile and Douven argue – conditionals are to be thought of as *leaky pipes*, where the leakiness can vary in degree. The argument they embody

---

14 Specifically, endorsement rates ranged between 89 and 100%.
15 In this experiment, there were 120 participants. In the analysis, Mirabile and Douven fit a number of Bayesian cumulative ordinal regression models to the data from these participants, all models having endorsement rates as dependent variable. The model that did best had both inference strength and conditional probability as predictors, but that model showed the former to have a much bigger impact on the data than the latter. For details, see Mirabile and Douven (2021, sec. 6.2).

may not be strong enough to carry over *all* the support we have or may have for the antecedent to the consequent. The part aimed at measuring inference strength can be thought of as having measured the degree of leakiness, and the degree of leakiness of the major premise of an MP argument turned out to predict with high accuracy whether a participant was to endorse the conclusion of that argument.

2.4 Open Questions

Inferentialism, in the version described in the foregoing, is still a young position, and there remain a number of questions to be answered. We mention two in particular. One concerns the learning of conditionals. It consists of two sub-questions, to wit, the question of how people actually adapt their beliefs to the receipt of conditional information, and the question of how they ought to adapt their beliefs to the receipt of such information. The learning of conditionals is badly understudied, both in philosophy and in psychology. As shown in Douven (2012), standard mechanisms for updating our beliefs can give counterintuitive results when applied to conditionals. A worked-out proposal for an update rule that does give satisfactory results for such applications is still lacking. A good approach may be to first gather more data on how people actually react when they learn a conditional. Work on this has just begun.

We know, for instance, that upon receiving a testimony of the form "If A, C", which we will refer to as a "conditional testimony", the participants increase their conditional probability ratings. Moreover, the participants' posterior conditional probability ratings are higher when they receive the conditional testimony from a highly reliable speaker, for instance, a professor of medicine making assertions about a patient's prognosis, than when the same conditional is asserted by a less reliable speaker, such as a medical student (Collins et al. 2020). But it is not only the conditional probability that people adjust upon receiving a conditional testimony. In a follow-up to the paper from Collins and colleagues, Krzyżanowska, Collins, and Hahn (2020) report that the perceived strength of the (probabilistic) relevance relation, estimated as the difference between $\Pr(C\,|\,A)$ and $\Pr(C\,|\,\neg A)$, also increases in response to someone's assertion of a conditional, and the extent of this increase depends on the reliability of the speaker, too. Furthermore, Collins (2017) found that people's conditional probability judgments increase to a greater extent when the same testimony comes from multiple sources than when the conditional is asserted by a single speaker. Collins and colleagues (2020) collected not only the conditional probability ratings but also the probability estimates of the relevant antecedents and consequents on their own. Perhaps unsurprisingly, the participants did not adjust their probability ratings for the antecedents and consequents if, prior to receiving the conditional testimony, they found them as likely as not, that is, both the prior and posterior probability estimates for these antecedents and consequents were close to 0.5. However, participants did increase their probability ratings for the antecedents and consequents whose prior probability was judged to be low.[16] Interestingly, while these results present a rather unsurprising and intuitive data pattern, they turned out to pose a significant modeling challenge. In their extensive theoretical discussion, Collins and colleagues conclude that none of the mainstream theories of conditionals can account for all of the reported findings in a straightforward way.[17]

The other question we want to mention concerns nested conditionals. Philosophers have been struggling to come to grips with such conditionals, and empirical studies devoted to nested conditionals are far and few between. There is some work relevant to the so-called Import–Export principle, according to which a nested conditional of the form "If A then if B, C" is equivalent to the simple conditional "If A and B, then C", but the results are mixed (Douven and Verbrugge 2013, van Wijnbergen-Huitink, Elqayam, and Over 2015), calling for further studies. van Wijnbergen-Huitink, Elqayam, and Over (2015) used abstract conditionals such as "If the chip is square, then if it is large, it is white" in a betting task, with two tasks, a probability task and a categorical truth task, both presented in a betting format. They found no differences between the probabilities of the iterated versus the imported form. However, in the categorical task, more imported forms than iterated forms were consistent with the defective truth table (according to which a conditional with an antecedent that is either false or has an indeterminate "truth value" is itself indeterminate), an effect attributed to processing difficulty.

3 Further Topics

We have focused on the experimental philosophy of conditionals and conditional reasoning because, first, it is an area that has seen a lot of recent activity, and second, much of that activity consisted of collaborative projects involving both philosophers and psychologists. We firmly believe that such collaborations have the best chance of leading to high-quality work in experimental philosophy and so we recommend that philosophers interested in doing experiments try to team up with colleagues from the psychology department.

In this section, we briefly mention some other research examining empirically topics that are of direct concern to logicians and formal epistemologists. The first topic we want to mention is the study of the Liar paradox ("This sentence is false" – which is false if it is true and true if it is false). While the roots of the Liar go way back, it is

---

16 Collins and colleagues (2020) also looked at high probability antecedents and consequents, but found only a slight, non-significant decrease in the probability ratings. However, the prior probability estimates for what was supposed to be high probability antecedents and consequents were less extreme – that is, farther away from the end point of the scale – than the estimates for their low-probability counterparts.

17 Though see Hartmann and Hahn (2020) for a new formal proposal devised specifically to account for the empirical data on updating with conditionals.

in the twentieth century that philosophers such as Tarski (1944) and Kripke (1975) famously used it as a focal consideration in theories of truth. Notwithstanding the massive impact this work had on philosophy, little psychological work has been done with the Liar. Elqayam (2006; see also Elqayam et al. 2008) embedded Liar-type propositions in truth-table tasks, with the Truthteller ("This sentence is true") as a control. Conditionals with a Liar component tended to be evaluated as indeterminate, whereas conditionals with the Truthteller (equally indeterminate but not paradoxical) were "collapsed", that is, they were treated as if the Truthteller were simply true. In terms of processing, this is evidence to the difficulty people have in effort-laden computations such as those required in tracking multiple iterations.

Another interesting example is what has been dubbed in the psychological literature "logical intuitions". The idea is that people are able to provide fast, automatic logical responses (e.g., Handley et al. 2011), or at least identify when their responses went wrong (De Neys 2012), even if they were powerless to revise them. The term "logical intuitions" can be misleading, insofar as it might create the misapprehension that humans might have intuitions for classical logic implanted in their brains. As more recent work identified (Ghasemi et al. 2022), such intuitions are anything but logical; rather, they are generated by fast processing of superficial cues, whose outputs happen to correlate with logical responding.

Another topic we want to mention is the experimental study of various forms of non-deductive reasoning, such as work on analogical reasoning (e.g., Spellman and Holyoak 1992), or informal reasoning and argumentation (e.g., Hahn and Oaksford 2007, Mercier and Sperber 2011). A substantial body of work has gone into probabilistic reasoning. As intimated, it is a core tenet of both formal epistemology and the New Paradigm psychology of reasoning that reasoning is, most fundamentally, probabilistic in nature. Psychologists have been mainly interested in the extent to which "probabilistic" can be taken literally, that is, the extent to which people obey the postulates of probability theory in their reasoning. Famously, Tversky and Kahneman (1983) published results showing that people sometimes assign a probability to a conjunction that exceeds the probability they assign to the (in their eyes) least probable conjunct, in violation of probability theory. Collaboration between philosophers and psychologists led to a series of papers defending a plausible explanation of Tversky and Kahneman's results (see Crupi, Tentori, and Gonzalez 2007, Crupi, Fitelson, and Tentori 2008, as well as Tentori, Crupi, and Russo 2013). According to these authors, people often attend more closely to probabilistic confirmation than to probability per se, but because the notions are so closely related, they can get easily conflated in people's minds.

Work on abductive reasoning – a form of non-deductive reasoning guided by explanatory considerations – is reported in Douven and Schupbach (2015a, 2015b).[18] Philosophers have long argued that we may be justified in believing something because it

---

[18] See also Lombrozo (2016), Walker et al. (2017), Wojtowicz and DeDeo (2020), Douven (2021), as well as Jern, Derrow-Pinion, and Piergiovanni (2021).

best explains the evidence in our possession (see, e.g., Boyd 1985, McMullin 1992, Lipton 2004). More recently, Bayesian philosophers of science have rejected this idea as – according to them – it can lead to probabilistic incoherence, which they see as a token of irrationality (van Fraassen 1989). Douven and Schupbach showed experimentally that judgments of explanation quality had a significant impact on their participants' belief updates and explained why those updates tended to deviate from Bayesian prescriptions. Whereas that might just go to show that Bayesianism is not descriptively adequate, Douven (2022) argues that people may be right to update their beliefs on the basis of explanatory considerations and that there is no reason to view this as a sign of irrationality, even if it leads to discrepancies with Bayesian norms.

We already briefly touched upon analogical reasoning, which relies on similarity relations. So far, there has been little contact between philosophers and psychologists studying this form of reasoning. Carnap (1980), Kuipers (1988), Niiniluoto (1988), and other philosophers have been mainly concerned with trying to formalize analogical reasoning, whereas psychologists have – much of it under the heading of "category-based induction" – experimentally investigated the role of similarity in inference (e.g., to what extent people's willingness to infer that cows have a certain property from the premise that horses have that property depends on how similar they judge cows to be to horses). Osta-Vélez and Gärdenfors (2020) make an explicit attempt to connect philosophical work on analogical reasoning with the aforementioned psychological research. The main result of their paper is an account of analogical reasoning based on the so-called conceptual spaces framework (Gärdenfors 2000). Douven and colleagues (2022a) report empirical support for this new proposal.

Finally, formal epistemologists have expended much time and effort on analyzing the notion of coherence. In mainstream epistemology, Bonjour (1985) and other had proposed that coherence was key to a theory of justification. Specifically, the idea was that the more coherent a set of beliefs is – the more those beliefs hang together – the more justified we are in holding those beliefs. This idea was challenged on the grounds that there was nothing to suggest that coherence is truth-conducive and that it hence was unclear that coherence can play any role in a theory of justification (see, e.g., Klein and Warfield 1994). That, at the time, we only had an informal understanding of the notion of coherence made the challenge hard to address. Realizing this, various researchers set out to make coherence formally precise, which led to a great number of probabilistic measures of coherence; see, among many other publications all proposing different measures, Shogenji (1999), Olsson (2002), Bovens and Hartmann (2003), Fitelson (2003), Douven and Meijs (2007), Schippers (2014), as well as Schippers and Schurz (2017).

Most authors working on probabilistic measures of coherence supported their proposals by arguing that they gave verdicts about cases that aligned with our intuitions about those cases. It is unfortunate that, to this day, few attempts have been made to subject the various proposals to empirical testing. Two notable exceptions are Harris and Hahn (2009) and Koscholke and Jekel (2017). An exception of sorts is Angere (2008), which uses computer simulations to determine which of the measures is most conducive to the truth. Whereas computer simulations have not gained any prominence so far in experimental philosophy, it is arguable that they can give empirical support of sorts, much in the way in which they can in physics and the natural sciences generally (Galison 1997).

Bibliography

Adams, Ernest (1975): *The logic of conditionals*. Dordrecht: Reidel.
Angere, Stefan (2008): "Coherence as heuristic", *Mind* 117, pp. 1–26.
Berto, Francesco, and Aybüke Özgün (2021): "Indicative conditionals. Probabilities and relevance", *Philosophical Studies* 178, pp. 3697–3730.
Bonjour, Laurence (1985): *The structure of empirical knowledge*. Cambridge: Harvard University Press.
Bonnefon, Jean-François (2009): "A theory of utility conditionals. Paralogical reasoning from decision-theoretic leakage", *Psychological Review* 116 (4), pp. 888–907.
Bovens, Luc, and Stephan Hartmann (2003): *Bayesian epistemology*. Oxford: Oxford University Press.
Boyd, Richard (1985): "Lex orandi est lex credendi", in: Paul Churchland and Clifford Hooker (Eds.): *Images of science. Essays on realism and empiricism*. Chicago: University of Chicago Press, pp. 3–34.
Braine, Martin, and David O'Brien (1991): "A theory of if. Lexical entry, reasoning program, and pragmatic principles", *Psychological Review* 98 (2), pp. 182–203.
Carnap, Rudolf (1980): "A basic system of inductive logic. Part II", in: Richard Jeffrey (Ed.): *Studies in inductive logic and probability*. Berkeley: University of California Press, pp. 7–155.
Collins, Peter (2017): *Rationality, pragmatics, and sources*. Doctoral dissertation. Birkbeck: University of London.
Collins, Peter, Karolina Krzyżanowska, Stephan Hartmann, Gregory Wheeler, and Ulrike Hahn (2020): "Conditionals and testimony", *Cognitive Psychology* 122, 101329.
Crupi, Vincenzo, Branden Fitelson, and Katya Tentori (2008): "Probability, confirmation, and the conjunction fallacy", *Thinking & Reasoning* 14 (2), pp. 182–199.
Crupi, Vincenzo, and Andrea Iacona (2022): "The evidential conditional", *Erkenntnis* 87, pp. 2897–2921.
Crupi, Vincenzo, Katya Tentori, and Michel Gonzalez (2007): "On Bayesian measures of evidential support. Theoretical and empirical issues", *Philosophy of Science* 74 (2), pp. 229–252.
De Finetti, Bruno (1995): "The logic of probability", *Philosophical Studies* 77 (1), pp. 181–190.
De Neys, Wim (2012): "Bias and conflict. A case for logical intuitions", *Perspectives on Psychological Science* 7 (1), pp. 28–38.
Douven, Igor (2012): "Learning conditional information", *Mind & Language* 27 (3), pp. 239–263.
Douven, Igor (2016): *The epistemology of indicative conditionals. Formal and empirical approaches*. Cambridge: Cambridge University Press.
Douven, Igor (2017): "How to account for the oddness of missing-link conditionals", *Synthese* 194 (5), pp. 1541–1554.
Douven, Igor (2021): "How explanation guides belief change", *Trends in Cognitive Sciences* 25 (10), pp. 829–830.
Douven, Igor (2022): *The art of abduction*. Cambridge: The MIT Press.
Douven, Igor, Shira Elqayam, Peter Gärdenfors, and Patricia Mirabile (2022a): "Conceptual spaces and the strength of similarity-based arguments", *Cognition* 218, 104951.
Douven, Igor, Shira Elqayam, and Patricia Mirabile (2022b): "Inference strength predicts the probability of conditionals better than conditional probability does", *Journal of Memory and Language* 123, 104302.
Douven, Igor, Shira Elqayam, and Karolina Krzyżanowska (2023): "Inferentialism. A manifesto", in: Stefan Kaufmann, David Over, and Ghanshyam Sharma (Eds.): *Conditionals. Logic, linguistics, and psychology*. London: Palgrave Macmillan, pp. 175–221.

Douven, Igor, Shira Elqayam, Henrik Singmann, and Janneke van Wijnbergen-Huitink (2018): "Conditionals and inferential connections. A hypothetical inferential theory", *Cognitive Psychology* 101, pp. 50–81.

Douven, Igor, Shira Elqayam, Henrik Singmann, and Janneke van Wijnbergen-Huitink (2020): "Conditionals and inferential connections. Toward a new semantics", *Thinking & Reasoning* 26 (3), pp. 311–351.

Douven, Igor, and Sara Verbrugge (2010): "The Adams family", *Cognition* 117 (3), pp. 302–318.

Douven, Igor, and Sara Verbrugge (2013): "The probabilities of conditionals revisited", *Cognitive Science* 37 (4), pp. 711–730.

Elqayam, Shira (2006): "The collapse illusion effect. A pragmatic–semantic illusion of truth and paradox", *Thinking & Reasoning* 12 (2), pp. 144–180.

Elqayam, Shira, and Jonathan Evans (2011): "Subtracting 'ought' from 'is'. Descriptivism versus normativism in the study of human thinking", *Behavioral and Brain Sciences* 34 (5), pp. 233–248.

Elqayam, Shira, Simon Handley, Jonathan Evans, and Alison Bacon (2008): "On some limits of hypothetical thinking", *Quarterly Journal of Experimental Psychology* 61 (5), pp. 784–808.

Elqayam, Shira, and David Over (2013): "New paradigm psychology of reasoning", *Thinking & Reasoning* 19 (3–4), pp. 249–265.

Evans, Jonathan, and David Over (2004): *If*. Oxford: Oxford University Press.

Fitelson, Branden (2003): "A probabilistic theory of coherence", *Analysis* 63 (3), pp. 194–199.

Fugard, Andrew, Niki Pfeifer, Bastian Mayerhofer, and Gernot Kleiter (2011): "How people interpret conditionals. Shifts toward the conditional event", *Journal of Experimental Psychology – Learning, Memory, and Cognition* 37 (3), pp. 635–648.

Galison, Peter (1997): *Image and logic. A material culture of microphysics*. Chicago: University of Chicago Press.

Gärdenfors, Peter (2000): *Conceptual spaces. The geometry of thought*. Cambridge: The MIT Press.

Ghasemi, Omid, Simon Handley, Stephanie Howarth, Ian Randal Newman, Valerie Thompson (2022): "Logical intuition is not really about logic", *Journal of Experimental Psychology – General* 151 (9), pp. 2009–2028.

Griggs, Richard, and James Cox (1982): "The elusive thematic materials effect in the Wason selection task", *British Journal of Psychology* 73 (3), pp. 407–420.

Hahn, Ulrike, and Mike Oaksford (2007): "The rationality of informal argumentation. A Bayesian approach to reasoning fallacies", *Psychological Review* 114 (3), pp. 704–732.

Handley, Simon, Stephen Newstead, and Dries Trippas (2011): "Logic, beliefs, and instruction. A test of the default interventionist account of belief bias", *Journal of Experimental Psychology – Learning, Memory, and Cognition* 37 (3), pp. 28–43.

Harris, Adam, and Ulrike Hahn (2009): "Bayesian rationality in evaluating multiple testimonies. Incorporating the role of coherence", *Journal of Experimental Psychology – Learning, Memory, and Cognition* 35 (5), pp. 1366–1373.

Hartmann, Stephan, and Ulrike Hahn (2020): "A new approach to testimonial conditionals", in: Stephanie Denison, Michael Mack, Yang Xu, and Blair Armstrong (Eds.): *Proceedings of the 42nd annual conference of the Cognitive Science Society*. Red Hook: Curran, pp. 981–986.

Jern, Alan, Austin Derrow-Pinion, and Alan Jern Piergiovanni (2021): "A computational framework for understanding the roles of simplicity and rational support in people's behavior explanations", *Cognition* 210, 104606.

Klein, Peter, and Ted Warfield (1994): "What price coherence?", *Analysis* 54 (3), pp. 129–132.

Kneale, William, and Martha Kneale (1962): *The development of logic*. Oxford: Oxford University Press.

Koscholke, Jakob, and Mark Jekel (2017): "Probabilistic coherence measures. A psychological study of coherence assessment", *Synthese* 194 (4), pp. 1303–1322.

Kripke, Saul (1975): "Outline of a theory of truth", *Journal of Philosophy* 72 (19), pp. 690–716.

Krzyżanowska, Karolina (2015): *Between "if" and "then"*. Doctoral dissertation. University of Groningen.

Krzyżanowska, Karolina, Peter Collins, and Ulrike Hahn (2017): "Between a conditional's antecedent and its consequent. Discourse coherence vs. probabilistic relevance", *Cognition* 164, pp. 199–205.

Krzyżanowska, Karolina, Peter Collins, and Ulrike Hahn (2020): "… that P is relevant for Q. Indicative conditionals and learning from testimony", in: Stephanie Denison, Michael Mack, Yang Xu, and Blair Armstrong (Eds.): *Proceedings of the 42nd annual conference of the Cognitive Science Society*. Red Hook: Curran, pp. 987–993.

Krzyżanowska, Karolina, Peter Collins, and Ulrike Hahn (2021): "True clauses and false connections", *Journal of Memory and Language* 121, 104252.

Krzyżanowska, Karolina, Sylvia Wenmackers, and Igor Douven (2014): "Rethinking Gibbard's riverboat argument", *Studia Logica* 102 (4), pp. 771–792.

Kuipers, Theo (1988): "Inductive analogy by similarity and proximity", in: David Helman (Ed.): *Analogical reasoning. Perspectives of artificial intelligence, cognitive science, and philosophy*. Dordrecht: Kluwer, pp. 299–313.

Kyburg, Henry, Choh Teng, and Gregory Wheeler (2007): "Conditionals and consequences", *Journal of Applied Logic* 5 (4), pp. 638–650.

Lewis, David (1976): "Probabilities of conditionals and conditional probabilities", *Philosophical Review* 85 (3), pp. 297–315.

Lipton, Peter (2004): *Inference to the best explanation*. 2nd edition. London: Routledge.

Lombrozo, Tania (2016): "Explanatory preferences shape learning and inference", *Trends in Cognitive Sciences* 20 (10), pp. 748–759.

Mackie, John (1973): *Truth, probability and paradox. Studies in philosophical logic*. Oxford: Oxford University Press.

Marr, David (1982): *Vision. A computational investigation into the human representation and processing of visual information*. San Francisco: Freeman.

McDermott, Michael (1996): "On the truth conditions of certain 'if'-sentences", *Philosophical Review* 105 (1), pp. 1–37.

McGee, Vann (1985): "A counterexample to modus ponens", *Journal of Philosophy* 82 (9), pp. 462–471.

McMullin, Ernan (1992): *The inference that makes science*. Milwaukee: Marquette University Press.

Mercier, Hugo, and Dan Sperber (2011): "Why do humans reason? Arguments for an argumentative theory", *Behavioral and Brain Sciences* 34 (2), pp. 57–74.

Mill, John Stuart (1843/1872): *A system of logic. Ratiocinative and inductive*. 8th edition. London: Longmans, Green, Reader, & Dyer.

Mirabile, Patricia, and Igor Douven (2020): "Abductive conditionals as a test case for inferentialism", *Cognition* 200, 104232.

Niiniluoto, Ilkka (1988): "Analogy and similarity in scientific reasoning", in: David Helman (Ed.): *Analogical reasoning. Perspectives of artificial intelligence, cognitive science, and philosophy*. Dordrecht: Kluwer, pp. 271–298.

Oaksford, Mike, and Nick Chater (2003): "Conditional probability and the cognitive science of conditional reasoning", *Mind & Language* 18 (4), pp. 359–379.

Oaksford, Mike, and Nick Chater (2007): *Bayesian rationality. The probabilistic approach to human reasoning*. Oxford: Oxford University Press.

Oaksford, Mike, and Nick Chater (2010): "Causation and conditionals in the cognitive science of human reasoning", *The Open Psychology Journal* 3, pp. 105–118.

Oaksford, Mike, and Nick Chater (2013): "Dynamic inference and everyday conditional reasoning in the new paradigm", *Thinking & Reasoning* 19 (3–4), pp. 346–379.

Oaksford, Mike, and Nick Chater (2014): "Probabilistic single function dual process theory and logic programming as approaches to non-monotonicity in human vs. artificial reasoning", *Thinking & Reasoning* 20 (2), pp. 269–295.

Oaksford, Mike, and Nick Chater (2017): "Causal models and conditional reasoning", in: Michael Waldmann (Ed.): *The Oxford handbook of causal reasoning*. Oxford: Oxford University Press, pp. 327–346.

Oaksford, Mike, and Nick Chater (2020): "Integrating causal Bayes nets and inferentialism in conditional inference", in: Shira Elqayam, Igor Douven, Jonathan Evans, and Nicole Cruz (Eds.): *Logic and uncertainty in the human mind. A tribute to David E. Over.* London: Routledge, pp. 116–132.

Oberauer, Klaus, Andrea Weidenfeld, and Katrin Fischer (2007): "What makes us believe a conditional? The roles of covariation and causality", *Thinking & Reasoning* 13 (4), pp. 340–369.

Olsson, Erik (2002): "What is the problem of coherence and truth?", *Journal of Philosophy* 99 (5), pp. 246–272.

Osta-Vélez, Matias, and Peter Gärdenfors (2020): "Category-based induction in conceptual spaces", *Journal of Mathematical Psychology* 96, 102357.

Over, David (2009): "New paradigm psychology of reasoning", *Thinking & Reasoning* 15 (4), pp. 431–438.

Over, David, Igor Douven, and Sara Verbrugge (2013): "Scope ambiguities and conditionals", *Thinking & Reasoning* 19 (3–4), pp. 284–307.

Over, David, and Jonathan Evans (2003): "The probability of conditionals. The psychological evidence", *Mind & Language* 18 (4), pp. 340–358.

Over, David, Constantinos Hadjichristidis, Jonathan Evans, Simon Handley, and Steven Sloman (2007): "The probability of causal conditionals", *Cognitive Psychology* 54 (1), pp. 62–97.

Paris, Jeffrey, and Alena Vencovská (2017): Combining analogical support in pure inductive logic", *Erkenntnis* 82 (2), pp. 401–419.

Ramsey, Frank (1990): "General propositions and causality", in: Frank Ramsey: *Philosophical Papers.* Ed. by David Hugh Mellor. Cambridge: Cambridge University Press, pp. 145–163.

Rostworowski, Wojciech, Natalia Pietrulewicz, and Marcin Będkowski (2021): "Conditionals and specific links. An experimental study", *Synthese* 199, pp. 7365–7399.

Ryle, Gilbert (1950): "'If', 'so', and 'because'", in: Gilbert Ryle: *Philosophical analysis. A collection of essays.* Ed. by Max Black. Ithaca: Cornell University Press, pp. 323–340.

Schippers, Michael (2014): "Probabilistic measures of coherence. From adequacy constraints towards pluralism", *Synthese* 191 (16), pp. 3821–3845.

Schippers, Michael, and Gerhard Schurz (2017): "Genuine coherence as mutual confirmation between content elements", *Studia Logica* 105, pp. 299–329.

Schurz, Gerhard, and Ralph Hertwig (2019): "Cognitive success. A consequentialist account of rationality and cognition", *Topics in Cognitive Science* 11, pp. 7–36.

Shogenji, Tomoji (1999): "Is coherence truth-conducive?", *Analysis* 59 (4), pp. 338–345.

Skorupski, John (1989): *John Stuart Mill.* London: Routledge.

Skovgaard-Olsen, Niels, Henrik Singmann, and Klaus Klauer (2016): "The relevance effect and conditionals", *Cognition* 150, pp. 26–36.

Spellman, Barbara, and Keith Holyoak (1992): "If Saddam is Hitler then who is George Bush? Analogical mapping between systems of social roles", *Journal of Personality and Social Psychology* 62 (6), pp. 913–933.

Spohn, Wolfgang (2015): "Conditionals. A unifying ranking-theoretic perspective", *Philosophers' Imprint* 15 (1), pp. 1–30.

Stalnaker, Robert (1975): "Indicative conditionals", *Philosophia* 5 (3), pp. 269–286.

Stenning, Keith, and Michiel van Lambalgen (2008): *Human reasoning and cognitive science.* Cambridge: The MIT Press.

Tarski, Alfred (1944): "The semantic conception of truth and the foundations of semantics", *Philosophy and Phenomenological Research* 4 (3), pp. 341–376.

Tentori, Katya, Vincenzo Crupi, and Selena Russo (2013): "On the determinants of the conjunction fallacy. Probability versus inductive confirmation", *Journal of Experimental Psychology – General* 142 (1), pp. 235–255.

Tversky, Amos, and Daniel Kahneman (1983): "Extensional versus intuitive reasoning. The conjunction fallacy in probability judgment", *Psychological Review* 90 (4), pp. 293–315.

van Fraassen, Bas (1989): *Laws and symmetry.* Oxford: Oxford University Press.

van Rooij, Robert, and Katrin Schulz (2019): "Conditionals, causality and conditional probability", *Journal of Logic, Language and Information* 28, pp. 55–71.
Walker, Caren, Tania Lombrozo, Joseph Williams, Anna Rafferty, and Alison Gopnik (2017): "Explaining constrains causal learning in childhood", *Child Development* 88 (1), pp. 229–246.
Wojtowicz, Zachary, and Simon DeDeo (2020): "From probability to consilience. How explanatory values implement Bayesian reasoning", *Trends in Cognitive Sciences* 24 (12), pp. 981–993.

Jonathan Waskan
Experimental Philosophy of Science: Scientific Explanation

Abstract: This chapter discusses the achievements and potential of broad and narrow approaches to experimental philosophy of science with a specific focus on scientific explanation. Proponents of the broad approach attempt to enrich the philosophical investigation of science with an array of empirical findings about human cognition. Most philosophers of science claim, however, that such findings hold little relevance to their own inquiries. The newer, narrow approach to experimental philosophy of science utilizes tools from social psychology and bibliometrics to directly study scientists and their written output. Among its findings is that the above claims for the autonomy of philosophy of science (i.e., from cognitive science) rest on judgments that are unjustifiably out of step with those of practicing scientists. A thoroughly interdisciplinary investigation of the nature and value of science may thus be warranted after all. Possible future contributions from this type of research are discussed in closing.

Keywords: Ceteris Paribus Conditions; Data Mining; Demand Characteristics; Ecological Validity; Explanation; Philosophy of Science; Reasoning; Understanding

1 Introduction

By forcing a much-needed self-examination of how analytic philosophy works and what it promises to reveal, experimental philosophy (x-phi) has done as much to reinvigorate the discipline as anything in the past 50 years. This contribution will show how recent work in x-phi of science, which attempts to breach a longstanding barrier to interdisciplinarity, may just warrant a major shake-up to how mainstream philosophy of science is practiced, particularly as concerns the study of one of science's central goals: providing explanations. Section 2 begins with an account of how philosophy of science came, in terms of both subject-matter and methodology, to take on its current, self-contained form (Section 2.1). It then outlines the more interdisciplinary alternatives offered by the broad and narrow approaches to x-phi of science (Section 2.2) and describes a set of findings generated through the narrow approach that undercut longstanding philosophical arguments against interdisciplinarity, particularly as concerns the study of explanation (Section 2.3). The chapter closes with an exploration of the many other ways in which philosophy of science might benefit from the scientific study of laypeople and scientists (Section 3).

Note: Many thanks to Alexander Max Bauer and Stephan Kornmesser for their helpful comments on earlier drafts of this chapter.

2 X-phi of Explanation

To speak sensibly about x-phi's possible contributions to the study of scientific explanation, it is useful to first review philosophy's troubled history with this topic. We can gain some useful traction in this regard by first taking a historical look at the backbone of the entire field – namely, its inquiry into the nature and testing of theories.

2.1 The History of "Why?"

Philosophy of science took on its contemporary form around the turn of the twentieth century through attempts to *demarcate* that paragon of epistemic virtue, science, from such putative forms of intellectual skullduggery as splatiomancy, religion, Freudian psychology, or Hegelian and Marxists philosophy. There arose in this period a new group of *logical* empiricists (named for their reliance on newly developed formal machinery) who, like their predecessors, hoped to distinguish the meaningful claims of science from the meaningless claims of (broadly speaking) metaphysics. While science and metaphysics do both appeal to unseen goings-on, it was thought that only the theoretical claims of science could be logically reduced to meaningful claims about the observations that would confirm them. Scientific theories came in this way to be viewed as having only descriptive and predictive functions, and empiricists consequently lost interest in explanation (the *sine qua non* of metaphysics). By the 1930s to 1940s, it was thus commonly held that science is only about answering "what?" not "why?" As Walter Terence Stace (1935, p. 413) put it, "'why?' does not really express a desire for information at all. It expresses a feeling. It does not proceed from the intellect, but from the emotions". Such subjective, affect-laden states are no use to science, says Stace, and thus "the function of science is not explanation at all" (Stace 1935, p. 415).

The prospective, verificationist account of theoretical claims faced numerous challenges, one being that the requisite verifications are beyond the reach of science. The focus thus turned from theories of meaning to proposals about how science evaluates claims. Appealing to famous episodes of theory change, Popper (1959, originally published in 1935) concluded that science's most distinctive strategy is, through so-called crucial tests, to falsify theories and thereby winnow down the range of plausible positions. Further consideration of cases (both actual and hypothetical), however, convinced the bulk of the field that testing never truly falsifies a theory, for seemingly damning evidence can be explained away by rejecting auxiliary assumptions (e.g., concerning background conditions, instrumentation, or observers) or through subtle modifications to the theory itself (see Quine 1953, Lakatos 1970). In response, Popper tried to subtly modify his own theory, but it nevertheless fell from favor. Popper's research did, however, put a spotlight on the important fact that theoretical claims are tested not in isolation but *en masse*, which led some to reject the demarcation project altogether (Quine 1953).

Though the founding goal of the field proved elusive, a great deal was learned in this way about the local and global logic of scientific investigation (see Lakatos 1970) and about science's important sociological dimension. For instance, though one may hang onto any theory "come what may" (Quine 1953, p. 43), the professional clustering of those new to a field ultimately arbitrates which theories are further pursued (Kuhn 1970). Moreover, the founding goals of philosophy of science spun off in countless ways, leading to debates about the very nature of theories, the relevance of simplicity, the possible superiority of the physical over the social sciences, the reducibility of high- to low-level sciences, alternatives to realism, how theory affects observation, the role of extra-scientific values, and so on.

There were also discussions focused on specific disciplines, including many incarnations of the following schema: *What does the scientific concept x* (e.g., function) *amount to, or at least what must it amount to if it is to serve its designated role in a particular field* (e.g., biology or anthropology)? This schema would also be applied to more general concepts (see Colombo 2017). For instance, one question that took on great importance after the demise of verificationism concerned what the concept of explanation amounts to, or what it must amount to if it is to serve the role slated for it in science. Answering "why?" it finally came to be seen, is (alongside prediction and control) a central goal of science. Using real and hypothetical cases as data, philosophers tried to determine both what sorts of things scientific explanations are and how they are structured.

2.1.1 Philosophical Theories of Explanation

The kinds of concerns about explanation raised by Stace (1935) led Hempel (1965) to model the philosophical investigation of explanation after Frege's (1884) investigation of logical inference. To capture the principles of logic (the claim went), we must focus neither on the contents of particular inferences nor on the psychological states they involve; we must focus instead on abstract logical form. Hempel maintained that all this holds, *mutatis mutandis*, for the study of explanation, otherwise we risk equating explanations with inconstant and nonrational *feelings*. The approach was complicated by the connection between explanation and understanding, a *prima facie* psychological state, and so Hempel distinguished *genuine* (non-psychological) understanding (more on which below) from the *feeling* of understanding, which he took to involve familiarity or empathy (Hempel 1965, pp. 256–257, 430). Hempel took accounts tying explanation to the latter to be refuted by some simple considerations. First, many of the most ground-breaking explanations appeal to principles that are unfamiliar (e.g., the law of gravity) and evoke no feelings of empathy (Hempel 1965, pp. 257, 431). In addition, some proposals do evoke such feelings (e.g., the teleological theory of freefall) but are not explanations.[1] This double dissociation, offering a putative falsification of psychologism about explanation, is textbook analytic philosophy at work.

As for what explanations are, Hempel claimed initially that they comprise statements describing laws and (sometimes) specific conditions from which can be deduced a statement describing the occurrence one wishes to explain. For instance, an explanation for why a shadow has a particular length might take the form of the deduction of a statement describing the shadow from further statements describing the particular conditions at play (e.g., the height/orientation of a flagpole and the position of the sun in the sky) and one or more laws (e.g., of geometrical optics). Unfortunately for Hempel, there were more dissociations to be had. To start with, there seemed to be legitimate cases of non-deductive (viz., statistical) explanation. Like Popper, Hempel tried to salvage the core of his model in the face of seemingly falsifying evidence, amending the approach to allow for high-probability statistical explanations. Even so, there were still cases it seemed to misclassify as non-explanations, including the low-probability case where prior syphilis explains paresis (Scriven 1959), and cases it misclassified as explanations, such as a deduction of the sun's position from the laws of optics and facts about a flagpole and its shadow (Bromberger 1966).

Says Hempel of his covering-law account, "[l]ike any other explication, the construal here put forward has to be justified by [...] [showing that it] does justice to such accounts as are generally agreed to be instances of scientific explanation" (Hempel 1965, p. 489). There is a bit of wiggle room allowed, for the ultimate goal of "explication" is to settle upon norms of use for a term that will maximize precision and fecundity while (even if some gerrymandering is required) subsuming the bulk of what the term had pre-theoretically been taken to denote (Maher 2007). But the covering-law model failed to live up to even this relaxed standard, and its effective demise was thought by many to stem from its failure to exclude causation from the formula (e.g., it left out that the shadow does not cause the position of the sun and that a prior bout of syphilis may cause paresis). Subsequent models of explanation – including the causal-mechanical, statistical-relevance, pragmatic, unificationist (for a summary, see Salmon 1989) and counterfactual-intervention (Woodward 2003) models – would be proposed that either embraced and explicated or sought ways of avoiding the fraught notion of causation. All the while, the list of critical test cases kept growing.

While Hempel's model of explanation attracted few new adherents, his anti-psychologism arguments (which delimited the space in which the detailed explication project was to be effected) took hold of the mainstream of the field.[2] For instance, in pioneering the causal-mechanical and, later, statistical-relevance models, Wesley Salmon maintained that psychologistic theories equate explanation with the feeling of under-

---

[1] Hempel also offers arguments concerning not what explanations are but how they should be assessed.

[2] The main exception here was Achinstein (1984), though his work was more about the act of explaining than what makes something an explanation.

standing, which he took to involve overcoming uneasiness and achieving satisfaction (Salmon 1998, p. 90). He contends that tying explanation to those feelings leads to the misclassification of both genuine explanations (e.g., subatomic theory) and non-explanations (e.g., feeling satisfied that barometers cause storms). Based on this double dissociation, claims Salmon (1984, p. 13), "[t]he psychological interpretation of scientific explanation is patently inadequate". He advocated instead for an *ontic* account which equates explanations with objective facts rather than descriptions (Salmon 1989, p. 121).[3]

More recent dissociation arguments emphasize cases where a legitimate explanation defies all human comprehension. According to Craver, who also favors the ontic account, explanations are at best imperfectly correlated with such states as intellectual satisfaction, insight, and *aha* feelings (Craver 2007, pp. IX, 21). He argues for this as follows:

> Some phenomena might be so complex that they overwhelm our limited cognitive systems. Perhaps a mechanism [e.g., a neural system] has so many parts with so many interactions that it is impossible to understand. [...] It would be wrong to say that the phenomena produced by such complex mechanisms have no explanation. The explanations exist even if we cannot represent them cognitively. (Craver 2007, pp. 33 f.; also see Craver 2014)

Trout (2007) similarly takes the psychological correlates of explanation to be feelings of confidence, insight, and *aha* feelings and dissociates explanation from them by claiming that the complexity of certain explanatory descriptions (e.g., of the speciation of certain salamanders) often exceeds the limits of human comprehension. Trout claims that to deny these descriptions constitute explanations because they fail to evoke such feelings "seems suspiciously ad hoc. They certainly behave like other explanations, and they are treated as such by scientists" (Trout 2007, p. 584).[4] Trout, like Craver, thus singly dissociates explanations from psychological states by invoking hyper-complex processes that defy comprehension and that, consequently, fail to elicit any relevant feelings. Completing the double dissociation, Craver cites putative cases (e.g., Ptolemy's model of retrograde motion) where the relevant feelings are present without explanation (2007, 2014). Trout's (2007) take on such cases is that they prove that feelings are a poor indicator of accuracy, which seems beyond dispute.

Hempel's distinction between the psychological *feeling* of understanding and *genuine* understanding has also been embraced by his successors. To speak as vaguely as the literature seems to require, the genuine sort is said to involve representations that do things such as show, exhibit, reveal, display, elucidate, or enable one to grasp things about the world (e.g., see Hempel 1965, Salmon 1989, Machamer, Darden, and Craver 2000, Grimm 2010, Strevens 2013, Baumberger, Beisbart, and Brun 2017). Insofar as gen-

---

[3] It bears mentioning that when discussing good versus bad explanations Salmon and other ontic theorists tend to slip back to a representational construal (Waskan 2011).

[4] Trout, to be fair, claims that explanation sometimes result from unconscious, implicit learning, and he allows that they sometimes even comprise psychological representations (Trout 2007, p. 581).

uine understanding of some phenomenon precludes being radically mistaken about it – that is, insofar as understanding is *factive* – it is no surprise that many philosophers (e.g., Hempel 1965, Salmon 1998, Humphreys 1989, Craver 2007, Grimm 2010) also maintain that explanations are necessarily accurate.

2.1.2 Constraints on Theories of Explanation

If we take a big-picture look at the philosophical method for studying explanation (and countless other topics), we find striking similarities with science itself. Theories are evaluated in terms of existing data, new "crucial" tests, and coherence with surrounding theories; a "failed" test can always be handled by rejecting claims apart from those at the theory's core; over time, the branching space of possible theories is mapped out and parceled between theorists; and the field as a whole determines which branches to pursue, in part through the clustering of theoretically uncommitted newcomers.

Importantly, though, where the study of explanation is concerned, science and philosophy play very different roles. There is a pecking order. Science is the rat, and philosophy wears the white coat. This might seem odd given that the psychological sciences also study, among other shared topics, prediction, explanation, causation, mechanistic and probabilistic reasoning. And the scientific study of explanation is at an advanced stage, revealing much about the developmental progression of explanation-seeking (Keil and Wilson 2000), the functions (Simon 1966, Gelman and Wellman 1991, Keil 2006, Lombrozo and Carey 2006, Lombrozo 2006) and forms (Brewer, Chinn, and Samarapungavan 2000, Brewer 2001, Hickling and Wellman 2001, also see Keil 2006, Lombrozo and Carey 2006) of explanation, the preference for simplicity (Lombrozo 2007), and so forth. At least nominally, there is a strong overlap here between the two disciplines.

There are differences, however. One is that when psychologists study explanation, they mostly focus on children and lay adults. They also seem primarily interested in the effect explanation has on memory, pattern detection, and other cognitive processes crucial to our everyday judgments and activities, or, in philosophical parlance, its functional profile. Philosophers, on the other hand, focus on hypothetical examples and examples from the past and present of science. Their primary goal is to devise a single, unified model (or even a pluralist model) that reveals the internal structure (or intrinsic nature) of scientific explanation. They are also interested in the kinds of normative considerations discussed above concerning what could rationally justify the acceptance or rejection of a given explanatory theory.

Viewed in this manner, it is harder to see how philosophical models of scientific explanation and psychological models of everyday explanatory reasoning are connected, and it is thus unclear how the two sets of inquiries might relate. Thus, if there is to be an accepted unification of the two fields, it would help if we first knew whether "explanation" (as used by psychology) and "explanation" (as used by philosophy) co-refer or, failing that, refer to aspects of the world that overlap greatly enough for the two fields to enrich, inform, and constrain one another. The dissociation arguments discussed above, however, seem to put this very much into doubt.

But what if those arguments are misguided? What if the two cannot be cleanly dissociated? In that case, the barriers to interdisciplinary collaboration ought to crumble.

To show that these arguments fail, one might try playing by the old rules, citing new cases that seem to falsify the accepted theory. Except there is no real theory involved here. At the heart of the case are some fairly bald claims of the form, *x is an explanation* and *y is not*. If one should deny those claims (and their implications), it would thus help to have an outside arbiter of some sort capable of settling the dispute.

This is where x-phi enters the story.

2.2 Broad versus Narrow X-phi of Explanation

To see x-phi's potential here, we should first note that (as discussed further in Section 3.3) there have been many philosophers of *cognitive* science who take there to be a need for a scientifically informed investigation of explanation (and of science more generally). We might term this a *broad* x-phi approach to explanation. One might place psychological and other cognitive-scientific inquiries into explanation under this heading as well, except their relevance to philosophy is here precisely what is at issue (cf. Sytsma and Livengood 2015).

There is also what might be called *narrow* x-phi of science, which is constitutive of a recent, broad-based movement in philosophy that borrows behavioral methods from psychology (to study a population's judgments about cases, often presented as vignettes) and from fields such as bibliometrics (to study concepts, theories, and norms of terminology use). These methods are currently being deployed to supplement or correct traditional philosophical analyses. While narrow x-phi as a whole is thriving, however, its investigation of science remains comparatively underdeveloped. To see how it might nevertheless contribute, it helps to first understand the potential shortcomings of the old-school, analytic alternative (see also Griffiths and Stotz 2008, Machery 2016, Colombo 2017).

As discussed, philosophers of science often appeal to hypothetical cases (e.g., hexed salt) and cases from the historical record (e.g., Ptolemaic astronomy) to support their explicatory views. Well-justified tweaking aside, a good explication must sort cases in a generally agreed-upon manner. But agreed upon by whom? The relevant population here is clearly that of practicing scientists, though philosophers of science often view themselves as reasonable proxies. While such philosophers do commonly have extensive exposure to science, there is still some risk that their judgments might not reflect science's sociolinguistic norms. A philosopher's judgments might, for instance, be influenced by the very theories they aim to prove (Cummins 1998). This, mind you, is the very worry that motivates the use of theoretically naïve coders for classifying qualitative data in psychology. In addition, one should prefer it if the classifications issued from a representative sampling of the population (or at least proxies therefor), but when a philosopher is moved by consideration of a given case, they are relying upon a sample size of one (Griffiths and Stotz 2008). There is also the matter of which cases are selected and how many. This too involves a sample (of science), and ideally one wants it to be large, unbiased, and representative, but such samples are instead often tiny, hand-picked (or even cherry-picked), and concern either revolutionary developments or cases about which a philosopher has special knowledge (Thagard 2012).

While all of this is concerning, it does not render analytic philosophy of science irrelevant or justify its elimination in favor of an approach with greater empirical rigor. To start with, there is much more to philosophy of science than studying terms (or concepts). It (like the rest of analytic philosophy) is also often focused on determining which sets of claims can be coherently maintained, a task for which the scientific method is simply the wrong tool. There is also an important normative dimension to the philosophy of science. Sometimes this involves the explicatory project of determining if we should revise the application conditions for a term – whether that term be discipline-specific (e.g., "gene") or generic (e.g., "cause") – so that it can better serve its intended ends (see Colombo 2017, Woodward 2019). While one must begin with an accurate description of actual usage, the normative component of the enterprise is not to be resolved by experiment. There are, in addition, deeper normative questions concerning, for instance, the rational way to analyze evidence. There is, to be sure, much psychological research on such matters, but it often concerns whether humans, in their day-to-day lives, adhere to rational norms gleaned independently from the (roughly put) a priori inquiries of philosophy, mathematics, and statistics.[5]

Even setting normative issues aside, there is still much to like about analytic philosophy of science. As we saw, while its founding objective (demarcation) has proved elusive (an insight in itself), the field has uncovered much about theory change and, in the process, greatly pruned the tree of viable accounts of how science works. Indeed, if anything counts as a major success story for analytic philosophy more generally, progress made during the above historical sequence is it.

Likewise, regarding the structure of scientific explanation, analytic philosophy has done much to map out the branching space of plausible theories, testing each against a collection of real and hypothetical cases. Philosophers have covered tremendous ground in this way, and it would be excessive to demand that narrow x-phi or some other approach either replicate or supplant every purported philosophical result. For instance, there may be no need to revisit the field's nearly uniform conclusions from the flagpole case that mere deduction from statements of laws and specific conditions does not suffice for explanation. Assessing the covering-law model based on that case amounts to something like a crucial test (i.e., with the usual post-Popperian caveats). One prefers more than one such test (and those have been provided), but re-

---

[5] Garry Ebbs first drove this simple point home to me.

quiring a large, unbiased, representative, sample of crucial tests before rejecting a theory is clearly overkill in any domain.

There is, however, still the potentially devastating worry that reaching a conclusion based on a particular case is to rely upon a sample of a single intuiter (i.e., oneself). Indeed, the power of, say, the flagpole case to convince you (or me) that the covering-law model is inadequate does seem on its face to be limited in this way. But as in science, such tests must be regarded as compelling by the vast majority of the profession to cause a particular theoretical branch to wither. In that respect, the sample size needs to be, and in this case was, much larger.

All of this is just to say that the above concerns about analytic philosophy of science should not trouble us so much as to trigger attempted scientific replications of each and every influential result. One may, however, still be legitimately concerned about whether philosophers of science are letting their theories influence their case judgments and about whether those judgments are useful proxies for the relevant target population (in the present case, scientists). These matters become most important precisely when the judgment *is* widely shared and is, consequently, influential. If one suspects that some critical philosophical judgment is not representative of the relevant target population – or alternatively, if one suspects that there are varying standards between, or even within, linguistic communities (see Griffiths and Stotz 2008) – then the techniques of narrow x-phi become particularly useful and important.

Applying this to this study of explanation, recall that a critical set of philosophical judgments, the ones behind the above dissociation arguments, led to conclusions that had bearing not just on some theory of explanation or other, but on how the field ought even to go about investigating explanation. Those judgments (concerning barometer readings, hyper-complex models, and the like) helped to turn the philosophical investigation of a central goal of science into a walled garden. If those judgments were erroneous or unjustifiably idiosyncratic, then there is a high risk that the field has taken an entirely wrong turn.

2.3 The Psychological Concept of Explanation

A closer look at the psychological study of explanation does much by itself to heighten these suspicions. Consider first that the affective states that philosophers have historically decried as irrelevant for explanation are not regarded as constitutive of explanation by psychologists either. Explanations are, instead, identified with non-affective, representation-comprising states.[6] Alison Gopnik, for instance, tells us that the intense feelings that accompany explanations are what lead us to seek them out (much as sexual orgasm leads us to seek opportunities for procreation) and that explanation itself is

---

6 Some philosophers reach the same conclusion on analytic grounds (see de Regt 2004, Grimm 2010, Baumberger, Beisbart, and Brun 2017).

the product of the "operation of a special representational system", namely, "the 'theory formation system'" (Gopnik 2000, p. 300). Likewise, Brewer, Chinn, and Samarapungavan (2000) describe the application of different explanatory frameworks as something that, while perhaps leading to, is quite distinct from various forms of affect. This view is widely shared among both cognitive scientists (e.g., Simon 1966, Brewer 200, Vosniadou 2002, Keil 2006, Lombrozo and Carey 2006) and philosophers of cognitive science who study explanation (e.g., Churchland 1989, Giere 1990, Waskan 2003, Bechtel and Abrahamsen 2005, Thagard and Litt 2008).

As for understanding, while psychologists tend to view it as crucial, they are typically concerned with *neither* the feeling of understanding nor so-called genuine (factive) understanding. The latter's success requirement is far too stringent. After all, the explanations studied by psychologists can be naïve, fragmented, shallow, or simply incorrect. Research thus focuses instead on a slightly different form of understanding, something that in daily life we often term finding a happening intelligible, understandable, sensible, or comprehensible (see Simon 1966, Brewer, Chinn, and Samarapungavan 2000, Berland and Reiser 2009).[7] To find a happening comprehensible, one need not genuinely comprehend it. Put differently, to possesses an explanation on this view, one must understand not how or why a phenomenon occurred *simpliciter*, but how or why *possibly*.[8] This, again, requires neither rectitude nor any of explanation's affective correlates. In philosophical terminology, to have an explanation is to have a belief (or set thereof) of a certain sort, a belief about what at least might have produced an occurrence and in virtue of which one understands how- or why-possibly.[9] It could even be a species of knowledge insofar as what is known are the conditions (however implausible) that could have produced the occurrence.[10]

---

[7] Hempel's forerunners likewise emphasized intelligibility (see Bridgman 1927, Lovell 1931, Benjamin 1941, Miller 1946, Miller 1947). While de Regt (2009) does as well, his view is that explanation requires intelligible *theories*.

[8] Machamer, Darden, and Craver (2000) introduce this terminology for discussing explanations in the representational-artifact sense (more on which below).

[9] Craver finds talk of a psychological sense of "explanation" to be nonsensical on the basis of cases (whose protagonist is strangely familiar) such as, "Jon's mental representation of the mechanism of the action potential explains the action potential" (Craver 2014, p. 33). His putative linguistic counterexamples, however, all refer to the act (explaining) rather than the entity (explanation), and the present account takes representations to be merely *constituents* of the relevant psychological states (i.e., beliefs).

[10] This approach dispenses with some widely discussed concerns about the role of understanding, *qua* factive state, in science (see Wilkenfeld 2015, Baumberger, Beisbart, and Brun 2017). We can say, for instance, that Ptolemy understands how-possibly the planets move, and thus has an explanation, even if he is wrong about how they actually move.

2.3.1 Hypotheses Regarding Explanation

Between philosophy and cognitive science, we have so far come across three senses of the term "explanation" in use (Waskan 2011, 2014b; also see Grimm 2010). One sense refers to representational artifacts (typically written descriptions), one refers to objective conditions (typically causes), and one refers to psychological states (typically beliefs about causes). All three seem to echo common practice. To illustrate, in the representational-artifact sense (call it explanation$_{R-A}$), one might say, "There is an aquatic-ape explanation for human furlessness on page 37 of *The Naked Ape*." In the ontic sense (explanation$_O$), one might say, "The explanation for combustion is oxidation." And in the psychological sense (explanation$_P$), one might say, "The pre-verbal child has an explanation for the meowing coming from behind the door." Notice also that the above dissociation arguments mainly concern the representational-artifact sense and that the moment (per necessity) philosophers begin talking about good and bad explanations and about inference to the best explanation, a representational construal of some sort is required. And having now introduced a conception of explanation$_P$ that more faithfully reflects the views of cognitive science (i.e., one whereby affect is a mere byproduct), it becomes a very live possibility that explanation$_P$ is *at least as* critical a goal of science as explanation$_{R-A}$. This already spells bad news for the anti-psychologistic viewpoint that dominates (and insulates) mainstream philosophy of science, but the case against psychologism will truly collapse if it turns out that "explanation" in the representational-artifact sense refers to something that is *constituted by* the psychological state of understanding how- or why-possibly, a state that cognitive science takes to be at the core of explanation$_P$. As concerns this possibility, any one of the following three hypotheses may turn out to be true (i.e., with respect to a given population):

Objectivity Hypothesis: Explanation$_{R-A}$ is regarded as in no way psychological.

Actual Intelligibility Hypothesis: It is taken to be required for explanation$_{R-A}$ that the artifact in question has rendered the target intelligible to someone.

Potential Intelligibility Hypothesis: It is taken to be required for explanation$_{R-A}$ that the artifact in question possesses the capacity, whether exercised or not, to render the target intelligible to someone.

Note that to say that a representational artifact has the capacity to render intelligible is to say that were one to comprehend it (by which is meant something akin to linguistic comprehension) one would thereby understand how- or why-possibly the phenomenon occurred. Notice also that according to both intelligibility hypotheses, if there is something about a representation (e.g., its unimaginable complexity or utterly exotic constructs) that positively precludes it from ever rendering the target intelligible to anyone, then the relevant population ought to be much less inclined to regard it as an explanation$_{R\text{-}A}$.[11]

2.3.2 Explanation Studies

With these three hypotheses in hand, conditions are perfect to invoke the kinds of methods characteristic of (the behavioral branch of) narrow x-phi (see Section 2.2).

2.3.2.1 Intelligibility

As concerns the above hypotheses, dissociation arguments that invoke hyper-complex models are particularly important, for they might show that explanation$_{R\text{-}A}$ is constituted by neither affective *aha*-type states nor the intellectual state of finding a phenomenon intelligible. Responses to such cases were the primary focus of my own research group's experiments.

In one experiment (Waskan et al. 2014a), we presented participants of varying levels of scientific training with a brief story (a vignette) about a scientist who studies the mysterious astronomical phenomenon of gamma-ray bursts. The vignette states that the scientist eventually produces a complex series of calculations concerning the evolving interiors of type-B2 stars, calculations that are well-grounded in accepted theory and observations and that imply the occurrence of gamma-ray bursts in those stars. We presented participants with three variants of the vignette, yielding the following three conditions:

Intelligible: The model renders the gamma-ray bursts intelligible to the scientist.
Potentially Intelligible: The model has the as-yet unexercized capacity to render gamma-ray bursts intelligible to someone (viz., anyone with knowledge of the field willing to devote sufficient time and effort).
Never Intelligible: The model is so prohibitively complex that it is incapable of rendering the target intelligible to anyone.

The objectivity, actual intelligibility, and potential intelligibility hypotheses each predict a unique pattern of results regarding participants' judgments in these three conditions. On the objectivity hypothesis, varying intelligibility should make no difference, so explanation judgments should be comparable across the three conditions; on the actual intelligibility hypothesis, explanation judgments should be higher in the Intelligible

---

[11] The capacity to bring about understanding is assumed here to be a non-accidental feature of the representation.

condition than in the others (which should not differ); and on the potential intelligibility hypothesis, explanation judgments should be higher in the Potentially Intelligible and Intelligible conditions (which should not differ) than in the Never Intelligible condition.

Per Mishra and Brewer (2003), we encouraged close reading of the materials by forewarning participants of an impending comprehension test. After reading the vignette, participants were asked to rate on a seven-point Likert scale (ranging from "strongly disagree" to "strongly agree") the extent to which they agree that the model in the vignette is an explanation.[12] They then completed a comprehension test and supplied demographic information.

The comprehension results indicated that participants understood the vignettes they read, including the extent to which the calculations described enable understanding how- or why-possibly gamma-ray bursts occur. We also found that participants were significantly more likely to regard a model as an explanation in the Intelligible condition than in either the Potentially Intelligible or Never Intelligible conditions, though no difference was detected in their responses in the Potentially Intelligible and Never Intelligible conditions (Figure 1). Our data were thus consistent with the actual intelligibility hypothesis. We also found that one's level of scientific training is a poor predictor of participants' explanation ratings, which is at least suggestive that science training does not affect the extent to which one regards intelligibility as constitutive of explanation.

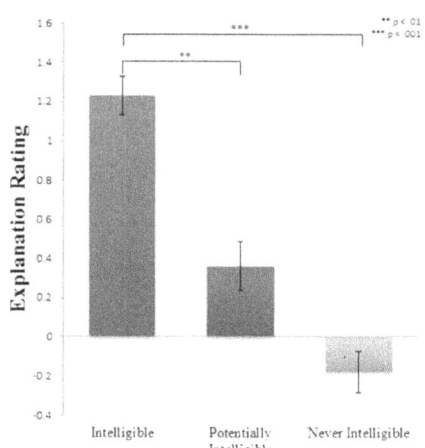

Figure 1: Mean "constitutes an explanation" ratings by condition after dummy coding qualitative scale with –3 corresponding to "strongly disagree" and +3 corresponding to "strongly agree" (from Waskan et al. 2014a)

All of this might be taken to indicate that common philosophical judgments about hyper-complex models are out of step with those of both laypeople and scientists. However, to be truly convincing, it would be necessary to investigate professional scientists

---

[12] Following Lombrozo and Carey (2006), we took measures to limit the extent to which participants might confuse this question with that of whether the model constitutes a good or satisfying explanation.

directly. When we piloted the same material and methods on a group of professional scientists (members of a prestigious multidisciplinary science institute), however, ratings on all conditions clustered towards the midpoint of the scale. Feedback from participants suggested that they were forming an interpretation of the intent of the experiment according to which their professional opinions as scientists were being solicited. They were thus hesitant to pass judgment about the model without knowing its specific contents. A new method was thus needed to reduce these demand characteristics.

To this end, we devised a new set of materials and instructions that far better hid the goals of the experiment (Waskan et al. 2014a). The story utilized was adapted from an article on the mystery of gamma-ray bursts from a popular-science website and thus had greater ecological validity. It included information about the history of research into gamma-ray bursts and culminated in mention of how a noted astrophysicist, Dr. Brown, produced a computer model of this phenomenon and a report thereupon. The model, well-grounded in existing theory and observations, was described as having generated a very surprising prediction (a brief, spherical burst of gamma rays), one later confirmed by telescopic observation. The model was also said to be extremely complex, such that Dr. Brown had, at least initially, difficulty using it to understand the origin of gamma-ray bursts. The final part of the vignette varied per the Intelligible, Potentially Intelligible, and Never Intelligible conditions.

After reading the story, participants were asked to take a true-false comprehension test based on what they read. Mixed in with standard comprehension prompts were statements about whether the model constituted an explanation, was plausible, and made a surprising prediction. Importantly, "explanation" was never used in the vignettes, and so we regarded responses to the true-false prompt using this term as providing an implicit measure of participants' underlying views about the relevance of understanding how- or why-possibly to explanation. We believe this approach adds an important tool to the narrow x-phi arsenal, for it occludes the goals of the experiment both in terms of the materials presented (which contained many irrelevant details) and the crucial measure (disguised within a broader comprehension task).

We first administered these materials to a sample from the general population and were able to corroborate the findings of the previous experiment (Figure 2, left side). We then turned to scientists. Here too our data were consistent with the intelligibility hypothesis (Figure 2, right side). Importantly, responses to the "explanation" prompt did not track whether participants thought that the model was plausible, as a high percentage across all three conditions claimed that it was. Our data thus lend support to the actual intelligibility hypothesis and, given that the same pattern obtained for both laypeople and scientists, were at least suggestive that the scientific conception of explanation is, where intelligibility is concerned, of a piece with commonsense.

In sum, though the objectivity hypothesis may be true of many philosophers who study explanation, the actual intelligibility hypothesis better characterizes lay and scientific conceptions of explanation. In classifying hyper-complex models that defy comprehension as explanations, philosophers may thus be relying too heavily on their own theories, concepts, or tacit beliefs about explanations, ones which (without any discern-

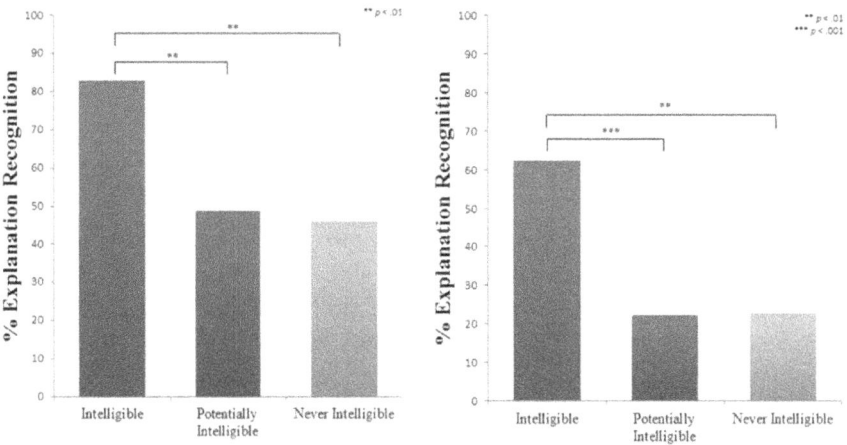

Figure 2: Percentage of lay (left) and scientific (right) participants remembering that an explanation was provided (from Waskan et al. 2014a)

ible justification) may be out of step with the population at large and, more importantly, scientists. This is critically important to the philosophy of science *as a whole*, for arguments based upon such cases have done much to keep the philosophical investigation of a central goal of science walled off from research in other disciplines. And insofar as having an explanation in the sense studied by cognitive science is having a belief (or beliefs) in virtue of which one understand how- or why-possibly, we have grounds for thinking that the philosophical investigation of explanation$_{R-A}$ and the cognitive scientific investigation of explanation$_p$ are intimately related and that there needs to be greater integration between the disciplines involved.

Conceivably there is a similar underlying psychological component to explanation$_o$. For instance, it could be that an objective process is only regarded as the explanation for a phenomenon if someone understands how it brought the phenomenon about. Accordingly, our study investigated the connection between intelligibility, explanation$_{R-A}$, and explanation$_o$ (Waskan et al. 2014b). We used similar methods as the previous experiment, only this time a lengthy distractor (about neuroscience) was interposed between the target materials concerning gamma-ray bursts and the comprehension test. This brought our methods into closer alignment with Powell, Horne, and Pinillos' (2014) semantic integration paradigm, an indispensable addition to the x-phi toolkit which relies on the fact that, when remembering a passage of text after a delay, participants' memories often reflect their semantic interpretations rather than the actual sentences read. Demand characteristics, moreover, are in this way concealed to an even greater degree.

We presented both lay and professional science participants with Actually Intelligible and Never Intelligible versions of the gamma-ray vignette. As before, "explanation" appears in neither version of the vignette. We included in our true-false comprehension test one or the other of the following prompts:

Brown's paper and the accompanying computer model constitute an explanation for why type-B2 stars produce gamma-ray bursts.

The explanation for gamma-ray bursts is a physical process which also produces gamma-ray bubbles.

The first statement references a set of representational artifacts, and so we take responses to it to provide an implicit measure of the semantic activation of participants' concept of explanation$_{R-A}$. The second refers to an objective, physical process, and so we take responses to it to provide a measure of the activation of participants' concept of explanation$_O$. One of the remaining items measured if participants correctly remembered whether Dr. Brown was able to understand a way in which gamma-ray bursts may be produced.

We found the same pattern of results among both lay and scientific populations. Specifically, memory for whether Dr. Brown understands how-possibly varies appropriately across the Actually Intelligible and Never Intelligible conditions. In addition, while memory for the explanation$_{R-A}$ statement varies significantly between the two conditions (Figure 3, top), memory for the explanation$_O$ statement does not (Figure 3, bottom). In short, unlike memory for explanation$_{R-A}$, memory for explanation$_O$ appears unaffected by manipulating intelligibility, suggesting that intelligibility is not considered a constituent of ontic explanation. All of this also provides reason, independent of philosophical analysis, for thinking that "explanation" is ambiguous between representational-artifact and ontic senses.

2.3.2.2 Factivity

There is, lastly, the question raised above (Section 2.1.1) of whether the kind of understanding that seems constitutive of explanation$_{R-A}$ is regarded as strongly factive (i.e., such that an explanation$_{R-A}$ must accurately represent the explanation$_O$). If this *accuracy hypothesis* is correct, manipulating the accuracy of the relevant representational artifacts should alter both memory for explanation$_{R-A}$ and memory for whether the physical processes those artifacts represent constitute the explanation$_O$ for the occurrence. Alternatively, explanation$_{R-A}$ might only be regarded as weakly factive in that it must merely represent a possible reason for an occurrence. If this *possibility hypothesis* is correct, manipulating accuracy should alter memory for explanation$_O$, but it should not alter memory for explanation$_{R-A}$.

To alter accuracy judgments, in our next experiment (Waskan et al. 2014b) we varied whether the materials supplied by Dr. Brown survive (again with the usual caveats) a crucial test. We added a comprehension question measuring memory for whether the materials Brown supplied are accurate. Among both laypeople and scientists, the crucial test manipulation did influence memories concerning the accuracy of the materials. But while it did not significantly affect memory for whether the materials constitute an explanation$_{R-A}$ (Figure 4, top), it did alter memories for whether the process

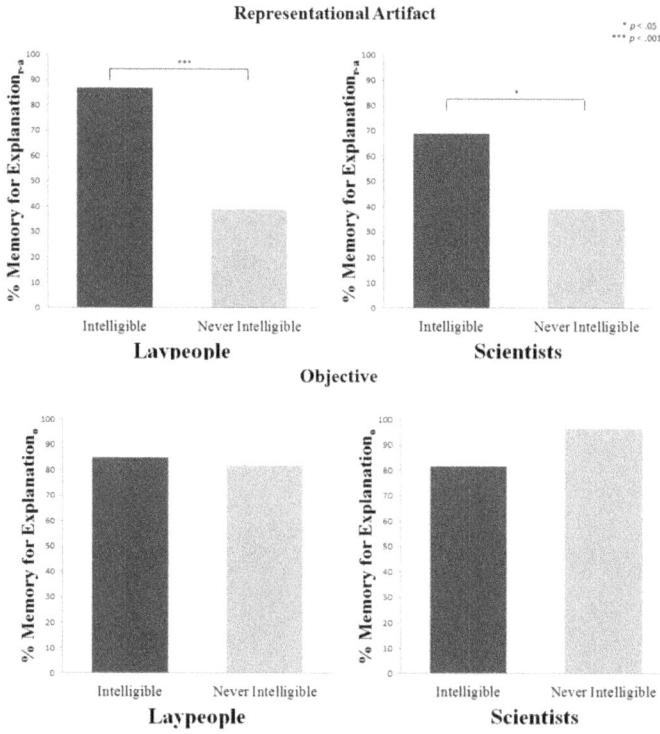

Figure 3: Percentage of laypeople and professional scientists remembering that the materials constitute an explanation$_{R-A}$ (top) and that the process described is the explanation$_O$ (bottom) under the Intelligible and Never Intelligible conditions (from Waskan et al. 2014b)

they designate constitute the explanation$_O$ (Figure 4, bottom). These data thus lend support to the possibility hypothesis and at the same time undermine the mainstream philosophical assertion that accuracy is necessary for explanation$_{R-A}$.

It bears mentioning that the above studies found the same pattern of results among both laypeople and scientists. This brings to mind Wilfred Sellars' (1956, p. 313) claim that "science is continuous with common sense, and the ways in which the scientist seeks to explain empirical phenomena are refinements of the ways in which plain men, however crudely and schematically, have attempted to understand their environment and their fellow men". Some words of caution are in order, however. The scientists who participated in the study all speak English and all were employed at a single, albeit large and fairly diverse, U.S. research institute. Conceivably, these results do not generalize to the broader population of U.S. scientists, though the fact that the same effects were found among laypeople should temper this concern. However, the results might not generalize outside of the U.S. or to researchers from other linguistic communities, and in this regard more research is needed.

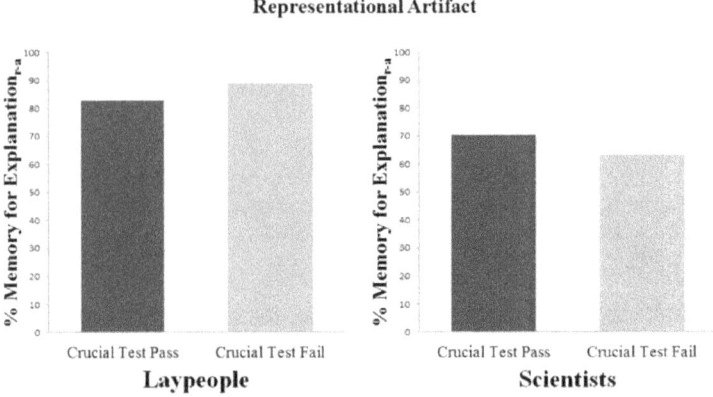

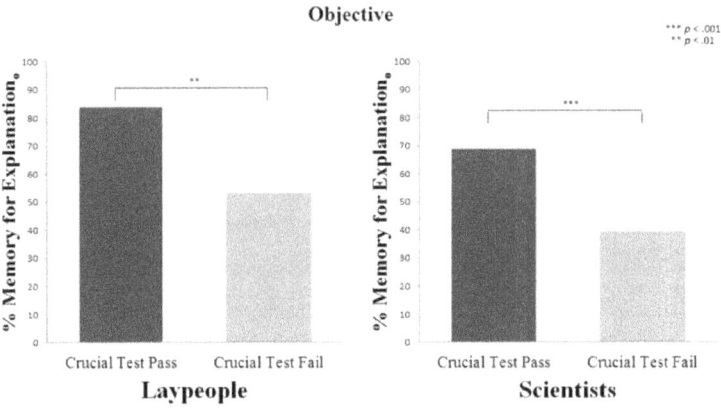

Figure 4: (4a) Percentage of laypeople and professional scientists remembering that the materials constitute an explanation$_{R-A}$ (top) and that the process described is the explanation$_O$ (bottom) under the Crucial Test Pass and Crucial Test Fail conditions (from Waskan et al. 2014b)

In addition, while the above studies provide what we consider powerful support for the view that understanding how- or why-possibly is constitutive of explanation$_{R-A}$, Wilkenfeld and Lombrozo (2020) note that our participants' memories for explanation$_{R-A}$ could conceivably be tracking something else (not mentioned in the vignettes or questions) that they associate with understanding. To rule out this possibility and thereby strengthen the case that understanding is constitutive of what I have been calling explanation$_{R-A}$, they cleverly adapt the side-effect effect (SEE) methodology developed by Knobe (2003), for it provides a robust marker of mental state ascriptions. They show, first, that explanation$_{R-A}$ judgments are sensitive to speaker and audience mental states and, second, that explanation$_{R-A}$ judgments are sensitive to speaker and audience level of understanding, specifically. This effectively shores up the case that understanding is the primary psychological driver of explanation$_{R-A}$ attributions and, by using a wholly distinct method, demonstrates that the above results are themselves at least somewhat robust.

3 Further Topics and Future Directions

Philosophers often study the particular terms (as well as categories and concepts) used in science with any of various goals in mind. Per Colombo (2017), some of these terms (e.g., "explanation", "cause", and "time") are broad in scope. Most of these have origins independent of science but are used so pervasively within it that we cannot hope to understand science unless we know what scientists mean by them and to what they do or might refer. Other terms are narrower in scope (e.g., "innate", "function", and "concept") and, whatever their origins, play important roles in specific fields that philosophers wish to understand. As mentioned above, philosophers often wish to determine whether various terms or concepts can serve the roles they are meant to in scientific discourse (a somewhat normative concern) and, if not, if there is a way to refine or alter them so that they can. Philosophers also sometimes wish to know if our pretheoretic, folk image accords with the scientific image of our place in the world (Sellars 1963). All such projects have an important descriptive component, which presents a perfect opportunity to bring the tools of narrow x-phi online. As mentioned, however, the approach should not be used scattershot, but only with a specific goal in mind, such as showing (per the above) that widely accepted philosophical analyses have led the field astray.

3.1 Behavioral Studies

A fine illustration of how narrow x-phi can contribute to the philosophy of science is Machery et al.'s (2019) investigation of the scientific and vernacular concept of innateness. They find that scientists use the vernacular concept when asked to think about traits even though this differs from the explicit characterizations of innateness found in print. They suggest on this basis that a revision to scientific practice is needed (such as eliminating the term from scientific discourse). Similarly, by using traditional survey instruments administered to university students working both in economics and other disciplines, Nagatsu and Põder (2019) find that whereas the folk concept of choice concerns conscious volition, the economic concept appears justifiably more concerned with objective incentive structures (conscious or not). This result, they claim, undermines calls to render the economic concept more psychologically realistic.

While these two studies shed light on facts about terms and concepts in ways that have normative implications, there are ways to use the tools of narrow x-phi to tackle even deeper normative questions, for these too often have an important descriptive dimension. Rudner (1953), for instance, famously worries that extra-scientific (e.g., political) values unduly influence scientific deliberations. A study by Sikimić and colleagues

(2021) goes some way towards addressing this concern. They studied scientists working in different fields and found that at least where political values are concerned (e. g., degree of conservatism), such values negligibly impact scientists' epistemic attitudes (e. g., their openness to alternatives).

3.2 Quantitative Text Analysis

The above studies on explanation and the studies of Machery et al. (2019) and Sikimić et al. (2021) are some of the very few that specifically apply the methods of behavioral experimentation to the population of professional scientists (also see Griffiths and Stotz 2008, Knobe and Samuels 2013). In some ways, this is not surprising. Working scientists can be difficult to recruit and (per Section 2.3.2.1) difficult to study. As we have seen, alternatives include treating those studying particular sciences as proxies and determining the extent to which level of science training predicts a particular effect. Another increasingly popular alternative is to exploit the fact that the written output of science is itself a rich source of data, one that can readily be mined using techniques recently developed in library science and other fields. These methods enable researchers to cull vast datasets for information that had previously been inaccessible. Indeed, Malaterre, Chartier, and Pulizzotto (2019) show that these methods may offer the first unbiased window onto the unfolding history of philosophy of science itself.

Examples of this new data-driven trend in x-phi of science include Overton's (2013) study suggesting that the precise nature of what counts as explanation varies across disciplines in ways that are at least somewhat reflective of various philosophical theories of explanation (see Section 2.1.1). Similarly, Malaterre and Chartier (2021) used text-mining of more than 30,000 scientific articles in defense of the view that there is no single scientific construal of life nor, consequently, any clear living-nonliving divide; rather there is a "lifeness space" involving varying properties that are indicative of the degree to which something is considered living.

In data mining, too, there are studies that tackle deep normative issues directly. Mizrahi, for instance, has conducted studies on the relevance of truth, knowledge, and understanding to the goals of science (2021) and on the epistemic relevance of theoretical virtues such as simplicity and consistency (forthcoming). Similarly, Beebe and Dellsén (2020) investigate how scientists' attitudes about whether science reveals the actual workings of the universe (i. e., their endorsement of realism) are impacted by their areas of specialization (e. g., philosophy of science, natural science, or social science) and by their awareness that even widely accepted theories can be overturned. Lastly, it is worth mentioning that although Hansson's (2006) analysis of a year's worth of articles from *Nature* was not automated, he found compelling evidence that so-called crucial tests may be less important than even holists about theory change have supposed (see Section 2.1).

3.3 Further Readings and New Directions

To learn more about narrow x-phi of science, a good place to start is with Griffiths and Stotz' (2008) seminal essay discussing the role of conceptual analysis in the philosophy of science and illustrating how narrow x-phi might serve as a corrective. With the field having had by then time to mature, Machery (2016) offers a deep and broad survey of progress to date while also doing much to defend and motivate this form of research. Colombo (2017), likewise, discusses the field's motivations and addresses concerns while focusing on scientific explanation, specifically. After a further period of maturation, Wilkenfeld, Samuels, and Beebe (2019) produced the field's first anthology. Though clear progress has been made, this work paints a collective portrait of a field still wide open for significant discoveries in the domains of analysis and explication, the reconciliation of folk and scientific visions, and those deeply normative questions about why science is such an exemplary epistemically enterprise.

As for broad x-phi (Section 2.2), there is need for a more thorough integration of philosophy of science and relevant areas of cognitive science. In large part due to the barriers discussed above, this need has seldom been acknowledged by the mainstream of the field. Apart from breaching those barriers directly, the best way to alter the course of philosophy is to show by doing, and this is already well underway. I would direct readers, in particular, to Giere (1990, 1992), Carruthers, Stich, and Segal (2002), Keil and Wilson (2002), Brown (2003), Nersessian (2008), and Thagard (2012). Bearing special mention is Lombrozo (2016), which offers pointers to some of this researcher's many behavioral studies that bear directly on issues dear the hearts of philosophers of science.

Though broad x-phi of science has already made great strides in terms of deploying models and findings to inform our understanding of science, there are still major areas that need attention. There are, for one, too few studies focusing directly on the cognitive activities of scientists. Most simply, one could re-run many of the same experiments used to study the population at large. Regarding the philosophical study of explanation, however, to be truly relevant, cognitive scientists must turn from studying the functional profile of explanations (e.g., conditions leading to their formation and their effects on things like categorization and probability judgments) and instead work to reveal the inner structure of explanation, for only this will resolve the effective deadlock between the many competing models (see Section 2.1.1). What is required, specifically, is an account of the structure of the representations underlying the so-called grasping of explanatory connections.

To be successful, any such model must be able to account for how we use explanations$_p$ to (a) predict the consequences of countless novel alterations to a system (finding some that are testable) and (b) determine the countless *ceteris paribus* conditions under which those predictions might fail.[13] Using explanations in this way is, we saw

---

[13] Some equate the ability to find these implications with understanding itself (see Baumberger, Beis-

(Section 2.1), critical to the process of evaluating them and holding onto them "come what may". For my part, I favor the mental-model-based approach to (our foundational mode of) everyday practical and explanatory reasoning first proposed by Craik (1943). It fits well with many findings and, in computational form, avoids the frame problem of artificial intelligence, which is just a rediscovery of desiderata (a) and (b) above (see Waskan 2006, 2008, 2017).

Lastly, for the truly ambitious, the greatest prize of all awaits those able to discover the intrinsic cognitive basis of our ability to reach, through so-called a priori reasoning, the kinds of deep normative conclusions about math, probability, and logic discussed in Section 2.2. There could surely be no greater contribution to philosophy as a whole than for science to finally explain this peculiar means of "grasping" connections. Thus, while some such as Woodward (2019) wonder "how discoveries about how people in fact reason could be relevant to these normative concerns", for my part, I wonder, how could they not?

Bibliography

Achinstein, Peter (1984): "The pragmatic character of explanation", *Proceedings of the Biennial Meeting of the Philosophy of Science Association* 2, pp. 275–292.

Baumberger, Christoph, Claus Beisbart, and Georg Brun (2017): "What is understanding? An overview of recent debates in epistemology and philosophy of science", in: Stephen Grimm, Christoph Baumberger, and Sabine Ammon (Eds.): *Explaining understanding. New perspectives from epistemology and philosophy of science.* New York: Routledge, pp. 1–34.

Bechtel, William, and Adele Abrahamsen (2005): "Explanation. A mechanist alternative", *Studies in History and Philosophy of Science – Part C* 36 (2), pp. 421–441.

Beebe, James, and Finnur Dellsén (2020): "Scientific realism in the wild. An empirical study of seven sciences and history and philosophy of science", *Philosophy of Science* 87 (2), pp. 336–364.

Benjamin, Cornelius (1941): "Modes of scientific explanation", *Philosophy of Science* 8 (4), pp. 486–492.

Berland, Leema Kuhn, and Brian Reiser (2009): "Making sense of argumentation and explanation", *Science Education* 93 (1), pp. 26–55.

Brewer, William (2001): "Models in science and mental models in scientists and nonscientists", *Mind & Society* 2 (2), pp. 33–48.

Brewer, William, Clark Chinn, and Ala Samarapungavan (2000): "Explanation in scientists and children", in: Frank Keil and Robert Wilson (Eds.): *Explanation and cognition.* Cambridge: The MIT Press, pp. 279–298.

Bridgman, Percy (1960): *The logic of modern physics.* New York: Macmillan.

Bromberger, Sylvain (1966): "Why-questions", in: Robert Colodny (Ed.): *Mind and cosmos.* Pittsburgh: University of Pittsburgh Press, pp. 86–111.

---

bart, and Brun 2017), but this seems another incarnation of the old strategy of conflating conditions for verifying x with x itself (cf. analytic behaviorism, the coherence theory of truth, the Turing test, the statistical-relevance theory of causation, and so forth). This ability is better viewed as a *consequence* of possessing the representations constitutive of understanding (Waskan 2008, Wilkenfeld 2015, Strevens 2016), a proposal that better fits with psychological research on the intrinsic and instrumental value of explanations (Lombrozo 2011).

Brown, Theodore (2003): *Making truth. Metaphor in science.* Urbana: University of Illinois Press.
Carruthers, Peter, Stephen Stich, and Michael Siegal (Eds.) (2002): *The cognitive basis of science.* Cambridge: Cambridge University Press.
Churchland, Paul (1989): *A neurocomputational perspective. The nature of mind and the structure of science.* Cambridge: The MIT Press.
Colombo, Matteo (2017): "Experimental philosophy of explanation rising. The case for a plurality of concepts of explanation", *Cognitive Science* 41 (2), pp. 503–517.
Craver, Carl (2007): *Explaining the brain. Mechanisms and the mosaic unity of neuroscience.* New York: Clarendon Press.
Craver, Carl (2014): "The ontic account of scientific explanation", in: Marie Kaiser, Oliver Scholz, Daniel Plenge, and Andreas Hüttemann (Eds.): *Explanation in the special sciences. The case of biology and history.* Dordrecht: Springer, pp. 27–52.
Cummins, Robert (1998): "Reflections on reflective equilibrium", in: Michael DePaul and William Ramsey (Eds.): *Rethinking intuition. The psychology of intuition and its role in philosophical inquiry.* New York: Rowman & Littlefield, pp. 113–128.
de Regt, Henk (2004): "Making sense of understanding", *Philosophy of Science* 71 (1), pp. 98–109.
de Regt, Henk (2009): "The epistemic value of understanding", *Philosophy of Science* 76 (5), pp. 585–597.
Frege, Gottlob (1884): *Grundlagen der Arithmetik.* Breslau: Koebner.
Gelman, Susan, and Henry Wellman (1991): "Insides and essences. Early understandings of the non-obvious", *Cognition* 38 (3), pp. 213–244.
Giere, Ronald (1990): *Explaining science. A cognitive approach.* Chicago: University of Chicago Press.
Giere, Ronald (1992): *Cognitive models of science.* Minneapolis: University of Minnesota Press.
Gopnik, Alison (2000): "Explanation as orgasm and the drive for causal knowledge. The function, evolution, and phenomenology of the theory formation system", in: Frank Keil and Robert Wilson (Eds.): *Explanation and cognition.* Cambridge: The MIT Press, pp. 299–324.
Griffiths, Paul, and Karola Stotz (2008): "Experimental philosophy of science", *Philosophy Compass* 3 (3), pp. 507–521.
Grimm, Stephen (2010): "The goal of explanation", *Studies in History and Philosophy of Science – Part A* 41 (4), pp. 337–344.
Hansson, Sven Ove (2006): "Falsificationism falsified", *Foundations of Science* 11 (3), pp. 275–286.
Hempel, Carl Gustav (1965): *Aspects of scientific explanation.* New York: Free Press.
Hickling, Anne, and Henry Wellman (2001): "The emergence of children's causal explanations and theories. Evidence from everyday conversation", *Developmental Psychology* 37 (5), pp. 668–683.
Humphreys, Paul (1989): "Scientific explanation. The causes, some of the causes, and nothing but the causes", *Minnesota Studies in the Philosophy of Science* 13, pp. 283–306.
Keil, Frank (2006): "Explanation and understanding", *Annual Review of Psychology* 57 (1), pp. 227–254.
Keil, Frank, and Robert Wilson (Eds.) (2000): *Explanation and cognition.* Cambridge: The MIT Press.
Knobe, Joshua (2003): "Intentional action and side effects in ordinary language", *Analysis* 63 (3), pp. 190–194.
Knobe, Joshua, and Richard Samuels (2013): "Thinking like a scientist. Innateness as a case study", *Cognition* 126 (1), pp. 72–86.
Kuhn, Thomas (1970): *The structure of scientific revolutions.* Chicago: University of Chicago Press.
Lakatos, Imre (1970): "Falsification and the methodology scientific research programmes", in: Imre Lakatos and Alan Musgrave (Eds.): *Criticism and the growth of knowledge.* Cambridge: Cambridge University Press, pp. 91–195.
Lombrozo, Tania (2006): "The structure and function of explanations", *Trends in Cognitive Sciences* 10 (10), pp. 464–470.
Lombrozo, Tania (2007): "Simplicity and probability in causal explanation", *Cognitive Psychology* 55 (3), pp. 232–257.
Lombrozo, Tania (2011): "The instrumental value of explanations", *Philosophy Compass* 6 (8), pp. 539–551.

Lombrozo, Tania, and Susan Carey (2006): "Functional explanation and the function of explanation", *Cognition* 99 (2), pp. 167–204.

Lovell, Tasman (1931): "Explanation", *Australasian Journal of Psychology and Philosophy* 9 (3), pp. 214–221.

Machamer, Peter, Lindley Darden, and Carl Craver (2000): "Thinking about mechanisms", *Philosophy of Science* 67 (1), pp. 1–25.

Machery, Eduard (2016): "Experimental philosophy of science", in: Justin Sytsma and Wesley Buckwalter (Eds.): *A companion to experimental philosophy*. Chichester: Wiley-Blackwell, pp. 475–490.

Machery, Eduard, Paul Griffiths, Stefan Linquist, and Karola Stotz (2019): "Scientists' concepts of innateness. Evolution or attraction?", in: Daniel Wilkenfeld, James Beebe, and Richard Samuels (Eds.): *Advances in experimental philosophy of science*. London: Bloomsbury, pp. 172–201.

Maher, Patrick (2007): "Explication defended", *Studia Logica* 86 (2), pp. 331–341.

Malaterre, Christophe, and Jean-François Chartier (2021): "Beyond categorical definitions of life. A data-driven approach to assessing lifeness", *Synthese* 198 (5), pp. 4543–4572.

Malaterre, Christophe, Jean-François Chartier, and Davide Pulizzotto (2019): "What is this thing called philosophy of science? A computational topic-modeling perspective, 1934–2015", *The Journal of the International Society for the History of Philosophy of Science* 9 (2), pp. 215–249.

Mishra, Punyashloke, and William Brewer (2003): "Theories as a form of mental representation and their role in the recall of text information", *Contemporary Educational Psychology* 28 (3), pp. 277–303.

Mizrahi, Moti (2021): "Conceptions of scientific progress in scientific practice. An empirical study", *Synthese* 199, pp. 2375–2394.

Mizrahi, Moti (forthcoming): "Theoretical virtues in scientific practice. An empirical study", *The British Journal for the Philosophy of Science*.

Nagatsu, Michiru, and Kaire Põder (2019): "What is the economic concept of choice? An experimental philosophy study", *Economics and Philosophy* 35 (3), pp. 461–478.

Nersessian, Nancy (2008): *Creating scientific concepts*. Cambridge: The MIT Press.

Overton, James (2012): "'Explain' in scientific discourse", *Synthese* 190 (8), pp. 1383–1405.

Popper, Karl (1935): *Logik der Forschung*. Vienna: Springer.

Popper, Karl (1959): *The logic of scientific discovery*. London: Hutchison.

Powell, Derek, Zachary Horne, and Ángel Pinillos (2014): "Semantic integration as a method for investigating concepts", in: James Beebe (Ed.): *Advances in experimental epistemology*. London: Bloomsbury, pp. 119–144.

Quine, Willard Van Orman (1953): *From a logical point of view*. Cambridge: Harvard University Press.

Rudner, Richard (1953): "The scientist qua scientist makes value judgments", *Philosophy of Science* 20 (1), pp. 1–6.

Salmon, Wesley (1984): *Scientific explanation and the causal structure of the world*. Princeton: Princeton University Press.

Salmon, Wesley (1989): *Four decades of scientific explanation*. Minneapolis: University of Minnesota Press.

Salmon, Wesley (1998): *Causality and explanation*. New York: Oxford University Press.

Scriven, Michael (1959): "Explanation and prediction in evolutionary theory. Satisfactory explanation of the past is possible even when prediction of the future is impossible", *Science* 130 (3374), pp. 477–482.

Sellars, Wilfred (1956): "Empiricism and the philosophy of mind", in: Herbert Feigl and Michael Scriven (Eds.): *The foundations of science and the concepts of psychoanalysis*. Minneapolis: University of Minnesota Press, pp. 253–329.

Sellars, Wilfred (1963): *Science, perception and reality*. London: Routledge & Kegan Paul.

Sikimić, Vlasta, Tijana Nikitović, Miljan Vasić, and Vanja Subotić (2021): "Do political attitudes matter for epistemic decisions of scientists?", *Review of Philosophy and Psychology* 12, pp. 775–801.

Simon, Herbert (1966): "Thinking by computers", in: Robert Colodny (Ed.): *Mind and cosmos. Essays in contemporary science and philosophy*. Pittsburgh: University of Pittsburgh Press, pp. 3–21.

Sosa, Ernest (2006): "Experimental philosophy and philosophical intuition", *Philosophical Studies* 132 (1), pp. 99–107.

Stace, Walter (1935): "Science and the explanation of phenomena", *Philosophy* 10 (40), pp. 409–427.
Strevens, Michael (2013): "No understanding without explanation", *Studies in History and Philosophy of Science – Part A* 44 (3), pp. 510–515.
Sytsma, Justin, and Jonathan Livengood (2015): *The theory and practice of experimental philosophy.* Peterborough: Broadview.
Thagard, Paul (2012): *The cognitive science of science. Explanation, discovery, and conceptual change.* Cambridge: The MIT Press.
Thagard, Paul, and Abninder Litt (2008): "Models of scientific explanation", in: Ron Sun (Ed.): *The Cambridge handbook of computational cognitive modeling.* Cambridge: Cambridge University Press, pp. 549–564.
Trout, John Dewain (2007): "The psychology of scientific explanation", *Philosophy Compass* 2 (3), pp. 564–591.
Vosniadou, Stella (2002): "Mental models in conceptual development", in: Lorenzo Magnani and Nancy Nersessian (Eds.): *Model-based reasoning. Science, technology, values.* Berlin: Springer, pp. 353–368.
Waskan, Jonathan (2006): *Models and cognition.* Cambridge: The MIT Press.
Waskan, Jonathan (2008): "Knowledge of counterfactual interventions through cognitive models of mechanisms", *International Studies in the Philosophy of Science* 22 (3), pp. 259–275.
Waskan, Jonathan (2011): *Intelligibility and the CAPE. Combatting anti-psychologism about explanation.* Manuscript.
Waskan, Jonathan (2017): "From neural circuitry to mechanistic model-based reasoning", in: Lorenzo Magnani and Tommaso Bertolotti (Eds.): *Springer handbook of model-based science.* Berlin: Springer, pp. 671–692.
Waskan, Jonathan, Ian Harmon, Zachary Horne, Joseph Spino, and John Clevenger (2014a): "Explanatory anti-psychologism overturned by lay and scientific case classifications", *Synthese* 191 (5), pp. 1013–1035.
Waskan, Jonathan, Ian Harmon, Andrew Higgins, and Joseph Spino (2014b): "Three senses of 'explanation'", in: Paul Bello, Marcello Guarini, Marjorie McShane, and Brian Scassellati (Eds.): *Proceedings of the 36th annual conference of the cognitive science society.* Austin: Cognitive Science Society, pp. 3090–3095.
Wilkenfeld, Daniel (2015): "MUDdy Understanding", *Synthese* 194 (4), pp. 1273–1293.
Wilkenfeld, Daniel, and Tania Lombrozo (2020): "Explanation classification depends on understanding. Extending the epistemic side-effect effect", *Synthese* 197 (1), pp. 2565–2592.
Wilkenfeld, Daniel, Robert Samuels, and James Beebe (Eds.) (2019): *Advances in Experimental Philosophy of Science.* London: Bloomsbury.
Woodward, James (2003): *Making things happen.* New York: Oxford University Press.
Woodward, James (2019): "Causal judgment. What can philosophy learn from experiment? What can it contribute to experiment?", in: Daniel Wilkenfeld, Robert Samuels, and James Beebe (Eds.): *Advances in experimental philosophy of science.* London: Bloomsbury, pp. 205–244.

Mark Phelan
Experimental Philosophy of Mind: Conscious State Attribution

Abstract: Two key questions dominate the experimental philosophy of mind literature: Do ordinary people possess a concept of phenomenal consciousness? What features of an entity lead people to attribute phenomenally conscious (and non-phenomenally conscious) mental states? Five responses to one or both of these questions are discussed: (1) an Embodiment View, which claims that agents capable of phenomenal consciousness are thought by the folk to possess a certain kind of biological body; (2) a Valence View, which emphasizes the importance of considerations of affective valence in mental state attribution; (3) a "Naïve" View, which claims that pains and colors are just thought by the folk to be physically localized properties; (4) a Functionalist View, which argues that functionalist considerations predominate ordinary peoples attributions of all varieties of mental states; and (5) a Dual-Systems View, which claims that all of the other views are investigating rational mental state attributions and have missed the significant part of the story involving automatic mental state attributions. Experimental philosophical evidence for and against each response is considered. The chapter concludes with some brief remarks about other projects in the experimental philosophy of mind.

Keywords: Consciousness; Embodiment; Experimental Philosophy; Functionalism; Mental State Attribution; Mind Perception

1 Introduction – Experimental Philosophy of Mind, Positive and Negative

Philosophers have used a variety of experimental methods to investigate topics squarely within the philosophy of mind. Indeed, in one of the earliest and most influential papers of contemporary experimental philosophy, Knobe (2003) investigated how people attribute the mental capacity of intentionality and uncovered a now famous asymmetry in our attributions of intentional states. Much experimental philosophy of mind has followed this early example, investigating folk theory of mind, in general, and when and why people attribute mental states of different kinds, in particular. In an important early paper, Knobe and Prinz (2008) investigated the attribution of mental states as such, and posited the existence of a folk psychological concept of phenomenal consciousness. They argued that such a posit was needed to explain their finding that people were less willing to attribute presumed phenomenal mental states, such as feeling sad, to group entities, such as corporations, than they were to attribute non-phenomenal mental states, such as thinking (whereas they were willing to attribute both kinds of states to other, non-group entities). In recent years, numerous other works of experimental philosophy have expanded and complicated our understanding of mental state attribution.

If one is inclined to accept that the identity conditions for at least some mental states are imposed by our intuitive folk psychological theories, then one will likely regard the results of the previous examples of experimental philosophy of mind as of instrumental value. Experimental philosophical projects of this kind purport to augment the philosopher of mind's toolbox with the tool of scientifically-informed experimental studies of people's intuitions about mental states. Thus, they can be seen as of a piece with more traditional, non-experimental, analytic philosophy of mind, since both have as their primary goal the investigation and further understanding of the metaphysics of minds and the epistemology of mental state attribution and since both typically appeal to philosophical intuitions to advance their arguments.[1] Such projects, then, make positive contributions to analytic philosophy of mind. However, there also exists a negative project in experimental philosophy of mind, which aims to undermine arguments that appeal to philosophical intuitions. Negative projects intend to show that some purportedly generally held philosophical intuition, to which some philosophical argument appeals, is not, in fact, generally held, or is not generally held in such a way as to support the argument it is intended to support. Because both non-experimentalists and positive experimentalists appeal to intuitions in making their arguments, either may end up as the target of a negative experimental philosopher of mind (as we shall see below).

In this chapter, I will focus, first and primarily, on the experimental philosophy of conscious state attribution. A mental state may be said to be conscious in a variety of ways, but experimental philosophers of mind have primarily been interested in phenomenal consciousness. As I explain below, experimental philosophers of mind have asked whether there are folk correlates to the philosopher's concept of phenomenal consciousness and when and why we attribute phenomenally conscious mental states to some entities but not others. In Section 2, the main part of this chapter, I examine several different accounts of phenomenal state attribution that have emerged from the experimental philosophy literature. In Section 3, I will briefly introduce several other topics of interest in the experimental philosophy of mind.

2 The Experimental Philosophy of Conscious State Attribution

Theorists have distinguished between mental states that are, in some sense, conscious and other states that are not conscious, in that sense. For example, Freud claimed that

---

[1] Recently, a number of theorists have argued for the surprising thesis that analytic philosophers don't actually use intuitions as evidence, including Williamson (2007) and Cappelen (2012). However, a number of others have offered compelling challenges to this position, including Nado (2015) and Climenhaga (2018).

repressed mental attitudes are not first-person accessible, and hence are unconscious, in that sense. At this point, many psychological studies have partially vindicated Freud and demonstrated that individuals often lack first-person awareness of various mental attitudes and processes (e.g., judgments, decisions, belief formation processes) that are, nonetheless, operative in their behavior.[2] The idea that people possess mental attitudes that are unconscious – in the sense of first-person inaccessible – is now widespread in Western culture, to the point that we routinely attribute unconscious attitudes, as when we attribute implicit bias to someone.

However, many philosophers of mind have been interested in so-called phenomenal consciousness. According to Block (1995, p. 228), "phenomenal consciousness is experience; what makes a state phenomenally conscious is that there is something 'it is like' (Nagel 1974) to be in that state". Chalmers (1995, p. 201) writes of the "subjective aspect" of experience, claiming that sensory states, bodily sensations, emotions, and mental images are all united in that "there is something it is like to be in them. All of them are states of experience". Not only do philosophers of mind such as these countenance phenomenal consciousness, but they also further maintain that its existence is manifestly obvious to anyone who experiences phenomenally conscious states – that is, to all of us. For example, Chalmers (1995, p. 206) goes on to claim that "experience is the most central and manifest aspect of our mental lives". Also, Jackson's (1986) *Knowledge Argument* relies on the undefended premise that Mary will come to know about the phenomenal experience of seeing red upon her release from her monochromatic internment. Presumably, Jackson supposes that his readers will find this just obvious. Finally, these philosophers of mind are committed to the assumption that people attribute phenomenally conscious mental states to some but not all other entities. For example, Jackson goes on to claim that

> after Mary sees her first ripe tomato, she will realize how impoverished her conception of the mental life of *others has been all along.* [...] All along their experiences (or many of them, those got from tomatoes, the sky, ...) had a feature conspicuous to them but until now hidden from her... (Jackson 1986, pp. 292 f.)

And Nagel's "What Is It Like to Be" Argument relies on our tacit acceptance that it *is* like something to be a bat (but maybe not some other living things):

> I assume we all believe that bats have experience. After all, they are mammals, and there is no more doubt that they have experience than that mice or pigeons or whales have experience. I

---

[2] Nisbett and Wilson (1977, p. 232) cover numerous studies demonstrating that "we may have no direct access to higher order mental processes such as those involved in evaluation, judgment, problem solving, and the initiation of behavior". More recently, arguments by analogy from research on commissurotomy ("split-brain") subjects (see especially Gazzaniga 1995, 2000) to the conclusion that we quite generally lack first-person awareness of our attitudinal states have been offered by Carruthers (2013, pp. 39–45; see also Carruthers 2010).

> have chosen bats instead of wasps or flounders because if one travels too far down the phylogenetic tree, people gradually shed their faith that there is experience there at all. (Nagel 1974, p. 438)

Presumably, neither Jackson nor Nagel would maintain that we attribute phenomenally conscious states to a stone, a dead person, or a plant. Block's (1978) Nation of China Argument appeals to our intuition that the citizens of the nation of China, organized so as to instantiate the machine-table description of, say, the state of pain, would not thereby instantiate a pain state.

As these quotations suggest, some prominent analytic philosophers of mind suppose that there is a class of phenomenally conscious mental states that are obvious to those who experience them and are also attributed by those who experience them to some but not all other entities. Inspired by these discussions of phenomenally conscious mental states, experimental philosophers of mind have investigated two main questions:

1. Do ordinary people possess a concept analogous to the concept of phenomenal consciousness employed by analytic philosophers of mind?
2. What features of an entity lead people to attribute the mental states that philosophers identify as phenomenally conscious mental states?

In the remainder of this section, I'll survey some projects that have attempted to answer one or both of these questions.

2.1 The Embodiment Hypothesis

An early inspiration for the experimental philosophy of conscious state attribution was provided by the psychologists Gray, Gray, and Wegner (2007a), who surveyed ordinary people's preferential attributions of different sorts of mental states to different sorts of entities. They had thousands of participants complete one survey each, consisting of 78 assessments as to which of two characters was more capable of a particular mental state. Participants selected the state they would assess, out of 18 possibilities (e.g., feeling pain, experiencing pride, exercising restraint, telling right from wrong). Each participant assessed half of the 156 possible pairings of 13 different characters (e.g., an infant, a chimpanzee, a robot, a dead woman, God). So, if a participant had selected the survey on the affective state of *pride*, they might be asked whether and to what degree a robot is more capable of experiencing pride than an infant, then asked whether a chimpanzee is more capable of experiencing pride than a person in a persistent vegetative state, and so on. Gray and colleagues subjected these results to a principle component factor analysis, and identified a two-factor model that accounted for 97% of the variance in people's assessments. One factor, which they called "Experience", explained 88% of the variance and included capacities such as feeling fear and feeling hunger. Another factor, which they called "Agency", explained 8% of the variance and included capacities such as self-control and moral reasoning.[3] As shown in Figure 1, participants assessed some entities (a five-year old girl, the family dog) as more capable of experiential states than some other entities (a robot, God). And they assessed some entities (God, an adult woman) as more capable of agentic states than some other entities (a fetus, a dead woman).

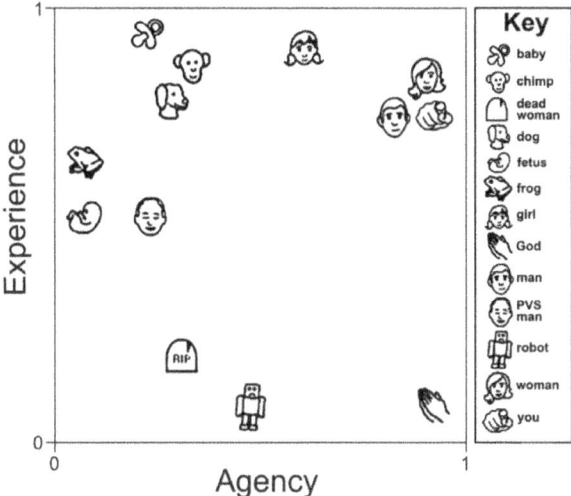

Figure 1: Adjusted character factor scores on the dimension of mind perception (from Gray, Gray, and Wegner 2007a)

One thing that stands out about Gray, Gray, and Wegner's findings is that the entities assessed as least capable of experiential states – a dead woman, a robot, and God – are all alike in lacking a functioning biological body. But, despite lacking a biological body, God was still deemed highly capable of agentic states. The experiential states used by Gray and colleagues are bodily sensations and emotions, so, they are prototypical phenomenally conscious mental states (and their agentic states are not). Their results, then, seem to suggest that considerations of bodily constitution weigh heavily in ordinary attributions of at least some phenomenally conscious mental states, but not in the attribution of other, non-phenomenally conscious mental states.

Building on these results, Knobe and Prinz used a series of experimental studies to argue that ordinary people possess an implicit concept of phenomenal consciousness and that "information about physical constitution plays a special role in those ascriptions that require phenomenal consciousness – a role it does not play in other kinds of mental state ascription" (Knobe and Prinz 2008, p. 71). Knobe and Prinz's studies fo-

---

[3] The experience dimension was subsequently confirmed in replications by Takahashi, Ban, and Asada (2016) as well as Weisman, Dweck, and Markman (2017), though the agency dimension has proved less robust. See Malle (2019) for further discussion.

cused on people's attributions of mental states to groups – to corporations, specifically. They pointed out that groups, being composed of individual agents, have a radically different constitution than a human being. Yet we seem willing to attribute some mental states to group entities – we are perfectly willing to talk about what Apple thinks or what the Republican Party wants, for example. In one study Knobe and Prinz gave participants sentences that ascribed phenomenal states or (purportedly non-phenomenal) intentional states (such as believing or intending) to a fictional *Acme Corporation*. They then asked participants to rate how natural each sentence sounded on a scale anchored at "sounds natural" and "sounds weird". Group phenomenal state ascriptions sounded significantly weirder than group intentional state ascriptions to these participants. Knobe and Prinz inferred that these results "seem to indicate that people are unwilling to ascribe to group agents states that require phenomenal consciousness" (Knobe and Prinz 2008, p. 75). In another study, Knobe and Prinz showed that utterances such as "Acme Corp. is feeling upset" or "Acme Corp. is feeling regret" are judged to sound much weirder than utterances such as "Acme Corp. is upset about the court's recent ruling" or "Acme Corp. regrets its recent decision". They concluded from this result that, in addition to the folk psychological concepts of *regret* and *upset*, ordinary people also possess a concept of phenomenal consciousness, or *feeling*. And that, "people's reluctance to say that a group agent 'feels upset' stems not from the criteria associated with their concept of upsetness, but rather from the criteria associated with their concept of phenomenal consciousness" (Knobe and Prinz 2008, p. 78).[4]

Reflecting on the results from Gray, Gray, and Wegner (2007a) as well as Knobe and Prinz (2008),[5] we may ask ourselves what common feature a robot, God, and a corporation share that inhibits people's attributions of phenomenally conscious mental states to them? According to Knobe and Prinz, this cannot be a feature related to how these entities function, since "a state of a corporation easily could have a functional role similar to one that people ordinarily associate with feeling depressed" (Knobe and Prinz 2008, p. 73). Intuitively, God or a robot could react to their environment in exactly the same way as an enraged person. At least *prima facie*, then, it seems that these three entities can occupy states functionally equivalent to the ordinary humans to whom we reflexively attribute phenomenal states. What God, a robot, and a corporation lack, however, and what a human possesses, is a unified, biological body. These findings, then, may support an Embodiment Thesis, which regards unified biological embodiment as a psychological cue to attributions of phenomenally conscious mental states. The Embodiment Hypothesis claims that ordinary people tacitly possess a con-

---

[4] Knobe and Prinz use these and additional results to argue for a somewhat radical conception of human nature. They accept that information about the non-phenomenal, intentional mental states of other entities – information about their beliefs and desires – is useful for predicting and explaining behavior. But they maintain that we primarily exploit information about the phenomenal mental states of other entities to determine what our moral obligations to those entities are, and not primarily to predict and explain their behavior.

[5] See also Knobe (2008) as well as Robbins and Jack (2006).

cept of phenomenal consciousness roughly equivalent to the one philosophers of mind use and that they preferentially apply it to entities that exhibit the non-functional feature of unified, biological embodiment.

Evidence for the Embodiment Hypothesis has been challenged. For example, Huebner, Bruno, and Sarkissian (2009) presented versions of Knobe and Prinz's corporation probes to students at Hong Kong University, who were significantly more comfortable attributing phenomenal states to distributed group entities than were their American counterparts. Embodiment tendencies, then, insofar as they exist, seem to be malleable and mutable, not universally held. Sytsma and Machery (2009) challenged the idea that people possess a concept of phenomenal consciousness that they express with the word *feeling*. They claimed that the sentence, "Acme Corp. is upset about the court's recent ruling", sounds more natural than the sentence, "Acme Corp. is feeling upset", simply because the mental state attribution is contextualized with a prepositional phrase in the former but not the latter. They were able to reverse the effect Knobe and Prinz found, getting participants to judge that the sentence "Acme Corporation is feeling upset about the court's recent ruling" sounds more natural than the sentence "Acme Corporation is upset". Similarly, Arico (2010) found no difference between people's naturalness assessments of "McDonalds is upset" and "McDonalds is feeling upset" when each was contextualized with the addition of the prepositional phrase "about the court's recent ruling". Finally, Phelan and colleagues (2013) found that participants were equally likely to choose "they" (rather than "it") to paraphrase a group name in group phenomenal state attributions and group intentional (non-phenomenal) state attributions. They were significantly more likely to choose "it" to paraphrase a group name in non-mental state attributions. This suggests that people understand *all* group mental state attributions – phenomenally conscious or not – distributively, as attributions of states to the constituents of groups. If correct, Knobe and Prinz's results tell us very little about how people think about the mental states of groups, as opposed to how they think about the people who constitute groups.[6]

Despite these challenges to the Embodiment Hypothesis, the role that an entity's body plays in our attributions of emotions, perceptual states, bodily sensations, and other phenomenally conscious states has remained a topic of interest. For example, Forstmann and Burgmer (forthcoming), have recently purported to provide evidence that people conceptualize consciousness as a spatio-temporally located process in the human brain. Though, it is doubtful that their method of asking people to color the part(s) of a two-dimensional picture of a brain that they think "contribute" to consciousness delivers much evidence as to where people think consciousness is located, since something can clearly contribute to a process without being collocated with it. Meanwhile, Díaz has presented experimental evidence that "people report anger, sad-

---

6 Concurrently, with these negative projects, positive projects within experimental philosophy of mind seemed to demonstrate that, contra Knobe and Prinz, people are perfectly happy to attribute phenomenally conscious states to entities that lack a biological body. We'll review such projects in Sections 2.2 and 2.3 below.

ness, and fear in the absence of bodily feelings" (Díaz 2022, p. 24). If correct, this suggests that bodily responses are not essential to ordinary people's conception of emotions and, thereby, undermines one source of support for a sort of embodiment view.

2.2 The Valence View and the Naïve View

The Embodiment Hypothesis answered the first of experimental philosophy of mind's key questions affirmatively. People tacitly employ a concept of phenomenal consciousness analogous to that employed by analytic philosophers of mind, it claimed. Further, it maintained an answer to the second question that when we decide to predicate phenomenally conscious mental states to entities, we do not merely consider the functional capacities of those entities. We also consider physical properties that are irrelevant to functional capacities. The Valence View and the Naïve View, however, are alike in giving a negative answer to the first of experimental philosophy of mind's key questions. Both maintain that ordinary people do not employ a concept of phenomenal consciousness analogous to that employed by analytic philosophers of mind. Instead, they contend that the diverse set of sensory states, bodily sensations, emotions, and mental images that analytic philosophers have identified as phenomenally conscious are conceptualized in a variety of different ways by ordinary people, no one of which approximates the analytic philosopher's concept of a phenomenally conscious mental state. Both views maintain that the analytic philosopher's commitment to the manifest obviousness of phenomenal consciousness was, in fact, the product of biased post-theoretic reflection on what is pre-theoretically obvious. However, none of this means that the Valence View or the Naïve View are off the hook when it comes to the second question. In fact, they have complicated the task, since either view would seem to entail that we need a variety of different accounts for how people apply each of the motley set of mental states philosophers mistakenly unify under the heading "phenomenally conscious states".

According to the philosophically prominent conception of phenomenal consciousness described above, we must accept the existence of phenomenal consciousness because its existence is obvious to anyone who experiences it and we all continually experience it. Proponents of this prominent conception have, further, identified both bodily sensations (e.g., the experience of physical pain) and sensory states (e.g., the state of seeing something red) as prototypical instances of phenomenally conscious mental states. According to this view, then, it seems that anyone who occupies the mental state of physical pain should experience that state as phenomenally conscious – that is, as a state that it is like something to occupy. And the same follows for anyone who occupies the state of seeing something red. Presumably, given the obviousness of phenomenal consciousness, after a little experience of bodily sensations and sensory states like these, most everyone would associate the two sorts of mental states together as being phenomenally conscious – that is, as being like something to occupy. Thus, Sytsma and Machery (2010) argue that ordinary people should tend to treat attributions of paradigmatic examples of phenomenally conscious mental states similarly and similarly to how people with philosophical training treat them.

With this argument in mind, Sytsma and Machery designed a set of vignettes to test whether ordinary people attribute bodily sensations and sensory states in the same way as philosophers. In their first study, Sytsma and Machery split their sizable sample into two groups: "Philosophers" – including undergraduate majors and participants with some graduate training in philosophy – and "Non-Philosophers". Participants in each group were presented with one of four vignettes. Two vignettes described a normal human (Timmy), the other two described a simple, non-humanoid robot (Jimmy). In every vignette, the agent was instructed to place a red box in front of a door as part of a psychological experiment. The agent successfully completed the task in two of the vignettes. In the other two, the box gave the agent "a strong electric shock" and, "He let go of the box and moved away from it" (Sytsma and Machery 2010, p. 306). For each vignette, the participant was asked whether the agent "saw red" or "felt pain when he was shocked" and answered on a 7-point scale anchored at 1 with "clearly no", at 4 with "not sure", and at 7 with "clearly yes". As the results in Figure 2 show, the responses of the philosophers diverged from those of the non-philosophers when it came to the purported phenomenal states of seeing red.

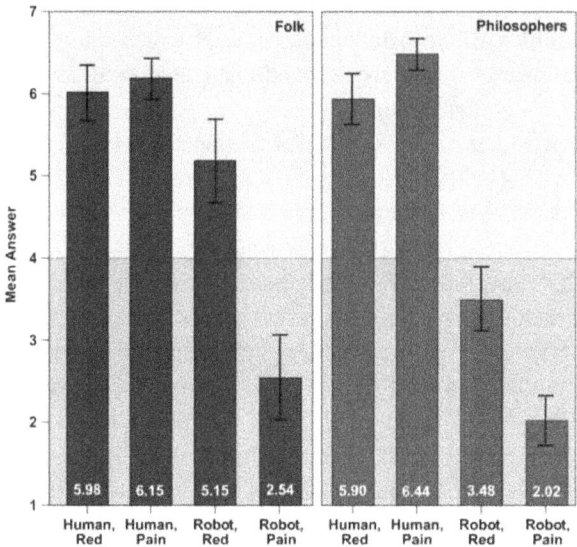

Figure 2: Mean attributions of the mental states of feeling pain and seeing red (from Sytsma and Machery 2010)

As Sytsma and Machery report, philosophers' mean attributions of the mental states of feeling pain and seeing red were significantly above the midpoint for Timmy, the normal human, and significantly below the midpoint for Jimmy, the simple robot. For non-philosophers, mean attributions of both mental states were significantly above the midpoint for Timmy, as was the mean attribution of seeing red to Jimmy. Only attributions of feeling pain to Jimmy were below the midpoint for non-philosophers.

On the basis of their first study, Sytsma and Machery tentatively conclude that non-philosophers lack the philosopher's concept of phenomenal consciousness. They then strengthen this tentative conclusion with a series of experiments that serve to develop their positive view of how people think about sensory states and bodily sensations. They ultimately conclude that philosophers and ordinary people agree that simple robots are not capable of what we may describe as subjectively rich experiences. It's just that philosophers and ordinary people part ways on what counts as "subjectively rich". Philosophers identify the category of phenomenally conscious mental states with subjectively rich experiences. Ordinary people, on the other hand, sort experiential states according to their valence and identify positively or negatively valenced mental states with subjectively rich experiences.[7]

This Valence View explains Sytsma and Machery's findings. Because feeling pain is negatively valenced, ordinary people, like the philosophers operating with their concept of phenomenal consciousness, regard this as a subjectively rich experience to be denied a simple robot. But ordinary people are willing to attribute the state of seeing red to the simple robot because they do not regard it as a subjectively rich (that is, valenced) experience. Philosophers, though, are unwilling to attribute seeing red to the robot, because they see it as a subjectively rich (that is, phenomenally conscious) experience.[8] Sytsma and Machery (2010, p. 319) conclude that, "in clear contrast to philosophers, the folk do not seem to believe that there is something common to all these mental states – namely that they are phenomenal".

Several studies have challenged the Valence View. For example, Buckwalter and Phelan (2013), designed a pair of studies based on the simple robot vignettes. In their first study, they asked participants whether a robot smelled something, either isoamyl acetate, bananas, or vomit. These sensory states were chosen because, in one of their studies, Sytsma and Machery had found that participants were more inclined to say the robot smelled isoamyl acetate (presumably unknown to these participants, and, so, unvalenced) than either vomit or bananas. However, Buckwalter and Phelan varied the functional complexity of the robot and the functional role the robot was designed to perform across conditions. They also had participants rank the valence of the three sensory objects and found that participants attributed little positive or negative valence to isoamyl acetate, a slight positive valence to bananas, and a strong negative valence to vomit. They then compared the degree to which participants rated the valence for each

---

[7] Sytsma and Machery (2010) helpfully clarify their use of the term "valence" in a footnote: "mental states have a valence if and only if they have a hedonic value for the subject. That is, mental states have a valence if and only if they are pleasurable (they then have a positive valence) or disagreeable (they then have a negative valence). Not all mental states have a valence, and valenced states are more or less pleasurable or disagreeable" (Sytsma and Machery 2010, p. 350).

[8] A similar explanation can be applied to the results Sytsma and Machery find in their other studies for the mental states of smelling vomit, bananas, and isoamyl acetate.

smell with the degree to which they attributed the subjective experience of smelling the object to the robot. Contra the Valence View, no relationship was found between the intensity of positive or negative valence ratings and smell attributions. However, there was a strong relationship between the functional role a robot was designed to perform and people's attributions of sensory states. When the robot was designed to make smoothies, people were more likely to say that he smelled the chemical and the banana but not the vomit. Conversely, when his functional role was to clean up biomedical waste, mean scores where higher for vomit than for the chemical (and to a lesser extent the banana), as can be seen in Figure 3.

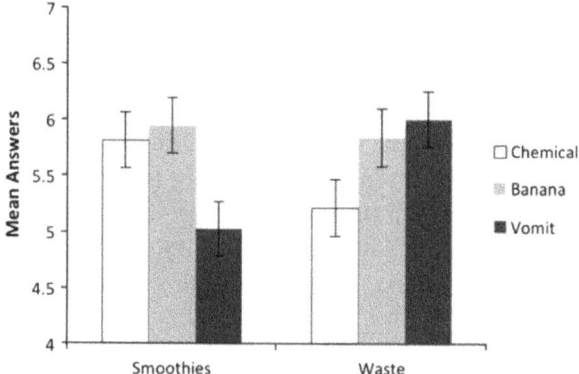

Figure 3: Interaction effect of object and function on smell attribution ratings (from Buckwalter and Phelan 2013)

In their first study, Buckwalter and Phelan did not find an effect for complexity of the robot. However, in a second study, participants' assessments of whether or not a robot could feel guilt were influenced both by its complexity and its specified functional role. But, again, in this study, participants' valence assessments for the emotional state of guilt were not predictive of their guilt attributions. Finding no evidence of a valence effect, Buckwalter and Phelan explained Sytsma and Machery's results by referencing participant's assumptions about function, rather than valence. Specifically, they argue that participants likely assumed that a simple robot in a psychological study that was directed to move a red box was designed to satisfy the functional role of detecting colors and with the mechanical complexity to do so. Such a robot was probably not designed to feel pain when it is damaged, especially since the shock it sustains is likely to be interpreted as the result of an accident, rather than a planned intervention by its designers.[9]

---

9 See also Fiala, Arico, and Nichols (2014), who provide evidence that few people describe the robot in Sytsma and Machery's (2010) vignettes as "seeing green" when given options to describe it, instead, as "detecting green" or "identifying the green box" (whereas most people describe the person as seeing green). As they explain, "These results suggest that the overly narrow choice format might artificially

To his credit, after his own further studies failed to present additional evidence in favor of the Valence View, Sytsma abandoned it, arguing from previous research and original experiments to the conclusion that ordinary people tend to "hold a naïve view of both colors and pains" (Sytsma 2012, p. 190). According to this Naïve View, ordinary people take "colors to be mind-independent qualities of worldly objects" and pains "to be mind-independent qualities of certain body parts" (Sytsma 2012, p. 188). The Naïve View offers an explanation of Sytsma and Machery's findings. Ordinary people thought the simple robot was incapable of feeling pain but not seeing red because they thought that it could see the mind-independent color inherent in the box in front of it, whereas they also thought it lacked the appropriate, fleshy body, in which a pain state might occur.[10] Sytsma (2012) offers three additional studies supporting the Naïve View. The first reveals that participants are more willing to attribute pain to someone who burns their bio-engineered, fleshy prosthetic hand, than to someone who burns their robotic, synthetic prosthetic hand, supporting the idea that people tend to view pain as a mind-independent quality of certain kinds of body parts. In the second, he finds that participants are just as willing to attribute the experience of seeing red to someone with robotic eyes as to someone with bio-engineered eyes, suggesting that bodily constitution doesn't matter for seeing red. In the third study, he shows that the results for pain generalize to robot agents, by showing that participants are more willing to attribute pain states to a robot agent with fleshy, bio-engineered hand than to a robot agent with hard, metallic hands.

While the Naïve View is similar to the Embodiment Hypothesis in advocating that considerations of physical makeup play an important role in ordinary attributions of some prototypical phenomenal mental states, it differs from the Embodiment Hypothesis in claiming that this is true only for pain states and other states that ordinary people regard as adhering in particular types of bodies. The Naïve View, like the Valence View, and contra the Embodiment Hypothesis, also maintains that ordinary people lack a concept of phenomenal consciousness, for at least two reasons. First, as Sytsma concludes:

> While philosophers tend to treat the qualities at issue for ascriptions of seeing red and feeling pain as mind-dependent qualia [...] lay people understand [these] two prototypical examples of (supposed) phenomenally conscious mental states in a way that is fundamentally different from the standard philosophical account. (Sytsma 2012, p. 195)

---

inflate the attributions of perceptual experience to robots in Sytsma and Machery's (2010) studies" (Fiala, Arico, and Nichols 2014, p. 39).

10 While the Naïve View doesn't explain Buckwalter and Phelan's (2013) findings, those findings are at least compatible with the Naïve View, since the Naïve View itself is consistent with a broadly functionalist picture, offering, as it does, only a metaphysical thesis about the kinds of things ordinary people take pains and colors to be.

Second, though not noted by Sytsma (2012), while a Naïve View may be plausible for the supposed phenomenal states of seeing red or feeling pain, it is implausible to suppose that other states that philosophers identify as prototypically phenomenal are thought by ordinary people to be mind-independent qualities of worldly objects. In what worldly object or part of the body would sadness reside, for example? What about a hallucination of a pink elephant? Thus, ordinary people do not think of all the states that philosophers group under the heading "phenomenally conscious mental states" in the same way.

In other papers, Sytsma and colleagues have deepened the case for the Naïve View of colors and pains. Sytsma (2010) included numerous findings that could be seen as consistent with the Naïve View. In one study, participants tended to answer in a way that suggested they think of the redness they experience when they see a ripe tomato as not in their minds, but out there, on the tomato, an objective property that is sure to be experienced in the same way by any normal-sighted individual. In another set of studies, participants tended to respond that two agents who share a body part (e.g., conjoined twins) experience the same pain when they injure their shared part, challenging the analytic philosopher of mind's conception of pain as a private mental state locked away in each individual's mind. Another set of studies found that participants were likely to judge there was an unfelt pain, when presented with vignettes describing seriously injured patients who reported they hadn't been aware of pain while watching an engrossing movie or reading a compelling book, suggesting that ordinary participants don't think of pain as a necessarily conscious state. Reuter and Sytsma (2020) deepened this last result through 17 additional studies, which demonstrated that ordinary participants are happy to say that people experience unfelt pains. In another vein of research, Reuter, Phillips, and Sytsma (2014) offered a series of studies suggesting that ordinary people think it's possible to hallucinate a pain – i.e., to have an experience as of a pain when no pain is, in fact, present. This accords with a perceptual model of pains, since perceptions are subject to an appearance-reality distinction, and it runs counter to the views of analytic philosophers of mind, such as Hillary Putnam, who claims that "any situation that a person cannot discriminate from a situation in which he himself has a pain *counts* as a situation in which he has a pain" (Putnam 1963, p. 218). An appearance-reality distinction for pain is further supported by an argument Reuter (2011) as well as Sytsma and Reuter (2017) make from their findings that ordinary English and German speakers preferentially use the phrase "having pain" (or its German analogue) to express mild pains and "feeling pain" (or one of its three German analogues) to express large pains. If we can take these attributions literally (as Sytsma and Reuter argue we can), then ordinary people seem to acknowledge pains you have but don't feel. In yet another project, Reuter, Sienhold, and Sytsma (2019) present a challenge to the "finger in mouth" argument against the Naïve View of Pain. According to that argument, if a pain is actually located in my finger (as the Naïve view would claim) and I put that finger in my mouth, then it should follow that I have a pain in my mouth. But it seems incorrect to say that I have a pain in my mouth in that situation. Reuter and colleagues contend that, even though it follows that one does have a pain in one's mouth in this situation, we would be hesitant to say that, because having a pain in a body part – like having tissue damage in a body part – tends to imply something (a pain) adhering in the substance of the body part, but the premises of the argument do not suggest that there is pain adhering in the mouth's substance. They provide evidence that, if you cancel these implications, people are happy to say there is a pain in the person's mouth. Finally, Kim and colleagues began to make the case that the naïve conception of pain is a cultural universal, by presenting data from two studies suggesting that Americans and South Koreans "overwhelmingly conceive of pains as bodily states" (Kim et al. 2016, p. 163).

At this point, proponents of the Naïve View have compiled a great deal of evidence for the claim that ordinary people sometimes think of pains as mind-independent qualities of certain body parts and a bit of evidence for the claim that they sometimes think of colors as mind-independent qualities of worldly objects. But what exactly is the scope of these claims? Is it simply that ordinary people *sometimes* think of pains and colors in a mind-independent way? Or is it the much stronger claim that ordinary people *only* think of pains and colors in this way? Or is it some middle view that is being suggested? Unfortunately, the above papers are not very clear on this point. Sytsma and Reuter (2017) is typical. In their conclusion, the authors claim that "the accumulated research suggests that people tend to conceive of pains not as mental states, but as bodily states" (Sytsma and Reuter 2017, p. 23), which seems to suggest a folk *tendency* towards the Naïve View, but to also leave open the possibility that people sometimes think of pains in other ways. In fact, this conclusion seems to be well supported by the data, since, in each study on pain attributions a (sometimes sizable) minority of participants seemed to endorse a mentalistic view of pain. However, Sytsma and Reuter also refer to the Naïve View as "*the* commonsense conception of pains" (Sytsma and Reuter 2017, p. 23, emphasis added). And if proponents of the Naïve View want to maintain, as Sytsma (2012, p. 183) did, that ordinary people "lack the philosophical concept of phenomenal consciousness", then they will have to adopt the additional assumption that the common-sense concept of pain they have identified operates to the exclusion of other, mentalistic conceptions of pain. But Sytsma and colleagues have not defended this additional assumption. And recent work by Borg, Salomons, and Hansen (2019) as well as Salomon and colleagues (2021) suggests considerable conceptual diversity in the ways in which ordinary people can and do think of pain.

2.3 Functional Considerations and the Agency Model

Though radically different in a variety of ways, the previous accounts of phenomenal state attribution are alike in offering definitive (though distinct) responses to the question of whether ordinary people possess a concept of phenomenal consciousness. They are also alike in applying only to attributions of states that philosophers would consider phenomenally conscious (or to subsets of those states), not to attributions of mental states in general. The views I will consider in this section differ from the previous ones on both counts. These views claim that we are not yet in a position to say whether people possess a concept of phenomenal consciousness. They also claim that our attributions of states that philosophers would consider phenomenally conscious are guided by the same sorts of considerations that guide our attributions of mental states in general. We'll consider the second of these claims first.

It is worth noting that, before the analytic philosopher's conception of phenomenal consciousness came to prominence, many philosophers tended to emphasize quite different aspects of our ordinary understanding of experiential states such as pain. These philosophers did not emphasize the, purportedly obvious, qualitative aspects of experiential states, instead they suggested that ordinary conceptions of experiential states (like other mental states) centered on the functional roles those states played. So, for example, Lewis contends that, "the definitive characteristic of any experience as such is its causal role. The definitive causal role of an experience is expressible by a finite set of conditions that specify its typical causes and its typical effects under various circumstances" (Lewis 1966, pp. 19 f.). And he goes on to assert that this is, "an account of the parlance common to all who believe that experiences are something or other real and that experiences are efficacious outside their own realm" (Lewis 1966, p. 20). Armstrong (1993, p. 79) suggests "that what we mean when we talk about the mind, or about particular mental processes, is nothing but the effect within a man of certain stimuli, and the cause within a man of certain responses". Braddon-Mitchell and Jackson offer a succinct, yet detailed, statement of this sort of view of ordinary mental state concepts:

> We distinguish the roles that matter for having a mind, and matter for being in one or another mental state, by drawing on what is common knowledge about mental states. We extract the crucial functional roles from the huge collection of what is pretty much common knowledge about pains, itches, beliefs, desires, intentions, and so on and so forth, focusing on what is most central to our conception of what a pain is, what a belief is, what it is to desire beer and all the rest. And we can group the common knowledge into the three clauses distinctive of the functionalist approach. The input clauses will contain sentences like "Bodily damage causes pain" and "Chairs in front of people in daylight cause perceptions as of chairs"; the output clauses will contain sentences like "Pain causes bodily movement that relieves the pain and minimizes damage" and "Desire for beer causes behavior that leads to beer consumption"; the internal clauses will contain sentences like "Perception as of beer in front of one typically causes belief in beer in front of one" and "Belief that if p then q typically causes belief that q on learning p". (Braddon-Mitchell and Jackson 1996, p. 46)

Philosophers who have introduced this conception of our ordinary understanding of mental states have sometimes used it to argue that the entities that occupy the functional roles specified by our common-sense understandings of mental states are brain states, and thereby defended an identity between minds and brains (as do Armstrong 1993 and Lewis 1966). As Fiala, Arico, and Nichols (2014, p. 45, fn. 3) point out, "it is doubtful whether ordinary people are committed (even implicitly) to a theory like this". However, those who suggest a functionalist answer to the question of what features lead people to attribute phenomenally conscious mental states do not attribute

this metaphysical theory to ordinary people. Instead, they use empirical methods to argue for two claims:
1. We have good evidence that people exploit information about the functional roles an entity can and does occupy in deciding what mental states (including phenomenally conscious states) it is (or is capable of) occupying, and
2. We have no good evidence that people exploit information that does not contribute to information about the functional roles an entity can and does occupy in deciding what mental states (including phenomenally conscious states) it is (or is capable of) occupying.[11]

If these two claims are correct, they contend, it would be unsurprising if it turned out that people's attributions of mental states – phenomenal states included – were typically mediated by their beliefs about an entity's functional capacities and the functional roles it currently occupies and nothing else.

Direct evidence for the first claim has been provided by Huebner (2010), who had participants assess their agreement with various mental state attributions to four sorts of entities: A normal human with a Central Nervous System (CNS); a human with a CPU in place of a CNS, a robot with a CNS in place of a CPU, and a robot with a CPU. In a reasonable attempt to standardize the functional capacities of each of these entities (and so to isolate the role of constitution) Huebner (2010, p. 138) described each as behaving "in every respect like a person on all psychological tests". He found that while people were somewhat inconsistent in their attributions of some paradigmatic phenomenal states to either the robot or the cyborgs, they strongly agreed with attributions of intentional (non-phenomenal) states to all four entities. This suggests that people exploit functional information in attributing intentional mental states, at least. Additional evidence that people exploit information about functional roles in deciding what mental states an agent is capable of occupying is provided by Buckwalter and Phelan (2014). They investigated people's attributions of the emotional states of happiness and sadness to embodied and disembodied agents across five studies. While they found no effect for whether or not the agent was embodied in any of these studies, each study revealed a strong effect for how the entity was functionally described. In their third study, for example, participants were presented with a vignette describing either a forest-dwelling hermit or an entirely disembodied forest-dwelling spirit. The agent was then described as responding to encroaching developers by breaking their equipment. Finally, the developers were either turned away by the retaliation or else the agent was driven out of the forest by the developers. As (the left half of) Figure 4 shows, participants strongly agreed with attributions of feelings of sadness to the embodied hermit *and* the disembodied spirit in the sad situation of being forced from

---

11 Information that contributes to information about functional roles is here understood to include information about functional roles and any other information that implies information about functional roles. For example, information about the purpose for which some devise was designed may imply information about the functional roles it might occupy.

their home, but not in the happy situation of driving away the developers. Conceptually equivalent results were found for happiness attributions.

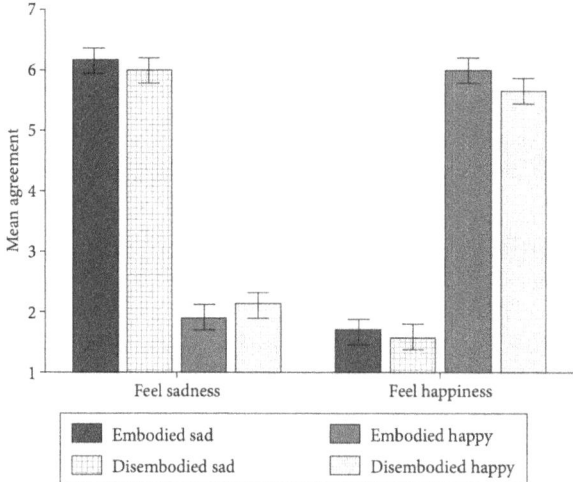

Figure 4: Assessments of attributions of feelings of sadness or happiness for an embodied or disembodied sophisticated entity in a happy or sad situation (from Buckwalter and Phelan 2014)

These results suggest that people exploit and, indeed, prioritize functional information in deciding what mental states – including phenomenally conscious mental states – an entity is occupying. But perhaps few would deny this claim. The functionalist's second claim, however, asserts something additional, specifically, that there isn't good evidence that people exploit information that does not contribute to information about functional roles in deciding what mental states an entity is capable of occupying. But how can the functionalist defend this claim in light of the studies above that seem to suggest that people exploit non-functional information about entities in deciding what mental states to attribute to them?

As should be clear from the previous discussion, functionalists have often answered this question by presenting empirical evidence of their own to support a functionalist interpretation of results initially interpreted as supporting an anti-functionalist account of mental state attributions. For example, in responding to Knobe and Prinz's (2008), Phelan, Arico, and Nichols (2013) found that participants were significantly more likely to choose "they" paraphrases for group names in sentences that attributed a phenomenal *or* non-phenomenal mental state to a group, compared with sentences that attributed a non-mental state. They argued from these results that attributions of mental states to groups are typically understood distributively, as attributions of states to the members that make up the relevant group *qua* members of that group. Such mental state ascriptions are thought to be appropriate, they contend, insofar as the relevant input, output, and internal clauses associated with the relevant mental state are satisfied and insofar as the mental state is saliently associated with the role of being a member of the relevant group. If correct, Knobe and Prinz's (2008) findings are explicable functionally, along the following lines: Participants found it appropriate to say that "Acme Corp. believes that its profit margin will soon increase" or "intends to release a new product this January" because they understood these as attributions to the employees that make up Acme Corp. (in their role as Acme Corp. employees) and they associated beliefs about profit margins and intentions to release products with the role of being a corporate employee. They also understood "Acme Corp. is getting depressed" or "is feeling excruciating pain" as attributions to the employees that make up Acme Corp. in their role as Acme Corp. employees, but they did not associate feelings of depression or excruciating pain with the role of being a corporate employee, and so they judged these attributions inappropriate.[12] Tellingly, Sytsma and Machery (2009) as well as Arico (2010) both found that the addition of a prepositional phrase further contextualizing a group phenomenal state attribution led participants to judge that attribution more natural. This is explicable on the current functionalist approach, since feelings of depression over a recent court ruling are more saliently associated with being a corporate employee than are simply free-floating feelings of depression.

Similarly, reconsider Sytsma and Machery's (2010) simple robot studies, now that we have a more fully articulated functionalist view on the table. Note that whether or not an entity can satisfy a specific, functional input condition depends not only on considerations of what is impinging on it, but also on considerations of that entity's functional capacities. Chairs in front of people in daylight are taken to cause perceptions as of chairs. But, of course, chairs in a forest devoid of anything but trees are not taken to cause perceptions as of chairs, even when the sun is shining. This is because trees are not generally regarded as the right sorts of entities to satisfy the functional input conditions for visual states and experiences. They lack the appropriate sensory apparatus. Sytsma and Machery may have inadvertently manipulated people's assumptions about the sort of sensory apparatus their simple robot was equipped with by putting it in the context of what appeared to be a psychological study that required it to see colors but not feel pains. This interpretation is supported by Buckwalter and Phelan's (2013) finding that when you make assumptions about design more explicit, by giving the robot a job it was built to perform, attributions of experiential, sensory states associated with that job go up.

In addition to this experimental work, proponents of the functionalist perspective have also offered non-experimental arguments for functionalist interpretations of purportedly anti-functionalist results. Consider, for example, Gray and colleagues' (2007a) finding that God was deemed less susceptible to experiences than a host of other en-

---

[12] If this functionalist explanation is correct, then we might expect participants to find attributions of phenomenal states to groups such as ISIS or the capital mob more appropriate, since phenomenal states are more saliently associated with being a member of such a group.

tities. Phelan and Buckwalter (2012) argue that this is likely the result of people's beliefs about the kinds of functional roles an all-powerful God might occupy, rather than their beliefs about God's physical constitution. After all, Gray and colleague's (2007b, p. 7) study describes God as "the creator of the universe and the ultimate source of knowledge, power, and love". It is unsurprising for purely functional reasons that such a God was deemed less susceptible to hunger, fear, pain, pleasure, and rage compared with a bunch of mere mortals.[13] Think of the many plausible input and internal clauses for "fear" to which a mere mortal is susceptible that make no sense to apply to an all-powerful, eternal deity.

To these arguments against anti-functionalist interpretations of specific experimental results, we can add a general consideration: It is unclear how experimental manipulations to an entity's physical constitution impact people's understanding of the sorts of functional clauses to which that entity is subject. Clearly, *some* manipulations to physical constitution influence what functional clauses we think an entity capable of satisfying. We accept that chairs in front of people in daylight cause perceptions as of chairs, but not if those people's eyes have been gouged out. We suppose that an eye (or some other sensory apparatus) is required for certain functional capacities related to visual states. So, those without eyes are incapable of satisfying this input clause and others like it, and, if satisfying such input clauses is requisite for having visual experiences, then those without eyes are incapable of having visual experiences on functional grounds. However, little is known about how ordinary people think specific aspects of physical constitution bear on functional capacities. Do people think fleshy hands are required to occupy the functional roles associated with haptic sensations? Do they think stomachs are required to occupy the functional roles associated with feeling hungry? We don't know the answer to questions such as these, so we don't know how manipulations of an entity's physical constitution influence ordinary people's understanding of that entity's capacity to fill various functional roles. Nor have experimental philosophers typically included probes to assess people's inferences about functional capacities.

An intriguing twist to these functional considerations is offered by Arico and colleagues (2011) as well as Fiala, Arico, and Nichols (2014), in the form of their model of mental state attribution, the Agency Model. Arico and colleagues (2011) subjected participants to a reaction time study in which they agreed or disagreed with various state attributions – including phenomenally conscious state attributions ("feels anger", "feels happy", "feels pain", "feels pride") – to various entities (mammals, birds, insects, plants, artifacts, vehicles, inanimate natural objects such as mountains, and moving natural objects such as clouds). They found that significantly more people responded affirmatively to phenomenal state attributions to insects than to plants, vehicles, or natural moving objects. They also found that it took participants longer to deny phenomenal states to insects than to vehicles or natural moving objects. On reflection, it may

---

[13] Malle (2019) points out that these were the highest loading experiential traits in Gray et al. (2007a).

seem somewhat surprising that people were willing to attribute states such as feeling anger or pride to insects at all. However, Arico and colleagues (2011) use these results to argue for a dual-process model of mental state attribution.[14] Fiala, Arico, and Nichols (2014) further support this dual process model through a wider survey of the literature on mental state attribution. According to these researchers' Agency Model, there is a high road and a low road to mental state attribution. When asked for their considered judgment about whether an entity has mental states (as in the previous vignette studies), people depart on the high road and end up producing a reasoned assessment based, in large part, on functional considerations. But, if forced to make a speeded judgment (as by Arico and colleagues 2011) or a judgment under cognitive load, people go down the low road and manifest a more fundamental tendency to attribute a whole host of mental states – including fairly complex emotional states – to any entity that triggers the "agent" concept, where an agent is any entity that possesses one or more simple features, including eyes, particular motion trajectories, or contingent interaction. This view doesn't contradict the Functionalist view (or other of the views we have considered), but it does entail that those views have missed a significant part of the story by focusing on higher level processing rather than more automatic judgments about mental state attribution.

The Functionalist and Agentic views are alike in claiming that our attributions of phenomenal states to other entities are guided by the same sorts of considerations that guide other of our mental state attributions. The functionalist emphasizes only functional considerations, whereas proponents of the agentic view suggest that simpler considerations come into play in more automatic, unreasoned responses. These views are also alike in not taking a stand on the question of whether ordinary people possess a concept of phenomenal consciousness. People may possess such a concept, but, if they do, it appears not to be reflected in their practice of mental state attribution.

2.4 Further Readings on the Experimental Philosophy of Conscious State Attribution

Sytsma (2014a) provides an excellent review of the literature on conscious state attribution up to 2014, which emphasizes different perspectives than the current review. A number of influential articles in the experimental philosophy of mind are also contained in Sytsma (2014b). Sytsma and Buckwalter (2016) includes a section on experimental philosophy of mind with several important chapters on different aspects of the literature. Wyrwa (2020) provides a careful analysis of most of the studies discussed in this section and suggests a number of important limitations of this research.

---

[14] Dual-process models posit two, overlapping processes for a particular domain of cognition, where one of the processes is automatic and fast, and the other is deliberate and slow. Such models have been offered to explain mental heuristics (Kahneman 2011), moral reasoning (Greene 2013), and other cognitive phenomena.

Huebner (2015) raises a compelling challenge directed at Buckwalter and Phelan (2013) and some other experimental philosophical work. He argues, inspired by Suppes (1962), that experimentalists must develop and defend "plausible models of the data that are collected, the scales that are used, and the statistical analyses that are carried out" (Huebner 2015, p. 3274). He further contends that experimental philosophers have not typically done this and that they are therefore unable, quite generally, to justify the conclusions they draw from their own data (presumably, Huebner includes his own experimental work in this assessment). However, Huebner also concedes that, since experimental philosophers use the same "methodologies that have been successful in cognitive and social psychology" (Huebner 2015, p. 3287), the problem he raises would apply to much of psychology.

Malle (2019) revisits the approach to thinking about mental state attribution pioneered by Gray, Gray, and Wegner (2007a). He points out a number of limitations of their original study and conducts his own study, addressing these limitations. Ultimately, he rejects Gray and colleagues' two-dimensional (agentic, experiential) view of the folk conception of mind, in favor of a three-dimensional account, encompassing an Affective Dimension, a Moral and Mental Regulation Dimension, and a Reality Interaction Dimension. He also develops a 20-item measure for dimensions of mind perception, which will prove useful in future research.

3 Further Topics

Other projects in the experimental philosophy of mind do not directly address either of our previous questions about phenomenal consciousness. One such project attempts to undercut a central discourse in consciousness studies altogether. As discussed previously, Chalmers (1995), among others, assumes that the experiential dimension of our mental lives is manifestly obvious. He goes on to argue that explaining this fact – that we have phenomenally conscious experiences – constitutes the "Hard Problem" of consciousness, since phenomenal consciousness is not explicable via the sorts of functional accounts that are common to the sciences. In arguing for this position, he asks that his readers

> note that even when we have explained the performance of all the cognitive and behavioral functions in the vicinity of experience [...] there may still remain a further unanswered question: *Why is the performance of these functions accompanied by experience?* A simple explanation of the functions leaves this question open [...]. (Chalmers 1995, p. 203)

Elsewhere, Chalmers (1996) and others have appealed to a version of the Modal Argument against physicalism to motivate the claim that functional explanations will leave questions about phenomenal experience open.[15] This argument relies on the intuition

---

15 See Kripke (1980, pp. 148–155).

that philosophical zombies – beings who lack experiential states but are physically and behaviorally just like us – are conceivable. It follows, these philosophers go on to argue, that philosophical zombies are possible, and, therefore, that experiential states are not identical to physical or functional states, since identity claims are necessarily true, if true at all. Thus, physicalism is false.

However, experimental philosophers have presented challenges for both the general intuition that a complete explanation of functions will leave open questions about experience *and* the Modal-Argument-supporting intuition that philosophical zombies are legitimately conceivable. For example, building on work from Fischer and Engelhardt (2016) as well as Fischer and colleagues (2021), Fischer and Sytsma (2021) argue that the source of (at least some) purported zombie intuitions is not of the appropriate cognitive sort to support the conclusion that philosophical zombies are legitimately conceivable. Specifically, Fischer and Sytsma argue that some of these intuitions are due to certain, shallow linguistic associations with the popular concept of a "zombie", and not to actual, considered judgments about whether something lacking experiential states could really be physically and behaviorally identical to us. They report a main effect whereby people are significantly more likely to agree with attributions of conscious states to "duplicates" who "are all dark inside", but are physically and behaviorally just like us, as opposed to "zombies" who "are all dark inside", but are physically and behaviorally just like us. Similarly, Díaz (2021) finds evidence that the general intuition that a complete explanation of functions will leave open questions about experience is not widespread. Further, he purports to demonstrate that when such intuitions do arise, they are often due to extraneous factors not related to consciousness, such as a general skepticism about whether science can formulate a complete explanation of functions. These studies undercut the Hard Problem's preeminent role in consciousness studies by providing evidence that many of the judgments supporting the problem are due to irrelevant factors and unconsidered assessments.

Other experimental projects investigate how conscious states relate to other states of philosophical interest. For example, Nahmias and colleagues (2020) found that people who responded yes to a dichotomous question about whether some humanoid robots could have conscious experiences were more likely to attribute free will and moral responsibility to those robots. This effect on will and responsibility attributions was mediated by attributions of emotional states, which led Nahmias and colleagues to conclude that,

> the ability to feel emotions and have things actually matter to the individual is important in Free Will attributions, yet the ability to have conscious sensations (e.g., the ability to experience sounds or smells) specifically plays no significant role. (Nahmias et al. 2020, p. 76)

In another project, Díaz and Reuter (2021) investigated the role of normative considerations on attributions of emotional states. They found that an agent described as behaving fearfully in response to a friendly dog was assessed as less afraid than an indistinguishable agent described as behaving fearfully in response to a fearsome dog. And they found that an agent who thinks herself happy in a possessive relationship was assessed as less happy than an indistinguishable agent who thinks herself happy in a non-possessive relationship. These findings seem to support the hypothesis from moral psychology that there are normative fittingness conditions for emotional states.

Eschewing the topic of phenomenal consciousness altogether, some experimentalists have also investigated attributions of attitudinal states. Intentional states have been the most extensive target of such investigations.[16] But recent work on belief attribution is also important. For example, a series of papers by John Turri and co-authors argue that the folk accept a voluntary view of belief, whereby people can come to believe some proposition simply because they want to believe it. Turri and colleagues (2018), for example, offer six studies exploring the dimensions of folk voluntarism. They find that people preferentially assent to attributions of voluntary "immediate" belief, even when they could attribute mere acceptance. The extent to which people are willing to make such attributions is influenced by factors such as the willfulness of the believing agent and the evidential domain to which the belief relates (i.e., inferential versus perceptual belief). Rose and colleagues (2017) report a robust cross-cultural finding that people prioritize sincere assertions of belief, over behavioral counter-evidence, when attributing belief.

Finally, we may ask how people conceive of the targets of their mental state attributions. Strohminger and colleagues (2017) summarize research suggesting a bifurcated view of other minds. People seem to think some mental traits and attributes are more authentic than others, such that we can refer to a "true self", the aspect of a person that is who they really are, hiding under the superficial self an individual presents to the world. This research also suggests that we have a bias in attributing mental states to the true self; we tend to think that the true self is morally good, such that even though a person may behave in immoral ways, deep down, they know their behavior is wrong and want to do better (for whatever we individually think it is to do better). But if we conceive of others as consisting of a superficial and a true self, then, for any belief, desire, or feeling we might attribute to another, we might also attribute that belief, desire, or feeling's opposite to that other's true self. And this, indeed, will complicate our picture of mental state attribution.

Bibliography

Arico, Adam (2010): "Folk psychology, consciousness, and context effects", *Review of Philosophy and Psychology* 1 (3), pp. 371–393.

Arico, Adam, Brian Fiala, Robert Goldberg, and Shaun Nichols (2011): "The folk psychology of consciousness", *Mind & Language* 26 (3), pp. 327–352.

Armstrong, David (1993): *A materialist theory of the mind*. 2nd edition, with new preface. London: Routledge.

---

16 See Cova (2016) for a useful review.

Block, Ned (1978): "Troubles with functionalism", in: Wade Savage (Ed.): *Perception and cognition. Issues in the foundations of psychology*. Minneapolis: University of Minnesota Press, pp. 261–326.

Block, Ned (1995): "On a confusion about a function of consciousness", *Behavioral and brain sciences* 18 (2), pp. 227–247.

Borg, Emma, Tim Salomons, and Nathaniel Hansen (2019): "The meaning of pain expressions and pain communication", in: Simon van Rysewyk (Ed.): *Meanings of pain*. Cham: Springer, pp. 261–282.

Braddon-Mitchell, David and Frank Jackson (1996): *Philosophy of mind and cognition*. Oxford: Blackwell.

Buckwalter, Wesley and Mark Phelan (2013): "Function and feeling machines. A defense of the philosophical conception of subjective experience", *Philosophical Studies* 166 (2), pp. 349–361.

Buckwalter, Wesley and Mark Phelan (2014): "Phenomenal consciousness disembodied", in: Justin Sytsma (Ed.): *Advances in experimental philosophy of mind*. London: Bloomsbury, pp. 45–74.

Cappelen, Herman (2012): *Philosophy without intuitions*. Oxford: Oxford University Press.

Carruthers, Peter (2010): "Introspection. Divided and partly eliminated", *Philosophy and Phenomenological Research* 80 (1), pp. 76–111.

Carruthers, Peter (2013): *The opacity of mind. An integrative theory of self-knowledge*. Oxford: Oxford University Press.

Chalmers, David (1995): "Facing up to the problem of consciousness", *Journal of Consciousness Studies* 2 (3), pp. 200–219.

Climenhaga, Nevin (2018): "Intuitions are used as evidence in philosophy", *Mind* 127 (505), pp. 69–104.

Cova, Florian (2016): "The folk concept of intentional action. Empirical approaches", in: Justin Sytsma and Wesley Buckwalter (Eds.): *A companion to experimental philosophy*. Hoboken: Wiley, pp. 121–141.

Díaz, Rodrigo (2021): "Do people think consciousness poses a hard problem? Empirical evidence on the meta-problem of consciousness", *Journal of Consciousness Studies* 28 (2–4), pp. 55–75.

Díaz, Rodrigo (2022): "Emotions and the body. Testing the subtraction argument", *Philosophical Psychology* 35 (1), pp. 47–65.

Díaz, Rodrigo, and Kevin Reuter (2021): "Feeling the right way. Normative influences on people's use of emotion concepts", *Mind & Language* 36 (3), pp. 451–470.

Fiala, Brian, Adam Arico, and Shaun Nichols (2014): "You, robot", in: Edouard Machery and Elizabeth O'Neill (Eds.): *Current controversies in experimental philosophy*. New York: Routledge, pp. 31–47.

Fischer, Eugen, and Justin Sytsma (2021): "Zombie intuitions", *Cognition* 215, 104807.

Fischer, Eugen, and Paul Engelhardt (2016): "Intuitions' linguistic sources. Stereotypes, intuitions, and illusions", *Mind & Language* 31 (1), pp. 67–103.

Fischer, Eugen, Paul Engelhardt, and Justin Sytsma (2021): "Inappropriate stereotypical inferences? An adversarial collaboration in experimental ordinary language philosophy", *Synthese* 198, pp. 10127–10168.

Forstmann, Matthias, and Pascal Burgmer (forthcoming): "The Cartesian folk theater. People conceptualize consciousness as a spatio-temporally localized process in the human brain", *Journal of Experimental Psychology – General*.

Gazzaniga, Michael (1995): "Consciousness and the cerebral hemispheres", in: Michael Gazzaniga (Ed.): *The cognitive neurosciences*. Boston: The MIT Press, pp. 1391–1400.

Gazzaniga, Michael (2000): "Cerebral specialization and inter-hemispheric communication", *Brain* 123 (7), pp. 1293–1326.

Gray, Heather, Kurt Gray, and Daniel Wegner (2007a): "Dimensions of mind perception", *Science* 315 (5812), p. 619.

Gray, Heather, Kurt Gray, and Daniel Wegner (2007b): "Supporting Online Material for 'Dimensions of Mind Perception'", *Science* 315. https://www.science.org/doi/suppl/10.1126/science.1134475/suppl_file/gray.som.pdf, last accessed May 19, 2023.

Greene, Joshua (2013): *Moral tribes. Emotion, reason, and the gap between us and them*. New York: Penguin.

Huebner, Bryce (2010): "Commonsense concepts of phenomenal consciousness. Does anyone care about functional zombies?", *Phenomenology and the Cognitive Sciences* 9 (1), pp. 133–155.

Huebner, Bryce (2015): "What is a philosophical effect? Models of data in experimental philosophy", *Philosophical Studies* 172 (12), pp. 3273–3292.

Huebner, Bryce, Michael Bruno, and Hagop Sarkissian (2009): "What does the nation of China think about phenomenal states?", *Review of Philosophy and Psychology* 1 (2), pp. 225–243.

Jackson, Frank (1986): "What Mary didn't know", *The Journal of Philosophy* 83 (5), pp. 291–295.

Kahneman, Daniel (2011): *Thinking, fast and slow*. New York: Farrar, Straus, and Giroux.

Kim, Hyo-Eun, Nina Poth, Kevin Reuter, and Justin Sytsma (2016): "Where is your pain? A cross-cultural comparison of the concept of pain in Americans and South Koreans", *Studia Philosophica Estonica* 9 (1), pp. 136–169.

Knobe, Joshua (2003): "Intentional action and side effects in ordinary language", *Analysis* 63 (179), pp. 190–194.

Knobe, Joshua (2008): "Can a robot, an insect or God be aware?", *Scientific American* 19, pp. 68–71.

Knobe, Joshua, and Jesse Prinz (2008): "Intuitions about consciousness. Experimental studies", *Phenomenology and the Cognitive Sciences* 7 (1), pp. 67–83.

Kripke, Saul (1980): *Naming and necessity*. Cambridge: Harvard University Press.

Lewis, David (1966): "An argument for the identity theory", *Journal of Philosophy* 63 (1), pp. 17–25.

Malle, Bertram (2019): "How many dimensions of mind perception really are there?", in: Ashok Goel, Colleen Seifert, and Christian Freska (Eds.): *Proceedings of the 41st annual meeting of the cognitive science society*. Montreal: Cognitive Science Society, pp. 2268–2274.

Nado, Jenny (2016): "The intuition deniers", *Philosophical Studies* 173 (3), pp. 781–800.

Nagel, Thomas (1974): "What is it like to be a bat?", *The Philosophical Review* 83 (4), pp. 435–450.

Nahmias, Eddy, Corry Allen, and Bradley Loveall (2020): "When do robots have free will? Exploring the relationships between (attributions of) consciousness and free will", in: Bernard Feltz, Marcus Missal, and Andrew Sims (Eds.): *Free will, causality, and neuroscience*. Leiden: Brill, pp. 57–80.

Nisbett, Richart, and Timothy Wilson (1977): "Telling more than we can know. Verbal reports on mental processes", *Psychological Review* 84 (3), pp. 231–259.

Phelan, Mark, Adam Arico, and Shaun Nichols (2013): "Thinking things and feeling things. On an alleged discontinuity in the folk metaphysics of mind", *Phenomenology and the Cognitive Sciences* 12 (4), pp. 703–725.

Phelan, Mark, and Wesley Buckwalter (2012): "Analytic functionalism and mental state attribution", *Philosophical Topics* 40 (2), pp. 129–154.

Putnam, Hillary (1963): "Brains and behavior", in: Ronald Butler (Ed.): *Analytical philosophy. Second series*. Oxford: Blackwell, pp. 24–36.

Reuter, Kevin (2011): "Distinguishing the appearance from the reality of pain", *Journal of Consciousness Studies* 18 (9–10), pp. 94–109.

Reuter, Kevin, Dustin Phillips, and Justin Sytsma (2014): "Hallucinating pain", in: Justin Sytsma (Ed.): *Advances in experimental philosophy of mind*. London: Bloomsbury, pp. 75–100.

Reuter, Kevin, Michael Sienhold, and Justin Sytsma (2019): "Putting pain in its proper place", *Analysis* 79 (1), pp. 72–82.

Robbins, Philip, and Anthony Jack (2006): "The phenomenal stance", *Philosophical Studies* 127 (1), pp. 59–85.

Rose, David, Edouard Machery, Stephen Stich, Mario Alai, Adriano Angelucci, Renatas Berniūnas, Emma Buchtel, Amita Chatterjee, Hyundeuk Cheon, In-Rae Cho, Daniel Cohnitz, Florian Cova, Vilius Dranseika, Ángeles Eraña Lagos, Laleh Ghadakpour, and Maurice Grinberg (2017): "Behavioral circumscription and the folk psychology of belief. A study in ethno-mentalizing", *Thought* 6 (3), pp. 193–203.

Salomons, Tim, Richard Harrison, Nat Hansen, James Stazicker, Astrid Grith Sorensen, Paula Thomas, and Emma Borg (2021): "Is pain 'all in your mind'? Examining the general public's views of pain", *Review of Philosophical Psychology* 13, pp. 683–698.

Strohminger, Nina, Joshua Knobe, and George Newman (2017): "The true self. A psychological concept distinct from the self", *Perspectives on Psychological Science* 12 (4), pp. 551–560.

Sytsma, Justin (2009): "Phenomenological obviousness and the new science of consciousness", *Philosophy of Science* 76 (5), pp. 958–969.

Sytsma, Justin (2010): "Folk psychology and phenomenal consciousness", *Philosophy Compass* 5 (8), pp. 700–711.

Sytsma, Justin (2012): "Revisiting the valence account", *Philosophical Topics* 40 (2), pp. 179–198.

Sytsma, Justin (2014a): "Attributions of consciousness", *WIREs Cognitive Science* 5 (6), 635–648.

Sytsma, Justin (Ed.) (2014b): *Advances in experimental philosophy of mind.* Oxford: Bloomsbury.

Sytsma, Justin, and Edouard Machery (2009): "How to study folk intuitions about consciousness", *Philosophical Psychology* 22 (1), pp. 21–35.

Sytsma, Justin, and Edouard Machery (2010): "Two conceptions of subjective experience", *Philosophical Studies* 151 (2), pp. 299–327.

Sytsma, Justin, and Kevin Reuter (2017): "Experimental philosophy of pain", *Journal of Indian Council of Philosophical Research* 34 (3), pp. 611–628.

Takahashi, Hideyuki, Midori Ban, and Minoru Asada (2016): "Semantic differential scale method can reveal multi-dimensional aspects of mind perception", *Frontiers in Psychology* 7, 1717.

Turri, John (2018): "Choosing and refusing. Doxastic voluntarism and folk psychology", *Philosophical Studies* 175 (10), pp. 2507–2537.

Weisman, Kara, Carol Dweck, and Ellen Markman (2017): "Rethinking people's conceptions of mental life", *Proceedings of the National Academy of Sciences of the United States of America* 114 (43), pp. 11374–11379.

Williamson, Timothy (2007): *The philosophy of philosophy.* New York: Routledge.

Part 3: Topics from Practical Philosophy

Justin Bruner
Experimental Political Philosophy: Social Contract

Abstract: This chapter provides an overview of recent work in experimental political philosophy. It begins with a brief discussion of methodology: unlike many areas of experimental philosophy, experimentalists in political philosophy often draw on laboratory protocols from economics and forgo questionnaires and vignettes. The chapter then turns to recent experimental work on the social contract and suggest further avenues for exploration.

Keywords: Experimental Philosophy; Game Theory; Political Philosophy; Rational Choice; Social Contract

1 Introduction

Like many areas of experimental philosophy, experimental political philosophy benefits directly from theoretical and empirical work done in neighboring disciplines. Specifically, philosophically minded economists have made important contributions to both political theory (Roemer 1996, 1998; Fleurbaey 2008; Binmore 2006; Basu 2000; Skaperdas 1992) and experimental political philosophy (Powell and Wilson 2008, Smith, Skarbek, and Wilson 2012). Furthermore, interdisciplinary work at the border of economics and philosophy lends itself to a level of formal rigor that is somewhat uncommon in philosophy. For instance, economists and philosophers have developed game-theoretic models of the state of nature (Chung 2015, Vanderschraaf 2006, Skaperdas 1992, Bruner 2020, Kogelmann and Ogden 2018), drawn on axiomatic bargaining theory to model the social contract (Gauthier 1986, Vanderschraaf 2018), and employed mathematical models of learning and cultural evolution to better understand the emergence of conventions and social norms (Binmore 2006, Sugden 1986, Bicchieri 2004, Skyrms 1996, Basu 2000). These formal tools not only allow philosophers to get a better handle on central issues and thought experiments, but models yield concrete predictions that can then be tested in the experimental laboratory. In this sense, experimental political philosophy benefits from a rich and generative theory (the theory of rational choice) and much of the work in experimental political philosophy reflects this.

This brings us to yet another way in which experimental political philosophy differs from more traditional avenues of experimental philosophy. Experimental political

Note: Thanks to the editors for detailed feedback on a previous draft.

philosophers often draw on the methods and tools of experimental economics.[1] This is a departure from standard practice, as most experimental philosophers rely on the protocols and techniques common to psychology. To briefly illustrate the difference, a psychologist might present subjects with a vignette, inviting their subjects to imagine a scenario and then elicit the subjects' opinion or intuitions. Experimental economists try to avoid hypotheticals and instead design an experiment which – to the best of the experimenter's ability – places the individual in the scenario of interest. So, for instance, a psychologist may present the subject with a short story about a community tasked with monitoring a common pool resource. They would then ask the subject to report how they believe they would behave in such circumstances. Economists, on the other hand, would attempt to recreate the strategic scenario of interest in the lab and then observe how individuals actually behave. This is done by ensuring subjects participate in a game or decision problem where real money is at stake. That is, payment is tied to behavior in the lab in a way that reflects the underlying theory being tested. The difference in experimental practices can be explained by the fact that economists are often interested in testing the predictions of their core theory: rational choice theory. Rational choice theory makes predictions about how individuals behave, not how they believe they will behave.

It is thus unsurprising that experimental political philosophers have by and large adopted experimental methods from economics: much work in political philosophy draws on rational choice theory, and those political philosophers most inclined to run experiments tend to also be disposed to the "economic approach". That said, there is room for both kinds of experiments, and recently questionnaires have explored pressing issues in analytic political philosophy such as desert (Frieman and Nichols 2011) and relational egalitarianism (Inoue et al. 2019). Since survey work is less prevalent, we will focus on much of the work done by economists and economic-minded philosophers (although some survey-based experiments will be considered). This is not to say that one method is better than the other, just that experimentally minded political philosophers have tended to draw on techniques from economics.

2 The Social Contract

At its core, we can conceive of the social contract as a "system of cooperation designed to advance the good of those taking part in it" (Rawls 1999, p. 4). Mutual benefit is possible because the contract comes with a set of rules or shared understandings that "allow the citizens of a society to coordinate their efforts" (Binmore 2006, p. 3). Even at this rather abstract level, a number of crucial questions immediately come to mind. We outline three central concerns here (stability, efficiency, and fairness) and

---

[1] For an overview of the methods of experimental economics and the ways in which they can inform philosophy and experimental philosophy, see Rubin, O'Connor, and Bruner (2019).

address each in more detail (with reference to the experimental literature) in the following sections.

First: What, if anything, ensures citizens adhere to the rules that govern the "system of cooperation"? This is known as the *problem of compliance* and gets to the heart of a central topic in political philosophy: the stability of the social contract. Second: What is the relationship between efficiency and the social contract? While successful social cooperation makes possible a better life for all compared to the situation where each were to live solely by their own efforts, alternative arrangements could nonetheless allow for an *even better* life for all involved. What are the prospects of an efficient social contract? We shall refer to this as the *problem of efficiency*. Finally, we come to the *problem of fairness*: While all benefit from social cooperation, there is a conflict of interest "since persons are not indifferent as to how the greater benefits produced by their collaboration are distributed" (Rawls 1999, p. 4). This is one of the most discussed problems in the literature and not surprisingly much of the empirical literature on the social contract speaks to the problem of fairness.

2.1 Stability

Individuals must have incentive to adhere to the rules governing social cooperation. Yet compliance is difficult to achieve: There are scenarios where citizens may stand to gain from violating the terms of the social contract. We can think of this scenario as a game (Vanderschraaf 2018, Kavka 1986, Gauthier 1986). Specifically, individuals can restrain their behavior (comply) or flout the rules (defect). Restraint is individually costly but to the benefit of one's counterpart. And while flouting the rules is often in one's immediate material interests, mutual compliance is preferable to mutual defection. This strategic scenario, broadly speaking, maps on to the so-called *prisoner's dilemma*. In the prisoner's dilemma, two criminals are captured by the authorities. Each accomplice can either remain silent (Cooperate) or "rat out" (Defect) their counterpart. If both prisoners select to keep quiet they both receive a light sentence. If one prisoner remains quiet while his colleague sings, the former is given a heavy sentence, while the latter is set free. Alternatively, if both confess to the authorities, they are both given a moderate sentence. Table 1 represents this strategic scenario game-theoretically with a payoff table. Alf selects a row (Cooperate or Defect), while Betty picks a column. Numbers in the cells represent ordinal utilities associated with each of the four possible outcomes. So, for example, the outcome where Alf selects to Cooperate while Betty plays Defect ensures Alf ends up with a utility of one and Betty a utility of four.

Note that in the prisoner's dilemma, defection strictly dominates compliance, but mutual defection is inefficient. The pressing question, then, is: How can we ensure widespread compliance? One obvious solution is the creation of a state with a monopoly on the use of force. This entity then ensures that violators of the terms of social cooperation are punished. This essentially transforms the prisoner's dilemma into what is often referred to as a prisoner's delight (see Table 1). With the introduction of punishment, compliance now strictly dominates defection (Skyrms 2007).

Table 1: Prisoner's dilemma (top) and prisoner's delight (bottom)

		Betty	
		Comply (Cooperate)	Flout (Defect)
Alf	Comply (Cooperate)	2, 2	1, 4
	Flout (Defect)	4, 1	1, 1
		Betty	
		Comply (Cooperate)	Flout (Defect)
Alf	Comply (Cooperate)	2, 2	1, 1
	Flout (Defect)	1, 1	0, 0

Alternatively, what are the prospects of addressing the compliance problem when no third-party is available? Answering this question is a driving force in much of the literature. One natural thought is that community enforcement (via peer-to-peer punishment) can secure high levels of compliance. Peer-to-peer punishment has the same effect as state-administered punishment (the dilemma is transformed into a delight) but importantly does not require the apparatus of the state. That said, administering punishment is costly as the punisher must spend time and effort monitoring the behavior of others. Furthermore, risk of retaliation is omnipresent. Yet costly punishment of this kind has been observed time and time again in the laboratory, even occurring in one-shot interactions where punishers have no self-interested reason to discipline their counterpart. Yet while many experimental subjects do appear to have a proclivity to punish rule-breakers, some have argued that peer-to-peer punishment is of limited importance in enforcing norms in actual decentralized communities (Francesco Guala 2012, provides a compelling critique of this literature). Finally, recent experimental work on anti-social punishment calls into question the effectiveness of peer-to-peer punishment. An Experiment by Nikos Nikiforakis (2008) indicates that punishment no longer solves the compliance problem when free-riders can retaliate and "counter-punish". Cross-cultural work by Benedikt Herrmann, Christian Thöni, and Simon Gächter (2008) finds that a sizable fraction of participants direct punishment at both contributors and defectors alike.

Luckily, costly peer-to-peer punishment is not the only viable solution to the compliance problem. One popular and often discussed method is direct reciprocity. Consider Amir and Bing, who both decide to comply with the rules so long as their counterpart does so as well. Amir (Bing) has incentive to continually comply because non-compliance will be met with by non-compliance by Bing (Amir) in future rounds. Thus, the "shadow of the future" ensures continued compliance. This informal argument is supported by modeling work (see the so-called *Folk Theorem*)[2] as well as experimental work on the repeated prisoner's dilemma. On the latter point, Pedro Bo (2005) finds a positive correlation between the continuation probability and level of cooperation in the laboratory. However, cooperation is less likely for larger groups. Urs Fischbacher, Simon Gächter, and Ernst Fehr (2001) find that universal defection occurs in the lab when groups of individuals must play the N-person prisoner's dilemma, despite the fact that subjects repeatedly interact with the same set of participants. Some, such as Herbert Gintis and Samuel Bowles, take this to mean that direct reciprocity on its own is not enough to achieve a stable social contract. Other mechanisms, such as peer-to-peer punishment or group competition, must be present (Bowles and Gintis 2011).

There are a host of other social mechanisms that have been thoroughly explored in the laboratory, such as reputation tracking (Seinen and Schram 2006, van Apeldoorn and Schram 2016) where individuals can observe their counterpart's dealings with others before they play the prisoner's dilemma and partner choice (Barclay and Raihani 2016, Stromland, Tjotta, and Torsvik 2018) where individuals can continue to interact with cooperative partners and sever those who attempt to exploit them. In general, cooperation is possible if the social benefits of compliance are directed at like-minded individuals. This intuition has been formalized by William Hamilton (1964) and is known as *Hamilton's Rule*, which stipulates that compliance outperforms defection when $rb > c$. That is, cooperators secure a higher payoff than defectors when the cost of compliance (c) is less than the weighted communal benefit (rb). The crucial parameter r is known as the correlation coefficient and captures the extent to which interactions are correlated – that is, the probability benefits of compliance are directed at fellow compliers. Many purported solutions to the prisoner's dilemma work because they, at base, ensure r is sufficiently high. As a result, Hamilton's Rule lays out general conditions for a stable social contract (Skyrms 2014).

2.2 Efficiency

Ideally, citizens want to adopt an efficient system of cooperation. But this might be more difficult to do than it initially appears. Why? Kenneth Binmore (2004, sec. 4.6) provides an insightful discussion of efficiency, drawing on the so-called *stag hunt game*. In its simplest form, the stag hunt involves two hunters. If both make efforts to hunt the stag, the hunt is a success and they split a large bounty. However, hunting stag comes with great risk because both hunters must participate in the endeavor for it to be a success. Hunting stag independently is a waste of time. Complicating this scenario is the fact that each hunter can independently track down and capture a hare. Thus, hunting stag is risky (but highly rewarding) while hunting hare is safe (but less rewarding). This strategic scenario is represented game-theoretically in Table 2. Once again, num-

---

[2] See Fudenberg and Tirole (2000, sec. 5.1) for more on the Folk Theorem.

bers correspond to ordinal utility. Both prefer mutual stag hunting to mutual hare hunting (three is greater than two), but hunting hare is preferred to unilaterally hunting stag (two is greater than zero). Binmore argues that the stag hunt nicely captures the strategic considerations involved with institutional reform (that is, the process of moving from an inefficient system of cooperation to a stable and efficient system of cooperation). One can expend time and effort advocating for reform or instead stick with the status quo. Reform is no guarantee but, if successfully pulled off, is to the benefit of all. Hence, attempting to bring about an efficient social contract is a risky endeavor. Remaining at the middling status quo (hunt hare) is sub-optimal but does not require citizens to go out on a limb.

Put in these terms, successful institutional reform involves a move from the hare-hunting equilibrium to the stag-hunting equilibrium. Is such a transition possible? A number of experiments have explored the stag hunt game, with disappointing results. Van Huyck, Battalio, and Beil (1990) found many experimental subjects inevitably end up at the sub-optimal hare-hunting equilibrium, and once there, continue to play hare for the foreseeable future.[3] That said, the picture changes if individuals are allowed to communicate prior to playing the stag hunt. Gary Charness (2000) as well as Kenneth Clark, Stephen Kay, and Martin Sefton (2000) find that when communication is permitted individuals signal their desire to play stag and can overcome the sub-optimal hare-hunting equilibrium. Pre-game communication allows citizens to coordinate on their desired system of cooperation, thus ensuring the efficiency of the social contract. Yet communication is not the only way to grease the wheels of institutional reform. As we saw in the previous section, correlation is key. If reformers are more likely than chance to find one another, stag hunting will soon thrive. This insight is explored by Brian Skyrms (2004), and a number of different correlative mechanisms are shown to lead to efficient outcomes in social contract games such as the stag hunt.

Table 2: The Stag Hunt Game

		Betty	
		Stag	Hare
Alf	Stag	3, 3	0, 2
	Hare	2, 0	2, 2

2.3 Fairness

Our final concern pertains to the terms of social cooperation – that is, the content of the social contract. There are a host of stable and efficient contracts. Which, if any, are

---

[3] Although see Rankin, Van Huyck, and Battalio (2000), who find that individuals are able to coordinate on playing stag.

fair? And what principles should regulate social cooperation? Following Brian Barry (1989), we consider two related but distinct approaches: justice as mutual advantage and justice as impartiality. According to the former, justice is the result of a bargain among rational individuals. David Gauthier (1986) is a lodestar of this tradition. Alternatively, thinkers in the justice-as-impartiality persuasion are wed to the idea that the principles of justice are those that will be agreed to in an original position. To ensure some level of impartiality, individuals will often be denied crucial information about themselves in the original position. We discuss each approach in what follows, with special focus on related laboratory experiments.

2.3.1 Mutual Advantage and Bargaining

David Gauthier (1986) has forcefully argued the social contract should be conceived of and modeled as a bargaining problem. Following Richard Braithwaite (1954), Gauthier draws on John Nash's pathbreaking work on axiomatic bargaining theory. A bargaining problem is defined as a feasible set – a collection of utility pairs – and a disagreement point specifying the utility for both agents should bargaining break down. A bargaining solution takes as input a bargaining problem and outputs an element of the feasible set. Normative criteria are then invoked to evaluate various solutions. For instance, if the selected utility pair is always efficient, then the solution satisfies the *Pareto* condition. Gauthier, contra Nash, argues for the so-called minimax relative concessions solution, which selects the element of the feasible set that minimizes the maximum concession made by either bargainer.[4] The relative merits of minimax relative concessions and competing solutions is the subject of ongoing debate (see Vanderschraaf 2018, Moehler 2018, Gauthier 1993, Bruner 2021, Young 1995).

Which solution do experimental subjects find most compelling? Kenneth Binmore and colleagues (1993) designed an experiment where individuals were repeatedly confronted by bargaining problems. Their results seem to provide strong evidence for the so-called Nash bargaining solution, which selects the utility pair that maximizes the product of the bargainer's utility. Specifically, subjects initially primed on competing solutions (egalitarian, minimax relative concessions) slowly gravitate toward the Nash solution and ultimately report that those agreements approximating the Nash solution strike them as fair. While this experiment is highly suggestive, additional work comparing bargaining solutions is needed. Furthermore, no extant experiments interrogate subject's attitudes toward the axioms themselves. An experiment exploring how compelling subjects find both agreements approximating various solutions and axioms

---

[4] This is a variant of the better known Kalai-Smorodinsky solution (Kalai and Smorodinsky 1975). Interestingly, neither Gauthier's favored solution nor the Kalai-Smorodinsky solution satisfy the Pareto axiom when there are more than two bargainers.

underlying these solutions would allow subjects to engage in a kind of reflective equilibrium.

Before we turn to justice as impartiality, it is worth mentioning that Gauthier (1986) also has a solution to the compliance problem. Recall that agreement does not entail widespread compliance: Since everyone has incentive to flout the rules on occasion, widespread compliance is no guarantee. Gauthier's solution to this problem is intriguing, although, as we shall see, it is effective because it ensures – à la Hamilton (1964) – that the benefits of cooperation are more likely than chance to go to others willing to cooperate. Gauthier imagines two kinds of individuals, straightforward maximizers and constrained maximizers. Straightforward maximizers embody the orthodox account of rationality (*homo economicus*) and defect in the one-shot prisoner's dilemma. Constrained maximizers, on the other hand, constrain their behavior (and thus comply in the prisoner's dilemma) when they have reason to suspect that they are interacting with a fellow constrained maximizer. If they do not have such assurances, then they defect in the prisoner's dilemma. Constrained maximizers outperform straightforward maximizers when individuals are transparent (that is, one can determine the strategic type of one's counterpart with ease). However, transparency is obviously not possible in many circumstances. Instead, individuals are translucent, meaning constrained maximizers may often, but not always, correctly identify their counterpart as a fellow constrained maximizer.[5] Gauthier shows that under certain conditions constrained maximizers secure a higher expected payoff than straightforward maximizers.[6] It should now be somewhat clear why translucency is not a distinct solution. Translucency is effective because it allows constrained maximizers to direct their cooperative efforts at other constrained maximizers. That is, it ensures cooperation is more likely to be met with cooperation in the prisoner's dilemma, thereby satisfying Hamilton's inequality $rb > c$.

That said, it is unclear whether Gauthier's account is effective because the expected utility secured by constrained maximizers crucially hinges on just how difficult it is to determine another's strategic type. This has prompted a number of studies investigating the extent to which individuals can successfully predict the strategic behavior of their counterpart. The evidence is mixed. Robert Frank, Thomas Gilovich, and Dennis Regan (1993) find evidence supporting the claim that individuals can discern the cooperative intentions of their partner. Following up on this, Brosig (2002) finds cooperators are likely to identify one another but only if ample time for verbal communication is allowed. Contra these findings, Axel Ockenfels and Reinhard Selten (2000) uncover that individuals are only slightly better than chance. Overall, it appears the empirical literature weakly supports the claim that individuals are discerning. However, it is unclear

---

[5] See also Robert Frank's (1986) account of the strategic role of the emotions.
[6] Gauthier (1986) spells these conditions in *Morals by Agreement*, although see Franssen (1994) for a more careful game-theoretic treatment.

whether the level of translucency – if any – uncovered in the lab is enough to ensure that constrained maximizers outperform straightforward maximizers.

2.3.2 Justice as Impartiality

Principles of justice are those that would be selected in some privileged choice situation (an "original position"), and defenders of "justice as impartiality" contend that the circumstances of choice must be engineered so as to ensure some level of impartiality. John Harsanyi (1953) and John Rawls (1971) both famously considered decisions being made from behind a veil of ignorance.[7] Of course, Harsanyi and Rawls have slightly different articulations of the veil. Harsanyi's equiprobability model assigns an equal chance to being any member of society. Rawls, on the other hand, considers choice under uncertainty: Individuals are unable to assign probabilities to the various outcomes. These differences have real purchase. On Harsanyi's veil, rational individuals gravitate to social states that maximize average utility. According to Rawls, individuals behind his version of the veil will be attracted to more egalitarian arrangements (and to be precise, they will endorse the *difference principle*, which dictates that inequalities are justified insofar as they are to the benefit of the worst off). As Michael Moehler (2018) has convincingly argued, different articulations of the veil track the different moral commitments of the authors. We do not consider which formulation of the veil is best, but instead, discuss empirical work done on impartial decision-making.

The first systematic empirical study of the veil was conducted by two political scientists, Norman Frohlich and Joe Oppenheimer (1987). Frohlich and Oppenheimer invited students into the experimental lab and split them into small groups. Each group was then presented with several distributive principles. The principles were explained to them, and example distributions were provided. The individuals were then given time to discuss the various principles and, at the end of the discussion period, select one principle as a group. Experimental subjects were told ahead of time that the principle selected by their group will be used to determine their income (payment) in the experiment. Importantly, individuals were not told where on the income distribution they would land.

Frohlich and Oppenheimer observed several noteworthy things. First, impartiality appears to promote consensus. The principle selected by the group was, in almost all cases, done so unanimously. This speaks to the role impartiality plays in the veil framework: Agreement is possible in large part because individuals cannot advocate for principles that directly benefit them. Second, almost none of the groups endorsed Rawls' preferred principle. This may be due to the fact individuals were deciding under

---

[7] Pre-dating both publications is the economist William Vickery, who in the 1940s invoked the veil of ignorance framework to judge alternative income distributions. Finally, James Buchanan and Gordon Tullock (1962) construct a variant of the veil they refer to as the veil of uncertainty.

risk as opposed to uncertainty (recall that John Harsanyi's equiprobability framework – which supports average utilitarianism – models decision under risk, while Rawls assumes a more radical form of uncertainty). Third, most groups did not find utilitarianism to be particularly attractive either. Instead, they selected a restricted form of utilitarianism, "utilitarianism with a floor". This principle ensures a baseline level of income for all in society and above this threshold utilitarianism kicks in.[8] Thus, Frohlich and Oppenheimer's findings do not appear to support Harsanyi's contention that average utilitarianism will be endorsed from behind the veil. Instead, individuals will sacrifice some level of efficiency in order to buy security, in the form of an income floor.[9] Follow-up experiments have confirmed this, and Frohlich and Oppenheimer's finding has been replicated in cross-cultural studies as well (see Lissowski et al. 1991).

While illuminating, it is fair to note that the above study misses many important features of the Rawlsian veil of ignorance. Primary goods – not income – is Rawls' preferred currency of justice. Furthermore, the experiment only investigates Rawls' distributive principle (the difference principle), ignoring the *liberties principle* and fair equality of opportunity. While it is unclear how something like the liberties principle can be studied experimentally (especially if one wants to adhere to the norms of experimental economics), a number of experiments have focused on the opportunity principle.[10] Scott and colleagues (2001) as well as Mitchelbach and colleagues (2003) investigate the support fair equality of opportunity (FEO) garners. According to FEO, morally arbitrary features such as one's skin color, gender, and family background should not influence one's life prospects. Instead, opportunities are sensitive to natural talent and effort alone. Thus, two individuals with comparable motivation and talent should have (in expectation) similar life prospects. The experiments conducted in both papers suggest an interesting relationship exists between FEO and utilitarianism. Namely, individuals are more inclined to favor utilitarian distributions when FEO is said to hold, and individuals are more egalitarian in spirit when FEO is violated. This makes sense: When FEO is violated, individuals can be seen as perhaps trying to rectify unfair inequalities by enforcing a more egalitarian distribution of resources. When FEO holds, individuals are much more comfortable with the potentially large inequalities dictated by utilitarianism.

As interesting as these experiments are, there are a few things to point out. First, these experiments do not technically explore decision-making behind the veil. Individ-

---

[8] Note that in this experiment (as in many experiments on the veil), utility is not measured. Instead, income is a proxy for utility and the utilitarian aims to maximize the average income of society.

[9] As mentioned in the previous footnote, these experiments are cashed out in terms of income and not utility. Thus, it is possible that individuals believe an income floor will be the best way to secure high average utility.

[10] Although there are many empirical investigations of opportunity, we focus on just those experiments that consider opportunity and the veil. For those interested in the folk's views regarding merit and opportunity see Cappelen et al. (2007). See also work done by Alexander Max Bauer and colleagues (Bauer et al. 2022).

uals are asked to rank different societies and told they are not a member of said societies. Thus, the experiment is less of an investigation of the veil and more of an exploration of Smith's impartial spectator model (for more on Smith, see below). Second, individuals were not allowed to directly compare societies satisfying FEO to those not satisfying FEO. As a result, these experiments were unable to register whether individuals even support Rawls' opportunity principle. To address these shortcomings, Bruner (2018) asks individuals to rank a number of distributions from behind the veil. Distributions vary with respect to the extent socially arbitrary factors and effort affect individual prospects. Individuals are also administered an effort-measuring task in the laboratory. Bruner finds an interesting relationship between FEO and utilitarianism. Like Rawls, individuals have a lexical ordering of distributive principles. Utilitarian distributions are ranked most favorably, and the opportunity principle is invoked when deciding between two distributions with the same level of average utility.

While ample experimental work exists on the veil, several experiments also explore alternative models of impartial decision-making. James Konow (2009), for instance, has done the most to understand Smith's so-called impartial spectator. Spectators are disinterested third parties asked to make a moral judgment. Interestingly, Konow uncovers a counterintuitive link between information and consensus: The more information subjects have about a particular case, the more likely they are to arrive at similar moral judgments. This is in stark contrast with the veil, where consensus is thought to be possible *because* individuals are denied relevant information. Relatedly, Herne and Mård (2008, also see Herne and Suojanen 2004) examine whether impartial spectators and "veiled stakeholders" endorse similar distributive principles. Interestingly, they find that spectators tend to be more egalitarian, while, as we have seen, decision-makers from behind the veil gravitate toward utilitarian principles of justice. Herne and Mård also consider a model of impartial decision-making that is loosely inspired by Thomas Scanlon's (1998) contractualism. Subjects are asked to select principles they believe no one can reasonably reject, and in practice, individuals in the Scanlonian original position endorse egalitarian distributions. Somewhat ironically, then, Rawlsian distributive principles of justice receive strongest support from subjects embedded in the Smithian and Scanlonian frameworks.

Taking stock: Individuals by and large endorse the same distributive principle behind the veil (restricted utilitarianism). Furthermore, as James Konow and others have shown, impartial spectators also converge in their moral judgments. Bruner and Lindauer (2020) refer to these different circumstances of choice designed to ensure some level of impartiality as an impartiality frame. As discussed in the previous paragraph, Herne and Mård's experiments indicate that while unique principles are selected within a particular impartiality frame, there is a significant divergence across impartiality frames (veiled stakeholders gravitate to utilitarian distributions while impartial third parties prefer egalitarian distributions). Bruner and Lindauer explore how compelling subjects find these various frames. Their questionnaire strongly suggests that there is no uniquely choiceworthy impartiality frame. While subjects rated the veil frame and impartial spectator frame significantly higher than the Scanlonian frame, a runoff involving just the veil and spectator frames found that neither impartiality frame was uniquely choiceworthy. Bruner and Lindauer argue that their findings blunt the force of the contractarian approach in political philosophy. Namely, if no frame is uniquely choiceworthy, then "neither are the principles of justice which follow from them" (Bruner and Lindauer 2020, p. 473).

Lastly, Bruner and Lindauer consider whether there is a robust connection between subject's preferences over distributive principles and preferences over impartiality frame. Intuitively, one would expect that an individual's preferences fit together in the right way. For instance, a utilitarian would likely find the utilitarian-friendly impartiality frame to be especially appealing. Interestingly, Bruner and Lindauer do not find evidence for coherence of this kind: One's distributive preferences are not correlated with one's ranking of impartiality frames.

2.4 Agreement and Compliance

We now briefly return to the compliance problem. Recall that while agents might agree on rules, they might not always have incentive to follow said rules. Solving this compliance problem is, as we have seen, a major endeavor in the social contract tradition. In a series of fascinating articles, Marco Faillo and Lorenzo Sacconi along with a number of co-authors, ask whether the act of agreement in and of itself helps alleviate the compliance problem.[11] That is, is a group of individuals who actively discuss and then agree to rules more or less likely to adhere to said rules? Interestingly, Faillo and Sacconi answer in the affirmative: Their experiments indicate that individuals are *more* likely to abide by rules when they were involved in the same process of ex ante agreement. The explanation given by Faillo and Sacconi is that individuals have a conditional preference for conformity. That is, a subject will adhere to the rule if she both expects others to adhere to said rule and believes others expect her to comply.[12] The process of actual agreement establishes such expectations, thereby generating widespread compliance.

Relatedly, we can consider what effect compliance has on the agreement stage. Does the content of the agreed-upon distributive principle hinge on how the compliance problem is solved (if at all)? According to Kenneth Binmore (2006), the answer is "yes". Binmore contends that a utilitarian social contract will be selected behind the veil if a third-party is tasked to enforce the contract once the veil is lifted. If instead the community is responsible for solving the compliance problem, then, Binmore argues, utilitarianism is no longer viable. Egalitarian principles are now agreed to behind the veil because egalitarianism is re-negotiation proof and, as a result, stable. It is un-

---

[11] See Sacconi and Faillo (2010), Sacconi, Faillo, and Ottone (2016), as well as Faillo, Ottone, and Sacconi (2015).
[12] As Faillo and Sacconi themselves note, the similarities to Bicchieri's (2006) account of social norms is obvious.

clear whether this argument generalizes beyond Binmore's specific model of the social contract. That said, Binmore has his finger on an intriguing question: Does the solution to the compliance problem influence the agreement stage of the social contract? There has yet to be an attempt to address this question empirically, although modifying the experimental design of Faillo and Sacconi is a natural place to start. In their experiments, Faillo and Sacconi consider a variant of the dictator game, where one individual (the dictator) is given resources and can allocate some portion to their counterpart. Behind the veil, subjects discuss various distributive principles and how a dictator should behave. Faillo and Sacconi find that groups tend to settle on an equal division rule. This is in line with Binmore's claim that egalitarianism is ex post stable when agreements are self-enforced. It would not be too difficult to test Binmore's second claim about utilitarianism and third-party enforcement: If agreements are enforced by a third-party (the experimenter), are subjects now drawn to utilitarian principles?

2.5 More to Explore

Those interested in the experimental approach to the social contract will benefit from recent theoretical work which brings game theory and other tools from economics to bear on matters of justice. In particular, Kenneth Binmore's (1994, 1998) two-part series *Game Theory and the Social Contract* as well as Brian Skyrms's (1969, 2004) *The Evolution of the Social Contract* and *The Stag Hunt and the Evolution of Social Structure* are excellent starting points. Samuel Bowles and Herbert Gintis's (2011) *A Cooperative Species* is less philosophical but provides the reader with a taste of recent evolutionary work of relevance to the social contract. Bowles and Gintis also reference empirical work relevant to the problem of compliance, stability, and fairness.

3 Further Topics

One area we were not able to discuss at length is the exciting work done in democratic theory on deliberation and preference aggregation. Some guiding questions relate to the supposed transformative power of deliberation, how discussion should be structured, and the relationship between deliberation and aggregation. On this latter point, Christian List and John Dryzek (2003) argue on the basis of data from a deliberative poll that while deliberation does not lead to consensus, it transforms preferences in helpful ways. Namely, post-discussion preferences are more likely to be single-peaked. This is significant: If preferences are single-peaked, one can avoid some of the famous impossibility results of social choice (Arrow 1951). In other words, deliberation makes preferences more amenable to aggregation, or so the data suggests.

On a slightly different note, Helen Landemore (2012) and others have considered the epistemic benefits of deliberation. Discussion is heavily informed by case studies (such as the crowd sourcing of the Icelandic constitution) as well as the rich theoretical literature on epistemic voting and epistemic networks (see Lu Hong and Scott Page 2004, as well as Robert Goodin and Kai Spiekermann 2018). The theoretical literature provides a host of predictions that can then be further explored in the context of the laboratory. Kevin Zollman (2010), for instance, has argued that deliberation is more likely to arrive at the truth when certain restraints are placed on the discussion phase which limit the flow of information. Specifically, groups are more likely to arrive at a true consensus when it is not possible for each individual to share their evidence and reasons with everyone else. Stifling the communication network has epistemic benefits because it results in a longer period of deliberation and evidence-gathering, which makes it all the more likely the group will ultimately arrive at the truth. Erik Olsson and colleagues (Jönsson, Hahn, and Olsson 2015) confirmed these predictions in the laboratory, suggesting that there really are epistemic benefits to hampering deliberation (although see Rosenstock et al. 2017 for another perspective).

Looking beyond democratic theory, another strain of empirical work explores the emergence of distributive and social norms. Game-theoretic work on the dynamics of distributive norms suggest that when two groups repeatedly meet to divide a resource, a divisional norm favoring the larger group is likely to emerge (Bruner 2019). This effect is known as the "Cultural Red King effect", and has been explored empirically by Mohseni, O'Connor, and Rubin (2021). Mohseni, O'Connor and Rubin test the Red King effect in the laboratory and find that those in the minority end up with fewer resources than those in the majority, thereby lending support to the effect. Furthermore, philosophers have conducted many laboratory experiments to better understand the role social norms play in our social interactions. Starting with Cristina Bicchieri's (2006) pathbreaking work *The Grammar of Society*, norms can be understood as addressing the compliance problem (Section 2.1). Namely, individuals have a conditional preference to conform. That is, individuals prefer to conform on condition they that others will conform, and that others believe one ought to conform. According to Bicchieri, norms of this kind can effectively translate a prisoner's dilemma into a stag hunt game, making the problem of compliance that much more tractable. Cristina Bicchieri, along with many co-authors, has conducted many laboratory experiments to better understand the nature of social norms (Bicchieri, Xiao, and Muldoon 2011; Bicchieri and Chavez 2009, 2013).

Bibliography

Arrow, Kenneth (1951): *Social choice and individual values*. New York: Wiley.

Barclay, Pat, and Nichola Raihani (2016): "Partner choice versus punishment in human prisoner's dilemmas", *Evolution and Human Behavior* 37 (4), pp. 263–271.

Bauer, Alexander Max, Frauke Mayer, Jan Romann, Mark Siebel, and Stefan Traub (2022): "Need, equity, and accountability. Evidence on third-party distribution decision from a vignette study", *Social Choice and Welfare* 59, pp. 769–814.

Bicchieri, Cristina (2006): *The grammar of society. The nature and dynamics of social norms*. Cambridge: Cambridge University Press.

Bicchieri, Cristina, and Alex Chavez (2009): "Behaving as expected. Public information and fairness norms", *Journal of Behavioral Decision Making* 23 (2), pp. 161–178.

Bicchieri, Cristina, and Alex Chavez (2013): "Norm manipulation, norm evasion. Experimental evidence", *Economics & Philosophy* 29 (2), pp. 175–198.

Bicchieri, Cristina, Erte Xiao, and Ryan Muldoon (2011): "Trustworthiness is a social norm, but trusting is not", *Politics, Philosophy & Economics* 10 (2), pp. 170–187.

Binmore, Kenneth (1993): "Bargaining and morality", in: David Gauthier and Robert Sugden (Eds.): *Rationality, justice and the social contract. Themes from morals by agreement*. Ann Arbor: University of Michigan Press, pp. 131–156.

Binmore, Kenneth (1994): *Game theory and the social contract. Vol. 1. Playing fair*. Cambridge: The MIT Press.

Binmore, Kenneth (1998): *Game theory and the social contract. Vol. 2. Just playing*. Cambridge: The MIT Press.

Binmore, Kenneth (2006): *Natural justice*. Oxford: Oxford University Press.

Binmore, Kenneth, Joe Swierzbinski, Steven Hsu, and Chris Proulx (1993): "Focal points and bargaining", *International Journal of Game Theory* 22, pp. 381–409.

Bowles, Samuel, and Herbert Gintis (2011): *A cooperative species. Human reciprocity and its evolution*. Princeton and Oxford: Princeton University Press.

Braithewiate, Richard (1954): *Theory of games as a tool for moral philosophy*. Cambridge: Cambridge University Press.

Bruner, Justin (2015): "Diversity, tolerance and the social contract", *Philosophy, Politics & Economics* 14 (4), pp. 429–448.

Bruner, Justin (2018): "Decision behind the veil. An experimental approach", in: Tania Lombrozo, Joshua Knobe, and Shaun Nichols (Eds.): *Oxford Studies in Experimental Philosophy* 2, pp. 167–180.

Bruner, Justin (2019): "Minority (dis)advantage in population games", *Synthese* 196 (1), pp. 413–427.

Bruner, Justin (2020): "Locke, Nozick and the state of nature", *Philosophical Studies* 177 (1), pp. 705–726.

Bruner, Justin (2021): "Convention, correlation and consistency", *Philosophical Studies* 178 (5), pp. 1707–1718.

Bruner, Justin, and Matthew Lindauer (2020): "The varieties of impartiality, or, would an egalitarian endorse the veil?", *Philosophical Studies* 177 (2), pp. 459–477.

Bruner, Justin, Cailin O'Connor, Hannah Rubin, and Simon Huttegger (2018): "David Lewis in the lab. Experimental results on the emergence of meaning", *Synthese* 195 (2), pp. 603–321.

Chung, Hun (2015): "Hobbes's state of nature. A modern game-theoretic Bayesian analysis", *Journal of the American Philosophical Association* 1 (3), pp. 485–508.

Chung, Hun (forthcoming): "Locke's state of nature and its epistemic deficit. A game-theoretic analysis", *Synthese*.

Chung, Hun (forthcoming): "When utilitarianism dominates justice as fairness. An economic defense of utilitarianism from the original position", *Economics & Philosophy*.

Dryek, John, and Christian List (2002): "Social choice theory and deliberative democracy. A reconciliation", *British Journal of Political Science* 33 (1), pp. 1–28.

Faillo, Marco, Stefania Ottone, and Lorenzo Sacconi (2015): "The social contract in the laboratory. An experimental analysis of self-enforcing impartial agreements", *Public Choice* 163 (3–4), pp. 225–246.

Fehr, Ernst, and Simon Gächter (2000): "Cooperation and punishment in public goods experiments", *The American Economic Review* 90 (4), pp. 980–994.

Fehr, Ernst, and Simon Gächter (2002): "Altruistic punishment in humans", *Nature* 415, pp. 137–140.

Fleurbaey, Marc (2008): *Fairness, responsibility and welfare*. Oxford: Oxford University Press.

Franssen, Maartin (1994): "Constrained maximization reconsidered. An elaboration and critique of Gauthier's modelling of rational cooperation in a single prisoner's dilemma", *Synthese* 101, pp. 249–272.

Freiman, Christopher, and Shaun Nichols (2011): "Is desert in the details?", *Philosophy and Phenomenological Research* 82 (1), pp. 121–133.

Frohlich, Norman, Joe Oppenheimer, and Cheryl Eavey (1987): "Laboratory results on Rawls' distributive justice", *British Journal of Political Science* 17 (1), pp. 1–21.

Fudenberg, Drew, and Jean Tirole (2000): *Game theory*. Cambridge and London: The MIT Press.

Gauthier, David (1986): *Morals by agreement*. Oxford: Claredon Press.

Gauthier, David (1993): "Uniting separate persons", in: David Gauthier and Robert Sugden (Eds.): *Rationality, justice and the social contract. Themes from morals by agreement*. Ann Arbor: University of Michigan Press, pp. 176–192.

Goodin, Robert, and Kai Spiekermann (2018): *An epistemic theory of democracy*. Oxford: Oxford University Press.

Guala, Francesco (2012): "Reciprocity. Weak or strong? What punishment experiments do (and do not) demonstrate", *Behavioral and Brain Sciences* 35 (1), pp. 1–15.

Herne, Kaisa, and Maria Suojanen (2004): "The role of information in choices over income distributions", *Journal of Conflict Resolution* 48 (2), pp. 173–193.

Herne, Kaisa, and Tarja Mård (2008): "Three versions of impartiality. An experimental investigation", *Homo Oeconomicus* 25 (1), pp. 27–53.

Herrmann, Benedikt, Christian Thöni, and Simon Gächter (2008): "Antisocial punishment across societies", *Science* 319 (5868), pp. 1362–1367.

Inoue, Akira, Kazumi Shimizu, Daisuke Udagawa, and Yoshiki Wakamatsu (2019): "Luck vs. capability? Testing egalitarian theories", *Review of Philosophy and Psychology* 10 (2), pp. 809–823.

Jönsson, Martin, Ulrike Hahn, and Erik Olsson (2015): "The kind of group you want to belong to. Effects of group structure on group accuracy", *Cognition* 142, pp. 191–204.

Kalai, Ehud, and Meir Smorodinsky (1975): "Other solutions to Nash's bargaining problem", *Econometrica* 43 (3), pp. 513–518.

Kogelmann, Brian, and Benjamin Ogden (2018): "Enough and as good. A formal model of Lockean first appropriation". *American Journal of Political Science* 62 (3), pp. 682–694.

Konow, James (2000): "Fair shares. Accountability and cognitive dissonance in allocation decisions", *The American Economic Review* 90 (4), pp. 1072–1091.

Konow, James (2009): "Is fairness in the eye of the beholder? An impartial spectator analysis of justice", *Social Choice and Welfare* 33, pp. 101–127.

Konrad, Kai, and Stergios Skaperdas (2012): "The market for protection and the Origin of the state", *Economic Theory* 50, pp. 417–443.

Landemore, Helene (2012): *Democratic reason. Politics, collective intelligence and the rule of the many*. Princeton: Princeton University Press.

Lissowski, Grzegorz, Tadeusz Tyszka, and Wlodzimierz Okrasa (1991): "Principles of distributive justice. Experiments in Poland and England", *Journal of Conflict Resolution* 35 (1), pp. 98–119.

Michelbach, Philip, John Scott, Richard Matland, and Brian Bornstein (2003): "Doing Rawls justice. An experimental study of income distribution norms", *American Journal of Political Science* 47 (3), pp. 523–539.

Moehler, Michael (2010): "The (stabilized) Nash bargaining solution as a principle of distributive justice", *Utilitas* 22 (4), pp. 447–473.

Moehler, Michael (2018): *Minimal morality. A multilevel social contract theory*. Oxford: Oxford University Press.

Mohseni, Aydin, Cailin O'Connor, and Hannah Rubin (2021): "On the emergence of minority disadvantage. Testing the cultural red king hypothesis", *Synthese* 198 (6), pp. 5599–5621.

Nash, John (1950): "The bargaining problem", *Econometrica* 18 (2), pp. 115–162.

Nash, John (1953): "Two-person cooperative games", *Econometrica* 21 (1), pp. 128–140.

Rankin, Frederick, John Van Huyck, and Raymond Battalio (2000): "Strategic similarity and emergent conventions. Evidence from similar stag hunt games", *Games and Economic Behavior* 32 (2), pp. 315–337.
Rawls, John (1958): "Justice as fairness", *Philosophical Review* 67 (2), pp. 164–194.
Roemer, John (1998): *Equality of opportunity*. Cambridge and London: Harvard University Press.
Roemer, John (1998): *Theories of distributive justice*. Cambridge and London: Harvard University Press.
Rosenstock, Sarita, Justin Bruner, and Cailin O'Connor (2017): "In epistemic networks, is less really more?", *Philosophy of Science* 84 (2), pp. 324–352.
Rubin, Hannah, Cailin O'Connor, and Justin Bruner (2019): "Experimental economics for philosophers", in: Eugen Fischer and Mark Curtis (Eds.): *Methodological advances in experimental philosophy*. London and New York: Bloomsbury, pp. 175–206.
Sacconi, Lorenzo, and Marco Faillo (2010): "Conformity, reciprocity and the sense of justice. How social contract-based preferences and beliefs explain norm compliance. The experimental evidence", *Constitutional Political Economy* 21 (2), pp. 171–201.
Sacconi, Lorenzo, Marco Faillo, and Stefania Ottone (2016): "Contractarian compliance and the 'sense of justice'. A behavioral conformity model and its experimental support", *Analyse & Kritik* 33 (1), pp. 273–310.
Scanlon, Thomas (1998): *What we owe to each other*. Cambridge and London: Harvard University Press.
Scott, John, Richard Matland, Philip Michelbach, and Brian Bornstein (2001): "Just deserts. An experimental study of distributive justice norms", *American Journal of Political Science* 45 (4), pp. 749–767.
Seinen, Ingrid, and Arthur Schram (2006): "Social status and group norms. Indirect reciprocity in a repeated helping experiment", *European Economic Review* 50 (3), pp. 581–602.
Skaperdas, Stergios (1992): "Cooperation, conflict and power in the Absence of property rights", *The American Economic Review* 82 (4), pp. 720–739.
Skyrms, Brian (1996): *The evolution of the social contract*. Cambridge: Cambridge University Press.
Skyrms, Brian (2004): *The stag hunt and the evolution of social structure*. Cambridge: Cambridge University Press.
Skyrms, Brian (2010): *Tanner lectures on human value*. Utah: University of Utah Press.
Stromland, Eirik, Sigve Tjotta, and Gaute Torsvik (2018): "Mutual choice of partner and communication in a repeated prisoner's dilemma", *Journal of Behavioral and Experimental Economics* 75, pp. 12–23.
Sugden, Robert (1986): *The economics of rights, cooperation and welfare*. Oxford: Basil Blackwell.
van Apeldoorn, Jacobien, and Arthur Schram (2016): "Indirect reciprocity. A field experiment", *PLOS ONE* 11, e0152076.
Van Huyck, John, Raymond Battalio, and Richard Beil (1990): "Tacit coordination games, strategic uncertainty, and coordination failure", *The American Economic Review* 80 (1), pp. 234–248.
Vanderschraaf, Peter (1995): "Convention as correlated equilibrium", *Erkenntnis* 42 (1), pp. 65–87.
Vanderschraaf, Peter (2006): "War or peace? A dynamical analysis of anarchy", *Economics & Philosophy* 22 (2), pp. 243–279.
Vanderschraaf, Peter (2018): *Strategic justice. Convention and problems of balancing divergent interests*. New York: Oxford University Press.
Young, Peyton (1994): *Equity. In theory and in practice*. Princeton: Princeton University Press.
Zollman, Kevin (2010) "The epistemic benefit of transient diversity", *Erkenntnis* 72 (1), pp. 17–35.

Raff Donelson

Experimental Legal Philosophy: General Jurisprudence

Abstract: This chapter offers an overview of experimental legal philosophy with a special focus on questions in general jurisprudence, that part of legal philosophy that asks about the concept and nature of law. Much of the experimental general jurisprudence work has tended to follow the questions that have interested general jurisprudence scholars for decades, that is, questions about the relation between legal norms and moral norms. Wholesale criticism of experimental general jurisprudence is scant, but, given existing debates about experimental philosophy generally, one can anticipate where disagreement is likely to occur. Outside of experimental general jurisprudence, there is plenty of vibrant discussion about how experimental results can enrich our understanding of various concepts that figure in everyday legal thought such as causation, intention, consent, or meaning. In the future, experimental legal philosophers should continue to consider the degree to which their project is purely descriptive or whether it is revisionary or pragmatic in its ambitions. Also, future work might consider whether to focus more attention on legal experts.

Keywords: Causation; Consent; Empirical Legal Studies; Experimental Jurisprudence; Experimental Philosophy; Expertise Defense; General Jurisprudence; Legal Positivism; Natural Law Theory; Pragmatist Jurisprudence

1 Introduction

Legal philosophy has a long and storied history. At least as far back as Plato, one finds Western philosophers wondering whether we have a general obligation to follow the law (Plato, *Crito*) and making claims about which kinds of activities require legal regulation (Plato, *Republic* IV, 425b – d). Experimentalists today are adding a new chapter to that story. In just the past few years, experimental legal philosophy has flourished, and this new work has mainly taken the form of using the tools of cognitive psychology to explore "how core legal concepts are understood by laypeople who know little about the law" (Sommers 2021, p. 394).[1] At first blush, it would seem that such investigation, however interesting, is irrelevant to legal philosophy. This chapter aims to assuage this

---

Note: This chapter has benefited greatly from the research assistance of Nick Gonano as well as comments from the editors of this volume.

[1] To be sure, some work examines experts, rather than laypeople, see, e.g., Donelson and Hannikainen (2020).

worry or, at the least, aims to explain why a number of well-trained philosophers think their work is continuous with the traditional concerns of legal philosophy.

Like other subfields in philosophy, legal philosophy does not have a singular focus. Some of the work is normative or normative-adjacent. For instance, some thinkers explore our supposed obligation to follow the law (Raz 2009b, Mackie 1981); some focus on whether certain acts should be criminalized (Nussbaum 1998, Husak 2002); some think about free will and responsibility as they relate to the law (Levy 2019, Caruso 2021). Another stream of work is more analytical; thinkers working in this stream are concerned to offer the correct analysis of *law, legal system*, or any of the varied legal concepts that surface in everyday legal thought such as *intention, cause, consent*, and so on. Most of the recent work in experimental legal philosophy, usually styled *experimental jurisprudence* (or "ex-jur" or "XJur"), concerns these analytical projects. This chapter, which seeks to capture a part of the field as it presently stands, similarly focuses on experimental jurisprudence in the analytical vein.

Though this chapter focuses narrowly on experimental work that seeks to advance conversations in legal *philosophy*, and specifically *analytical* projects within legal philosophy, there is plenty of experimental work about other legal matters. Some of this research adopts the "ex-jur" label; some of it embraces the broader *empirical legal studies* banner. There are thousands of articles that fit this description such that any overview will be woefully inadequate. Nevertheless, exemplary works include Kassin and Norwick (2004), which explains why people waive their right against self-incrimination, Wilkinson-Ryan (2015), which explains why people breach contracts (and why they don't, even when it would be efficient), as well as Kugler and Strahilevitz (2017), which shows that people's expectations of privacy from government intrusion are not much affected by court decisions about privacy rights.[2]

2 Experimental General Jurisprudence

Even within analytical projects in experimental jurisprudence, there is great diversity. One can distinguish between two streams of research. First is research that focuses on understanding the nature or concept of law. A second strand is research that focuses on

---

[2] For someone looking for this sort of work, instead of experimental legal philosophy, there are many, many potential sources. The *Journal of Empirical Legal Studies* has perhaps broadest appeal, while plenty of other journals have particular disciplinary concentrations. For instance, *Law and Human Behavior* is a periodical which highlights psychology, the *Journal of Experimental Criminology* centers on crime, and the *American Law and Economics Review* focuses on economics (and not all of it is empirical, let alone experimental). Also, one sometimes finds experimental work in generalist outlets like the *Journal of Legal Studies* and many student-edited American law reviews such as the *Harvard Law Review* or the *Northwestern University Law Review*, the latter of which currently has an annual empirical issue. For some writing on the rise of empirical legal studies in American law reviews, see Diamond and Mueller (2010).

what one might call *everyday legal concepts*, concepts that regularly figure in legal reasoning, especially in legal doctrines. Everyday legal concepts include concepts such as *legal cause, intention, punishment*, and the like. The former project is what many call *general jurisprudence* because it treats law at its most general. This chapter concentrates on experimental approaches to general jurisprudence, while briefly mentioning some of the experimental work about everyday legal concepts.

To get a handle on how experimentalists add to the discussion, it is important to first understand the main conversations in general jurisprudence, much of which proceeds in a non-empirical, or armchair, fashion. Perhaps the most famous cluster of debates within general jurisprudence is the controversy over whether there are moral criteria that something must satisfy in order to be a (full) legal norm. Some thinkers – sometimes called *natural law theorists*, sometimes called *legal non-positivists* – claim that membership among the class of legal norms requires that the norm comport with some standard, usually a moral standard. Examples of this view include Finnis (1980). On the simplest version of the thesis, a norm is not a legal norm if it requires behavior that is morally impermissible. For instance, then, the American Fugitive Slave Act of 1850, which required people to assist in the return of runaway slaves, is a paradigmatically unjust law that required morally impermissible behavior. Natural law theorists typically claim that legislation like that is not genuine law. Opponents of this kind of view – often called *legal positivists* – contend that a norm can be a legal norm, even it requires morally impermissible behavior. Examples of this view include Kelsen (1967), Hart (2009), and Shapiro (2011).

It is fitting to call this a *cluster* of debates because natural law theorists and legal positivists each have their own intramural debates.

Natural law theorists divide over two main questions. The first is whether failure to comport with the strictures of morality fully disqualify a norm from membership in the class of legal norms or whether the immorality just means the norm fails to be a legal norm in *the fullest sense*. This debate is sometimes called the debate between strong and weak versions of natural law theory. The classical view, espoused by folks like Martin Luther King Jr. (1986) and Thomas Aquinas (1994) is a strong version of natural law theory, and its adherents contend that an immoral law is no law at all. Meanwhile, contemporary natural law theorists like M. Murphy (2011) tend to embrace the weak version, which claims that immoral laws fail to be laws in the full sense.

A second controversy within the natural law theory camp concerns the debate between substantive natural law theory and procedural natural law theory. Substantive natural law theory holds that a norm is not a (full) legal norm if that norm requires any morally impermissible behavior. By contrast, procedural natural law theory, championed by Fuller (1969), holds that some legal norms may require immoral conduct, so long as the norms adhere to certain morally desirable procedural standards. For instance, for Fuller, legal norms must be prospective, rather than retrospective, in order to give legal subjects fair notice because providing fair notice is morally desirable. If a set of norms failed to give this fair notice, it would fail to be a legal system or fail to be a legal system in the fullest sense.

These two debates within natural law theory have no overlap. It is, therefore, possible to occupy one of four different positions: (1) strong, substantive natural law theory, (2) a weak, substantive natural law theory, (3) strong, procedural natural law theory, or (4) weak, procedural natural law theory.

Legal positivists have their own internecine squabbles. While all legal positivists contend that, in general, some norm can be a legal norm even if it is morally iniquitous, inclusive legal positivists contend that some legal systems include or incorporate moral norms (see, e.g., Hart 2009). For instance, the Eighth Amendment to the American Constitution purports to outlaw cruel punishments. If "cruel" is a thick ethical term, encoding both normative and descriptive elements, this suggests that this particular law incorporates a moral stricture, a prohibition on what is in fact cruel. This, at least, is the official story of the inclusive legal positivist. By contrast, exclusive legal positivists deny that legal systems actually incorporate moral norms; instead, they incorporate what the legal officials *think* morality requires (see, e.g., Raz 2009b).

This summary of important debates within general jurisprudence has necessarily been quick, and discussion of many valuable contributions has been omitted. The point, however, was not to offer a comprehensive overview of the field. Instead, the point is to offer sufficient summary to set up a new question, *the question of relevance*.

2.1 The Question of Relevance

The most pressing question for experimental philosophy is the question of relevance. In essence, the question demands that experimentalists explain why results from cognitive psychology, the paradigmatic kind of evidence garnered by x-phi researchers, have any bearing on philosophical questions. Since philosophers typically care about how the world is, and not how people believe the world to be, psychological data seems irrelevant. Before any review of experiments in general jurisprudence, it is important to consider head-on this most important challenge to the experimentalist turn.

For some experimental work, the argument for relevance is relatively straightforward and well-known. For instance, some experimentalist work, to borrow from Nadelhoffer and Nahmias (2007), is of the *Restrictionist* variety. Restrictionists often deploy a kind of master argument. First, they claim that philosophical work that traffics in thought experiments requires uniform, well-reasoned responses to the hypothetical cases described. Next, Restrictionists present evidence that the folk (or experts) differ in their responses to philosophical thought experiments or that the folk (or experts) seem to be affected by irrelevant factors in their responses to those thought experiments. Finally, Restrictionists conclude that all philosophical projects that rely on intuitive responses to hypothetical cases are suspect. Because general jurisprudence abounds in such intuition-pumping projects, Restrictionist experimental work is clearly relevant to general jurisprudents. Of course, the Restrictionist reproach is not peculiar to general jurisprudence. For this reason, jurisprudence scholars feel no particular compunction to address such work.

The tricky case for establishing the relevance of experimental results concerns, not the blunt negative program of the Restrictionist, but rather the positive program that Nadelhoffer and Nahmias (2007) call *Experimental Analysis*. The Analysts offer experimental results with the aim of defending (or rebutting) particular claims about the proper analysis of some object of philosophical concern, and that analysandum might be *knowledge, causation, the self,* or indeed *law*. In short, the Experimental Analyst who works in general jurisprudence claims that she can tell us specifically about the nature or concept of law using experiments, and the question is how. Some recent papers provide answers.

Donelson and Hannikainen (2020) offer one answer to the question of relevance. This paper begins with the suggestion that general jurisprudential claims may be interpreted in at least two ways, as quasi-empirical claims about our shared concept[3] or as metaphysical claims about the referent of our law-talk. If general jurisprudence is rightly understood in the first sense, the entire enterprise is about how people understand the world, and cognitive psychology is of immediate relevance. Many legal philosophers reject this psychologistic reading of general jurisprudence, however. If general jurisprudence is rightly understood in the second sense, as a metaphysical enterprise, probing folk intuitions is still indirectly relevant. According to Donelson and Hannikainen, in proposing a theory about something as ubiquitous as law, theorists labor under a presumption against error theories. This presumption provides that a theory which most would reject as false must, as an epistemic matter – not just as a practical matter – adduce more evidence than theories that are widely believed to be true. If this presumption is sound, "determining what people believe is essential to determining whether the presumption against error theories weighs for or against" a particular theory of law (Donelson and Hannikainen 2020, p. 11).

In addition to this claim about the presumption against error theories, Donelson and Hannikainen also briefly suggest that widespread and reliable support for a theory may bolster it. The widespreadness condition should be both easy to understand and easy to motivate. Reliability is another story. For Donelson and Hannikainen, an intuition is reliable insofar as it will be elicited consistently by the same, or substantially the same, stimuli, and if the response pattern is not much affected by irrelevant factors. To illustrate reliability and explain how its absence means that widespread support for a theory is epistemically valueless, consider an example. Suppose that an overwhelming majority of the folk were inclined to support, say, legal positivism when an experiment is run on a Monday, but when the study is re-run on Tuesday, an equally large majority is inclined not to support legal positivism. This response pattern is inconsistent and seemingly affected by an irrelevant factor, namely the day of the

---

[3] This appears to be the view of Raz (2009a). To be clear, Raz does think that investigating our shared concept will tell us some about the referent of that concept. For worries about whether that project can be pulled off, see Nye (2017).

week in which the study is conducted. Thus, widespread support for a theory bolsters it only when that support is also reliable.

Flanagan and Hannikainen (2022) indicate a related basis for the relevance of experimental analysis of law. They point out that many legal philosophers themselves take the intuitiveness of a view as some evidence in the view's favor: "A brief review of prominent positivist and natural law contributions establishes the folk concept's role as a ground on which to defend a theory of [...] legality" (Flanagan and Hannikainen 2022, p. 166). No doubt, one need not to accept that the folk intuition is direct evidence to make a limited case for the relevance of x-phi. Insofar as some jurisprudents accord folk intuitions epistemic weight, it is important to know what those folk intuitions are so that legal philosophers can judge their arguments by the standards they accept as normative.

Donelson (2023) supplies yet another answer to the question of relevance. In this paper, Donelson begins by noting that philosophical conversation relies on unproven premises. Even if foundationalism about knowledge and justification turns out to be true, as a practical matter, philosophical discussion must proceed with unproven premises. If philosophical practice is to continue, philosophers must adhere to the following epistemic principle: In making arguments, one should only rely on those premises that can be expected to be generally acceptable to interlocutors. Donelson does allow for a weaker version of this principle according to which we have more reason to accept arguments with generally acceptable premises than premises without generally acceptable premises. Those acceptable premises are what Donelson calls "common ground propositions". As Donelson sees it, results from cognitive psychology can help establish what is, or is not, common ground in legal philosophy.

Taken together, these answers proclaim that what others think has epistemic value. If everyone disagrees with one's theory, this is some reason to doubt that theory. If everyone supports one's theory, this is some extra reason to have confidence in that theory. If philosophical practice is to continue producing knowledge, or approximations thereof, which is epistemically valuable, we need to meet interlocutors on common ground, which is determined by what others think. If what others think has epistemic value for conversations in legal philosophy, discovering others' thoughts – the work of ex-jur – is philosophically relevant. This collection of arguments, which are independent but mutually supportive, vindicates experimental analysis of law. Having concluded the case for relevance, we can turn to the experiments themselves.

2.2 Summarizing the Recent Work

One of the earliest examples of experimental analysis of law is found in Donelson and Hannikainen (2020). This paper evaluates Lon Fuller's version of procedural natural law theory. According to Fuller (1969), a set of norms fails to be a legal system if those norms do not adhere to eight procedural principles which together ensure that the law treats legal subjects with a minimal level of respect. For Fuller, laws must be consistent, general, intelligible, possible to comply with, prospective, public, stable, and enforced in a manner consistent with the official, public version. Donelson and Hannikainen perform a set of surveys to determine whether ordinary folk and legal experts agree that legal systems must observe these Fullerian principles.

The results of these studies show that, although a few Fullerian principles garner broad support, many of these principles do not, and, averaging across the set of principles, they jointly do not have widespread support from either the folk or experts. This suggests that Fullerian principles are not common ground. If Fullerian principles are best understood as premises in support of procedural natural law theory more generally, these results cast doubt on Fuller's argument for procedural natural law theory. However, because the principles do enjoy modest support, the presumption against error theories does not imperil Fuller's conclusions.

The study by Donelson and Hannikainen also reveals that support for Fullerian principles is unreliable. "Participants were much more likely to endorse Fuller principles in the abstract" (Donelson and Hannikainen 2020, p. 21). That is, when asked if a hypothetical legal system must observe Fullerian principles, survey respondents were likely to agree. On the other hand, when asked about actual legal systems or asked to think about *both* hypothetical and actual legal systems, respondents were far less likely to affirm Fullerian principles. Donelson and Hannikainen (2020, p. 24) claim that the abstract construal is the less epistemically ideal setting because "our intuitions are sharpest when considering more everyday things". Even if this were not so, the fact that there is a construal effect at all presents a problem that advocates for Fuller's view should address. If Fuller's view aims to represent our shared understanding of law, these conflicting reports lend some credence to the worry that we have no shared conception of law in the first place, or a very limited shared conception, a worry voiced by L. Murphy (2005) and Priel (2011). If Fuller's theory aims to describe law itself, these construal effects – the fact that the folk agree with the theory when construed one way and disagree with it when construed another way – may not *undercut* his theory, but they offer no support for it either.

Published as a follow-up to Donelson and Hannikainen (2020), Hannikainen et al. (2021) is a cross-cultural, cross-linguistic analysis. This study focused on an odd finding in the original study: Survey respondents, as a whole,[4] both said that laws must obey Fuller's criteria and that actual laws do not obey Fuller's criteria. This is curious because "must", understood as a modal term rather than a deontic term, designates what is necessarily the case, and if laws necessarily obey Fullerian criteria, then it cannot also be that there are laws in the actual world that fail to obey the criteria. In short,

---

[4] When one set of subjects was only asked the more abstract question, about whether a hypothetical legal system must obey the Fullerian principles, they agreed, and when another set of subjects was only asked the concrete question, about whether actual legal systems do obey Fullerian principles, they disagreed. However, when yet another set of subjects was asked both about hypothetical and actual legal systems, they tended to disagree with Fuller. Thus, the group as a whole had the seemingly conflicting intuitions, but individual subjects did not exhibit this conflict.

the folk seems to be in contradiction with itself. The 2021 study sought to discover whether this response pattern would hold for a more diverse set of respondents. Whereas Donelson and Hannikainen (2020) relied on Anglophone respondents from the United States, Hannikainen et al. (2021) selected speakers from the United States, the United Kingdom, and nine non-Anglophone countries. In those non-Anglophone countries, experiments were conducted in a non-English language commonly spoke in the relevant country. For instance, Portuguese was the experimental language in Brazil, Khmer was the experimental language in Cambodia, and Dutch was the experimental language in the Netherlands. Remarkably, Hannikainen and his co-authors found that the response pattern held in all 11 nations: Respondents said that no law could flout the Fullerian principles and that actual laws do flout those same principles.

While the 2021 study offers "limited insight into the psychological processes that engender conflicting beliefs about actual versus possible laws" (Hannikainen et al. 2021, p. 10), Hannikainen and his co-authors note that several interpretations are consistent with these findings. Among them is the thought that law is a dual-character concept (Hannikainen et al. 2021, p. 11). To better understand dual-character concepts, consider a concept like *philosopher*. In one sense of the word, *philosopher* covers anyone employed by a philosophy department to teach philosophy classes. There is, however, another sense of the word, such that one can ask of any particular philosophy teacher whether they are a *true* or *real* philosopher. The true philosopher exhibits intellectual curiosity, argues in good faith about philosophical questions, and holds genuine convictions about certain philosophical claims. But many a person employed to teach philosophy is an uncurious charlatan. *Law* might be the kind of concept that also has two senses. Perhaps *law* in the more pedestrian sense is any norm recognized as law by the procedures specified in a constitution that a majority of officials accept, but a *true* law must be part of a set of norms that jointly obey Fullerian principles.[5]

Even though Hannikainen and his co-authors decline to draw the link, their study may lend some modest support for weak natural law theory. If the shared conception of law is as a dual-character concept, this understanding of law would fit easily with the weak natural law theorist's contention. Recall that weak natural law theory provides that laws failing to meet certain moral criteria fail to be law in the full sense. Weak natural law theory is a theory of what law itself is, and law-as-dual-character-concept is a theory of how we conceive law, but the latter can offer some support for the former in part because of the presumption against error theories. If further investigation does vindicate the conjecture from Hannikainen and his co-authors that law is usually conceived as dual-character, someone attacking weak natural law theory has a bit of an uphill battle. That theorist would need to explain why everyone else is wrong and why the theorist is in such a better epistemic position to see what everyone

---

5 For a more thoroughgoing explication of dual-character concepts, see Knobe and colleagues (2013) as well as Leslie (2015).

else has missed. Of course, this is getting ahead of ourselves. The evidence from Hannikainen and his co-authors merely suggests that this a possibility.

Another recent paper worth noting is Flanagan and Hannikainen (2022). This piece is unique in that the authors seek to determine the nature of law via experiments testing folk intuitions about grammaticality, which is a proxy for the folk's conceptual frameworks. They tested five main hypotheses. Following their nomenclature, the five hypotheses are as follows:

(1) **Strong classical natural law:** an unjust rule is not a law in any sense,
(2) **Weak classical natural law:** a grossly unjust rule is not a law in any sense,
(3) **Strong neo-classical natural law:** an unjust rule is not a law in the true sense,
(4) **Weak neo-classical natural law:** a grossly unjust rule is not a law in the true sense,
(5) **Positivism:** a grossly unjust rule is no less a law than is a just one.

Important for the authors is the widespread assumption that the positivist has commonsense on her side. They claim their study shows just the opposite: "A large majority (64.4%) rejected the view that, ultimately, law is just a matter of concrete social facts" (Flanagan and Hannikainen 2022, p. 175). Ultimately, the authors conclude that the folk concept of law is intrinsically moral and that the folk concept is a hybrid between strong and weak natural law theses, in the traditional senses of those terms, or, in their nomenclature, a hybrid between classical and neo-classical nature law theory.

As mentioned above, Flanagan and Hannikainen hold that results such as theirs are valuable because they can tell us who has commonsense on their side. Positivism may still be true, but if these results are to be trusted, the positivist has an uphill battle, or at least more of an uphill battle than one might have thought.

While Flanagan and Hannikainen suggest that their results are a resounding victory for natural lawyers, there is another interpretation of their data worth nothing. In looking over their results, one finds that roughly a third of respondents offer answers suggesting weak natural law theory, another third affirms strong natural law theory, and the last third affirms positivism. Perhaps, this is no victory for anyone.

2.3 Criticisms

Since its inception, experimental philosophy has been subject to many sorts of criticism. Philosophers have tried to deflect Restrictionist arguments and deny Restrictionist conclusions in various ways, by claiming that philosophers do not rely on intuitions in the first place (for an overview of such work, see Nado 2016), by arguing that use of intuition is indispensable (see, e.g., Nagel 2012), and even by suggesting that a master argument against any use of intuitions in philosophy is unscientific (Tobia 2015). Less critical attention has been paid to the Analytic project,[6] and even less attention has been focused specifically on experimental analysis of law.

Jimenez (2021) offers an interesting version of an expertise defense that specifically targets experimental general jurisprudence. Before looking more specifically at Jimenez's version of it, it is worth saying something general about the "expertise defense" (also see Chapter 3 of this book). At its most general, an expertise defense is a criticism of experimental work which seeks to ascertain folk attitudes; the proponent of an expertise defense holds that the folk attitudes are irrelevant, for what really matters are the attitudes of experts of the relevant kind. The expertise defense often arises in response to Restrictionist work because those experimentalists are keen to show that folk responses to philosophers' thought experiments diverge from the expected intuitive response either as a general matter or because folk intuitions on the question are unreliable. Those offering up the expertise defense tell Restrictionists to ignore those folk attitudes, whatever they are. Of course, one could raise the expertise defense with respect to analytical work, and this is precisely what Jimenez does.

For Jimenez, law is the kind of concept, and accordingly the kind of thing, that is shaped by certain kinds of legal experts, particularly those who apply the law. As such, we best learn about the law, not by asking the person on the street, but by asking one of these legal officials. As he puts it, "questions about the concept of law [...] might be illuminated by armchair speculation about certain agents' intuitions or by empirical evidence about their actual views – but only to the extent those agents are involved in the interpretation and application of legal concepts and, more broadly, in the operation of the legal system" (Jimenez 2021, p. 8).

The trouble with this iteration of the expertise defense is that it depends on seeing law as a rarefied concept, when it arguably is not. For certain rarefied concepts, it seems odd to seek out folk opinions. If one wants to learn about neutron stars, post-structuralism, or stereotype threat, seeking out the folk intuitions, if there are any, seems unlikely to yield anything of theoretical value. When an astronomer's conception of a neutron star differs from that of the folk, this does nothing to diminish the astronomer's justification in holding that conception because we have no reason to believe the folk were in a good position to know the truth. Or, another way of putting it, explaining why the folk would misunderstand the nature of a neutron star is a simple task. The same goes with philosophers' conceptions of post-structuralism or psychologists' conceptions of stereotype threat. For these and other rarefied concepts, most people are unfamiliar with the concepts and the referents. Law is not like that. Nearly every adult on earth has knowingly lived under a legal system for decades and has used and applied the concept of law on a regular basis throughout their lives. In democratic systems, adults are regularly called upon to select the people that create laws in their society, and they are asked to evaluate the laws created by those people. Some democratic systems even permit the populace to make laws directly. There are also

---

6 But see Kauppinen (2007, 2014) for such critiques. Also see Donelson (2023) for a reply.

myriad detailed depictions of legal systems in popular media, from courtroom dramas or to works focusing on the day-to-day struggles of elected officials and law enforcement. For better or worse, there are no movies about neutron stars or post-structuralism.

In rejecting the expertise defense offered by Jimenez (2021), one must be careful not to overstate the disagreement. Law is an arena where expert intuitions are important too. This is a topic for further discussion in Section 4.1, below.

3 Further Topics

While this chapter focuses on experimental general jurisprudence, there is also new work which employs experimental techniques to analyze everyday legal topics, such as consent and causation. Reviewing some of this interesting work is valuable because it is some of the most visible scholarship under the experimental jurisprudence heading. Also, this works reveals the wide variety of purposes to which experimental results can be put.

3.1 Consent

Sommers (2020) is a groundbreaking study on the folk conception of consent. The paper focuses on a puzzle in American law. On most scholarly accounts of the concept of consent, deception vitiates consent. However, there are cases where judges, from time to time, find consent where there was deception. According to Sommers, this is not puzzling when one recognizes that there is a reliable understanding of consent that is compatible with the possibility of deception: the folk conception of consent.

In a series of experiments, Sommers shows a few things about the folk conception of consent. The major conclusion, of course, is that the folk think that a deceived person still consents. For instance, if A deceives B with respect to A's HIV status in order to have B agree to sex, the folk think that B still consented. This is surprising, and for some, disturbing. Sommers also shows that this view of consent is a reliable intuition that crops up not just when the folk consider consent to sexual activity; the view is reliably elicited in cases about consent to medical treatment and consenting to a search by law enforcement. Next, Sommers amply shows that the best explanation of the folk response pattern is a genuine folk belief that deception does not undermine consent. The pattern is not best explained by the folk finding the offeree unsympathetic, by the mere fact that "consenter" said yes, et cetera. Finally, Sommers shows that on those occasions in which the folk was inclined to find consent incompatible with deception this owes to a distinction they implicitly draw between being deceived about what is happening (fraud in factum) and being deceived about the balance of reasons for engaging in the deed (fraud in inducement). Only the former sort of deception is thought, by the folk, to vitiate consent.

What is most interesting about this work is Sommers's explanation of its relevance for the law of consent. For Sommers (2020, p. 2301), it is not the case that legal systems should mirror the folk conception of consent simply because the folk hold that view. Instead, the primary value of such work, for Sommers, may well be explanatory. Having uncovered this understanding of consent, one can employ it to better understand the American judges who claim to find consent where there was deception. Perhaps these judges are influenced by the folk conception of consent (Sommers 2020, p. 2297). Knowing that this explains judicial conduct, as opposed to something else, is of great practical value.

In addition to explaining judicial behavior, these findings have upshots for ordinary people too. Knowing how ordinary people think about consent will be useful information when thinking about how to help people in their interactions with the law as jurors and as private citizens.

3.2 Causation

As a preliminary remark, it is important to note that there are two major causal notions under American law, actual causation and proximate causation. Roughly, actual causation asks a descriptive question about whether x causes y; whereas, proximate causation asks whether the causal relation is sufficient to conclude that A is responsible for y given that A did x which causes y in the actual causation sense. This distinction is important to bear in mind, for the two studies discussed below attempt to reveal the folk notion of legal cause, but one study examined actual causation while the other study examined proximate causation (also see Chapter 9 of this book for experimental work on causation in non-legal contexts).

Macleod (2019) is one of the earlier experimental papers to explore legal causation in any sense,[7] and it focuses on actual causation. The starting point of the paper is the fact that American judges often, though not invariably, claim to rely on the ordinary meaning of causal phrases like "because of" or "results from" when interpreting statutes containing such language. To recover the ordinary meaning of these phrases, judges rely on their own understandings or use dictionaries, but Macleod suggests that one might instead rely on survey data to determine ordinary meaning. Accordingly, Macleod employs this technique to determine the conception of causation held by most Americans.

The most significant finding of Macleod (2019) is that the folk strongly disagree with the courts about what "cause" means. American courts often suggest that a legal cause is, per definition, a necessary condition for an event's occurrence, or to put it in the courts' terms, a legal cause is a *but-for cause*. To be clear, but-for causation

---

[7] However, see Kominsky and colleagues (2015). This paper is not specifically about legal cause, but the motivating example is a legal case about causation.

does not look for *logically* necessary conditions for the event. In asking "but for *x*, would *y* have happened?" one is looking for conditions that are physically necessary for the event, given that certain other antecedents to the event remain fixed. With that said, Macleod's (2019, pp. 999 f.) survey results amply show that "the but-for test appears to be overly restrictive: most people confidently allege that *y* 'resulted from' *x*, and that *y* occurred 'because of' *x*, while simultaneously and confidently alleging that *x* was not a but-for cause of *y*". If there are reasons to follow the folk understanding, whether from one's general approach to adjudication or from specificities about particular legal doctrines, these results present a major problem to judges who apply a different understanding of legal cause.

Knobe and Shapiro (2021) is another work about causation, this time about proximate causation. The starting point for this paper is an age-old debate about proximate causation.[8] For Knobe and Shapiro, legal formalists claimed that judges employed the term *proximate cause* as just the ordinary, descriptive notion of cause; whereas, legal realists claimed that, for judges, proximate cause is not so much a doctrine to be used in reasoning as a legal conclusion. For the realist, a judge first reaches the moral judgment that someone is morally responsible for, and thus liable for, a harm, and then the judge employs the "doctrine" of proximate cause to justify the legal outcome, post-hoc. Knobe and Shapiro argue that there is a middle path between these views, and that view is the folk conception of cause. This folk conception has two major benefits: it not only avoids certain theoretical pitfalls, but it also best explains a spate of judicial decisions which employ the concept of proximate cause.

For Knobe and Shapiro, the folk conception of causation works in the following way. The folk have a normative understanding of cause which they in turn apply to reach a normative conclusion about whether someone is liable. To be more perspicacious, the authors argue that the folk begin with normative judgments, specifically judgments about what is normal versus abnormal conduct. Abnormal conduct might be statistically abnormal, or it might violate some deontic standard. Armed with this peculiar kind of normative judgment, the folk make determinations of causation. A faculty member causes a receptionist to miss taking down an important message if the faculty member and someone else took the last two pens, but only the faculty member was forbidden by rule from taking the receptionist's pens. After making this causal judgment, the folk make the ultimate, normative judgment of who is liable for the problem. Knobe and Shapiro draw attention to the fact that the folk are making two distinct normative judgments, one about normality and the other about ultimate liability. These both go into reasoning about proximate causation.

What is most interesting about this study, beyond the experimental results themselves, is the use to which these results are put. Knobe and Shapiro, like Sommers (2020), use their work to give cover to judges. It is hard to understand and justify some bit of judicial conduct. The formalist understanding of the conduct makes judges

---

[8] This chapter does not endorse this framing of that age-old debate.

good rule-followers, but the formalist implausibly claims that no moral judgment is involved in reaching the causal judgment. The realist understanding of the conduct allows that judges use moral judgment, but then the judges seem to be completely unrestrained, which has some major democratic difficulties. The Knobe-Shapiro account explains how judges can be rule-followers and use moral judgment. Of course, if this is the biggest upshot of the paper, it is unclear why it matters that the best explanation happens to comport with the folk conception of causation.[9]

4 Prospective Outlook

In considering the future of experimental jurisprudence, particularly work in the analytical vein, there are two main issues that advocates might consider, whether the work is general jurisprudence or the analysis of everyday legal concepts. First, experimentalists should consider whether to consider the intuitions of legal experts, rather than – and sometimes in addition to – the folk. Second, the experimentalists should think more broadly about how their work can enrich legal philosophy and legal practice.

4.1 Probing the Experts

Above, a version of the expertise defense from Jimenez (2021) was considered and rejected. Recall that Jimenez suggested that law is a rarefied concept such that the folk is unlikely to know much about it. In addition to arguing that this is likely mistaken, there are two other points to make.

First, instead of insisting that folk and expert intuitions about the nature of law diverge or converge, it would be better to gather and inspect empirical data. In other words, the best defense against the expertise defense may well be an experimental one. There is some work that seeks out expert intuitions (see, e.g., Donelson and Hannikainen 2020), but there should be more of this work.

Second, the Jimenez suggestion about rarefied concepts is much more plausible when one thinks, not of the concept of law, but of certain everyday legal concepts that are anything but "everyday" for most people. Jimenez actually makes this point too. The law abounds in concepts that are unfamiliar such as "due process of law" and "the rule against perpetuities". Even terms that are familiar might be given a different legal meaning, terms like *hearsay*, *search*, and even *consent.* How should experimentalists react to this version of an expertise defense? Examining a recent paper may point the way.

---

9 This point is made more eloquently by Jimenez (2021).

Klapper (2021) offers a range of arguments against using surveys to find the correct analysis of everyday legal concepts. Some of these worries are more technical ones about whether surveys can be designed to do what experimentalists want. For instance, Klapper wonders if surveys can uncover reliable response patterns, if enough context can be given to respondents, and if respondents know whether they are being asked descriptive versus normative questions. While these difficulties are genuine, they likely can be surmounted by technically trained experimentalists. Klapper also raises harder questions about when asking contemporary ordinary folks seems inappropriate. If the term under investigation is not ordinary but is instead a term of art,[10] or if the term's meaning has considerably changed from the time of enactment, surveys of the folk have limited applicability. The deeper worries are perhaps best seen as a version of the expertise defense. Legal experts are well-suited to understand legal terms of art and to understand which legal terms have drifted over time.

If Klapper (2021) is understood to raise a version of the expertise defense, an obvious answer is in the offing. While Klapper takes his expertise worries to fell the entire survey approach, these worries might be appropriately read more narrowly. There are times when it would be more appropriate to survey experts instead of the folk. Borrowing from Macleod (2019), one can develop an argument on why expert surveys may be helpful. Sometimes the courts are looking to ordinary, plain meaning as a first pass. If there is an unambiguous plain meaning, it must control, but if there is not, there are other consequences. Consider the rule of lenity, a principle for adjudicating criminal matters. According to the rule of lenity, if it is unclear that some behavior is contemplated for criminalization by the criminal statute, the criminal defendant found to have engaged in the behavior cannot be convicted under the relevant criminal statute. Applying the rule of lenity, then, requires understanding the ordinary meaning of criminal statutes. However, as Klapper points out, "ordinary meaning" perhaps does not refer to what the person on the street thinks, but what the ordinary person *with legal training* thinks. If that were so, surveying legal experts could uncover just how clear or unclear a given criminal statute is. If a sufficient number of legal experts were divided, one might conclude, as a matter of law, that the rule of lenity requires acquittal.

As this example from Macleod (2019) makes clear, surveying experts may hold considerable value for applying legal doctrine in particular cases. If, as a doctrinal matter, one must know whether experts disagree about the meaning of a legal text, discovering whether experts agree or disagree is important. There might, however, be different ways that expert (or, for that matter, folk) intuitions are legally or philosophically significant.

---

[10] What Klapper (2021) calls the "Drax problem" is really just another version of the worry that the term is a term of art.

4.2 A Broader Vision

For both experimental work seeking to further conversations in general jurisprudence and work seeking to uncover the meaning of everyday legal concepts, richer conversations might be had about the conclusions one can draw from this work.

For experimental general jurisprudence, much of the research has only argued *in passing* that the results would enrich debates in general jurisprudence. A more sustained conversation would be good to see. In addition to more theoretical conversation, it would be great to have more experiments on the familiar topics in general jurisprudence. There has been no work on different versions of legal positivism, for instance. Also, it would be nice to see analytical work with a wider focus. Most of the experimental work narrowly centers on vindicating or vanquishing particular claims about the relation between legal norms and moral norms. This is the heart of general jurisprudence, as presently understood, so this exclusive focus is forgivable, but there are other conversations to which experimentalists might turn. There are, for example, other conversations about the necessary conditions of a legal systems, such as conversations on whether legal systems require coercion, conversations on whether law is a system of rules or imperatives, and conversations on the difference between legal officials and mafiosos.

Beyond considering new studies on the necessary conditions for legal systems, there are meta-debates to which experimentalists can contribute. As one example, some legal philosophers contend that we lack a shared concept of law which could be the focus of philosophical discussion (see, e.g., L. Murphy 2005, Priel 2011). While one can interpret some experimental findings in ways that support that view (Flanagan and Hannikainen 2022), no work yet has made that issue its primary focus. This would be of interest. Also, some legal philosophers contend that the point of general jurisprudence should not be to discover the nature of law, but instead to settle on, or *engineer*, a conception of law to satisfy certain practical aims (for an overview, see Donelson 2021). Experiments may be helpful in carrying out that engineering work.

Moving from experimental general jurisprudence to experimental takes on divining everyday legal concepts, there is much more work those experimentalists can do too. In its most modest incarnation, experimental work on everyday legal concepts seeks to discover information that legal doctrine already requires lawyers and judges to have. Sometimes legal doctrine explicitly demands the ordinary folk or expert view on something, and experimentalists are just doctrine's handmaidens. In more ambitious forms, experimentalists may insist on totally *a priori* grounds that most or all everyday legal concepts ought to cohere with ordinary understandings. If such normative arguments can be sustained, this would certainly broaden the range of everyday legal concepts that experimentalist should study. However, there is an underexplored middle path between waiting to see if legal doctrine already calls for experimental interventions and having a more "activist" stance.[11] For instance, maybe research will reveal

---

11 A thought akin to this is developed by Sommers (2020, pp. 2302–2306).

that conceptions of certain everyday legal concepts are sticky or relatively impervious to correction. If so, and if these are concepts that laypeople have to employ, either as a juror or as a private citizen conducting their affairs, maybe these legal concepts ought to cohere with folk understandings. In this example, experimental results themselves supply part of the explanation for when folk understandings ought to receive reliance.

In closing, then, I implore experimentalists both to continue performing studies and to search out new ways to ply their trade. There are cogent arguments about why such research would advance jurisprudence. It remains for researchers (and their funders) to produce the work.

Bibliography

Aquinas, Thomas (1994): *The treatise on law.* Ed. by Robert Henle. Notre Dame: University of Notre Dame Press.

Caruso, Gregg (2021): *Rejecting retributivism. Free will, punishment, and criminal justice.* Cambridge: Cambridge University Press.

Diamond, Shari Seidman, and Pam Mueller (2010): "Empirical legal scholarship in law reviews", *Annual Review of Law and Social Science* 6 (1), pp. 581–599.

Donelson, Raff (2021): "The pragmatist school in analytic jurisprudence", *Philosophical Issues* 31 (1), pp. 66–84.

Donelson, Raff (2023): "Experimental approaches to general jurisprudence", in: Stefan Magen and Karolina Prochownik (Eds.): *Advances in experimental philosophy of law.* London: Bloomsbury, pp. 27–43.

Donelson, Raff, and Ivar Hannikainen (2020): "Fuller and the folk. The inner morality of law revisited", in: Tania Lombrozo, Joshua Knobe, and Shaun Nichols (Eds.): *Oxford studies in experimental philosophy.* Vol. 3. Oxford: Oxford University Press, pp. 6–28.

Flanagan, Brian, and Ivar Hannikainen (2022): "The folk concept of law. Law is intrinsically moral", *Australasian Journal of Philosophy* 100 (1), pp. 165–179.

Fuller, Lon (1969): *The morality of law.* Rev. edition. New Haven: Yale University Press.

Hannikainen, Ivar, Kevin Tobia, Guilhermeda de Almeida, Raff Donelson, Vilius Dranseika, Markus Kneer, Niek Strohmaier, Pyotyr Bystranowski, Kristina Dolinina, Bartosz Janik, Sothie Keo, Egle Lauraitytė, Alice Liefgreen, Maciej Próchnicki, Alejandro Rosas, and Noel Struchiner (2021): "Are there cross-cultural legal principles? Modal reasoning uncovers procedural constraints on law", *Cognitive Science* 45 (8), e13024.

Husak, Douglas (2002): *Legalize this! The case for decriminalizing drugs.* London and New York: Verso.

Kassin, Saul, and Rebecca Norwick (2004): "Why people waive their Miranda rights. The power of innocence", *Law and Human Behavior* 28 (2), pp. 211–221.

Kelsen, Hans (1967): *Pure theory of law.* Transl. by Max Knight. Berkeley: University of California Press.

King, Martin Luther (1986): "Letter from Birmingham City Jail", in: Martin Luther King: *A testament of hope.* Ed. by James Washington. New York: Harper & Row, pp. 289–302.

Klapper, Shlomo (2021): "Mechanical Turk jurisprudence", *Brooklyn Law Review* 86 (2), pp. 291–319.

Knobe, Joshua, Sandeep Prasada, and George Newman (2013): "Dual character concepts and the normative dimension of conceptual representation", *Cognition* 127 (2), pp. 242–257.

Knobe, Joshua, and Scott Shapiro (2021): "Proximate cause explained. An essay in experimental jurisprudence", *The University of Chicago Law Review* 88 (1), pp. 165–236.

Kominsky, Johnathan, Johnathan Phillips, Tobias Gerstenberg, David Lagnado, and Joshua Knobe (2015): "Causal superseding", *Cognition* 137, pp. 196–209.

Kugler, Matthew, and Lior Jacob Strahilevitz (2017): "The myth of fourth amendment circularity", *University of Chicago Law Review* 84 (4), pp. 1747–1812.

Leslie, Sarah-Jane (2015): "'Hillary Clinton is the only man in the Obama administration'. Dual character concepts, generics, and gender", *Analytic Philosophy* 56 (2), pp. 111–141.

Levy, Ken (2019): *Free will, responsibility, and crime. An introduction.* New York: Routledge.

Mackie, John (1981): "Obligations to obey the law", *Virginia Law Review* 67 (1), pp. 143–158.

Macleod, James (2019): "Ordinary causation. A study in experimental statutory interpretation", *Indiana Law Journal* 94 (3), pp. 957–1029.

Murphy, Liam (2001): "The political question of the concept of law", in: Jules Coleman (Ed.): *Hart's Postscript. Essays on the Postscript to "The concept of law"*. Oxford: Oxford University Press, pp. 371–409.

Murphy, Liam (2005): "Concepts of law", *Australian Journal of Legal Philosophy* 30 (1), pp. 1–19.

Murphy, Mark (2011): "The explanatory role of the weak natural law thesis", in: Wil Waluchow and Stefan Sciaraffa (Eds.): *Philosophical foundations of the nature of law*. Oxford: Oxford University Press, pp. 3–21.

Nadelhoffer, Thomas, and Eddy Nahmias (2007): "The past and future of experimental philosophy", *Philosophical Explorations* 10 (2), pp. 123–149.

Nado, Jennifer (2016): "The intuition deniers", *Philosophical Studies* 173 (3), pp. 781–800.

Nagel, Jennifer (2012): "Intuitions and experiments. A defense of the case method in epistemology", *Philosophy and Phenomenological Research* 85 (3), pp. 495–527.

Nussbaum, Martha (1998): "'Whether from reason or prejudice'. Taking money for bodily services", *The Journal of Legal Studies* 27 (S2), pp. 693–723.

Nye, Hillary (2017): "A critique of the concept-nature nexus in Joseph Raz's methodology", *Oxford Journal of Legal Studies* 37 (1), pp. 48–74.

Plato (1997a): "Crito", in: Plato: *Complete works*. Ed. by John Cooper and Douglas Hutchinson. Indianapolis and Cambridge: Hackett, pp. 37–49.

Plato (1997b): "Republic", in: Plato: *Complete Works*. Ed. by John Cooper and Douglas Hutchinson. Indianapolis and Cambridge: Hackett, pp. 971–1224.

Priel, Dan (2011): "Is there one right answer to the question of the nature of law?", in: Wil Waluchow and Stefan Sciaraffa (Eds.): *Philosophical foundations of the nature of law*. Oxford: Oxford University Press, pp. 322–350.

Raz, Joseph (2009a): "Can there be a theory of law?", in: Joseph Raz: *Between authority and interpretation. On the theory of law and practical reason*. Oxford: Oxford University Press, pp. 17–46.

Raz, Joseph (2009b): *The authority of law. Essays on law and morality*. 2nd edition. Oxford: Oxford University Press.

Shapiro, Scott (2011): *Legality*. Cambridge: Harvard University Press.

Sommers, Roseanna (2020): "Commonsense consent", *Yale Law Journal* 129 (8), pp. 2232–2324.

Sommers, Roseanna (2021): "Experimental jurisprudence", *Science* 373 (6553), pp. 394–395.

Stoljar, Natalie (2012): "In praise of wishful thinking. A critique of descriptive/explanatory theories of law", *Problema – Anuario de Filosofía y Teoría del Derecho* 6, pp. 51–79.

Tobia, Kevin (2015): "Philosophical method and intuitions as assumptions", *Metaphilosophy* 46 (4–5), pp. 575–594.

Tobia, Kevin (2020): "Testing ordinary meaning. An experimental assessment of what dictionary definitions and linguistic usage data tell legal interpreters", *Harvard Law Review* 134 (2), pp. 726–806.

Wilkinson-Ryan, Tess (2015): "Incentives to breach", *American Law and Economics Review* 17 (1), pp. 290–311.

Thomas Nadelhoffer
Experimental Philosophy of Action: Free Will and Moral Responsibility

Abstract: During the past 20 years, researchers have become increasingly interested in how people ordinarily think about free will and moral responsibility. One central issue that has been explored by experimental philosophers is whether people believe that determinism threatens their commonsense views about moral agency. A related issue that has been explored is whether people believe that advances in neuroscience and other cognate fields pose a similar threat. In this chapter, I will first survey some of the findings on these two compatibility questions. I will then discuss two error theories that experimental philosophers have developed to explain away findings that conflict with their preferred views about commonsense intuitions (namely, bypassing and indeterministic intrusion). As we will see, the gathering evidence suggests that comprehension errors are far more common than researchers have previously assumed. Having discussed the recent work on this issue, I will briefly consider some strategies for addressing it and explain why I am cautiously optimistic that experimental philosophers will find a way forward. Finally, I will highlight some further topics that experimental philosophers have explored when it comes to people's beliefs about free will and moral responsibility that I did not have space to explore in this chapter.

Keywords: Determinism; Experimental Philosophy; Folk Intuitions; Free Will; Moral Responsibility

1 Introduction

Of the perennial philosophical questions, whether or not we have free will is one of the most popular in the eyes of the public. Consider, for instance, the following array of articles published in the popular press just in the past five years: "The Clockwork Universe – Is Free Will an Illusion?" (*The Guardian* in 2021), "Science Hasn't Refuted Free Will" (*Boston Review* in 2020), "Yes, Free Will Exists" (*Scientific American* in 2020), "Quantum Mechanics, Free Will and the Game of Life" (*Scientific American* in 2020), "A Famous Article about Free Will Has Been Debunked" (*The Atlantic* in 2019), "Does Belief in Free Will Make Us More Ethical?" (*The Wall Street Journal* in 2017), and "There's No Such Thing as Free Will" (*The Atlantic* in 2016). One won't find similar coverage of other venerable philosophical debates in leading magazines and newspapers.

Why the abiding public interest in free will? On the one hand, it's because people already have a pre-theoretical concept of free will (however ill-defined and inconsistent it may be). And so, when they read about free will, they take themselves to understand both what is being discussed and what is at stake when it is threatened. On the other hand, and more importantly, people care about free will because it is bound up with their religious and cultural traditions, their experience of their own agency, their self-understanding, and how they judge moral behavior (both their own and that of others). The connection between free will and moral responsibility is especially important. After all, some philosophers claim that the kind of up-to-usness that is at stake in the debate about free will just is the kind of control that is relevant to (or even required by) moral responsibility (Double 1992, Ekstrom 2000, Fischer 1994, Levy 2011, Mele 2006, Nelkin 2011, Pereboom 2014, Smilansky 2000, Vargas 2007, McKenna and Widerker 2003, Wolf 1990; cf. Rossi and Warfield 2017, van Inwagen 2008).

Given the connection between our metaphysical views about free will and our more pedestrian moral beliefs and practices, it is perhaps unsurprising that it has been commonplace for both parties to the free will debate to align their respective theories with popular opinion. Frank Jackson, for instance, claims that the fundamental issue in the free will debate should be "whether free action according to our ordinary conception, or something suitably close to our ordinary conception, exists and is compatible with determinism" and he suggests that to identify our ordinary conception we must "appeal to what seems to us most obvious and central about free action [...] as revealed by our intuitions about possible cases" (Jackson 1998, p. 31). As we will see, Jackson is not alone in having these metaphilosophical commitments. Appeals to folk intuitions are standard fare in the literature on free will.

In this chapter, I will first discuss some of the research from experimental philosophy on whether people think that determinism threatens free will and moral responsibility (Section 2.1). I will then turn my attention to the related debate about whether people think that advances in neuroscience and other cognate fields pose a similar threat (Section 2.2). Next, I will discuss two error theories that experimental philosophers have developed to explain away findings that conflict with their preferred views about commonsense intuitions; namely, bypassing and indeterministic intrusion (Section 2.3). As we will see, the gathering evidence suggests that comprehension errors are far more common than researchers have previously assumed. So, I will briefly consider some strategies experimental philosophers could adopt in an effort to address the comprehension problem (Section 2.4). I will end this section on a cautiously optimistic note since I believe that the very empirical methods that have unearthed the comprehension problem can help experimental philosophers find a way forward. Finally, I will highlight some further topics that experimental philosophers have explored when it comes to people's beliefs about free will and moral responsibility that I did not have space to explore in this chapter (Section 3). The breadth of these issues makes it clear just how much interdisciplinary work remains to be done.

2 Folk Intuitions about Free Will

2.1 The (Potential) Threat of Determinism

The traditional debate about free will focuses on the potential threat of determinism, which philosophers have conceptualized in several related ways. For instance, van Inwagen (1983, p. 3) defines determinism as the thesis that "there is at any instance exactly one physically possible future", while Mele (2006, p. 3) defines determinism as the thesis that "at any instant exactly one future is compatible with the state of the universe at that instant and the laws of nature". The key metaphysical question is whether determinism, thusly defined, is compatible with free will and/or moral responsibility. In shedding light on this issue, philosophers often rely on what they take to be the intuitive responses to thought experiments, thereby adopting the kind of "possible cases" method favored by Jackson (1998). This intuition-driven approach naturally gives rise to the question of which theories of free will and moral responsibility best capture people's ordinary intuitions.

According to philosophers who defend *natural incompatibilism*, most people intuitively believe that free will and/or moral responsibility are incompatible with determinism (see, e.g., Cover and O'Leary-Hawthorne 1996, Ekstrom 2000, Kane 1999, Nichols 2015, O'Connor 2000, Pereboom 2001, Searle 1984, Smilansky 2003, Strawson 1986). For instance, van Inwagen claims that:

> It has seemed obvious to most people who have not been exposed (perhaps "subjected" would be a better word) to philosophy that free will and determinism are incompatible. It is almost impossible to get beginning students of philosophy to take seriously the idea that there could be such a thing as free will in a deterministic universe. Indeed, people who have not been exposed to philosophy usually understand the word "determinism" (if they know the word at all) to stand for the thesis that there is no free will. And you might think that the incompatibility of free will and determinism deserves to be obvious because it is obvious. (van Inwagen 2009, p. 257)

According to philosophers who defend *natural compatibilism*, on the other hand, most people intuitively believe that free will and/or moral responsibility are compatible with determinism (see, e.g., Ayer 1954, Dennett 1984, Fischer and Ravizza 1998, Lycan 2003, Nahmias 2014, Nowell-Smith 1949, Wolf 1990). For instance, Stace claims that:

> Acts freely done are those whose immediate causes are psychological states in the agent. Acts not done freely are those whose immediate causes are states of affairs external to the agent. It is plain that if we define free will in this way, then free will certainly exists, and the philosopher's denial of its existence is seen to be what it is – nonsense. For it is obvious that all those actions of men which we should ordinarily attribute to the exercise of their free will, or of which we should say that they freely chose to do them, are in fact actions which have been caused by their own desires, wishes, thoughts, emotions, impulses, or other psychological states. (Stace 1952, pp. 408f.)

Figuring out which of these claims about how people ordinarily think about free will and responsibility is correct is ultimately an empirical task.

Unfortunately, the extant data from experimental philosophy are mixed and open to multiple interpretations. On the one hand, there are findings that (appear to) support natural incompatibilism (e.g., Chan, Deutsch, and Nichols 2016; Deery, Bedke, and Nichols 2013; Feltz and Milan 2013; Nadelhoffer, Yin, and Graves 2019; Nadelhoffer, Rose, Buckwalter, and Nichols 2020; Nichols 2004, 2006a, 2006b; Nichols and Knobe 2007; Rose and Nichols 2013; Rose, Buckwalter, and Nichols 2017; Roskies and Nichols 2008; Sarkissian et al. 2010; Wisniewski, Deutschländer, and Haynes 2019). On the other hand, there are findings that (appear to) support natural compatibilism (e.g., Andow and Cova 2016; Deery, Davis, and Carey 2014; Feltz 2013; Hainnikainen et al. 2019; Miller and Feltz 2011; Monroe and Malle 2009; Murray and Nahmias 2014; Nahmias, Coates, and Kvaran 2007; Nahmias, Morris, Nadelhoffer, and Turner 2005, 2006; Nahmias and Murray 2011; Nahmias, Shepard, and Reuter 2014; Sripada 2012; Turner and Nahmias 2006; Turri 2017; Woolfolk, Doris, and Darley 2006).

In some of the earliest work in experimental philosophy on folk intuitions about free will, Nahmias and colleagues (2005, 2006) set out to shed light on the debate about natural incompatibilism.[1] So, they ran three studies that used vignettes with different descriptions of determinism. Consider, for instance, their supercomputer scenario, which involves an algorithm that can predict the future with 100% accuracy based on deductions from the "laws of nature and the current state of everything in the world" (Nahmias et al. 2005, p. 559). Nahmias and colleagues asked two main questions – one about whether Jeremy acted of his own free will and one about whether Jeremy was morally responsible. Despite the determinism that was built into the scenario, 76% of participants judged that Jeremy robbed the bank of his own free will and 83% judged that he was morally responsible. These findings were consistent across cases involving neutral actions (e.g., going jogging), positively valenced actions (e.g., saving a child from a burning building), and negatively valenced actions (e.g., robbing a bank).

In another study, involving a so-called "rollback" scenario modeled on van Inwagen's widely discussed thought experiment (2000), participants read a scenario whereby the universe is "re-created over and over again, starting from the exact same initial conditions and with all the same laws of nature" (Nahmias et al. 2006, p. 38). In this scenario, an agent named Jill stole a necklace every time the universe was recreated. Participants were then asked whether "Jill decided to steal the necklace of her own free will" and whether "it would be fair to hold her morally responsible (that is, blame her) for her decision to steal the necklace". Whereas 66% judged that Jill decided of her own free will, 77% judged her to be blameworthy for her decision. Collectively, the findings from the supercomputer and rollback studies provided some intriguing preliminary

---

[1] The first paper published in experimental philosophy in this area was Nichols (2004) which provided evidence that children operate with an agent causal conception of human agency.

evidence that people may be more compatibilist than philosophers have traditionally assumed.

However, shortly thereafter, Nichols and Knobe (2007) provided evidence that problematized the conclusions drawn by Nahmias and colleagues. In the studies by Nichols and Knobe, participants were randomly assigned to either an abstract condition that describes a deterministic Universe A and an indeterministic Universe B or a concrete condition that describes these two universes but also describes a person in Universe A, Bill, who murders his wife and family to be with his secretary. Participants were first asked which one of these two universes was more like their own. Nearly all participants (90%) selected Universe B – indicating that most participants believe that the world we live in is indeterministic. Then, participants in the abstract condition were asked whether it was possible for a person in Universe A to be "fully responsible for their actions" while participants in the concrete condition were asked whether Bill is "fully morally responsible for killing his wife and children". Whereas 72% of subjects in the concrete condition gave the *compatibilist* response that Bill is fully morally responsible in Universe A, 84% in the abstract condition gave the *incompatibilist* response that it is not possible for people in Universe A to be fully morally responsible.

On the surface, these findings appear to put pressure on the claim that people's intuitions are robustly compatibilist. Instead, whether people are inclined to give compatibilist answers may depend less on the presence (or absence) of determinism and more on other features of the vignettes. Whereas people tend to display compatibilist leanings when asked to make judgments concerning the responsibility of specific agents, when they are asked instead to think about responsibility in the abstract, their intuitions lean towards incompatibilism. Nichols and Knobe take their results to show that while people have an incompatibilist theory of free will, when they consider a concrete, emotionally charged, situation, they are led to make a performance error that doesn't reflect their dispassionate incompatibilist view about free will.

There is an on-going debate about how to best explain (away) the conflicting findings from Nahmias and colleagues and Nichols and Knobe (e.g., Bear and Knobe 2016; Björnsson 2014; Björnsson and Pereboom 2014; Bourgeois-Gironde, Cova, Bertoux, and Dubois 2012; Clark, Winegard, and Baumeister 2019; Cokely and Feltz 2010; Cova and Kitano 2014; Feldman, Wong, and Baumeister 2016; Feltz and Cokely 2009; Feltz, Cokely, and Nadelhoffer 2009; Feltz and Cokely 2012; Feltz, Perez, and Harris 2012; Feltz and Cova 2014; Knobe 2014; Lim and Chem 2018; Mandelbaum and Ripley 2012; May 2015; Murray and Nahmias 2014; Nadelhoffer et al. 2020; Nahmias and Murray 2011; Phillips and Knobe 2009; Rose and Nichols 2013; Rose et al. 2017; Roskies and Nichols 2008; Shepherd 2012, 2015; Sinnott-Armstrong 2008; Weigel 2011). I will discuss some of this research in Section 2.3. But first I want to discuss some related findings on how people think about the tension (or lack thereof) between advances in neuroscience and cognate fields and our traditional picture of human agency.

2.2 The (Potential) Scientific Threat to Free Will

On New Year's Day, 2012, evolutionary biologist Jerry Coyne made the following remarks in the widely-read pages of *USA Today*:

> Perhaps you've chosen to read this essay after scanning other articles on this website. Or, if you're in a hotel, maybe you've decided what to order for breakfast, or what clothes you'll wear today. You haven't. You may feel like you've made choices, but in reality, your decision to read this piece, and whether to have eggs or pancakes, was determined long before you were aware of it – perhaps even before you woke up today. And your "will" had no part in that decision. So, it is with all of our other choices: not one of them results from a free and conscious decision on our part. There is no freedom of choice, no free will. And those New Year's resolutions you made? You had no choice about making them, and you'll have no choice about whether you keep them. (Coyne 2012)

What Coyne says here is representative of how free will, responsibility, and advances in neuroscience are often discussed in the popular press. One of the recurring themes is that as researchers learn more about the biopsychosocial causes of human action, they will uncover increasingly compelling evidence that free will is a "complete illusion". Unfortunately, overly sensationalized editorials serve only to generate more confusion than clarity. With so much at stake, we owe it to ourselves and the public more generally to proceed with caution. After all, as Coyne (2012) himself acknowledges, "the issue of whether we have free will is not an arcane academic debate about philosophy, but a critical question whose answer affects us in many ways: how we assign moral responsibility, how we punish criminals, how we feel about our religion, and, most important, how we see ourselves – as autonomous or automatons".

Scientific skeptics about free will often claim that most laypersons are (a) dualists about the relationship between the mind and the brain, and (b) libertarians about free will (e.g., Cashmore 2010, Greene and Cohen 2004, Harris 2012, Haynes 2011, Montague 2008). These assumptions enjoy empirical support. For instance, researchers have argued that the belief in dualism and/or the soul may be hard-wired into the parts of our cognitive architecture that facilitate how we distinguish agents from non-agents (Bloom 2004, Bering 2006). Relatedly, researchers have found that neuroscientific explanations of mental phenomena that were designed to be convincing *decreased* the belief in the soul while neuroscientific explanations of mental phenomena designed to be unconvincing *increased* the belief in the soul (Preston, Ridder, and Hepler 2013). Finally, a recent large-scale cross-cultural study of people's intuitions about free will, determinism, and dualism found that the belief in dualism is very common and also strongly correlated with beliefs in libertarian free will (Wisniewski, Deutschländer, and Haynes 2019).

Having assumed that folk dualism and folk libertarianism are core elements of the ordinary concept of free will, scientific skeptics conclude that as researchers continue to learn more about the purely physical causes of human thought and behavior, this will leave increasingly less room for the soul and free will to do any explanatory work. For instance, Greene and Cohen claim that:

> Neuroscience will challenge and ultimately reshape our intuitive sense(s) of justice. New neuroscience will affect the way we view the law, not by furnishing us with new ideas or arguments about the nature of human action, but by breathing new life into old ones. Cognitive neuroscience, by identifying the specific mechanisms responsible for behavior, will vividly illustrate what until now could only be appreciated through esoteric theorizing: that there is something fishy about our ordinary conceptions of human action and responsibility. (Greene and Cohen 2004, p. 1775)

According to Greene and Cohen, while current legal doctrine requires only the sorts of cognitive, emotional, and volitional capacities championed by compatibilists, "the law's intuitive support is ultimately grounded in a metaphysically overambitious, libertarian notion of free will that is threatened by determinism and, more pointedly, by forthcoming cognitive neuroscience" (Greene and Cohen 2004, p. 1776). Because they believe that the kind of determinism and reductionism revealed by cognitive neuroscience means that all actions are traceable to forces beyond our control, they conclude that the commonsense belief in dualism and libertarianism will lose its appeal. As they say, "when we look at people as physical systems, we cannot see them as any more blameworthy or praiseworthy than bricks" (Greene and Cohen 2004, p. 1782).

For present purposes, the key question is whether commonsense intuitions about free will and responsibility support the view promulgated by scientific skeptics like Coyne, Greene, Cohen, and others. In order to shed light on this issue, Nahmias, Coates, and Kvaran (2007) explored people's judgments about reductive materialism in addition to their judgments about determinism (which need not go together). Their working hypothesis was that while most people appeared to endorse incompatibilism in the earlier studies by Nichols and Knobe, it was only because participants mistakenly inferred that determinism entails bypassing – that is, the view that "our deliberations and conscious purposes are bypassed by forces that are out of our control" (Nahmias et al. 2007, p. 220).[2] Nahmias and colleagues suggested that by telling participants that the decisions of people in a deterministic universe "had to happen", Nichols and Knobe may have unwittingly primed participants to make the bypassing error. According to Nahmias and colleagues, it is this mistaken judgment and not determinism per se that explains why so many participants sometimes express judgments that appear on the surface to support natural incompatibilism.

To test this hypothesis, Nahmias and colleagues (2007) presented participants with a deterministic scenario that they were told took place either on Earth or on an alternative universe Erta that is very similar to our own.[3] These scenarios described human behavior in either folk psychological terms or in reductionistic neurological terms.

---

[2] I am going to discuss bypassing in much more detail in Section 2.3.
[3] Nahmias et al. (2007) included the Earth and Erta conditions because they thought that the latter way of framing determinism might make it easier for participants to reason counter-factually (under the assumption that most participants would view our universe through the lens of indeterminism).

Here is relevant passage from one of the scenarios that highlights the difference between these two elements:

> For instance, neuroscientists [psychologists] have discovered that whenever an Ertan is trying to decide what to do, the decision the Ertan ends up making is completely caused by the specific chemical reactions and neural processes [thoughts, desires, and plans] occurring in his or her brain [mind]. The neuroscientists [psychologists] have also discovered that these chemical reactions and neural processes [thoughts, desires, and plans] are completely caused by the Ertan's current situation and the earlier events in his or her life. (Nahmias et al. 2007, p. 223)

Nahmias and colleagues used these scenarios to explore participants' intuitions about several related issues – e.g., were the agents' decisions up to them, were they able to make decisions of their own free will, should they be held morally responsible, do they deserve to be blamed for doing something bad, is it possible for them to have deep personal relationships and/or lead meaningful lives, and so forth?

The primary finding by Nahmias and colleagues (2007) is that participants in both the Earth and Erta conditions attributed more free will and moral responsibility when the agent's behavior was described in folk psychological terms rather than in neuro-reductive terms (even though both conditions were deterministic). Nahmias and colleagues claim that these results show that most people don't find determinism per se threatening to free will so long as it is described as operating at the level of people's beliefs, desires, decisions, and so forth. It is only when the determinism is presented in a way that conflates determinism with epiphenomenalism that people's belief in free will and moral responsibility is weakened. Epiphenomenalism is the thesis that "one's (conscious) mental events or processes have no causal effect on physical events, including one's behaviors" (Murray and Nahmias 2014, p. 439). On this view, while it feels like my conscious desires and intentions to *x* explains why I *x*-ed, this is an illusion. Instead, all actions are ultimately explicable in terms of unconscious mental states.

This is germane to our present discussion because both compatibilists and incompatibilists alike agree that epiphenomenalism, if true, threatens free will and moral responsibility. Moreover, they also agree that determinism does not entail epiphenomenalism – that is, just because all of our conscious beliefs, desires, decisions, and intentions are completely determined, it doesn't follow that these mental states don't play a causal role in our behavior. This means that researchers must be careful to make sure that the scenarios they use don't encourage participants to confound determinism with epiphenomenalism.[4]

In some follow-up research, Nahmias, Shepard, and Reuter (2014) explored people's intuitions about "perfect prediction", a term coined by Harris (2012) who had readers envision the following scenario:

---

4 I will also say more about this is Section 2.3.

> Imagine a perfect neuroimaging device that would allow us to detect and interpret the subtlest changes in brain function. [...] [T]he experimenters knew what you would think and do just before you did it. You would, of course, continue to feel free in every preset moment, but the fact that someone else could report what you were about to think and do would expose this feeling for what it is: an illusion. (Nahmias, Shepard, and Reuter 2014, pp. 10f.)

Nahmias and colleagues conducted three experiments to see whether people shared Harris' view about the purportedly antagonist relationship between neuroprediction, free will, and moral responsibility. While the scenarios in Experiments 1 and 2 are couched in physicalist language, the scenarios in Experiment 3 are coached in dualistic language. As Nahmias and colleagues (2014, p. 504) point out, "under the view that the ordinary understanding of free will requires a specific metaphysics of mind (e.g., dualism), one would expect to find different patterns of results among these experiments (e.g., low attributions of free will in the scenarios that rule out dualism)".

Across all three experiments, Nahmias and colleagues (2014) found that neuroprediction did not tend to undermine attributions of free will and moral responsibility so long as it was made clear that the agents' behavior was the result of their own practical deliberation. Whether the scenarios described neuroprediction in terms of neural activity in the brain (Experiments 1 and 2) or in terms of mental activity in the mind or soul (Experiment 3), participants who made the bypassing error were less likely to attribute free will and moral responsibility. These findings suggest that participants tend to judge that agents can be free and responsible in the face of neuroprediction so long as they aren't encouraged to interpret the scenarios through the lens of epiphenomenalism.

However, even if Nahmias and colleagues (2014) are right that some of the apparent support for natural incompatibilism is predicated on a misunderstanding of determinism, physicalism, or both, this doesn't mean that the prediction by Greene and Cohen (2004) won't come to pass. After all, it could be that developments in neuroscience and cognate fields might slowly erode our traditional beliefs about agency and responsibility even if the erosion is caused, at least in part, by mistaken assumptions about the relationship between determinism, reductive physicalism, epiphenomenalism, and so forth. There are at least two questions at work on this front. The first is normative – namely, *should* advances in neuroscience erode people's beliefs in free will and moral responsibility? The second is purely descriptive – namely, *will* advances in neuroscience likely erode people's beliefs in free will and moral responsibility (and if so, why)? The answer to the latter question could be yes even if the answer to the former question is no.

As we saw, Greene and Cohen (2004) answer both of these questions in the affirmative – that is, they believe that advances in neuroscience and other cognate fields both *will and should* challenge our traditional views about human agency. Because only the descriptive question is amenable to the methods of experimental philosophy, that will be my focus here. Consider, for instance, the recent work by Shariff and colleagues (2014). As they note, purely natural phenomena, such as viruses and hailstorms, are not held morally responsible for the damage they cause because they are not perceived as freely choosing their actions. The rejection of free will for humans could similarly undermine attributions of responsibility, both for oneself and for others, rendering human actions akin to other natural phenomena. (Shariff et al. 2014, p. 2)

In order to shed light on this issue, Shariff and colleagues ran four studies, predicting that exposing people to neuroscientific primes would diminish their beliefs in free will, which would, in turn, diminish their support for retributive punishment.

In Study 1, Shariff and colleagues explored the relationship between free will beliefs and attitudes toward consequentialist punishment (e.g., punishing someone because it serves as a deterrent) and retributivist punishment (e.g., punishing someone because they deserve it), and found that individual differences in free will beliefs correlated with support for retributive punishment. In Study 2, they tried to manipulate people's belief in free will using neuroscientific scenarios and found that challenging beliefs in free will diminished retributive punishment. In Studies 3 and 4, they exposed participants to research concerning the neural mechanisms underlying human action (either by reading popular press articles about neuroscience and human behavior or by having participants take an introductory class in neuroscience) and found that exposing participants to mechanistic explanations for human action also correlated with weakened support for retributive punishment.

In light of their findings, Shariff and colleagues (2014, p. 7) claim that "the mere exposure to modern neuroscience can be sufficient to reduce retributivist motivations", which supports one of the main predictions by Greene and Cohen.[5] However, Nahmias and colleagues could nevertheless be right that these findings are driven by misunderstanding about the stimuli that researchers have used. Because this issue has the potential to undermine a number of the findings on folk intuitions about free will, moral responsibility, and the two compatibility questions we have discussed thus far, I want to take a closer look at the nature and potential scope of the (mis-)comprehension problem.

2.3 A Tale of Two Error Theories – Bypassing Versus Intrusion

2.3.1 Epiphenomenal Bypassing and Fatalistic Bypassing

The most widely discussed strategy that has been employed to explain away (seemingly) incompatibilist intuitions was first developed by Eddy Nahmias and colleagues

---

[5] It is an open question whether society would be better or worse off if people lost their zeal for retributive punishment in the wake of neuroscientific advances. I side with Greene and Cohen (2004) in thinking that we'd be better off if our society moved away from backward-looking approaches to punishment and adopted instead forward-looking alternatives.

(Nahmias et al. 2007, Nahmias and Murray 2011, Murray and Nahmias 2014). Their key claim is that the modal language found in some of the more widely used scenarios that have elicited incompatibilist intuitions – e.g., the Universe A/B scenario states that events in "had to happen" in the deterministic universe – could lead participants to draw problematic inferences about the agents in those scenarios. Nahmias and colleagues focus on the spurious inference that determinism entails bypassing – which comes in two forms.

The first is fatalistic bypassing – that is, the thesis that "certain things will happen no matter what one wants, decides, or tries to do, such that nothing could happen other than what actually happens even if one's past mental states, such as one's desires, had been different" (Murray and Nahmias 2014, p. 439). But it is a mistake to conflate determinism with fatalism – e.g., in a deterministic universe, it is possible that events could have unfolded differently whereas in a fatalistic universe, there are no possible alternative sequences of events. As Nahmias and Murray (2011, p. 197) point out, fatalism (unlike determinism) "negates a compatibilist understanding of the ability to do otherwise, because one's actions have to happen even if the past (e.g., one's reasons) had been different". Consequently, fatalism generates problems for free will and moral responsibility that are not generated merely by determinism – which is why even compatibilists about determinism ought to be incompatibilists about fatalism.

The other form of bypassing is epiphenomenalism. As we saw earlier, while determinism does not entail epiphenomenalism, if epiphenomenalism is true, our conscious selves are left out of the causal loop. This explains why all parties to the free will debate believe that epiphenomenalism undermines free will. After all, if I cannot exercise conscious control over what I believe, decide, intend, and do, then it doesn't make sense to say that I am free or responsible. As such, *everyone* ought to be an incompatibilist about epiphenomenalism regardless of where they come down on the debate about determinism. That's because epiphenomenalism – much like fatalism – generates metaphysical problems that go above and beyond the problems associated with determinism.

As Murray and Nahmias (2014, p. 440) point out, while some participants may mistakenly judge that determinism entails fatalism or epiphenomenalism, this is not a mistake that philosophers tend to make. As such, in order for an intuition to count for or against natural incompatibilism about determinism *as philosophers understand it* – rather than natural incompatibilism about fatalism and/or epiphenomenalism – efforts must be made to control for bypassing. After all, intuitions predicated on mistaken inferences about the nature and implications of determinism aren't philosophically probative even if they may nevertheless be psychologically probative.

Because the findings by Nichols and Knobe (2007) are the most often cited in support of natural incompatibilism, Nahmias and colleagues make these findings their central target. On their view, the stimuli used in these earlier studies encourage participants to infer that determinism entails bypassing (e.g., participants are told that in the deterministic universe, "given the past, each decision has to happen the way that it does", Murray and Nahmias 2014, pp. 442f.). To explore this issue, Murray and Nahmias designed two studies to test whether their error theory could help explain away the empirical support for natural incompatibilism.

In Study 1, there were four conditions – which included abstract and concrete versions of the supercomputer scenario and abstract and concrete versions of the Universe A/B scenario. Having read one of these scenarios, participants then reported their intuitions about the agent's free will, moral responsibility, and deservingness of blame. Participants also reported their intuitions about four items that were specifically designed to see whether participants were making the bypassing error.[6] Murray and Nahmias found a very strong negative correlation between intuitions about free will, responsibility, desert, and the bypassing error (collapsing across all four conditions): $r(247) = -0.734$, $p < 0.001$. They then used mediation analysis, which showed that once they controlled for bypassing errors, there was no longer a difference between responses to the supercomputer conditions and the Universe A/B conditions. In light of these findings, Murray and Nahmias claim:

> These data suggest that most people judge that agents in deterministic scenarios lack moral responsibility, free will, and blameworthiness only when they conflate determinism with bypassing – that is, when they interpret the description of determinism in a scenario to mean that agents' beliefs, desires, and decisions have no effect on what they end up doing and that agents have no control over what they do. When they do not confuse determinism with bypassing, most people do not offer incompatibilist intuitions. (Murray and Nahmias 2014, p. 449)

In Study 2, Murray and Nahmias wanted to extend their earlier findings by trying to reduce the prevalence of the bypassing error to see whether participants would then be more likely to attribute free will and responsibility in response to scenarios that normally elicit (seemingly) incompatibilist judgments. They also wanted to make sure that participants did not make a different error in modal reasoning – namely, the error of misunderstanding what determinism actually does entail (e.g., "that it is impossible, holding fixed the past and the laws, for future events to occur otherwise than they actually do", Murray and Nahmias 2014, p. 450). So, Murray and Nahmias altered the scenarios so that they explicitly stated both what determinism *does not* entail (namely, bypassing) and what determinism *does* entail. The overarching goal was to make sure that they were only analyzing the data from "competent participants", that is, "those who do not conflate determinism with bypassing, but who understand what determinism does properly preclude" (Murray and Nahmias 2014, p. 450).

---

[6] Here are examples of the bypassing items from Study 2 (abstract cases first with variations in brackets; concrete cases in parentheses): (a) In Universe [A/B], a person's decisions have no effect on what they end up doing. (Bill's decision to steal the necklace has no effect on what he ends up doing.), (b) In Universe [A/B], what a person wants has no effect on what they end up doing. (What Bill wants has no effect on what he ends up doing.), (c) In Universe [A/B], what a person believes has no effect on what they end up doing. (What Bill believes has no effect on what he ends up doing.), and (d) In Universe [A/B], a person has no control over what they do. (Bill has no control over what he does.)

As Murray and Nahmias predicted, the modified language of the stimuli in Study 2 led to lower agreement with the bypassing items and higher agreement with the items measuring free will, responsibility, and desert in response to the abstract scenarios. As for the other question they explored, they found that the overwhelming majority of participants did not make any modal errors in forming judgments about what determinism entails. Taking these findings together, Murray and Nahmias think that they have shown that the bypassing error largely explains why some earlier findings on free will beliefs suggested that incompatibilism enjoyed broadscale popular support. On their view, by focusing on competent (rather than confused) participants, they were able to produce more reliable and probative data about common beliefs about free will and moral responsibility – beliefs that they claim support natural compatibilism.

In follow-up research, Rose and Nichols (2013, p. 600) claim that the earlier findings on the bypassing error have been "systematically misinterpreted". In an effort to support this claim, they discuss two different models that one might use to explain the data. The first is the bypassing model favored by Murray and Nahmias whereby deterministic scenarios lead people to mistakenly infer bypassing, which in turns leads people to judge that the agents in these scenarios are less free and responsible. But as Rose and Nichols point out, a single mediation analysis by itself does not establish causal directionality. As a result, while the mediation analysis used by Murray and Nahmias is consistent with their bypassing model, it is also consistent with the rival MR/FW (moral responsibility and free will) incompatibilist model favored by Rose and Nichols. So, they ran a new study to test which of these two models does a better job of explaining the data. Rose and Nichols predicted that deterministic scenarios would lead people to make incompatibilist judgments about free will and responsibility, which would in turn lead people to make the bypassing error.

Whereas Murray and Nahmias (2014) compared responses to the supercomputer scenario with responses to the abstract version of Universe A/B scenario claiming that the latter elicited more bypassing errors than the former – Rose and Nichols chose instead to limit themselves to the Universe A/B scenario while varying whether participants were asked about the deterministic or indeterministic universe. Then, using structural equation modeling, they found that the best performing model indicates that determinism judgments influence MR/FW judgments which then influence bypassing judgments. Moreover, once Rose and Nichols (2013, p. 606) factored in how people responded to the MR/FW items, scores on the determinism item no longer predicted scores on the bypassing item.

Rose and Nichols then ran a second study to shed further light on the causes of the bypassing error. Their main hypothesis was that bypassing is more likely to occur when practical reasoning is involved (as it often is in moral decision-making) than when theoretical reasoning is involved (e.g., doing arithmetic). They wanted to explore this issue because decision-making – which has been the focus of much of the work on bypassing – is a paradigmatic example of practical reasoning. After all, while being bad at math or physics needn't make one any less free and responsible, having impairments in practical rationality might. As such, Rose and Nichols predicted that scenarios involving practical reasoning would be more likely to elicit bypassing intuitions than scenarios involving theoretical reasoning – which could help explain why people tend to have incompatibilist responses to these scenarios. Rose and Nichols also predicted that people who are presented with a deterministic scenario will be more likely to say that practical reasoning is impossible than theoretical reasoning.

For this study, Rose and Nichols modified the Universe A/B scenario so that there were three conditions: an agent engaged in practical reasoning, an agent engaged in theoretical reasoning, and a non-agential natural event (which served as control condition). Having read one of the scenarios, participants were then asked to report their level of agreement (using a 7-point scale) with the following statements:

- Practical reasoning: "In this universe, when people make decisions, what they think and want has no effect on what actions they end up performing."
- Theoretical reasoning: "In this universe, when people solve math problems, the numbers they add has no effect on the answers they end up giving."
- Physical event: "In this universe, the earth's shaking has no effect on whether trees fall over."

Moreover, in each condition, participants were asked a forced-choice question about the nonexistence of the relevant type of event:

- Practical reasoning: "In this universe, people make decisions."
- Theoretical reasoning: "In this universe, people add numbers."
- Physical event: "In this universe, trees fall over."

The main finding was that people judged determinism to be more threatening to practical reasoning than theoretical reasoning and natural events. Moreover, Rose and Nichols found that participants who attributed less practical reasoning had higher bypassing scores, which they take to provide more evidence that the MR/FW incompatibilism model does a better job of explaining the data than the bypassing model.

Rose and Nichols claim that their findings highlight just how deeply incompatibilist people's intuitions go. On their view, the commonsense view of agency is ruggedly indeterministic. When presented with deterministic scenarios, people (correctly) judge that the agents don't have the sort of agency that they associate with free will and responsibility, which then leads them to make the bypassing error. If this is right, Nahmias and colleagues got things precisely backwards. Bypassing intuitions don't distort beliefs about free will and moral responsibility; rather, intuitions about the latter distort the former.

Björnsson and Pereboom (2014) take a different tact in criticizing the work on bypassing by Nahmias and colleagues. Rather than accepting the earlier findings at face value and trying to show that a different causal model best explains them, Björnsson and Pereboom claim that the sorts of measures for bypassing used by Nahmias and colleagues can be given an incompatibilist reading that doesn't constitute a misunderstanding of determinism. According to Björnsson and Pereboom (2014, p. 31), "traditional incompatibilism has it that because propositions detailing the natural laws and the remote past entail propositions describing every subsequent event, and agents can't render propositions about the laws and the remote past false, agents cannot make a difference to whether any such event occurs". As they point out, this is the kind of reasoning that underlies the widely discussed Consequence Argument (van Inwagen 1993).

On this view, "difference making requires that the difference maker is an independent variable in the causal system of the universe, that is, a variable the value of which is not determined by the value of other variables in that system" (Björnsson and Pereboom 2014, p. 31). Björnsson and Pereboom claim that the sorts of items used by Nahmias and colleagues to measure bypassing can be reinterpreted in this way. Consider, for instance, the following two items: (a) "In Universe A, a person has no control over what they do", and (b) "In Universe A, a person's decisions have no effect on what they end up being caused to do". According to Björnsson and Pereboom (2014), these items can plausibly be viewed through the lens of ultimate difference making. In the case of (a), they claim that this could be taken to mean that "the strings have no control over the marionette because their movement is completely dependent on the manipulator. It is not confused to think that our beliefs, desires, or decisions have no such ultimate control in a deterministic system" (Björnsson and Pereboom 2014, p. 32). In the case of (b), they claim that if participants agree with this item "because they deny that human decisions […] are ultimate difference makers in a deterministic universe, they need not be confused about the nature of determinism" (Björnsson and Pereboom 2014, p. 32). Björnsson and Pereboom give similar treatment to the other measures for bypassing used by Nahmias and colleagues. If their criticisms hit the mark, then Nahmias and colleagues cannot take their findings to speak against natural incompatibilism without begging the question against a plausible incompatibilist interpretation.

In light of their analysis, Björnsson and Pereboom (2014) make the following observation: "It seems to us, then, that the five statements designed to test for bypassing can be plausibly understood in ways allowing that determination of actions passes through rather than bypasses agents' decisions, desires, and belief" (Björnsson and Pereboom 2014, p. 33). To test their "throughpass" hypothesis, they ran a study that used the Universe A/B scenario. Having read the scenario, participants were then presented with two throughpass items (e.g., "In Universe A, when earlier events cause an agent's action, they do so by affecting what the agent believes and wants, which in turn causes the agent to act in a certain way"). Average agreement with the two throughpass items was just above the midpoint ($M = 4.17$), providing limited evidence that participants' intuitions supported the throughpass hypothesis – that is, people tended to correctly agree with the throughpass items and this agreement did not correlate with their judgments about free will and moral responsibility.

The work by Pereboom and Björnsson extended the earlier work on the throughpass hypothesis done by Björnsson (2013), who reported the results from another study that used the abstract and concrete versions of the Universe A/B scenario. In addition to making some changes to the way Nahmias and colleagues worded the measures for people's judgments about the agent's decisions, wants, and beliefs, Björnsson removed the bypassing item about control and added the following throughpass items to each condition:

> **Abstract:** In Universe A, when earlier events cause an agent's action, they typically do so by affecting what the agent believes and wants, which in turn causes the agent to act in a certain way.
>
> **Concrete:** When earlier events caused Bill's action, they did so by affecting what he believed and wanted, which in turn caused him to act in a certain way.

As Björnsson notes, Nahmias and colleagues ought to predict that scores on the bypassing and throughpass items would be *negatively* correlated since the bypassing items specifically rule out a causal role for mental states to play while the throughpass items make it clear that mental states do play a causal role. But if instead people interpret the bypassing items to mean that the agent's mental states in the scenario had no *independent* effect on what the agent did (rather than meaning that the mental states have *no causal role* whatsoever), then one ought to predict that the bypassing and throughpass items would *not* be negatively correlated (Björnsson 2013, p. 107) – which would support the view that throughpass and bypass items are being interpreted similarly, thereby providing evidence for an incompatibilist interpretation of the bypassing items.

As predicted, Björnsson (2013) found that responses to the throughpass items were (a) above the midpoint in the deterministic condition ($M = 4.38$; 95% CI: [4.15, 4.62]), (b) significantly (albeit weakly) correlated with the bypassing items ($r = 0.250$, $p = 0.002$), and (c) not correlated with responses to the responsibility items. In light of these results, Björnsson concludes that we ought to reject the bypassing hypothesis put forward by Nahmias and colleagues. On his view, the reason that scores on bypassing items are consistently negatively correlated with scores on responsibility items is that participants who have incompatibilist intuitions take the "no effect" language of the bypassing items to indicate that the mental states of the agents in the scenarios do not provide any independent input into what the agents do (not that the mental states of the agents are causally inert). In light of these findings, Björnsson takes himself to have thwarted the attempt by Nahmias and colleagues to explain away the empirical support for natural incompatibilism.

2.3.2 Indeterministic Intrusion

As we saw in the previous section, it is imperative that participants adequately understand the nature and implications of the determinism that is built into the scenarios used by experimental philosophers. The aforementioned work on bypassing highlights one way that participants might fail to comprehend determinism. But the potential for misunderstanding cuts in the other direction as well. For instance, there is gathering evidence for what has been called indeterministic intrusion – that is, when people judge that it is possible for agents in *deterministic* universes to have capacities that are only possible in *indeterministic* universes such as the unconditional ability to do otherwise. Both incompatibilists and compatibilists alike agree that this is an ability that is ruled out by determinism. But if participants fail to comprehend that the agents in deterministic scenarios don't have the unconditional ability to do otherwise, they might be more inclined to judge the agents to be free and responsible. If this kind of mistake is common enough, it provides a potential avenue for explaining away compatibilist intuitions.

This is an issue that was first explored by Rose and colleagues (2017). Given that folk metaphysics about human agency is largely indeterministic (Monroe, Dillon, and Malle 2014, Nichols 2012, Nichols and Knobe 2007, Rose and Nichols 2013, Sarkissian et al. 2010, Stillman, Baumeister, and Mele 2011), Rose and colleagues hypothesized that this might interfere with people's ability to understand the deterministic features of the kinds of scenarios used by experimental philosophers. If people's indeterministic beliefs intrude on their intuitions about deterministic scenarios, then their responses cannot provide evidence for natural compatibilism. As Nahmias and colleagues have made clear in their own work on bypassing errors, only the intuitions of competent participants are philosophically probative.

So, in a series of studies, Rose and colleagues used the neuro-deterministic vignettes from Nahmias, Shepard, and Reuter (2014) along with some more fine-grained comprehension questions designed specifically to detect the potential influence of an intrusive indeterministic metaphysics. They found intrusion effects across all six studies, which suggests that many participants who appeared, on the surface, to give compatibilist answers were failing to adequately track the determinism built into the scenarios. Rose and colleagues concluded that to the extent that natural compatibilists have failed to adequately control for indeterministic intrusion, they have failed to provide evidence for their preferred theory about the nature of ordinary intuitions about free will and responsibility.

Nadelhoffer, Rose, Buckwalter, and Nichols (2020) built on the earlier work on indeterministic intrusion. In a large, preregistered study (with more than 1,000 participants), they used a between subject design that varied the following factors between conditions: Scenario (Supercomputer, Rollback), Action (Good, Bad), Case Type (Abstract, Concrete), and Entity (Agent, Robot). Having read one of the versions of the supercomputer or rollback scenarios, participants were then asked to state their level of agreement with a battery of statements that were designed to measure judgments about free will, praise/blame, moral responsibility. They also included several items designed to measure indeterministic intrusion.

For instance, there was a single-item measure which participants used to report what they thought the chances are that the agent in the deterministic scenarios will do something differently than predicted by the supercomputer (or do something differently after the rollback). Participants responded using a sliding 100-point scale (ranging from 0 = very unlikely to 100 = very likely). This item is important because, if determinism is true, then the kind of openness required for chance is impossible. If a supercomputer in a deterministic universe really could perfectly predict what an agent will do at a particular time and place based on the past and the laws, then there is no chance that the agent could do something else at that time. So, if participants wrongly think that deterministic universes are metaphysically open in this way, they have misunderstood determinism. As such, their intuitions cannot be used to support natural compatibilism.

Collapsing across the cases in the concrete conditions, Nadelhoffer and colleagues found that 50% of participants gave a rating of greater than 0 on the single-item measure of chance. Similarly, collapsing across the cases in the abstract conditions, 68% of participants gave a rating of greater than 0 on single-item measure of chance. When Nadelhoffer and colleagues treated the chance item as a genuine comprehension check, excluding those who displayed indeterministic intrusion, only 39% of the remaining participants judged that the agent had free will (collapsing all other variables). These findings problematize the earlier work by Nahmias and colleagues (2005, 2006). After all, not only did Nadelhoffer and colleagues find that comprehension failures about determinism are common using the very same deterministic scenarios, they also found that people who are prone to indeterministic intrusion are far more likely to judge that the agents in these scenarios are free and responsible.

Nadelhoffer, Murray, and Murray (2021) more recently combined the insights from the research on bypassing and indeterministic intrusion. Their goal was to develop improved measures for the three different types of errors that we've discussed: (a) epiphenomenal bypassing, (b) fatalistic bypassing, and (c) indeterministic intrusion.[7] So, Nadelhoffer and colleagues ran two preregistered studies. One used the supercomputer scenario and the other used the Universe A/B scenario. In each condition, participants read the scenario and responded to questions about free will and responsibility. Then, depending on the condition, participants responded to four items about (a) epiphenomenalism (e.g., "In Universe A, what people want and believe has no effect on what they do"), (b) fatalism (e.g., "In Universe A, John would have ended up having French Fries no matter what he tried to do"), or (c) intrusion ("In Universe A, what people decide to do could have been different even if everything leading up to the decision had been exactly the same").

Of the 585 participants who successfully completed the two studies by Nadelhoffer and colleagues, 81% (475) misinterpreted determinism by falsely believing either that it entails epiphenomenalism or fatalism or that it is compatible with fundamentally indeterministic capacities such as the unconditional ability to do otherwise. Moreover, Nadelhoffer and colleagues found that while bypassing errors make people less likely to attribute free will and moral responsibility to agents in deterministic scenarios, indeterministic intrusion has the opposite effect. Finally, Nadelhoffer and colleagues also

---

[7] It's worth noting that we solicited feedback from experimental philosophers on the wording of these items before we ran the studies. Eddy Nahmias and Gunnar Björnsson both sent us their suggestions and concerns, which we tried to address. For instance, we tried to word the bypassing items in a way that was incompatible with the throughpass items used by Björnsson.

found that different scenarios tend to elicit different comprehension mistakes. The supercomputer scenario is more likely to elicit indeterministic intrusion, which artificially inflates how many people give seeming compatibilist responses, while the Universe A/B scenario is more likely to elicit bypassing, which artificially inflates how many people give seeming incompatibilist responses.

Given how rampant comprehension failures were across the two studies, the findings by Nadelhoffer and colleagues suggest that there may be enough confusion concerning determinism baked into the existing evidence on folk intuitions about free will that these intuitions can't reliably be used to shed light on the debate about natural incompatibilism.[8] If that's right, experimental philosophers may need to go back to the drawing board when it comes to the best way to get at the intuitions they're trying to probe.

2.4 Addressing the Comprehension Problem

Above, I wanted to first familiarize readers with some of the research on people's intuitions about free will and moral responsibility. So, we looked at two related issues: Do people think that determinism threatens free will and moral responsibility? Do people think that recent advances in neuroscience and cognate fields threaten free will and moral responsibility? As we saw, the findings on both of these fronts are mixed. This empirical stalemate has prompted experimental philosophers to develop rival error theories in order to explain (away) the conflicting findings. The problem is that this strategy has led to a crisis. Once researchers started taking a closer at whether people adequately understand the stimuli and measures being used, it turned out that comprehension failure is more prevalent than anyone realized. Until this issue has been adequately addressed, experimental philosophers will remain at an impasse about the contours of commonsense.

So, what are some of the potentially promising avenues for righting the empirical ship when it comes to the comprehension problem? First, researchers might opt for using psychometric scales for measuring beliefs about determinism, dualism, free will, responsibility (Deery et al. 2015, Nadelhoffer et al. 2014, Paulhus and Carey 2011, Wisniewski, Deutschländer, and Haynes 2019). Second, researchers could use more realistic and mundane stimuli rather than scenarios involving supercomputers, rollback universes, etc. (Monroe, Dillon, and Malle 2014, Monroe and Malle 2010, Nadelhoffer and Monroe forthcoming, Turri 2017). Third, researchers could collect data on how people view their past, present, and future actions (and also perhaps how they view their lives in relation to the lives of others) when it comes to free will (Pronin and Kugler

---

[8] Murray, Murray, and Nadelhoffer (forthcoming) have collected similar data using several other scenarios from the literature. The results are the same, namely, the overwhelming majority of participants fail to understand determinism.

2010, Stillman, Baumeister, and Mele 2011). Finally, researchers could ask people to describe the phenomenology of their experiences of their own agency (Deery, Bedke, and Nichols 2013, Nahmias et al. 2004). These approaches are not mutually exclusive. But for researchers who choose to forgo these approaches and forge ahead using fantastical deterministic scenarios, the onus is on them to develop adequate comprehension checks to ensure that participants are understanding the stimuli as intended by the researcher. Otherwise, the probative philosophical value of their findings will remain uncertain.

While some readers might find this situation disconcerting, I believe that it ought to be a source for guarded optimism. Experimental philosophy is still in its infancy. It has barely been 15 years since the first papers about natural incompatibilism were published. It is to be expected that there would be some steep learning curves and growing pains along the way. It's hard enough just doing philosophy or psychology independently. Doing the latter in order to shed light on the former is doubly difficult. The important thing is that the empirical nature of this enterprise has the potential both to expose problems with the research that has been done and to help us find solutions to these problems. Even if the comprehension problem has raised concerns about the extant findings on intuitions about free will and responsibility, this doesn't undermine the value of the work done by experimental philosophers on this front.

3 Further Topics

In this chapter, I provided an overview of some of the most influential research in experimental philosophy when it comes to folk intuitions about free will and moral responsibility, I considered some concerns that have arisen about this research, and I offered a forecast of some potential future directions experimental philosophers might take in allaying these concerns. However, owing to space limitations, there are a number of other important areas of research that I was lamentably unable to explore. In closing, I want to briefly survey some of these other topics so that the reader has a better sense of the breadth of the work that experimental philosophers are doing when it comes to how people think about free will and moral responsibility.

First, there is the research on intuitions about the unconditional and conditional abilities to do otherwise (e.g., Deery, Bedke, and Nichols 2013, Nadelhoffer, Yin, and Graves 2020, Nahmias, Morris, Nadelhoffer, and Turner 2004). The unconditional ability to do otherwise is the ability to act differently even if everything leading up to one's decision had been exactly the same. The conditional ability requires instead that in order for a different decision to have been possible, something leading up to the decision must have been different. According to incompatibilists, this unconditional ability is both required for free will and *incompatible* with determinism. Compatibilists, on the other hand, tend to think that free will requires only the conditional ability to do otherwise which is *compatible* with determinism. Experimental philosophers have explored which of these two abilities to do otherwise best captures commonsense thinking about free will and responsibility.

Second, there is the research inspired by the work of Harry Frankfurt (e.g., Miller and Feltz 2011, Woolfolk, Doris, and Darley 2006). According to Frankfurt (1969), moral responsibility doesn't require that the agent had alternative possibilities (and hence doesn't require that the agent had the ability to do otherwise – whether conditional or unconditional). Instead, so long as the agent identifies with what he does – that is, the decision flows from the agent's own desires and intentions – then the agent can be responsible even if he could not have avoided what he did. In arguing for this view, Frankfurt constructed some now famous cases involving nefarious neuroscientists, mind control devices, and the like. Experimental philosophers have designed vignettes based on these cases in an effort to explore the role played by alternative possibilities in people's intuitions about moral agency.

Third, there is the related research on whether or not laypersons tend to think manipulated agents can be free (e.g., Sripada 2012, Feltz 2015). The interest in this issue has been fueled by famous arguments for incompatibilism that are based on manipulation – e.g., Alfred Mele's (2006) *Zygote Argument* and Derk Pereboom's (2001) *Four Case Argument*. That commonsense morality suggests that manipulated agents tend to be unfree is reflected in the criminal law where duress can be an excuse. Agents who are brainwashed, propagandized, or hypnotized might also plausibly be construed as unfree. But how are manipulated agents any different from agents who inhabit deterministic universes? If manipulated agents are unfree because their actions are caused by forces beyond their control, why not think that determined agents are unfree for the very same reason? Experimental philosophers have designed vignettes based on cases from the debate on manipulation to explore whether (and if so, when) people find manipulation and/or determinism exculpating.

Fourth, there is the research on people's intuitions about the relationship between free will, dualism, and the soul. As we saw earlier, a number of scientific skeptics about free will assume that most people are libertarians, dualists, and retributivists. It's because skeptics assume that dualism is the commonsense view that they believe that neuroscience poses a threat to how people normally think about free will and responsibility. There are some recent findings which support this view (e.g., Nadelhoffer et al. 2014, Wisniewski, Deutschländer, and Haynes 2019). But not all researchers share this view. Instead, they claim that the commonsense notion of moral agency does not require an immaterial soul, dualism, etc. (e.g., Forstman and Bergmer 2015, 2018; Monroe, Dillon, and Malle 2014; Vonasch, Baumeister, and Mele 2018).

Fifth, there is growing interest in cross-cultural intuitions about free will and responsibility (e.g., Hannikainen et al. 2019, Sarkissian et al. 2010, Wisniewski, Deutschländer, and Haynes 2019). The extant findings make it clear that while some intuitions are cross-culturally stable (e.g., the belief in free will is very strong everywhere philosophers have looked), there are some important differences (e.g., people in the United States believe more strongly in libertarian free will and dualism than people in Singapore). This research raises important metaphilosophical questions. For instance, if the intuitions of philosophers from countries that are Western, Educated, Industrialized, Rich, and Democratic (WEIRD; Henrich, Heine, and Norenzayan 2010) are largely idiosyncratic, what does that say about the evidential value of these intuitions?

These five areas that are being explored by experimental philosophers themselves represent just another subset of the work that is being done when it comes to people's intuitions about free will and responsibility. Indeed, it's amazing how much experimental philosophers have done in such a short amount of time. And while a lot of progress has been made, there are still a number of unanswered questions and problems to be addressed. Luckily, this interdisciplinary endeavor is a marathon and not a sprint. We will learn from our mistakes, improve our experimental designs, and get back to the task of understanding how people ordinarily think about free will and responsibility.

Bibliography

Andow, James, and Florian Cova (2016): "Why incompatibilist intuitions are not mistaken. A reply to Feltz and Millan", *Philosophical Psychology* 29 (4), pp. 550–566.

Ayer, Alfred Jules (1954): "Freedom and necessity", in: Alfred Jules Ayer: *Philosophical essays*. London: Macmillan, pp. 271–284.

Bear, Andrew, and Joshua Knobe (2016): "What do people find incompatible with causal determinism?", *Cognitive Science* 40 (8), pp. 2025–2049.

Björnsson, Gunnar (2014): "Incompatibilism and 'bypassed' agency", in: Alfred Mele (Ed.): *Surrounding free will*. New York: Oxford University Press, pp. 95–112.

Björnsson, Gunnar, and Derk Pereboom (2014): "Free will skepticism and bypassing", in: Walter Sinnott-Armstrong (Ed.): *Moral psychology. Vol. 4. Free will and moral responsibility*. Cambridge: The MIT Press, pp. 27–36.

Bourgeois-Gironde, Sacha, Florian Cova, Maxime Bertoux, and Bruno Dobois (2012): "Judgments about moral responsibility and determinism in patients with behavioral variant of frontotemporal dementia. Still compatibilists", *Consciousness and Cognition* 21 (2), pp. 851–864.

Chan, Hoi-Yee, Max Deutsch, and Shaun Nichols (2016): "Free will and experimental philosophy", in: Justin Sytsma and Wesley Buckwalter (Eds.): *A companion to experimental philosophy*. Hoboken: John Wiley & Sons, pp. 158–172.

Clark, Cory, Bo Winegard, and Roy Baumeister (2019): "Forget the folk. Moral responsibility preservation motives and other conditions for compatibilism", *Frontiers in Psychology* 10, 215.

Cokely, Edward, and Adam Feltz (2010): "Questioning the free will comprehension question", in: Stellan Ohlsson and Richard Catrambone (Eds.): *Proceedings of the 32nd annual conference of the cognitive science society*. Austin: Cognitive Science Society, pp. 2440–2445.

Cova, Florian, and Yasuko Kitano (2014): "Experimental philosophy and the compatibility of free will and determinism. A survey", *Annals of the Japan Association for Philosophy of Science* 22, pp. 17–37.

Cover, Jan, and John O'Leary-Hawthorne (1996): "Free agency and materialism", in: Jeff Jordan and Daniel Howard-Snyder (Eds.): *Faith, freedom and rationality*. Lanham: Roman and Littlefield, pp. 47–71.

Coyne, Jerry (2012): "Why you don't really have free will", *USA Today*. www.usatoday.com/news/opinion/forum/story/2012-01-01/freewill-science-religion/52317624/1, no longer accessible.

Deery, Oisín, Matt Bedke, and Shaun Nichols (2013): "Phenomenal abilities. Incompatibilism and the experience of agency", in: David Shoemaker (Ed.): *Oxford studies in agency and responsibility*. New York: Oxford University Press, pp. 126–150.

Deery, Oisín, Taylor Davis, and Jasmine Carey (2015): "The Free-Will Intuitions Scale and the question of natural compatibilism". *Philosophical Psychology* 28 (6), pp. 776–801.

Dennett, Daniel (1984): "I could not have done otherwise. So what?", *Journal of Philosophy* 81 (10), pp. 553–565.

Double, Richard (1991): *The non-reality of free will.* New York: Oxford University Press.

Ekstrom, Laura (2000): *Free will.* Boulder: Westview.

Feldman, Gilad, Kin Fai Ellick Wong, and Roy Baumeister (2016): "Bad is freer than good. Positive-negative asymmetry in attributions of free will", *Consciousness and Cognition* 42, pp. 26–40.

Feltz, Adam (2013): "Pereboom and premises. Asking the right questions in the experimental philosophy of free will", *Consciousness and Cognition* 22 (1), pp. 53–63.

Feltz, Adam, and Edward Cokely (2009): "Do judgments about freedom and responsibility depend on who you are? Personality differences in intuitions about compatibilism and incompatibilism", *Consciousness and Cognition* 18 (1), pp. 342–350.

Feltz, Adam, and Edward Cokely (2012): "The philosophical personality argument", *Philosophical Studies* 161 (2), pp. 227–246.

Feltz, Adam, Edward Cokely, and Thomas Nadelhoffer (2009): "Natural compatibilism versus natural incompatibilism", *Mind & Language* 24 (1), pp. 1–23.

Feltz, Adam, and Florian Cova (2014): "Moral responsibility and free will. A meta-analysis", *Consciousness and Cognition* 30, pp. 234–246.

Feltz, Adam, and Melissa Millan (2015): "An error theory for compatibilist intuitions", *Philosophical Psychology* 28 (4), pp. 529–555.

Feltz, Adam, Ashley Perez, and Maegan Harris (2012): "Free will, causes, and decisions. Individual differences in written reports", *The Journal of Consciousness Studies* 19 (9), pp. 166–189.

Figdor, Carrie, and Mark Phelan (2015): "Is free will necessary for moral responsibility? A case for rethinking their relationship and the design of experimental studies in moral psychology", *Mind & Language* 30 (5), pp. 603–627.

Fischer, John (1994): *The metaphysics of free will.* Oxford: Blackwell.

Fischer, John, and Mark Ravizza (1998): *Responsibility and control.* New York: Cambridge University Press.

Forstmann, Matthias, and Pascal Burgmer (2015): "Adults are intuitive mind-body dualists", *Journal of Experimental Psychology – General* 144 (1), pp. 222–235.

Forstmann, Matthias, and Pascal Burgmer (2018): "A free will needs a free mind. Belief in substance dualism and reductive physicalism differentially predict belief in free will and determinism", *Consciousness and Cognition* 63, pp. 280–293.

Frankfurt, Harry (1969): "Alternate possibilities and moral responsibility", *Journal of Philosophy* 66 (23), pp. 829–839.

Hannikainen, Ivar, Edouard Machery, David Rose, Stephen Stich, Christopher Olivola, Paulo Sousa, Florian Cova, Emma Buchtel, Mario Alai, Adriano Angelucci, Renatas Berniūnas, Amita Chatterjee, Hyundeuk Cheon, In-Rae Cho, Daniel Cohnitz, Vilius Dranseika, Ángeles Eraña Lagos, Laleh Ghadakpour, Maurice Grinberg, Takaaki Hashimoto, Amir Horowitz, Evgeniya Hristova, Yasmina Jraissati, Veselina Kadreva, Kaori Karasawa, Hackjin Kim, Yeonjeong Kim, Minwoo Lee, Carlos Mauro, Masaharu Mizumoto, Sebastiano Moruzzi, Jorge Ornelas, Barbara Osimani, Carlos Romero, Alejandro Rosas López, Massimo Sangoi, Andrea Sereni, Sarah Songhorian, Noel Struchiner, Vera Tripodi, Naoki Usui, Alejandro Vázquez del Mercado, Hrag Vosgerichian, Xueyi Zhang, and Jing Zhu (2019): "For whom does determinism undermine moral responsibility? Surveying the conditions for free will across cultures", *Frontiers in Psychology* 10, e2028.

Henrich, Joseph, Steven Heine, and Ara Norenzayan (2010): "The weirdest people in the world?", *Behavioral and Brain Sciences* 33 (2–3), pp. 61–83.

Jackson, Frank (1998): *From metaphysics to ethics. A defense of conceptual analysis.* New York: Oxford University Press.

Kane, Robert (1999): "Responsibility, luck, and chance. Reflections on free will and indeterminism", *Journal of Philosophy* 96 (5), pp. 217–240.

Knobe, Joshua (2014): "Free will and the scientific vision", in: Edouard Machery and Elizabeth O'Neill (Eds.): *Current controversies in experimental philosophy*. New York: Routledge, pp. 69–85.

Levy, Neil (2011): *Hard luck. How luck undermines free will and moral responsibility*. New York: Oxford University Press.

Lim, Daniel, and Ju Chen (2018): "Is compatibilism intuitive?", *Philosophical Psychology* 31 (6), pp. 878–897.

Lycan, William (2003): "Free will and the burden of proof", in: Anthony O'Hear (Ed.): *Minds and persons*. Cambridge: Cambridge University Press, pp. 107–122.

Mandelbaum, Eric, and David Ripley (2012): "Explaining the abstract/concrete paradoxes in moral psychology. The NBAR hypothesis", *Review of Philosophy and Psychology* 3 (3), pp. 351–368.

McKenna, Michael, and David Widerker (2003): "Introduction", in: David Widerker and Michael McKenna (Eds.): *Moral responsibility and alternative possibilities*. Aldershot: Ashgate, pp. 1–16.

Mele, Alfred (2006): *Free will and luck*. New York: Oxford University Press.

Miller, Jason, and Adam Feltz (2011): "Frankfurt and the folk. An empirical investigation", *Consciousness and Cognition* 20, pp. 401–414.

Monroe, Andrew, and Bertram Malle (2009): "From uncaused will to conscious choice. The need to study, not speculate about people's folk concept of free will", *Review of Philosophy and Psychology* 1 (2), pp. 211–224.

Murray, Dylan, and Eddy Nahmias (2014): "Explaining away incompatibilist intuitions", *Philosophy and Phenomenological Research* 88 (2), pp. 434–467.

Murray, Samuel, Elise Murray, and Thomas Nadelhoffer (forthcoming): "Do people understand determinism? The tracking problem for measuring free will beliefs", in: Joshua Knobe and Shaun Nichols (Eds.): *Oxford studies in experimental philosophy*. Vol. 5. Oxford: Oxford University Press.

Nadelhoffer, Thomas, and Andrew Monroe (forthcoming): "Folk jurisprudence and judgments about free will and responsibility", in: Thomas Nadelhoffer and Andrew Monroe (Eds.): *Advances in experimental philosophy of free will and responsibility*. New York: Bloomsbury.

Nadelhoffer, Thomas, Samuel Murray, and Elise Murray (2021): "Intuitions about free will and the failure to comprehend determinism", *Erkenntnis*.

Nadelhoffer, Thomas, David Rose, Wesley Buckwalter, and Shaun Nichols (2020): "Natural compatibilism, indeterminism, and intrusive metaphysics", *Cognitive Science* 44 (8), e12873.

Nadelhoffer, Thomas, Jason Shepard, Eddy Nahmias, Chandra Sripada, and Lisa Ross (2014): "The free will inventory. Measuring beliefs about agency and responsibility", *Consciousness and Cognition* 25, pp. 27–41.

Nadelhoffer, Thomas, Siyuan Yin, and Rose Graves (2020): "Folk intuitions and the conditional ability to do otherwise", *Philosophical Psychology* 33 (7), pp. 968–996.

Nahmias, Eddy (2014): "Is free will an illusion? Confronting challenges from the modern mind sciences", in: Walter Sinnott-Armstrong (Ed.): *Moral psychology. Vol. 4. Freedom and responsibility*. Cambridge: The MIT Press, pp. 1–25.

Nahmias, Eddy, Justin Coates, and Trevor Kvaran (2007): "Free will, moral responsibility, and mechanism. Experiments on folk intuitions", *Midwest Studies in Philosophy* 31 (1), pp. 214–242.

Nahmias, Eddy, Stephen Morris, Thomas Nadelhoffer, and Jason Turner (2004): "The phenomenology of free will", *The Journal of Consciousness Studies* 11 (7–8), pp. 162–179.

Nahmias, Eddy, Stephen Morris, Thomas Nadelhoffer, and Jason Turner (2005): "Surveying free will. Folk intuitions about free will and moral responsibility", *Philosophical Psychology* 18 (5), pp. 561–584.

Nahmias, Eddy, Stephen Morris, Thomas Nadelhoffer, and Jason Turner (2006): "Is incompatibilism intuitive?", *Philosophy and Phenomenological Research* 73 (1), pp. 28–53.

Nahmias, Eddy, and Dylan Murray (2011): "Experimental philosophy on free will. An error theory for incompatibilist intuitions", in: Jesús Aguilar, Andrei Buckareff, and Keith Frankish (Eds.): *New waves in philosophy of action*. New York: Palgrave Macmillan, pp. 189–216.

Nahmias, Eddy, Jason Shepard, and Shane Reuter (2014): "It's OK if 'my brain made me do it'. People's intuitions about free will and neuroscientific prediction", *Cognition* 133 (2), pp. 502–516.

Nelkin, Dana (2011): *Making sense of freedom and responsibility*. New York: Oxford University Press.

Nichols, Shaun (2004): "The folk psychology of free will. Fits and starts", *Mind & Language* 19 (5), pp. 473–502.

Nichols, Shaun (2006a): "Folk intuitions on free will", *Journal of Cognition and Culture* 6 (1–2), pp. 57–86.

Nichols, Shaun (2006b): "Free will and the folk. Response to commentators", *Journal of Cognition and Culture* 6 (1–2), pp. 305–320.

Nichols, Shaun (2015): *Bound*. Oxford: Oxford University Press.

Nichols, Shaun, and Joshua Knobe (2007): "Moral responsibility and determinism. The cognitive science of folk intuition", *Noûs* 41 (4), pp. 663–685.

Nowell-Smith, Patrick Howard (1949): "Free will and moral responsibility", *Mind* 57 (225), pp. 45–65.

O'Connor, Timothy (2000): *Persons and causes. The metaphysics of free will*. New York: Oxford University Press.

Paulhus, Delroy, and Jasmine Carey (2011): "The FAD-Plus. Measuring lay beliefs regarding free will and related constructs", *Journal of Personality Assessment* 93 (1), pp. 96–104.

Pereboom, Derk (2001): *Living without free will*. Cambridge: Cambridge University Press.

Pereboom, Derk (2014): *Free will, agency, and meaning in life*. Oxford: Oxford University Press.

Phillips, Jonathan, and Joshua Knobe (2009): "Moral judgments and intuitions about freedom", *Psychological Inquiry* 20 (1), pp. 30–36.

Preston, Jesse Lee, Ryan Ritter, and Justin Hepler (2013): "Neuroscience and the soul. Competing explanations for the human experience", *Cognition* 127 (1), pp. 31–37.

Pronin, Emily, and Matthew Kugler (2010): "People believe they have more free will than others", *Proceedings of the National Academy of Sciences* 107 (52), pp. 22469–22474.

Rose, David, and Shaun Nichols (2013): "The lesson of bypassing", *Review of Philosophy and Psychology* 4 (4), pp. 599–619.

Rose, David, Wesley Buckwalter, and Shaun Nichols (2017): "Neuroscientific prediction and the intrusion of intuitive metaphysics", *Cognitive Science* 41 (2), pp. 482–502.

Roskies, Adina, and Shaun Nichols (2008): "Bringing moral responsibility down to earth", *The Journal of Philosophy* 105 (7), pp. 371–388.

Rossi, Benjamin, and Ted Warfield (2016): "The relationship between moral responsibility and freedom", in: Kevin Timpe, Meghan Griffith, and Neil Levy (Eds.): *The Routledge companion to free will*. New York: Routledge, pp. 612–622.

Sarkissian, Hagop, Amita Chatterjee, Felipe de Brigard, Joshua Knobe, Shaun Nichols, and Smita Sirker (2010): "Is belief in free will a cultural universal?", *Mind & Language* 25 (3), pp. 346–358.

Searle, John (1984): *Minds, brains, and science*. Cambridge: Harvard University Press.

Shariff, Azim, Joshua Greene, Johan Karremans, Jamie Luguri, Cory Clark, Jonathan Schooler, Roy Baumeister, and Kathleen Vohs (2014): "Free will and punishment. A mechanistic view of human nature reduces retribution", *Psychological Science* 25 (8), pp. 1563–1570.

Sinnott-Armstrong, Walter (2008): "Abstract + concrete = paradox", in: Joshua Knobe and Shaun Nichols (Eds.): *Experimental philosophy*. New York: Oxford University Press, pp. 209–230.

Smilansky, Saul (2000): *Free will and illusion*. Oxford: Oxford University Press.

Smilansky, Saul (2003): "Compatibilism. The argument from shallowness", *Philosophical Studies* 115 (3), pp. 257–282.

Sripada, Chandra (2012): "What makes a manipulated agent unfree?", *Philosophy and Phenomenological Research* 85 (3), pp. 563–593.

Stace, Walter Terence (1952): *Religion and the modern mind*. Philadelphia: Lippincott.

Strawson, Galen (1986): *Freedom and belief*. Oxford: Oxford University Press.

Turner, Jason, and Eddy Nahmias (2006): "Are the folk agent-causationists?", *Mind & Language* 21 (5), pp. 597–609.

Turri, John (2017): "Compatibilism can be natural", *Consciousness and Cognition* 51, pp. 68–81.

van Inwagen, Peter (1983): *An essay on free will*. Oxford: Oxford University Press.

van Inwagen, Peter (2000): "Free will remains a mystery", *Philosophical Perspectives* 14, pp. 1–19.

van Inwagen, Peter (2008): "How to think about the problem of free will", *The Journal of Ethics* 12 (3–4), pp. 327–341.

van Inwagen, Peter (2009): *Metaphysics*. 3rd edition. New York: Routledge.

Vargas, Manuel (2007): "Revisionism", in: John Martin Fischer, Robert Kane, Derk Pereboom, and Manuel Vargas: *Four views on free will*. Malden: Blackwell, pp. 126–164.

Vierkant, Tillmann, Robert Deutschländer, Walter Sinnott-Armstrong, and John-Dylan Haynes (2019): "Responsibility without freedom? Folk judgements about deliberate actions", *Frontiers in Psychology* 10, 1133.

Weigel, Christina (2011): "Distance, anger, freedom. An account of the role of abstraction in compatibilist and incompatibilist intuitions", *Philosophical Psychology* 24 (6), pp. 803–823.

Wisniewski, David, Robert Deutschländer, and John-Dylan Haynes (2019): "Free will beliefs are better predicted by dualism than determinism beliefs across different cultures", *PLOS ONE* 14, e0221617.

Wolf, Susan (1990): *Freedom within reason*. New York: Oxford University Press.

Woolfolk, Robert, John Doris, and John Darley (2006): "Identification, situational constraint, and social cognition. Studies in the attribution of moral responsibility", *Cognition* 100 (2), pp. 283–301.

Rodrigo Díaz

Experimental Philosophy of Emotion: Emotion Theory

Abstract: Are emotions bodily feelings or evaluative cognitions? What is happiness, pain, or "being moved"? Are there basic emotions? In this chapter, I review extant empirical work concerning these and related questions in the philosophy of emotion. This will include both (1) studies investigating people's emotional experiences and (2) studies investigating people's use of emotion concepts in hypothetical cases. Overall, this review will show the potential of using empirical research methods to inform philosophical questions regarding emotion.

Keywords: Basic Emotions; Being Moved; Cognitive Theory; Emotion; Experimental Philosophy; Happiness; Pain; Somatic Theory

1 Introduction

Philosophers often ground their arguments on claims that are empirical or "intuitive" (i.e., pre-theoretical, commonsense), and the philosophy of emotion is no exception. In order to decide which cases count as cases of emotion and to develop an account of what emotions are, philosophers have traditionally appealed to intuitions about the application of emotion concepts, as well as to our everyday experience of emotion. This approach seems to be appropriate. Indeed, our theories of emotion should account for people's emotional experiences, and we rely on ordinary language to pinpoint those experiences. However, different authors use intuitions and everyday experiences of emotion to defend opposing claims, and that makes progress difficult.

The good news is that, given the use of empirical and intuitive claims in the philosophy of emotion, experimental philosophy understood either in a broad sense (i.e., using empirical research methods to test philosophical claims) or a narrow sense (i.e., using vignette studies to test laypeople's intuitions regarding cases) can readily inform debates in the field. In this chapter, I will review studies that are relevant for questions regarding the nature of emotion.

Note that, despite the methodological similarities with other areas of philosophy, the (experimental) philosophy of emotion might, nonetheless, constitute an exception. While some might be tempted to make a sharp distinction between (1) empirical studies on *people's emotional experiences* and (2) empirical studies on *people's intuitions about emotion*, the boundaries are rather blurry. To date, the only method to measure

---

Note: This work was funded by the Swiss National Science Foundation (SNF; research project P2BEP1_200040). I would like to thank Sabrina Coninx, Florian Cova, Markus Kneer, and Kevin Reuter for their comments on early drafts of this chapter.

https://doi.org/10.1515/9783110716931-016

people's emotional experience is self-report (Quigley et al. 2014). That is, asking participants whether they are afraid, sad, angry, and so forth. Thus, many studies on emotion are testing people's use of emotion concepts, just as studies on intuitions about emotion. The relation between emotion and emotion concepts (Reisenzein 2022, Díaz 2022b, Johnson-Laird and Oatley 1989, Fontaine, Scherer, and Soriano 2013, Scherer 2005) will not be discussed at length here, but it motivates the decision to consider both studies on emotion and studies on intuitions about emotion.

The structure of this chapter is as follows. First, I will introduce the core topic: the nature of emotion. I will briefly introduce (some of) the main theories of emotion and reconstruct central arguments in favor of these theories. This reconstruction will allow us to identify the empirical premises contained in those arguments and review studies testing those claims. In the last section, I will review further studies testing claims regarding specific emotions and affective states.

2 What is an Emotion?

While most of us agree that things such as joy, sadness, fear, or anger are emotions, it is not so clear what makes them emotions. Emotions seem to be a specific kind of reaction to our environment. But what kind of reaction? Sweating is also a reaction to our environment. Nevertheless, sweating is not an emotion. Perhaps emotions are not physiological but psychological reactions to our environment. However, we psychologically react to the environment every single moment of being awake, and not all these reactions are emotional. Emotions seem to be associated with certain facial expressions: we smile when we are joyful and wrinkle our noses when we are disgusted. However, we also smile to pose for pictures and wrinkle our noses when the beat drops in our favorite rap song. The question, as we can see, is not an easy one.

There are at least three main (families of) theories of emotion: Cognitive, Somatic, and Componential theories. Let us have a brief look at those theories.

According to *Cognitive theories*, to fear darkness is to believe that darkness is dangerous, being angry at Donald Trump is evaluating Donald Trump as offensive, grieving the death of someone is believing that their death is an irrevocable loss, and so on. To have an emotion, then, is to hold certain judgments or beliefs [1] about the value of particular objects and events. Thus, the core claim of Cognitive theory is: Emotions are evaluative beliefs.

According to *Somatic theories*, to be afraid is to feel one's body shivering, to be angry is to feel one's "blood boiling", to be sad is to feel one's body drain out of energy,

---

[1] To avoid repetition, I will from now on talk about beliefs and judgments interchangeably (Nussbaum 2004). But note that some authors have argued that evaluative beliefs and evaluative judgments should be distinguished as non-identical mental states, and that emotions should be identified with the latter but not the former (Solomon 2002). Furthermore, as we will see, some Cognitive theories identify emotions with other types of evaluative states.

and so on. Importantly, those bodily changes have to be registered by the subject, so the emotion can be felt.[2] This way, the core claim of Somatic theories is that emotions are perceptions of one's own bodily changes or, in short: Emotions are bodily perceptions.

Componential theories posit that emotions are constituted by the combination of two or more elements, including cognitive evaluations, bodily reactions, action tendencies, and/or motor expressions. Different Componential theories hold different views about how these features come together to constitute emotions, most importantly: Via affect programs (Ekman 1999), appraisal processes (Scherer 2009), or psychological construction (see Gendron and Feldman Barrett 2009).

In this section, I will present four central arguments in favor of Cognitive and Somatic theories of emotion. These arguments can be divided into four categories, based on whether they concern the claim that: (1) bodily perceptions are necessary for emotion, (2) bodily perceptions are sufficient for emotion, (3) evaluative beliefs are necessary for emotion, or (4) evaluative beliefs are sufficient for emotion. But before introducing the arguments, some clarifications are due.

First, note that claims (1) to (4) do not refer to necessity and sufficiency in a metaphysical sense (i.e., what emotions are in all possible worlds), but rather in a nomological sense (i.e., what emotions are in our world, given the laws of nature). Thus, "Xs are necessary for emotion" means that worldly emotions will always involve Xs; and "Xs are sufficient for emotion" means that it will always be possible to identify emotions in our world by their respective Xs. Most emotion researchers would probably settle for these "modally modest" claims (Machery 2017). But some researchers might want more. For those, this author cannot offer more than good wishes.

Second, note that claims (1) and (3) are also relevant for Componential theories of emotion, as long as they regard bodily perceptions and evaluative beliefs as necessary constituents of emotion. Furthermore, slight modifications of claims (3) and (4) would make them fit modern versions of Cognitive theories, which argue that emotions are not *judgments* of value but rather *perceptions* of value (Roberts 2003, Döring 2007, Tappolet 2016). The same is the case for claims (1) and (2) and modern versions of Somatic theories of emotion, which argue that emotions are not attitudes *directed* at bodily changes but rather attitudes *constituted* by bodily changes (Deonna and Teroni 2012, 2015, 2017).

After presenting each argument, I will review empirical studies testing their premises. This will allow us to determine whether the arguments are sound or not.

---

[2] From now on, I will sometimes use bodily perceptions and sometimes bodily changes to avoid repetition. Please take into account that, unless otherwise noted, those bodily changes are considered to be perceived by the subject.

2.1 Are Bodily Perceptions Necessary for Emotion?

Emotions commonly involve certain bodily changes, such as heart pounding, muscle contraction, and so forth. Somatic theories claim that those changes are not mere accompaniments of emotions. Instead, those bodily changes are a constitutive part of the emotion. To see this, consider a case of anger. Would it be anger without accelerated heartbeats, shallow breathing, muscle clenching, or any other bodily disturbances? It seems like such a case would appear to be rather unemotional. One cannot experience emotion without experiencing bodily disturbances. In other words, emotions *necessarily* involve bodily perceptions (James 1884, Prinz 2004, Hufendiek 2016, Deonna and Teroni 2017). According to Somatic theories, the best way of accounting for this is to claim that emotions are bodily perceptions:

(P1) When someone does not [bodily perception], she is not [emotion].
(P2) Emotions are bodily perceptions" is the best explanation for (P1).
(C1) Emotions are bodily perceptions (Somatic theory).

There are two ways of supporting (P1): using hypothetical cases of absence of bodily perceptions or actual cases of absence of bodily perceptions (e. g., spinal cord injuries).

Patients with spinal cord injuries lack awareness of their own bodily changes. This deficit occurs in different degrees, depending on the position (e. g., cervical or lumbar) and severity of the injury (e. g., complete or partial). Hohmann (1966) conducted a series of interviews with spinal cord injury patients, asking them about their emotional experiences before and after the injury. Patients with spinal cord injuries reported decreases in their experience of emotion after the injury. And, importantly, these decreases were larger for patients with more severe or higher injuries. Although none of the patients completely lacked bodily feedback, the results are in line with (P1).

Other studies, however, have found that patients with spinal cord injuries *do not* report decreases in their experience of emotion after their injuries (Cobos et al. 2002). Importantly, this was the case even for complete cervical injuries. Against (P1), these results suggest that, at least in some cases, emotions can be experienced in the absence of (normal) bodily perceptions.

To account for the evidence against (P1), proponents of Somatic theories of emotion have stressed the fact that spinal cord injuries (and other clinical conditions that impair the perception of one's own bodily changes) do never constitute cases of a *complete* lack of bodily feelings (Hufendiek 2016). William James (1884) was already aware of this problem,[3] and he relies on a thought experiment, known as the Subtraction Argument, to support (P1).

---

[3] "It must be confessed that a crucial test of the truth of the hypothesis [that emotions are bodily perceptions] is quite as hard to obtain as its decisive refutation. [...] Hysterical anesthesias seem never to be complete enough to cover the ground. Complete anesthesias from organic disease, on the other hand, are excessively rare" (James 1884, p. 203).

In the Subtraction Argument, we are told to imagine an emotion (e.g., fear) and subtract from it all the feelings of bodily changes that it involves (e.g., accelerated heartbeat, sweaty palms, shivering). After the subtraction, we are invited to think about whether the resulting state is an emotional state. According to William James (1884), the outcome is clear. After subtracting the feelings of bodily changes, "we have nothing left behind" and "most people, when asked, say that their introspection verifies this statement" (James 1884, p. 193). But do people's (introspective) intuitions really support the claim that there is no emotion in the absence of bodily perceptions, as (P1) suggests?

In a recent study, Díaz (2021) tested people's intuitions regarding the Subtraction Argument. Participants were guided to imagine themselves experiencing either fear, sadness, or anger. After this, they were told to imagine that they don't feel the bodily changes associated with the emotion at hand and asked whether they would still consider themselves to be afraid (sad, angry). Contrary to James' claims, most participants (77.3%) answered that they would still have the emotion. Furthermore, there was no significant relationship between participants' answers and individual differences in cognitive reflection or interoceptive awareness, ruling out some alternative interpretations of the results. In a second study, these results were replicated using an emotion induction task (autobiographical recall) instead of making participants imagine an emotion. Once again, and against (P1), the results suggest that emotions persist in the absence of bodily feelings. Hence, bodily perceptions are not necessary for emotion.

2.2 Are Bodily Perceptions Sufficient for Emotion?

Sometimes, we perceive changes in our bodies without experiencing emotion. For example, I can feel my heart racing because I'm playing basketball, and not because I have an emotion. Here, it is important to note that Somatic theories do not identify emotions with the perception of *any kind of* bodily changes. The bodily changes involved in emotion are reliably caused by challenges in our environment and prepare us to quickly deal with these challenges (Prinz 2004). But even if bodily changes can help us distinguish emotional and unemotional states (see Barlassina and Newen 2014 for a skeptical view), can bodily changes account for the differences between emotion types such as, for example, anger and fear?

At first sight, it seems like the same bodily changes can characterize several distinct emotion types. Accelerated heartbeat, for example, can indicate both fear and anger. The picture gets even more blurry when we consider other emotions such as disgust, sadness, shame, pride, joy, contempt, amusement, and so forth. It seems there are not enough bodily changes to distinguish all these different emotions (Cannon 1927). This challenges the capacity of Somatic theories to account for the assumption that emotion types are distinct from each other.

Proponents of Somatic theories, however, are aware of this worry. In response, it has been claimed that each emotion has a *prototypical* pattern of bodily feelings (Prinz

2004, p. 72). The prototypical pattern of bodily changes might appear very few times. But all instances of, e.g., fear, are similar enough to the prototype of fear to be perceived as fear and not as, say, anger. Whether a bodily pattern constitutes fear or anger, then, is a matter of degree. But this does not preclude distinguishing between emotion types in terms of bodily changes. Thus, bodily perceptions are sufficient to individuate emotions:

(P1)   Emotion types are distinct from each other.
(P2)   (Prototypical) bodily perceptions are different across emotion types.
(C1)   Bodily perceptions are sufficient to individuate emotions.

The claim that prototypical bodily perceptions are different across emotion types (P2) is supported by studies on "bodily maps" of emotions. Nummenmaa, Glerean, Hari, and Hietanen (2014) presented a group of participants with emotional stimuli (written stories) along with two silhouettes of bodies. Participants used the body silhouettes to color the regions where they felt an increase or decrease in activity while reading the stories. Based on participants' drawings, researchers could predict the story that participants read in 48 % of the cases. As they used seven different stories (inducing anger, disgust, fear, happiness, sadness, surprise, and neutral states, respectively), this percentage was way above chance levels (14 %). These results have been replicated using short movies as emotional stimuli (Nummenmaa et al. 2014), in children (Hietanen et al. 2016) and adults across different cultures (Volynets et al. 2020).

2.3 Are Evaluative Beliefs Necessary for Emotion?

Most would agree that emotions typically involve evaluative beliefs. When I'm angry, I typically think that something is offensive. But, according to Cognitive theories, the relationship between emotions and evaluative beliefs is not a sheer coincidence. To illustrate this, consider the following case. You go through a reviewer's comments on your paper, and a remark on your writing angers you. Would you be angry if you thought that the remark was friendly and helpful? Probably not. It seems like one cannot be angry if one doesn't believe something is offensive. Similarly, one cannot be afraid if one doesn't believe that something is dangerous. In other words, emotions *necessarily* involve evaluative beliefs (Kenny 1963; Nussbaum 2001, 2004; Solomon 1976). The best way to explain this, according to Cognitive theories, is to hold that emotions *are* evaluative beliefs.[4] This argument takes the following form:

---

4 Alternatively, we could explain this in terms of evaluative beliefs causing emotions, but not constituting them.

(P1) When someone does not [evaluative belief], she is not [emotion].
(P2) "Emotions are evaluative beliefs" is the best explanation for (P1).[5]
(C1) Emotions are evaluative beliefs (Cognitive theory).

(P1) is sometimes taken as a matter of logic (see Solomon 1976, p. 118). In this view, the concept of emotion implies evaluative belief, and it is thus impossible to conceive emotion without it. However, the relation between emotion and evaluative belief can also be taken as an empirical issue. This way, some have claimed that emotions disappear in the absence of the relevant evaluative beliefs. With regards to anger, Martha Nussbaum (2001, pp. 28 f.) claims that "If I should discover that not A but B had done the damage, or that it was not done willingly, or that it was not serious, we could expect my anger to modify itself accordingly, or go away".

Siemer (2008) presents some experimental results that are relevant for (P1). The main goal of this study is to test the centrality of evaluative beliefs versus behavioral expressions in people's understanding of emotion. Participants in the study were presented with vignettes in which someone is described as having (anger-, fear-, or sadness-related) evaluative beliefs and behavioral expressions (e.g., *crying* and *talking little* in the case of sadness). In one of the conditions of the study, participants answered the question "Would [person described in scenario] still feel [emotion described] if not [described evaluative beliefs]?" on a scale from 1 ("definitely not true") to 5 ("definitely true"). Most participants gave a negative response to this question ($M = 1.99$), while most participants gave a positive response when asked the same question about behavioral expressions ($M = 3.96$). These results suggest that, in line with (P1), people think that one would not experience emotion absent the relevant evaluative beliefs.

In a series of studies, Díaz (2022a) tested people's use of emotion concepts utilizing vignettes in which the presence (absence) of evaluative cognitions (e.g., "you see the situation as dangerous"), bodily feelings (e.g., "you feel your body trembling"), and action tendencies (e.g., "you feel the urge to get away") were independently manipulated. Participants judged whether the vignettes depicted cases of emotion. Results across four studies showed that the presence or absence of evaluative cognitions had the biggest impact on people's use of emotion concepts (explaining between 15% and 44% of the variance in participants' emotion ratings), followed by bodily feelings and action tendencies (explaining between 5% and 9% of the variance). Furthermore, participants tended to infer the presence of evaluative cognitions from the presence of bodily feelings (action tendencies) more so than the other way around. In other words, people seem to think that, if someone is having emotional bodily feelings or action tendencies, they must also have the relevant evaluative cognitions. Overall, these results are in line with the claim that emotions depend on evaluative beliefs (P1).

---

[5] Please note that this premise is included to show that the argument at hand is not a deductive argument, but rather an inference to the best explanation.

Against (P1), some have noted that emotions sometimes persist "against our better judgment". For example, it is possible to believe that planes are a highly safe means of transportation and nevertheless be afraid of flying. These emotions are sometimes referred to as "recalcitrant emotions" (Greenspan 1981, Roberts 1988, D'Arms and Jacobson 2003, Grzankowski 2017, Naar 2018). Cases of recalcitrant emotion constitute counterexamples to (P1). Consider the case of recalcitrant fear of flying. In this case, the person does not believe that flying is dangerous (to the contrary, she believes that flying is safe) but she is nevertheless afraid of flying.

That recalcitrant emotions do not involve the relevant evaluative beliefs is usually taken as commonplace in the philosophical literature. However, the literature in clinical psychology offers a very different picture of phobias, the paradigmatic case of emotional recalcitrance (see de Jong 2015). One of the most studied phobias is aerophobia (i.e., the above-mentioned fear of flying). Across studies, the reports of flying phobics tell us that they indeed believe that flying is dangerous, as Cognitive theories would predict. For example, Walder and colleagues (1987) found that flying phobic participants were worried about being enclosed (37%), crashing (34%), heights (13%), or had multiple worries (16%). Similarly, McNally and Louro (1992) found that flying phobics report a high concern about external aspects of flying (e.g., crashing). These results suggest that the phenomenon of emotional recalcitrance has been inadequately described in the philosophical literature (Díaz n.d.).

2.4 Are Evaluative Beliefs Sufficient for Emotion?

Some evaluative beliefs are not emotional. For example, I might believe that someone's remark is offensive without being angry. To constitute emotions, evaluative beliefs have to be about things that are important for the subject. In the example above, I probably believe that the remark does not constitute an *important* offense or is not offensive *for me*, and thus remain calm. These two aspects: importance and self-reference, are usually included as essential characteristics of the beliefs that constitute emotions (Nussbaum 2001, pp. 40–42; Solomon 1976, p. 127). But in order to be sufficient for emotion, evaluative beliefs should not only distinguish emotions from non-emotions, but also between emotion types.

Cognitivism posits that each emotion type is constituted by a specific evaluative belief. Fear is the belief that something is dangerous, anger is the belief that something is offensive, and so on. Thus, it seems like Cognitive theories can easily account for the assumption that emotion types are distinct from each other. For example, I can be afraid that Sarah came to the party, or angry that Sarah came to the party. In these cases, the object of my emotion is the same (that Sarah came to the party). The difference lies in how I evaluate the event in each case. If I am afraid, I believe that there is an upcoming danger, perhaps because Sarah is an aggressive person. If I am angry, I take her coming to the party as an offense, perhaps because I didn't invite her. Since evaluative beliefs are different across emotion types, they are sufficient to individuate emotions:

(P1) Emotion types are distinct from each other.
(P2) Across emotion types, evaluative beliefs are distinct from each other.
(C1) Evaluative beliefs are sufficient to individuate emotions.

(P2) finds empirical support in a study by Scherer and Meuleman (2013). In this study, participants recalled a past emotional experience and reported their evaluations of the emotion-eliciting event. Using participants' reported evaluations and theoretical assumptions about the relation between emotions and evaluative beliefs, the authors were able to predict the emotion that participants experienced in 51% of the cases. Taking into account that they considered 13 different emotion types, this prediction is way above chance levels (7.7%).

Other studies have obtained similar results using machine learning models and cross-cultural data regarding people's explicit associations between emotions and evaluative beliefs (Meuleman and Scherer 2013, Meuleman et al. 2019). For example, Meuleman and colleagues (2019) found that evaluative beliefs predict specific emotion types with a probably between 68% (for guilt and sadness) and 23% (for anxiety). As they considered 24 different emotions, this prediction is again above chance levels (4.2%). Thus, it seems like evaluative beliefs do a relatively good job of differentiating emotion types, supporting (P2).

2.5 Further Readings

Apart from the references already provided in the text, readers interested in the nature of emotion can dig deeper into the topic by consulting the edited collections *Thinking about Feeling – Contemporary Philosophers on Emotions* (Solomon 2004) and *The Ontology of Emotions* (Naar and Teroni 2017), as well as the *Stanford Encyclopedia of Philosophy* entry on emotion (Scarantino and de Sousa 2018). The first two compile the work of philosophers, while the latter integrates emotion research in both philosophy and psychology.

3 Further Topics

The studies reviewed in the previous section aim to inform questions regarding emotions in general. Other experimental-philosophical studies have focused on specific phenomena that could be understood as emotional but deserve special attention. In particular, much work has been devoted to studying happiness, pain, "being moved", and basic emotions.

3.1 Happiness

In a series of papers, Phillips and colleagues (2011, 2014, 2017) present compelling evidence that the folk concept of happiness encodes not only descriptive information regarding the psychological states of the agent but also normative considerations about the moral value of her life (as other authors had suggested, e.g., Foot 2001). The design of these studies consists of presenting participants with vignettes describing an agent who lives either a morally good or a morally bad life. In both cases, the agent experiences high pleasure, low pain, and is highly satisfied with her life. Results consistently show that people are less likely to attribute happiness to the morally bad agent, despite her having the same psychological states as the morally good agent.

The findings above have been interpreted as evidence that the folk concept of happiness is partially moral. However, Díaz and Reuter (2021) have argued that the effect recorded in these studies is better explained in terms of fittingness rather than moral norms. In a series of studies considering both happiness and fear, they show that people are more willing to attribute emotion when the emotion fits the situation in which it is experienced (e.g., happiness about something good versus happiness about something bad), even when the situation is morally neutral (e.g., fear towards something dangerous versus fear towards something harmless). In line with this idea, Kneer and Haybron (2019) present a set of studies suggesting that the folk concept of happiness includes both internal (psychological) and external (situational) factors. Importantly, however, they found that the folk concept of happiness is much less sensitive to external factors than the folk concept of wellbeing.

Further studies have recently investigated the descriptive content of our concepts of happiness and wellbeing. Cova and Deplanque (2021) asked participants to define the terms "happiness" and "wellbeing" in their own words using open-ended text questions. After coding participants' definitions, they found some notable differences in people's understanding of happiness versus wellbeing. While many participants mentioned health (~55%) and quality of life (~25%) in their definition of wellbeing, these aspects were absent in most of the participants' definitions of happiness. Conversely, many participants mentioned positive feelings (~80%) and satisfaction (~35%) in their definition of happiness, but very few participants mentioned these in their definition of wellbeing. In line with this latter result, Reuter and colleagues (2022) found that people understand happiness mostly in terms of positive feelings. In a series of studies, they show that people tend to attribute happiness to a person if she feels good most of the time, regardless of whether she is satisfied with her life or not.

3.2 Pain

Many studies have investigated people's use of the concept of pain (for a review, see Sytsma and Reuter 2017). The main question being tested in these studies is whether pain is considered to be mental (i.e., an experience) or bodily (i.e., a physical condition). Several arguments have been put forward to defend either view.

A much-discussed argument in the (experimental) philosophy of pain is the so-called pain-in-the-mouth argument (Block 1983). The argument goes as follows: There is a pain in my fingertip; the fingertip is in my mouth; therefore, there is a pain in my mouth. Intuitively, the argument fails. But why? According to some, the conclusion doesn't follow because pain is a (non-spatially located) mental state. Against this, Reuter and colleagues (2019) provide evidence that the argument fails because the conclusion (although technically correct) pragmatically implies that "there is something wrong with the speaker's mouth". This interpretation supports a bodily view of pain. However, Liu (2020) presents evidence that the conclusion does not *imply* but rather *entails* that the speaker's mouth hurts because people understand pain as a mental state.

Other arguments build on the existence of different types of pain. For example, if there are unfelt or shared pains, this will go against the idea that pain is essentially a (subjective, private) experience. The same is true for the existence of pain hallucinations, which would also suggest that pains are bodily rather than mental. Using vignette studies and text analyses, it has been shown that people accept the possibility of unfelt pains (Reuter and Sytsma 2020), pain illusions (Reuter 2011, Reuter et al. 2014), and shared pains (Sytsma 2010). Thus, it seems that people have a body-centric view of pain. However, recent studies have shown that people's attributions of pain are subject to context effects and, depending on the wording of the vignettes we use, these attributions can fit either a body- or a mind-centric view of pain. This suggests that the folk concept of pain is a hybrid of bodily and mental aspects (Borg et al. 2019, Salomons et al. 2022), although some have argued that the best interpretation of the results is that pain terms are polysemous (Liu 2021).

Finally, we should not overlook the vast number of empirical studies on people's pain experiences. Some of these studies have already been used for philosophical purposes. For example, studies on the correlates of pain have been used to question the claim that pain is a unitary phenomenon; although there is disagreement regarding whether this makes "pain" unsuitable for scientific inquiry (Corns 2016, 2020) or we can nevertheless make progress in explaining, predicting, and treating pain (Coninx 2020). Empirical studies on people's experience of pain have also been used to argue against specific theories of pain (Casser 2021, Coninx 2021), and there is much empirical work that is philosophically relevant and has not received attention yet (Corns 2018).

3.3 Being Moved

The phenomenon we refer to by using the expression "being moved" has also been the object of much empirical work (see Cova et al. 2017 and Cullhed 2020 for reviews). The main questions here concern whether "being moved" can be considered a distinctive emotional state (Cova and Deonna 2014) or rather a blend of other emotions (Kuehnast et al. 2014, Menninghaus et al. 2015), and how we should characterize its eliciting conditions. In particular, researchers have investigated whether being moved is a response to instantiations of positive core values (Cova and Deonna 2014), attachment (Menninghaus et al. 2015), communal sharing (Fiske et al. 2017), or depth and profundity (Cova et al. 2017).

In a seminal paper, Cova and Deonna (2014), present some evidence regarding people's descriptions of episodes in which they felt moved. In particular, they collected responses regarding features that are diagnostic of emotional episodes: evaluative appraisals, bodily feelings, and action tendencies. Their results suggest that "being moved" is a distinctive emotional state, involving all the characteristic features of emotion. Others, however, have collected evidence showing that people often mention other positive (joy) and negative (sadness) emotions when describing their "moving" experiences (Kuehnast et al. 2014, Menninghaus et al. 2015), suggesting that "being moved" refers to a mix of different emotions.

The studies above approach the topic by collecting people's descriptions of their past experiences, either in free-text or forced-choice questionnaires. But studies on "being moved" have also used emotion induction techniques (i.e., presenting participants with evocative stimuli) to elucidate what situations evoke being moved (Landmann et al. 2019), or the physiological responses associated with these experiences (Zickfeld et al. 2020). These studies help us further understand the phenomenon of being moved. At a more general level, debates around the nature of "being moved" highlight the problem of finding agreed-upon criteria to carve the emotional domain.

3.4 Basic Emotions

According to basic emotion theory (Ekman 1999), there is a subset of emotions (typically anger, sadness, fear, disgust, and joy) that are the result of evolutionary pressures and have their roots in hard-wired mechanisms in the brain. If this is the case, each basic emotion must be associated with activity in a specific brain region or network of regions. In other words, there should be distinct "basic emotion circuits" in the brain (but see Scarantino and Griffiths 2011).

To test the above-mentioned claim, Lindquist and colleagues (2012) conducted a meta-analysis of the results from neuroimaging studies investigating the neural correlates of (the perception and experience of) anger, sadness, fear, disgust, and joy. Their results show significant overlap between the neural correlates of these emotions, suggesting that there are no basic emotion circuits in the brain (but see Celeghin et al. 2017, Loaiza 2021). For example, the amygdala, which is sometimes taken to be the "fear area", or at least the most important hub in a fear circuit, was also consistently recruited by the experience and perception of anger, sadness, disgust, and joy.

Other studies, however, have shown that it is possible to neurally distinguish between basic emotions if we look at distributed (versus localized) patterns of brain activity (see Kragel and LaBar 2016, for a review). This suggests that there are basic emotion circuits in the brain. However, it has been noted that the success of these studies in discriminating between basic emotions has to do with predictive power, and predictive power does not necessarily involve the existence of dedicated neural networks (Hebart and Baker 2017, Ritchie et al. 2017). Indeed, the distributed patterns of brain activity identified in these studies are not necessarily present in any of the individual instances of emotion (Clark-Polner et al. 2016). Thus, this type of evidence would not support the existence of hard-wired mechanisms for basic emotions (Díaz 2019).

3.5 Other

In an early study on people's understanding of emotion, Reisenzein (1995) tested semantic claims about the relationship between non-basic and basic emotions. In particular, Reisenzein tested whether non-basic emotions are understood as modifications or combinations of basic emotions (Johnson-Laird and Oatley 1989). For example, whether euphoria is just intense happiness rather than a distinct emotion. Participants' judgments regarding the conditional probability of having [basic emotion] given [non-basic emotion], as well as the possibility of having [non-basic emotion] without [basic emotion], did not support the claim that non-basic emotions can be reduced to basic emotions.

Kurth, Kosacz, and Díaz (n.d.) tested people's judgments regarding the possibility of emotional error. That is, cases in which someone is wrong about the emotion she is feeling. According to some versions of constructivist and feeling theories of emotion, it is not possible to be mistaken about one's own emotions; either because there is no matter of fact about emotions, or because first-person judgments are authoritative. Their results show that people think it is possible to be mistaken about one's own emotions, and that extant alternative interpretations in terms of a lack of attention or understanding, on the one hand, or self-deception, on the other, cannot explain away these results.

Díaz and Reuter (n.d.) present a series of studies showing that people can distinguish between the intentional (world-directed) and phenomenal (felt) aspects of emotion by using the expressions "being [emotion]" and "feeling [emotion]", respectively. In two corpus linguistic analyses, they show that (1) proponents of Cognitive theories of emotion show a stronger preference for using the expression "being [emotion]" versus "feeling [emotion]" than proponents of Somatic theories of emotion, and (2) laypeople show the same preference when specifying the intentional object of their emotions versus specifying the cause of their emotions. Vignette studies depicting situations of cognitive evaluation (and no somatic feel) versus somatic feel (and no cognitive evaluation) showed the same asymmetry. The authors use this data to support a conceptual separation between (non-phenomenal) emotional attitudes and (non-intentional) emotional feelings.

Bibliography

Barlassina, Luca, and Albert Newen (2014): "The role of bodily perception in emotion. In defense of an impure somatic theory", *Philosophy and Phenomenological Research* 89 (3), pp. 637–678.

Block, Ned (1983): "Mental pictures and cognitive science", *Philosophical Review* 92 (4), pp. 499–541.

Borg, Emma, Nathaniel Hansen, and Tim Salomons (2019): "The meaning of pain expressions and pain communication", in: Simon van Rysewyk (Ed.): *Meanings of pain*. Dordrecht: Springer, pp. 261–282.

Cannon, Walter (1927): "The James-Lange theory of emotions. A critical examination and an alternative theory", *American Journal of Psychology* 39 (3), pp. 106–124.

Casser, Laurenz (2021): "The function of pain", *Australasian Journal of Philosophy* 99 (2), pp. 364–378.

Celeghin, Alessia, Matteo Diano, Arianna Bagnis, Marco Viola, and Marco Tamietto (2017): "Basic emotions in human neuroscience. Neuroimaging and beyond", *Frontiers in Psychology* 8, 1432.

Clark-Polner, Elizabeth, Timothy Johnson, and Lisa Feldman Barrett (2016): "Multivoxel pattern analysis does not provide evidence to support the existence of basic emotions", *Cerebral Cortex* 27 (3), bhw028.

Cobos, Pilar, María Sánchez, Carmen García, María Nieves Vera, and Jaime Vila (2002): "Revisiting the James versus Cannon debate on emotion. Startle and autonomic modulation in patients with spinal cord injuries", *Biological Psychology* 61 (3), pp. 251–269.

Coninx, Sabrina (2020): *Experiencing pain. A scientific enigma and its philosophical solution*. Berlin and Boston: De Gruyter.

Coninx, Sabrina (2021): "Strong representationalism and bodily sensations. Reliable causal covariance and biological function", *Philosophical Psychology* 34 (2), pp. 210–232.

Corns, Jennifer (2016): "Pain eliminativism. Scientific and traditional", *Synthese* 193 (9), pp. 2949–2971.

Corns, Jennifer (2018): "Recent work on pain", *Analysis* 78 (4), pp. 737–753.

Corns, Jennifer (2020): *The complex reality of pain. The complex reality of pain*. New York and London: Routledge.

Cova, Florian, and Julien Deonna (2014): "Being moved", *Philosophical Studies* 169 (3), pp. 447–466.

Cova, Florian, Julien Deonna, and David Sander (2017): "'That's deep!' The role of being moved and feelings of profundity in the appreciation of serious narratives", in: Donald Wehrs and Thomas Blake (Eds.): *The Palgrave handbook of affect studies and textual criticism*. London: Palgrave Macmillan, pp. 347–369.

Cova, Florian, and Sylvain Deplanque (2021): "The everyday concept of well-being". Manuscript.

Cullhed, Eric (2020): "What evokes being moved?", *Emotion Review* 12 (2), pp. 111–117.

D'Arms, Justin, and Daniel Jacobson (2003): "The significance of recalcitrant emotion (or, anti-quasijudgmentalism)", *Royal Institute of Philosophy Supplement* 52, pp. 127–145.

de Jong, Peter (2015): "Danger-confirming reasoning and the persistence of phobic beliefs", in: Niall Galbraith (Ed.): *Aberrant beliefs and reasoning*. London and New York: Psychology Press, pp. 132–153.

Deonna, Julien, and Fabrice Teroni (2012): *The emotions. A philosophical introduction*. New York: Routledge.

Deonna, Julien, and Fabrice Teroni (2015): "Emotions as attitudes", *Dialectica* 69 (3), pp. 293–311.

Deonna, Julien, and Fabrice Teroni (2017): "Getting bodily feelings into emotional experience in the right way", *Emotion Review* 9 (1), pp. 55–63.

Díaz, Rodrigo (2019): "Using fMRI in experimental philosophy. Exploring the prospects", in: Eugen Fischer and Mark Curtis (Eds.): *Methodological advances in experimental philosophy*. London: Bloomsbury, pp. 131–152.

Díaz, Rodrigo (2022a): "What do people think is an emotion?", *Affective Science* 3, pp. 438–450.

Díaz, Rodrigo (2022b): "Emotions and the body. Testing the subtraction argument", *Philosophical Psychology* 35, pp. 47–65.

Díaz, Rodrigo (n.d.): "How to understand recalcitrant emotions". Manuscript.

Díaz, Rodrigo, and Kevin Reuter (2021): "Feeling the right way. Normative influences on people's use of emotion concepts", *Mind & Language* 36 (3), pp. 451–470.

Díaz, Rodrigo, and Kevin Reuter (n.d.): "Engineering affect. Emotional feelings vs. emotional attitudes". Manuscript.

Döring, Sabine (2007): "Seeing what to do. Affective perception and rational motivation", *Dialectica* 61 (3), pp. 363–394.

Ekman, Paul (1999): "Basic emotions", in: Tim Dalgleish and Mick Power (Eds.): *Handbook of cognition and emotion*. Chichester: John Wiley & Sons, pp. 45–60.

Fiske, Alan Page, Thomas Schubert, and Beate Seibt (2017): "'Kama muta' or 'being moved by love'. A bootstrapping approach to the ontology and epistemology of an emotion", in: Julia Cassaniti and Usha Menon (Eds.): *Universalism without uniformity. Explorations in mind and culture*. Chicago: The University of Chicago Press, pp. 79–100.

Fontaine, Johnny, Klaus Scherer, and Cristina Soriano (2013): *Components of emotional meaning. A sourcebook*. Oxford: Oxford University Press.

Foot, Philippa (2001): *Natural goodness*. New York: Oxford University Press.

Gendron, Maria, and Lisa Feldman Barrett (2009): "Reconstructing the past. A century of ideas about emotion in psychology", *Emotion Review* 1 (4), pp. 316–339.

Greenspan, Patricia (1981): "Emotions as evaluations", *Pacific Philosophical Quarterly* 62 (2), pp. 158–169.

Grzankowski, Alex (2017): "The real trouble with recalcitrant emotions", *Erkenntnis* 82 (3), pp. 641–651.

Hebart, Martin, and Chris Baker (2017): "Deconstructing multivariate decoding for the study of brain function", *Neuroimage* 180 (A), pp. 4–18.

Hietanen, Jari, Enrico Glerean, Riitta Hari, and Lauri Nummenmaa (2016): "Bodily maps of emotions across child development", *Developmental Science* 19 (6), pp. 1111–1118.

Hohmann, George (1966): "Some effects of spinal cord lesions on experienced emotional feelings", *Psychophysiology* 3 (2), pp. 143–156.

Hufendiek, Rebekka (2016): *Embodied emotions. A naturalist approach to a normative phenomenon*. New York: Routledge.

James, William (1884): "What is an emotion?", *Mind* 9 (34), pp. 188–205.

Johnson-Laird, Philip, and Keith Oatley (1989): "The language of emotions. An analysis of a semantic field", *Cognition and Emotion* 3 (2), pp. 81–123.

Kenny, Anthony (1963): *Action, emotion and will*. London: Routledge.

Kneer, Markus, and Daniel Haybron (2019): "Happiness and well-being. Is it all in your head? Evidence from the folk". Manuscript.

Kragel, Philip, and Kevin LaBar (2016): "Decoding the nature of emotion in the brain", *Trends in Cognitive Sciences* 20 (6), pp. 444–455.

Kuehnast, Milena, Valentin Wagner, Eugen Wassiliwizky, Thomas Jacobsen, and Winfried Menninghaus (2014): "Being moved. Linguistic representation and conceptual structure", *Frontiers in Psychology* 5, 1242.

Kurth, Charlie, Daniel Kosacz, and Rodrigo Díaz (n.d.): "Emotion and error". Manuscript.

Landmann, Helen, Florian Cova, and Ursula Hess (2019): "Being moved by meaningfulness. Appraisals of surpassing internal standards elicit being moved by relationships and achievements", *Cognition and Emotion* 33 (7), pp. 1387–1409.

Lindquist, Kristen, Tor Wager, Hedy Kober, Eliza Bliss-Moreau, and Lisa Feldman Barrett (2012): "The brain basis of emotion. A meta-analytic review", *Behavioral and Brain Sciences* 35 (3), pp. 121–143.

Liu, Michelle (2020): "The intuitive invalidity of the pain-in-mouth argument", *Analysis* 80 (3), pp. 463–474.

Liu, Michelle (2021): "The polysemy view of pain", *Mind & Language* 38 (1), pp. 198–217.

Loaiza, Juan (2021): "Emotions and the problem of variability", *Review of Philosophy and Psychology* 12 (2), pp. 329–351.

Machery, Edouard (2017): *Philosophy within its proper bounds*. Oxford: Oxford University Press.

McNally, Richard, and Christine Louro (1992): "Fear of flying in agoraphobia and simple phobia. Distinguishing features", *Journal of Anxiety Disorders* 6 (4), pp. 319–324.

Menninghaus, Winfried, Valentin Wagner, Julian Hanich, Eugen Wassiliwizky, Milena Kuehnast, and Thomas Jacobsen (2015): "Towards a psychological construct of being moved", *PLOS ONE* 10 (6), e0128451.

Meuleman, Ben, Agnes Moors, Johnny Fontaine, Olivier Renaud, and Klaus Scherer (2019): "Interaction and threshold effects of appraisal on componential patterns of emotion. A study using cross-cultural semantic data", *Emotion* 19 (3), pp. 425–442.

Meuleman, Ben, and Klaus Scherer (2013): "Nonlinear appraisal modeling. An application of machine learning to the study of emotion production", *IEEE Transactions on Affective Computing* 4 (4):, pp. 398–411.

Naar, Hichem (2018): "The real issue with recalcitrant emotions. Reply to Grzankowski", *Erkenntnis* 85, pp. 1035–1040.

Naar, Hichem, and Fabrice Teroni (Eds.) (2017): *The ontology of emotions*. Cambridge: Cambridge University Press.

Nummenmaa, Lauri, Enrico Glerean, Riitta Hari, and Jari Hietanen (2014): "Bodily maps of emotions", *Proceedings of the National Academy of Sciences of the United States of America* 111 (2), pp. 646–651.

Nussbaum, Martha (2001): *Upheavals of thought. The intelligence of emotions*. Cambridge: Cambridge University Press.

Nussbaum, Martha (2004): "Emotions as judgments of value and importance", in: Robert Solomon (Ed.): *Thinking about feeling. Contemporary philosophers on emotions*. New York: Oxford University Press, pp. 183–199.

Phillips, Jonathan, Julian de Freitas, Christian Mott, June Gruber, and Joshua Knobe (2017): "True happiness. The role of morality in the folk concept of happiness", *Journal of Experimental Psychology – General* 146 (2), pp. 165–181.

Phillips, Jonathan, Luke Misenheimer, and Joshua Knobe (2011): "The ordinary concept of happiness (and others like it)", *Emotion Review* 71 (3), pp. 929–937.

Phillips, Jonathan, Sven Nyholm, and Shen-Yi Liao (2014): "The good in happiness", in: Tania Lombrozo, Shaun Nichols, and Joshua Knobe (Eds.): *Oxford Studies in Experimental Philosophy*. Vol. 1. Oxford: Oxford University Press, pp. 253–293.

Prinz, Jesse (2004): *Gut reactions. A perceptual theory of emotion*. New York: Oxford University Press.

Quigley, Karen, Kristen Lindquist, and Lisa Feldman Barrett (2014): "Inducing and measuring emotion and affect. Tips, tricks, and secrets", in: Harry Reis and Charles Judd (Eds.): *Handbook of research methods in social and personality psychology*. New York: Cambridge University Press, pp. 220–252.

Reisenzein, Rainer (1995): "On Oatley and Johnson-Laird's theory of emotion and hierarchical structures in the affective lexicon", *Cognition and Emotion* 9 (4), pp. 383–416.

Reisenzein, Rainer (2022): "Tasks for a theoretical psychology of emotion", *Cognition and Emotion* 36 (2), pp. 171–187.

Reuter, Kevin (2011): "Distinguishing the appearance", *Journal of Consciousness Studies* 18 (9–10), pp. 94–109.

Reuter, Kevin, Michael Messerli, and Luca Barlassina (2022): "Not more than a feeling. An experimental investigation into the folk concept of happiness", *Thought* 11 (1), pp. 41–50.

Reuter, Kevin, Dustin Phillips, and Justin Sytsma (2014): "Hallucinating pain", in: Justin Sytsma (Ed.): *Advances in Experimental Philosophy of Mind*. London: Bloomsbury, pp. 75–100.

Reuter, Kevin, Michael Sienhold, and Justin Sytsma (2019): "Putting pain in its proper place", *Analysis* 79 (1), pp. 72–82.

Reuter, Kevin, and Justin Sytsma (2020): "Unfelt pain", *Synthese* 197 (4), pp. 1777–1801.

Ritchie, Brendan, David Kaplan, and Colin Klein (2017): "Decoding the brain. Neural representation and the limits of multivariate pattern analysis in cognitive neuroscience". Manuscript.

Roberts, Robert (1988): "What an emotion is. A sketch", *Philosophical Review* 97 (2), pp. 183–209.

Roberts, Robert (2003): *Emotions. An essay in aid of moral psychology.* Cambridge: Cambridge University Press.

Salomons, Tim, Richard Harrison, Nat Hansen, James Stazicker, Astrid Grith Sorensen, Paula Thomas, and Emma Borg (2022): "Is pain 'all in your mind'? Examining the general public's views of pain", *Review of Philosophy and Psychology* 13, pp. 683–698.

Scarantino, Andrea, and Paul Griffiths (2011): "Don't give up on basic emotions", *Emotion Review* 3 (4), pp. 444–454.

Scarantino, Andrea, and Ronald de Sousa (2018): "Emotion", in: Edward Zalta (Ed.): *The Stanford Encyclopedia of Philosophy.* Summer 2021 edition. https://plato.stanford.edu/archives/sum2021/entries/emotion/, last accessed May 19, 2023.

Scherer, Klaus (2005): "What are emotions? And how can they be measured?", *Social Science Information* 44 (4), pp. 695–729.

Scherer, Klaus (2009): "Emotions are emergent processes. They require a dynamic computational architecture", *Philosophical Transactions of the Royal Society B – Biological Sciences* 364 (1535), pp. 3459–3474.

Scherer, Klaus, and Ben Meuleman (2013): "Human emotion experiences can be predicted on theoretical grounds. Evidence from verbal labeling", *PLOS ONE* 8 (3), e58166.

Solomon, Robert (1976): *The passions. Emotions and the meaning of life.* New York: Anchor.

Solomon, Robert (2004): *Thinking about feeling. Contemporary philosophers on emotions.* Oxford: Oxford University Press.

Sytsma, Justin (2010): "Dennett's theory of the folk theory of consciousness", *Journal of Consciousness Studies* 17 (3–4), pp. 107–130.

Sytsma, Justin, and Kevin Reuter (2017): "Experimental philosophy of pain", *Journal of Indian Council of Philosophical Research* 34 (3), pp. 611–628.

Tappolet, Christine (2016): *Emotions, values, and agency.* New York: Oxford University Press.

Volynets, Sofia, Enrico Glerean, Jari Hietanen, Riitta Hari, and Lauri Nummenmaa (2020): "Bodily maps of emotions are culturally universal", *Emotion* 20 (7), pp. 1127–1136.

Walder, Cristine, Jim McCracken, Michael Herbert, Peter James, and Norman Brewitt (1987): "Psychological intervention in civilian flying phobia. Evaluation and a three-year follow-up", *British Journal of Psychiatry* 151, pp. 494–498.

Zickfeld, Janis, Patrícia Arriaga, Sara Vilar Santos, Thomas Schubert, and Beate Seibt (2020): "Tears of joy, aesthetic chills and heartwarming feelings. Physiological correlates of Kama Muta", *Psychophysiology* 57 (12), e13662.

Ian M. Church

Experimental Philosophy of Religion: Problem of Evil

Abstract: While experimental philosophy has fruitfully applied the tools and resources of psychology and cognitive science to debates within epistemology, metaphysics, and ethics, relatively little work has been done within philosophy of religion. And this isn't due to a lack of need! Philosophers of religion frequently rely on empirical claims that can be either verified or disproven, but without exploring whether they are. And philosophers of religion frequently appeal to intuitions which may vary wildly according to education level, theological background, and so on, without concern for whether or not the psychological mechanisms that underwrite those intuitions are broadly shared or reliable. In this chapter, I explore some of the fruit and possibilities for the emerging field of experimental philosophy of religion. First, in Section 1, I motivate and outline the chapter. Then in Section 2, I briefly consider how the tools and resources of experimental philosophy might be fruitfully applied to a seminal topic within philosophy of religion, namely, the problem of evil. In Section 3, I'll sketch some broader applications of experimental philosophy of religion.

Keywords: Experimental Philosophy; Philosophy of Religion; Problem of Evil; Psychology of Religion; Religious Epistemology

1 Introduction

From its very conception, philosophy of religion has arguably been accompanied by questions concerning why people form the religious beliefs that they do. Consider the following famous passage from the pre-Socratic philosopher, Xenophanes:

> Homer and Hesiod have attributed to the gods everything that is a shame and reproach among men, stealing and committing adultery and deceiving each other. But mortals consider that the gods are born, and that they have clothes and speech and bodies like their own. The Ethiopians say that their gods are snub-nosed and black, the Thracians that theirs have light blue eyes and red hair. But if cattle and horses or lions had hands, or were able to draw with their hands and do the work that men can do, horses would draw the forms of the gods like horses, and cattle like cattle, and they would make their bodies such as they each had themselves. (translation by Kirk and Raven 1960, p. 168 f.)

Note: This research was made possible by the generous support of the John Templeton Foundation (ID 61886). Justin Barrett, Isaac Warchol, and Rebecca Carlson were all helpful interlocutors while conducting research for this paper, and I'm also enormously grateful to the editors of this anthology for their patient feedback and guidance.

Such an observation is often taken as a serious objection to various religious beliefs. Given the cultural genesis of many religious beliefs, we might justifiably suspect that people are simply inclined to worship gods of their own making; an observation that obviously casts doubt on such beliefs.

And we have good reason to think that Xenophanes' critique is still with us today. For example, ever since Karl Barth famously gave the doctrine of the Trinity preeminence in his magisterial *Church Dogmatics* – developing the Trinity as a lens through which we must see and develop distinctively Christian theology – many theologians have followed suit and tried to develop theological insights by extrapolating from the Trinity. In practice, however, it often looks like the Trinity is used as a mirror for reflecting whatever theological conclusions a theologian wants to arrive at. As Stephen Holmes (2009), notes in his article "Three versus One? Some Problems of Social Trinitarianism", theologians with different leanings regarding ecclesiology, for example, can sometimes come to radically (but predictably!) different conclusions regarding what lessons we can learn from reflecting on the Trinity. A theologian with high-church leanings will likely find hierarchical ecclesiology to be supported by their doctrine of the Trinity. A theologian with low-church leanings will likely find the Trinity to be a foundation for more egalitarian conclusions. Such insights raise challenging questions: to what extent is our theology (or atheology) predicated on our prior commitments? Are our conceptions of God of our own making? Xenophanes' worry still lingers.

Psychology has had a long history of exploring the empirical foundations of religious beliefs;[1] however, despite the recent flourishing of philosophy of religion within the Anglophone world,[2] most scholars working within philosophy of religion have only rarely explored how the empirical literature might shed light on the field.[3] And while experimental philosophy has fruitfully applied the tools and resources of psychology and cognitive science to debates within epistemology, metaphysics, and ethics, scholars within philosophy of religion have been slow to follow suit.[4] And this isn't due to a lack of need! Philosophers of religion frequently rely on empirical claims that can be either verified or disproven, but without exploring whether they are. And philosophers of religion frequently appeal to intuitions which may vary wildly according to education level, theological background, and so on, without concern for whether or not the psychological mechanisms that underwrite those intuitions are broadly shared or reliable.

---

1 Freud himself was frequently explaining religious beliefs in terms of "illusions" or "wish-fulfillment" (Freud 1953, p. 30). Some other seminal works in this area include Durkheim (2008), Evans-Pritchard and Gillies (1976), Malinowski (2015).
2 As Nicholas Wolterstorff (2011, p. 155) noted in his article "How Philosophical Theology Became Possible within the Analytic Tradition of Philosophy", "Never since the late Middle Ages has philosophical theology so flourished as it has during the past thirty years".
3 This is perhaps especially surprising given that experimental philosophy can be seen as a continuation of very traditional philosophical projects. See Knobe and Nichols (2007, p. 3).
4 That said, work within experimental philosophy of religion is starting to proliferate. Some of it is even quite favorable to various forms of theism. See, e.g., Barrett and Church (2013), Church, Carlson, and Barrett (2020), De Cruz and De Smedt (2015), De Cruz (2015, 2017), Green (2015).

And while quite a few contemporary scholars working within philosophy of religion have been interested in looking to the psychological literature for philosophical insights (see, e.g., Barrett and Church 2013, De Cruz 2015, De Cruz and De Smedt 2015, Green 2015), relatively little work has been done conducting empirical research in the spirit of experimental philosophy as it has been done within epistemology, metaphysics, and ethics.[5] This is all starting to change. Thanks to generous funding from the John Templeton Foundation, a number of projects on the theme of experimental philosophy of religion are being funded; as such, we should expect a proliferation of literature on experimental philosophy of religion in the coming years.[6]

In this chapter, we'll explore some of the fruit and possibilities for this emerging field. In Section 2, I want to briefly consider how the tools and resources of experimental philosophy have been fruitfully applied to a seminal topic within philosophy of religion, namely, the problem of evil. For the sake of reducing the word-count, my focus here will primarily be on simply summarizing the results. Finally, in Section 3, I'll briefly sketch some broader applications of experimental philosophy of religion.

But before we get started, it's worth considering the following question: Why is it important to extend experimental philosophy to philosophy of religion? After all, philosophy of religion has seen an almost unparalleled flurry of activity over the past 50 years; what is experimental philosophy going to bring to the table? Let me briefly point to two motivations for experimental philosophy of religion: First, while philosophy of religion has indeed flourished over the past few decades in many regards, it's public image within the field more broadly is still somewhat suspect. As Draper and Nichols (2013, p. 421) explain: "[In] spite of the recent expansion of work in philosophy of religion, it exhibits at least four symptoms of poor health: it is too partisan, too polemical, too narrow in its focus, and too often evaluated using criteria that are theological or religious instead of philosophical". They go on to suggest that the contemporary philosophy of religion literature is permeated by scholars who "suffer from cognitive biases and group influences" (Draper and Nichols 2013, p. 420). One of the central benefits of experimental philosophy of religion is that it might help us better understand the biases of scholars working within the field (myself included!) and perhaps even facilitate intellectual modesty. Here, I like to quote David Hume (who can, I think, in places be read as a proto-experimental philosopher):

> The greater part of mankind are naturally apt to be affirmative and dogmatical in their opinions; and while they see objects only on one side, and have no idea of any counterpoising argument, they throw themselves precipitately into the principles, to which they are inclined; nor have they any indulgence for those who entertain opposite sentiments. To hesitate or balance perplexes their understanding, checks their passion, and suspends their action. They are, therefore, impatient till they escape from a state, which to them is so uneasy: and they think, that they could never remove themselves far enough from it, by the violence of their affirmations and obstinacy

---

[5] A prominent exception to this trend has been some of the work of Helen De Cruz. See, e.g., De Cruz (2017).
[6] This is the "Launching Experimental Philosophy of Religion Project" (Project ID 61886).

> of their belief. *But could such dogmatical reasoners become sensible of the strange infirmities of human understanding, even in its most perfect state, and when most accurate and cautious in its determinations; such a reflection would naturally inspire them with more modesty and reserve, and diminish their fond opinion of themselves, and their prejudice against antagonists.* (Hume 1975, p. 161, emphasis added)

If we (i.e., philosophers of religion) could better understand the cognitive, social, and psychological mechanisms that underwrite our beliefs, we *might* (as Hume ultimately suspects) find that human understanding "is by no means fitted for such remote and abstruse subjects" (Hume 1975, p. 12); however, more hopefully, we might simply learn a better way forward in the field – a way that's perhaps not so plagued with "cognitive biases and group influences", a way that's accompanied by more "modesty and reserve".

Secondly, experimental philosophy of religion might also push the field towards greater pluralism. A lot of work that is done in philosophical theology and philosophy of religion is done from the perspective of Western academia, along with Western academic intuitions. And in many cases, that might be just fine. (If the subject under consideration is a technical Western concept, then it might make sense to take seriously the intuitions of technical Westerners.) The problem, however, is that academic Western intuitions are often assumed to be *everyone's* intuitions, and this is particularly problematic when arguments are being made that aim to apply far beyond Western academia, across religions and across cultures. It's not at all obvious that philosophers and theologians should prioritize the intuitions of Western academics when it comes to many central debates (like the debates surrounding the problem of evil, natural law, purpose, and so on). As such, one hope for experimental philosophy of religion is that it will expand the religious and cultural insights that are relevant to the contemporary debates, breaking down cultural barriers, and better revealing (and perhaps honestly owning) the presuppositions that shape our view of ourselves, the divine, and evil.[7]

---

[7] This, of course, also connects with the previous point about modesty. The problem of "echo-chambers" in contemporary religious debates – where people only listen to pundits "on their side" while ignoring or caricaturing any opposition – is arguably antithetical to intellectual modesty, the honest exchange of ideas, and academic progress. If viable, divergent opinions are ignored, silenced, or simply overlooked, then it's all too easy to be intellectually arrogant – to think that our views are the only viable views, to just assume that our idiosyncratic ideas and intuitions are accurate representations of objective reality. As such, one hope of experimental philosophy of religion is that by opening the doors to a wide range of perspectives and intuitions regarding human nature, evil, and the divine, philosophers and theologians will be able to take a humbler and more reflective stance toward their own presuppositions and insights.

2 The Problem of Evil

From 2018 through 2020, Justin Barrett, Oliver Crisp, undergraduate research assistants, and myself worked on the "Problem of Evil and Experimental Philosophy of Religion" project (generously funded by the John Templeton Foundation; Project ID 61095), which explicitly aimed to apply the tools and resources of experimental philosophy to a seminal issue within the philosophy of religion, namely, the problem of evil. The hope was that this research would lead to and motivate further work within experimental philosophy of religion. While the research here is ongoing, in this section I will briefly report on some of what we have been finding. First, I'll consider Rowe's formulation of the problem (Section 2.1), and then I'll sketch some applications from experimental philosophy (Section 2.2). After that, I'll summarize our results (Section 2.3).

2.1 Rowe's Formulation of the Problem

While our 2021 article, "Evil Intuitions? The Problem of Evil, Experimental Philosophy, and the Need for Psychological Research" (co-authored with Rebecca Carlson and Justin Barret) pointed to broader applications, our research thus far has focused predominantly on William Rowe's seminal 1979 formulation of the problem of evil, which will be our central focus in this section. Here is Rowe's (1979) central argument:

1. There exist instances of intense suffering which an omnipotent, omniscient being could have prevented without thereby losing some greater good or permitting some evil equally bad or worse.
2. An omniscient, wholly good being would prevent the occurrence of any intense suffering it could, unless it could not do so without thereby losing some greater good or permitting some evil equally bad or worse.
3. [Therefore,] there does not exist an omnipotent, omniscient, wholly good being. (Rowe 1979, p. 336)

Given (a) that Rowe frequently uses the shorthand "pointless" to refer to suffering where allowing it to happen doesn't either afford some greater good or prevent some other evil equally bad or worse and (b) a traditional conception of God as omnipotent, omniscient, and omnibenevolent, we can simplify Rowe's argument to something like this:
1. There exists pointless suffering.
2. If there is a God, then there won't be pointless suffering.
3. Therefore, there is no God.

A fairly straightforward *Modus tollens* argument. But why should we think the premises are true? Rowe takes premise (2) – or (5), respectively – to be relatively uncontroversial; as Rowe (1979, p. 336) notes, "This premise (or something not too distant from it) is, I think, held in common by many atheists and nontheists". Agreed; if there is an all-good, all-powerful, all-knowing God, we wouldn't expect there to be genuinely pointless suffering in the world. That premise won't be our focus here. But what about premise (1) – or (4), respectively? Why should we think there is indeed pointless suffering in the world?[8]

Here, Rowe introduces a brief vignette, showcasing what appears to be an example of pointless suffering:

> **FAWN:** Suppose in some distant forest lightning strikes a dead tree, resulting in a forest fire. In the fire a fawn is trapped, horribly burned, and lies in terrible agony for several days before death relieves its suffering. (Rowe 1979, p. 337)

According to Rowe (1979, p. 337), "so far as we can see, the fawn's intense suffering is pointless". Now, whether the suffering is genuinely pointless is up for debate, but Rowe's central point here is that such suffering *seems* pointless. And that certainly seems to be the case! While an omnipotent, omniscient, all-good being certainly could have prevented such an event, it's extremely difficult to imagine how permitting something like the suffering of FAWN could either prevent a greater evil from occurring or might usher in some greater good. Given this case, premise (1) – or (4), respectively – looks extremely plausible!

To be sure, this doesn't amount to a proof. As Rowe is quick to point out, for all we can tell there *is* a greater evil that allowing FAWN prevents or perhaps there *is* a greater good that allowing FAWN affords. The problem, as Rowe sees it, is that given "*our experience and knowledge of the variety and profusion of suffering in our world*" it *seems like* evils like those manifest in the example above are wholly avoidable and more or less pointless; and while the above argument doesn't amount to a *proof*, it does, according to Rowe, provide "rational support for atheism, that it is reasonable for us to believe that the theistic God does not exist" (Rowe 1979, p. 338, emphasis added).

2.2 Applying Experimental Philosophy

So how might experimental philosophy apply to Rowe's argument? One straightforward application is to see if the intuitions that underwrite Rowe's argument are shared across a wide range of demographics. When epistemologists talk about "our intuitions" regarding Gettier counterexamples, experimental philosophers wonder, "whose intuitions?"; similarly, when Rowe talks about "our experience and knowledge of the variety and profusion of suffering in our world" we might also easily wonder "whose ex-

---

[8] Notice how already the argument has an empirical component to it, since it seems to clearly rest on the world being (or at least appearing) a certain way, namely as having instances of pointless suffering within it.

perience?" or "whose knowledge?"[9] Similarly, when Rowe says that the suffering of the fawn "does not appear" to have a point or that it doesn't "seem" reasonable to believe that the suffering of the fawn has a point, we might plausibly ask "does it 'appear' or 'seem' this way to everyone?"(Rowe 1979, p. 337).

If not, then we might wonder if we have any reason to champion one set of intuitions over another. And maybe we do, maybe those of us who feel the weight of Rowe's argument are drawing from intuitions that have been honed by years of training and expertise; maybe the divergent intuitions are simply reflecting a degree of ignorance. But if no such story can be plausibly told, then there is a legitimate worry that the philosophical import of Rowe's intuitions regarding the FAWN case might be significantly diminished.[10]

Along these lines, we predicted that intuitions regarding the FAWN case would indeed diverge across various demographics. Quoting from our forthcoming article, we came up with the following hypotheses about the demographics of intuitions regarding the FAWN case:

Religion: Intuitions regarding Rowe's case will significantly diverge according to the respondents' religious beliefs. More specifically, people who report being atheists or agnostics will, on average, agree with Rowe's intuitions regarding the FAWN case; whereas, people who are not atheists or agnostics will, on average, disagree with Rowe's intuitions regarding the FAWN case.

Gender: Relatedly, given that men are statistically more likely to be atheists or agnostics than women (Cragun 2016, p. 307), we predicted that men would, on average, agree with Rowe's intuition more than women.

Education: Additionally, given that education levels negatively correlate with religiosity (Beit-Hallahmi 2006, p. 313) – such that the more educated someone is the more likely they are to be an atheist or an agnostic –, we predicted that more educated people will report greater agreement with Rowe's intuition, on average, than less educated people.

Nationality: Given that Rowe is working within the American academy, we expected that Americans might, on average, be more likely to agree with Rowe than other nationalities.

Ethnicity: Given that Rowe is working within the Anglophone academic world, a world that has historically been predominantly populated by people of European descent, we expected that people who identify as White would, on average, be more likely to agree with Rowe than other ethnicities. (McAllister et al., sec. 2.1)

---

9 For such work on the Gettier problem, see Weinberg, Nichols, and Stich (2001).
10 Critically, it's our intuitions regarding FAWN that are the driving force for thinking that premise (1) – or (4), respectively – is true. As Plantinga (2000) elucidates Rowe's argument in *Warranted Christian Belief*, if it *seems* as though the suffering in FAWN is pointless, then that gives us a reason for thinking that the suffering in FAWN is pointless; and insofar as we have evidence for thinking that the suffering in FAWN is pointless, then that will give us evidence against theism (given Rowe's argument; Rowe 1979, p. 465 f.). As such, if we don't think that the suffering of the FAWN is pointless, contrary to Rowe, then the evidence in favor of thinking that premise (1) – or (4), respectively – is true greatly diminishes. And if our evidence in favor of thinking that premise (1) – or (4), respectively – is greatly diminished, then, as Rowe rightly acknowledges, the evidence the argument generates against theism greatly diminishes too.

Let's call these the *religion-hypothesis*, *gender-hypothesis*, and so on, respectively.

We might also inquire into the psychological mechanisms that underwrite intuitions regarding the FAWN case. In addition to directly testing the stability of key philosophical intuitions across various demographics, it is also worth exploring what factors might contribute to people having the intuitions that they do. We might think of this as the *psychology of philosophy* or the *psychology of philosophers* (heaven help us!). For example, given that fawns are exceptionally cute animals (just think of Bambie!), we might wonder if cuteness is a driving factor behind our intuitions regarding the FAWN case. Would horrific death of a less cute animal – for example, perhaps a boar or a vulture – be seen as any less pointless? And what if we tried to bring the cuteness to the fore by presenting people with the picture of a cute fawn along with the standard FAWN case? Or if they're reading a version of the vignette with a boar or vulture instead, what if we included a less than flattering picture of the boar or vulture respectively? Call this the *cuteness-hypothesis*. If cuteness is driving the perception of pointlessness (when it comes to the suffering), then that might give us a reason to wonder how veridic such intuitions are.[11]

Finally, we might also wonder if the brevity of the FAWN case – being only two sentences long – is what's contributing to the perception of pointlessness (again, when it comes to the suffering). Many scholars have highlighted the importance of context and narrative when wrestling with the problem of suffering,[12] so we might wonder if the presence of some background information as context might diminish the perception of pointlessness. Call this the *context-hypothesis*.

2.3 Summary of Results

Justin Barrett and I (along with some undergraduate research assistants) began exploring these hypotheses during the "Problem of Evil and Experimental Philosophy of Religion" project, and we've started to submit our findings to various academic journals. Some of the results were published open access in our article "The Context of Suffering" (forthcoming), but others are still awaiting publication. In either case, I can only briefly summarize our findings here.

Quoting from "The Context of Suffering" (forthcoming), we tested the above hypotheses via the following methods:

---

[11] To be sure, the goal here isn't to commit the genetic fallacy; in other words, the goal here is *not* to suggest that if we can explain why someone believes something, then that their belief must be false. (After all, if we can explain why someone loves their spouse, that doesn't mean that they don't love their spouse!) However, there can be something deeply revealing about explaining why people have the beliefs and intuitions that they do. And, in at least some circumstances, if we know that the psychological mechanisms that drive a target intuition are not sufficiently truth-sensitive, then that can give us pause to reflect on the philosophical import of those intuitions.

[12] Eleonore Stump's 2012 work, *Wandering in Darkness*, is particularly relevant here.

To investigate these questions, we developed an experimental study with a 2x2x3 between-subjects factorial design. 1,506 participants were recruited from Amazon's Mechanical Turk online workforce. After completing an informed consent form, participants provided demographic information including: age, gender, ethnicity, religious affiliation, nationality, income, and education level. Participants then read Rowe's vignette of the fawn from the 1979 paper. Participants were presented with the vignette in one of several manners. To half of the participants the vignette was accompanied by a description of the role of wildfires in a forest ecosystem to provide context to the suffering. This description, approximately a paragraph in length, discussed the role occasional, small forest fires have in the health of the ecosystem by clearing away dead organic material and helping the forest recovery by leaving behind a topsoil dense in organic materials. The other half of the participants read the vignette without context, just as it appeared in Rowe's 1979 paper. The subject of the vignette varied as either a fawn, a boar, or a vulture. Finally, in half of the cases a picture of the subject of the vignette accompanied the vignette. Thus, this experiment contained three variables: context (High or low) picture (Picture or no picture) and animal (Fawn, boar, or vulture).

After reading the vignette, participants rated several statements designed to assess their degree of agreement or disagreement with Rowe's intuition that the suffering described in the vignette is pointless. These statements read, "The story you just read is an example of pointless suffering," "Some equal or greater evil could have been prevented because of the situation in the story," and "Some equal or greater good could be accomplished because of the situation in the story." Participants responded on a 7 point Likert scale ranging from 1, Strongly Disagree to 7, strongly agree. We initially intended to measure the degree to which participants shared Rowe's intuitions through an index compiled of the score of these three statements, however, we found that whereas scores of the last two questions were highly correlated ($r = .478, p < 0.01$) the first question was not highly correlated in the expected direction with the last two questions ($r = .071, p < 0.01$ and $r = -.171, p < 0.01$). Therefore, we measured agreement with Rowe through an index of the reverse scored second and third questions. Finally, the participants answered questions about their intuitions concerning pointlessness and suffering more broadly and about how often the butchered or killed animals for food. (Church, Warcol, and Barrett forthcoming)

The demographics of our participants:

After excluding participants who failed attention checks, rushed through the survey (in under 90 seconds), or abandoned the survey (left more than 10 % of the survey incomplete), we had a sample size of $n = 1,506$. Of these 476 where female, 1,014 were male, 16 had another gender identity. The sample consisted of 846 White participants, 363 Asian participants, 146 Black or African American participants, 105 Hispanic participants, and 46 participants belonging to other ethnicities. 201 participants were agnostic, 161 atheist, 464 Catholic, 261 Hindu, 181 Protestant, 100 were another denomination of Christian, and 138 participants reported another religious affiliation. 4 participants had a 9th grade education or less, 117 participants had a high school education or G.E.D., 158 had some college or specialized training, 82 had associates degrees, 899 had Bachelor's degrees, 246 had a Master's degree or higher. (Church, Warcol, and Barrett forthcoming)

So, what did we find? Let's start with the hypotheses regarding whether or not intuitions regarding the FAWN case diverge across various demographics (the *religion-hypothesis*, the *gender-hypothesis*, and so on). Please note that in the following results, a score of 8 represents a midpoint of neither agreeing or disagreeing with Rowe. Anything above 8 (up to a maximum of 14) represents agreement with Rowe on average. Anything below 8 (to a minimum of 2) represents disagreement with Rowe on average.

Across those five demographic variables – gender, education, ethnicity, religion, and nationality – we saw significant divergences from Rowe's intuition regarding the FAWN case; however, not always in ways we predicted. Some results weren't terribly surprising; religious beliefs did indeed seem to have a significant ($p < 0.001$) impact on people's intuitions. Where atheists ($M = 8.58$, $SD = 3.20$) and agnostics ($M = 8.22$, $SD = 2.92$) on average agreed with Rowe's intuitions regarding the FAWN case, all religious groups with a sufficient amount of data (Protestants, $M = 7.29$, $SD = 2.67$; Catholics, $M = 6.10$, $SD = 2.50$; Hindus, $M = 5.32$, $SD = 2.32$; and "other Christians", $M = 6.53$, $SD = 2.49$) disagreed with Rowe's intuitions on average.[13] Other intuitions were more surprising. While intuitions do seem to diverge according to gender, it's women ($M = 7.09$, $SD = 2.94$, $p < 0.001$), not men ($M = 6.66$, $SD = 2.85$, $p < 0.001$), who are significantly ($p = 0.007$) more likely to agree with Rowe regarding the FAWN case. Our research also revealed a significant relationship between Rowe agreement and level of education ($p < 0.001$); however, it was the least educated (not the most educated) who were most likely to agree with Rowe (those with only a high-school education, $M = 8.51$, $SD = 2.76$; those with some college or specialized training, $M = 8.05$, $SD = 3.10$; those with an associate degree, $M = 7.70$, $SD = 2.96$; a bachelor degree, $M = 6.48$, $SD = 2.77$; or a postgraduate degree, $M = 6.05$, $SD = 2.57$).

But perhaps what is most striking from all of this research is the fact that so few people across all of these demographics agree, on average, with Rowe's intuition regarding the FAWN case. Ethnicity was indeed significant factor in perceptions of pointlessness ($p < 0.001$). While White ($M = 7.31$, $SD = 2.90$) and Hispanic ($M = 7.17$, $SD = 3.12$) participants were significantly more likely to agree with Rowe's intuition than, say, Asian ($M = 5.89$, $SD = 2.55$) participants, Whites and Hispanics nevertheless, on average, still disagreed with Rowe's intuition. Nationality too was significant ($p < 0.001$). While Americans ($M = 7.10$, $SD = 2.88$) and Brazilians ($M = 8.47$, $SD = 2.96$) were significantly more likely to agree with Rowe's intuition than Indians ($M = 5.41$, $SD = 2.41$), Americans, on average, nevertheless still disagreed with Rowe's intuition regarding the FAWN case. While women were significantly more likely to agree with Rowe's intuition than men, women, on average, nevertheless still disagreed with Rowe's intuition.

What does this mean for Rowe's seminal formulation of the problem of evil? Does such a variety in response to FAWN really threaten Rowe's argument? After all, a defender of Rowe's argument might argue that their conclusions about FAWN are not driven by intuition but are the result of a rational assessment of the possibility of rational justification of the target suffering! To be sure, many philosophers (see, e.g., Wykstra 1984, Russell and Wykstra 1988, Inwagen 1988, Alston 1991, Plantinga 2000) have already cast doubt on such a response; however, given the details of our empirical research, such a response now might seem especially implausible. Do we have a good reason for thinking that as people become more educated, they become generally less able to rationally assess the FAWN case? Do we have a good reason to think that Brazil-

---

[13] Though the divergence between agnostics and Protestants was less significant ($p = 0.015$).

ians are better at rationally assessing the FAWN case than Indians? That people of European descent are better at rationally assessing the FAWN case than Blacks or Asians? Surely not. Minimally, then, these empirical findings might raise serious concerns about the ultimate success of Rowe's formulation of the problem of evil, since it seems to suggest that Rowe's response to FAWN might be underwritten by cognitive mechanisms and influences that are not nearly as reliable, universal, or objective as we might have previously hoped.

What about the cuteness-hypothesis? Does the cuteness of an animal have a significant impact on the perception of pointless suffering in FAWN-style cases? No, it doesn't seem to. We didn't see any significant differences between people's responses whether or not they received the case with a fawn in the vignette, or with a boar, or with a vulture. It also didn't seem to matter whether or not we included a picture of the target animal.

What did matter, however, was context. With some of the variations of Rowe's FAWN case, we included the following paragraph of information before showing the target vignette:

> Forest fires are often viewed as some of the most dangerous and destructive natural disasters. While some fires of catastrophic size can be detrimental to forests and endanger human lives and infrastructure, smaller forest fires are actually an essential aspect of the forest ecosystem. It may seem counterintuitive that fires could be beneficial to the life of a forest, however, recent ecological research has shown that small burns play a major role in the health of an ecosystem as a whole. Fires, often resulting from lightning strikes, quickly and efficiently clear away thick undergrowth, dying trees, and the dead material that congregates on the forest floor. If left unchecked, dead organic material and undergrowth will prevent new trees and plants from taking root and being able to grow. The burnt organic material such as plants, shrubs, and animals, leave behind topsoil that is rich in nutrients from which new plant life can easily grow. Small forest fires also play an important role in preventing fires from reaching catastrophic sizes. When a fire is small, it is usually confined to burning the undergrowth and dead material on the forest floor and does not burn the tree canopy or kill the large trees of the forest. However, if a forest goes too long without a fire, the undergrowth will become so thick that when it does burn it will easily ignite not only the forest floor but also the trees themselves. Many experts attribute the record-setting fires that have been seen in recent years to decades of fire suppression in forests, which has left entire ecosystems vulnerable to catastrophic fires. Many species of plants have adapted to occasional fires and can quickly regrow burnt branches. Some trees even need fire to reproduce due to seed-cones that will only open when exposed to extreme temperature.

We then gave participants a variation of Rowe's FAWN case (some with boars, some with vultures, some with pictures, and so on). Across the board, participants who received the context paragraph reported (on average) significantly less "pointlessness" in the target case than participants who did not receive the context paragraph ($p < 0.001$).[14] Consider the graph (Figure 1) from Church, Warcol, and Barrett (2022).

---

[14] And, to be sure, no interaction effects across the different variables were statistically significant.

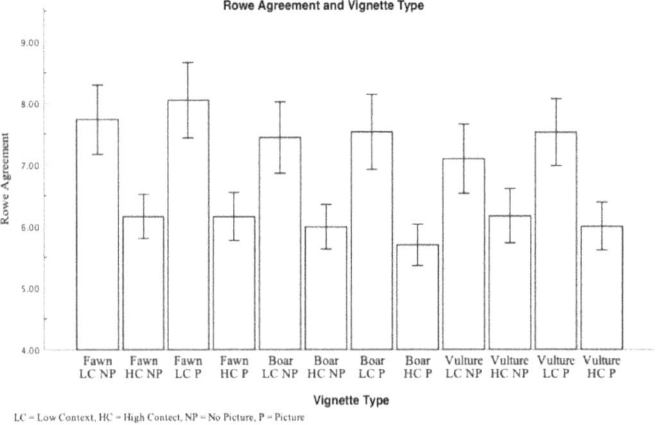

Figure 1: Vignette Type and Agreement with Rowe; anything above 8 (up to a maximum of 14) represents agreement with Rowe on average; anything below 8 (to a minimum of 2) represents disagreement with Rowe on average

In this graph, it's easy to see that the type of animal (fawn versus boar versus vulture) or the inclusion of a picture had no significant effect; that said, however, the effect of context on perceptions of pointlessness is (in our opinion) genuinely remarkable.[15]

To be sure, more research is needed before we can know what philosophical conclusions to draw from this result. Maybe the significance of context is a result of "points" being found in context; if that were the case, it wouldn't be surprising that Rowe's original case seemed pointless, because it was only two sentences long! That said, the significance of context might also be a result of some other factor. Given that we're pattern loving critters, maybe context gives us the resources to imagine a "point" where there isn't one. Again, more research is needed before we can draw any firm conclusions.[16]

2.4 Further Readings

Given that new subfield of experimental philosophy of religion is still in its infancy, works applying empirical tools to the problem of evil are extremely rare (most being either cited above or in progress). Under the umbrella of experimental philosophy of religion regarding the problem of evil, both Silverman and colleagues (2020) as well as Teehan (2013) and Teehan (2016) are examples of work in this area.

---

[15] For more information on this result, please see "The Context of Suffering" by Church, Warchol, and Barrett (forthcoming).
[16] Please see Church, Carlson, and Barrett (2020, sec. 3) for further empirical dimensions of the problem of evil that could be explored.

Thus far, the psychological literature has been more generous. Some literature has directly focused on the problem of evil; see, e.g., Sanford (198), Saxton (2006), and Betageri (2008). There is also an extensive literature on perceptions of suffering; see, e.g., Carrere (1989), Dunning and Hajcak (2009), Sibley and Bulbulia (2012), Barry (2013), Govrin (2018), and Jong (2021). A lot of psychological literature could also help explain variations in intuitions that are salient to religious belief; two examples would be both Bruneau, Dufour, and Saxe (2012) as well as Timm (2016). Dunbar et al. (2016), Tarr et al. (2015), Mueller-Pfeiffer et al. (2010), Crossley (2000), as well as Qureshi et al. (2011) are just a few examples of work that can give us insights into better understanding the psychological mechanisms underwriting pain and suffering.

It is also worth noting that the broader psychological literature also has resources that might plausibly be extremely helpful when bringing empirical tools to bear on the problem of evil – from the literature surrounding the now defunct Stanford Prison Experiment (Haney, Banks, and Zimbardo 1973), to Satisfaction with Life research (see, e.g., Krause and Hayward 2015), to research linking attachment styles to conceptions of the divine (see, e.g., Davis, Moriarty, and Mauch 2013), to research on suffering more generally (see, e.g., Wilt et al. 2016), all the way to the psychology of how humans process large numbers (see, e.g., Slovic, Västfjäll, and Gregory 2012). But the umbrella of "also plausibly relevant" is too broad for us to explore further here.

3 Further Topics

While our research has primarily focused on applying empirical tools to seminal formulations of the problem of evil, experimental philosophy has promising applications more broadly within philosophy of religion. This new field of experimental philosophy of religion is proliferating and has already made valuable contributions in a number of areas, including: religious disagreement (De Cruz 2017, De Cruz 2019, Woudenberg and Eyghen 2017); applications of cognitive science to philosophy of religion (Barrett and Church 2013, De Cruz and De Smedt 2015, De Smedt and De Cruz 2020); religious concepts and beliefs (Heiphetz et al. 2016, Shtulman and Lindeman 2016, De Cruz 2014, Leeuwen 2014); along with arguments for the general need for experimental philosophy of religion (Lim 2017, Mizrahi 2020, Tobia 2016, Draper and Nichols 2013). In this final section, I'd like to simply point to a few additional areas for future research.

3.1 Theological Methodology

One of the great effects experimental philosophy has had on contemporary philosophy is to generate a healthy amount of angst over what philosophers are doing when doing philosophy. Shortly after work in experimental philosophy started challenging the theoretical import of so many intuitions that undergird central projects in philosophy, the academic literature saw a flurry of interest in philosophical methodology (see, e.g.,

Williamson 2007, Cappelen, Gedler, and Hawthorne 2016, De Cruz 2015b). Where do our intuitions come from? Are they a reliable foundation for theory-building? Are some intuitions better than others? Why or why not? Are our philosophical intuitions simply a reflection of our worldview, our upbringing, our culture, or our personal experiences? What are philosophers doing when they do what they do?! Angst indeed.

But angst loves company. And experimental theology might very well give theologians reason to take a long look in the mirror and further reflect on their own methodology. And as we saw in the introduction of this chapter, from Xenophanes' classic critique of religious belief being made in our own images to the predictable responses to Barth's emphasis on the Trinity, questions concerning theological methodology can be of central interest for experimental philosophy of religion. Where do our theological intuitions come from? Are they a reliable foundation for theory-building? Are some theological intuitions better than others? Are our theological intuitions simply a reflection of our worldview, our upbringing, our culture, or our personal experiences? Further empirical research is needed.

3.2 Theodicies

While the above considerations regarding Rowe's formulation of the problem of evil arguably takes some pressure off of traditional brands theism, it's worth noting that applying resources from experimental philosophy to philosophy of religion or philosophical theology is a double-edged sword. In this instance, the result might take some pressure off of theism; however, additional work on experimental philosophy of religion might very well cut against various theological or religious projects. One immediately relevant project, of course, is the project of trying to develop a theodicy to justify God's allowing for the evils of this world. In his landmark work, *Evil and the Love of God*, John Hick (1966) identifies several seminal theodicies (or families of theodicies) within the relevant philosophical and theological literature, and the literature has only continued to expand. The worry here then is that, in addition to potentially undermining the evidential problem of evil, experimental philosophy of religion might also call into question seminal explanations for why God allows for the evil we see in the world.

Consider, for example, Alvin Plantinga's (2004) influential *felix culpa* theodicy as found in his work "Supralapsarianism, or 'O Felix Culpa'". In that paper, Plantinga argues that any possible world that contains features of divine *incarnation* and *atonement* (in the way that the Christian religion describes)[17] will be better than any other possible world that doesn't contain these features. Even if we're comparing a uto-

---

[17] There is, no doubt, tremendous disagreement regarding how we should understand the atonement and the incarnation within the Christian religion; however, let's put these disagreements to the side for the time being.

pian world where there is no sin or death or suffering to a world that is wallowing in depravity and sadness, if the broken world contains divine incarnation and atonement, it is a better world than the utopian world.[18] A strong view indeed! But if this is right, then this can account for the broken and fallen world that we find ourselves in; after all, if the world wasn't fallen, broken, and in need of redemption, then there wouldn't be a need for divine incarnation and atonement (at least on the Christian picture of things).

One of the difficulties for theodicies like this comes in knowing how we should weigh the value of different possible worlds. Just like we might wonder how our observations of the distribution of pain and pleasure in the world would be more plausible based on theism or a hypothesis of indifference (see Draper 1989), so too might we wonder how best to weigh the value of possible worlds and how we might know if features like incarnation and atonement really have the *decisive* value Plantinga attributes to them. Plantinga, no doubt, has arguments to support his view; however, many people (perhaps especially non-Christians) might find his theodicy counter intuitive. And it's for this reason, we might wonder if many theodicies, like Plantinga's *felix culpa* theodicy, rest on intuitive insights that might diverge across many demographics. And as such, this could potentially be another area of fruitful research in experimental philosophy of religion.

3.3 Argument from Design

Another important argument in philosophy of religion where the tools of experimental philosophy seem particularly apt is the argument from design, especially because the argument (at least as it is typically formulated) fundamentally relies on particular interpretations of empirical phenomena. As the *Internet Encyclopedia of Philosophy* nicely summarizes the typical structure of the argument:

> Design arguments typically consist of (1) a premise that asserts that the material universe exhibits some empirical property F; (2) a premise (or sub-argument) that asserts (or concludes) that F is persuasive evidence of intelligent design or purpose; and (3) a premise (or sub-argument) that asserts (or concludes) that the best or most probable explanation for the fact that the material universe exhibits F is that there exists an intelligent designer who intentionally brought it about that the material universe exists and exhibits F. (Himma n.d., par. 2)

So, to put it roughly, arguments from design typically rest on appeals to elements of the natural world that seem to manifest the hallmarks of design; and given such design, we can seemingly conclude that there must be a designer. While the devil is in the details, of course – especially in terms of how the aforementioned "hallmarks of design" are

---

18 For some of the ongoing conversation on Plantinga's *felix culpa* theodicy, see, e.g., Diller (2008), Adams (2008).

fleshed out – many formulations of the argument from design make fairly bald appeals to elements in the natural world that simply appear to be designed. And because of this, it's easy enough to see where work in experimental philosophy might be fruitfully done. After all, is the appearance of design in the natural world common to everyone? Or is it the case that where some people see order and design, others see the result of chaotic, natural processes?[19]

Following Hume in his *Enquiries*, we might also ask what kind of design we see in the natural world? As Hume (1975, p. 136) noted, "When we infer any particular cause from an effect, we must proportion the one to the other, and can never be allowed to ascribe to the cause any qualities, but what are exactly sufficient to produce the effect". And this can radically affect how we think about the Argument from Design. Again, quoting Hume:

> Allowing, therefore, the gods to be the authors of the existence or order of the universe; it follows, that they possess that precise degree of power, intelligence, and benevolence, which appears in their workmanship; but nothing farther can ever be proved, except we call in the assistance of exaggeration and flattery to supply the defects of argument and reasoning. (Hume 1975, p. 137)

As such, if we see a flawed design we can, at best, only conclude that there might be a flawed designer. Here it's helpful to think of some human creations to make this point. Whoever honestly considers a pug, for example, cannot but conclude that such an animal – with its constant struggle to breath, its propensity to pop its eyes out of their sockets whenever it sneezes, and so forth – is not meant for this world and a sin against nature. And whoever is responsible for the creation of such a creature – most saliently, human beings in this case – is surely deranged! And, depending on how misanthropic you're feeling, that might seem like a very plausible conclusion. So even if the appearance of design is resilient to humans across a wide range of cultures and demographics, we might still wonder how individual "appearances" might diverge (whether the appearance is of perfect design or not) in order to further assess what conclusions we might draw.

And there are a host of important questions on the psychology behind the argument from design that are worth asking here. For example, when and why do people attribute design to natural phenomena when they do? Human beings, it seems, are naturally inclined to look for and recognize patterns in nature (see, e. g., Kelemen and Rosset 2009). Is this what drives us to see the design patterns that we think we see? Human beings might also be inclined to attribute design to a natural phenomenon that they can't otherwise explain. (And arguably, something like this has happened throughout human history. We'd see a natural phenomenon that we didn't understand, and attribute that phenomenon to the hand of the divine; only later recognizing it had a natural cause all along.) Is our attribution of design in nature at all connected with a need for cognitive closure?

---

[19] Helen De Cruz and Johan De Smedt (2015, ch. 4) have made similar observations.

3.4 Divine Hiddenness

In his seminal works, *Divine Hiddenness and Human Reason* (1993) and *The Hiddenness Argument – Philosophy's New Challenge to Belief in God* (2015), John Schellenberg powerfully argued, in sum, that if God is perfectly loving, he would make it so that anyone capable of having a personal relationship with him would be able to reasonably believe that God exists. Given that some people do *not* believe in the existence of God – even after careful, sincere, and open investigation – then such a perfectly loving God does not exist. Such an argument rests on two seemingly uncontroversial assumptions. First, the assumption that because God is perfectly loving he would make his existence sufficiently manifest to everyone or at least everyone capable of having a relationship with him. Call this the *perfectly-loving assumption.* The second assumption, the one I'm more interested in here is that someone can sincerely and honestly consider the question as to whether or not God exists and non-culpably maintain non-theistic belief, that someone can be non-resistant in their non-belief. Call this the *non-resistant non-belief assumption.* Importantly, this is an empirical assumption – in a way, it seems as if we can go and see if there really is non-resistant non-belief. That said, it's nevertheless an empirical assumption that is very easy to grant for the sake of argument. Various social norms might even make it taboo to deny that someone can be non-resistant in their non-belief. After all, if an atheist tells us that they've sincerely and honestly considered the arguments for and against belief in God and have concluded in atheism, who are we to deny their sincerity and honesty, their non-resistant evaluation of the various arguments? To be sure, some philosophers *have* responded to the problem of divine hiddenness by rejecting the non-resistant non-belief assumption on theoretical grounds; however, such a move often seems very uncharitable and unfriendly, at the very least. But interestingly, no work exploring the empirical viability of the non-resistant non-belief assumption has been done.

Here is another area where empirical methods – like those used by experimental philosophers – might be fruitfully applied to an important debate in philosophy of religion. To what extent is non-resistance possible from a psychological point of view? Is it really the case that anyone is entirely sincere and objective when they are considering a debate as monumental and potentially life changing as the question of whether or not God exists? Current psychological literature on heuristics and biases might already cast doubt on this assumption – numerous studies have shown that we evaluate arguments that support our views much higher than arguments that go against our views and that we are much more inclined to find objections to conclusions that might impinge on us.[20] That said, however, further empirical research connecting this literature

---

[20] See, e.g., Gilovich (1991) for an accessible introduction to this area of research. And belief in a personal God who makes significant moral demands on us, requires that we appreciate our own sinfulness, fallenness, and so forth, certainly can impinge on us.

to the problem of divine hiddenness and additional research into the non-resistance assumption itself are both needed.

4 Conclusion

Over the past 50 years, analytic philosophy of religion has experienced a renaissance of activity that is arguably unmatched in the Western philosophical tradition. And along with this renaissance of analytic philosophy of religion, analytic philosophers have started to increasingly speak into theology – utilizing the analytic passion for clarity and logical rigor to try to develop and shed light on longstanding theological debates.[21] About the same time, however, analytic philosophy itself has gone through some changes. In the past 20 years, experimental philosophy has increasingly spoken into analytic philosophy – highlighting how empirical data can and should inform and indeed shape our philosophizing. The goal of this chapter has been to better see how these two trends might be brought together, to see how experimental philosophy might speak into analytic philosophy of religion, with work on the problem of evil serving as a proof of concept.

While empirical questions have arguably always attended philosophical reflections on religion, experimental philosophy of religion – as an expansion of the experimental philosophy projects of the last 20 or so years – is still an emerging area of research. In this chapter, we explored some of the fruit and possibilities for this emerging field. First, I elucidated some of the motivation for experimental philosophy of religion. Then, in Section 2, we considered how the tools and resources of experimental philosophy have been fruitfully applied to a seminal topic within philosophy of religion, namely, the problem of evil (more specifically, Rowe's 1979 formulation of the problem). Finally, in Section 3, I sketched some broader applications of experimental philosophy of religion.

Given that the "Launching Experimental of Religion" project is due to run from September 2021 through August 2024, we can reasonably expect the field to significantly expand in the coming years. It will truly be exciting to see how the field evolves and develops.

---

[21] In his article "Theology as a Bull Session", Randal Rauser (2011) aptly (and very amusingly!) sketches some of the reasons why the analytic theology movement has picked up so much traction recently. That said, analytic theology hasn't always been welcomed with open arms. Mike Rea (2011), a leading advocate in favor of analytic theology, wrote an introduction to analytic theology that, in my view, best outlines some of the worries someone might have against applying analytic methods and tools within the context of theology.

Bibliography

Adams, Marilyn McCord (2008): "Plantinga on 'felix culpa'", *Faith and Philosophy* 25 (2), pp. 123–140.
Alston, William (1991): "The inductive argument from evil and the human cognitive condition", *Philosophical Perspectives* 5, pp. 29–67.
Barrett, Justin, and Ian Church (2013): "Should CSR give atheists epistemic assurance? On beer-goggles, BFFs, and skepticism regarding religious beliefs", *The Monist* 96 (3), pp. 311–324.
Barry, Peter Brian (2013): *Evil and moral psychology.* London: Routledge.
Barth, Karl (1975): *Church dogmatics.* Edinburgh: T. & T. Clark.
Beit-Hallahmi, Benjamin (2006): "Atheists. A psychological profile", in: Michael Martin (Ed.): *The Cambridge companion to atheism.* Cambridge: Cambridge University Press, pp. 300–318.
Betageri, Ankur Prahlad (2008): "Psychology and the problem of evil", *Europe's Journal of Psychology* 4 (2).
Bruneau, Emile, Nicholas Dufour, and Rebecca Saxe (2012): "Social cognition in members of conflict groups. Behavioral and neural responses in Arabs, Israelis and South Americans to each other's misfortunes", *Philosophical Transactions of the Royal Society B – Biological Sciences* 367 (1589), pp. 717–730.
Cappelen, Herman, Tamar Szabó Gedler, and John Hawthorne (Eds.) (2016): *The Oxford handbook of philosophical methodology.* Oxford: Oxford University Press.
Carrere, Robert (1989): "Psychology of tragedy. A phenomenological analysis", *Journal of Phenomenological Psychology* 20 (2), pp. 105–129.
Church, Ian, Rebecca Carlson, and Justin Barrett (2021): "Evil intuitions? The problem of evil, experimental philosophy, and the need for psychological research", *Journal of Psychology and Theology* 49 (2), pp. 126–141.
Church, Ian, Isaac Warcol, and Justin Barrett (forthcoming): "The context of suffering. Empirical insights into the problem of evil", *TheoLogica – An International Journal for Philosophy of Religion and Philosophical Theology.*
Cragun, Ryan (2016): "Nonreligion and atheism", in: David Yamane (Ed.): *Handbook of religion and society.* Cham: Springer, pp. 301–320.
Crisp, Oliver (2011): "On analytic theology", in: Oliver Crisp and Michael Rea (Eds.): *Analytic theology. New essays in the philosophy of theology.* Oxford: Oxford University Press, pp. 33–54.
Crossley, Michele (2000): "Narrative psychology, trauma and the study of self/identity", *Theory & Psychology* 10 (4), pp. 527–546.
Davis, Edward, Glendon Moriarty, and Joseph Mauch (2013): "God images and God concepts. Definitions, development, and dynamics", *Psychology of Religion and Spirituality* 5 (1), pp. 51–60.
De Cruz, Helen (2014): "Cognitive science of religion and the study of theological concepts", *Topoi* 33 (2), pp. 487–497.
De Cruz, Helen (2015a): "Divine hiddenness and the cognitive science of religion", in: Adam Green and Eleonore Stump (Eds.): *Hidden divinity and religious belief. New perspectives.* Cambridge: Cambridge University Press, pp. 53–68.
De Cruz, Helen (2015b): "Where philosophical intuitions come from", *Australasian Journal of Philosophy* 93 (2), pp. 233–249.
De Cruz, Helen (2017): "Religious disagreement. An empirical study among academic philosophers", *Episteme* 14 (1), pp. 477–504.
De Cruz, Helen (2019): *Religious disagreement.* Cambridge: Cambridge University Press.
De Cruz, Helen, and Johan De Smedt (2015): *A natural history of natural theology. The cognitive science of theology and philosophy of religion.* Cambridge: The MIT Press.
De Smedt, Johan, and Helen De Cruz (2020): "Cognitive science of religion and the nature of the divine. A pluralist non-confessional approach", in: Jerry Marin (Ed.): *Theology without walls. The transreligious imperative.* New York: Taylor and Francis, pp. 128–137.

Diller, Kevin (2008): "Are sin and evil necessary for a really good world? Questions for Alvin Plantinga's felix culpa theodicy", *Faith and Philosophy* 25 (1), pp. 87–101.

Draper, Paul (1989): "Pain and pleasure. An evidential problem for theists", *Noûs* 23 (3), pp. 331–350.

Draper, Paul, and Ryan Nichols (2013): "Diagnosing bias in philosophy of religion", *The Monist* 96 (3), pp. 420–446.

Dunbar, Robin Ian MacDonald, Ben Teasdale, Jackie Thompson, Felix Budelmann, Sophie Duncan, Evert van Emde Boas, and Laurie Maguire (2016): "Emotional arousal when watching drama increases pain threshold and social bonding", *Royal Society Open Science* 3 (9), 160288.

Dunning, Jonathan, and Greg Hajcak (2009): "See no evil. Directing visual attention within unpleasant images modulates the electrocortical response", *Psychophysiology* 46 (1), pp. 28–33.

Durkheim, Emile (2008): *The elementary forms of religious life*. Abridged edition. Ed. by Mark Cladis. Transl. by Carol Cosman. Oxford: Oxford University Press.

Evans-Pritchard, Edward Evan, and Eva Gillies (1976): *Witchcraft, oracles and magic among the Azande*. Abridged edition. Oxford: Oxford University Press.

Freud, Sigmund (1953): *The standard edition of the complete psychological works of Sigmund Freud*. 24 vols. Ed. and transl. by James Strachey. London: Hogarth.

Gilovich, Thomas (1991): *How we know what isn't so. The fallibility of human reason in everyday life*. New York: Free Press.

Govrin, Aner (2018): "The cognition of severe moral failure. A novel approach to the perception of evil", *Frontiers in Psychology* 9, 557.

Green, Adam (2015): "Hiddenness and the epistemology of attachment", in: Adam Green and Eleonore Stump (Eds.): *Hiddenness and the epistemology of attachment*. Cambridge: Cambridge University Press, pp. 139–154.

Haney, Craig, Curtis Banks, and Philip Zimbardo (1973): "A study of prisoners and guards in a simulated prison", *Naval Research Review* 30, pp. 4–17.

Heiphetz, Larisa, Jonathan Lane, Adam Waytz, and Liane Young (2016): "How children and adults represent God's mind", *Cognitive Science* 40 (1), pp. 121–144.

Hick, John (1966): *Evil and the God of love*. Stuttgart: Macmillan.

Himma, Kenneth (n.d.): "Design arguments for the existence of God", *Internet Encyclopedia of Philosophy*. https://www.iep.utm.edu/design/, last accessed May 19, 2023.

Holmes, Stephen (2009): "Three versus one? Some problems of social trinitarianism", *Journal of Reformed Theology* 3 (1), pp. 77–89.

Hume, David (1975): *Enquiries concerning human understanding and concerning the principles of morals*. 3rd edition. Oxford: Clarendon.

John Templeton Foundation (2021a): "The problem of evil and experimental philosophy of religion". https://www.templeton.org/grant/the-problem-of-evil-and-experimental-philosophy-of-religion/, last accessed May 19, 2023.

John Templeton Foundation (2021b): "Launching experimental philosophy of religion". https://www.templeton.org/grant/launching-experimental-philosophy-of-religion/, last accessed May 19, 2023.

Jong, Jonathan (2021): "Death anxiety and religion", *Current Opinion in Psychology* 40, pp. 40–44.

Kelemen, Deborah, and Evelyn Rosset (2009): "The human function compunction. Teleological explanation in adults", *Cognition* 111 (1), pp. 138–143.

Kirk, Geoffrey, and John Raven (1960): *The presocratic philosophers*. Cambridge: Cambridge University Press.

Knobe, Joshua, and Shaun Nichols (2007): "An experimental philosophy manifesto", in: Joshua Knobe and Shaun Nichols (Eds.): *Experimental philosophy*. Oxford: Oxford University Press, pp. 3–14.

Kornblith, Hilary (1998): "The role of intuition in philosophical inquiry. An account with no unnatural ingredients", in: Michael Raymond DePaul and William Ramsey (Eds.): *Rethinking intuition. The psychology of intuition and its role in philosophical inquiry*. London: Rowman & Littlefield, pp. 129–141.

Krause, Neal, and David Hayward (2015): "Assessing whether practical wisdom and awe of God are associated with life satisfaction", *Psychology of Religion and Spirituality* 7 (1), pp 51–59.

Lim, Daniel (2017): "Experimental philosophy and philosophy of religion", *European Journal for Philosophy of Religion* 9 (3), pp. 139–158.

Malinowski, Bronislaw (2015): *Magic, science and religion.* Mansfield Centre: Martino Fine Books.

McAllister, Blake, Ian M. Church, Paul Rezkalla, and Long Nguyen (forthcoming): "Empirical challenges to the evidential problem of evil", in: Joshua Knobe and Shaun Nichols (Eds.): *Oxford studies in experimental philosophy.* Oxford: Oxford University Press.

Mizrahi, Moti (2020): "If analytic philosophy of religion is sick, can it be cured?", *Religious Studies* 56 (4), pp. 558–577.

Mueller-Pfeiffer, Christoph, Chantal Martin-Soelch, Robert James Blair, Alois Carnier, Nicole Kaiser, Michael Rufer, Ulrich Schnyder, and Georg Hasler (2010): "Impact of emotion on cognition in trauma survivors. What is the role of posttraumatic stress disorder?", *Journal of Affective Disorders* 126 (1–2), pp. 287–292.

Plantinga, Alvin (2000): *Warranted Christian belief.* New York: Oxford University Press.

Plantinga, Alvin (2004): "Supralapsarianism, or 'o felix culpa'", in: Peter van Inwagen (Ed.): *Christian faith and the problem of evil.* Grand Rapids: Eerdmanns, pp. 1–25.

Qureshi, Salah, Mary Long, Major Bradshaw, Jeffrey Pyne, Kathy Magruder, Timothy Kimbrell, Teresa Hudson, Ali Jawaid, Paul Schulz, and Mark Kunik (2011): "Does PTSD impair cognition beyond the effect of trauma?", *The Journal of Neuropsychiatry and Clinical Neurosciences* 23 (1), pp. 16–28.

Rauser, Randal (2011): "Theology as a bull session", in: Oliver Crisp and Michael Rea (Eds.): *Analytic theology.* Oxford: Oxford University Press, pp. 70–84.

Rea, Michael (2011): "Introduction", in: Oliver Crisp and Michael Rea (Eds.): *Analytic theology.* Oxford: Oxford University Press, pp. 1–30.

Russell, Bruce, and Stephen Wykstra (1988): "The 'inductive' argument from evil. A dialogue", *Philosophical Topics* 16 (2), pp. 133–160.

Sanford, John (1980): "The problem of evil in Christianity and analytical psychology", *Psychological Perspectives* 11 (2), pp. 112–132.

Saxton, Calvin (2006): "The social psychology of good and evil", *The Journal of Nervous and Mental Disease* 194 (4), pp. 306–307.

Schellenberg, John (1993): *Divine hiddenness and human reason.* Ithaca: Cornell University Press.

Schellenberg, John (2015): *The hiddenness argument. Philosophy's new challenge to belief in god.* Oxford: Oxford University Press.

Shtulman, Andrew, and Marjaana Lindeman (2016): "Attributes of God. Conceptual foundations of a foundational belief", *Cognitive Science* 40 (3), pp. 635–670.

Sibley, Chris, and Joseph Bulbulia (2012): "Faith after an earthquake. A longitudinal study of religion and perceived health before and after the 2011 Christchurch New Zealand earthquake", *PLOS ONE* 7 (12), e49648.

Silverman, Eric Jason, Elizabeth Hall, Jamie Aten, Laura Shannonhouse, and Jason McMartin (2020): "Christian lay theodicy and the cancer experience", *Journal of Analytic Theology* 8 (1), pp. 344–370.

Slovic, Paul, Daniel Västfjäll, and Robin Gregory (2012): "Informing decisions to prevent genocide", *SAIS Review* 32 (1), pp. 33–47.

Stump, Eleonore (2012): *Wandering in darkness. Narrative and the problem of suffering.* Oxford: Oxford University Press.

Tarr, Bronwyn, Jacques Launay, Emma Cohen, and Robin Dunbar (2015): "Synchrony and exertion during dance independently raise pain threshold and encourage social bonding", *Biology Letters* 11 (10), 20150767.

Teehan, John (2013): "The cognitive bases of the problem of evil", *The Monist* 96 (3), pp. 325–348.

Teehan, John (2016): "Cognitive science, evil, and God", in: Helen De Cruz and Ryan Nichols (Eds.): *Advances in religion, cognitive science, and experimental philosophy.* London: Bloomsbury, pp. 39–60.

Timm, Simon Christopher (2016): "Moral intuition or moral disengagement? Cognitive science weighs in on the animal ethics debate", *Neuroethics* 9 (3), pp. 225–234.

Tobia, Kevin (2016): "Does religious belief impact philosophical analysis?", *Religion, Brain and Behavior* 6 (1), pp. 56–66.

van Inwagen, Peter (1988): "The place of chance in a world sustained by God", in: Peter van Inwagen (Ed.): *God, knowledge, and mystery*. Ithaca: Cornell University Press, pp. 42–65.

van Leeuwen, Neil (2014): "Religious credence is not factual belief", *Cognition* 133 (3), pp. 698–715.

van Woudenberg, René, and Hans van Eyghen (2017): "Most peers don't believe it, hence it is probably false", *European Journal for Philosophy of Religion* 9 (4), pp. 87–112.

Weinberg, Jonathan, Shaun Nichols, and Stephen Stich (2001): "Normativity and epistemic intuitions", *Philosophical Topics* 29 (1–2), pp. 429–460.

Williamson, Timothy (2007): *The philosophy of philosophy*. Oxford: Blackwell.

Wilt, Joshua, Julie Exline, Joshua Grubbs, Crystal Park, and Kenneth Pargament (2016): "God's role in suffering. Theodicies, divine struggle, and mental health", *Psychology of Religion and Spirituality* 8 (4), pp. 352–362.

Wolterstorff, Nicholas (2011): "How philosophical theology became possible within the analytic tradition of philosophy", in: Oliver Crisp and Michael Rea (Eds.): *Analytic theology*. Oxford: Oxford University Press, pp. 155–169.

Wykstra, Stephen (1984) "The Humean obstacle to evidential arguments from suffering. On avoiding the evils of 'appearance'", *International Journal for Philosophy of Religion* 16 (2), pp. 73–93.

Florian Cova
Experimental Philosophy of Aesthetics: Aesthetic Judgment

Abstract: Experimental philosophy of aesthetics is the attempt of using empirical methods to make progress in traditional questions in philosophical aesthetics and philosophy of art. While psychology of aesthetics and neuroaesthetics have mainly focused on aesthetic experiences and aesthetic appreciation, experimental philosophy of aesthetics explores people's conceptions of the aesthetic and artistic realms. Thus, one of its main topics of investigation has been "folk meta-aesthetics", i.e., whether people consider aesthetic properties to be objective rather than subjective. In this chapter, I begin by presenting a comprehensive survey of this debate and how it engages a wide variety of topics in philosophical aesthetics: the nature of guilty pleasures and aesthetic taste, the possibility of aesthetic disagreement, and the value of aesthetic testimony. I then illustrate the breadth and variety of empirical research in the field of experimental philosophy of aesthetics by summarizing past and present research on topics as diversified as the definition of art, the ontology of musical works of arts, the nature of aesthetic adjectives, the interaction between aesthetic and non-aesthetic evaluations, the paradox of fiction, and the puzzle of imaginative resistance.

Keywords: Aesthetic Realism; Art; Beauty; Empirical Aesthetics; Experimental Philosophy; Objectivism

1 Introduction

Compared to other fields in experimental philosophy, experimental philosophy of aesthetics (including experimental philosophy of art) is quite a late comer (Cova, Garcia, and Liao 2017). This is all the more surprising because there is a long-standing tradition of empirical research in aesthetics, from Wundt's (1910–1911) and Fechner's (1876) first works on aesthetic appreciation to contemporary neuroaesthetics (Zeki 1999, Chatterjee 2014). Some might argue that this is the case because, at least at its beginnings, experimental philosophy tended to focus on intuitions about thought experiments, while philosophical aesthetics do not generally rely on such methods (Arielli 2018; see also Monseré 2015a). This would mean that the rise of an experimental philosophy of aesthetics had to wait for a broader conception of experimental philosophy to be accepted, according to which experimental philosophy is not restricted to the study of folk intuitions. To some, this move away from intuitions and abstract thought experiments even constitutes a strength that allows experimental philosophy of aesthetics to escape some

---

Note: The work on this chapter was supported by an Eccellenza Professorial Fellowship of the Swiss National Science Foundation (SNSF project "Eudaimonic emotions and the (meta-)philosophy of well-being").

of the traditional objections raised against experimental philosophy (Torregrossa 2017, Weinberg 2019). However, some people disagree with this idea and argue that intuitions play an important role in certain debates in philosophical aesthetics (Mikalonytė forthcoming). A more trivial explanation might simply be that the "founding fathers" of experimental philosophy were not particularly aware of debates in philosophical aesthetics, or that aesthetics tend to be disregarded by philosophers outside the field (Turri 2016).

One question concerns the distinction between experimental philosophy of aesthetics and other types of empirical approaches to aesthetics. One simple answer might be that experimental philosophy of aesthetics is driven by traditional philosophical questions that have eluded other forms of investigations. Another might be that other forms of empirical investigations have mainly focused on processes by which people come to appreciate aesthetic objects, while experimental philosophy of aesthetics is free to investigate people's aesthetic concepts and theories (Arielli 2018).

Whatever the reasons for its late emergence and the best ways to set its boundaries, experimental philosophy of aesthetics is alive and thriving (Cova and Réhault 2019). Though the number of papers in the domains in this area is low compared to other areas of experimental philosophy, the breadth of topics that have already been covered is staggering. I will first focus on the topic of folk meta-aesthetics, which have been at the heart of numerous debates in Section 2, before highlighting the diversity of questions experimental philosophers have addressed in the field of aesthetics in Section 3.

2 Folk Aesthetic Objectivism

2.1 Aesthetic Realism and Folk Objectivism about Aesthetic Judgments

Aesthetic realism is the claim that aesthetic properties (such as beauty) exist independently from our minds and perceptions: when we perceive an artwork as "beautiful" or "elegant", we do not confer these properties to the artwork, but discover them, in the same way we discover its size and shape. To put it otherwise: aesthetic realism claims that beauty is *not* in the eye of the beholder, but in objects themselves.

One argument in favor of aesthetic realism is that it is supposed to be in line with the way we spontaneously think about aesthetic properties. For example, Caroll (1999, p. 243) writes that "the supposition that aesthetic properties are objective also explains better how we talk about them". But why think that common sense is realist about aesthetic properties?

Zangwill (2001) puts forward the following argument: supposing that common sense is realist about aesthetic properties is the best explanation for the *normativity* of aesthetic judgment. Indeed, since Hume (1985) and Kant (1928), it is generally accepted that aesthetic judgments differ from other judgments of taste (e.g., from judgments about whether some food is tasty or not) to the extent that they claim some sort of *intersubjective validity* (Cova 2019). The idea is the following: when I claim that the hamburger I am eating is tasty, I speak only for myself and don't think that people who have a different opinion are wrong. However, when I say that something (such as an artwork) is beautiful, I claim that this judgment is valid for every other human being and that any human being who would disagree with me would simply be *wrong*. As Zangwill (2019a, p. 291) puts it: "a feature that characterizes judgments of beauty, but not judgments of agreeableness, is their normative aspiration: they aspire to correctness".

That we treat aesthetic judgments differently from other judgments of taste is a commonplace assumption in philosophical aesthetics (see Zangwill 2019b). But is this assumption justified? To find out, Cova and Pain (2012) presented participants with five kinds of disagreements: disagreements about non-evaluative facts, disagreements about the beauty of natural objects, disagreements about the beauty of artworks, disagreements about the beauty of human individuals, and disagreements about questions of taste (e.g., whether pasta with ketchup is good). For each of the disagreements, participants had to indicate which of the following options was the best way to describe the situation:

(A) One of the interlocutors is right while the other is wrong.
(B) Both are right.
(C) Both are wrong.
(D) Neither is right or wrong. It makes no sense to speak in terms of correctness in this situation. Everyone is entitled to his own opinion.

Answer (A) can be called the *objectivist*[1] answer: it is the one participants should select if they think that aesthetic judgments aspire to some sort of intersubjective correctness. However, very few participants actually chose this option, and most of them chose option (D) instead. This suggests that, *pace* Hume and Kant, common sense does not consider aesthetic judgments to demand intersubjective validity.

Cova and Pain (2012) conducted a second experiment in which they focused on disagreement about whether something was ugly (rather than beautiful). In a third study, they asked participants to think about an artwork they found beautiful and to imagine they disagreed with someone about this artwork's beauty. However, both studies yielded similar results, with most participants answering that neither interlocutor was right or wrong. It was all a matter of personal taste.

---

[1] I actually don't think that *objectivism* is the best label for this option. Cova and Pain (2012) call it the *normativist* option instead, and I think this label is more accurate. However, most other authors have opted for *objectivism* and I decided to follow their decision in this chapter, for the sake of simplicity.

2.2 Objectivism and Aesthetic Comparisons

One objection that can be leveraged against Cova and Pain's studies is that they presented participants with aesthetic judgments about single artworks rather than comparisons between artworks from very different qualities. However, Hume (1985) famously argued that our commitment to aesthetic normativism is more easily detected when we attempt such comparisons (see also Zangwill 2019a). What if we presented people with the claim that "Shakespeare was a better writer than Dan Brown" or that "Miles Davis was a better musician than Britney Spears"? Would participants still think that such claims are neither right nor wrong? This is something Goodwin and Darley (2008) tested (though the main focus of their study was the objectivity of moral judgment). They found that most people considered such claims to be "a matter of opinion".

Similarly, Rabb and colleagues (2020) sought to determine to which extent participants' subjectivism about aesthetic properties was stable. Through three studies, they presented participants with comparative aesthetic judgments and asked them to rate whether they concerned "matters of opinion" or "matters of fact".[2] They also used factual judgments, moral judgments, and judgments about color preferences as comparison points. In their first study, they manipulated to which extent the artworks that were compared differed from each other: whether one of the artworks was older than the other, whether it was generally regarded as better, or both. In their second study, they presented statements with or without a photograph of the artwork in question, to control for the role of acquaintance. In their third study, they had participants rate to which degree they liked each of the artwork before being presented with the comparative statements. This allowed experimenters to present them with comparisons between artworks they liked most and artworks they liked least. However, none of these manipulations had any impact on participants' judgments regarding the objectivity of aesthetic judgments. Through all three studies, aesthetic judgments were considered as much more subjective than factual statements, and on par with judgments about color preferences.

2.3 Aesthetic Normativism in a Cross-Cultural Perspective

Another criticism that can be leveraged against Cova and Pain's (2012) original study was the limitation of their sample: not only was the sample size quite small, but it was mostly composed of Parisian students, who can be hardly considered representative of common sense in general (Réhault 2013). Fortunately, later studies investigated folk aesthetic objectivism in wider and more diverse samples.

---

2 See Moss and Bush (2021) for a methodological criticism of this way of operationalizing aesthetic objectivism.

Beebe and colleagues (2015) investigated moral objectivism in a cross-cultural perspective (comparing participants from China, Poland, and Ecuador), while Beebe and Sackris (2016) investigated how intuitions about the objectivity of moral statements evolved across the lifespan. As comparison classes for moral statements, they used statements about non-evaluative facts and statements about taste. Statements about taste included, but were not limited to, aesthetic judgments such as "classical music is better than rock music". Participants had to rate to which extent they agreed with each statement and, for each of them, were asked the following question:

> If someone disagrees with you about whether (one of the test statements is true), is it possible for both of you to be correct or must one of you be mistaken?
>
> - It is possible for both of you to be correct.
> - At least one of you must be mistaken.

The first answer was interpreted as a rejection of objectivism, while the second was interpreted as an endorsement. Overall, they observed that judgments about taste were consistently considered as less objective than moral judgments and non-evaluative judgments. Moreover, participants tended to be even less objectivists when they considered that there was a lot of disagreement about the quality of the target artworks.[3] However, it should be kept in mind that their judgments about taste were not limited to aesthetic judgments but also included items about food.

As part of an international research project on the variability of philosophical intuitions, Cova and colleagues (2019) investigated folk aesthetic objectivism across 19 countries. They asked participants to name something they found very beautiful, and to imagine that someone disagreed with them by claiming that this same object was not beautiful at all. Then participants had to choose between the three following options:

> (A) One of you is correct while the other is not.
> (B) Both of you are correct.
> (C) Neither is correct. It makes no sense to talk about correctness in this situation.

There were significant cultural variations: some geographical areas (such as East Asia) favored answer (B), while others (such as South America) favored answer (C). But, across all areas, answer (A) was always the least selected (between 4.8% and 22%), suggesting that folk aesthetic subjectivism is a widespread phenomenon.

---

[3] Beebe and Sackris (2016) also observed that age negatively correlated with objectivism about taste ($r = -0.07$).

2.4 Methodological Issues in the Measure of Folk Aesthetic Normativism

However, Zangwill (2019) raised methodological objections to this conclusion. According to him, the measures employed by experimental philosophers might not adequately capture aesthetic objectivism, and might measure something else instead. Zangwill is particularly worried about the fourth option in Cova and Pain's (2012) studies. He claims that this option "does not separate correctness from the right to make a claim" and "confuses correctness and justification" (Zangwill 2019, p. 293). The idea, here, is that people might think that there is a correct answer to aesthetic debates but still answer that, in the case of Cova and Pain's imaginary disagreements, no one is right or wrong because both interlocutors lack reasons that would justify their claim. More precisely, if we think that "being right" involves not only making a true assertion but also having good epistemic reasons to make this assertion, it is possible that neither interlocutor is right because they both lack good reasons, even when one says something true while the other says something false.

There is some plausibility to Zangwill's criticism. For example, Beebe and colleagues introduced among their non-evaluative statements a statement about a fact "whose truth value was not only unknown but practically unknowable" (Beebe et al. 2015, p. 393). The statement was "Confucius did not eat soup on his 21st birthday" and this statement received very low objectivity ratings (between 47% and 52% depending on the country). These puzzling results can be easily explained by Zangwill's objection, suggesting that the methods used by experimental philosophers might indeed confuse people's belief that there is no objective fact of the matter with their belief that no one can be right because both interlocutors lack justification.

As an alternative method, Zangwill advises to ask participants whether one aesthetic judgment can be better than another. He makes the following prediction: "Some judgments (of beauty) are better than their opposites; and this is not true of judgments about the agreeable" (Zangwill 2019, p. 302).

Cova (2019) put this prediction to test. He asked participants to describe something they considered to be (1) beautiful, (2) agreeable, or (3) made of steel, depending on the condition they were assigned to. Then, they were asked to imagine that they met someone who claimed that this thing was *not* beautiful, agreeable, or made of steel, and to choose among the following options the one that would best describe the two judgments made in this situation:

(A) One judgment is better than the other.
(B) Both judgments are equally good.
(C) Neither.

In the "beautiful" condition, 37.9% of participants chose the first, objectivist answer (A), compared with 71.4% in the "steel" condition. Even if less than half of participants chose the objectivist answers, this was still a way higher rate of objectivist answers than in previous studies. Should we then consider that previous studies had underestimated the prevalence of aesthetic normativism? Not really since, contrary to Zangwill's expectations, 44.7% of participants chose the alleged objectivist answer in the "pleasant" condition. On the basis of these results, Cova (2019) argued that, when participants claimed that one judgment was better than the other, they only did so to express their agreement with one of both judgments, and not to express their commitment to some aesthetic norm that would make one of these judgments more objectively correct than the other. Thus, it is likely that the method Zangwill advocated tends to overestimate the rate of objectivist answers, by conflating objectivism with mere agreement.[4]

However, it is not because the method suggested by Zangwill is inadequate that his methodological worries are not legitimate. To investigate to which extent previous results can be explained by a confusion between subjectivism and a lack of justification, I presented each participant with a total of six disagreements (see Cova 2022, for more details on the materials and methods):

- A disagreement about a non-evaluative claim in which one of the interlocutors has good justification for his claim: "Mars is a smaller planet than Jupiter".
- A disagreement about a non-evaluative claim in which none of the interlocutors has good justification for their claim: "Cesar ate soup on his 21st birthday".
- A disagreement about a judgment the truth value of which depends on the interlocutor: "It is hard to run two miles straight without taking a break".
- A disagreement in which both participants' claims capture part of the truth: one says that a certain building is ancient and the other says that this same building is not ancient, while the building actually is a mix of ancient and recent architecture.
- A disagreement about a question of taste: "This hamburger is tasty."
- A disagreement about aesthetics: "The Leonardo da Vinci's *Mona Lisa* is beautiful".

For each disagreement, participants were asked to select which of the following options best described the situation:

(A) One is right and the other is wrong, since there is a single universal answer to their disagreement.
(B) Neither is right. There is a single universal answer to their disagreement, but, since they have no way of knowing which answer is the right one, the one who says the truth cannot be said to be right.
(C) They are both right because it depends on the person and/or the situation.
(D) They are both right because, even if none of them is completely right, they both capture some part of a more complex truth.
(E) Neither is right or wrong. It makes no sense to speak in terms of being right or wrong in this situation, since there is no fact of the matter.
(F) Other.

---

[4] On the basis of similar results, Cova (2019) argues that the method consisting in asking participants whether one judgment is true and the other false falls prey to the same limitations.

Table 1: Percentage of participants who selected each answer (A to E) for each of the six types of disagreement

	A	B	C	D	E
Planets	**97.2%**	01.9%	00.9%	0%	0%
Cesar	15.0%	**45.8%**	02.8%	05.6%	30.8%
Running	04.7%	01.8%	**70.1%**	10.3%	13.1%
Building	18.7%	11.2%	09.3%	**52.3%**	07.5%
Hamburger	01.9%	00.9%	**61.7%**	08.4%	26.2%
Art	02.8%	02.8%	**41.1%**	11.2%	40.2%

Results are described in Table 1. Answer (B) was supposed to capture the intuition of participants who think that neither interlocutor is right, not because there is no objective fact, but because both interlocutors lack justification. As predicted, it was the most selected answer in the disagreement about whether Cesar ate soup on his 21st birthday. This vindicates Zangwill's criticism according to which certain participants choose the "neither is right" option for reasons that have to do with lack of justification. But does lack of justification explain participants' seemingly anti-normativist answers to aesthetic disagreements? Not likely, as answer (B) was rarely selected in the case of aesthetic disagreement. Thus, even if Zangwill's methodological criticism was sound, it does not explain away the results previous studies observed: participants seem to endorse strong anti-objectivist views about aesthetic judgment.

2.5 Are Folks Implicitly Objectivists about Aesthetic Properties?

Another objection to this conclusion is that people might not be *aware* that they tacitly endorse some sort of objectivism about aesthetic properties (Zangwill 2019a). Thus, even if they explicitly deny endorsing objectivism about aesthetic properties, their explicit stance might still run contrary to the tacit commitments that they express through behavior.

2.5.1 Guilty Pleasures

One phenomenon that might reveal some sort of implicit endorsement of aesthetic objectivism are *guilty pleasures* (i.e., the fact of feeling bad for enjoying certain artworks). Indeed, an easy explanation for this phenomenon is that people feel bad because they consider these artworks to lack the aesthetic qualities that would justify their enjoyment (Frierson 2014). But is it the right explanation? Goffin and Cova (2019) empirically investigated the nature of guilty pleasures. First, they asked participants to think about and describe a work of art they considered to be one of their "guilty pleasure", before asking them how bad they felt about liking this work of art. They found that a lot of people used the expression "guilty pleasure" to refer to works of art they liked but did not hold in high aesthetic praise, but that they did not really feel bad about liking them. In a second study, they thus focused on people who felt bad about enjoying certain artworks to determine the source of their discomfort. They asked participants to describe a work of art that they liked but was such that they felt bad about liking it. Then, they asked participants to rate their agreement with a series of statements that probed possible reasons for their discomfort: lack of aesthetic value ("From a purely artistic and aesthetic point of view, there is objectively speaking nothing good about this object"), fear of social disapproval ("If someone else learns that I enjoy this kind of work, this would reflect poorly on me"), or personal ideals ("The person I aspire to be would not enjoy this kind of work"). Goffin and Cova found that participants' negative feelings about their aesthetic enjoyment (that were closer to shame than guilt) were predicted not by participants' considerations about the aesthetic worth of artworks, but by their social and personal norms.

2.5.2 Distinction between Good and Bad Taste

Another reason to think that people implicitly endorse some sort of objectivism is that they seem to draw a distinction between "good" and "bad" aesthetic taste, which seems to indicate that they perceive some kind of normativity in the aesthetic realm. But what do people mean by "good" and "bad taste"? In a qualitative study, Humbert-Droz and colleagues (forthcoming) asked participants whether they made a difference between good and bad aesthetic taste and, if they answered positively, to define what they meant by "good" and "bad" taste. They also asked participants whether taste could be improved and, if yes, how. Most participants answered that they indeed made a difference between good and bad taste, and that aesthetic taste *could* be improved. At first sight, this seems to suggest that people might indeed endorse some kind of objectivism about aesthetic properties. However, experimenters then went through participants' open-ended answers and sorted them in different categories. It turned out that a non-negligible proportion of participants defined people with "good taste" as people who shared their preferences or the majority's preferences. In the end, participants tended to be equally split between those who defined taste in an apparent subjective way, as the fact of sharing their or someone else's preference, and those who defined taste in an apparent objective way, as the capacity to perceive certain aesthetic properties.

Additionally, in subsequent questions, Humbert-Droz and colleagues asked participants whether it made sense to speak of good and bad taste for a whole list of domains. They found out that most participants considered that it made sense to speak of good taste for food, wine and, to a lesser extent, beer. Should we conclude that people are also implicitly objectivist about such things? If not, then the inference from talk of "good" and "bad" taste to implicit objectivism is compromised.

2.5.3 Aesthetic Disputes

A third phenomenon that might reveal an implicit endorsement in laypeople is the existence of aesthetic disputes, in which people argue about the aesthetic merits of a given artwork. Caroll (1999, p. 117) makes the following argument: "people involved in disputes about aesthetic properties act as though they think that they are disagreeing about the real properties of objects […]. So, they, at least, must believe that aesthetic properties are objective".

One way to interpret this argument is the following: (1) people involved in aesthetic disputes think they disagree, (2) but they must also think that disagreement involves that one side of the dispute is right while the other is wrong, therefore (3) people involved in aesthetic disputes think (at least at an implicit level) that one of them is right while the other is wrong. However, it is not clear that premise (2) holds. Murray (2020) investigated people's conception of disagreement. He asked participants to imagine that they heard an agent make a judgment about whether something was delicious (versus disgusting) or beautiful (versus ugly) and they disagreed. Participants then had to tell whether (1) they disagreed with this agent and (2) whether the agent was incorrect. Results showed that most participants were happy to say that they "disagreed" with the agent without deeming the agent's judgment "incorrect". Thus, the existence of disagreement does not seem to entail the presupposition that there is some objective fact of the matter.

Another way to interpret this argument is to see it as an inference to the best explanation: why would people argue about aesthetic matters if they did not think that there was an objective fact of the matter? To answer this question, further studies on the motivations behind aesthetic disputes are needed. One possibility would be that people argue to show that their judgment is not true, but reasonable, and that they would be motivated to do so by the fact that they consider aesthetic taste to be an important component of their personal identity (Fingerhut et al. 2021).

2.6 Folk Aesthetic Subjectivism and Attitudes towards Aesthetic Testimony

Finally, one argument *for* folk aesthetic subjectivism might draw on our attitudes towards "aesthetic testimony". The expression "aesthetic testimony" refers to cases in which we are told by someone else about the aesthetic properties of an object (e.g., "this painting was beautiful", "this movie was great"). Traditionally, philosophers working on aesthetic testimony have argued that people tend to consider aesthetic testimony as epistemically inferior to other kinds of testimonies. Sure, we do read reviews before deciding whether we are going to watch a movie, but we don't usually claim to *know* that a movie is good or bad before watching it ourselves.

One possible explanation for the alleged inferiority of aesthetic testimony is simply aesthetic *relativism*: indeed, if aesthetic properties are response-dependent and vary depending on who is appreciating a certain work of art, it would make sense to conclude that not much can be learned from the aesthetic appreciation of others (unless we can be certain that others always react in the same way as we do). Of course, this is not the only possible explanation for the inferiority of aesthetic testimony, but the fact that this phenomenon is readily explained by aesthetic relativism provides one more reason to reject the idea that we are aesthetic realists at heart.

But is aesthetic testimony really considered epistemically inferior? Andow (2019) conducted a series of experiments on aesthetic testimony. In a first study, he asked participants whether it was *permissible* and *legitimate* to adopt a certain belief about a particular painting (e.g., "a particular painting is beautiful") in the light of a certain evidence. The nature of evidence was manipulated across conditions: either it was first-hand experience, an expert's testimony, or a friend's testimony. The nature of the property the belief was about was also manipulated: it was either an aesthetic property ("beautiful" or "ugly") or a non-aesthetic one ("large", "costing $14 millions to create"). As a result, Andow observed that most participants considered that it was neither permissible nor legitimate to form beliefs about aesthetic properties on the basis of testimony, even when an expert's testimony was involved, while they considered it more permissible and legitimate to form beliefs about non-aesthetic properties on the basis of testimony. Thus, it seems that people do tend to consider aesthetic testimony as epistemically inferior.

But why do people consider aesthetic testimony as epistemically inferior? In a second study, Andow used a similar design but, in addition, asked participants questions similar to the one used by Cova and Pain (2012) to assess their degree of aesthetic objectivism. Andow did not find any relationship between participants' normativism about aesthetic properties and their judgments about the value of aesthetic testimony, leading him to conclude that the difference people make between aesthetic and non-aesthetic testimony might not be the result of relativism. In a third and final study, Andow provided an alternate explanation for the apparent inferiority of aesthetic testimony. He asked participants about the amount of disagreement in people's aesthetic judgments (e.g., "People disagree about whether a particular painting is beautiful") and the frequency of deception in people's aesthetic claims (e.g., "People lie about liking art"). He found that, in participants who tended to think that there was little disagreement and deception on aesthetic judgments, the difference between aesthetic and non-aesthetic judgments tended to disappear.

However, the conclusion we can draw from these results should be qualified in light of the fact that Andow only tested whether participants' normativism about aesthetic properties predicted individual differences in the value they gave to aesthetic testimony. However, he did not test whether the difference between aesthetic and non-aesthetic testimony was due to the fact that participants were less normativist for aesthetic claims than for non-aesthetic claims, which would be the proper test for the relativist explanation of the inferiority of aesthetic judgment.

In fact, in a later study, Andow (2020) investigated the value people gave to *moral* testimony, while using aesthetic and descriptive testimonies as comparison class. But

Andow did not only ask participants whether it is legitimate to form a moral, aesthetic or descriptive belief on the sole basis of a friend's testimony: he also measured participants' normativism about moral, aesthetic and descriptive claims and investigated to which extent normativism mediated the impact of testimony type (moral versus aesthetic versus descriptive) on the epistemic value of testimony. He found that normativism was indeed a significant mediator of this effect, along with participants' perceptions of disagreement and deception. This suggests that the difference in epistemic value between aesthetic and descriptive varies along participants' beliefs in the objectivity of aesthetic properties. Thus, the fact that we tend to perceive aesthetic testimony as inferior might be one more reason to think that most people are not realists about aesthetic properties.

3 Further Topics

3.1 Definitions of Art

Unsurprisingly, one traditional question in aesthetics and philosophy of art is simply: "what is art?" Many different answers (i.e., philosophical definitions of art) have been offered to this question. In these debates, it is often assumed that a good definition of art is a definition that would accommodate most of which we consider as art, while leaving aside most of which we do *not* consider as art – which means that our intuitions about whether certain objects count as artworks constitute the evidence by which these definitions are to be judged. This is why Kamber (2011) went to explore people's intuitions about a large series of specific artifacts, from William Blake's poem *The Sick Rose* and Duchamp's *Fountain* to a grade school rhyme, a Bugatti and a painting made by a female elephant. For each artifact, participants were asked to check one of three responses: "It is art", "It is not art", and "I am not sure". Participants included both laypeople and art experts. Kamber's conclusion was that none of the main philosophical definitions of art could accommodate all his results. Kamber and Enoch (2019) conducted a similar survey on both laypeople and art experts but, in addition, asked participants to justify their answer. After classifying a certain item as art or non-art, participants were presented with a list of 14 possible justifications and asked to indicate for each of them to which extent this consideration played a role in their answer. Justifications corresponded to different philosophical definitions of art. Across the survey, the most frequently selected justifications were "it was [not] made or selected by a conscious agent" and "it was [not] intended by its maker(s) or selector(s) to be an object of aesthetic interest or appreciation". Though Kamber and Enoch conclude once again that none of the definitions they tested could successfully track the judgments and justifications of art experts, they argue that the most successful definition was Beardley's "aesthetic definition of art" according to which art is something that has been created or selected to be an object of aesthetic appreciation (Beardsley 1983).[5]

However, the apparent impossibility of finding a definition of art that would be able to account for all our intuitions might come from the fact that "art" is a dual-character concept. The expression "dual-character concept" has been introduced by Knobe, Prasada, and Newman (2013) to refer to concepts for which it makes sense to say that something "can be X without being a true or real X". For example, it makes sense to say that Didier "is a scientist" (because he works in lab and publishes a lot of papers in scientific journals) but that "he is not a true or real scientist" (because he does not care about the truth and about following the scientific method, only about becoming famous). Such concepts are dubbed "dual-character" because it seems that their application depends on two criteria: a *descriptive* one and an *evaluative* one (i.e., not whether a certain instance is good in any sense, but whether it embodies the precise values that are supposed to be characteristic of a true X). Though many instances will fulfill (or fail to fulfill) both criteria at the same time, some cases will fulfill one criterion without fulfilling the other, leading to disagreement (is Didier a scientist or not?).

Liao, Meskin, and Knobe (2020) argue that the concept of "art" (and many other art-related concepts) are dual-character concepts in this sense. Thus, they asked participants whether it sounds natural to say something like this:

> There is a sense in which that is clearly *art*, but ultimately, when you think about what it really means to be *art*, you would have to say that it is not *art* at all. (Liao, Meskin, and Knobe 2020, p. 12)

In this case, most participants answered that it was appropriate to say something like that, which, according to Liao, Meskin, and Knobe, means that "art" is indeed a dual-character concept. They used the same procedure on a wide array of art-related concepts and observed that some were treated as dual-character concepts ("street art", "literature") while others tended to be treated as purely descriptive concepts ("comic", "architecture"). They conclude that, since "art" is a dual-character concept, there might be robust disagreement about certain instances of art, even when people share the same concept of "art" (e.g., because different weights to the two corresponding criteria).

3.2 Ontology of Musical Works

When it comes to the ontology of art, musical works raise specific ontological puzzles that are not shared by simpler cases such as paintings and sculptures. Indeed, while paintings, sculptures or buildings have a determinate, concrete existence that can be easily delineated in space and time, this is not the same for works of music. Are musical works abstract objects that are instantiated by specific musical performances, or concrete objects such as a set of particular performances? Are musical works created

---

[5] For a theoretical and methodological criticism of Kamber's work, see Monseré (2015b).

or discovered? When do two slightly different performances count as the same (or different) musical works? These are only a few examples of the numerous ontological questions raised by the nature of musical works. But how exactly are we to answer these questions? What is the criterion that allows us to decide between two competing philosophical accounts? Mikalonytė (forthcoming) surveyed the philosophical literature on the ontology of musical works and compiled a list of almost 100 hypotheses about common intuitions about musical works, suggesting that these debates heavily rely on people's intuitions and their everyday musical practices. However, as she points out, philosophers tend not to agree on what exactly is intuitive, which opens the door to philosophically relevant empirical investigations.

In line with this suggestion, Bartel (2018) investigated people's intuitions about the *repeatability* of musical works, in the context of pop songs. His results suggest that most people have the intuition that a song can be repeated, but that conditions for repetition are particularly stringent: modifications in the message or emotions conveyed by the song is enough to shift intuitions to the conclusion that one is dealing with two different songs. Similarly, Mikalonytė and Dranseika (2020) investigated people's intuitions about the individuation of musical works in the context of classical music. Using vignettes, they examined the role of six factors: the identity of the composer, the method used to compose the music, emotional and representational properties of the music, instrumentation (whether different instruments were used), timbral properties of the music, and score. Their results suggest that emotional and representational properties, timbral properties, and instrumentation play little role in intuitions about individuation. Rather, much of the variation was explained by musical score, composer's identity, and – less prominently – by the method used to create the music. In a later paper, Mikalonytė and Dranseika (forthcoming) also investigated the role played by teleological considerations in people's intuitions. They presented participants with cases of musical works being modified, while manipulating three variables: whether the purpose of the work was modified, whether the musical score was modified, and whether the composer was different. They found that all three factors had an impact on participants' intuitions, suggesting that teleological considerations do inform (albeit weakly) people's judgments about the identity of musical works.

3.3 Aesthetic Adjectives

Experimental philosophers have also investigated the semantics of aesthetic adjectives. Since we can easily say that some things are *more* beautiful *than* others, it seems that aesthetic adjectives are gradable (i.e., that they accept certain degrees). However, linguists typically distinguish between *relative* gradable adjectives (the application of which requires a comparison class that depends on context, such as "tall") and *absolute* gradable adjectives (such as "flat"). So, are aesthetic adjectives *absolutely* or *relatively* gradable? Through a series of studies, Liao, McNally, and Meskin (2016) found that aesthetic adjectives such as "beautiful" and "elegant" fit neither category: they behave as *absolute* adjectives on certain tests (e.g., it makes sense to ask "is this beautiful?" without specifying a comparison class), but as *relative* adjectives on others (i.e., saying that A is more beautiful than B does not imply that B is not beautiful). Similarly, Liao and Meskin (2017) submitted aesthetic adjectives to a test supposed to discriminate between absolute and relative gradable adjectives: the *presupposition assessment task*. For example, they presented two objects to participants and asked them to "select the beautiful one", a task that would not make sense to most participants in the case of absolute gradable adjectives. They observed that aesthetic adjectives (such as "beautiful", "ugly", or "elegant") behaved neither as absolute nor as relative gradable adjectives: some participants refused to comply with the task but others did pick one of the two items. Thus, it seems that aesthetic adjectives differ in specific ways from other gradable adjectives.

3.4 "Impure Aesthetics" and the Interaction Between Aesthetic and Non-Aesthetic Domains

In other works, experimental philosophers have investigated to what extent appreciation of works of art and attributions of aesthetic properties could be influenced by factors and considerations that seem (at least at first sight) to be irrelevant to aesthetic matters. For example, Seidel and Prinz (2018) report studies in which they influenced participants' aesthetic appreciation by manipulating the size and position of artworks. Liao, Meskin, and Fletcher (2020) investigated to which extent participants' judgments of an artwork could be influenced by the artwork's uniqueness (whether there is one or several copies) and its relationship to the artist (whether it was directly made by the artist or produced according to the artists' instructions). They argued that certain of these effects (such as the importance of uniqueness) might depend on the context of appreciation (in a lab versus a museum setting).

Such results might seem to cast a doubt about the reliability of aesthetic judgment. However, experimental philosophers have also defended aesthetic judgment against such skeptical doubts. Against the claim that our aesthetic preferences have nothing to do with the qualities of artworks but are mainly the product of a "mere exposure" effect (i.e., the fact of liking what we are familiar with), Meskin and colleagues (2013) argue, based on the results of an experiment, that the effect of "mere exposure" depends on the qualities of artworks: while it increases liking for good art, it decreases liking for bad art. Thus, the effect of mere exposure does not exclude the possibility that artworks' aesthetic qualities play a major role in our preferences: mere exposure might only help to appreciate them.

Among the non-aesthetic factors explored by experimental philosophers, moral considerations have attracted particular attention. Liao (n.d.) investigated to which extent moral defects in an artwork (such as immoral content) contributed to lower its aesthetic value. He found that moral considerations had an impact, with immoral artworks being less appreciated. However, this impact was mitigated by the artworks' genre (e.g., the presence of immoral themes had less impact on participants' appreciation of a music when the music was presented as hip hop rather than a ballad). Doran investigated the claim that there are such things as moral beauty and ugliness, and more particularly the claim that "if a person is morally good then, to this extent, they are beautiful; or, conversely, if a person is morally bad then, to this extent, they are ugly" (Doran 2021, p. 396). To test this claim, he presented participants with faces of female models (that had been rated as more or less attractive in previous studies) and a vignette describing the model's alleged moral character (morally good or bad). Participants were then asked to indicate to which extent they agreed that the model was beautiful. As a result, participants tended to rate the model as more beautiful when she was supposed to have a good moral character.

3.5 Paradox of Fiction

Fiction and people's engagement with fiction are the source of numerous puzzles in philosophy of art. The most famous is probably the so-called *paradox of fiction*, that can be summarized by a series of three statements that might appear plausible at first sight, but cannot be all true at the same time:
(1) We feel emotions for fictional characters and their predicament.
(2) To feel emotion for a person being in a certain situation, we must believe that this person exists and that this person is indeed in this situation.
(3) We do not believe that fictional characters exist and/or that they actually are in the situation described by the fiction.

Premise (2), according to which one has to believe in the existence of an entity to feel emotions for it, is often considered to be the weakest premise, as there are strong empirical reasons to reject it (Tullmann and Buckwalter 2014). Moreover, Cova and Teroni (2016) have found that, though participants tend to consider this premise to be intuitive, they also tend to reject it as false anyway. Does this mean that we can easily get rid of the paradox by rejecting premise (2)?

Cova and Teroni (2016) argue that this won't suffice, because it won't solve the initial problem that is hidden by the paradox. According to them, the paradox is grounded in a genuine psychological puzzle: how is it that, in everyday life, our emotions seem sensitive to the existence of their object, while they are not when we engage with fiction? After all, if we were shocked by learning of a gruesome murder then learned that this murder did not happen and the victim did not even exist, our emotional state would surely change. But knowing that the victims of a killer in a slasher movie do not really exist does not seem to have the same effect. One solution to this problem has been to argue that emotions we feel for emotional characters follow different rules because they are of a different kind: they are not genuine emotions but *quasi-emotions* (Currie 1990, Walton 1978).

Sperduti and colleagues (2016) tried to empirically assess the truth of the quasi-emotions thesis. They had participants watch a series of short (4 to 5 seconds) video clips, the content of which they presented as either real (documentary or amateur video) or fictional (mockumentary, films depicting fictional events as real and shot in a documentary style). The emotional content of video clips could be positive, negative, or neutral. In the first phase of the experiment, participants were only presented with video clips, without being asked any questions, but their electrodermal activity was measured. In the second phase, they were presented each video clip a second time (without any indication of whether they were real or fictional) and, after each clip, were asked to indicate the intensity of their emotional reaction, the valence of their emotional reaction, to which extent they associated a precise personal memory with the scene, and the nature of the scene (real or fictional).

When it came to electrodermal activity (a physiological measure of emotional arousal), Sperduti and colleagues found no difference between the real and fictional video clips. For self-reported emotional reactions, they found a significant difference for negative video clips: participants tended to report more intense emotional reactions for negative video clips presented as real, compared to video clips presented as fictional. However, this difference was not presented for positive video clips. From the lack of difference in physiological reactions, Sperduti and colleagues conclude that their data "seem to suggest that the fiction-directed emotions are physically robust, as witnessed by a physiological arousal comparable to real material, and can be seen as genuine emotions" (Sperduti et al. 2016, p. 58).[6]

However, another series of studies suggest that this conclusion might be premature. Indeed, Humbert-Droz and colleagues (2020) report the results of two other studies on the difference between "real" and "fictional" emotions, conducted by Sennwald and colleagues (2021). While Sperduti and colleagues only used short, silent video clips, Sennwald and colleagues used lengthier stimuli: either five-minutes long videos (video condition) or one-page long texts (text condition). Videos and texts were matched in content, as texts based on the content of videos. Video clips were taken from documentaries and were either neutral or sad in content.

In a first study, Sennwald and colleagues presented participants with a series of either videos or texts. Participants were told that some of the stimuli were real (documentaries and journal articles) while others were fictional (mockumentaries and fictions under the form of journal articles), but they were not told which stimuli were real or fictional. Participants went through all video clips or all texts (depending on the condition they were assigned to) and, for each of them, were asked to indicate to which extent they experienced negative feelings while watching or reading it, and to which extent they believed it was real or fictional. They were also asked to highlight the most emotional moments of the video or text, to prepare for the second study. Sennwald and colleagues observed that the more participants considered stimuli as

---

[6] Interestingly, one of the authors of this study seems to disagree and argues elsewhere (Pelletier 2019) that these results actually support the conclusion that emotions directed towards fictional characters are indeed quasi-emotions, though in a very specific sense.

real (as opposed to fictional), the more they experienced negative feelings. This suggests that perception of a story as real or fictional might influence participants' emotional reactions, though it could also be that emotions themselves influence to which extent participants perceive a stimulus as real or fictional (thus, Sperduti and colleagues also observed that neutral clips tended to be rated as more fictional than positive and negative ones).

Thus, to determine the causal direction of this relationship, Sennwald and colleagues conducted a second study in which they presented participants with videos or texts but, for each of them, told participants whether they were real or fictional. For each stimulus, they asked participants to indicate to which extent they experienced negative emotions. Also, focusing on the moments identified as the most emotional in their first study, they measured participants' physiological responses (heart rate and electrodermal activity) and motor expressions (corrugator activity). They found that, for negative stimuli, participants reported more negative emotions when stimuli were presented as real, both for videos and texts. They also found that participants' electrodermal activity was higher for videos presented as real, compared to videos presented as fictional. This suggests that appraising the same content as real rather than fictional can have an impact on emotional experience, beyond self-reported emotional experience.

Should we then oppose Sperduti and colleagues and conclude that empirical data support the claim that emotions elicited by fictions are not genuine emotions, or at least differ in nature from everyday emotions? Humbert-Droz and colleagues (2020) argue that such a conclusion would be premature. Indeed, they point to the fact that these studies investigate to which extent "real" and "fictional" emotions differ from each other from a phenomenological point of view (subjective experience and bodily response), and thus presuppose that phenomenology is a relevant criterion to adjudicate the debate. However, going through the literature, they argue that proponents of quasi-emotions have tended to consider phenomenology as irrelevant to the debate and, for some, have even claimed that quasi-emotions are phenomenologically indistinguishable from genuine emotions. Thus, they conclude that the results of these studies might not have important implications for the philosophical debate about quasi-emotions.

3.6 Imaginative Resistance

Another puzzle raised by our interactions with fiction is the puzzle of *imaginative resistance*. The expression "imaginative resistance" refers to cases in which we find it hard or impossible to imagine certain things, even when a fiction asks us to (Gendler 2000). Typical examples in the philosophical literature include fictional worlds in which moral norms or values are different from ours: though we have no trouble imagining worlds full of flying, fire-breathing dragons, certain philosophers argue that it is almost impossible (or at least very hard) to imagine a world in which it would be morally good to torture newborns for fun. However, other philosophers deny the existence of imaginative resistance, arguing that the alleged difficulty to imagine such worlds comes from the brevity and artificiality of examples produced by philosophers: According to them, it is possible to imagine such worlds in the context of a genuine, full-fledged fiction.

In the past years, philosophers have empirically investigated imaginative resistance, and the data they collected suggest that it is indeed a genuine phenomenon. Liao, Strohminger, and Sripada (2014) gave their participants a vignette describing a questionable action performed in the context of Greek mythology. The more participants disapproved of said action, the more they had trouble imagining and accepting that this action was right *in the fictional world of the story*. Going beyond the simple method of vignette presentation, Black and Barnes (2020) asked participants to describe in writing morally deviant, dystopian, and fantastical worlds. After each writing task, participants were asked whether they had successfully completed the task, and if not, why not. They were also asked to report how easy it was for them to imagine the corresponding fictional world. Black and Barnes found that, even though participants produced more words in the morally deviant condition, they were more likely to believe they had failed to the task and found it harder to imagine the corresponding world than in the two other conditions. Thus, it seems that morally deviant worlds are indeed *harder to imagine*. Moreover, emotions seem to play a role in this phenomenon. Black and Barnes (2020) found that disgust sensitivity predicted higher difficulty to imagine dystopian and morally deviant worlds. And Campbell and colleagues (forthcoming) found that imaginative resistance was greatest among participants who experienced more negative affect while reading the fictional vignettes and were lower in trait anxiety and trait psychopathy. However, Black and Barnes (2017) found no connection between imaginative resistance and empathic concern.[7]

However, imaginative resistance might depend on certain aesthetic properties of fictions. Liao, Strohminger, and Sripada (2014) investigated the impact of literary genre on imaginative resistance. They gave their participants a story describing a mother giving her baby for sacrifice. The story came in two versions: either as a police procedural, or as an Aztec myth. Participants were more likely to agree with the claim that what the mother did was right *in the context of the fiction* in the case of the Aztec myth than in the case of the police procedural.[8] This suggests that imaginative resistance is modulated by people's expectations, as those differ across fictional genres.

But imaginative resistance is not limited to morally deviant worlds. Barnes and Black (2016) presented participants with brief scenarios that pictured either morally

---

[7] Black and Barnes (2017) have developed and validated a scale supposed to measure participants' tendency to oppose imaginative resistance (the *Imaginative Resistance Scale*). However, it is not clear whether this scale really captures what philosophers understand by imaginative resistance, rather than a desire to avoid fictions that convey messages incompatible with one's moral norms.

[8] Those results were replicated in the context of the *XPhi Replicability Project* (see Phelan 2018, Cova et al. 2021).

deviant, factually unlikely, or conceptually contradictory fictional worlds. Participants considered morally deviant worlds (e.g., worlds in which committing murder is the right thing to do) as harder to imagine than factually unlikely worlds (e.g., worlds in which wolves roamed the streets of England), but as easier to imagine than conceptually contradictory worlds (e.g., a world in which 7 + 5 is both equal and unequal to 12). Contrasting descriptively and evaluatively deviant fictions, Kim, Kneer, and Stuart (2019) did not limit themselves to morally deviant fictions, but also introduced vignettes that explored aesthetically and humorously deviant fictions. Again, they found that evaluatively deviant worlds triggered more imaginative resistance than descriptively deviant ones. However, they also found that evaluatively deviant worlds were also judged "weirder" than descriptively deviant ones. This led them to wonder whether the difference they observed between descriptively and evaluatively deviant worlds was really due to the type of fiction (descriptively versus evaluatively deviant) rather than their content (to which extent they were weird). They thus assessed the impact of fiction type on imaginative resistance while controlling for the weirdness of fiction content (i.e., to which extent the fiction requested participants to imagine something unusual, surprising and different from the actual world). They found that, when imagine resistance was assessed by asking participants how difficult and possible it was to imagine a certain fiction world, controlling for the weirdness of content tended to make the impact of fiction type on imaginative resistance disappear. However, when imaginative resistance was assessed by asking participants whether they agreed that the target statement was true in the fictional world, the impact of fiction type on imaginative resistance remained even after controlling for the weirdness of content.

Thus, people's interactions with fictions open fascinating avenues of research to experimental philosophers. Some long-standing philosophical debates about how we come to appreciate fiction, such as the "paradox of tragedy" and the "paradox of horror" are still open to investigation and are yet to receive attention from experimental philosophers. Of course, this might be because there already is relevant evidence from other academic fields (see, e.g., Cova, Deonna, and Sander 2018, for the paradox of tragedy as well as Andersen et al. 2020, for the paradox of horror), but my intuition is that there is still plenty of work to do in these areas.

Bibliography

Andersen, Marc Malmdorf, Uffe Schjoedt, Henry Price, Fernando Rosas, Coltan Scrivner, and Mathias Clasen (2020): "Playing with fear. A field study in recreational horror", *Psychological Science* 31 (12), pp. 1497–1510.

Andow, James (2019): "Aesthetic testimony and experimental philosophy", in: Florian Cova and Sébastien Réhault (Eds.): *Advances in experimental philosophy of aesthetics.* London: Bloomsbury, pp. 33–58.

Andow, James (2020): "Why don't we trust moral testimony?", *Mind & Language* 35 (4), pp. 456–474.

Arielli, Emanuele (2018): "Is beauty in the folk intuition of the beholder? Some thoughts on experimental philosophy and aesthetics", *Rivista di Estetica* 69, pp. 21–39.

Barnes, Jennifer, and Jessica Black (2016): "Impossible or improbable. The difficulty of imagining morally deviant worlds", *Imagination, Cognition and Personality* 36 (1), pp. 27–40.

Bartel, Christopher (2018): "The ontology of musical works and the role of intuitions. An experimental study", *European Journal of Philosophy* 26 (1), pp. 348–367.

Beardsley, Monroe (1983): "An aesthetic definition of art", in: Hugh Curtler (Ed.): *What is art?* New York: Haven, pp. 15–29.

Beebe, James, and David Sackris (2016): "Moral objectivism across the lifespan", *Philosophical Psychology* 29 (6), pp. 912–929.

Beebe, James, Runya Qiaoan, Tomasz Wysocki, and Miguel Endara (2015): "Moral objectivism in cross-cultural perspective", *Journal of Cognition and Culture* 15 (3–4), pp. 386–401.

Black, Jennifer, and Jessica Barnes (2017): "Measuring the unimaginable. Imaginative resistance to fiction and related constructs", *Personality and Individual Differences* 111, pp. 71–79.

Black, Jennifer, and Jessica Barnes (2020): "Morality and the imagination. Real-world moral beliefs interfere with imagining fictional content", *Philosophical Psychology* 33 (7), pp. 1018–1044.

Bonard, Constant, Florian Cova, and Steve Humbert-Droz (forthcoming): "De gustibus est disputandum. An empirical investigation of the folk concept of aesthetic taste". In Jeremy Wyatt, Julia Zakkou, and Dan Zeman (Eds.): *Perspectives on taste*. London: Routledge.

Campbell, Dylan, William Kidder, Jason D'Cruz, and Brendan Gaesser (forthcoming): "Emotion in imaginative resistance", *Philosophical Psychology*.

Caroll, Noël (1999): *Philosophy of art. A contemporary introduction*. London: Routledge.

Chatterjee, Anjan (2014): *The aesthetic brain. How we evolved to desire beauty and enjoy art*. Oxford: Oxford University Press.

Cova, Florian (2019): "Beyond intersubjective validity. Recent empirical investigations into the nature of aesthetic judgment", in: Florian Cova and Sébastien Réhault (Eds.): *Advances in experimental philosophy of aesthetics*. London: Bloomsbury, pp. 13–32.

Cova, Florian (2022): "Calibrating measures of folk objectivism". Manuscript. University of Geneva.

Cova, Florian, Julien Deonna, and David Sander (2018): "'That's deep!' The role of being moved and feelings of profundity in the appreciation of serious narratives", in: Donald Wehrs and Thomas Blake (Eds.): *The Palgrave handbook of affect studies and textual criticism*. Cham: Palgrave Macmillan, pp. 347–369.

Cova, Florian, Amanda Garcia, and Shen-yi Liao (2015): "Experimental philosophy of aesthetics", *Philosophy Compass* 10 (12), pp. 927–939.

Cova, Florian, Christopher Olivola, Edouard Machery, Stephen Stich, David Rose, Mario Alai, Adriano Angelucci, Renatas Berniūnas, Emma Buchtel, Amita Chatterjee, Hyundeuk Cheon, In-Rae Cho, Daniel Cohnitz, Vilius Dranseika, Ángeles Lagos, Laleh Ghadakpour, Maurice Grinberg, Ivar Hannikainen, Takaaki Hashimoto, Amir Horowitz, Evgeniya Hristova, Yasmina Jraissati, Veselina Kadreva, Kaori Karasawa, Hackjin Kim, Yeonjeong Kim, Minwoo Lee, Carlos Mauro, Masaharu Mizumoto, Sebastiano Moruzzi, Jorge Ornelas, Barbara Osimani, Carlos Romero, Alejandro Rosas, Massimo Sangoi, Andrea Sereni, Sarah Songhorian, Paulo Sousa, Noel Struchiner, Vera Tripodi, Naoki Usui, Alejandro del Mercado, Giorgio Volpe, Hrag Vosgerichian, Xueyi Zhang, and Jing Zhu (2019): "De Pulchritudine non est Disputandum? A cross-cultural investigation of the alleged intersubjective validity of aesthetic judgment", *Mind & Language* 34 (3), pp. 317–338.

Cova, Florian, and Sébastien Réhault (2019): *Advances in experimental philosophy of aesthetics*. London: Bloomsbury.

Cova, Florian, Brent Strickland, Angela Abatista, Aurélien Allard, James Andow, Mario Attie, James Beebe, Renatas Berniūnas, Jordane Boudesseul, Matteo Colombo, Fiery Cushman, Rodrigo Díaz, Noah N'Djaye Nikolai van Dongen, Vilius Dranseika, Brian Earp, Antonio Gaitán Torres, Ivar Hannikainen, José Hernández-Conde, Wenjia Hu, François Jaquet, Kareem Khalifa, Hanna Kim, Markus Kneer, Joshua Knobe, Miklos Kurthy, Anthony Lantian, Shen-yi Liao, Edouard Machery, Tania Moerenhout, Christian Mott, Mark Phelan, Jonathan Phillips, Navin Rambharose, Kevin Reuter, Felipe Romero,

Paulo Sousa, Jan Sprenger, Emile Thalabard, Kevin Tobia, Hugo Viciana, Daniel Wilkenfeld, and Xiang Zhou (2021): "Estimating the reproducibility of experimental philosophy", *Review of Philosophy and Psychology* 12 (1), pp. 9–44.

Cova, Florian, and Fabrice Teroni (2016): "Is the paradox of fiction soluble in psychology?", *Philosophical Psychology* 29 (6), pp. 930–942.

Currie, Gregory (1990): *The nature of fiction*. Cambridge: Cambridge University Press.

Doran, Ryan (2021): "Moral beauty, inside and out", *Australasian Journal of Philosophy* 99 (2), pp. 396–414.

Fechner, Gustav Theodor (1876): *Vorschule der Ästhetik*. Leipzig: Breitkopf & Härtel.

Fingerhut, Joerg, Javier Gomez-Lavin, Claudia Winklmayr, and Jesse Prinz (2021): "The aesthetic self. The importance of aesthetic taste in music and art for our perceived identity", *Frontiers in Psychology* 11, 4079.

Frierson, Patrick (2014): "Affective normativity", in: Alix Cohen (Ed.): *Kant on emotion and value*. Hampshire: Palgrave Macmillan, pp. 166–190.

Gendler, Tamar Szabó (2000): "The puzzle of imaginative resistance", *The Journal of Philosophy* 97 (2), pp. 55–81.

Goffin, Kris, and Florian Cova (2019): "An empirical investigation of guilty pleasures", *Philosophical Psychology* 32 (7), pp. 1129–1155.

Goodwin, Geoffrey, and John Darley (2008): "The psychology of meta-ethics. Exploring objectivism", *Cognition* 106 (3), pp. 1339–1366.

Humbert-Droz, Steve, Amanda Garcia, Vanessa Sennwald, Fabrice Teroni, Julien Deonna, David Sander, and Florian Cova (2020): "Lost in intensity. Is there an empirical solution to the quasi-emotions debate?", *Aesthetic Investigations* 4 (1), pp. 54–76.

Hume, David (1985): "Of the standard of taste", in: David Hume: *Essays. Moral, political and literary*. Ed. by Eugene Miller. Indianapolis: Liberty, pp. 226–249.

Kamber, Richard (2011): "Experimental philosophy of art", *The Journal of Aesthetics and Art Criticism* 69 (2), pp. 197–208.

Kamber, Richard, and Taylor Enoch (2019): "Why is that art?", in: Florian Cova and Sébastien Réhault (Eds.): *Advances in experimental philosophy of aesthetics*. London: Bloomsbury, pp. 79–102.

Kant, Immanuel (1928): *Critique of judgment*. Transl. by James Meredith. Oxford: Oxford University Press.

Kim, Hanna, Markus Kneer, and Michael Stuart (2019): "The content-dependence of imaginative resistance", in: Florian Cova and Sébastien Réhault (Eds.): *Advances in experimental philosophy of aesthetics*. London: Bloomsbury, pp. 143–165.

Knobe, Joshua, Sandeep Prasada, and George Newman (2013): "Dual character concepts and the normative dimension of conceptual representation", *Cognition* 127 (2), pp. 242–257.

Liao, Shen-yi (n.d.): "Genre moderates morality's influence on aesthetics". Manuscript.

Liao, Shen-yi, Louise McNally, and Aaron Meskin (2016): "Aesthetic adjectives lack uniform behavior", *Inquiry* 59 (6), pp. 618–631.

Liao, Shen-yi, and Aaron Meskin (2017): "Aesthetic adjectives. Experimental semantics and context-sensitivity", *Philosophy and Phenomenological Research* 94 (2), pp. 371–398.

Liao, Shen-yi, Aaron Meskin, and Jade Fletcher (2020): "The vanity of small differences", *Aesthetic Investigations* 4 (1), pp. 6–21.

Liao, Shen-yi, Aaron Meskin, and Joshua Knobe (2020): "Dual character art concepts", *Pacific Philosophical Quarterly* 101 (1), pp. 102–128.

Liao, Shen-yi, Nina Strohminger, and Chandra Sripada (2014): "Empirically investigating imaginative resistance", *British Journal of Aesthetics* 54 (3), pp. 339–355.

Meskin, Aaron, Mark Phelan, Margaret Moore, and Matthew Kieran (2013): "Mere exposure to bad art", *British Journal of Aesthetics* 53 (2), pp. 139–164.

Mikalonytė, Elzė (forthcoming): "Intuitions in the ontology of musical works", *Review of Philosophy and Psychology*.

Mikalonytė, Elzė, and Vilius Dranseika (2020): "Intuitions on the individuation of musical works. An empirical study", *The British Journal of Aesthetics* 60 (3), pp. 253–282.

Mikalonytė, Elzė, and Vilius Dranseika (forthcoming): "The role of teleological thinking in judgments of persistence of musical works", *Journal of Aesthetics and Art Criticism*.

Monseré, Annelies (2015a): "The role of intuitions in the philosophy of art", *Inquiry* 58 (7–8), pp. 806–827.

Monseré, Annelies (2015b): "Experimental philosophy and intuitions on what is art and what is not", *Teorema – Revista Internacional de Filosofía* 34 (3), pp. 159–176.

Moss, David, and Lance Bush (2021): "Measuring metaaesthetics. Challenges and ways forward", *New Ideas in Psychology* 62, 100866.

Murray, Dylan (2020): "Maggots are delicious, sunsets hideous: false, or do you just disagree? Data on truth relativism about judgments of personal taste and aesthetics", in: Tania Lombrozo, Joshua Knobe, and Shaun Nichols (Eds.): *Oxford studies in experimental philosophy*. Vol. 3. Oxford: Oxford University Press, pp. 64–96.

Pelletier, Jérôme (2019): "Being quasi-moved. A view from the lab", in: Florian Cova and Sébastien Réhault (Eds.): *Advances in experimental philosophy of aesthetics*. London: Bloomsbury, pp. 123–141.

Phelan, Mark (2017): "XPhi Replicability Project. Replication of 'Liao, S., Strohminger, N., and Sripada, C.S. (2014), Empirically Investigating Imaginative Resistance. British Journal of Aesthetics 54: 339–355'", *Open Science Framework*. https://osf.io/7e8hz/, last accessed May 19, 2023.

Rabb, Nathaniel, Alex Han, Lucy Nebeker, and Ellen Winner (2020): "Expressivist to the core. Metaaesthetic subjectivism is stable and robust", *New Ideas in Psychology* 57, 100760.

Réhault, Sébastien (2013): *La beauté des choses*. Rennes: Presses Universitaires de Rennes.

Seidel, Angelika, and Jesse Prinz (2018): "Great works. A reciprocal relationship between spatial magnitudes and aesthetic judgment", *Psychology of Aesthetics, Creativity, and the Arts* 12 (1), pp. 2–10.

Seidel, Angelika, and Jesse Prinz (2019): "Impure aesthetics", in: Florian Cova and Sébastien Réhault (Eds.): *Advances in experimental philosophy of aesthetics*. London: Bloomsbury, pp. 59–76.

Sennwald, Vanessa, Florian Cova, Amanda Garcia, Patrizia Lombardo, Sophie Schwartz, Fabrice Teroni, Julien Deonna, and David Sander (2021): "Is what I'm feeling real?". Manuscript. University of Geneva.

Sperduti, Marco, Margherita Arcangeli, Dominique Makowski, Prany Wantzen, Tiziana Zalla, Stéphane Lemaire, Jérôme Dokic, Jérôme Pelletier, and Pascale Piolino (2016): "The paradox of fiction. Emotional response toward fiction and the modulatory role of self-relevance", *Acta Psychologica* 165, pp. 53–59.

Torregrossa, Clotilde (2017): "A defence of experimental philosophy in aesthetics", *Inquiry* 63 (8), pp. 885–907.

Tullmann, Katherine, and Wesley Buckwalter (2014): "Does the paradox of fiction exist?", *Erkenntnis* 79 (4), pp. 779–796.

Turri, John (2016): "Perceptions of philosophical inquiry. A survey", *Review of Philosophy and Psychology* 7 (4), pp. 805–816.

Walton, Kendall (1978): "Fearing fictions", *Journal of Philosophy* 75 (1), pp. 5–27.

Weinberg, Jonathan (2019): "Are aestheticians' intuitions sitting pretty?", in: Florian Cova and Sébastien Réhault (Eds.): *Advances in experimental philosophy of aesthetics*. London: Bloomsbury, pp. 267–288.

Wundt, Wilhelm (1910–1911): *Grundzüge der physiologischen Psychologie*. Vol. 2 and 3. 6th edition. Leipzig: Engelmann.

Zangwill, Nick (2001): *The metaphysics of beauty*. Ithaca: Cornell University Press.

Zangwill, Nick (2019a): "Beauty and the agreeable. A critique of experimental aesthetics", in: Florian Cova and Sébastien Réhault (Eds.): *Advances in experimental philosophy of aesthetics*. London: Bloomsbury, pp. 289–308.

Zangwill, Nick. (2019b): "Aesthetic judgment", in: Edward Zalta (Ed.): *The Stanford Encyclopedia of Philosophy*. Fall 2022 edition. https://plato.stanford.edu/archives/fall2022/entries/aesthetic-judgment/, last accessed May 19, 2023.

Zeki, Semir (1999): *Inner vision. An exploration of art and the brain.* Oxford: Oxford University Press.

Supplementary Materials: Materials and data for the new results reported in this chapter can be found at https://osf.io/4z2qa/, last accessed May 19, 2023.

List of Contributors

Theodore Bach is associate professor of philosophy at Bowling Green State University's Firelands College. His research addresses issues in the philosophy of science, social ontology, and metaphilosophy. His recent journal articles in *Erkenntnis* and *Theoria* defend the epistemic virtue of expert philosophical theorizing and intuiting. His journal articles in *The Monist*, *Synthese*, and *Ethics* provide a naturalized epistemology and ontology for social categories generally and gender categories specifically.

Alexander Max Bauer is research associate at the University of Oldenburg's Department of Philosophy, where his work revolves around experimental philosophy, need-based distributive justice, and causation. Formerly, he has been working in the Research Group 2104 "Need-Based Justice and Distribution Procedures" of the German Research Foundation (DFG) and at the Helmut Schmidt University's Department of Economics. Besides journal contributions (e.g., in *Philosophy of Science*, *Social Choice and Welfare*, or *Judgment and Decision Making*), he has recently published *Empirical research and normative theory* (co-edited with Malte Ingo Meyerhuber; De Gruyter 2020).

James R. Beebe is professor of philosophy, director of the Experimental Epistemology Research Group, and member of the Center for Cognitive Science at the University at Buffalo. He works primarily on topics in experimental philosophy (e.g., folk epistemology, folk metaethics) and mainstream epistemology (e.g., skepticism, reliabilism) and hopes to write a lot about conspiracy theories (unless his plans are thwarted by an evil cabal of saboteurs).

Justin Bruner is associate professor in the Department of Political Economy and Moral Science at the University of Arizona. He was previously assistant professor in the Department of Theoretical Philosophy at the University of Groningen and lecturer in the School of Politics and International Relations at the Australian National University. His research focuses on social and political philosophy as well as the philosophy of science.

Ian Church is associate professor of philosophy at Hillsdale College and the director of the Arete Research Center for Philosophy, Science, and Society. He's co-author of *Intellectual humility – An introduction to the philosophy and science* (with Peter Samuelson; Bloomsbury 2017) and co-editor of *The Routledge handbook of the philosophy and psychology of luck* (with Bob Hartman; Routledge 2019). He is also principal investigator of the project "Launching experimental philosophy of religion", generously funded by the John Templeton Foundation (ID 61886), which supports this research.

Florian Cova is assistant professor at the University of Geneva. He works at the intersection of philosophy and psychology on topics such as action theory, aesthetics, free will, moral judgment, and political philosophy.

Rodrigo Díaz is SNSF post-doctoral fellow at the Centre for Research in Ethics at the University of Montreal. He is an empirically minded philosopher working on emotion, morality, and the philosophy of psychology and neuroscience.

Raff Donelson is associate professor at the Chicago-Kent College of Law at the Illinois Institute of Technology. His research focuses on metaethics, American criminal justice, and methodological questions about legal philosophy. Donelson has published widely in peer-reviewed journals such as *Philosophia*, *Philosophical Issues*, *Metaphilosophy*, *Cognitive Science*, and *Contemporary Pragmatism*. Donelson has also published in a number of law reviews such as the *North Carolina Law Review*, the *Saint Louis University Law*

Journal, and the *Canadian Journal of Law and Jurisprudence*. Donelson holds a JD and a PhD in philosophy from Northwestern University, a MA from the University of Chicago, and a BA from Williams College.

Igor Douven is CNRS research professor at the Panthéon-Sorbonne University and works in cognitive science and formal epistemology. Recent publications include *The epistemology of indicative conditionals* (Cambridge University Press 2016) and *The art of abduction* (The MIT Press 2022).

Shira Elqayam is professor of cognitive psychology and cognitive science at De Montfort University, with research interests in reasoning, decision-making, and rationality. Recent publications include articles in *Cognitive Psychology, Cognition, Journal of Memory and Language*, as well as *Synthese*.

Eugen Fischer (DPhil Oxford) is reader in philosophy at the University of East Anglia. He is the author of *Linguistic creativity* (Springer 2000) and *Philosophical delusion and its therapy* (Routledge 2011). He has co-edited several volumes including *Experimental philosophy, rationalism, and naturalism* (with John Collins; Routledge 2015) and *Methodological advances in experimental philosophy* (with Mark Curtis; Bloomsbury 2019).

Chad Gonnerman is associate professor of philosophy and the philosophy program coordinator at the University of Southern Indiana.

Paul Henne is assistant professor of philosophy and neuroscience at Lake Forest College. He is also the principal investigator of the RAD Lab.

Joachim Horvath is junior professor for metaphilosophy and experimental philosophy at the Institute for Philosophy II at Ruhr University Bochum, and principal investigator of the Emmy Noether Independent Junior Research Group "Experimental philosophy and the method of cases – Theoretical foundations, responses, and alternatives (EXTRA)", funded by the German Research Foundation (DFG; project number 391304769). He was previously post-doctoral researcher at the University of Cologne and managing director of the German Society for Analytic Philosophy (GAP). Horvath's main areas of research are epistemology, metaphilosophy, experimental philosophy, and argumentation theory. His work has been published in journals like *Mind, Philosophical Studies*, as well as *Philosophy and Phenomenological Research*.

Stephan Kornmesser is research associate at the University of Oldenburg's Department of Philosophy. He works on the philosophy of science, philosophy of linguistics, experimental philosophy, and philosophy of language. Currently he is principal investigator of the project *The diversity of scientific concepts*, funded by the German Research Foundation (DFG; project number 456636934).

Karolina Krzyżanowska is assistant professor in philosophy of language and cognition at the Institute for Logic, Language and Computation of the University of Amsterdam. Her research concerns various issues at the intersection of analytic philosophy, psychology of reasoning, and linguistic pragmatics. Recent publications include articles in *Philosophical Studies, Journal of Memory and Language*, as well as *Cognitive Psychology*.

Edouard Machery is distinguished professor in the Department of History and Philosophy of Science at the University of Pittsburgh and the Director of the Center for Philosophy of Science at the University of Pittsburgh. He is senior research fellow at the African Centre for Epistemology & Philosophy of Science of the University of Johannesburg. Machery is the author of *Doing without concepts* (Oxford University Press 2009) and of *Philosophy within its proper bounds* (Oxford University Press 2017).

Thomas Nadelhoffer is associate professor of philosophy at the College of Charleston. His research focuses primarily on moral psychology, neuroethics, free will, psychopathology, and the criminal law.

Mark Phelan is associate professor of philosophy, chair of the Philosophy Department, and director of the Program in Cognitive Science at Lawrence University in Appleton, Wisconsin. He received his PhD from the University of North Carolina, Chapel Hill, in 2010. Phelan works primarily in the philosophies of mind and language.

Justin Sytsma (PhD University of Pittsburgh) is associate professor in the philosophy program at Victoria University of Wellington. He is co-author of *The theory and practice of experimental philosophy* (with Jonathan Livengood; Broadview 2015), co-editor of *A companion to experimental philosophy* (with Wesley Buckwalter; Wiley-Blackwell 2016), and editor of *Advances in experimental philosophy of mind* (Bloomsbury 2014).

Joseph Ulatowski is senior lecturer in philosophy at the University of Waikato. His research in experimental philosophy focuses upon the nature and value of truth, facts, and action.

Jonathan Waskan is formerly associate professor of philosophy at the University of Illinois, Urbana-Champaign. His work in the philosophy of science, cognitive science, and experimental philosophy largely concerns the nature and role of cognitive models in both everyday human thought processes and science. He has also written extensively about artificial intelligence, consciousness, and folk psychology.

Index

Action   3f., 40, 44, 46, 48, 56f., 84, 133f., 136f., 139–146, 148–150, 153, 194, 246, 327–334, 336f., 340–343, 345, 347, 355, 359, 364, 373, 411, 417, 419
– Intentional action   40
Aesthetics   4, 17, 21, 393–395, 399, 404, 407, 417
– Aesthetic judgment   4, 393–398, 400, 403, 407
– Aesthetic realism   393f.
– Aesthetic testimony   4, 393, 402–404
Agency   4, 266f., 276, 281f., 327f., 330f., 335, 340, 343, 346f.
Analytic philosophy   20, 26, 31, 41f., 237, 240, 244f., 264, 372, 388, 418
Anger   230, 269, 281f., 354, 356–360, 364
Argument   3f., 9, 12, 14f., 19, 21, 28f., 31, 46, 48–54, 60f., 72, 74, 76f., 87–96, 104, 109, 111–115, 117, 119, 121, 123f., 205, 212, 215, 218–223, 225–227, 237, 240f., 243, 245, 247f., 251, 264–266, 271, 275f., 280f., 283f., 295, 303, 312, 314f., 317, 323–325, 333, 341, 347, 353–359, 363, 373–377, 380, 383, 385–387, 394, 402
– Argument from design   385f.
Armchair philosophy   15, 29
Art   22, 323, 393, 400f., 403–405, 407f., 418
Attitude   11, 20, 23, 29, 31, 62, 91, 123, 176, 256, 265, 297, 318, 336, 355, 365, 402
Attribution   14, 40, 43f., 46, 50, 55–59, 138, 151, 163f., 168f., 177–179, 254, 263f., 266–285, 335f., 363, 386, 407

Bargaining   291, 297
Beauty   393–395, 398, 408
Behavior   11f., 14–16, 72, 115, 134, 137, 175f., 205, 215, 265, 268, 277, 285, 292–294, 298, 310f., 320, 323, 328, 332–336, 400
– Behavioral studies   255, 257
Being moved   4, 353, 361, 363f.
Belief   3f., 19, 21, 24f., 42, 48–50, 52, 61f., 72, 91f., 102, 117f., 124, 163–166, 168–178, 187, 195, 198f., 218, 226f., 230, 246f., 250f., 265, 268, 277f., 280f., 285, 316, 319, 327f., 332–336, 338–343, 345, 347, 354, 360, 372, 374, 377f., 383, 387, 398, 403f.
– Evaluative belief   4, 354f., 358–361
– Religious belief   371f., 377, 380, 383f.
Bypassing   4, 327f., 333, 335–345

Causation   1–4, 13, 20, 26, 40, 48, 54–59, 83f., 95, 106, 133–137, 139–142, 145–153, 223, 240–242, 244f., 247, 255, 258, 277, 280f., 309–311, 313, 319–322, 329, 332, 336, 339, 341f., 365, 386, 417
Cognition   41, 50, 54, 75, 77, 84, 115, 148, 152, 175, 237, 282, 353, 359, 418
– Cognitive science   3, 9f., 39, 46f., 102, 145, 149, 237, 243, 246f., 251, 257, 371f., 383, 417–419
– Cognitive theory   353f., 359
Common sense   25, 43, 49, 250, 253, 276, 317, 327f., 333, 340, 345, 347, 353, 394–396
Compatibilism   61, 84, 329f., 339, 343f.
– Incompatibilism   61, 329–331, 333, 335, 337–342, 345–347
Compliance   293–295, 298, 302–304
Compositionality   152
Comprehension   47, 50, 52, 108, 241, 247, 249–252, 327f., 336, 343–346
Concept   3f., 39, 42–46, 55–60, 74f., 82f., 103, 109, 111f., 116–118, 122f., 141, 149, 151–153, 163, 166f., 174f., 211, 239, 243–245, 250, 252, 255, 263f., 266–270, 272, 274, 276f., 282, 284, 309–311, 313f., 316–319, 321–325, 332, 353f., 359, 362f., 374, 383, 388, 394, 405, 418
– Pre-theoretical concept   84, 327
Conceptual analysis   23, 29f., 43–47, 71, 112, 215, 257
Conditional   3, 109, 205, 211–229, 302, 304, 346f., 365, 418
Confirmation   17, 101, 104, 107, 122, 229
Consciousness   43, 46, 85, 263, 269, 283f., 419
– Conscious state attribution   4, 263f., 266, 281f.
– Phenomenal consciousness   4, 263–270, 272, 274, 276f., 282f., 285
Consent   4, 309f., 319f., 322, 379
Context   24, 50, 53f., 58f., 75, 103, 105f., 111, 115, 117–120, 122, 124, 164, 183, 185, 201f., 204, 213, 217f., 220, 223, 280, 304, 320, 323, 363, 378f., 381f., 388, 406f., 411
– Contextualism   40, 205
Corpus analysis   2, 11, 21f., 39, 42, 55, 57f., 152
Criticism   2f., 101, 103f., 108–111, 113f., 119, 122, 124f., 309, 317f., 341, 396, 398, 400, 405
Culture   12–14, 61, 79, 122, 164, 169, 175, 183, 187f., 191f., 194, 202, 205, 265, 358, 374, 384, 386

– Cross-cultural research   3, 27, 154, 163–165, 167, 170f., 175–177, 183, 189–192, 194, 285, 294, 300, 315, 332, 347, 361, 397

Data   10, 12, 15, 21f., 24, 26, 28f., 49, 57–59, 101, 107f., 111, 113, 124, 138, 166f., 173, 178, 186–188, 190, 193f., 204, 215, 221, 223, 225–228, 239, 242f., 249f., 253, 256, 276, 283, 303, 312, 317, 320, 322, 330, 338–340, 345, 361, 365, 380, 388, 409–411
– Data mining   237, 256
Debunking   42, 46, 49, 61f.
Descriptivism   184–186
Determinism   4, 30, 327–335, 337–347
– Indeterminism   333
Digital humanities   2, 28, 39, 42
Distance   53, 165, 219–221
Divine hiddenness   387f.
Dualism   332f., 335, 345, 347

Economics   1, 4, 255, 291f., 300, 303, 310, 417
Efficiency   4, 292f., 295f., 300
Embodiment   263, 266, 268–270, 274
Emotion   4, 238, 265, 267, 269f., 284, 298, 329, 353–365, 393, 406, 408–411, 417
Empirical legal studies   309f.
Empirical philosophy   28, 40
Empirical science   1, 9
Epistemology   40, 77, 83, 89f., 116–120, 122, 125, 163–166, 169, 172, 178, 230, 264, 371–373, 417f.
– Epistemic internalism   164, 177
– Experimental epistemology   3, 163–165, 170f., 176–179, 417
– Folk epistemology   163, 165, 174–177, 179, 417
– Formal epistemology   3, 211f., 229, 418
Essentialism   154, 196
Ethics   12, 40, 77, 83f., 371–373, 417
Evidence   3, 9, 11, 13–15, 17, 29, 42, 44f., 47, 52, 54f., 58, 71f., 74–76, 79–83, 85–90, 93–95, 103, 108, 111–113, 116, 119, 123, 135–139, 141, 145f., 150–154, 165f., 169–172, 174f., 189f., 192, 194, 205, 211, 213, 219, 229f., 238, 240, 244, 256, 263f., 269, 273f., 276, 278f., 284f., 297f., 302, 304, 312–314, 317f., 327f., 330–332, 340–343, 345, 356, 362–365, 377, 385, 403f., 412
– Apparent evidence   163, 171–177
– Authentic evidence   3, 163, 171–173, 175, 177

Evil   19, 374–376, 379, 384, 417
– Problem of Evil   4, 371, 373–375, 378, 380–384, 388
Experience   14f., 17, 19, 51, 82, 84f., 107, 173, 265–267, 270, 272–275, 277, 280f., 283f., 328, 346, 353f., 356, 359, 361–364, 376f., 384, 393, 403, 410
Expertise   17, 71, 74, 76–87, 94f., 101, 107, 114, 116f., 119–122, 174, 204, 323, 377
– Expertise defense   2f., 71, 73f., 76–78, 82–85, 87, 95, 106, 110, 119, 121, 174, 309, 318f., 322f.
Explanation   10, 22, 25, 30, 40, 42, 46f., 49f., 52, 57, 60–62, 89, 117, 133, 136–142, 145, 148, 150–154, 176, 205, 213, 219, 223, 229f., 237–258, 272, 274, 280, 283f., 302, 319f., 322, 325, 332, 336, 356, 359, 384f., 394, 400, 402f.
– Scientific explanation   3, 237–242, 244, 257
Externalism   164, 177, 195–198, 200, 203
Eye tracking   1, 53

Fairness   4, 292f., 296, 303
Fiction   184, 196, 408–412
– Paradox of fiction   393, 408
Folk   2, 10, 13, 44f., 49, 52, 55f., 59–61, 116, 118, 121, 164, 172f., 175, 178, 255, 257, 263f., 268, 272, 276, 283, 285, 295, 300, 311–325, 327–330, 332–334, 336, 343, 345f., 362f., 393f., 396–398, 400, 402, 417, 419
Free will   4, 21, 27, 30, 40, 43, 46, 48, 61, 75, 84, 104, 284, 310, 327–341, 343–348, 417, 419
Functionalism   263, 274, 277, 279–282

Game theory   291, 303
Guilty pleasure   4, 393, 400f.

Happiness   4, 21, 278f., 353, 358, 361f., 365
History   2, 9, 11–13, 16–18, 20f., 23, 25, 31, 42, 104, 118, 121, 173, 178, 200, 238, 250, 256, 309, 372, 386, 418
Human nature   12, 19, 268, 374

Identity   25, 40, 154, 203, 264, 277, 284, 379, 402, 406
Illusion   21, 49–52, 60f., 327, 332, 334f., 363, 372
Impartiality   297–299, 301f.
Inferentialism   3, 216, 218f., 221, 223, 225–227
Intelligibility   246–252
Intention   43f., 46, 191–193, 277, 280, 298, 309–311, 334, 347
Internalism   195, 197

Intuition   2f., 10f., 17, 27–30, 40, 42–47, 49f., 61, 71–74, 76f., 80, 83f., 87–96, 101–103, 105, 107f., 110–114, 117, 123, 151, 163–167, 169f., 173–178, 184, 187, 190, 192, 204, 215, 225, 229f., 264, 266, 283f., 292, 295, 312–315, 317–319, 322f., 327–334, 336–338, 340–348, 353f., 357, 371f., 374–380, 383f., 393f., 397, 400, 404–406, 412

Judgment   2–4, 10, 13, 23f., 28f., 31, 40–50, 54f., 57, 61, 71–96, 101–103, 105–124, 133–138, 140–142, 144–153, 163f., 166f., 171–174, 176, 183f., 186f., 189–194, 197f., 200–205, 214, 217, 222, 225–227, 230, 237, 242f., 245, 248–250, 252, 254, 257, 265, 282, 284, 301, 321f., 331, 333, 338f., 341–343, 354f., 360, 365, 395–399, 402–404, 406f., 417
Jurisprudence   4, 309–313, 318f., 322, 324f., 418
Justice   105, 240, 297–303, 333, 417
Justification   13f., 91, 94, 112, 122, 168f., 178, 215, 219, 230, 251, 314, 318, 380, 398–400, 404

Knowledge   3, 14, 19, 21f., 24–27, 40, 42–44, 46, 50, 72, 75, 80, 82, 88, 91f., 102, 104f., 107, 111, 114, 117f., 121, 163–179, 223–225, 244, 246, 248, 256, 265, 277, 281, 313f., 376f.
– Justified true belief   27, 72, 88, 119, 163–165, 167f., 170, 172–174, 176f.

Language   3, 11, 20–23, 40f., 43, 47, 50, 52, 60, 79f., 83, 109, 115, 135, 149, 167, 169, 176, 183, 191, 195, 204f., 214, 216, 222, 316, 320, 335, 337, 339, 342, 353, 418f.
Law   4, 76, 135, 211, 213f., 217, 239f., 244f., 309–320, 322–324, 329f., 333, 338, 341, 344, 347, 355, 417–419
Lay people   83, 274
Linguistics   10, 39, 55, 57f., 60, 80, 152, 204, 418
Linguistic turn   26
Logic   3, 15, 19, 21f., 117, 211–215, 229, 239, 258, 359, 418

Mastery   78–80, 82f., 86, 95
Meaning   59, 108, 163f., 184, 195f., 204f., 214, 218, 222f., 238, 298, 309, 320, 322–324, 342
Mental state   4, 14, 77, 104, 254, 263–272, 274–283, 285, 334, 337, 342, 354, 363
Mereology   154
Metaphilosophical naturalism   2, 39, 41, 49

Metaphilosophy   9, 28f., 39, 71, 90f., 93, 96, 101, 167, 417f.
Metaphysics   2f., 11, 23, 40, 77, 83, 120, 133, 136, 151, 153f., 238, 264, 335, 343, 371–373
Method of cases   2f., 42–45, 71–74, 76f., 87–91, 93–96, 101–103, 108f., 112–115, 121, 418
Mind   4, 12, 16, 19–21, 28f., 40, 48, 78, 104, 115, 120, 140, 152, 229, 243, 253, 255, 263–267, 269–271, 274–277, 282f., 285, 292, 320, 332, 334f., 347, 363, 394, 397, 418f.
Mischaracterization objection   2f., 71, 74, 87–93, 95f., 115
Music   147f., 221, 397, 405f., 408

Naturalism   39–41, 112, 418
Natural kind   103, 124, 183, 195, 197f., 201–205
Natural law   309, 311f., 314–317, 341, 374
Neuroscience   4, 40f., 251, 327f., 331–333, 335f., 345, 347, 417f.
Normality   3, 133f., 136, 146, 321
Normativism   396, 398f., 403f.

Objectivism   393–397, 399–401
– Aesthetic objectivism   394, 396–398, 400, 403
Omission   3, 113, 133, 141–146, 149, 152f.
Ontology   20, 116, 361, 393, 405f., 417
Ordinary language philosophy   12, 23, 39, 41, 47–50, 54f., 60
Overdetermination   3, 140, 145–149

Pain   4, 25, 41, 263, 266, 270–277, 280f., 346, 353, 361–363, 383, 385, 395f., 398, 403
Paradox   48, 50, 228, 408, 412
Perception   4, 15, 19–21, 41, 48–52, 55, 59–61, 77, 145, 154, 263, 267, 275, 277, 280f., 283, 355–358, 364, 378, 380–383, 394, 404, 410
Person   15, 24, 26, 84f., 91, 102, 113, 118, 135, 139, 144, 163, 166f., 169, 171, 175, 178, 184, 186f., 192, 198, 213, 218, 265f., 268, 273, 275f., 278, 285, 293, 295, 316, 318f., 323, 331, 338, 341, 359f., 362, 365, 399, 401, 408
Phenomenology   346, 410
Physicalism   283f., 335
Positivism   309, 313, 317, 324
Pragmatics   211, 418
Predicate   3, 23, 183, 195–201, 203–205, 270
Prediction   12, 72, 81, 105, 139f., 145f., 164, 172, 175, 186, 239, 242, 250, 257, 291f., 304, 334–336, 361, 398
Preemption   3, 133, 139, 146–150

Prisoner's dilemma   293–295, 298, 304
Probability   78f., 139, 192, 211–215, 217, 222–229, 240, 257f., 295, 365
Proof   43, 45, 107, 302, 376, 388
Proper name   3, 30, 80, 106, 176, 183–185, 189–191, 193–197, 204f.
Protagonist projection   169f., 205
Psycholinguistics   2, 28, 39, 42, 48, 52, 72
Psychology   1, 3, 9, 12, 20–22, 40f., 47, 60, 83f., 102, 105, 108, 114, 116, 125, 164, 173, 176, 186, 211–213, 215–218, 227–229, 237f., 242f., 283, 285, 292, 309f., 312–314, 346, 360f., 371f., 378, 383, 386, 393, 417–419
Punishment   294f., 311f., 336

Rational choice   291f.
Realism   15, 22, 49, 52, 61, 239, 256
Reason   1, 9, 15, 22, 42, 45, 58, 73, 79, 88f., 91–94, 106f., 112, 114, 120, 135f., 141, 143, 151, 166–168, 172, 176–178, 186, 200, 212, 214, 218, 222, 230, 252, 258, 274, 281, 294, 298, 304, 312, 314, 318f., 321, 333, 337, 342, 347, 372, 377f., 380, 384f., 387f., 394, 398, 400f., 403f., 408
Reference   2f., 23, 27f., 30, 46f., 52, 58, 80, 103, 106, 108, 114f., 123, 183–186, 189–191, 193–197, 204f., 252, 293, 303, 360f.
Religion   4, 94, 238, 332, 371–375, 377–380, 382–385, 387f., 417
Replication   27, 92, 108, 167, 190, 245, 267
– Replication crisis   84, 188
Responsibility   4, 43, 46, 55, 57–59, 84, 137f., 142–145, 152, 284, 310, 327–348

Sadness   270, 275, 278f., 354, 357–359, 361, 364, 385
Science   3f., 9, 12, 15, 17–20, 22, 24, 29, 39f., 60, 79, 81–84, 95, 102, 145, 148, 151, 188, 196f., 200, 216, 230f., 237–239, 242–247, 249–251, 253, 255–258, 283f., 327, 353, 393, 417–419
Self   11, 13f., 17f., 46, 75f., 84, 86, 91, 101, 103f., 108, 110, 112, 122, 176, 217, 237, 267, 285, 294, 303, 310, 313, 328, 354, 360, 365, 409f.
Semantics   3, 15, 183, 197, 204f., 211, 215–217, 219, 221, 406
– Experimental semantics   183, 193, 204f.
– Semantic externalism   80, 183
– Semantic internalism   183
– Semantic intuitions   183, 190
– Semantic reference   108f., 191f.

Slur   205
Social contract   2, 4, 291–293, 295–297, 302f.
Social sciences   1f., 42, 108, 164, 239
Somatic theory   353, 356
Soul   14, 16, 332f., 335, 347
Speaker   28, 40, 43f., 57, 184f., 190–193, 195–199, 202–205, 211f., 227, 254, 275, 316, 363
– Speaker's reference   108f., 191f.
Stability   4, 84, 292f., 303, 378
Subjectivism   396f., 399, 402
Suffering   4, 375–383, 385
Survey   10, 14, 18, 41, 71, 74, 85, 91, 101–103, 107–109, 111–113, 115f., 119, 122, 165, 179, 255, 257, 266, 282, 292, 315, 320f., 323, 327, 346, 379, 393, 404

Taste   4, 15, 196, 201, 205, 303, 393, 395, 397, 399, 401f.
Teleology   154
Temporality   3, 146, 148
Testimony   16, 171, 177, 218, 227, 403f.
Theodicy   384f.
Theology   372, 374, 384, 388
Theory   3, 11, 15f., 19, 21, 23, 28, 42, 104, 114f., 117–119, 123f., 178, 183–186, 195, 203, 211–213, 216, 229f., 238–246, 248, 250, 256, 258, 263, 277f., 291f., 297, 303f., 309, 311–317, 331, 343, 353, 364, 384, 417–419
– Error theory   338
Thought experiment   2, 10, 27, 42, 71f., 74, 76f., 79–82, 84, 87–89, 91, 95f., 104, 109, 111, 113, 115, 117, 120, 122, 164, 166–168, 173f., 178, 184–186, 189, 196–198, 200–202, 204, 291, 312, 318, 329f., 356, 393
Time   9, 11, 13, 16, 18, 20–23, 26, 28–31, 43, 47, 53–55, 61, 76, 111, 113, 115, 120, 124, 135, 138, 140–142, 146f., 149, 151, 154, 163, 165, 170–173, 175, 177, 187f., 191, 199f., 212f., 216, 218, 222, 230, 242, 248, 251, 253, 255, 257, 281, 294–296, 298f., 319, 321, 323, 330, 344, 348, 358, 362, 384, 388, 405, 408f.
Truth   23–27, 44f., 56, 72, 82, 94, 103, 105f., 114, 166, 179, 184, 193f., 200, 203, 211f., 214f., 217, 219, 221–226, 228–231, 256, 258, 304, 318, 356, 378, 398f., 405, 408, 419

Universality   165, 167, 170, 176

Valence   40, 44, 58, 263, 270, 272–274, 409

Vignette   1, 28, 56, 108 f., 134, 137 f., 141 – 143, 146 f., 150, 152 f., 164, 186, 188, 190 – 192, 194, 198 – 200, 204, 243, 248 – 251, 254, 271 – 273, 275, 278, 282, 291 f., 330 f., 343, 347, 353, 359, 362 f., 365, 376, 378 f., 381 f., 406, 408, 411 f.

www.ingramcontent.com/pod-product-compliance
Lightning Source LLC
Chambersburg PA
CBHW080406230426
43662CB00016B/2328